Marketing Communications

A behavioral approach to men, messages, and media

The Wiley Marketing Series

WILLIAM LAZER, Advisory Editor
Michigan State University

MARTIN ZOBER, *Marketing Management*

ROBERT J. HOLLOWAY AND ROBERT S. HANCOCK,
The Environment of Marketing Behavior—
Selections From The Literature

GEORGE SCHWARTZ, Editor.
Science in Marketing

EDGAR CRANE
Marketing Communications:
A behavioral approach to men, messages, and media

Marketing Communications

*A Behavioral Approach
to Men, Messages, and Media*

Edgar Crane

College of Business Administration
University of Notre Dame

New York • London • Sydney   John Wiley & Sons, Inc.

Library of Congress Card Number: 65-21444
Printed in the United States of America

To Lois

and Larry, Margaret Ann, and Richard

Preface

These are exciting times. Knowledge in marketing and communications is increasing at so rapid a pace that the businessman finds it hard to keep up, even in areas where he already has competence. The teacher is acutely aware of the torrent of new discoveries. He has the added burden of screening material for students whose time and data-processing abilities are even more limited than his own. This very outpouring of knowledge may cause both businessman and teacher to hesitate when faced with an attempt, as in this book, to extend the horizons of the traditional business disciplines to include the behavioral sciences. Teachers, in particular, will ask how they can find room in their syllabi for new material, and which of the old must give way to the new.

Yet I feel neither businessman, nor teacher, nor student actually has any choice in the matter. Or rather, that they have no choice as to *whether* to apply the insights of the behavioral sciences to their problems, only a question as to *how* to do so. Businessmen, in fact, have been receptive to these insights, even eager for them, although an ad hoc, piecemeal, unsystematic approach has often led them from one catchword to another. Their expectations have frequently been too high and their demands too great, so that their subsequent disillusionment has been disheartening. Some educators, on the other hand, have been slow to adopt the new because of the value they placed upon the old. As a teacher, I share this respect for the conventional wisdom: I do not feel, however, that one need be the enemy of the other. (This text, for example, has been used for six terms at the University of Notre Dame in what was once a conventional course in advertising; a traditional text is still used as a companion volume.) If knowledge is increasing today, so is the ability of our students to handle more substantial intellectual fare; more students die of boredom than are killed by overwork. Unless we in business challenge our students with more substantial content, I feel we may lose the best of them. The alert and able students, who the business firm of today needs and whose careers in business would benefit all society, will turn from us to other disciplines which make demands commensurate with their abilities and aspirations.

The need for the behavioral sciences in business was recognized by Bossard and Dewhurst more than 30 years ago, and it was reiterated in 1959 in both the Gordon and Howell and the Pierson reports. Yet, as recently as December 1964, members of the American Marketing Association were told that of nineteen universities reporting on their doctoral programs in marketing, only three required a course in the behavioral sciences. Some of us have tried to meet the need by sending our students to established departments in the behavioral sciences, only to have them come back without the insights, integration, and application to their careers which would illuminate their understanding and inspire their imagination. I am convinced that business students do not and probably cannot schedule enough conventional courses in psychology, sociology, and the other behavioral sciences to meet their needs. Nor do I feel that many business schools will be able to lure first-rate behavioral scientists from their parent disciplines. I *do* believe that we can and must do the job ourselves. Many marketing teachers, themselves trained in traditional approaches, have added the insights of a systematic study of human behavior to those gained from experience in business and in teaching the business disciplines.

Having found such teachers, today's business school must then provide them with the tools they need, tools which enable them to add their own experiences and insights to those of the behavioral scientist, rather than duplicating his efforts. Is not the day past when we can afford to save students the effort of careful study of a text by using up class time in a repetition of its contents? This text is designed for study, freeing the teacher to explicate a conventional text in his lectures or to illustrate its lessons with case discussions, audiovisual materials, and examples of his own first-hand experience in marketing, in advertising, and in salesmanship. This text, in short, is a tool designed for the modern student and the conditions of the classroom of today.

Even the best of teachers using the most modern tools will not find the task ahead a simple one, however. The behavioral sciences are far from integrated themselves; integrating them with marketing and the other business disciplines requires an adventuresome spirit willing to generalize and speculate, in a calling where caution is often preferred to creativity. Educators must be willing to satisfice, to recognize the heuristic need for imperfect approximations to the truths we may ultimately attain, and to accept the businessman's needs for decisions now with what information is available. Businessmen, in their turn, must develop that tolerance for ambiguity which we are told accompanies creativity, and to be content without the kind of closure which is, at least for the present, beyond the grasp of the behavioral sciences. Students, along with the rest of us, must learn to walk on shifting sands, with change the order of the day and the "rules" and "principles" of today subject to continuing qualification and revision. They must realize, with us, that obsolescence in education is occurring at an ever-increasing rate. They may, indeed, see the day when the diploma is not issued for life but must be renewed like a pilot's license, and they, like the pilot, must be reexamined periodically and "checked out" on new equipment, or the day when every diploma carries a series of coupons which can be cashed-in at 5-year intervals to pay refresher-course tuition.

Until that day and in anticipation of that day, we teachers, the students in our classrooms, and the businessmen in their refresher courses must be less concerned with the static history of what men have discovered, decided, and done and more attentive to the methods of discovery, the processes of decision, and the analysis of doing. Students must be encouraged to ask of every text and lecture: "How do you know? So what?" They must learn to ask us these questions and then, as their skills grow, to provide their own answers. We must expose them to some of the sources in which evidence can be found, to some of the techniques by which evidence may be gathered and analyzed, to some of the methods by which research can be made relevant to life, and life can stimulate research.

Such imperatives as these have guided the writing of this book.

Undergraduates who plan to seek an advanced degree may find the summaries of research articles in each chapter a painless introduction to the exciting world of research which they will enter upon graduation. These summaries have three advantages; they are available, they are brief, and they are relatively free of scholarly jargon. The teacher whose primary interest lies in research may find these summaries (and an annotated list of nearly 100 additional studies in the instructor's manual) a useful platform from which to launch his students on a broader or more intensive search of the literature. The primary target of these summaries, however, is the student who will not continue beyond the bachelor's degree and the businessmen who left college some years ago. It is their time spent tracking down research articles I wish to save. It is for their sake that I have reduced the number of words that must be read. It is for them that I have tried to translate into a simpler tongue the specialized and diverse dialects of the psychologist, sociologist, and social psychologist. It is they who I hope will be encouraged to report, relate, reconcile, and replicate the fascinating, often puzzling diversity of the research literature. It is within them, by constant passage back and forth between text and research, that I hope to develop the realization that generalizations become meaningful only when we know the data on which they are based.

Many other articles might have served as well as those I chose to summarize. I have sought to produce a kind of Whitman's Sampler, with a diversity of subject matter and research techniques, and a balance between studies which illustrate important variables in the behavioral sciences and those which apply behavioral science techniques or principles to marketing problems. In every instance, students will benefit by looking at the more complete original article and by preparing summaries of their own.

Books do not teach, however; men must do this. Teaching, in turn, is not a goal in itself but a means to learning, and learning is the responsibility of the student. And the student is himself a preliminary stage in the development of the businessman. All of us—author, teacher, student, businessman—must communicate with one another, for only through our communication and cooperation can any of us achieve our ends. Thus I have made communications the means by which the behavioral sciences can be introduced into marketing and integrated with it. In similar fashion, communications can serve as a means of integrating behavioral sciences with accounting, with finance, and with production; management in all these areas is concerned with influencing human behavior. Some day, I hope, books like this will not be needed, for the behavioral sciences will be so well integrated throughout the business curriculum that their insights will be as much a part of man as his breath and his speech. Perhaps, as an intermediate stage, we may see the day when all business students are required to take, as a matter of course, a core sequence in the behavioral sciences which stresses what our functional fields in business have in common rather than our differences. This book is designed as a stepping stone toward these ends. In the meantime, however, since patterns are stubborn in education and change is slow, I have written a book which can be fitted into the existing framework of the marketing curriculum. We have been teaching communications or promotion as an art and we must continue to do so. It is time to recognize that communications is also on the verge of becoming a science.

May 1965   *Edgar Crane*
Notre Dame, Indiana

Acknowledgments

The "basic library" suggested at the end of this text and the detailed bibliography include as many of the printed sources as I can now recall, although there must be within these covers many an echo of sources now forgotten or, because they came to me through others, never known. Similarly, I cannot begin to list all of the persons who have shaped my own approach to communications. Let those listed then represent many others, some of whom may be astonished at the interpretation I have given their teachings, many of whom I hope will give me the benefit of their criticisms, but none of whom may be held responsible for the contents of this book.

Teachers: First of all to Nathan Maccoby of Stanford, a living link with the great Hovland research tradition, without whom my dissertation and doctor's degree would not have been possible; and, for the same reason, to Richard F. Carter. Next, to the creative mind of John Malone who as head of marketing management at the University of Notre Dame originally suggested this book, but who, as assistant dean of the College of Business Administration, found that his duties prevented him from participating in its authorship. To Kenneth Boulding, who has set an example for all of us, by combining the creativity of the poet, the analytic skills of the economist, and the social responsibility of the Quaker. To Leon Festinger, who gave me the privilege of listening-in while he planned a study and of running subjects for him that emphasized once more to me the educational significance of guided experience.

Colleagues: On newspapers, to Carl Rowan, at present head of the United States Information Agency, whose reporting in our days on the *Minneapolis Tribune* showed that facts have meaning only when their emotional consequences are recognized. On magazines, to Lauren K. Soth, now of the *Des Moines Register and Tribune,* who showed me how to translate economic research for a farm audience in our days on the *Iowa Farm Economist.* In public relations, to headquarters staff of the American Friends Service Committee whose worldwide activities I once helped interpret. In research, to Macolm S. MacLean, Jr., with whom I have explored the problems of educational television and radio; to the late Paul Deutschmann, under whom

I served in the Communications Research Center at Michigan State University, and to a master teacher, David K. Berlo.

Students: To the students who taught me both content and method as I tried to aid their learning at the Universities of Minnesota, Iowa, and North Carolina and Michigan State and Notre Dame.

And, finally, to the four persons to whom this book is dedicated: my wife, whose training as a child psychologist has helped her cope with a husband in the throes of authorship and whose example has taught me that we human beings must communicate with our hearts as well as our heads; and to my children, who have forced me to develop my skills of persuasive communication to their utmost.

E. C.

Contents

Contents for Section A

SECTION A

The Behavioral Science Approach to Communications

IN DELIGHTFUL anecdotal fashion, Matthews, Buzzell, Levitt, and Frank have described the process of decision making in the purchase of a new car.

Their story is presented in the left column; in the right I have analyzed it as an event in communications. The behavior they regard as a keystone in marketing thus may serve as an introduction to the behavioral science approach to communications used in this text.

CAR-BUYING DECISIONS*

A new, medium-sized Buick sits in the Wilsons' two-car garage, next to Mr. Wilson's commuting car. The idea of a new car had been **discussed for almost a year.**[1] It had first arisen when the old family car, a 1958 model, had to have new shock absorbers and a front end transmission seal **within a 30-day period.**[2] Mr. Wilson had pointed out that they could expect more repair bills because the car had run over 50,000 miles, and he said that **his experience with run-down machinery**[3] at his company's plant had convinced him that in the long run, it would be wiser to get a new car than to keep repairing the old one.

BEHAVIORAL ANALYSIS

1. All three members are involved and as often happens with consumer durables, the decision-making process takes a long time.
2. The process begins when two events occur close together in time and thus aid attention and perception.

3. The process could end abruptly, if the family decided just to repair the old car, but one member brings to bear his experience in another group.

*From *Marketing, An Introductory Analysis* by John B. Matthews, Jr. et al., Copyright, 1964, McGraw-Hill Book Company. Used by permission. (pp. 40–43).

Bill was **enthusiastic**[4] about the idea of a new car from the beginning, although he said that American cars were **too big and expensive**[5] to operate. Mr. Wilson said that he had a lot of **faith in all the big Detroit companies.**[5] Bill agreed in general, but said they ought to switch brands because the old car hadn't run too well.

Mrs. Wilson was **lukewarm**[6] at first. She rather liked the old car. She also said she could put **a new roll-out refrigerator**[7] to much better use and mentioned that they had never been to Hawaii. Her friend, Mrs. Huff, had given the **bridge club a lecture about Hawaii**[8] and had shown some colored slides, and Mrs. Wilson had been a bit envious. She suggested that they put off buying a new car until they had done some of the things they had talked about doing for so many years.

The men dropped the subject for a while, although Mr. Wilson was surprised to learn that his wife harbored ideas about travel. He was also **somewhat resentful**[9] at the implication that he might not be able to afford a new car in addition to other things. He and Bill discussed the subject privately on several occasions, and **they agreed**[10] that a new car made a great deal of sense. The more Mr. Wilson thought about it, the better he liked the idea. Bill was an ever-present source of encouragement. Mrs. Wilson had been stubborn on previous occasions, however, and the men were puzzled as to how to overcome her objections.

Several months passed before the family could agree that a new car was desirable. On one occasion, Mr. and Mrs. Wilson went to a potluck

4,5. Certain values are characteristic of age and sex: innovation for the young, old ways for the older person. These values are also appropriate to the roles of father and of son in the family.

6. True to *her* role in the family, Mrs. Wilson proposes two alternatives.

7. One arises from her role as housewife.

8. The other from her desire to maintain her family's status in an important reference group—the bridge club.

9. Mr. Wilson is also conscious not only of his family's status but of his own status as bread winner within the family.

10. Some sociologists say the three-person group is unstable, tending to break down in a coalition and an isolate. This happened here. How are the men to prepare messages which will win Mrs. Wilson over?

8. A reference group influenced Mrs. Wilson *against* car purchase.

supper at their church[11] and parked the old car near those of **several friends.**[12] The nearest car belonged to the Beckwiths. It was a white convertible and during the evening the **Beckwiths mentioned many of the car's advantages**[13] to the Wilsons. The Wertheims also had a new car that they had brought back from a European trip. When the evening ended, Mr. Wilson **had difficulty starting the family car,**[14] and Mrs. Wilson was noticeably silent during the ride home.

At dinner two weeks later, Mrs Wilson said that she had been thinking it over. She had decided that she would go along, but she still hoped that any car they bought would not be **flashy and showy.**[15] Mr. Wilson and Bill agreed.

The next decision was **what type of car**[16] and what **brand** to buy. The Wilsons knew that many of their friends had been loyal for many years to certain manufacturers and had always either **bought the same makes**[17] of cars or chosen a different make by the same manufacturer. Bill, however, encouraged his parents to try something new. After considerable discussion, Mr. and Mrs. Wilson decided that the new car would be a four-door type like the old one.

Although Mr. Wilson did not say so, he thought that **a two-door car might look strange**[18] to some of their friends.

The Wilsons had trouble deciding how much to spend on the new car. Mr. Wilson said they could afford anything "within reason." Mrs. Wilson and Bill were **unable to understand what that phrase meant,**[19] except that it had something to do with the trade-in price of the old

11. Now another reference group, composed of members of her church, influences her in favor.

12. These friends affect her in two ways: in terms of status and the question—if they can afford it, why can't we?

13. They affect her also through direct messages, through a channel which is second only to one's own experience: the informal group.

14. Did Mr. Wilson do this deliberately, or was his subconscious at work? Psychologists would suspect this difficulty was not just a coincidence.

15. Her connotative words indicate her attitude but what do they denote? As we see later, even members of her own family do not know the referents of Mrs. Wilson's terms.

16. The basic product decision is made; now the family must decide what brand; if brands are similar in features and price, then the decision may turn on company image (as a cue to probability of repairs and as a symbol of status).

17. Dissonance theory may help explain such "brand loyalty;" it also simplifies the difficult process of choice.

18. Note that Bill is now an isolate. Not only are there status implications here but, if all three are to ride in the car, two doors might be inconvenient.

19. As in the case of Mrs. Wilson's remark, her husband's connotative language has ambiguous referents.

car and the future **trade-in value**[20] of the new car. Mr. Wilson also talked about **depreciation and operating costs,**[20] and had figures on sheets of paper. Mrs. Wilson looked at them and decided to **leave the figuring to her husband.**[21] After getting nowhere on what they should pay, the Wilsons decided to **look at some cars.**[22] At this point all three admitted that they had been looking at **advertisements on television**[23] and in **magazines.**
Bill said that he had already **talked to two dealers.**[24] He had been smitten by the increased use of aluminum in some of the new cars and **explained its advantages**[25] to his parents. The older people were not very interested.
Mrs. Wilson wanted to look at a Rambler. She had seen a yellow one advertised in a magazine and had an idea that she had seen something about **free savings bonds**[26] if enough people bought Ramblers. Her husband asked if a yellow car wouldn't be too flashy and Mrs. Wilson said that a **nice yellow**[27] wasn't flashy at all. Mr. Wilson said he wanted to look at cars made by the Chrysler company because their cars had always been **well engineered.**[28] The Wilsons looked at Ramblers and at Plymouths and Dodges, but they were **not very enthusiastic**[29] about anything the dealers showed them.
One evening the family had a visit from **a car salesman**[30] whose company's showroom was near the supermarket where Mrs. Wilson did her shopping. At the door, the salesman said he had heard the Wilsons were thinking about a new car. He wanted them to see **some brochures.**[31] Mrs. Wilson thought

20. The husband's role specifies that he is the expert on financial questions.

21. His wife professes ignorance of the symbol system of numbers.

22. Now the family begins the process of search and comparison; this means a commitment, both to self and others, which will make a change-of-mind difficult. They look to formal channels, both (24) face-to-face and (23) mediated.

25. Bill, still favoring innovations, conveys information to his parents.

26. Was the practice of letting the housewife keep savings on household buying or the trading-stamp habit making her more alert to such premiums?
27. Obviously Mrs. Wilson is talking her own language and referring to differences her menfolk do not understand.

28. Engineering, like finances, is something the male sex role is assigned.

29. Is it possible the variety of choice fatigued them and made decision-making too formidable a task?
30. Word-of-mouth channels have alerted a salesman: the first seller-initiated contact so far on a face-to-face channel.

31. He uses a printed message.

the salesman was a pleasant young man, so she invited him in. Mr. Wilson was watching a baseball game on TV, and although he was polite to the young salesman, he paid very little attention. **Mrs. Wilson was embarrassed.**[32] When the young man went, he left his card and suggested the Wilsons drop into the showroom at their convenience. After he had gone, Mrs. Wilson said **they ought to visit the showroom**[32] because the salesman had taken his time to call on them, but her husband said the salesman had been a pest and he didn't like being bothered at home—**it was bad enough to have to see salesmen at the plant.**[33]

For the next several weeks, all three Wilsons **continued to look at advertisements.**[34] The old car was running well, however, and Mr. Wilson seemed to be losing some of his interest. On one occasion, he said that as far as he could see **there wasn't much real difference**[35] between the various kinds of cars and that all manufacturers were just interested in gewgaws and fancy accessories. **Bill disagreed**[36] and described a number of technical improvements made by Detroit and foreign manufacturers in recent years. Meanwhile, Mrs. Wilson began to **cut pictures**[37] of the new models from her favorite magazine and several times **asked her friends' reactions** to various **colors and styles**[38] of cars.

Several months after they had first talked about a new car, the family went on a Sunday drive. While passing **a large billboard**[39] advertising the **medium-sized Buick,**[40] Mr. Wilson announced that he expected to receive a fairly substantial bonus from his company in the near

32. Having invited the salesman into the house, Mrs. Wilson felt obliged to treat him as a guest. Indeed, she may be quite accustomed to dealing with door-to-door salesmen.

33. Her husband, however, seems to feel that he wants to initiate any sales conversation. He puts his business and home life in separate compartments, not allowing the two roles to mix.
34. Ads maintain a low level of interest, but they are not enough to precipitate action.

35. The strongest member of the triad seems to have lost interest—perhaps because he finds choice too difficult.

36. Meanwhile, wife and son now favor purchase.

37. Mrs. Wilson uses two channels—searching in magazines and asking friends to help in the task of comparison.
38. In the decision-making process, she assumes responsibility for areas in which her sex-role prescribes that she is expert.
39. An "intrusive" kind of ad provides the occasion for Mr. Wilson to announce that he has decided to buy a car now.
40. Complex problems of decision are sidestepped by deciding to buy the same make; recent repairs and Bill's earlier objections are overlooked.

future. **The bonus**[41] would be large enough to cover the cost of a new car and still leave **"something extra toward a trip."**[42] Mrs. Wilson reacted happily, but the son asked his father whether he was worried by the **current problems in the stock market.**[43] Mr. Wilson said that the market would go back up as soon as things picked up a bit and added that he wasn't as worried about the market as most people; as he put it, "Blue chips are blue chips, and **the company is basically sound."**[44]

The next morning, Mr. Wilson **called the owner**[45] of the Buick agency, who said that he would have the sales manager take care of them as soon as they arrived.

When the Wilsons got to the Buick agency, the sales manager was waiting. He **showed them**[46] several floor models and a number of brochures and offered to **let them test-drive**[47] any car the agency had. He **answered Mr. Wilson's questions**[48] about prices, trade-ins, delivery dates, and guarantees and helped Mrs. Wilson on questions of **color and fabric.**[49] During these conversations, he also **called in the service manager**[50] to talk to Bill about the **operating features**[51] of various models.

After an hour or so, the Wilsons retired to the family car for a **conference.**[52] It became quickly apparent that **all three preferred**[53] the medium Buick. The decision was made in 10 minutes, and the family returned to the sales manager's office, where Mr. Wilson arranged the delivery date and payment. He was obviously **in an expansive**

41. Mr. Wilson explains his action by mentioning the bonus.

42. He has not forgotten the implied criticism of his ability as a wage earner in his wife's "either/or" suggestion.

43. Now that the decision is made, Bill can express solidarity with his father's role of handling finances.

44. He allows Mr. Wilson to reward himself by posing as an expert.
45. No wonder Mr. Wilson was affronted by the door-to-door salesman; apparently he is an executive who deals with executives directly.

46. The salesman does all the proper things: shows models, offers to (47) demonstrate, and (48) answers questions.

50. When he feels out of his depth, he calls in an expert.
49–51. Note that each of the Wilsons specializes, acting as if each had a distinct part in the decision to be made.
52. Just as the salesman had a ritual to perform, so does the family.
53. Does this preserve the illusion that the family decides, when actually Mr. Wilson does? Is habit so strong that in fact there was no decision made, and the ritual merely allays guilt?

mood[54] and left for his office with Bill after telling his wife that she could choose the colors, but to remember that **they had agreed that flashy colors were out.**[55]

That night, as the family talked about the new car, all three Wilsons were surprised that they had been able to make the decision **so quickly**[56] and with **so little disagreement.**[57]

54. Mr. Wilson felt rewarded and the chances of satisfaction with the car are high. Why? Is he relieved at having settled a problem? Reducing dissonance following a decision?

55. But we thought Mrs. Wilson had made this decision; is this a way he emphasizes that she has only the power he delegates to her?

56. Why is the family's perception so different from ours?

57. Is harmony a fiction that must be maintained for family survival? How is harmony produced—by son and wife giving way to Mr. Wilson's power?

These Chapters Will Present Further Discussion of These Points:

Chapter	Relates to Points	Chapter	Relates to Points
1	8, 22	9	8, 10–12
2	15, 17, 19, 27, 28, 54	10	3, 4, 6, 20, 25, 26, 33, 38, 49, 51
3	1, 2	11	9, 18, 45
4	31	13	35, 36
5	5a	14	40, 42–44
6	5b, 16	15	14, 29, 54
7	13, 23, 24, 30–32, 34, 39, 46–48, 50	18	37

One

Marketing Communications: Who, What, and Why

This is a book on communications. Communications is the study of who says what to whom in what settings, by which channels, and with what purposes and what effects. It deals with messages designed to influence human behavior, the media that carry such messages, and the markets that respond to such messages. Messages, media, and markets, therefore, represent major concerns of this text.

This is specifically a book on marketing communications, a text in human behavior for students majoring in advertising, selling, or public relations. It is not concerned with the techniques of advertising, selling, or public relations but with the principles of human behavior to which such techniques must adapt themselves.

To familiarize themselves with these principles, students in most major universities would have to take a half dozen courses in as many departments, studying role and status in sociology, personality and motivation in psychology, language with the linguist, and meaning with the semanticist. Few students have the time to explore all these areas. Those who do find they have little time left to integrate the diverse material or to apply it to practical problems in such fields as advertising.

By assembling material from these fields in one place, this book seeks to give students and their teachers time to integrate and apply their learning. At the same time, it seeks to provide leads to the student who wants to pursue one or more of the fields and cover it in more depth. Recognizing that knowledge of human behavior is advancing at such a pace that today's graduate may have to re-educate himself three times before he reaches retirement age, this text also tries to introduce him to the methods by which knowledge is advanced and a few of the journals in which such advances are reported. This is done by including in each chapter brief summaries of journal articles, chosen to illustrate a variety of research techniques, by citing some of the evidence on which principles of human behavior are based, and by including some studies of the handful available made in marketing settings or of marketing problems.

Source, Message, Receiver

Three things are necessary for communication to take place: a source, a message, and a receiver. Both source and receiver must have goals; each must expect to receive some benefit if communication is to occur. All of us, as customers, receive a great many messages from advertisers and salesmen. All of us, as customers, also send a great many messages to advertisers and salesmen in the form of the questions we ask and, in that most effective form of all, the decision to buy or not to buy the product they are trying to sell.

This book, however, has been written from the standpoint of the marketing communicator, rather than that of the customer. There are two reasons for this. One is that most college courses and most of the students in them are source oriented. The typical college catalogue offers only a handful of courses that teach how to *receive* messages—courses such as music appreciation, consumer purchasing, or how to read a book. But this same catalogue offers a great many courses for the person who wants to *send* messages: courses in the performing arts, in salesmanship, in advertising, in journalism, in creative writing. The second reason that this book is written from the standpoint of the source is that most of the research that has been done to date has shared this viewpoint. There have been a great many studies on how to influence others; there have been very few studies on how to resist such influence.

This book is source oriented, therefore, in that it looks upon the purchaser as the target of influence attempts. It asks how messages can be designed which will cause prospects to move toward goals set by the advertiser. In trying to answer this question, however, the book devotes most of its content to characteristics of the receivers of marketing messages, to the prospects who represent a market for the product or service which the communicator is trying to sell. Thus the book is source-oriented in purpose and audience-oriented in content. It is a book *for* future sources, but it is a book *about* receivers.

First Task: Define Goals

The first task of any communicator is to define the goals which he seeks to attain. Before goals can be defined, however, we must indicate what functions the goals themselves have. Having described these functions, we can then specify the kind of goals which will perform such functions.

Goals have two functions to perform. The first is to guide our selection among alternative courses of action to those means which will achieve our goals most economically. The second is to indicate when we can cease to act, having achieved the end we sought.

To perform these functions, goals must be specific. They must indicate whose behavior is to be influenced, in what direction, to what degree, and within what time limits. A brewer, for example, may decide that he wants to increase his share of the market in his distribution area, from 6 to 9% during the next 18 months. To make sure that goals are specific, and to prevent arguments afterward, it is well to write them down and to agree, in advance, as to how one plans to go about measuring progress toward them. The brewer, for example, could define his goal as 9% of beer customers or 9% of beer purchases.

Setting goals is not easy. In theory, every firm seeks to maximize its profits, but even stockholders disagree on how profits are to be defined. Some are interested in current income; others long-range capital growth. And management, which actually determines the firm's goals, has still other alternatives. It may prefer high salaries to high profits or put prestige and power ahead of income. Deciding on the best means to achieve the goals is even more difficult. There are two reasons for this difficulty, each of which we want to examine at some length.

One reason is that, even after a goal has been achieved, it is difficult to say what means were responsible. The complexity of cause-effect relations makes this discovery a difficult scientific question. If the brewer achieves 9% of the market, for example, can he attribute it to his beer, his advertising, his salesmen, or the fact that his competitors failed to anticipate the rising consumption caused by an unusually hot summer? The second reason it is difficult to select the most efficient means to a goal is that these means are, themselves, subgoals, with three functions of their own to perform.

The first or *time* function is to provide indications along the way as to whether the original decision is working out. If our brewer finds, at the end of 6 months, that his market share is falling, not rising, he may want to revise his strategy.

The second or *source* function arises because most goals require the coordinated efforts of several persons, each of whom must have a goal of his own. The brewer's goal of a 9% market share is a *marketing* goal. To achieve it, his sales manager may have to increase retail outlets by 50% or his advertising manager may have to increase consumers' awareness or preference for the brand by 100%.

The third or *receiver* function of subgoals arises because not all receivers are at the same stage of persuasion. Some like our brewer's product, but advertising can encourage them to drink more of it. Others are not aware the beer exists; the goal of advertising for them may be to get them to sample a bottle.

Such audience differences mean that no single goal can guide communications strategy.

Four Levels of Decision

There are four levels of decision making in marketing communications, each of which limits all subsequent decisions concerning means and ends. The marketing manager makes the first two decisions and delegates the second two to his advertising agency, although he retains veto power over the agency's decision. The means of obtaining each goal thus become goals for decision makers lower on the list.

Marketing Mix

The marketing manager decides on price, place, product, and promotion (McCarthy 35, 872–874). He thus sets a goal for communications by indicating how much of the job of selling the product is to be done by promotion or, in the language of this book, by communications. At the same time, his decisions on price, place, and product limit the content of communications themselves. It is true that price, place, and product can have no effect upon a prospect's behavior unless he perceives them, and that communications can influence whether and how he perceives them. It is equally true that messages are not all-powerful. What a firm says about price, place, and product cannot diverge very far or very long from what it does without purchasers perceiving the discrepancy.

Communications Mix

The share of the selling task assigned to communications then is divided between advertising and personal selling.

Speaking to a group is cheaper than speaking to each of its members as individuals. It is also a gamble, since group support will increase a speaker's effectiveness and group opposition will decrease it. How can this risk be reduced?

Three Experiments in Group Discussion

During World War II, Kurt Lewin directed three experiments at the State University of Iowa in changing housewives' habits. In the first, three groups of 13 to 17 Red Cross home-nursing volunteers were given lectures advocating increased use of beef hearts, sweetbreads, and kidneys, for the sake of health, economy, and the war effort. Another three groups first discussed the change, including such obstacles as cooking smell and husbands' attitudes; only then did an expert offer her advice in overcoming the obstacles. A subsequent check showed that only 3% of the lecture audience compared with 32% of the discussion group started using the meats.

The second experiment compared lecture and discussion with sets of 6 to 9 housewives who knew one another but were not members of any group that held regular meetings. This time the purpose was to increase use of fresh or evaporated milk. Two check-ups were made this time, one at the end of two weeks, and the other at the end of four weeks. In both cases, use of both kinds of milk had increased more in the discussion groups.

In the third experiment, a state hospital nutritionist spent 25 minutes talking individually to farm mothers who had just had their first child at the university hospital. In each case the nutritionist urged use of cod liver oil and orange juice. The experiment consisted of meeting with the mothers six at a time and allowing group discussion. Again, even though most of the mothers had never met one another before and were not to see one another again, group discussion proved superior.

—Kurt Lewin, "Group Decision and Social Change," in Eleanor Maccoby et al., *Readings in Social Psychology* (New York: Holt, Rinehart and Winston, 1958).

A Closer Look at Group Discussion

"Group discussion," as used by Lewin, involved at least four different factors: discussion as a channel of information; a decision by individuals in the group; public announcement of the individual decisions; and members' perception of consensus in such committment. Which of these elements was responsible for the apparent superiority of group discussion?

An experiment at the University of Michigan divided 473 psychology students into 12 groups—all possible combinations of three kinds of influence attempt (lecture, discussion, and a control group involving no arguments) and 4 modes of committment (no decision at all, an anonymous decision, committment to the extent of raising one's hand, and committment by raising one's hand and giving one's name to be written down).

This time the lectures and discussions sought to get more students to volunteer as experimental subjects. A few days later all students received a letter asking them to sign up as subjects, and a week later a classroom questionnaire asked them whether they had committed themselves originally, whether they had actually signed up, and how many members of the group they thought had signed up.

The results showed that group discussion per se did not increase the number of students who signed up as subjects: about 75% in each group did so. Neither did public committment; students who raised their hands or gave their names were no more likely to sign up than students who wrote anonymous statements indicating a willingness to volunteer.

However, 22% of the 3 groups asked to make a decision did carry it out, as compared with only 15% of the no-decision group. Action was especially likely for individuals who thought other members of their group were going to volunteer. The actual proportions of subjects who had decided to volunteer varied from 41 to 100%, with 13 groups having proportions above the mean of 72.5%. In 10 of these 13 groups, members who actually signed up as volunteers assumed a higher level of volunteering than did other members of the same groups who did not themselves volunteer.

In all there were 131 subjects who were asked to make a decision and decided to volunteer in groups where a high proportion of members also decided to volunteer. Of these 131 subjects, 34% actually did sign up. In contrast, there were 135 students who were not asked to make a decision about volunteering; only 15% of them did sign up. The difference between these two groups is significant at the .001 level. These two variables, individual decision and individual perception of group consensus, appeared sufficient to have explained the results in the earlier studies directed by Lewin.

—E. B. Bennett, "Discussion, Decision, Commitment and Consensus in 'Group Decision,' " *Human Relations*, 8:251–274.

Media Mix

Advertising's share of the selling task is divided, in turn, among the several media—direct mail, newspapers, television, magazines, radio, and billboards.

Message Mix

Finally, someone decides how product characteristics are to be related to consumer benefits. He chooses appeals, selects symbols, and combines them in messages which express these appeals.

Since the goal of marketing is sales, why cannot sales themselves serve as subgoals for each of the subsequent levels of decision making, decisions as to the mix of communications, media, and messages? Some writers feel that they can and should. The author, however, feels that sales fail to perform the three functions of a subgoal.

1. *Time.* Sales come too late and in all-or-none fashion. They frequently do not permit us to measure progress at intermediate points in time, while it is still possible to alter our communications strategy.

2. *Receiver.* Sales are not sensitive enough to original differences in receivers or to changes in them brought about by communications. They ignore differences between the half-persuaded prospect and nonusers who are indifferent, unaware of the brand, or even antagonistic to it.

3. *Source.* This is the most serious objection of all. If sales are a good measure of the effectiveness of the marketing mix itself, they tend for that reason to be a poor measure of the effectiveness of its constituent parts.

It is true that, in theory, sales can measure the effectiveness of any of the mixes: communications, media, or message.

All we must do is find equivalent, isolated test markets sufficient in number to allow study of each combination of the variables we regard as relevant. (A marketer who must choose among three price alternatives, two pricing policies, four product variations, two different media schedules, and two kinds of messages would need to compare the effect on sales of $3 \times 2 \times 4 \times 2 \times 2$ or 96 different combinations. If he follows a rule of thumb that three test markets should be used for each combination, this would require 288 markets, all of which should be as similar as possible.)

By measuring sales "before" and "after" his entry into the market, the manager can make adjustments for original inequalities, provided (1) he is sure that there is no interaction between the original level and his own variables and (2) the "before" measure can be obtained without alerting retailers or consumers in such a way as to itself affect sales. In addition, using sales as a criterion runs the risk of tipping off one's competitors.

Observing the Prospect

Because of these difficulties in using sales as a measure of communications, communicators tend to go directly to the prospect himself, in telephone polls, mail surveys, or face-to-face interviews, to determine whether the media have exposed him to the advertiser's message, whether he can remember the message, and whether he prefers the brand. Or they lure the prospect into the laboratory, to determine his reaction to variations in the message, before it is turned over to the media.

If attitudes are highly correlated with behavior, they represent a way of predicting behavior, in time enough to take action that may influence behavior. But when are attitudes related to behavior?

Six Conditions Affecting Survey Validity

Dollard suggests six conditions under which attitude or opinion scores are likely to predict behavior:

1. If the subject is aware, when his attitude is measured, of all the elements which will affect his later behavior. (A man who has never faced an armed robber may not be aware of the unconscious tendencies which will come to the fore in him when this happens. The attitude test cannot make a respondent aware of relevant conditions within himself.)
2. Persons with poor verbal skills, those of low intelligence and the inarticulate, may not have the words needed to forecast their own behavior. (If one does not have the word "introvert" in his vocabulary, he cannot use it to describe himself—even though it might be a very useful description.)
3. Opinions of persons who think before they act, and seldom think without doing something concrete about their conclusions are likely to predict their behavior. (Some persons never move beyond the daydream, seeing no action they can take and no success possible if they do act.)
4. Previous experience with a given kind of behavior makes one's predictions of future behavior more likely to come true. (The attitude test itself cannot possibly mention or make real all of the conditions in the situation which will determine a respondent's future behavior. The closer it can come to doing so, however, the better predictions will be.)
5. The attitude test should not include behavior-influencing elements which will not be present when the behavior itself is to be evoked. (Penalties or rewards may be perceived in the attitude test situation itself, even such "subtle" ones as the approval or disapproval of the interviewer. Anonymity may protect a respondent against fears of retaliation from persons other than the interviewer.)
6. Prediction is best when no new experience that might affect behavior intervenes between the attitude test and the behavior itself. (The shorter the time between interview and behavior, the less time there is for such an experience to occur.)

To begin with, there is an arbitrary aspect to causes and effects, since each cause itself has a cause, and every effect produces other effects in its turn. A man's death may result from a gunshot and the gunshot, in turn, may be the result of an insult or an injury. The same man's death may also be viewed as the cause of a slayer's electrocution or of the sudden enrichment of a wastrel son.

Since a series of causes may precede any effect, the source must decide how far back in this chain he wants to go. The brewer finds, for example, that a hot spell in July causes his sales to soar. From his standpoint, however, this is an unsatisfactory kind of "cause." He has no way of producing a hot spell, and no businessman likes to feel that he is at the mercy of such vagaries of nature.

So he looks further. He may ask how many people, when a hot spell hits, seek solace in soft drinks or hard liquor, rather than beer. Or he may try to escape dependence on the weather, by appealing to other motives. Heat is not the only reason people drink. They must drink something at meals, even if it is only water. They must serve something, even if it is only coffee, when their friends drop in.

The brewer may ask why beer seems to be a lower-class drink: Is it solely a matter of price? Why does it tend to be a men's drink? Why does it tend to be a drink for young people? Why does he find some geographic areas are good markets: Is the ethnic background of their residents the explanation? Or, limiting himself to present beer drinkers, the brewer may ask why some people prefer nationally advertised, more expensive premium beers to his regional brand. Or even why some people drink his brand and others the competing regional brand.

To find answers to these questions, the brewer may have to look at people's motivations for drinking beer. If he finds that the more obvious demographic characteristics of social class and income don't help him separate beer drinkers from the hard liquor crowd, he may have to look to subtler personality differences. He may ask how a taste for beer or the beer-drinking habit was learned in the past, or ask how one's family, neighbors, and friends influence one's current decisions about beverages. Or he may ignore such differences and ask how his advertising and sales messages and his choice of media affect attitudes toward his beer.

There are advantages in not going any further back than one has to. The closer the causes one manipulates are to the effect one desires, the surer he is of getting the results he wants, of having them follow quickly upon his action, and of getting the results without undesirable side effects.

It is easier to determine cause-effect relationships when the causes are near to rather than remote from the desired effects. There are also disadvantages, however: when one concerns himself only with immediate causes, costs of research may rise and every decision may require a new study.

Once the brewer has answered these questions he must then decide whether to use an advertising campaign which builds a company or product image and creates favorable attitudes toward the firm or beer itself. He may concentrate, instead, on the brand image itself. It is difficult to compare these two strategies, since the effects of image-building are harder to measure, being smaller and occurring over a longer time span. The image-building campaign is likely to appear more costly in the short run. Its outcome is more affected by influences other than messages, including purchaser experience with the product. The effects, both desirable and undesirable, are more varied. At the same time, the costs of the campaign are spread over more products and the results may prove highly resistant to competition.

Which Is Cause, Which Effect?

A second reason for the difficulty in devising strategy in the behavioral sciences is that even when one has narrowed his concern to two variables, he often cannot be sure which is cause and which effect. Research has shown, for example, that a customer may buy a given brand of beer because he has read an advertisement, but that he may also read the advertisement because he has bought the brand (Festinger, 48-54). To determine which is the cause, one must determine which occurred first, either by taking "before" and "after" surveys or conducting an experiment in which the source can control the order of the two variables. Sometimes even time sequence is not sufficient to determine causality, since a person's behavior today may be caused by what he expects to happen tomorrow. Of course his anticipations do precede his behavior, but an economist who records only overt acts and does not probe into consumer attitudes will see only the purchase and, subsequently, the rise in prices.

A third factor which makes choice of means difficult is that human behavior has multiple causes. A single cause seldom serves as the sufficient explanation of any act. Since there are usually several substitutes for any given cause, it is rare for any single cause to be *necessary* to a given act. This means that the analyst of human behavior must compare combinations or "packages" of causes in deciding on a strategy, rather than comparing single causes.

Through research a communicator can try to determine how much each item in the package of causes contributes to the desired result. In more technical terms, he can try to discover what percentage of variance each item explains, hoping thereby to estimate what will happen if he changes one or more items in a given package.

Three Added Difficulties

Three added facts about cause-effect relationships in human behavior add to his difficulty. The first difficulty is that the items in a package of causes are seldom independent of one another. Variable *B* may be twice as effective, when combined with Variable *C*, as it was when combined with Variable *A*. These variables, of course, may be elements in the message itself, characteristics of the audience, or variations in the product itself. A drop in price may increase the brewer's sales to a low income group, for example, but it may cause sales to drop in a high income group if its members use price as an index of quality. Ads which talk about "gusto" may attract the hearty male drinker, but may suggest to women that beer is fattening.

There is a technical term for this phenomenon: the researcher says that the two variables *interact* with one another. Because of such interaction, the researcher must test all possible combinations of a given series of variables if he wants definitive results. Such tests may require a great many experimental subjects and be very costly.

The second difficulty arises because most variables can be quantified. Thus one must not only decide whether to include Variable *A* in his package of causes, but he must also decide how much of Variable *A* to include. Doubling the quantity may double the effects. It may produce more than double the effects or it may produce less.

Frequently the researcher finds that a *curvilinear relationship* exists. Up to a certain minimum level or threshhold, Variable *A* seems to have no effect. For a time, increasing the amount of *A* increases the effects. Then, beyond a certain ceiling, increasing the amount of Variable *A* has a diminishing effect, fails to have any effect at all, or even boomerangs by reducing the effects produced by a smaller amount. In beer, this curvilinear effect might operate in everything from flavor to price to repetition in advertising.

Up to a point, an increase in dryness may attract customers.

Up to a point, an increase in price may suggest a desirable increase in quality. Up to a point, repetition of a slogan or a jingle may increase retention of a brand name. But carried too far, dryness may be perceived as bitterness, a high price may be interpreted as extravagance, and repetition may either bring annoyance or indifference.

The third difficulty is that cause-effect relationships in the behavioral sciences are never certain, only probable. Even the best set of causative variables, each present to the optimum degree, cannot produce effects 100% of the time.

Predictions can be improved by increasing the number of variables studied, the number of subjects studied, or by extending the study over a longer period of time, but a source must first decide whether this gain in predictability is worth the extra costs it entails. If he decides it is, he must then choose, at a given level of costs, between probability and precision.

He can increase the probability of being right in his predictions, for example, from 95 times in 100 to 99 times in 100. Or he can increase the precision of his predictions. He can, for example, determine that readership of advertisement A is 9 to 11% higher than that of advertisement B, rather than contenting himself with the finding that advertisement A is 5 to 15% superior.

Increasing probability means decreasing precision, and vice versa, unless he wants to increase his costs. The source thus has to choose between these two conclusions:

> Chances are 95 out of 100 that the recognition score for advertisement A is 9 to 11% higher than the score of advertisement B.

> Chances are 99 out of 100 that the recognition score for advertisement A is 5 to 15% higher than the score of advertisement B.

Two Kinds of Causes

Having made all of these decisions and solved all of these problems, the source at last knows what package of causal variables is best. A closer look at the items in the package shows him that they fall into two classes: those he can manipulate and those he cannot. The latter of these are often called the "environment" of the decision-making process; these are the conditions which the decision maker must accept and to which he must adjust.

Some persons might argue that it is a waste of time to try to determine how much effect these environmental factors have upon results, since there is nothing the source can do about them anyway. This may be true in the short run. The source may, however, find that the variables he can manipulate account for such a small proportion of the variance that he is better advised to give up any attempt at communications. Or he may forget about immediate results and try to change the environment to create more favorable conditions for the changes he seeks and to give him a wider choice of alternatives.

The hot spell which led to increased sales of beer represents an environmental variable, a physical or natural one. The air conditioners which offset the hot spell are also part of the environment, a man-made part. The laws which limit when and where beer may be sold are an aspect of the social environment, as are the regulations and media policies which limit what the brewer's advertisements can say about his beer. Reactions of the brewer's competitors represent a special kind of environmental factor since he cannot control them, but his actions will have an effect on his competitors' behavior and often an effect which can be predicted in advance.

Functions of Subgoals

The complexity of cause-effect relations, which we have been discussing, is only one reason why choosing means appropriate to one's goals is difficult. These means, as we pointed out earlier, also serve as subgoals for all of the persons, including advertising agency and media employees, who must work together if the advertiser is to attain his goal. These subgoals, too, have functions to perform. They help each person to plan his work, help others check on it, and provides a basis for dividing rewards and penalties.

The job of the advertising medium, for example, is to expose prospects to an advertisement at the lowest possible cost. One test of its ability to reach this subgoal is the readership survey which counts the proportion of persons who say they recognize the advertisement. The job of the advertisement itself is to get the advertiser's message read, believed, and acted upon. Both surveys and laboratory tests can shed light on how well the advertisement has done its job, as well as which elements in the advertisement—headlines, illustrations or copy—have done most of the job.

By counting the number of magazine readers who recognize an advertisement, and then by asking all readers whether they have bought the advertised product within the last week, Daniel Starch obtains his "Netapps" (net-ad-produced-purchases) score.

Is Advertisement Recognition Related to Product Purchase?

Calculation of the Netapps score of advertising effectiveness requires four steps:

Step One

Readership score of ad	30%
Percentage of readers who bought product within week	15
Percentage of nonreaders who bought product within week	10

Step Two

Percentage of buyers among readers (30 × 15)	4.5
Percentage of buyers among nonreaders (10 × 70)	7.0
Total buyers	11.5

Step Three

Readership x percentage of readers who bought (30 × 15)	4.5
Readership x percentage of readers who would have bought even if they had not seen advertisement (30 × 10)	−3.0
Net percentage assumed to have bought because of advertisement	1.5

Final Step

Divide net percentage who bought because of advertisement by total number of buyers (1.5/ 11.5) to get—	13% Netapps Score

Starch suggests that this score can be used to compare new and old campaigns, or to compare competitors' campaigns, to compare media, and in deciding how often to repeat an advertisement. Comparisons become even more useful when advertisement costs and product prices are added to the analysis. Note that scores alone, even for a single product, do not predict effectiveness in dollar terms.

Colgate toothpaste

Theme	Seen-associated score	Netapps score	Sales return per ad dollar
Romance	15.5	.77	$3.80
Brush after eating	10.1	1.06	5.59
Romance and research	10.4	.71	4.23
Campbell's Soup			
Frozen soup	38	2.0	$2.99
New soup	64	6.5	6.56
Children	64	5.5	5.47
Ingredients	57	2.3	2.51
Large picture	64	5.1	5.21

The Netapps technique was applied to scores for some 45,000 advertisements in *Life* and the *Saturday Evening Post*, with 400,000 interviews over a 16-year period. As evidence of its validity, Starch reports that the average score for the 352 brands studied was 13.9%, which compares closely with scores in five other studies.

1. A 12.3% average rise in purchases found when a publication began to carry advertisements—ten products.
2. A 14% fall in purchases when a publication stopped carrying ads—80 products.
3. A rise of 11.3% in purchases by readers of an issue with ads as compared to an issue without advertisement—250 cases.
4. Sales 14.3% higher for advertisement readers than nonreaders—426 products.
5. Sales 14.5% higher for advertisement readers than nonreaders, the two groups being paired on pre-exposure buying rates—898 cases.

One caution in interpreting the Starch results is necessary: the reminder that correlation is not causation. Purchasing a product can lead to readership, or vice versa. Moreover, Netapps begins with recognition scores; a person who has bought a product may be more likely to remember an ad, memory of an ad may increase the chance that he will remember making the purchase. The two measures are not necessarily independent.

> —Daniel Starch and Staff, *Measuring Product Sales Made by Advertising* (Mamaroneck, New York: Starch, 1961).

It would be nice if these two "causes"—advertisement and advertising media—did not interact; one's conclusions then could be clear cut. But they do interact. Advertising media may deliver different people, but they may also deliver the same people in a different state of receptivity. Both belief and exposure then become subgoals by which the success of the advertising medium must be measured. Both headline and illustration may influence whether a person sees an advertisement, whether he reads it, whether he remembers it, and whether he believes it.

Frequently there is no single effect which can measure the total contribution made by media buyer or copywriter to an advertisement's success. Frequently the effect one measures has been produced by more than one cause. Causes and effects both tend to be multiple.

Conflict of Subgoals

Another difficulty is that the subgoals set up for different persons may conflict with one another. The brewery's vice-president for production, for instance, may seek to achieve his subgoal of reduced costs by eliminating minor-product differences. Its marketing vice-president, on the other hand, may seek to achieve his subgoal—increased sales—by increasing the number of product variations, so as to meet the tastes of different kinds of beer drinkers. Conflicts of this kind appear an inevitable result of specialization. They are made worse, however, when an executive is rewarded not only for his performance, but in proportion to the performance of other executives, as may happen when they are competing for larger departmental budgets, stock bonuses, or a crack at the presidency.

It is not easy to resolve such conflicts of subgoals. Some top executives may foster them on the grounds that if junior executives are fighting among themselves they represent less of a threat to their superiors. Others may tolerate them, feeling that nothing can be done about them, or because they are unwilling to make a decision which is bound to disappoint at least one of the contestants. Most persons involved would rather not talk about them, if they can avoid doing so. However, if specific goals are to be written down, there must be talk and there must be decisions. Here, then, is another reason why written goals of the kind we have said are needed often do not exist.

Not only do subgoals tend to conflict with one another but, sooner or later, they are likely to become irrelevant to the goal of the firm itself, or antagonistic to it. Once a man is assigned a subgoal, he may seek to attain it by means which his superiors did not foresee and, to the extent they can observe them, do not approve.

A stock clerk in a supermarket, for example, may be given the task of seeing that its shelves are always stocked. The supermarket wants shelves full so that customers will always be able to find what they want, so that sales and turnover will be high, and so that the supermarket's goal of profit can be attained. The clerk's rewards, however, do not depend upon sales, but on whether the shelves are kept full. As a result, customer purchases are not something good from the clerk's viewpoint, but something bad. The more items customers remove from the shelves, the harder he has to work, and the more risk he runs of being criticized. Human ingenuity being what it is, one should not be surprised if a stock clerk shrugs non-committally or even snarls at a customer who asks where to find a particular item.

One solution to this problem is close supervision—but close supervision tends to be self-defeating. Carried to its extreme, it turns the stock clerk or any other kind of employee into a mere robot, so that the firm fails to get the skill and brainpower it is paying for.

Moreover, close supervision itself tends to lower morale to the point where the worker either quits or becomes so skilled at evading supervision that the supervisor must spend more and more time watching him, until he might as well do the job himself.

A more appropriate solution to the problem is a system of rewards which induces the employee to attain his subgoal by means consistent with the overall goal of the firm. The difficulty of finding such a system of rewards represents another reason why businessmen, including communicators, often fail to specify their goals.

Conflict of goals occurs not only between employees of a given firm, as in the instances just cited, but between different firms engaged in a common task. Such conflict, whether recognized or not, is common in advertising, which requires the joint efforts of advertiser and advertising agency.

Both, we assume, are interested in making a profit. Our brewer can make his profit through increased sales. Having determined how much he will spend on advertising, he does not care whether this amount is spent on ten different advertisements in a single magazine or on a single advertisement in ten different magazines. The advertising agency, whose income is based on a 15% commission on media billings, gets the same gross income in each case. Its costs, however, are very different, for they depend on the number of advertisements which must be prepared: ten advertisements when a single magazine is used, one advertisement when ten magazines are used. With so marked a difference in costs and net income, one should not be surprised if the agency's subgoal became inconsistent with the goal of its client. Moreover, none of the ten magazines may be sufficiently alarmed at the loss of a single advertisement to spend time trying to sell itself to the agency or the advertiser. The threat of losing ten advertisements or the hope of gaining ten, on the other hand, may cause a magazine to support the advertising agency's own persuasive efforts.

Media Research

Thus far we have been asking one fundamental question: Having specified the effect one desires, what are some of the problems in determining what causes best produce this result? This, essentially, is the problem of goals as seen from the viewpoint of a top executive in the firm of the advertiser or client.

Much of the research used to guide his decisions, however, is produced in response to a very different question, one posed by the advertising medium which pays for the research. This question is: How can I show that this advertising medium—this cause—produces an effect which is superior to that produced by my competitors?

There are at last three ways in which a medium, or a vehicle* within a given medium, can show it is superior. One way is to show that it has more readers than its competitors. Another is to show that its readers are better than those of its competitors—richer, more likely to purchase the advertiser's product, more likely to influence other customers. The third is to show that its messages are more effective: more likely to be believed, perhaps, or more likely to induce favorable attitudes.

Thus *Life* magazine finances studies which show that its total readers outnumber its subscribers, because those who pay for the magazine hand it on to someone else when they have finished it. The *Saturday Evening Post*, which is less likely to be read in one sitting than is *Life*, will emphasize, through research, the number of separate occasions on which the average reader opens a single issue, even to counting the number of times a given page is exposed (Politz, 1958). *Better Homes and Gardens*, in turn, will show less concern with number of readers or number of exposures than with a reader's responses. It will count the number of readers who save back issues, or clip articles and advertisements from them, or say they follow the magazine's advice (Politz, 1956).

No one magazine supplies the advertiser with a comparison across the full range of possible effects, so that he can determine which of the media effects are the best means to his particular goal, or how best to assign functions among the media and media vehicles available to him. This is a job he must do for himself.

Receiver Function

To do this job, he must take a look at a factor we have ignored up to this point: the people whose behavior he wants to influence. He must take a look at the *receiver* function of subgoals.

We said earlier that subgoals represent signposts along the road by which a communicator can measure his progress. But not all the persons to whom messages are being sent start from the same point

* *True Story* and *Saturday Review* are separate vehicles in the magazine medium; the *New York Times* and *Podunk Weekly Gazette* vehicles in the newspaper medium; the ABC and CBS networks, or their individual affiliated stations, vehicles within the medium of TV.

on this road. Some are at the very beginning; others are well on their way. Different messages are needed with those who have come part way and those who are not sure they want to make the trip at all.

How do receivers differ? Some persons are prospects for our brewer's beer and others are not. The prospect is a person who has a need for the product, whether he realizes it or not, and the ability to pay for it. When the brewer chooses channels for his messages, it is not the total number of *persons* exposed to his message that is important, but the number of *prospects* exposed. Some publications argue that a high proportion of their readers are prospects because only prospects would pay for the publication. Others, both those that charge for subscriptions and those that are free, refuse to send the publication to nonprospects such as persons who do not live in a given region or follow a particular occupation.

Prospects, in turn, may be divided into those who have tried the product and those who have not, and each of these groups may be further subdivided. The brewer can distinguish between satisfied and dissatisfied users, and between nonusers who have a felt need for the product and those who feel no need for it. Each of these four groups calls for a different communications strategy:

1. *Satisfied users* may be sent messages which seek to increase the size of purchase and frequency of use.
2. *Dissatisfied users* represent a major problem, since their own unsatisfactory experience with the product is a much stronger influence on their behavior than any message about it. Moreover, each represents a possible source of messages hostile to the advertiser. Such sources are subject to few of the limits which the law or fear of retaliation place upon his competitors, another possible source of hostile messages. The advertiser is less likely to discover hostile messages produced by dissatisfied users, than those issued by his competitors, yet such messages are likely to be more trusted by the persons who receive them, than any messages which the advertiser himself may transmit.
3. Messages to *nonusers who feel a need for the product* may seek to create a preference for the advertiser's brand, as against the brands of his competitors, or to trigger actual purchase of the product. Messages, of course, are not the only way of influencing behavior of such nonusers. Free samples may induce trial of the product, and trial of the product shifts nonusers into the category of satisfied users.

4. The fourth group, *nonusers who do not feel a need for the product,* may be further subdivided into those who are aware of the product and those who are not. In either case, messages are needed which create a desire for the product; the unaware-nonuser group may require considerable information as well.

The behavior involved in measuring attitudes—often checking choices on a questionnaire—is often important because it is correlated with other behaviors which are difficult to measure or will occur at a later time.

Do People Who "Like" a Brand Buy That Brand?

A panel of 465 housewives in Chicago was interviewed twice during April and June, 1948. The first interview asked about eight products (listed below): what brands they had on hand, which they preferred, and which they intended to buy. The second interview, three weeks later, again asked their brand preferences for two of the products, cleanser and coffee, and their ratings of various such product attributes of these brands as package and price. Between the two interviews, housewives sent in weekly reports of their actual purchases. If intentions and preferences, or intentions and purchases failed to agree, housewives were asked why. Brand preferences were indicated on a 0 to 8 "very unsatisfactory . . . very satisfactory" scale.

Housewives rated only those brands that they had used and could remember well enough to rate: they varied most in knowledge and use of coffee and ice cream, where the number of brands being sold was large. The best predictors of actual purchase were the brand's share of intentions, weighted by *amount* to be purchased, or the brand on hand at the first interview. Most housewives gave the brands they intended to buy the top preference-score of 8 points; the number of such scores also proved a pretty good predictor of actual buying.

Correlation of Actual Purchase with—

Product	No. of Brands	No. of 8's	Inventory	Intentions
Cleanser	11	.93	.98	.99
Coffee	20	.67	.98	.90
Ice cream	15	.75	.87	.91
Peanut butter	11	.98	1.00	.99
Potato chips	10	.96	.99	.98
Mayonnaise	16	.95	.99	.99
Catsup	13	.97	.99	.99
Average		.92	.99	.98

As the author suggests, correlations of overall group behavior shown above would have been the same in the unlikely event of everyone doing the opposite of prediction: a tougher test is to see how individuals behaved. But 66% of the brands bought were those which a housewife gave the only top score in a product class, and 30% had tied for top score. Only 15% of those who stated their intentions made purchases that showed no relations to their intentions. An additional number, 22%, however, bought nothing during the three-week period, and 15% either bought only some of the brands or bought other brands in addition.

Purchases of brands which housewives had not rated, presumably because they did not know and had not seen them, occurred for ice cream and potato chips, both impulse goods. When housewives were asked why they had bought a different brand of cleanser than they had intended to, most said the brand was cheaper. When asked why they had switched brands for coffee, they said "out of stock." About 22% bought less than they had intended to, and 39% bought more. In terms of quantity, estimates were best for peanut butter, purchases exceeding predictions by 12%, and worse for ice cream, purchases being 2.6 times intentions.*

—Seymour Banks, "The Relationships Between Preferences and Purchase of Brands," *Journal of Marketing,* 15:145–157.

Six Stages of Persuasion

In addition to this four-fold classification based on product use and need, audiences can be classified, on the basis of brand knowledge and brand preference, into a six-stage measure of advance toward the advertiser's goal:

1. Some do not know the product exists.
2. Some know of the brand, but not what it claims to do.
3. Some know the claims, but do not accept them.
4. Some accept the claims, but prefer another brand.
5. Some prefer the brand, but have not yet purchased it.
6. And some, oh happy day, have actually bought the advertiser's brand!

Why do such differences in use, need, and awareness exist? Why does a baseline survey find persons scattered along the path of persuasion? One explanation is that some persons have just come into the market. They have just entered their teens and become interested in the latest teenage fad. Others are just married, have just had their first baby, or have just purchased their first set of false teeth.

* Data reprinted from the *Journal of Marketing,* national quarterly publication of the American Marketing Association.

Having entered the market as prospects, they now begin to pay attention to advertisements for products they formerly ignored. Second, persons differ as to the kind and number of advertising messages they are exposed to and the extent to which their behavior is influenced by such nonadvertising communications as the backfence comments of friends and neighbors. Finally, persons vary in their susceptibility to such messages; some are more persuasible than others.

Receivers Have Goals

We have, throughout this chapter, looked at communications, goals, and audiences from the standpoint of the advertiser, the person with something to sell. Communications, however, cannot take place without receivers, as well as sources, and receivers also have goals. Receivers, too, send messages. In many kinds of communication it is impossible to tell sources from receivers. Both the door-to-door salesman and the housewife have goals, and each expects to receive benefits from their communications. Each, in fact, has some minimum benefit which must be met or the communication process will be broken off. This minimum may be expressed in absolute terms. The housewife, for example, may require a reward in terms of information about the product, information about her neighbors, a compliment, or just a break in her daily chores. The minimum level may also be conceived in relative terms. The customer may be willing to let the seller have more than half the benefits of their interchange, however measured, but he may object if the seller tries to take 80 or 90 per cent.

In short, there is a final limit on the goals which a marketing communicator can set for himself. The source's goals must be contained within the range which his audience sees as allowing the audience to achieve minimum goals of its own.

Research Studies

Four of this chapter's studies concern the relation between attitudes and behavior. *Dollard* lists six conditions which affect the relationship; compare his suggestions with those of Hovland on page 516. *Banks* compares results of a taste test with actual sales in one study, tries to estimate brand choices shown on consumer diaries from preference ratings, inventories, and buying intentions in the other. *Starch* takes 16 years of magazine audience studies to relate ad readership to product sales. *Bennett* follows up *Lewin's* comparison of the effect on behavior of talking to and talking with women, in an example of how later studies may refine original insights as to cause and effect in communications.

SUMMARY

1. This is a text in human behavior for students of marketing, adver-

tising, and salesmanship. It seeks to serve the many students who lack time to explore the sociology and psychology of marketing for themselves and to help the few who have time to integrate and apply their knowledge. It also seeks to introduce students, through research summaries, to the journals which can help them keep their education up-to-date in years to come.

2. This is a text in communications and its three basic concepts: source, message, and receiver. Its aim is to show how the marketing manager, as source, achieves his goals through knowledge of his receivers, the purchasers and prospective purchasers of his products, both as individuals and in aggregates.

3. To communicate, the marketing manager must set specific goals: What behaviors of which persons are to be influenced in what direction, to what degree, and within what time limits? The goals must perform two functions: Help the marketer select the best means, and tell him whether he has failed or succeeded.

4. The marketing goals must, in turn, be broken into subgoals. Subgoals are needed to guide the manager's coworkers, to permit periodic check of progress to the main goal, and to recognize differences in the manager's receivers. The manager himself must make the first two levels of decisions, those as to the marketing mix and the communications mix, and retains veto power over decisions of his advertising agency concerning the other two, media mix and message mix.

5. Sales, which can serve as a goal of the marketing mix itself, cannot serve as goals of the three subsequent levels of decision-making since they fail to guide coworkers (the source function), permit check of progress (the time function) or recognize receiver differences (the receiver function). These levels require subgoals determined by direct study of the purchaser himself.

6. Such study finds that cause-effect relationships are complex: causes exist in a chain, the direction of causation may be uncertain, and causation in the behavioral sciences tends to be multiple. Difficulty increases when causes are not independent of one another, are only probable, and are quantifiable. Separation of causes into those the source can control and those, called environment, which he cannot tends to be arbitrary, being based on the time span in which the source chooses to operate.

7. The *source function* of subgoals is complicated because subgoals tend to conflict with one another and may conflict with the main goal itself, both within the marketing manager's firm and between his firm and other participants in the communications process. Much of the data on which the firm's decisions is based is gathered to serve subgoals of other participants.

8. The *receiver function* of subgoals arises because persons differ on whether they are present or potential users of a product, whether they are aware of it, feel a need for it, and have had satisfactory experience with it. These differences arise because of differences in time of entry into the market, in exposure to product messages, and in susceptibility to such messages. Receivers, as well as sources, have goals for communication which represent an additional limit on what the source can expect to achieve through communication.

Two

Goals of Communications: Meanings and Attitudes

Sales are the goal of the marketing manager. To achieve sales, he manipulates the marketing mix. He fashions a *product* whose features, he believes, will appeal to the purchaser. Then he offers it for sale at a *place* which, he hopes, the purchaser will find convenient and at a *price* which, he expects, the purchasers will find attractive. Finally, he seeks to devise messages which, he plans, will create a *perception* of price, product, and place that will cause prospects to purchase his brand.

The freedom of the marketing manager to manipulate the four elements of the marketing mix is not unlimited, however. First, the elements are not independent of one another. Price, for example, may be interpreted as a cue to product quality. Too low a price may hurt the sales of products, such as perfume and drugs, whose quality the purchaser is rarely able to judge. A high price may reassure him that the perfume is suitable as an anniversary gift to his wife or that the cough medicine is safe for his children.

Second, there are objective limits to the marketer's manipulation of price, product, and place. His price, for example, must be related to his costs, to his prospects' incomes, and to what his competitors are charging. Place is limited by the economics of transportation and his ability to persuade retailers to handle his brand. Technology, costs, and even the law may limit the features which can be built into his product.

In contrast to such limits, what the advertiser can *say* about his product seems virtually unlimited. The government, the media, and, to a limited extent, the industry itself bar outright untruth and fraud, but many messages deal with matters of taste, opinion, and psychological satisfaction, where objective (and enforceable) standards of "truth" are lacking. Moreover, the skepticism of the purchaser himself concerning advertising limits its effectiveness, although these limits are offset in turn by the purchaser's indifference. Thus the marketing manager has much freedom in devising messages to attain the subgoal assigned to communications.

Meanings and Attitudes

What is this subgoal assigned to communications?

The marketing communicator wants his messages to produce an internal response in the receiver—a belief or an attitude which will cause the receiver to purchase his product when the opportunity arises.

This internal response may be called the *meaning* of the message to the receiver, if we are talking about messages, or the *attitude* of the receiver, if we are talking about receivers. In this chapter we shall talk about both. Whichever term is used, meaning or attitude, it has three elements: a category, a value for the category, and a name which identifies the category and implies a value for it. When two or more persons use symbols to change ideas—another definition of communications—the "ideas" they exchange consist of categories, their labels, and their evaluations. The terms "corporate image," "product image," and "brand image" represent attitudes of receivers as seen from the marketer's viewpoint.

Thus a brewer wants receivers to put beer into the category of things-to-drink-when-thirsty and he wants his brand given a high value in that category, high enough so that when receivers become thirsty, they will choose it rather than lemonade, iced tea, gin and tonic, or one of the competing brands. The brewer does not expect his brand name to have the *same* meaning for others that it has for him. He, in fact, may be allergic to hops and prefer champagne. The brand, to the brewer, is something-which-moves-out-of-my-possession and something-which-puts-money-into-my-pocket. In a sense this is opposite to the meaning it has for the purchaser. The brewer's aim is not identity of meanings but to be able to specify that receivers have that meaning which will best serve his own goals.

The name of any category bears a close relationship both to the content of the category and its evaluation. The name both reflects and influences what items go into the category, and it both reflects and influences the way the category is valued. To a housewife, broccoli and Brussels sprouts may be part of the category she labels nutritious-green-vegetables-that-should-be-eaten-every-day. To her children, the two items may be just so much spinach-to-be-resisted-at-all-costs.

To change meanings, we must change the category itself, change the value attached to the category, or change both at once. A change in the name given the category may aid in changing the contents or value of the category or it may be a sign of our success in changing contents or value.

Before we can try to influence meanings through changing categories, we need to know something about how and why categories exist. It is the purpose of this chapter to provide that knowledge.

Categories and Expectations

Why do men form categories of things and people, events and ideas? To live at all, men must be able to predict, with more or less accuracy, a greater or lesser distance into the future. To predict, they must build up expectations, based on the observation that events repeat themselves.

Events, however, do not repeat themselves. They are unique. They appear to repeat themselves only because the observer groups them into categories as if they were identical. He stresses similarities and ignores differences. In a philosophical sense, however, two events cannot be identical. No man can step in the same river twice. Both man and river change with time and, indeed, the step itself changes both man and river.

This change may be visible, even drastic. If the river is seven feet deep and the man cannot swim, the single step may be the end of the man. If the man can swim, the depth of the river may be less important than its temperature or width. If the man wants a drink, the visible sediment or invisible bacteria in the water may be more important than the river's depth, width, or temperature.

In short, the attributes which a man observes and uses in constructing categories depend upon what use he plans to make of the categories after they are constructed. If he wants to hit someone on the head, granite and sandstone are both rocks; both can kill. If, on the other hand, he wants to carve a tombstone for his victim, the difference between sandstone and granite may require that they be put in separate categories.

Choice of Attributes

Every object, like the rock and the river, has several attributes. The significant attributes are those which are relevant to the use one wants to make of an object. This prospective use determines which objects are grouped together in a category as functionally equivalent.

A book, for example, may be put, at various times and by various persons, into the same category as a sofa cushion, a refrigerator,

---

Men group objects into categories as tools to some goal. If we know their goals, we can predict their categories, or vice versa. Here is a case of vice versa, based on a study of children in three different cultures.

Out of the Mouths of Babes—Insight into a Society

A professor at the American University of Beirut in Lebanon asked children what 16 different things are used for. His subjects included 120 American children, 58 Sudanese, and 900 Lebanese children.

Here are some of the larger differences found, object by object:

Mouth. Eating led, but 39% of Americans and only 14% of Sudanese said talking. On the other hand, 50% of the Sudanese said eating *and* drinking, but only 3% of the Americans.

Hands. For eating, said 33% of Sudanese but only 6% of Americans.

Mother. Providing food, said 51% of Lebanese, but only 16% of Americans.

Father. Working and earning money, said 76% of the Lebanese, but only 10% of Sudanese; providing care and assisting family said 45% of Sudanese but only 9% of Lebanese.

Boy. Going to school or working, said 61% of Lebanese, 39% of Americans, but only 24% of Sudanese. Playing, said 34% of Americans, none of the Sudanese, and only 9% of Lebanese.

Girls. Going to school or working, said 78% of Lebanese, 43% of Sudanese, and 40% of Americans.

Trees. Food, said 69% of Lebanese, (in a land of olives, dates, and almonds); and 34% of American children living in the same land. For climbing, said 12% of Americans but virtually none of the others.

Wood. Fire, said 43% of Americans and 5% of Sudanese; building, said 34% of Americans and 14% of Sudanese; gates, said 17% of Sudanese and none of the others.

Dogs. For guarding said more than 60% of Lebanese and Sudanese, but only 16% of American children, of whom 49% preferred the answer "pets."

Cats. For catching mice, said 50 to 60% of Lebanese and Sudanese; for pets, said 52% of Americans.

Birds. For eating, said 37% of Lebanese; for enjoyment, said 33% of Americans.

—Wayne Dennis, "Uses of Common Objects as Indicators of Cultural Orientations," *Journal of Abnormal and Social Psychology,* 55:21–28.

a newspaper, or a pail of sand. If one wants to prop open a door for example, either the book or the pail of sand will serve. If he wants to bring a youngster's head above his plate at supper, he can seat the child on a book or on a sofa cushion. If he wants to read while his wife does the dishes, he can hide behind a newspaper or bury his nose in a book. If he is paying a personal property tax, or collecting fire insurance, books and refrigerators will go down on the list together.

Thus the object "book" has as many meanings as there are purposes of people who want to use the book. Moreover, note that in each of the instances just cited, the category into which the book was put, was based on a different attribute. When the book was used to prop open a door, the important attribute was weight, which it shared with the pail of sand. When it was used to elevate a child at the table, the important attribute, shared with the cushion, was thickness. The book's verbal content became important when it was placed in the reading material category, along with the evening newspaper, and its cost became important for taxes and insurance.

Let us take another example. In marketing, an automobile may be an impulse good, a shopping good, a specialty good, a convenience good, or a consumer durable. Most of us treat it as a consumer durable and a shopping good; high in price, relative to our income, we buy carefully and use it for several years. A stunt driver, on the other hand, may treat it as a producer's raw material, using up a different car at each performance. A wealthy person may buy a car on impulse, as the rest of us buy popcorn or peanuts. Some persons treat the car as a specialty good, refusing to drive anything other than a Volkswagen or a Lincoln. Thus, the way we act toward the car determines the way we categorize it. The way we behave toward it determines the attributes we use to treat some cars as equivalent and others as different.

Experiments have shown that a person can construct a category without realizing he has done so or being able to tell what attributes he is using to form the category. By giving another person rewards, we can induce him to group objects into categories of our choosing, again without his being aware that he has done so. This method of category creation gives an advantage to the source, since the receiver who is unaware of what is happening is unable consciously to resist being influenced.

Most of our categories are learned from others, deliberately. Frequently we learn the label for the category first, and then more or less formally define the contents of the category it names. Sometimes a single attribute will indicate whether an object belongs in a given category. Sometimes one must combine attributes in one of at least three ways:

1. *Joint attributes.* Three sides *and* one 90-degree angle are needed to make a right triangle; a human being must be female *and* have a child to be a mother.

2. *Alternative attributes.* In baseball, a strike may be a pitch which the batter swings at and misses, *or* one which he hits but falls foul, *or* one that passes over the plate and is between knee-high and shoulder-high.

3. *Related attributes.* A fat man is a man whose weight is above a certain ratio to his height.

Two kinds of attributes are used, either alone or in combination, in making categories:

1. *Physical or formal.* All shovels fall within a range of shapes and sizes; color and weight may be critical attributes for other objects.

2. *Functional.* All shovels share certain uses; they can be used to dig holes or to fill them up.

Consumer reactions are important in determining what features should be put into a product and what features, already there, should be publicized. But how does one determine customer reactions?

What Kinds of Coffee and Cleanser Do Housewives Want?

Seymour Banks asked Chicago housewives what interested them most when they bought cleanser and coffee. From their responses he drew up a list of six attributes of cleanser and four of coffee. He then asked a panel of 465 other housewives to rate a series of cleanser and coffee brands on each of the attributes.

The attribute scores for eight leading brands of each product then were related to actual brands purchased by the housewives over a three-week period, and to their overall preferences for each brand on a 0 to 8 scale running from "very unsatisfactory" to "very satisfactory." Here are the results. (Banks does not report the actual correlation between attribute score and preference or purchase, but he gives the attribute showing highest correlation an arbitrary score of 1.00 and rates the others in terms of this base. Only statistically significant figures are reported in this table.)

Relation between Product Attribute and Brand Preferences

	Cleanser			Coffee	
	Preference	Purchase		Preference	Purchase
Package	.10	—	Package	—	—
Ability to			Flavor	1.00	1.00
clean	1.00	1.00	Many cups		
Grittiness	.25	—	per lb	.10	—
Harsh to hands	—	.27	Price knowl-		
Odor	—	—	edge	.05	.43
Price knowl-					
edge	.10	.41			

As Banks warns, these findings relate only to the range in attributes available in the market at the time. Very good or very bad coffee packages, for example, might make a difference not shown up here. Housewives made their ratings on the basis of what they remembered. They did not look at packages, feel cleanser, or taste coffee. And the attributes scored themselves are complex; a cleanser's efficiency may depend on detergent and abrasive effects.*

> —Seymour Banks, "The Relationships Between Preference and Purchase of Brands," *Journal of Marketing*, 15:145–157.

* Figures reprinted from the *Journal of Marketing*, national quarterly publication of the American Marketing Association.

Causes of Confusion

Trouble arises when attributes which are obvious are also irrelevant Two bright red cars—a Ford and a Chevrolet—may stand out in traffic, but if we are trying to identify different makes, their conspicuous color only gets in the way. Similarly, if we are looking for a secretary who can type, blonde hair and 36-24-33 dimensions may confuse our perception. Conspicuous categories may cause us to build categories around attributes which are imperfect, merely because they are obvious. For a long time, for example, we tended to think of books as having harder covers, more pages, and smaller pages than magazines. These attributes caused confusion when magazines like *Readers' Digest* began appearing with small pages, when magazines like *Heritage* began appearing in hard covers and paperback books appeared in soft covers. This confusion might easily have been avoided if we had used the single, perfect, criterion attribute employed by librarians and postal authorities: the appearance of a month, year, and volume number which characterizes each issue of a magazine as a "serial" publication, but which is lacking in a book.

Trouble also arises when people use the same object in different ways but refer to it by the same name. To a postal clerk, the significant thing about a stamp may be its face value, the nation of origin, and the fact that it has not been used previously. A philatelist, on the other hand, may also be interested in the stamp's color, cancellation, watermark, and perforations. To a home owner, the significant attribute of the object he calls a tree may be the shade its leaves provide. An artist, on the other hand, may be interested in the leaves' shape and color. An entomologist may be interested in the insects feeding on the leaves and an ornithologist in the concealment the leaves provide for nesting birds. A lumberjack may be so busy with other attributes that he may pay no attention to the leaves at all. Although each calls what he sees "leaves" the leaves each sees are not the same.

Names cause difficulty when persons apply different labels to the same category. If the names are in different languages, communication may break down completely. Since names cause difficulty, why do we use them?

Giving names to objects, putting labels on our categories, does save time. We do not have to go through the whole process of constructing a category every time we want to think or talk about it. Nor do we have to build up all of our own categories; we can "inherit" them from our fathers and pass them on to our children.

Of course we may mislead ourselves by seeing differences or identities where they do not exist, or we may mislead others. Sometimes this is done deliberately. A mystery writer, for example, depends upon such deception, delighting in the fact that objects with the same physical attributes may serve different functions. Thus the "icicle" of his first chapter turns out, in the last chapter, to have been used as a dagger. Often, however, the confusion is accidental. I may ask for a book, when I really "mean" that I want a door prop, and be disappointed when I am handed a thin volume of poetry. Or I may ask for a door prop in a home whose walls are covered with books only to be told that there are no door props to be had.

In similar fashion we can make our request for a book more specific by indicating the larger category to which it belongs: "I would like a book to use as a door prop." Or, beginning with the more general category, we can suggest a specific item in it: "I need a door prop;

an empty bottle would be fine." Suggesting attributes of both form and function help get our meaning across.

Cures for Confusion

One way of clearing up confusion is by putting the word in question in context. Context may tell us the part of speech involved, or it may suggest a specific word. Thus if we read the sentence, "The *bof nergled* all night long" we assume that *"bof"* is the name of something—boy, dog, or burbling brook—and that *nergled* represents an action. Similarly, when we see the sentences, "The car ran off the _____ into a ditch" or "That nasty _____ next door barked all night," we are very likely to supply "road" or "highway" for the first blank and "dog" for the second. We may be wrong, of course. The car may actually have run off a bridge, and the nasty animal next door could be a fox. Nevertheless, we play the probabilities, for words build up expectancies for one another, as well as for objects, people, and events.

Another way of clearing up confusion is to put the category itself in context by using the "ladder of abstraction"—a series of categories, each more inclusive than the previous one. Suppose we ask, for example, what a student *really* means when he says, "I do not like my course in calculus." We can enter this item at a midpoint on the ladder, and then proceed in either direction, as shown below.

1. I did not like today's lecture in calculus.
2. I do not like any of the lectures in calculus.
3. *I do not like this calculus course: lectures, text, exams.*
4. I do not like any mathematics course at this university.
5. I do not like any mathematics anywhere OR I do not like any of this university's courses, no matter what the subject.

Then, by a series of questions, we can begin to find out whether the student's objection is that which he originally stated, whether it is higher on this ladder (more specific), or lower (more general). Until we have done so, neither he nor we can be clear as to what to do about his original comment.

Communication sometimes breaks down because men fail to distinguish between the decisions they make about which attributes are to be used to form a category (and, therefore, which objects will land in a given category) and the decision they make as to which label to attach to the category. The reason for such confusion is apparent. Usually the formation of a category and its labeling occur simultaneously. Indeed, we do not create most of our categories, but learn from others, name and category together as if they were inseparable. Nor is it easy to find the physical objects on which a category is based, since so many of our categories are higher-order groups, made up of the names of lower-order categories.

To help reduce confusion, experts in meaning have developed certain symbols which bring labels into closer correspondence with categories (Chase, 139-142):

1. *Index numbers.* Thus a consumer may distinguish between *advertising*$_1$, such as the yellow pages, which he seeks, and *advertising*$_2$, such as the television commercial, which forces itself on him, whether he wants it or not. Index numbers may also be used to indicate change over time: the author $_{1966}$ is considerably balder than the author $_{1956}$. Index numbers may also indicate that the meaning of an event depends on the time at which it occurs: barking dog $_{3\ p.m.}$ is a less obnoxious beast than barking dog $_{3\ a.m.}$

2. *Quotation marks.* These may be used to indicate that the category referred to is so high on the ladder of abstraction, and has so many subcategories contained within it, that agreement between any two persons on the category's contents may be difficult. Examples are "free enterprise," "Americanism," and, for most readers of this book, "advertising" itself.

3. *etc.* When this useful abbreviation is added to the list of the objects that make up any category, or their attributes, the useful point is made that no such list can be complete. Some attribute not mentioned may be crucial to some individual, or may become so at some time in the future.

4. *Hyphens.* These are used to suggest that when we talk about the elements in a structure or process, the elements themselves represent arbitrary divisions we have forced upon reality. In life itself, body-mind and time-space do not occur separately; in communications, source-message-channel-receiver can exist only in combination with one another. To analyze, we must break up such processes; to act, however, we must put the pieces back together again.

These, and the other devices and techniques described in this chapter are useful when communication breaks down because the categories which people are using and the names they give them are too different from one another.

Ambiguity Is Needed

Categories can never be completely identical, however. People vary too much for that, both in their past experiences and in what they regard as important, true, beautiful, and good. Communication depends upon the optimum level of ambiguity, of categories which do not mesh completely. Too much precision can disrupt communication completely.

Do people differ in the kinds of categories they apply to the world about them? Yes, says this study—some people tend to use wide categories and others to use narrow categories.

How Fast Do Birds Fly, How Long Is a Turtle?

In this study, responses from 750 college students were used to develop a 20-item measure of *category width*. It consisted of items like the following, in which students were given the mean for some phenomenon and asked to pick one of four values as the top and the other as the bottom of the range from which the mean was derived.

Ornithologists tell us the best guess of the average speed of birds in flight would be about 17 mph. What do you think:
  a. Is the speed of the fastest bird 25, 105, 73, or 34 mph?
  b. Is the speed of the slowest bird 10, 2, 12, or 5 mph?
The average population of South American countries is 8.6 million. What do you think is the population of:
  a. The most populated country? 11.2, 54.7, 23.6, or 129.1 million?
  b. The least populated country? 7000, 6.2 million, 2.4 million, or 29,000?

Each of the alternatives was scored 0, 1, 2, or 3. The more distant it was from the mean, the higher the score. High scores were positively correlated (.26) with college entrance quantitative scores, the coefficient being significant at the .01 level.

Scores on the test also correlated with behavior: 26 subjects were asked to choose among lines drawn on a blackboard, among sets of weights, and among laboratory-produced sounds to estimate limits in the ranges of five categories not included in the scale: lengths of pheasants and turtles, weights of ostrich eggs, the pitch of women's voices, and factory whistles. Behavior and test scores gave a rank correlation coefficient of .57, significant at the .01 level. Subjects using wide categories also tended to choose more self-descriptive adjectives from a 300-word list; the correlation of .30 was low but significant at the .01 level.

A comparison of 218 men and 116 women gave men an average category-width score of 72, and women a score of 64, the difference being significant at the .001 level.

Using centroid factor analysis on scores of 270 subjects, the author found that there were actually two dimensions within his scale. One was quantitative, involving time and speed data like the first item cited above. The other, characterized by the second item cited, was nonquantitative, grouping such varied items as births, churches, and submarines.

—Thomas F. Pettigrew, "The Measurement and Correlates of Category Width as a Cognitive Variable," *Journal of Personality* 26: 532–533.

Most of us, for example, do not care whether the aunt whose funeral you just attended was your father's sister, mother's sister, father's brother's wife, or mother's brother's wife. Some societies, and the people in them, do care, however, and so the anthropologist who wants to study them has to develop such special terms as *FaBroWi*, thereby becoming incomprehensible to the rest of us by developing too fine a category system.

Most of us, on the other hand, do think it important to distinguish among aviators, the airplanes they pilot, and butterflies. We put them in separate categories and pin separate labels on the categories. To the Hopi-speaking Indian, the differences are unimportant; at least, one label suffices for all three.

Context, of course, can reduce the need for separate names, to the point where the dictionary can list more than 100 definitions for a word like "run" and more than 300 for "take." Context can change the meaning of a word drastically, so that a "few" snowflakes may mean thousands, but a "few" rubies may mean a half dozen or less.

Frequent use of a category, on the other hand, will increase the need to give it a separate label. Thus colloquial English, which lumps together parents' offspring without regard to sex in the word "children," lacks a convenient term for the children to use in referring to one another. They must use the phrase "brothers and sisters." The psychologist, however, who must refer to such relationships frequently, has invented the word "sibling," and the sociologist, who wants to refer to an individual's relations with persons of similar age or station in life uses the word "peers." With frequent use, phrases tend to collapse into single words. What started out as a "television receiving set" soon became "the TV," and in communications the reactions-of-an-audience-which-modify-the-subsequent-messages-produced-by-a-source was soon labeled "feedback."

When distinctions become important to us, we tend to give each

To think or to communicate to others, men must form categories and put labels on them. An individual is given both categories and labels when he learns his native tongue. How, then, does language influence what he sees and how he organizes his perceptions?

Language Affects Children's Perceptions

In the Navaho language, when one handles an object, the verb that describes his actions must vary with the shape of the object: a string, a stick, and a piece of paper thus require different verbs. Although the Navaho has no labels for the category of objects covered by each kind of verb, 3-year-olds use the verbs correctly, indicating that they must be sorting out objects on the basis of their shape. If so, they contrast with children in the United States and Europe who first learn to distinguish objects on the bases of size and color rather than shape.

To test this possibility, Joseph Casagrande took 135 Navaho children —59 of them Navaho-speaking, 43 English-speaking, and 33 bilingual. He showed them 10 pairs of objects, each of which differed in [two aspects, such as size, color, or shape. One pair, for example, consisted of a yellow stick and a piece of blue rope. Then he showed them a third object—a yellow rope—and asked the pupils which of the original pair it most resembled.

In the first four trials listed in the following table the third (test) object fell in the same verb category as the *a* object of the original pair. In all four cases many more Navaho-speaking pupils chose the *a* object, with a statistical significance beyond the .01 level by chi square in a 2×2 table. (Smaller differences, in the right direction but not statistically significant, were obtained in shape-size and shape-color comparisons.) When only size and color were involved, a difference not relevant to Navaho verb forms, both groups of pupils tended to pair on the basis of color, as shown by the two remaining cases in the table.

Original Pair		Test Object	Per cent of *a* Choices	
			Navaho Speech	English Speech
a	*b*		(*N* of 59)	(*N* of 43)
yellow rope	blue stick	blue rope	71%	40%
blue rope	yellow stick	yellow rope	71	40
yellow stick	blue cylinder	blue stick	71	44
yellow stick	blue oblong	blue stick	72	44
medium yellow cube	small blue cube	medium blue cube	21	23
medium white cube	large blue cube	medium blue cube	15	14

Since both groups of pupils came from a Navaho reservation, one might expect that a similar study of 47 Boston children would show an even more marked preference for color rather than form than did the English-speaking Navahos. Just the opposite occurred. Here are the results, with a breakdown by age of child. Figures represent the per cent of choices of *a* objects in the seven pairs in which shape is contrasted with size or color—those in which the Navaho-language is expected to induce a preference for shape.

Age of child	Navaho children who speak Navaho	English	Boston children
5	57	38	91
6	64	34	93
7	71	36	100
8	74	49	83
9–10	81	75	93

The Boston children out-Navahoed the Navahoes! The authors explain this by the likelihood that Boston's youngsters have played with formboard toys, which emphasize form and size over color, and that a preference for form has been found in the upper middle class from which these children come. In similar fashion, they say, increasing experience with *language* leads to increased preference for *a* pairings as shown by the rise in percentages for both columns of Indian children.

—John B. Carroll and Joseph B. Casagrande, "The Function of Language Classifications in Behavior," in Eleanor Maccoby et al., *Readings in Social Psychology* (New York: Holt, Rinehart and Winston, 1958.)

important and distinguishable object, event, person, or idea a name of its own. Once the distinction has a name, the difference itself seems easier to perceive. Thus Eskimos and skiers, to whom variations in snow are important, learn to identify differences which many of us do not care about and have no names for. If our attention is called to these snowy distinctions, we can see the differences. Lacking names for them, however, we have to resort to makeshift phrases. We are likely to disagree with one another in the phrases we apply to such occasionally glimpsed, unimportant differences and, indeed, to use one phrase ourselves this time and invent another the next time we have to refer to the phenomenon in question.

These conditions, in turn, make us highly susceptible to influence from any communicator who wants us to put the object in question into a particular category, to pin a particular label on it, and to evaluate it in a particular way. He does not have to displace an existing category, but he can supply one where none existed previously Television sets, for example, soon became something unique, not just modified radios or a new kind of movie theater. We developed attitudes toward television. If Martians were to land on earth, we might well develop a new category, not just treat them as a new variety of Africans or Chinese.

Labels Express Values

The name given a category does more than identify it; it also tends to suggest how the speaker feels toward the category. The adjectives "firm," "stubborn," and "pigheaded" may be applied to identical behaviors. The choice among them tells less about how the person being described actually behaved than how the speaker evaluates him and his behavior. Words vary in the extent to which they reflect the speaker's values for a category. Those which reveal little of his values and more about the contents of the category we call *denotative*. These are words like "six-foot," "soldier," and "walks." As the labels become more evaluative and reveal more of a speaker's feelings, we say they are *connotative*. These are words like "handsome," "hero," and "strides." If source and receiver agree on the objects which make up a category, the referents for the label, then the words they use to label the category are denotative—for them. Ordinarily it is easier to agree on values for objects which are physical than on ideas, so that the labels for categories of ideas tend to be connotative.

Although we speak of words themselves as denotative or connotative, this is only because on the average we use them in that way. In actuality connotation represents a relationship among category, label, and value. The word "soldier" becomes connotative if it is used to describe a resistance fighter to a member of the occupying forces, who regards this "soldier" as a "bandit." Words usually regarded as denotative may be selected and combined in such a way as to cause a receiver to attach a predetermined value judgement to the category they label. This technique is an effective one, insofar as it helps conceal the fact that the source is imposing his value upon the receiver. The clever advertiser selects the facts about the product and lets the purchaser supply the adjectives. The values given a category and its label may be positive values, negative or neutral. The position of neutrality, the point at which positive values change to negative, and vice versa, is an important one, and one that involves several complications.

Two Kinds of Neutrality

One must distinguish between two different kinds of neutrality—the neutrality of ambivalence and the neutrality of indifference. Some measures of meanings and attitudes make this distinction but many do not. The indifferent person may not have a category, or he may attach so little importance to it that he has no value for it. Ambivalent neutrality, in which pro's and con's are evenly balanced, is often unstable and temporary; messages, for example, may shift the balance one way or the other. On the other hand, if the category is an important one, the conflict of pro's and con's may cause the person in such a position to repress the attitude object, to force it out of his consciousness. Or the conflict may cause him to avoid or flee from situations in which the category is brought to his attention or in which he is under pressure to make and express a clearcut choice, pro or con.

Each type of neutrality requires a different communication strategy.

Selection of audiences occurs in at least two stages. First, each medium reaches only a part of the population. Second, the audience for each medium tends to select from its content that material of highest interest.

Self Selection and Mass Media Audiences*

In September 1947, two world affairs organizations in Cincinnati began a 6 months campaign to inform residents of facts about the United Nations. By March, every school child in the city had been given literature on the UN to take home, PTA programs had reached 12,868 members, and weekday church schools had reached 14,000 children. A single radio station broadcast 150 spot announcements a week on the UN, and nearly 60,000 pieces of literature were distributed; newspapers played up UN news for the entire 6 months.

At the start of the campaign and again at its end in March, the National Opinion Research Center took surveys; it interviewed 745 Cincinnatians in September and re-interviewed 80% of them in March, as well as reaching a new sample of 758 in March.

The second survey showed a sharp rise in interest in international affairs. When asked what first came to mind when they thought of problems facing the United States, only 47% mentioned an *international* problem in September, compared with 74% in March. However, a concurrent NORC nationwide survey showed the same thing happening in the United States. If one excluded Russia from the results, the number of persons expressing keen interest in international affairs was almost identical at the start and the end of the six-month campaign. It was the cold war, not the campaign, which caused the change in interest. Less than one-half of 1% claimed membership in either of the world affairs organizations. Only about 10% even knew they existed.

Respondents who indicated interest in the UN were more likely to express an "internationalist" belief. They expressed this belief at every level of information.†

	Well Informed		Poorly Informed		Uninformed	
	In- terest	No in- terest	In- terest	No in- terest	In- terest	No in- terest
1. Mentioned an inter- national problem	64%	43%	54%	40%	45%	27%
2. Favored United States taking active part in world affairs	86	62	82	65	55	37
3. Favored international control of atomic bomb	78	63	68	60	43	37

Moreover, beliefs which respondents expressed in September, were found related to the number of media in which they recalled seeing mention of the UN campaign over the next 6 months.

If they said in September . . . U.S. should take an active part in world affairs.	. . . then over the next 6 months, they reported exposure to campaign		
	In no medium	In at least one medium	In 3 or more media
	46%	73%	81%

Exposure (and interest) were related to certain demographic characteristics, with these percentages reporting exposure to the campaign in at least three media:

Education		Age		Sex	
College	68%	21–39 years	44%	Men	43%
High school	43	40 and more	32	Women	34
Grammar school	17				

—Shirley A. Star and Helen MacGill Hughes, "Report on an Educational Campaign: The Cincinnati Plan for the United Nations," *American Journal of Sociology*, 55:389–400.

* Information. 15% uninformed could name none of the main purposes of the UN, 50% poorly informed could identify no more than 3 of 6 items on UN responsibilities, and well informed could identify 4 or more. Interested persons expressed "keen interest" in at least two out of four international topics.

† Data reprinted from the *American Journal of Sociology* by permission of the University of Chicago Press. Copyright 1950 by the University of Chicago.

In the neutrality of indifference, the communicator may face very little competition; his main goal must be to show the receiver why this category is an important one. One way to do this is to show that it is a means to some goal which he already regards as important. In the neutrality of ambivalence, on the other hand, competition limits the communicator's freedom and effectiveness. His best tactic here may be to try to create a new category in which this conflict is less apparent.

The neutral point becomes important when we realize that positive and negative values exist in degrees. A small change which moves a person across the neutral point may be much more significant, practically, than a larger change which occurs on one side of the neutral point. A political candidate may not care if a supporter shifts from a strong to a mild or weak position. The supporter will still vote for him (though he may contribute less to the campaign chest). But a shift of the same size which moves a weak supporter across the line into the opposition camp may decide the election. Crossing the neutral point is especially important in communications since it brings into operation a tendency toward "selective exposure" to media and face-to-face messages.

Once committed, however lightly, to the opposition, the factor of "selective exposure" begins to operate. The person now tends to seek out messages and persons who support his new position, and avoid those who support his previous position. Over time, his new views are likely to become stronger—once he has crossed the neutral point.

In general, it appears easier to move a person away from the neutral point than across it. Usually we think of the process of attitude change as involving a gradual weakening of values, either negative or positive, and movement of the person toward and, finally, across the neutral point. However, there also appear to be cases of "conversion" in which an individual passes quickly from one extreme view to its "opposite." In such cases it may help to view the attitude scale not as a straight line but as a circle with a slight gap in it. The distance between the two ends of the line which makes up the circle thus is less than the distance from either end to the midpoint of the line; the person responds to attitude-changing influences by taking the shortest route—leaping across the gap itself.

The neutral point on an attitude scale can be designated in several ways. There is the arbitrary point designated by the scale maker; on a seven-point scale, the fourth position represents such a point. Three different locations are determined by the actual responses of the group to the scale. One is the midpoint of the range actually used; if actual ratings on a seven-point scale ranged from three to seven, then this midpoint will be position number five. If, on the other hand, we assume that most persons are neutral on most issues, we can designate the mode, the most popular value, as the midpoint of the scale. To find a third location, we correlate attitude scales with some behavior which the scale is supposed to predict. The neutral point then is that point on the scale which best separates persons who perform the criterion behavior from those who do not.

Ranges of Acceptance

Viewed from the standpoint of an individual receiver, the neutral point on a scale represents the breaking point between the positions he finds acceptable and those which he rejects.

Different persons designate different points on the scale as representing the breaking-point between "pro" and "con" positions. Thus they may differ markedly in the number of positions they find acceptable (Sherif and Hovland). Persons of extreme views, for example, tend to have very narrow ranges of acceptance and very wide ranges of rejection. Unless another's view comes very close to his own, such a person will tend to see him as an opponent, although persons of less extreme views would lump the two together. This rule appears to hold for many different kinds of attitudes and for extremists at both ends, pro and con.

Although the extremity of a view and the intensity with which it is held may be measured separately, persons at both extremes of an attitude scale tend to hold their views intensely. Those between these extremes vary in the intensity of their views, depending on the attitude and how it is measured. Thus, plotting the neutral point may be determined in still another way by intensity on a vertical scale and extremity of views on a horizontal scale. When this is done, we find some attitudes are V-shaped and others are U-shaped. In the former, intensity rises steeply on either side of the neutral breaking point between pro and con. In the latter, or U-shaped attitudes, intensity may be low for some distance on either side of the neutral point; it might be better to refer to neutrality as a zone rather than a point.

The neutral point, viewed as an index to a receiver's range of acceptance, helps answer the question of whether a source should advocate a large change, on the theory that his results represent a constant fraction of what he attempts, or ask a small change, on the theory that small steps are easiest to take and that, if he asks too much, he may get nothing.

Recent research suggests that the source should advocate the largest possible change that falls within his receiver's range of acceptance since the receiver will perceive positions within the range as closer to his own than they appear to an outside observer or to the source himself. At the same time, however, the source must avoid advocating a position which falls outside this range, since the receiver will magnify its distance from his own position. Since persons of extreme views have narrow ranges of acceptance, the source should advocate small changes for them. He can seek larger changes, however, with persons elsewhere on the scale.

Should a source ask for a bigger change than he expects to get, as much as he thinks safe, or the smallest amount that will serve his needs?

If You Want More, Demand More

Fifty-one high school pupils were asked to give their views on a dozen different questions ranging from the chances that atomic-produced electricity would be lighting homes within five years to the desirability of forcing persons to vote in presidential elections. They were also asked, for each issue, whose opinion they would respect most.

A month later, pupils got the same questionnaire again and, with it, a check mark indicating the views on each issue of the authority they said they would respect most. On any given issue, a third of the subjects were told that authorities were close to their own position; another third that authorities were a little further away; and a third that they were quite distant. Here's an example:

1. All things considered, Washington was a greater president than Lincoln.
   Agree strongly   (7-point scale)   Disagree strongly
2. Of the following authorities which group's opinion would you respect most in reference to this question?
   __Teachers __Historians __Parents

If a pupil *agreed strongly*, and checked *teachers*, then teachers would be shown as agreeing moderately for one-third of the subjects, as agreeing slightly for one-third, and as disagreeing slightly for one-third. If a pupil *disagreed moderately*, and checked *parents*, then the successive views attributed to parents would be: slight disagreement, slight agreement, moderate agreement. The absolute amount of change increased with the amount demanded, but the amount of change produced relative to that sought decreased with the amount demanded:

Amount of change advocated

	Slight	Moderate	Marked
Mean change score (after-before)	88	1.25	1.75
Change obtained as per cent of change sought	88%	62%	58%

This study avoids two problems: the likelihood that persons at extreme positions on a scale hold their views more fixedly and the chance that a ceiling effect obtains—that there is no room for them to move to a still more extreme position. The issues concerned were not ego involving and the communicators were all trustworthy ones.

—Carl I. Hovland and Henry A. Pritzker,
"Extent of Opinion Change as a Function
of Amount of Change Advocated," *Journal of Abnormal and Social Psychology*,
54:257–261.

Changing Categories

Changing the value attached to a category appears most easily done when we also change the category itself. This can be done in two ways. A source can show that an old category should be split up, some parts retaining the negative values, but others—those important to the source—being given favorable values. Or a source can show that the old, disliked category is actually part of a larger category which includes other attitude objects that his receivers like. The first of these two strategies usually appears to be the easier.

"Anchors" make a source appear less extreme, more trustworthy—but less effective.

"Extreme" Source Proves More Effective

One group of subjects read an appeal by an anonymous source for a punitive policy toward delinquents. Another group read the same message but preceded by two opinions statements, representing extreme attitudes—"anchors"—of leniency and punitiveness. Each subject then filled out two forms of a scale of attitudes toward punishment of delinquents: first to indicate what they thought the source's attitude was and second to indicate their own attitudes. A control group, which read no message, rated the first form in terms of the extremity of each item, and the second by giving their own attitudes.

Using a scale on which high scores indicated a punitive attitude, the experimenter found that the group given "anchors" judged the source as being more trustworthy and less extreme than the other group. This same group also was less affected by his message. (An after-only design was used with random assignment of subjects to conditions, so that all groups were assumed to start with the same pre-message attitudes.)

Group	Subjects' mean score	Relative change*	Estimate of source's score
"Anchors"	6.2	15%	10.7
"No anchors"	5.2	21%	13.3

—Walter Weiss, "The Relationship Between Judgments of a Communicator's Position and Extent of Opinion Change," *Journal of Abnormal and Social Psychology* 56:380–384.

*Average change divided by amount advocated.

It is the one used whenever a brewer suggests that his brand is new and different, without the bitterness or calories which made customers reject other brands. The second technique is that used whenever critics of advertising are told that, if they believe in free enterprise, they must accept advertising, since the two are inseparable.

An attitude object may be valued for itself or as a means of attaining another object. In the latter case, its value depends on (a) its efficacy in achieving the desired object and (b) the value of this end-object itself.

Should Communists Be Allowed to Address the Public?

Undergraduates at two institutions in Michigan checked a 5-point approve-opposed scale on the issue of allowing members of the Communist party to address the public: 17 were strongly opposed, 31 moderately opposed, 44 moderately approving, and 25 showed extreme approval. Then, 3 to 5 weeks later, they were given a set of 35 cards, each with a value on it such as "people being well educated" and "keeping promises made to others." They sorted these twice: first on a 21-point scale indicating how important each value was as a source of satisfaction, and second on an 11-point scale indicating whether allowing Communists to speak would aid or hinder the value in question. (All three scales produced reliability coefficients of .72 to .89, significant at or beyond the .01 level.)

A third score was produced by multiplying scores on the latter two scales. Thus a subject might rate "having a steady income" as having an importance of 10. If he thought that allowing Communists to speak would completely block his getting a steady income, he would have a −5 instrumental score; if he thought allowing Communists to speak would assure his getting a steady income, he would have an instrumental score of 5. In the first case, this would give a product score of −50, in the latter one of 50. Scores were summed for each subject algebraically over all 35 value items.

The results were put into three 3 × 4 tables, the four groups of the original 5-point scale being subdivided according to their "importance," "instrumentality," and "product" (instrumentality x importance) scores.

When importance was held constant, instrumentality proved a good predictor of attitude scores, producing chi squares significant at the .001 or .01 levels. When instrumentality was held constant, importance proved a good predictor with chi squares significant at or beyond the .05 level. When the two predictors were combined, chi squares were significant at the .001 level.

> —Milton J. Rosenberg, "Cognitive Structure and Attitudinal Affect," *Journal of Abnormal and Social Psychology,* 53:367–372.

Whenever we try to change the evaluation of one category by relating it to another, several questions of strategy arise which vary with the particular categories involved. Every act of communication, for example, forces the receiver to relate two attitude objects: the source himself and the object of his message (the brewer and his beer). The message may, in turn, urge a receiver to change his unfavorable or neutral attitude to one object because it is a means to another object, which he already favors. (Beer is advertised as a thirst quencher or weight reducer.) The source may have to create a relationship between the two objects or change one which already exists between them.

A different topic was used, and this experiment was repeated, to see whether messages could change subjects' perceptions of the instrumental value of an attitude in achieving some other value:

Should Negroes Be Allowed to Move into White Neighborhoods?

A group of 183 University of Michigan students served as experimental subjects and another 38 as controls. They first expressed their attitudes toward Negroes moving into white neighborhoods on a 16-point scale. Next, they expressed, on 11-point scales, the amount of satisfaction they would receive from 25 values, and the extent to which they saw Negroes in white neighborhoods as aiding or hindering the attainment of these values. Eight of the 25 items concerned four key issues, of which the following are examples:

America having high prestige in other countries
Having the value of property well protected
Being a person who is experienced, broadminded, and worldly wise
Everyone having opportunity to develop himself and his capacities

Then subjects were required to write messages indicating that allowing Negroes into white neighborhoods would lead to each of these four values, and to listen to a talk by the experimenter which made the same point. These messages did convince subjects, producing a chi square of 9.9, significant at the .01 level.

(However, subjects at either the anti-Negro or pro-Negro extremes of the original attitude scale showed least change: less than 50% changed positively, compared with 60 to 70 per cent of those of more moderate views.)

Moreover, subjects not at the extreme positions who became convinced that integrated housing would help them achieve the four values also came to favor integrated housing itself more than they had previously. A chi square of 24 for 69 subjects was significant at the .01 level. These same subjects, when compared with a control group which wrote and heard no messages, also became less prejudiced in regard to Jewish housing segregation, command of non-Jewish enlisted men by Jewish officers and white enlistees by Negroes. Two questions about Mexicans showed no difference between experimental and control groups.

> —Earl R. Carlson, "Attitude Change Through Modification of Attitude Structure," *Journal of Abnormal and Social Psychology*, 52:256–261.

A major problem in this process is that attitudes toward *both* objects are likely to change: attitudes toward the source and toward the object of his message or attitudes toward the object which is the end and that which is the means.

Which will change most? Scholars agree that when the two objects being related have opposite signs, one liked and one disliked, the new category or relationship tends to have a value somewhere between the two original positions. They disagree on what happens when the two objects are on the same side of the neutral point. Some say the value of the new category falls between the two original values, as an average of them. Others say that the new category acquires a more extreme value than either of the original two, representing the sum of their values.

When new meanings are created by combining old categories into a new category, what determines the evaluation which is attached to the new category? Some theorists suggest that the new valuation will be an average of those attached to the old categories, but this study disagrees.

Greeks and Americans Judge Six "Persons"

Experimenters chose the 13 "most prejudiced" and 12 "least prejudiced" subjects from each of two groups of subjects—91 students from the University of Illinois and 78 from the University of Athens.

Each student filled out a seven-point good-bad scale for a series of eight descriptive terms concerning color (white, Negro), occupation (bank manager, coal miner), nationality (French, Portuguese), and religion (same as the subject himself or different from the subject).

Then, using one term from each pair, descriptions of six different persons were prepared, as shown in the table below.

Next the experimenters attempted to predict how these persons would be rated on the good-bad scale, on the basis of students' original ratings of the individual descriptive terms themselves. Three separate predictions were made for each student and then each prediction correlated with the student's actual rating. One prediction was based on the occupation. A second, following Osgood's congruity theory, was based on the mean of ratings for the four descriptive terms, and the third was based on the sum of these ratings. This third prediction proved best, as shown by the means below.

Correlations between Predicted and Obtained Judgments

Method of Prediction

—25 Greek students—	Occu-pation	Mean	Sum
1. White—French bank manager, same religion	.54	.66	.67
2. Negro, French bank manager, same religion	.69	.54	.63
3. Negro, French bank manager, different religion	.27	.31	.40
4. White, Portuguese coal miner, same religion	.10	.29	.22
5. White Portuguese coal miner, different religion	.55	.12	.66
6. Negro, Portuguese coal miner, different religion	−.02	.38	.46
Mean correlation for Greek students	.38	.40	.52
—25 American students—			
1. White—French bank manager, same religion	.77	.80	.77
2. Negro, French *bank manager*, same religion	.31	.60	.70
3. Negro, French bank manager, different religion	.59	.41	.65
4. White, Portuguese coal miner, same religion	.74	.53	.73
5. White, Portuguese *coal miner*, different religion	.39	.63	.77
6. Negro, Portuguese coal miner, different religion	.66	.78	.84
Mean correlation for American students	.60	.65	.75
Grand mean for all 50 students	.50	.53	.65

The randomization test for both samples combined showed that predictions based on the sum of ratings was superior to those based on the mean beyond the .01 level.

Further analysis suggested that prejudiced students, when a term relevant to their prejudice was included in the description of a "person," were less likely to follow the "mean" or congruity predictions than unprejudiced students. (Religion was believed to be such a term for Greek students, and color for Americans.)

Correlations between obtained ratings and those predicted by the congruity principle exceeded .55 for unprejudiced students, but were only .35 to .40 for prejudiced students.

—Harry C. Triandis and Martin Fishbein, "Cognitive Interaction in Person Perception," *Journal of Abnormal and Social Psychology*, 67:446–453.

Only three signs are needed to express the source-object situation, because relationships of the person holding the attitude, usually designated as "ego," are defined by his attitudes toward the source and the object treated in his message. Thus, as shown below, only one relationship, that between the source and the object, can vary. (Ego is assumed to have a favorable attitude toward himself.)

Eliminate "ego" from the picture, and let the three points of the triangle indicate categories in his mind. It would take sixty-four such triangles to indicate all possible combinations of two objects and a source. (Each point of the triangle and each side of it may be either positive or negative: $2 \times 2 \times 2 \times 2 \times 2 \times 2 = 64$.) Here, for example, are just three of the possibilities involved in a "simple"

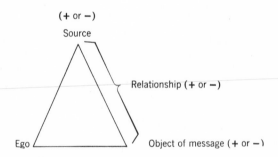

situation should an account executive suggest to our brewer that his firm use singing commercials.

Values at the points of the triangle represent the brewer's evaluation of the categories involved and his attitudes toward jingles, sales, and the account executive himself. Arrows on the sides of the triangle indicate the direction of the relationship. A plus sign means that one object likes or is the cause of the object toward which the arrow points. (The situation could be made more complex, of course, by allowing neutral as well as positive and negative relationships.)

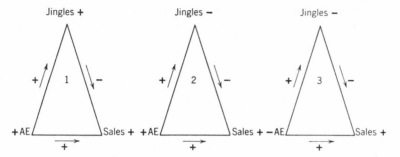

To use this mode of analysis, we assume that men seek, consciously or not, to balance their evaluation of the objects and the relationships among them. Balance is said to exist whenever elements of identical sign are linked by positive relationships and elements of opposite sign are linked by negative relationships (Roger Brown 1962). To see how this works out, let us first note that all three triangles agree in certain respects.

Three relationships do not vary. In each triangle the account executive is seen as having increased sales in the past (+), and as liking jingles (+), but jingles are seen as likely to hurt rather than help sales (—). In addition, the brewer's evaluation of one object, sales, remains constant. He favors them (+). This leaves two things free to vary. In triangle number 1, the brewer likes jingles. This makes the negative relationship between jingles and sales—his belief that jingles hurt sales—unbalanced. The right side of the triangle is imbalanced. In triangle number 2, he dislikes jingles; this creates imbalance on the left side of the triangle, since the account executive (who is liked) himself favors jingles (which are disliked). In triangle number 3, the brewer dislikes both jingles and the account executive. Imbalance now exists on the base of the triangle, since the account executive (disliked) now is seen as causing sales (liked).

Restoring Balance

Theory now suggests that in each case balance will be restored in the simplest possible manner—by changing a single sign. In triangle 1 this means the brewer changes his belief about the effect of jingles on sales from negative to positive. He switches to a belief that they actually help sales. In triangle 2 this means he changes his belief about the account executive's attitude toward jingles from positive to negative, telling himself that the advertising man does not really plan to use the jingles, after all. In triangle number 3, the simplest change requires changing the relationship on the base of the triangle from positive to negative. The brewer convinces himself that the account executive really has not increased sales.

There are more complicated ways of achieving balance. The negative relationship on the right side of triangle 1 can be left untouched for instance, if both the relationship on the left side, and the brewer's evaluation of jingles are changed from positive to negative. (If, that is, he decides that he dislikes jingles and that the account executive does not plan to use them.) Similarly, in triangle 2, balance can also be achieved by changing two signs rather than one. This means making sales negative (the brewer decides he does not want increased sales) and the jingles-sales relationship positive (deciding that jingles are likely to increase sales).

We must recognize that some objects may be so important that the brewer cannot take the simplest method of restoring balance by changing his evaluation of them. He is unlikely to decide, in the situation just described, that he really does not want to increase sales! Similarly, some relationships may be so clearly established that they will resist change. As long as one recognizes such limits, the triangles are useful devices that help him see a set of attitude objects, the relationships among them, and the various ways these relationships may change.

The difficulty just described could be avoided if the model distinguished the strength as well as the direction (plus or minus) of a value. The congruity model of attitude change, discussed in Chapter 6, does take account of the intensity of evaluation. It does so by assuming that two objects are in balance only if they are equidistant from the neutral point: both on the same side, if the relationship is positive, on opposite sides if the relationship is negative. It then hypothesizes that if the objects are not equidistant, both will move to a balanced position, but that the more distant object, that which has the more extreme value, will move least.

Two inferences can be drawn from this example. One is that by specifying his goal in attitude change, a communicator can find the most efficient means to that end. In triangle 3, for example, if the account executive wants the brewer to like him, he will first have to convince the brewer that the account man himself dislikes jingles. The brewer can achieve balance more easily by beginning to doubt that the account man has increased sales in the past. The second inference is that some evaluations, such as the brewer's liking for sales, are so central to the brewer's role itself, that they are amenable to change only when this individual can be approached while performing some other role, such as that of father or husband, to which profits are irrelevant.

Three Components of Attitude

For convenience, we have discussed balance solely in terms of beliefs—the technical word is *cognitions,* which are only one of the three parts which make up an attitude. The other two are feelings, the technical word being *affects,* and tendencies to action, which the psychologist sometimes calls *conations.*

The theory of balance or *homeostasis* can be extended to the relationships among these three parts, as well as to the relations among elements within each part. If change occurs in any one of the three—beliefs, feelings, or action tendencies—either or both of the others will change, too, until balance is restored. A communicator can work on all three, or he can try to influence the part which appears easiest to change, counting on subsequent change in the others. Usually he acts on beliefs, but not always.

In the laboratory an experimenter can manipulate *feelings* by giving suggestions to a hypnotized subject. In real life, a wife, about to announce a new dent in a fender, works on feelings by cooking a savory stew and employing sundry other wiles. If a man is forced to *act* in a way that is inconsistent with his feelings and beliefs, the feelings and beliefs may change, so as to become consistent with the fact that he has acted. In politics, this is the *fait accompli* effect. After a vote is taken, most persons accept it. (After a while, some of the original opponents even seem to think they always were in favor of it!) As Chapter Six points out, inducing a person to give a talk favoring one side of an issue will change his beliefs in that direction, although he was originally opposed.

We can induce a person to act by force, by bribery, or by messages which influence his feelings or beliefs. An interesting consequence of this, which Festinger's dissonance theory elaborates in a delightful series of experiments, is that the *less* force used to induce conformity and the *smaller* the rewards offered for compliant behavior, the greater the change that occurs in feelings and beliefs. In short, the three methods of inducing action combine; the less one of the three parts changes, the more change is required in the others.

The critical problem is to determine the minimum amount of reward or penalty needed. Use too little, so that the desired action does not follow, and beliefs will change in an opposite direction to that desired by the source. The source's message will boomerang. The same reasoning applies to this dissonant situation. The person who refuses to change knows what rewards he has missed and what penalties he has undergone for *not* complying with the source's demands; consistency requires that his beliefs be very strong to justify such sacrifices.

The three parts of attitude—beliefs, feelings, and action tendencies—differ in the extent to which they can be observed and be observed accurately, both by the individual himself and by others around him. This in turn means they differ in the extent to which they can be controlled, both by the individual and by others around him

Beliefs are ordinarily expressed in words which an individual can control. Feelings may be revealed through such nonverbal symbols as facial gestures and tones of voice. Action tendencies are inferred from actual physical movement or from a combination of words, gestures, and tones of voice. Because an individual can control what he says, because communication requires recognition of the receiver's attitudes, and because of pressures to conform with group beliefs, receivers are likely to put more trust in their observations of feelings and action tendencies as an index of beliefs than in the direct statement in words of those beliefs. At the same time, feelings are not expressed in words. The source has less control over the feelings themselves, and he is less able to conceal or disguise them from others.

Salience and Complexity

When we refer to the "extremeness" of an attitude, we are usually thinking of a belief which is at one end of a scale of beliefs. When we refer to the intensity of an attitude, we usually mean that a strong feeling of like or dislike is attached to it. We may also refer to the *salience* of an attitude. An attitude is salient if it is readily available, likely to be evoked by many cues, and likely to affect many of the things a person does. An attitude is likely to be salient if it is a large category containing many subcategories, and if it is highly complex.

The size of an attitude category depends, in part, on the goals of the person who measures it. Although he cannot impose upon his subjects a finer set of discriminable categories than they themselves possess, he can group their categories into larger units of whatever size best serves his purpose, creating an attitude of considerable *complexity.*

A customer, for example, may have attitudes toward a retail store's clerks, its prices, its assortment of merchandise, its location, and its delivery and credit policies. The store owner may desire to combine all of these separate attitudes into a single measure of "store image."

A consumer may have attitudes toward brands and products, toward individual salesmen and individual advertisements, toward types of salesmen and advertising media, and toward advertising and selling in general. He may have attitudes toward things that vary as widely as peace, tennis, his mother, and the practice of putting catsup on hamburgers. By using small categories when measuring attitudes, a researcher can obtain results which remain consistent over time and across people. By using small categories, a communicator can often find that his messages influence attitudes, where a more multidimensional kind of attitude might show no effect at all. The effects of an advertisement, for example, which change attitudes toward a store's delivery service might never be noticed if a measure determined attitudes toward the store in general. Whatever the size of the attitude categories used, there are two strategic advantages in knowing that attitudes toward two different objects are related to one another.

Attitudes toward religion and the family may be highly correlated, for example, in the persons being studied. If so, attitudes toward the family can be *measured* without running the risk that the measure itself will affect their attitudes toward religion. We can then use scores on attitudes toward the family as an index or predictor of their attitudes toward religion.

Similarly, a communicator interested in changing attitudes toward the family may fear that messages designed to accomplish this change will meet with resistance. To avoid this, he may frame messages on religion, hoping that any change here will cause a subsequent change in related attitudes.

Changing Attitudes

What have we said in this chapter?

The goal of the communicator is to change attitudes. He can do this in three ways. He may give existing categories new labels, affecting both their content and evaluation. He may change the categories themselves, by changing the attributes used in constructing them or by urging audiences to move toward larger or smaller categories. Or he may try to change the way that a category is evaluated, either directly or by influencing the values of related categories.

Attitudes are not easy to change. First, because there seems to be a tendency to restore balance when it is upset, and, second, because there is a tendency to prevent an upset by avoiding exposures to messages inconsistent with the existing attitude structure. Accidental exposure does occur, however. A communicator who knows existing attitude structures and the ways in which people react to their upset, can choose the method and point of attack most likely to produce, in the end, the new attitude structure most favorable to his objectives.

SUMMARY

1. The marketing manager seems freer to use messages to influence prospects' perceptions than he is to manipulate the other elements of the marketing mix: price, place, and product. The four elements are not independent of one another, and skepticism of the receiver does limit messages somewhat, however.

2. The goal of communications is an internal response, predisposing a prospect to product purchase, which we may call *meaning*. It has three parts: category, label, and evaluation. The label given a category reflects and influences both the category and the value put on it.

3. Only by grouping similar events and things into categories can men build the expectations which allow them to predict the future. To group events, they must stress some attributes and ignore others. The choice of attributes depends upon how the category is to be used.

4. There are two types of attributes—formal and functional—and three ways of combining them—joint, related, and alternative. Confusion arises when obvious attributes are irrelevant, when categories with the same function get different names, or those with different functions get the same name. Such confusion can often be overcome by using the ladder of abstraction, either by specifying the subcategory with which one is concerned or by putting the category into a still larger category. The word or the category itself can be put in context.

5. Confusion that arises through poor labeling of categories can be prevented through four devices: quotation marks, which indicate the category is very broad and its limits vague; "etc.," which reminds us that no listing of the objects in a category, or their attributes, can ever be exhaustive; index numbers, which indicate that two different categories of objects may bear the same label; and hyphens, which suggest that the elements into which a process or structure has been divided do not exist separate from one another in real life.

6. Communication will suffer if the source uses categories which make finer discriminations than his receivers know or are interested in or

if the discriminations made are not fine enough. A category used frequently will tend to be labeled with a short name rather than a phrase. The name helps persons perceive a category and agree on its content.

7. The name given a category also reflects the value attached to it, which may be positive, negative, or neutral. The neutral point is very significant in devising communications strategy. One must, for example, distinguish between the neutrality of ambivalence and of indifference. A small move which crosses this point is more significant than one which does not: it may decide elections, and it brings into operation the "selective exposure" factor in communications.

8. The neutral point separates friends from foes. Viewed from the standpoint of an individual receiver, it separates "acceptable" from "rejected" positions. Persons vary in the length of their range of acceptance; those at either end of an attitude scale tend to have narrow ranges. The source should advocate the largest possible change within his receiver's range of acceptance, since any change within this range will be perceived as closer to the receiver's range than it "really" is.

9. It is often easier to change the value of a category by a simultaneous change in the category itself, or in the relation of one category to another, as in source and object or means and ends. In such cases, however, one must anticipate that values of all objects being related to one another may change. Scholars hypothesize that men seek to balance their attitude structures.

10. Balance is said to exist when elements of identical sign (plus or minus) are linked by positive relationships (like or cause) and when elements of unlike sign are linked by negative relationships (dislike or prevent). When balance is upset, theory suggests it will be restored by changing the fewest number of signs possible, whether they be attached to objects or to the relations between objects.

Research Studies

Four of the studies summarized in this chapter deal with differences in category systems. *Dennis* discussed differences among cultures, *Banks* differences among products, and *Pettigrew* differences among people. *Carroll and Casagrande* presented evidence which suggests that the labels which language supplies for a people's categories influence the contents of those categories.

Three studies asked what happens when old categories are merged to form new ones. *Rosenberg* showed that a value for a category depends upon how efficient a means it is to a goal and how much that goal itself is valued. *Carlson* then used messages to change perceptions of the efficiency of a given means to a goal and found evaluation of the means itself changes. *Triandis and Fishbein* found that values for a new category do not represent an average of values for the old categories, as some theorists maintain, but a kind of weighted sum of the old values.

In trying to change the values attached to categories, should a source's messages be extreme or moderate? Extreme, said *Hovland and Pritzker; Weiss* agreed, in a study which varied perceptions of the source's position by the "anchors" provided. Finally, *Star and Hughes* showed how the phenomenon of audience self-selection or selective exposure to persuasive messages helps maintain values for category systems, once they have been attained.

Three

Targets of Communications: Markets and Audiences

The marketing communicator seeks to influence the attitudes which induce prospects to purchase his firm's product. This is his goal. It's easy to see why attitudes are his goal when a conscious choice among products or brands precedes purchase, since attitudes can influence such choice. It is harder to see why attitudes are important when a conscious choice among alternatives does *not* precede purchase.

Conscious choice is lacking under two very different circumstances: impulse buying and the kind of buying that occurs when brand loyalty is high. The "impulse" involved in impulse buying means that the decision to purchase the product is made so quickly and the purchase itself follows so swiftly that there is no chance for any true decision making to occur. But what enables the housewife's hand to swoop so swiftly when her eye perceives a shelf of competing brands of peanuts? A strong predisposition to buy the product and a preference for a particular brand, both aspects of what we have called *attitude*, must already exist in her mind.

Attitudes are also important in habitual purchases, which are estimated to constitute at least one third of consumer spending. Habits, we say, are the result of previous, satisfactory experience with the product. Marketing messages contribute to these habits in two ways. First, they precipitate the original decision to try the brand, necessary before there can be any experience with it, and second, they help ensure that the user perceives his product experience as rewarding.

Most marketing messages, however, are designed to break down *brand loyalty* rather than build it up, since only one source benefits from a purchaser's tendency to buy a given brand each time he makes a purchase. Each of the makers of competing brands is interested in replacing habit with decision making, hoping the decision will favor his brand, and lead to experience which, in turn, will produce loyalty to a new brand. Competitors must do two things: they must persuade purchasers to make a conscious decision and to make a decision which favors their brand. They must create a favorable attitude toward their products, and create, as well, an opportunity for those attitudes to affect behavior by getting the purchaser to redefine a situation where habit rules as one where a decision must be made.

Attitudes are important whether we are concerned with decision making by purchasers or in purchases made through habit or upon impulse. But *whose* attitudes? Who are the audiences of marketing communication? Before a communicator can devise messages or transmit them he must know who he wants as receivers. These audiences can be defined in several different ways. One way is to take a look at the hands through which a product must pass on its way to the purchaser—to compare the channels of distribution with the channels of communication.

Product Channel Definition

There are two basic patterns of product distribution: through middlemen or direct from the manufacturer via door-to-door salesmen, direct mail, or factory outlets, as shown below. (Arrows from the sides represent competition.)

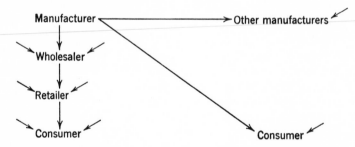

Messages, however, do not follow the pattern shown on the left. If they did, the manufacturer would find himself at the mercy of middlemen. Their interest and competence in passing along his message, not his own ability, would determine his success. Some part of his message would be lost at each step along the way. To keep this from happening, manufacturers communicate directly with each audience, in this fashion:

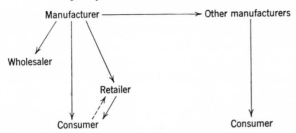

The manufacturer uses different channels and sends different kinds of messages to each of these audiences. He frequently sends salesmen with engineering training who can help solve technical production problems to other manufacturers. He sends salesmen to retailers to talk about markups and turnover. He advertises in such mass media as radio and television, newspapers and magazines, to reach the consumer.

Since failure to reach any of these audiences can prevent his product from reaching the purchaser, the manufacturer supplements these main channels for his message with others. He uses advertising in business papers, for example, to help the industrial salesman get a hearing or produce inquiries which the salesman can follow up. The retail sales clerk may tip the balance toward a sale, a product, or a brand even when advertising carries the main burden of communications by creating brand preference and getting the purchaser into the store.

The retailer is a critical link in this process, especially for the new firm, product, or brand. If consumers discover that their "friendly neighborhood drugstore" does not stock Toothpaste *A*, despite what their television set has told them, then the messages to consumers might better have not been sent. To obtain retail outlets, the manufacturer "pushes" his product through the channels by advertising to the retailer in business papers, and "pulls" it through channels by advertising which induces consumers to ask retailers for the brand (as shown in the dotted-line arrow above). He sends salesmen to call on retailers, to check on shelf displays, to show the retailer proofs of future consumer advertising, and to supply free point-of-purchase materials. Finally, through "cooperative advertising," he offers to pay part of the cost of the retailer's advertising if it mentions his brand.

In contrast to such complex patterns of communication, the direct manufacturer-to-consumer channels shown on the right have at least two advantages. One is that the manufacturer exercises more control over his messages; he controls their content and timing, and does not have to depend on anyone else's cooperation to get his message to its audience. Manufacturers of Fuller brushes and encyclopedias, of insurance policies, bottled milk, and newspapers also gain a chance to display their products to the purchaser in a setting free from comparison with competing brands. Thus the marketer enjoys an advantage other communicators ordinarily find only in totalitarian countries—a message monopoly.

Perhaps the most difficult task of a purchaser is to compare brands. The job is time consuming and often leaves him feeling frustrated and incompetent. But he feels guilty if he does not compare brands, for this, he has been told, is what the intelligent, provident householder must do. If the conflict becomes great enough, he may delay buying or refuse to make any purchase at all. The salesman who comes to his home frees the prospect from the burden and guilt of the brand-comparison dilemma. Thus the encyclopedia publisher who sends salesmen direct to the consumer enjoys two advantages. He frees himself from dependence upon the middleman, who may be uncooperative or incompetent, and he insulates himself from competition, so that both total sales of the product and his share of those sales increase. He pays for these two advantages by using a channel, face-to-face selling, which has a high cost per purchaser compared with the cost of advertising.

By selling through franchised outlets, automobile and appliance manufacturers also gain some insulation from competition. Although most purchasers feel they should see more than one dealer, any given retail salesman and any given retail advertisement for such outlets favor a single brand.

The content of messages to the consumer audience varies with the source. Manufacturers tend to talk about the product. The retailer emphasizes price and such characteristics of place as credit, free parking, fast delivery, friendly clerks—and a wide assortment of alternative brands. Thus the very thing which the manufacturer would like to avoid, comparison of his brand with its competition, becomes the means by which the department store and the supermarket attract customers.

Geographic Definition

Defining audiences by their position and function in the process of physical distribution is only one way of approaching this problem. It is just as important to distinguish among different kinds of consumer audiences. One important distinction among consumer audiences, itself related to physical distribution of the product, is geographic. Some products are distributed and advertised nationwide. Other products are limited to regional or even single-city markets.

In some instances, limited distribution is a temporary phase, as a new firm or a new product tries to establish itself. Messages to retailers may be very important at this phase, in persuading supermarkets and department stores to make room on their shelves for a brand or, in the case of franchised outlets, in finding a competent dealer. In other instances, place characteristics may limit distribution permanently: oil furnaces sell poorly in a hot climate. Price, too, may limit the geographic reach of the market. Some products are too bulky, in proportion to their price, to be transported far from the place they are produced. Unless a firm has plants scattered across the nation, its markets and its audiences must be sought within a limited geographic area. In addition to the geographic limits placed on distribution by price and place, there are other geographic limits imposed by differences in the purchaser himself. These differences may be ethnic. Beer buying tends to be high in German communities and pizza purchasing high in Italian communities. Income differences may be combined with regional causes; hominy grits and okra sell best below the Mason-Dixon line. Such purchaser-related limits are less restrictive than product-related limits, however, for people move about and messages can change preferences. When Southerners move to Chicago, they bring their food preferences with them, and in the postwar period pizza became a nationwide phenomenon.

Geographic limits on the size of the market, whatever their cause, affect communications channels and messages. Some channels, such as salesmen and newspapers, are themselves limited geographically, and thus suited to the product with limited distribution. To reach a nationwide market with such channels, a firm's sales manager must fit together the territories of a great many salesmen, and the media buyer in an advertising agency must fit together the circulation areas of many newspapers. Other channels, such as magazines and network television are essentially nationwide in scope, although general circulation magazines, as they have lost advertisers to television, have developed regional editions.

The quality of messages directed to a nationwide market tends to be better, if money spent on creating them is any guide, than that of messages directed to smaller markets. There are two reasons for this. One is obvious. More money can be spent to advertise a product bought by 160 million people than one bought by only 160,000.

STANDARD BREAKDOWNS FOR POPULATION DATA

Three organizations have approved the following breakdowns for population data, to permit use of census data and comparisons between studies. These groups are the American Association of Advertising Agencies, the Association of National Advertisers, and the American Marketing Association. Combinations should be made within the ruled lines shown.

1. Age Groups	*2. Economic Data A. Income*	*B. Rental*
Under 5	Under—$1,000	Under—$20.00
5–9	$1,000–$1,999	$20–$29.99
10–14	2,000– 2,999	30– 39.99
15–19	3,000– 3,999	40– 49.99
20–24	4,000– 4,999	50– 74.99
25–34	5,000– 6,999	75– 99.99
35–44	7,000– 9,999	100–149.99
45–54	$10,000 and over	150 and over
55–64		
65 and over		

C. Value of Owner-Occupied Homes

Under—$3,000
$3,000–$4,999
5,000– 7,499
7,500– 9,999
10,000–14,999
15,000 and over

3. Education

No school years completed

Less than 5 years of grammar school completed

5–8 years grammar school completed

1–3 years high school completed
4 years high school completed
1–3 years college completed
4 or more years college completed

4. Occupation

Professional and technical workers, nonfarm managers, officials, proprietors

Farmers and farm managers
Farm laborers and foremen

Clerical and kindred workers
Sales workers

Craftsmen, foremen and kindred workers
Operatives and nonfarm laborers

Service workers, including private household

Unemployed

Housewives

Students

Retired

Others not in labor force

5. *Community Size*

Rural farm
Rural nonfarm

Places 2,500–9,999
Places 10,000–24,999

Places 25,000–49,999
Places 50,000–99,999
Places 100,000–249,999

Places 250,000–499,999
Places 500,000–999,999
Places 1,000,000 and over

6. *Regions*

New England (Me., N.H., Vt., Mass., R.I., Conn.)
Middle Atlantic (N.Y., N.J., Pa.)

East North Central (Ohio, Ind., Ill., Mich., Wis.)
West North Central (Minn., Iowa, Mo., N.D., S.D., Neb., Kan.)

South Atlantic (Del., Md., D.C., Va., W.Va., N.C., S.C., Ga., Fla.)
East South Central (Ky., Tenn., Ala., Miss.)
West South Central (Ark., La., Okla., Texas)

Mountain (Mont., Idaho, Wyo., Colo., N.M., Ariz., Utah, Nev.)
Pacific (Wash., Ore., Cal.)

The other reason arises from a peculiarity of the advertising business. This peculiarity is that most advertising agencies are paid for their efforts by a 15 per cent commission on media billings, so that the more money spent to buy advertising space and time the more money there is available to prepare advertising messages.

In newspapers, the principal medium for retail advertising, the newspaper itself shares with local advertisers the task of message design, which national advertisers delegate to the advertising agency. At the same time most newspapers receive a lower rate of compensation for their efforts than does the advertising agency, since they charge a lower rate to local than to national advertisers. Add to this the fact already noted, that retailers tend to emphasize price and variety of brands available, and we see how product distribution limits message content and style.

In addition to market size, geographic concentration of purchasers has important implications for communications. A product does not need to have nationwide distribution or advertising to reach a large number of people. The advertiser can concentrate on the nation's cities. By directing his messages to only 199 standard metropolitan statistical areas, counties containing a city of at least 50,000 population, he can reach 64 per cent of the population, 65 per cent of the nation's households, and 69 per cent of its retail sales. To reach the remaining 31 to 36 per cent he will have to scatter his messages among some 2745 counties. He could do as well by concentrating on the twenty-two standard metropolitan areas which account for 36 per cent of the nation's population, 37 per cent of its households, and 40 per cent of its retail sales. Not only will this make physical distribution, selling, and advertising of the product easier, but there will be a much greater chance for the advertiser's formal communications to be supplemented by the informal messages exchanged when one satisfied user talks to another satisfied user or to a prospective purchaser. The opportunity for such contacts is greater when users are concentrated into twenty-two cities than when they are scattered across 2745 counties.

Demographic Definition

In large cities, some neighborhoods buy a lot of beer; others prefer pizza or okra. This suggests a third definition of audiences, the demographic. Demographic differences are the differences in people which cut across geographic boundaries. Differences in sex and age, in education and occupation, and in income and religion are demographic.

Specifying a market in geographic terms helps a source choose the channels for his message; specifying the market in demographic terms helps him devise the message itself and its context. Geography will tell him which newspapers to advertise in. Demographic patterns of purchase and readership will tell him whether his advertisement should appear in the society section, on the sports pages, or beside the comic strips.

Demographic variables have two advantages: they predict what purchasers will buy and the demographic data needed is usually available from the United States census. The more important variables follow.

Income

The first job of a salesman upon meeting a prospective customer is to "qualify" him—to determine whether he has the money needed to buy the product. For many products, of course, the ability to buy can be taken for granted. For other products, such as yachts and Cadillacs, income sharply restricts the list of potential buyers. At the same time, however, most persons today are above the minimum subsistence level of "a cave, a piece of meat, and, possibly, a fire." They have the money to buy the seller's product; the trouble is, they are spending it for something else!

In 1960, of some 352 billion dollars in after-tax incomes, it was estimated that 25 per cent had to be spent on fixed commitments, such as mortgages and 40 per cent to maintain existing living standards. This left 35 per cent as discretionary income. Whether people spent or saved this 35 per cent depended, in part, on the comparative effectiveness of banks and manufacturers in designing persuasive messages.

The amount of a family's income affects the kinds of products it buys. Higher income groups spend less on food and drink and more on furniture and automobiles. Here are figures from a study made by *Life* magazine in 1957 (Politz, 1957):

PERCENTAGE OF ANNUAL HOUSEHOLD EXPENDITURES

	Annual Income per Household		
	Under $2000	$3000 to $3999	$7000 to $9999
Food, drink, tobacco	36%	30%	26%
Furniture	7	8	9
Automobiles	11	15	15

Two kinds of changes in income are possible. The proportion of the population in various income groups may change, or an individual family may move up the scale. In the latter case, the effects of an increase in income are likely to be limited by the family's friends and neighbors. The full effects on purchasing of a rise in income may not take place until the family moves into a new neighborhood and acquires new friends.

Current spending does not quickly and automatically reflect current income. A man can spend more than he is earning, by dipping into savings or by borrowing; he can spend less, by saving more.

For individuals, the effect of a change in income depends on whether it is seen as permanent or temporary. A temporary fall in income or a permanent rise in income may lead a man to borrow and spend beyond his current income (Katona, 150). His willingness to buy depends partly upon his expectations concerning his own income and partly upon his expectations concerning general business conditions.

For society as a whole, however, a rise in income will produce predictable shifts from one kind of product to another. Here is how purchases changed between 1947 and 1954, with a 1 per cent rise in income (McCarthy, 112):

Airline travel	2.7%
Housing	1.5
Food	.9
Furniture	.6

The implications for communications are obvious. If furniture-makers want to maintain their share of consumer incomes as incomes rise, they will have to increase advertising effectiveness. Airlines can expect an increase with little effort on their part; they may want to use advertising to speed the process.

Occupation

A man's job affects his income, but it also influences where he lives and who he associates with, both on the job and off. All these things, in turn, affect his attitudes and purchases. The effects of job on income are shown in the bottom row of the table below; the effects of job and income on puchases are shown in the percentage figures.

PERCENTAGE OF ANNUAL HOUSEHOLD EXPENDITURES*

	Occupation of Household Head		
	Professional	Clerical, sales	Factory
Food, drink, tobacco	26%	27%	32%
Furniture	8	8	8
Automobiles	14	16	15
Total average annual spending in 1957	$5626	$4845	$4002

* *Life Study of Consumer Expenditures*. Conducted for *Life* by Alfred Politz Research, Inc. (c) Copyright 1957, by Time, Inc.

As with income, the proportion of the population in various occupational groups is changing; blue collar and farm jobs are decreasing and service trades are increasing. As with income, the type of movement makes a difference for attitudes and purchases. The individual who changes his occupational level may actually show a greater, quicker change in attitudes than were all of his associates to change simultaneously. An individual tends to adopt the attitudes of his associates, whereas attitudes of a group tend to remain fixed.

Education

The effects of education are two-fold. Like occupation, education affects the kinds of purchases a person makes: books, wine, travel, and hi-fi sets tend to be popular with college graduates. But education also directly affects the channels and messages a marketing communicator must use. Magazines in general and such specific magazines as *Harper's* and *Holiday* tend to reach the more educated purchaser who is likely to be more critical of advertising in general, more suspicious of it, and less dependent on it in making his decisions. He frequently judges the advertising message on its style and entertainment value, and he may resent its attempt to persuade.

As occupation is the chief determinant of income, so education is the chief means to a rise in the occupational scale in the United States today. As a result the proportion of college graduates is increasing, with some employers insisting on a high school diploma for jobs where a sixth grader's ability to read may be all that is necessary. Since occupation, income, and education are related to one another, marketing communicators often find it convenient to combine these three types of data into an index of social class.

Sex

Although the proportion of men and women tends to be equal at birth, subsequent events may cause changes. When wars were fought on battlefields to obliterate opposing armies instead of cities, they tended to produce a deficit of males. In peacetime, the tendency of men to die earlier seems to produce a surplus of women among the aged.

Sex differences affect both purchasing and communications behavior. Women use lipstick, listen to soap operas, and read the society sections of their newspapers. Men smoke cigars, watch westerns on television, and read the sports pages. The problem is more complex than this would suggest, however, since we must distinguish among three different steps in purchasing. It is possible, for example, for men to make the decision about a purchase, for women to do the actual buying, and for the entire family to use the product.

Age

Of all the demographic variables, age alone runs a continuous, predictable, progressive course. Desires for products change with age, as we move from the pablum market toward the market for false teeth. So does our role in purchasing. Children, for example, influence purchasing decisions long before they become old enough to do any purchasing themselves, as every toy and cereal manufacturer advertising on television knows. Age affects progress in schooling and entry

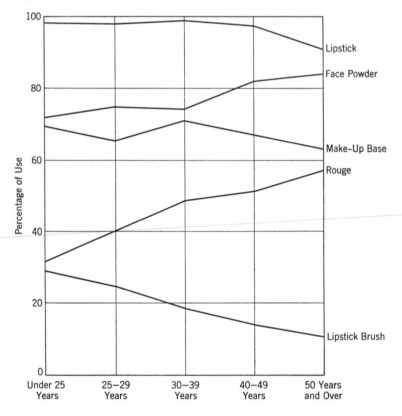

Fig. 3.1. Here is an interesting contrast between products of the same general type, some in general use and some in limited use. Note how the use of some rises with age and the use of others falls. (Reprinted from *Woman's Day Reports on Toiletries,* Volume 2, Fawcett Publications, Inc. New York, 1963).

into the job market, and, within any occupational level, it is not unrelated to income.

At least in the early years, age also determines the communications channels a marketer must use. Captain Kangaroo reaches preschoolers, situation comedy seems to work with preteens, and disc jockeys on portable transistor radios are fine for the teen-ager, off in a world of his own. As science lengthens life, the proportion of aged in the population increases. This is likely to decrease the total size of purchases, since both incomes and desires tend to diminish with age and to have marked effects on the kind of products desired. Purchasing habits may grow stronger with age, attitudes less amenable to change, and marketing messages less effective in influencing purchases. As our circle of friends constricts, informal influences on purchasing may also decrease.

Age and sex combined lead to marriage and the formation of a household, the basic decision-making unit in purchasing. In creating a two-person group, marriage itself leads to a great many new purchases. Housing, furniture, and insurance are prominent among them. The arrival of children intensifies these needs and, in turn, creates new needs, for such items as bottles and diapers.

All three of these demographic variables—age, marriage, and children—can be combined into a single index of purchasing behavior, called the *life cycle*.

Competitive Definition

So far in this chapter we have distinguished the consumer audience from retailer and manufacturer audiences and nationwide from regional consumer audiences, and we have discussed the ways in which demographic differences affect both purchases and messages. Now we move to a fourth way of defining audiences, based on purchasers' reactions to competition among marketers.

Competition, in fact, distinguishes most advertising from other types of communication. The teacher and minister face little direct opposition from competing brands; the door-to-door salesman also enjoys a communications monopoly. All products face competition in marketing, although the intensity of competition varies greatly. Even a legalized monopoly, such as Bell Telephone, loses some customers to the United States mails and to Western Union. If the degree of competition is slight, as between two items which are poor substitutes for one another, we think of the items as separate products. Oatmeal and

What kind of people represent the best market? One way of looking at this question is in terms of life cycle.

Effect of Life Cycle on Buying of Durables*

The concept of a six-stage life cycle, which begins with the young unmarried adult and ends with a widow or widower, reflects many different influences upon consumer behavior. Needs, produced by the arrival of children or a move from rented quarters to a home of their own, tend to be high in the couple, under 45 years of age, with children. A peak in income may be reached somewhat later, with credit filling the gap. Incomes are lowest at the beginning and end of the cycle.

Here is a table, using data taken from the 1956 Survey of Consumer Finances, showing how life cycle affects purchase of key durable goods.

Stage in life cycle	Percentage of house-holds in this stage	Relation between % of purchases and % of population*				Percentages of purchases made on installment plan
		New cars	Used cars	Stoves	Television sets	
Head below 45						
Unmarried	10%	60%	90%	30%	50%	40%
Md., no children	8	100	137	212	137	56
Md., children	35	126	140	117	134	65
Head over 45						
Md., children	12	100	116	125	100	53
Md., no children in home	21	109	47	95	85	27
Widow, widower	14	36	42	29	57	16

(* A figure of 100% means that this group's share of purchases was equal to its proportion in the population. A figure of 60% means it bought only 60% as much as one would expect in terms of its share of the population. A figure of 126 means it bought 26% *more* than one would expect.)

Unmarried persons under 45 did less than their share of buying of new cars. This group accounted for 10% of the population but bought only 6% of new cars sold in 1956 (6%/10% equals 60%). Married persons with children, however, bought 26% *more* new cars than one would expect on the basis of their share of the household studied.

Effect of Life Cycle on Dollars Spent

In 1955–1956, Alfred Politz Research studied some 15,000 households for *Life* magazine. Four interviews were sought with each household over a 13-week period, requiring some 8 hours of time per household. In addition, each household was asked to keep a daily record of its purchases during part of the period.

* Data from page 166 of *The Powerful Consumer* by George Katona. Copyright, 1960, McGraw-Hill Book Company. Used by permission.

Here is a table showing how families at each stage of the life cycle divided their budgets among 8 major items:

Stage in life cycle	Food, beverages	Home	Auto	Clothing	Furnishings	Medical	Recreation	Miscellaneous	Average budget	Average Number Persons
Head under 40, no children	26 %	19 %	17 %	12 %	10 %	4 %	7 %	5 %	$4,332	1.9
Children under 10	30	20	14	12	8	5	5	6	4,607	4.7
All children 10–19	30	15	15	13	8	6	5	8	4,881	3.8
No children under 20, head over 40, and										
Married	29	18	14	11	9	6	5	8	3,639	2.3
Single	28	23	10	13	7	6	5	8	2,350	1.4

The striking thing about this table as seen by reading down the columns is how similar spending is at various stages in the life cycle in proportion of income. Incomes, too, remain relatively alike, despite wide variation in the number of persons in the family, as shown in the last column.

—*Life Study of Consumer Expenditures.* Conducted for *Life* by Alfred Politz Research, Inc. (c) Copyright 1957, by Time, Inc. Data from Vol. I, pp. 30–32.

---

steak are both foods, for example, but a man has to be pretty hungry or steak must be extremely high priced before he will choose oatmeal. If the two items are very close substitutes for one another—Armour steaks and Swift steaks, for example—we tend to think of them as different brands of the same product.

The aim of a marketing communicator is to have people treat his brand as if it were a product. His messages aim at *product differentiation.* His success can be measured by the amount of effort consumers will spend searching for his brand rather than take a substitute, and by their lack of interest in comparing its price or other characteristics with those of competing brands. When purchasers compare prices, the marketer is at the mercy of his competitors. When they decide on the basis of place, his fate depends on the behavior of the middlemen. Only when they refuse to compare at all can he feel truly secure. When the communicator succeeds in product differentiation, we say that his brand has been categorized as a *specialty good* and that purchasers have formed the habit of *brand loyalty*

(McCarthy, 390–413). If, on the other hand, purchasers are willing to spend very little effort in either search or comparison but buy the first brand they find, we say that they have weak brand preference and that the product is a *convenience good*. When consumers spend a lot of time in comparing competing brands, we call the product involved *shopping goods*.

Although the terms used sound as if they described the things people buy, in actuality they are short-hand descriptions of the way buyers behave. Buyers are people and people differ, so it follows that the product which is a convenience good to one man may be a shopping good or a specialty good to his neighbor. This means that we can define audiences in terms of the amount of effort they are willing to spend in searching for and comparing the products treated in an advertiser's messages. Any given product may have a specialty goods audience, a shopping goods audience, and a convenience goods audience. The nature of a product's audience, in turn, affects the nature of the messages used to sell it.

If the audience treats the product as a shopping good, price is likely to play an important part in the messages, since this is one of the easiest types of comparisons to make, as well as one of the most important. If, on the other hand, buyers treat the product as a specialty good, we may need do nothing more than list our number in the yellow pages of the telephone book. Buyers who are willing to walk a mile for a Camel cigarette or to fight rather than switch brands will seek us out. For the purchaser of convenience goods who will buy the first brand he stumbles upon, consumer messages are important chiefly to the extent that they influence retailers to stock and display the brand.

In the short run, consumers' perceptions of the product as a specialty, shopping, or convenience good influence the messages sent to them. In the long run, messages affect perceptions. By manipulating product, place, or price, the marketer can counter competition when selling a shopping good or a convenience good. The main role of marketing communications, however, is to eliminate competition by shifting his brand from either of these categories to the category of specialty good, and make it stay there. The latter part of this task may be more difficult than the former.

Many brands begin life as an *unsought good*—something the purchaser does not know exists. Therefore, it has no meaning for the purchaser and he has no attitude toward it. It may take a great many messages to make the prospect feel a need for the product and to inform him where he can get it. For a brief time thereafter, the marketer may enjoy the bliss of a competition-free world. He seldom enjoys such a state for long, and the period seems to be growing shorter every year (McCarthy, 335). Although he may spend years in research, enjoy patent protection, and use the most elaborate security precautions, a rival all-purpose detergent or wrinkle remover is likely to hit the market within weeks of his. Since he enjoys so brief a period of real product distinctiveness, he must depend increasingly on communications to create preceptions of such exclusivity.

The history of a brand, as it progresses from *unsought good* to one of the other three types, has been summed up in a four-stage *product life cycle* (McCarthy, 332–336; 651–652), which reflects both the amount and nature of competition.

1. *Introduction*. Here, by definition, there are no competitors. The product is an unsought good and unusually unprofitable to the marketer, who must tell the prospect how and when to use it. Consumer messages are often supplemented by such *sales promotion techniques* as distributing free samples by mail or door-to-door, or by offering cents-off coupons. Messages to retailers are also important.

2. *Growth*. If the product catches on, profits tend to be highest at this stage. The marketer may set his price high to skim the cream or high-income purchasers, then drop it to pull in the others. Or he may set his price low to discourage competitors from entering the field. In either case, competitors do appear and for a time there is considerable variation as they vie to see which prices and product features are most popular. Brand differences exist and messages can exploit them.

3. *Maturity*. Now the market begins to settle down. Consumers have indicated what product features they want and what they will pay to get them. Competitive pressures and the economies of mass production and mass distribution reduce variations in brands. Messages which produce perceptions of product differentiation become harder to create at the same time that they become more necessary. Meanwhile, price competition begins and profits decline. If advertising budgets are geared to profits they also decrease.

4. *Decline*. Now sales themselves begin to decline, often because new products are displacing old ones. Effective messages become still more difficult to produce. Relying on them to hold customers may prove costly and ineffective. The marketer may be better advised to stop production, or to convert the declining product into a "new" product, either by changing the product itself or by finding new uses or new users for it. If he succeeds in this, the life cycle can begin

anew. One important strategic decision in communications, at this point, will be whether it is better to present the "new" product as an improved version of the old, and so capitalize on any residue of favorable attitudes or give it a new name, and play down associations with the old product.

Although the four-stage cycle is useful, it is very difficult to say how long any stage will last. One reason is that products vary. Hula hoops may run through the cycle in 90 days; automobiles may take 90 years. Another reason is that the distinction between old product and new is an arbitrary one. The record player can be regarded as a single product, originating with Edison, suffering a temporary eclipse when radio appeared, then adding new features, such as high fidelity and stereophonic sound, and regaining lost ground. On the other hand, we may with equal logic, regard the hi-fi or stereophonic set as a new product, which threatened to push such old products as concert tickets and books toward the fourth stage of their life cycles.

Decision-making Definition

One difficulty with all the definitions so far, useful as they are, is that none of them explicitly recognizes that purchasing decisions are frequently group decisions. They assume, without saying so, that purchasing decisions are made by individuals. This is true, sometimes. An adult buying cigarettes or a child buying a candy bar may not have to consult anyone about the purchase. On the other hand, husband and wife may spend a great deal of time in discussing the purchase of such high cost items as houses, cars, high fidelity sets, and washing machines. And even when it appears that one person makes the decision, others may influence it. A housewife may "decide" what cake mix or perfume to buy, yet she will certainly not ignore the reactions of the rest of the family to her choice.

The same range of decision making is found in industrial purchasing. Some decisions are made by a single individual. Others depend upon the complex discussions and power relationships of a purchasing committee. We must go behind the apparent routine award of a contract to the lowest bidder and ask how many persons participated in drawing up the specifications which limited the number of bidders and may even have predetermined the winner.

In any family, at least three different patterns of decision making can be distinguished. Some decisions are habitually delegated to the husband or the wife. Other decisions require thorough, joint discussion. One member may have more influence than the other, although each may have veto power. In still others, the decision-making process consists of a series of steps which may be delegated to one or another member.

The extent to which each of these patterns is used differs from family to family. Young couples report that they make many joint decisions, either because they think this is how families should behave, or because husband and wife have not had time to develop specialization of decision-making functions. In low-income families, the wife

---

One of the most important audiences in marketing is the family. How do husband and wife divide family tasks? Which decisions are made by each separately? When both make decisions, which has the most influence on them—and how are differences reconciled?

Family Chores and Family Decisions

Interviewers asked 731 Detroit housewives, an 89 per cent return of their original sample, who usually did eight different household chores. Here are results for the two chores most important in marketing.

Which person does the job of—

	Paying bills	Buying groceries
Husband	25%	14%
Both equally	34	29
Wife	41	56

Interviewers also asked housewives about 8 different kinds of decisions and found that 2 were left to the husband, 2 to the wife, and the rest were shared.

Choice made by—	Husband's job	Choice of car	Life insurance	Vacation site	Choice of house
Husband	94%	68%	42%	18%	18%
Both equally	3	25	41	68	58
Wife	1	5	14	11	23

	Wife's job	Which doctor	Food budget		
Husband	31%	10%	12%		
Both equally	18	45	32		
Wife	48	42	52		

On a 10-point scale, in which a score of 4 represents the "both equally" position, the average for all families fell at 5.09, slightly on the husband's side. In fact, 46 per cent of Detroit families fell in the 4-to-6 range, leaving 22 per cent with husband dominant, 22 per cent with wife dominant, and 10% unscorable.

Which were the families in which husbands were dominant? *Not* those such as the 178 farm families also studied, or recent immigrants, or Catholics, or older couples, or the uneducated which were expected to believe in male superiority as a matter of right and role definition. No, interviewers found a shift away from wife-dominance toward equal sharing of power, and a consequent move in overall scores toward the male end of the scale, when men showed high competence. Such competence might be measured by *occupation* (professional men: 5.52, unskilled 5.07), *income* (Under $3000, 4.58; over $10,000, 5.83), or *education* (husbands with 5 years less schooling than wives, 5.05; with 5 years more schooling than wives, 5.36).

Scores fell in families with working wives, and they were lower in the city of Detroit than in its suburbs (4.79 and 5.44). In lower-class families, there was less sharing of decisions, which tended to be delegated to either husband or wife. Dominance by the wife was more common in Negro families (44 per cent of the 115 studied) than in white families (20 per cent of the 616 studied).

> —Data reprinted with permission of The Free Press from *Husbands and Wives* by Robert O. Blood, Jr. and Donald M. Wolfe. Copyright (c) 1960 by The Free Press, a Corporation.

Husbands and Wives Agree on Role Definitions

Although the Detroit study summarized above was based on housewives' reports, other studies show little disagreement between husband and wife on such questions. Here are figures based on a succession of 5 interviews conducted over 2.5 years by the Survey Research Center on three household decisions. Note how close figures are for husbands and wives. (Percentages are based on about 300 to 350 cases, the number varying with the question.)

Decision: Report by:	When to Buy Car Husband	Wife	About Savings Husband	Wife	When to Buy Household Goods Husband	Wife
Wife decides	4%	4%	29%	32%	36%	35%
Joint decision	31	23	47	49	53	51
Husband decides	56	63	21	17	8	11

Specialization seemed to rise with income. Husbands took over in car-buying decisions: 61% being solely responsible in families of over $10,000 income, as compared with only 45% in families of under $3000. Wives became less important in decisions on savings: only 9% in top-income families made such decisions on their own as compared with 36% in low-income families. But wives made more household goods decisions: 31% were solely responsible in top-income families as compared with 24% in the under $3000 group.

Predictions that they would not buy something tended to be fairly accurate, regardless of which spouse made them. With figures for the husband given first, such predictions were accurate for automobiles (62%, 67%), refrigerators (92%, 93%), stoves (91%, 92%), washing machines (86%, 86%). However, although husbands are often supposed to have a veto power over spending, when it came to predictions of purchases, wives were much more accurate. Again, in these percentages showing fulfillment of plans, husbands appear first: cars (63%, 70%), home repairs (73%, 77%), appliances (38%, 57%), and televisions (39%, 76%).*

—Elizabeth H. Wolgast, "Do Husbands or
Wives Make the Purchasing Decisions?"
Journal of Marketing, 23:151–158.

---

tends to decide whether money will go into savings or be spent, since savings usually are delayed decisions to purchase. In high-income families, on the other hand, decisions to save are essentially decisions to invest and as such are delegated to the husband.

Merely asking husbands and wives who decides to buy a given product is likely to conceal the complexity of the process involved. It is more likely to indicate who society says should make the decision, rather than reveal who actually does make it. American couples, for example, say that the husband decides what automobile to buy and the wife decides what appliances and furniture (Katona, 156). Perhaps, if the decision-making were broken into stages, however, he might find that it is the wife, busy driving children to Cub Scout meetings and dancing class, who decides the family should buy a second car rather than a boat (George Brown). It may be the husband, who looks at his bank balance, that decides whether it was to be a new or used car. Husband and wife may decide jointly on seating capacity; husband on the brand; wife on the color. One way to discover such differences is to break the decision-making process into stages and ask about each separately. Another way to get behind the scenes is to ask each participant, in advance, what his preferences are and then see which preferences prevail in the actual decision. (Some authorities hold that any group, to survive, must see that each participant "wins" a fair share of the decisions.)

When members of a family find that their areas of responsibility overlap, or that a decision on color conflicts with an earlier decision to buy a used car, they can resolve the conflict through discussion. Business firms can use the same method, or pass the decision on to someone higher on the organization chart.

* Data reprinted from the *Journal of Marketing,* national quarterly publication of the American Marketing Association.

The decision-making definition of marketing audiences suggests that the most useful demographic or geographic data are based upon households rather than upon individuals, and upon family characteristics which affect patterns of decision making, such as its stage in the family life cycle. These data are of special value in predicting and influencing buying behavior. In some instances, of course, data about individuals become data about families. Thus families are often characterized by the husband's occupation and education, although considering these characteristics for both husband and wife might be more useful. Income figures certainly should report family earnings rather than those of the husband alone.

Media Definition

In a sense, all the definitions up to this point have been in terms of the audience a marketing man would like to have. They have been definitions of the market he wants to reach. The audience he can actually get for his messages may be something quite different.

In some cases, audiences can be custom built to the marketing man's specifications. Even the best mailing list or list of prospects he can get for his advertising or salesmen will include some who will not buy, however. This includes the readers of the specialized

---

Differences of opinion among decision makers in a household may be avoided by having each spouse specialize in decisions about certain products or certain parts of the decision process. If differences do arise, however, which spouse tends to prevail? How are their differences reconciled?

The One Who Talks Most Wins

Two individuals may have a similar experience, yet interpret it differently. What happens if they try to agree on a group interpretation?

Strodtbeck sought an answer to this question in communities, geographically close to one another in the American southwest, but poles apart culturally. His subjects consisted of 30 couples. Ten were Navaho Indians, in whose culture women are economically independent. Ten were Mormons, whose religion makes the husband head of the family. Ten were migrants from Texas, representing a kind of middle ground.

Each couple was asked to pick 3 families familiar to both husband and wife. Spouses were then separated and asked which of the 3 families was most religious, most ambitious, had the happiest children, and so on. Husband and wife were then brought back together and, in every instance of disagreement, asked to reconcile their differences. As shown in the following table, Navaho wives and Mormon husbands were most likely to win, the null hypothesis for the two groups combined being rejected at the .01 level.

Type of family	Total Number of Disagreements	Number of Decisions Won by Husband	Wife
Navaho	80	34	46
Texan	73	39	33
Mormon	71	42	29

But how did the "winner" exert his influence? Strodtbeck took a closer look at the 30 Southwest couples, and another 10 tested at Harvard. In 6 instances, decisions were split evenly. For the remaining 34 couples, the spouse who won most was likely to be the one who talked most—

Spouse Who Talked Most	Spouse Who Won Most Husband	Wife
Husband	14	5
Wife	5	10

Texas couples actually tried to split "victories" evenly between husband and wife. Navahos arrived at decisions with less talk, averaging only 8 acts of communication, compared with 30 for the other groups.

—Fred L. Strodtbeck, "Husband-Wife Interaction Over Revealed Differences," *American Sociological Review,* 16:468–473.

---

business paper, which refuses subscriptions from persons whose occupations make them poor prospects for its advertisers. The number of such "deadheads" increases steadily as we move to magazines of general circulation. (By providing a great many readers at a low cost per reader, such magazines hope to produce enough live prospects to make advertising in them worthwhile.) Newspapers and television assemble audiences suitable for products which nearly every reader buys and buys fairly frequently. Even they offer some selection, however; the type of news or the type of television program the advertisement appears next to may appeal to persons who differ in age, sex, or, occasionally, education.

The smaller the market and the more its members can be identified in terms of geographic and demographic characteristics, the easier it is, in theory, to assemble an audience which matches the market. In practice, of course, mistakes are made, as when children flocked to a comedy program advertising cigars and little old ladies in Dubuque were exposed to *New Yorker* night-club advertisements.

The nature of decision making also affects the type of media audience we want for our message. Ordinarily, a considerable process of search and comparison precedes the purchase of "big-ticket" items. Prospects spend a great deal of time with face-to-face channels, both formal (salesmen) and informal (friends and neighbors). Husband and wife may split up the information-gathering function, each reporting back what he has found to the family council. If prospects seek long, fairly detailed, informational messages, the print media are an effective device for assembling audiences of deliberate decision makers. A person who wants information badly enough will even pay for a catalogue. Radio and television, on the other hand, are useful in reaching the purchaser who is not actively searching for information and is uninterested in buying a product or in going through a careful decision-making process. The advertiser may need to embed his message in a context of news or entertainment which is rewarding in itself, and to make the commercial so short that its message gets across before the viewer can switch channels or leave the room.

Simulated Spending of $300 Windfall

Fifty college students and their wives were given a half hour to decide what they would buy with an assumed gift of $300; each couple's discussion was tape recorded. The items they chose were then classified as to which members of the family would use them. (Twenty per cent could not be fit into the 5 categories shown below.) The discussions were coded to see whether the amount and nature of either spouse's remarks bore any relationship to the final items chosen.

As this table shows, the husbands did more talking and did most of the "task-performance" talking (Bales' categories 4,5,6): giving suggestions, opinions, information. As expected, women dominated in "group maintenance" remarks (Bales' categories 1 and 2): rewarding the other discussant and releasing tension.

Percentage of Couples

	Total talk	Task Performance	Group Maintenance
Husband did most	42%	60%	20%
Wife did most	18	16	72
Both did equal amount	40	26	8

Each of the columns in this table was then used to construct a separate table showing how the differences in amount of these three kinds of

talking were related to final choice of items. In general, task performance appeared to have the least effect on choices.

Percentage items in category	Total Amount of Talking		
	Husband Led	Wife Led	Spouses Equal
Personal for wife's use (clothing, jewelry)	9%	11%	8%
Household for wife's use (washer, stove)	8	8	15
Husband's use (books, clothing)	18	24	15
Family use (furniture, television, car)	35	30	31
Children's use (clothing, toys)	16	23	13

	No. of Task-Performance Remarks		
	Husband Led	Wife Led	Spouses Equal
Wife's personal use	9%	7%	8%
Wife for household use	10	10	20
Husband's use	18	19	15
Family use	35	24	42
Children's use	17	21	14

	No. of Group Maintenance Remarks		
	Husband Led	Wife Led	Spouses Equal
Wife's personal use	12%	7%	3%
Wife for household use	6	14	13
Husband's use	21	17	31
Family use	22	35	38
Children's use	11	21	12

—William F. Kenkel, "Husband-Wife
Interaction in Decision Making and
Decision Choices," *Journal of Social Psy-
chology*, 54:255–262.

Stage-of-Persuasion Definition

In an earlier chapter, we spoke of audiences as representing collections of persons at a common stage in movement toward a purchase,

beginning with those who feel no need for the product and ending with those who have actually bought and used it. The media vary in their ability to attract audiences at each of these stages. Television, for example, may be best at making persons aware that a product exists. A magazine advertisement may sell them on a specific brand. The yellow pages may tell them where they can get it, and a newspaper may tell them what they will have to pay for it. Sampling through direct mail may give them experience with the brand without requiring them to actually hunt it down and pay for it.

Thus an individual purchaser, as he passes through the stages of persuasion may, over time, be a member of several different audiences, assembled by several different media. Moreover, it is quite possible that husband and wife have varying influence on one another at each stage in this process. Women may be most influential at the early, "awareness" stage; if so, the advertiser will not only want to use television but to surround his commercials with a woman's program, probably one broadcast during the day. If men make the actual purchase, then his newspaper advertisement for this same product will best appear on the sports pages.

Allow next for the possibility that families vary in the way they divide these responsibilities at each stage in decision making between husband and wife, and the problem of deciding which media audience we want becomes even more complex (Colley).

The stage-of-persuasion definition of audiences affects message style and content as well as choice of channel. When audience interest in a product is low, attention-getting devices must be provided in the message itself. Once interest in the product is aroused, messages need content which will build brand preference. Once brand preference is established, messages may take on the task of precipitating action.

Message Definition

Finally, receivers may be grouped on the basis of their reactions to the message itself. Some behave exactly as the source intended they should. Some come only part way down the course he has set for them. Some show no reaction at all. And some may even move in an opposite direction! Such after-the-fact groupings measure the effectiveness of the message.

The source would like, if possible, to group people in advance on the basis of their potential reactions to his messages. When this is possible, he can then prepare different messages for the easily persuaded and the highly resistant. He can cite the dangers of not using his brand to some receivers, and the rewards of using it to others. He can use logic or emotion, pictures or words, where they are most likely to be effective and make his language as simple or complex as it needs to be for a given set of receivers. The ability to group receivers on the basis of their reactions after they have received a message represents a measure of success. The ability to predict these reactions and group receivers in advance increases the chance of success, since it enables the preparation of different messages for each group.

Most of this book, in fact, is devoted to this very question of grouping people in terms of their responses to messages. Later chapters will take a look at how receivers perceive messages and learn their contents, at what motivation can be built into a message, and at how personality differences among receivers affect their reactions to a message. They will discuss the ways that groups affect receivers' reactions to a message and how a message directed to many receivers must differ from the message received by a single person.

A great deal of communications research has sought to find indices which will predict reactions to messages. Such demographic factors as sex and education have been related to receiver persuasibility. Receivers' preceptions of the product categories listed in the competitive definition of audiences represent guides for the message maker.

Grouping persons on the basis of their progress from unawareness that a product exists to actual use of the given brand, is as important in framing messages as it is in selecting media. Indeed, of the audience definitions in this chapter, only two—the geographic and the decision maker definitions—are chiefly designed to locate who the message should be aimed at, and therefore, are of use primarily in selecting channels. All the others are as important to the design of an effective message as they are to the selection of an effective channel for that message.

The first step in successful communications is to specify the goal: what attitudes you want to change, and whose attitudes. The second step is to specify the means to this goal: to select the symbols to be used and to combine them into messages. It is to this step we now turn.

SUMMARY

1. Attitudes are important whether conscious decision making precedes a purchase or not. Impulse buying is possible only if brand preferences have been established and habitual buying depends on experience which followed some past decision. A communicator who wants to change brand loyalties must precipitate a new decision-making situation.

2. Before messages can be devised or sent, their audiences must be defined. The *product-channel* definition distinguishes consumer and middleman audiences, which require different channels and message content. Direct manufacturer-consumer distribution is accompanied by two communications advantages: control and freedom from competitive messages.

3. Size of market and concentration of buyers, notes the *geographic* definition, affect both channels and message quality.

4. Cutting across geographic lines, *demographic* definitions of audiences are based on available census data and predict what people will buy. The important dimensions of this definition include income, occupation, education, sex, and age. The first three combine into an index of social class, and the last two into life cycle, which also correlates with size and nature of purchase.

5. Audiences can also be differentiated on the basis of their response to alternative brands, leading to the *competitive* definition. Both channels and message contents vary with the amount and kind of search and comparison that precedes a purchase. It must be remembered that a single product may, in time, be successively a specialty, shopping, and convenience good and, at any point in time, be each of these to different audiences.

6. The *decision-making* definition distinguishes between persons who make and those who influence decisions, and between those who make actual purchases and those who use the product. Decisions vary in the extent to which they are joint, delegated, and broken down into a series of subdecisions.

7. Audiences of salesmen and direct mail may be custom-made, but advertisers who use such mass media as newspapers and television must depend on ready-made audiences, many of which may not be good prospects. The *media* definition of audiences must be related to all the earlier definitions, including the decision-making definition, as we seek the media audience which best coincides with our target market.

8. The *stage-of-persuasion* definition affects both choice of channel and making of the message itself.

9. Finally, effects of communication may be measured by grouping persons according to their reactions to a *message*. Chances of success increase if we can predict, in advance, how they will react to message variables.

Research Studies

The summaries of this chapter dealt with attempts to predict purchasing by the use of demographic variables and with an examination of decision making within the household. After presenting standard breakdowns for such variables as age, income, job, and education, the chapter then presents work by *Katona* and by *Politz* showing how combinations of such variables in the concept of the "life cycle" shed light on many kinds of purchases.

Blood and *Wolfe* then report family decision making from the standpoint of the housewives they questioned. *Wolgast* compares the reports she received about decision making from husbands and wives. Two other authors then test these reports. *Strodtbeck* compares the original preferences of husbands and wives with their final decisions, and *Kenkel* analyzes tape recordings of the decision-making process itself to see how husbands and wives tried to influence one another.

Four

Tools of the Communicator
I: Symbol Systems

The first decision a marketing communicator must make concerns his goal. He must decide what behavior he wants his messages to produce. This goal can be defined from the standpoint of the object, usually a brand, treated in his messages: He wants this brand to have a particular meaning for his audiences. He can also define this goal from the standpoint of the audience: The communicator wants his audience to have a particular attitude toward the object.

The second decision a marketing communicator must make is to choose the audience he wants to influence. He must decide not only what attitudes but whose attitudes he wants to influence. The third decision a marketing communicator must make is that of method: *How* is he to make this audience adopt this attitude? Basically, there are three ways to influence human behavior. One way is to pay people, another is to punish them, and the third is to persuade them. The communicator's method is that of persuasion.

He persuades by using symbols. Words, numbers, and pictures do most of the work, although the communicator may, on occasion, use gestures or appeal to the senses of taste and smell. The purpose of this chapter is to indicate the wide variety of symbols available to the communicator, some of the limits upon his choices, and some of the effects of his choices.

Let us begin with a simple cartoon of a type used to measure housewives' attitudes toward a grocery store. It shows a person in slacks facing what appears to be a vegetable counter. The interviewer says, "Tell me what you see in this picture." The respondent is likely to reply: "A woman who is a good housewife is shopping. She is comparing prices because she wants to give her children good nutrition at the lowest possible cost."

One can change behavior through force, bribery, or by changing attitudes.
The less force and the smaller bribe one uses, the more attitude will change—
provided behavior is changed.

Boredom Disguised—for $1 and $20 "Bribes"

Sixty students at Stanford spent an hour at boring tasks: putting
spools in a tray and dumping them out again, turning pegs on a board.
Then 20 of the students were offered $1 and another 20 offered $20 to
tell another subject that the boring task they had just performed was
"enjoyable, a lot of fun, interesting, exciting." Finally, all 60 subjects
were interviewed about the experiment and rated it on four 11-point
scales (ranging from 0 to 10, or −5 to 5).

Mean Ratings

	Control Group	$1 Group	$20 Group
Were the tasks interesting and enjoyable?	−.45	1.35	−.05
Would you have any desire to participate in another similar experiment?	−.62	1.20	−.25
Did the experiment give you an opportunity to learn about your own ability?	3.08	2.80	3.15
Do you think the results may have scientific value?	5.60	6.45	5.18

Ratings in the $1 condition differed from those of the control group for
the first question (.02 level) and for the second question (.08).

—Leon Festinger and James M. Carl-
smith, "Cognitive Consequences of Forced
Compliance," *Journal of Abnormal and
Social Psychology*, 58:203–210.

Not one of these things actually appears in the picture! Every one
was supplied by the respondent herself. That, in fact, was why the
cartoon was used. It reveals what the respondent is thinking or how
she thinks a housewife should behave in a grocery store. To the
extent that housewives think differently they will see different things
in the picture.

Suppose, now that we wanted to communicate the message just
quoted. How could we increase the likelihood of getting this reply
and reduce the probability of having respondents read other meanings
into our cartoon?

More Symbols, Less Ambiguity

One way, certainly, is to increase the number of symbols in the picture. We can remove the possibility that the person is the supermarket manager by changing the slacks to a dress or showing the hair in curlers. We can convert the woman into a mother by surrounding her with children, the younger the better, or by putting one child in the cart we have supplied to indicate she is shopping and not just waiting for a friend. We can introduce the idea of nutrition by putting a poster on the wall, and we can suggest "lowest possible cost" by showing her counting the money in her purse or reaching for the carrots with the lowest price tag.

Thus we provide a few attributes; the respondent supplies the categories. Let us take another look at the sentence, this time with parentheses indicating the number of separate categories the respondent must form when she frames such a sentence:

$$\underset{1}{\text{"(A woman)}} \text{ who is a } \underset{2}{\text{(good)}} \underset{3}{\text{(housewife)}} \text{ is } \underset{4}{\text{(shopping)}}. \text{ She is}$$

$$\underset{5}{\text{(comparing prices)}} \underset{6}{\text{(because)}} \underset{7}{\text{(she wants to give)}} \underset{8}{\text{(her)}} \underset{9}{\text{(children)}}$$

$$\underset{10}{\text{(good nutrition)}} \text{ at the } \underset{11}{\text{(lowest possible cost)}}."$$

Objects (1, 9)

Using the psychologist's definition of objects to include people as well as things, there are two mentioned in the sentence: a woman and children. The children may be shown in the picture, or they may be an assumption of the viewer. If the attribute we supplied—the woman—is put in the category called "mother" then the children are a necessary part of that category.

Behaviors (4, 5)

One is partly physical, shopping; the other, comparing prices, is completely mental. Its existence is assumed by the viewer, not supplied by the artist.

Role (3)

The respondent attributes the role of housewife to the woman, probably because of the high probability that a woman who is shopping is a housewife.

Relationships (8, 10, 11)

Two kinds of relationships are involved. The children are seen as "belonging" to the housewife. The concept of lowest possible cost involves a complex relationship among price, quantity, and quality. That of good nutrition involves a complex balancing of vitamins, calories, and so on.

Evaluation (2)

With the highly connotative label "good," the respondent has revealed her attitude toward the woman in the picture. Having made this judgment, she then assigns other appropriate attributes—

Motivation (7)

The shopper, being a good housewife, naturally wants to give her children good nutrition. (It is fortunate that this is assumed, for it would be awfully hard to put motivation into a picture!)

Cause-and-effect (6)

The "because" that links the behavior of comparing prices to the motivation is the most difficult of all to determine and to picture. Both the behavior and the motivation may exist, but without being causally related to one another. The good housewife is also a woman, for instance, and may be comparing prices because she's saving money to buy a new hat!

Cues Create Expectancies

By using words to describe pictorial cues we have tried to show how a few attributes expressed as pictorial cues can suggest categories of people, behaviors, and relationships. They create expectancies of other attributes, much as the sight of eyes gleaming in the dark may suggest sharp teeth and a lashing tail to a timorous camper.

We might have done the same thing in words alone. We could, for example, describe a woman standing at the vegetable display as "a good houswife." It might be more effective, however, to describe her behavior and let the audience itself pin the label "good housewife" on our description. Thus we could report that this woman bakes her own bread, makes her own clothes, and still has time to play with her children and go fishing with her husband. (Of course, if we go too far, respondents may not believe us or may resent the woman.)

Thus we create expectancies with words. Words also create expectancies for one another. If I say "chair" about one listener in five will respond with "table," about 16 per cent with "sit" or "sitting" and 13 per cent with "seat" (Kent and Rosanoff). Similarly, "dog" tends to evoke "cat" and "knife" to evoke "fork." This method of *free association* is often used in marketing, to determine product images and select trade names. A "good" brand name, of course, is one which evokes favorable associations, which this method can determine.

Words create expectancies for one another, and these expectancies are consistent enough from one person to the next that they can be counted and graphed. The marketing communicator is interested in associations which have a high rate of agreement. The therapist finds deviant associations may provide clues to deviant personality traits.

What Are the Most Common Types of Word Associations?

Using 90 words and 1000 subjects, experimenters determined what types of word associations are most common. In this list, an asterisk which precedes the category indicates it is used more often by adults than by children; an asterisk which follows the label indicates it is used equally by both groups.

Class	Examples	Percentage of Adults Giving Responses
*Coordinate	table-chair; deep-low	10.9
*Contrasting	dark-light; sickness-health	10.6
Similar*	dark-black; sickness-illness	8.9
*Superordinate	table-furniture	7.6
Adjective-noun	deep-hole; soft-bed	6.9
Verbs	table-eat; dark-see	6.4
Contiguous	table-dish; dark-night	6.0
Noun-adjective	mountain-high; house-big	4.3
*Cause-effect	sickness-death; lamp-light	2.5
Whole-part	table-leg; mountain-rocks	2.1
*Participles	music-singing; chair-sitting	1.9
Subordinate	music-song; sickness-fever	1.6
*Part-whole	fruit-tree; soldier-army	1.1
Material*	table-wood; needle-steel	1.0
Verb-object	eating-bread; hammer-nails	.9
Compound words	table-cloth; spider-web	.8
Effect-cause*	sleep-tired; afraid-burglar	.4
*Noun-abstract attribute	mountain-height; eagle-flight	.3
Assonance	table-able; dark-mark	.1
Pronouns	woman-she; thirsty-me	.1
		74.2

Here are some comparisons of adult and child preferences for individual words, giving the three highest frequencies in each case:

Stimulus Word	Adult Responses	Children's Responses
Table	chair, wood, furniture	eat, dishes, legs
Sickness	health, death, illness	doctor, bed, ill
Man	woman, male, boy	work, hat, person
Joy	happiness, sorrow, pleasure	happy, glad, fun
Sheep	animal, lamb, wool	wool, animal, lamb
House	home, building, barn	live, warm, big

—Herbert Woodrow and Frances Lowell, "Children's Association Frequency Tables," *Psychological Monographs*, Vol. 22: No. 5, pages 81–96 and 106 (whole No. 97).

The more words we string together, the more cues to meaning we provide and the stronger expectancies we create. Expectancies may become so strong that we can drop out whole words. Most persons will not have any difficulty, for example, in filling in the blanks in these sentences:

"Now is the time for all good _____ to come to the aid of their party."

"_____'s taste good, like a cigarette should."

Expectancies become so strong, in fact, that even nonsense syllables suggest some meaning. When we report that "The nasty little fup next door yarped all night long," many of us will "hear" the words "pup" and "yapped" or "barked."

The communicator's problem in designing messages is to use the least number of symbols possible and still provide the desired degree of precision and probability that a given audience will end up with the attitude desired. Almost always there will be more than one cue to a given attribute, whether we are trying to transmit sounds or sentences or individual words. Most messages will employ several different symbol systems, as well as several different symbols. In English, for example, a written sentence can still be understood when 50 per cent of the letters in it are blanked out. The typical English sentence is said to be four to five times as long as it need be to convey information.

This abundance of cues permits a great variety of style and treatment in conveying any given denotative meaning. Very subtle distinctions can be made, as one cue modifies, denies, or contradicts another.

Use of many cues also means that some can provide information about the source, and reveal his attitude toward the object of a message. Many cues can convey connotative as well as denotative meaning. A third reason for using multiple cues is that communication occurs under a wide variety of circumstances, containing many competing stimuli which the communications expert terms "noise." Sometimes the communicators' noise is just that—physical noise. Sometimes it is interference from messages or other activities vying for a receiver's attention. Sometimes it is conditions within the receiver himself, such as hunger, headache, or fatigue, which get in the way of a source's message.

Multiple Cues Aid Communication

Language and other symbol systems have built into them a great number of multiple or "redundant" cues, either in the form of mere repetition of a symbol, or, more commonly, in the use of several different kinds of symbols to express a single attribute. A good communicator increases or reduces the amount of redundancy to match the ability and interest of his audience, his goals for that audience, and the circumstances in which communication must take place. Two examples, both using numbers, help illustrate how using "extra" cues can improve communication when noise is present.

The first, drawn from *information theory*, defines a minimum number of cues, so that we can determine when cues are, in fact, extra. Let us begin by setting up a situation in which we are looking for one coin in one hundred. We have the right to ask only one kind of question, "Is it in this pile or that pile?" The coin can be located in seven trials. On the first trial, we divide the one hundred coins into two equal piles. The answer we receive will eliminate fifty of them. On subsequent trials the alternatives will narrow to twenty-five, thirteen, seven, four, and two. Each trial reduces the alternatives by half and is said to contain "one bit" of information. Any message which enables us to pick the right coin on the first trial is the equivalent of seven trials and is said to contain "seven bits" of information. Provided that the alternative choices are equally likely and independent of one another, the amount of information is said to be proportional to the logarithm to the base two of the number of alternatives. Thus a message which enables us to pick one alternative out of ten contains a third of the information of the message which enables selection of one alternative out of 1000.

The second example shows how adding extra cues above this minimum can enable a message to get through despite noise. The artificial language used by a computer recognizes only two states: "current on" and "current off" and so has a language of two symbols: 0 and 1. These, of course, can produce four two-digit "words": 00, 01, 10, and 11. We can reduce errors in transmitting these four words by adding an extra digit, using three digits instead of two, and by accepting only four of the possible three-digit figures: 000, 110, 101, and 011. Thus two errors, not one, are necessary before any of those combinations can be converted into one of the others. Any two digits can carry the message: the first two, second two, or first and last. A single error will produce a word that does not exist in the language, and so will be detected immediately. We pay for this protection by making each message one-third larger than it would need to be in an errorless world. And we must choose carefully, avoiding three-digit numbers in which one digit, being identical, performs no function at all: 000, 100, 010, and 110.

Four Aids to Meaning

Spoken and written language both follow this same principle—providing extra cues to meaning—so that messages will get through. They do this in at least four different ways.

Variable Frequency
The first is to see that alternative choices are not equally likely. The letter *e* is more common than the letter *z* in English, and the word "mother" appears more frequently than the word "pother." If we are not quite sure which we heard or saw, our best bet is to pick the most frequent.

Dependence
The second is to see that alternatives are not independent of one another. If we see the letter *q*, for instance, we do not have to ask what letter comes next. We know that, in English, it must be a *u*. The same applies to words. Most adults can unscramble a mixed-up sentence such as "Shoes of trunk my six with pack pairs" in fairly short order.

Arbitrary Limits
The third is, as with computer language, to accept only a small number of the possible combinations of letters and sounds as meaningful. Some experts recognize seventy-two consonant sounds and forty-

two classes of vowel sounds (Miller, 19–20). If these were combined into simple consonant-vowel-consonant syllables, each of us could have a vocabulary of 217,728 one-syllable words (72 $\times$ 42 $\times$ 72). Actually, of course, only a few of these are found in English. Unless we are learning nonsense syllables in some psychologist's laboratory, when our ear hears something that sounds like "nef" our brain will run through a list of possible alternatives, such as "net" or "knife" and pick the most likely. We are aided in making a choice by the fourth form of redundancy—

Context

This fourth kind of multiple cue to meaning may involve subject matter. If we are talking about tennis, then "net" is the most likely choice; if about food, then "knife." Or the context may be what we call *syntax*—rules for combining sounds or their printed equivalents into words and for combining words into sentences. Grammar contains a great deal of redundancy. In the sentence, "A whale eats sardines," the order of the words tells us who does the eating, but even if the words were scrambled, the *s* on the verb would indicate that the eater is the singular and not the plural noun. In the sentence, "Most men have whiskers," there are no less than three cues to the fact that the subject is plural: The word "most," the use of "men" rather than "man," and the plural form of the verb. Multiple cues do more than help overcome noise, however. They serve three other functions, providing a repertoire of cues to fit various products, messages and media.

One of the marketing communicator's first tasks is to find some consumer benefit among the variety of product features available, which can be the basis of an advertising campaign. This is his "copy platform." He hopes it is a "unique selling proposition"—one that no other advertiser can use.

This feature may be air, whipped into a soap to make it float, so that a bather does not have to grope around on the bottom of the tub when the soap slips out of his hand. It may be a decay-preventing toothpaste ingredient which has the endorsement of the nation's dentists. It may be the fact, exploited by Volkswagen, that one year's model cannot be distinguished from another's, or the fact, exploited by other auto manufacturers, that each year's model is different. Once he has found such a feature, the communicator must find symbols which will convey his meaning to a receiver. These symbols may become a trademark, a slogan, a brand name, or the foundation of an advertising campaign. Frequently the same basic idea must be expressed in several different sets of symbols. To catch an audience's attention, to be believed, and to be remembered, the communicator may find he must express the same idea in different ways. Mere repetition may bore, whereas repetition with variation may be effective. Finally, the communicator may need to use several different media to reach his target audience. Each medium will limit his choice of symbols in different ways.

The Spoken Word

The two most important symbol systems available to the communicator are speech and print. Because both use words, we often act as if these were a single system, when in fact they are two quite different systems.

Speech is the more universal of the two systems, in both time and space. It is the first we learn, although very few of us study it formally. Instead we learn it informally in the home rather than in school. Of the two systems it requires less effort and its range of use, both as a means and as an end in itself, is very wide. On the other hand, it lacks the permanence of print, the cheapness of print, and the prestige of print. Speech, the original mode of teaching, now serves largely ceremonial and entertainment purposes in mass education. When we are really serious we turn to printed textbooks, journal articles, and written examinations. In marketing, on the other hand, when we are serious enough about selling to be willing to forego mass methods for a one-to-one relationship between seller and buyer, we send a salesman to talk—and listen—to the customer.

The salesman is superior only in part, however, because he is using the spoken rather than the written word, as can be seen if we contrast a salesman in person with a salesman on the telephone and with a salesman on television. In person, the salesman can evoke from us the special attitudes we show in dealing with people rather than things. In person and on the telephone he can adjust his message to our responses. In person and on television, he can employ the symbol systems of bodily and facial gesture. Only radio or a recording can eliminate these extraneous variables and let us concentrate on the effects of speech itself.

Two Limits on Speech

Basically, there are two physiological limits upon speech. A man's mouth must be able to produce sounds, and his ear must be able to receive them. In actuality, although speech appears to be an evolutionary afterthought imposed upon apparatus originally intended to handle breathing and eating, these are not very stringent limits.

Puffs of air, released through the Adam's apple or larynx atop the windpipe, are shaped into sounds, first by vibrating vocal cords in the larynx, then by the lips, tongue, teeth, and roof of the mouth (the articulators).* Air flow is also shaped by the resonating chambers of nose, mouth, and throat.

If air emitted from the larynx passes through the mouth without interruption, vowels are produced. If the stream of air is stopped completely, we get the explosive sounds indicated by the letters x, k, g, p, b, t, d—sounds like "*p* in pop" and "*g* in gag." Forcing the air through a narrow slit by teeth, by tongue, or by hard palate, produces the initial sounds of thin and then, sin and zin, shin and the *sh* shound in "measure." Air escaping around the sides of the tongue gives us the *l* sound in "let."

The possible variations in sounds run into the thousands, although in any given language only a few affect meaning. One system distinguishes forty-two vowel sounds. This system recognizes two positions of the lips (rounded or not), and three parts of the tongue (front, middle, and back) which can be raised to seven different heights: $2 \times 3 \times 7$ equals 42. (Still finer distinctions can be made if we note whether the entrance to the nasal cavity is open or closed, where the tongue is placed, and so on.) This system also identifies seventy-two consonant sounds based on five types of articulation (breath stopped, breath escaping through a narrow slit, breath escaping around the tongue, the trill, and the final nasal sounds heard in run and rung), and eight combinations of fixed and movable parts of the mouth (upper and lower lips, upper teeth and lower lip, tip of tongue and upper teeth, gum ridge or hard palate; front of tongue and hard palate, back of tongue and soft palate, vocal folds). In addition, consonant sounds may be voiced or voiceless. Voiced sounds, such as the *b* in "ban," require action by the larynx; voiceless sounds, such as the *p* in "pan," do not.

The ear is very sensitive to vibrations of the air which are sensed as sound. If a single-frequency tone in the most sensitive range of 2000 to 4000 cycles per second is sounded for a half-second, a person listening with both ears can detect vibrations so weak that they move the ear drum only .000 000 001 centimeter. (If the ear were slightly more sensitive, it could detect the random movements of air molecules.)

---

* This account and other content of this chapter is based on Chapters 2 and 3 of Miller.

The ear can distinguish some 1600 different frequencies and some 350 different intensities or some 340,000 tones, provided they are sounded in order. However, the human voice can produce only a part of what the human ear can sense. The voice produces not single frequencies but a frequency plus its multiples or harmonics: 125 cycles per second, 250, 375, and so on. As a result speech is limited to something like the eighty tones which the voice can produce rather than the 1600 tones which the ear can detect.

Of the 42 vowels some experts recognize, English uses only about 14 or 15, and of the 72 consonants only about 24. These speech sounds or *phonemes*, plus three types of stress, three pitches, and three types of pause or juncture, provide the labels for all our referent categories. Stress, for example, enables us to distinguish the noun per mit from the verb per mit'. Pitch enables us to distinguish a white ^{house} from the White $_{House.}$ A slight pause distinguishes the command "mark it" from the noun "market."

Moreover, all languages limit the way that these sounds may be combined. In English, certain sounds are never found at the beginning of a word, and others are never found at the end, and some are only found in combination with certain other sounds. The *t* formed by air escaping around the side of the tongue, for example, is never found at the start of a word, but only after a vowel, an *r*, an *l*, or an *n*, or before an *l*. Only six consonant sounds may precede an *l* at the beginning of a word: *p, k, b, g, f,* and *s;* and only nine consonant sounds may follow an initial *s*—*t, k, p, ph, th, m, l, w,* and *n*.

Denotative Cues Differ

Languages vary in the sounds they use to express denotative meanings. In English, for example, the distinction between voiced and voiceless sounds affects meaning, as the words "pan" and "ban" or "buzz" and "bus" indicate. In other languages, but not in English, a long vowel, such as the "o" sound in "toad," conveys a different meaning from a short vowel, such as the "o" sound in "tote." In some languages the difference between the initial sounds of "keep" and "cool" or "ski" and "school" has denotative significance. It does not in English, however; as a result, only the speech experts among us are likely to hear any difference in the sounds themselves. The difference is there, since the mouth operates differently to produce sounds, but our one ears have learned not to recognize the difference.

In other instances, our ears can hear a difference but our minds interpret what our ears report in other than denotative terms.

Differences in intensity, determined by the size of puffs of air emitted, for example, are interpreted as indicating the distance of the source of a sound, not the nature of the source.

Differences in frequency, the rate at which puffs of air are emitted, are interpreted as indicating the sex or age of the speaker, since women and children tend to have higher voices than men.

Thus language's use of only a small portion of the sounds which our mouths can produce and our ears can detect serves two functions. It allows the unused sounds to carry a nonreferent burden of information about the speaker himself, such as his age, sex, or distance from us. And it allows us to use several clues for every meaning we want to convey. As a result of this second function, messages can get through despite many different kinds of interference, among them these (Miller, 70–75):

Competing messages: The ear can detect several distinct sounds at once, or tune in one and tune out another. The two are not blended into a new sensation. (This ability breaks down, however, if a sound is too faint or if the frequencies of the two sounds are too close.)

Restricted frequency. Shifting pitch or frequency upward by as much as 400 cycles per second or downward by as much as 250 does not affect intelligibility.

Restricted loudness. Sounds actually become crisper and clearer if variations in air pressure are reduced by cutting off the tops of the peaks and the bottoms of the troughs. This tends to reduce the strength of vowels, which can be heard at an average intensity of twenty-five decibels, to that of consonants, some of which require sixty decibels. And consonants are more important to understanding.

Interruptions. If these are brief enough—ten per second—the complete message will get across although half the speech is cut off and although only one-syllable words are used.

Changes in speed. Paragraphs from reading comprehension tests can be read aloud at speeds ranging from 100 to 322 words per minute; even at top speed, some of the content is understood.

The Written Word

Most of us know more about words in print than we do about the spoken word, for much the same reason that when we learn a foreign language we are more conscious of its grammar than we are of the grammar of our own tongue. In each case formal teaching has made us aware of the underlying structure.

We tend to use different words in writing than we do in speaking, to use a greater variety of words, and to string them together in longer sentences. One reason is that there tends to be less "noise" present when we are writing or reading than when we are talking or listening. As noise increases, our vocabulary becomes more limited; we use fewer words, shorter words, and shorter sentences. The telephone, for example, is a "noisy" communications channel; of the 800 words used most frequently on the telephone, the top 100 are nearly all monosyllables and very few have as many as three syllables (Miller, 89). A pilot in a fighter plane, with the distractions of exploding flak, enemy planes, and his own churning viscera, to say nothing of the static on his radio, uses an even more limited vocabulary and repeats a lot of the little he uses. The writer of a television commercial, knowing it must compete with crying babies, slamming refrigerator doors, and churning dishwashers, tends to use similar techniques.

It takes a vocabulary of only fifty words to make up 60 per cent of what we say—and 45 per cent of what we write (Miller, 89). Ordinarily we can go only ten to fifteen words without repeating at least one word. This repetition is so common that it has been expressed in a formula, called Zipf's law, which predicts word frequency over a considerable range of content (Miller, 91). This formula says that if the most frequent word in a message occurs 1000 times, the second most common will appear about 500 times, the third 333, the fourth 250, and so on. In writing, the most common word is likely to be "the;" in a telephone conversation it is usually "I."

Sentences, too, tend to be shorter in speech than in writing. We have to make them short so that the person we are talking to can get a word in edgewise; if we do not, he will break in upon us, or leave. Although formal lecturers escape such pressure they often adopt some of the characteristics of informal conversation if only because a spoken sentence which becomes too long will cause the audience to forget the first half before the last half can be emitted. Verbs are more common in speech than in writing, and adjectives more common in writing than in speech. The ratio between the two has been found in one study to vary from nine verbs per adjective in drama, to five verbs per adjective in legal statutes, three verbs in fiction, 1.5 verbs in master's theses, and 1.1 in Ph. D. dissertations (Boder).

Not only do people tend to write differently than they speak, but they differ among themselves in the proportion of each which they do. Some persons write or read very little. We would expect their speech to show less resemblance to written language than the speech of those who are professional writers or inveterate readers.

The words a person uses, both spoken and written, can tell us a great deal about the place and times he is writing in, as well as about his age, sex, education, and social class. All of these things, in turn, may be important to an audience which is trying to decipher the source's attitudes and intentions toward them.

Both authors and their editors, of course, adjust their vocabularies and the length of their sentences to their intended audiences. *All-Story* magazine, for example, in one study averaged thirteen syllables per sentence compared with thirty-four syllables for the *Review of Reviews* (Miller, 125). Formulas to measure both reading ease or readability and human interest have been developed (Flesch).

At one time, a man's ability to spell correctly reflected his education, although today, with more lenient promotional policies, it may reflect his personal interest in language and spelling rather than that of his teachers. Spelling in English is a particularly good clue to formal education since it follows few sensible rules but has to be learned word by word. Just as spoken language carries a nonreferent burden of information about the person using it, so written language carries a nonreferent burden of information about where the words in it originated. Spelling provides few cues to how words should be pronounced, but carries considerable information as to what language we took them from: Anglo-Saxon or French, Latin or Spanish or Algonquin. Unfortunately, most of us do not care where they came from so these cues are wasted.

The Printed Word

Handwriting provides a great many clues to its author's age, sex, education, and even, if analyzed by an expert, to his personality or state of health. Print, on the other hand, tells nothing about the source of a message but, if chosen carefully, can contribute a good deal to its effect. It can help overcome noise in the communications, or add connotative dimensions to the message. Here are four important variations in the printed word:

Type size. Within limits, as type size increases, so do attention-getting power and legibility, the gains in which are offset by a decrease in the number of words which can be fitted into a given space.

Type family. Differences, often subtle, affect legibility and attention-getting power, and suggest connotative characteristics which may be suitable to the product, the medium, or the target audience. Although the customs of type use may be more important in creating associations than anything intrinsic to the type itself, some families are interpreted as being masculine and others as feminine. Some suggest high-priced and others inexpensive products.

Type face. The contrast among italic, bold, and condensed faces is often more obvious than the differences among families; the effects are often similar. Italics, for example, are often seen as feminine in nature, harder to read, but, if used in small quantities, likely to attract attention.

Experts assume that the choice of a type face affects the success of communication via the printed media. Do the experts agree with one another as to the shades of meaning which a particular type conveys—and, even more important, do the audiences agree with the experts?

Five Kinds of Meaning, 16 Kinds of Type

Three different audiences were asked to rate alphabets set in 16 different kinds of type on 25 semantic differential scales. Each audience included 25 persons: an expert audience, made up of editors and teachers of typography; a lay audience, made up of 25 university students; and an intermediate audience, consisting of students who had taken a one-semester course in typography.

The type included 2 "cases" (capital letters and lower case letters); 2 "inclinations" (italics and regular); and 4 type families (Bodoni, Garamond, Spartan, and Kabel): 2 × 2 × 4 or 16 combinations in all.

Factor analysis of the results showed that 5 factors accounted for at least 60% of the variance in all 3 audiences—but that the importance of the factors varied from one audience to the next. (Scales typical of each factor are shown in parentheses.)

Percentage of total variance explained by each factor

Factors	Experts	Students	Laymen
Evaluation	24%	17%	11%
("pleasant, good, beautiful")			
Potency	15	20	15
("rugged, masculine")			
Activity	9	13	21
("fast, young")			
Complexity	16	14	7
("fancy, complex")			
Physical aspects	6	6	5
("large, angular")			
Total variance	70%	70%	59%

Further analysis showed that the experts were most inclined to extreme and favorable judgments, avoiding the meaningless midpoint ratings of the bipolar scales. Laymen showed the least unanimity in their judgments.

The authors then resorted to analysis of variance to see which of the three variables being studied were responsible for differences on each dimension. This varied with the particular dimension of meaning—the factor—involved. Here are the most important differences in average factor scores; a score of "1" representing the most valued, potent, and active score possible:

	Evaluation	Potency	Activity
Family			
Garamond	2.8	4.98	
Spartan		3.35	3.22
Bodoni		3.40	
Kabel	4.1	2.37	3.95
Inclination			
Regular		3.30	3.96
Italic		3.70	3.11
Case			
Capital		3.30	
Lower case		3.80	

As the underlined figures indicate, the best way to indicate strength in a message would be to use regular, Kabel capitals, and the best way to indicate activity would be to use Spartan italics. Evaluative ratings were more complex; the meanings of both case and inclination varied with the family of type and, in addition, with the type of audience.

Nevertheless, anyone planning communication with laymen of the kind studied here might do well to note that both activity and potency scales "explain" more of their reactions than evaluation, and that ratings on these scales, in turn, seem to be more simply determined than the evaluative ratings.

—Percy H. Tannenbaum, Harvey K. Jacobson, and Eleanor L. Norris, "An Experimental Investigation of Typeface Connotations," *Journalism Quarterly*, 41: 1:65–73.

Layout. This dimension in turn has many elements that include the ratio of white space to illustration and type, and their arrangement on the page. It, too, has attention-getting, legibility, and connotative effects and is frequently used to direct the reader's gaze down a page.

The quality of paper on which a message is printed, and the color of ink and paper will also have an effect. It is not always clear whether the reader is responding to something intrinsic in print itself or merely recognizing current conventions in the use of print. If the latter is true, then an adventurous communicator may, on occasion, profit by running counter to convention.

Pictures

Next to words themselves, the most important symbol system in marketing communications is the system of pictures. In some instances, pictures carry the entire burden of the advertiser's message; in most consumer advertising they carry a large share of the burden.

Pictures, like words, can be highly denotative in content, as in the instructions for assembling a bicycle or in the contour map of a damsite, or they can be highly connotative, as in the typical *New Yorker* perfume advertisement. Some persons argue that advertising is most effective when it avoids words and persuades through pictures (Martineau). Words, they suggest, should be used only to give the guise of rational behavior to a man who has already been persuaded by a pictorial message. Pictures return high reward for little effort, and so are useful in communicating with the illiterate or, cross-culturally, with persons who speak a different language. They have not been associated as words have with the penalty-fraught situation of formal schooling.

Although pictures, like the spoken word, predate writing, and although writing itself began with pictures, we know very little of the vocabulary and syntax and the elements and structure of pictorial communication. Despite this lack of knowledge, pictures are performing these major functions in marketing communication:

Attention. In advertising, pictures, through contrast with a verbal context, attract attention. By presenting objects in unusual settings or content which contrasts with our expectations and experiences, they attract attention. The contrast between color and black and white attracts attention, too.

Mood. Well-composed pictures may, in themselves, be rewarding, aside from any reward implied by the objects they picture. Thus they can create moods, nonverbal feelings of pleasure or displeasure. Since most of us control our environment through the use of words, we may be less aware that pictures are influencing us than if words were used and less able to resist the influence even if we are aware of it. Before we can argue with a picture, we must express its meaning

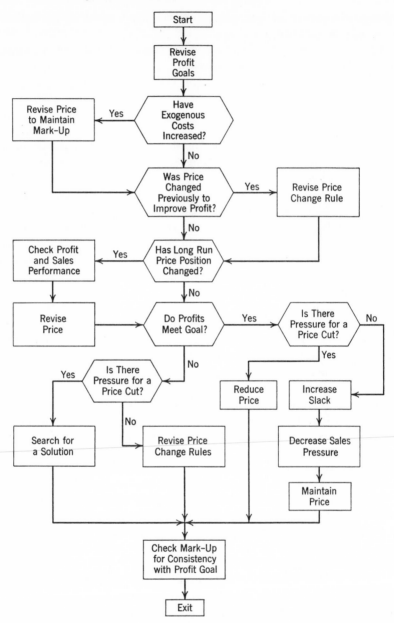

Fig. 4.1. This flow chart, one form of pictorial symbol, uses relations in space to show relations in time: successive stages of decision making about prices. (Richard M. Cyert and James G. March, *A Behavioral Theory of the Firm* (c) 1963, by permission of Prentice-Hall, Inc., Englewood Cliffs, New Jersey.)

in words. Even if we are willing to go to the effort of doing this, the very process of so doing tends to influence us.

Recognition. With the rise of self-service retailing, it is crucial that a customer be able to recognize a brand quickly. A picture of a package can develop this ability more easily than dozens of words.

Structure. If we want to describe how elements are related to one another in space, a picture is usually the most efficient way of doing so. Maps and organizational charts do this. So does every diagram which accompanies an assemble-it-yourself toy.

Process. Pictures are also useful in relating objects, or events, to one another in time. This can be done with moving pictures, as in the demonstration on a television commercial, or with still pictures, in which relations-in-space are used to symbolize relations-in-time. A flow chart of an industrial process or a sequence of pictures showing how to bake a cake are examples of the advantage over moving pictures because they can be studied in detail, over and over again, at one's own pace.

Numbers

In business and in science, numbers are steadily increasing in importance as a symbol system, whether they are numbers on the manager's balance sheet, on the computer program which directs an orbiting satellite, or in the table which forms the core of the behavioral scientist's article in a scholarly journal. Salesmen discussing purchase

---

Of all the variables that go into a message, which have most influence upon such an effect as readership? Here is an answer, found by using the techniques of factor analysis and multiple regression.

Size, Color, and Illustration Used in Formula

Taking 137 advertisements in the February 1950 issue of the 80,000-circulation business paper, *American Builder*, the author counted and measured 15 mechanical variables and 19 content variables. Out of these 34, he then chose the 19 which showed highest correlation with scores on "recall reading any part of this advertisement."

He correlated each of the variables with one another and subjected the resultant 19 × 19 matrix to centroid factor analysis, graphic rotation for orthogonal factors. This gave him the following factor table; the first 2 factors account for 53% of observed variance and 4 others for another 15 per cent.

Rotated Factor Loadings

Variable	Picture-Color	Size	Type	Information	Field	Prevs. Adv.	h²r
Readership	*64*	35	28	18	16	09	6766
Sq. in. illustration	*51*	48	25	06	23	04	6111
Pictures of Use	*51*	23	−18	09	10	−44	5571
Number of colors	*49*	−07	23	11	−15	01	3326
Size of Ad	18	*69*	26	45	45	04	9827
No. of Prod. Facts	20	*37*	−24	28	−12	−35	4498
Brad-Vern Schedules	21	*37*	−25	−01	07	34	3641
Largest Type	15	45	*62*	36	12	03	7543
Largest Prod. Ident.	18	34	*43*	21	−06	04	4277
Number Type Sizes	01	37	*47*	47	−16	−19	6405
Body Type Size	12	04	*46*	09	00	25	2982
Headline Size	26	24	*34*	30	14	27	4233
Number Words	05	46	−10	*71*	00	−03	7291
Number Copy Blocks	25	27	−13	*65*	10	−33	6937
Number Prod. Ident.	31	29	−20	*64*	19	06	6695
No. Prod. Benefits	14	52	−22	*57*	−06	−17	6658
Surround	−05	−13	61	10	*76*	17	1.0064
Previous Schedule	42	46	−21	19	14	*47*	7087
Pica Width	35	−01	34	14	05	*43*	4452
Number Illust.	36	17	−05	27	25	*−40*	4564

(Decimals omitted. Italics indicate factor on which each variable has its highest loading.)

Next he chose three of the original variables to represent the major factors, found they produced a multiple correlation coefficient with readership of .77, and constructed a multiple regression formula, which predicted readership on the basis of three variables.

His formula—Readership equals: 10.456 plus 8.29 (size of advertisement in pages) plus 3.87 (number of colors) plus .18 (square inches of illustration). Using this formula he predicted readership for advertisements in 6 different publications and got correlations of .58 to .80 between predicted and actual, and an average of .71.

—Dik Warren Twedt, "A Multiple Factor Analysis of Advertising Readership," *Journal of Applied Psychology*, 36:207–215.

of supplies, materials, or equipment with manufacturers ply their slide rules, and industrial advertising often makes its pivotal points with the aid of numbers.

Only in consumer advertising are numbers usually missing. Although we may be told that children have 23 per cent fewer cavities or that Ivory Soap is 99.44 per cent pure, we will find few graphs, few bar charts, few percentages, and few indices in most advertisements directed at consumers.

Conclusions from a study and the decisions to be based upon them will vary with the index number used to summarize the findings.

Same Data—Three Different Conclusions

Three to five days after an issue of the *Houston Chronicle* had appeared, the newspaper compared recall scores of advertisements in a split-run test in which some subscribers got the advertisements in black and white and some got them in color. Effects of color were compared for both full-page and smaller advertisements. Here are the 4 figures that resulted from the study—plus 3 different ways of summarizing the results:

| | Retention scores | | | Indices | |
| | Black- | Two- | | "Conven- | |
Ad size	white	color	Net diff.	tional"	Hovland
Small	13%	26%	13%	100%	14.3%
Full page	26	39	13	50	21.3

Subtracting black-and-white scores from color scores produces the "net difference" column which shows that color's superiority bore no relationship to size of advertisement. Dividing the "net difference" figures by the scores for black-and-white advertisements, to show how much better color was, produces the "conventional" indices. These suggest that color was more effective with small advertisements than with large ones.

The Hovland or "Effectiveness Index" is calculated by expressing color's advantage as a percentage of possible increase—dividing the net difference figures by 87 for small advertisements (100–13%) and 74 for full-page advertisements. This comparison suggests that color was more effective with full-page than with small advertisements.

Which interpretation will we choose? This depends on what use we want to make of the figures. A researcher who believes that retention scores increase easily once we reach a "threshold" indicated by 25% readership will deprecate the gains by color for the full-page and pick the "conventional" index. His colleague, who believes that 25% comes close to a readership ceiling, will value the full-page gains made by color and pick the "effectiveness index." And a businessman is likely to ask which page-color combination costs less in terms of readers-who-remember-his-advertisement-per-dollar; he is likely to prefer the "net difference" figures.

—Based on James C. Becknell, Jr., "Comment on Webb's Case for the Effectiveness Index," *Journal of Advertising Research*, 2:4:42–43 (1962).

This may change as the rising level of education and the increasing importance of mathematics in education make consumers feel more at ease with figures. Whether it does or not, the marketing communicator needs to know how to choose the number which best conveys his message, how to combine several numbers in a message and how to pick the best verbal label for the numbers he decides to use.

Since few persons are willing or able to extract meaning from a table of figures, and those few may extract a meaning other than that intended by the source, the communicator usually prefers to summarize it for them. Usually this means he tries to indicate a *central tendency* or average in a set of figures. He has his choice of three different measures of central tendency: the arithmetic mean, the median, and the mode. When the data form the normal, bell-shaped curve, beloved of statisticians and psychologists, all three measures will fall at the same place, at the midpoint of the curve. When the data are not "normal," however, each may fall at a different point and convey quite a different meaning. The mean will be distorted by extreme values: a mean income of $10,000 may reflect a neighborhood in which the range runs from $9000 to $11,000 or one which has a single millionaire and everyone else on relief. The median, on the other hand, will report the midpoint of the range, and the mode will report the most common income, regardless of either range of individual incomes or their actual size.

Instead of the central tendency of these data, a communicator may wish to indicate the *amount of variation* in them. The range is a simple measure of such variation. More precise measures which are keystones of inferential statistics are the *variance* and its square root, the *standard deviation*. A third possibility is that the communicator wants to show the *relationship* between two variables or between the values of a single variable at two different points in time. The task becomes complicated when he wants to show several relationships or the relation between relationships.

One way of doing this is to break a complex table into a series of smaller tables, so that the relationships are shown in sequence instead of all at once. Another way is to put the figures into the pictorial form of a bar diagram or a graph. A third way is to "throw away" some of the original detailed information and convert the data into a summary figure—a percentage, a ratio, an index, or a coefficient. (In actuality, information is "thrown away" only in the sense of data transmitted; in terms of data received by the audience, the amount conveyed by a summary figure may actually increase.)

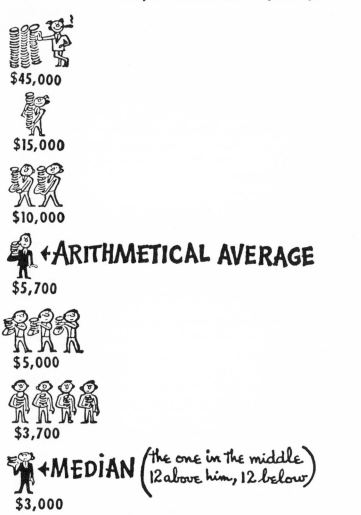

$45,000

$15,000

$10,000

←ARITHMETICAL AVERAGE

$5,700

$5,000

$3,700

←MEDIAN (the one in the middle, 12 above him, 12 below)

$3,000

←MODE (occurs most frequently)

$2,000

Fig. 4.2. (Darrell Huff, *How to Lie with Statistics*, W. W. Norton and Co., New York, 1954.)

The way one uses numbers depends both on his theories as to cause-effect relationships and on the nature of his data.

Tables Tell a Tale If Totals Tally Right Way

Here is a table, based on hypothetical figures for a small town in the Midwest, which provides very little information because the percentages are figured the wrong way:

Home Ownership and Income

	Own home	Rent
High income	25%	5%
Medium income	40	30
Low income	35	65
	100%	100%

What is wrong with this table? The *causal* variable should appear at the head of the columns, and in this instance it is clear that income determines home ownership rather than the reverse. Only if we happen to know that the high-income group represents about 10% of the population and the middle-income group about 30% can we see the effect of income on ownership.

Sometimes, however, either way of figuring percentages makes sense. Here is an example, with car-sale figures for a hypothetical midwestern town:

Make	Sedan	Model Convertible	Hardtop	Totals
Chevrolet	36	16	31	83
Ford	31	17	28	76
Plymouth	27	12	30	69
Totals	94	45	89	228

You, as an automobile dealer, may want to know which of your models is most popular. This table will tell you:

Percentage of Automobile Sales
by Make and Model

	Chevrolet	Ford	Plymouth
Sedan	43%	41%	39%
Convertible	19	22	17
Hardtop	38	37	44
Total	100%	100%	100%

On the other hand, you may be more interested in how big a share of market your brand of automobile gets. In that case, use models not makes to head your columns:

Percentage of Automobile Sales
by Make and Model

	Sedan	Convertible	Hardtop
Chevrolet	38%	35%	35%
Ford	33	38	31
Plymouth	29	27	34
Total	100%	100%	100%

Tables can be confusing if you try to pack too much information into them. Here is an example, based on a report made in 1962 for *Reader's Digest,* showing readership for the magazine by sex, age-group, and geographic region:

Percentage Who Receive *Reader's Digest*

Region	Age Group							
	10–17		18–34		35–54		55 and older	
	Men	Women	Men	Women	Men	Women	Men	Women
Northeast	15%	16%	16%	17%	21%	24%	23%	22%
Metropolitan New York	14	16	19	18	23	25	22	22
Great Lakes	12	14	14	16	21	24	21	21
Southern	7	10	10	11	15	18	18	17
North Central	12	12	14	16	20	25	23	24
Southwest	11	9	14	14	18	22	19	19
Pacific	15	20	16	16	25	29	27	32
Metropolitan Los Angeles	20	16	18	23	23	29	28	28

By going back to the original data, and calculating new percentages, this can be reduced to three summary tables, each of which considers only one of the three variables that might affect coverage:

Percentage Who Receive *Reader's Digest*

	By Region	By Age		By Sex	
Northeast	19%	10–17	13%	Men	17%
Metropolitan New York	21	18–34	15	Women	19
		35–54	22		
Great Lakes	18	55 up	22		
Southern	13				
North Central	19				
Southwest	16				
Pacific	23				
Metropolitan Los Angeles	24				

Or we can produce two-way tables such as this one:

	Percentage Who Receive *Reader's Digest*	
Region	Men	Women
Northeast	19%	20%
New York City	20	21
Great Lakes	17	19
Southern	12	14
North Central	18	20
Southwest	15	16
Pacific	21	25
Los Angeles	22	25

Another way of simplifying a complicated table is to report averages. Here, for example, is a comparison of one student's predictions with actual Starch measurement of readership for a series of advertisements in the *Saturday Evening Post:*

Student Estimates Compared with Readership of Selected Advertisements

Advertisement	Men		Women	
	Noted	Read Most	Noted	Read Most
Rambler	+ 8%	−13%	− 7%	−9%
Plymouth	−42	−15	−32	−5
Cadillac	−35	0	−22	+2
Longines	−13	+ 3	−19	+2
Admiral TV	−26	+ 3	−24	+2
Kent Cigarettes	+11	+14	+14	+8

It is hard to see any pattern in these scores, but mean scores show very quickly that the student underestimated "noted" scores, but did a fairly good job of predicting the "read most" scores which, of course, tend to be much smaller:

Average Discrepancy between Student Estimates and Actual Scores

	Noted	Read Most
Men	−16%	−1.3%
Women	−15	0

In addition to breaking a complex table into simpler sub-tables, various kinds of summary figures may be used.

It Is Often the Mode to Use the Mean

The firm which wants to reward the "most efficient" batsman on the Little League team it sponsors can do so on the number of home runs alone. Or it can try to take into account an overabundance of data like this:

Player	1 Base	2 Bases	3 Bases	Home Runs	Times at Bat
Maier	101	23	12	34	502
Dooley	133	36	11	9	578
Crabb	73	8	11	46	500

An index, the slugging average, reduces each boy's record to a single figure. It is calculated by multiplying each hit by the number of bases it won and dividing by total times at bat:

	Slugging Averages	
Maier	319/502	.635
Dooley	274/578	.474
Crabb	306/500	.612

Marketing communications rests on a host of such indices—ranging from the complex, even controversial, calculation of a consumer's price index to such equally controversial indices of media performance as readers-per-dollar, program ratings expressed as percentage of sets-in-use, and advertising costs as percentage of sales.

—Suggested by Hans Zeisel, *Say It With Figures* (New York: Harper and Brothers, 1947).

Both source and receiver should know the alternative ways in which a given set of data may be summarized, since each alternative may suggest a different relationship between cause-and-effect, a different strength in this relationship, or different implications for action. Speaking to a union audience, for instance, a public relations man may report that a firm suffered "a 40 per cent drop in profits as compared with last year" or "a return of only 2 per cent on sales." Using the same basic figures, he may then tell stockholders that the firm earned "a 10 per cent return on investment," made "a $15,000,000 profit," or experienced "a rise in profits of 30 per cent over the 10-year average." Same firm, same balance sheet, but different verbal labels.

Similarly, an identical amount of money paid to employees can be described as a fall in pay (that is, a lower rate per hour); no change in pay (that is, hours worked per day rose enough to offset the drop in hourly rate) or an increase in pay (that is, elimination of layoffs leads to a higher *annual* rate of pay). Union officials trying to win a pay increase would probably emphasize the per-hour figure. The same officials, attempting to persuade members to accept an offer from management, would probably use the annual rate.

Attitudes can be changed by persuading the people who hold them to change their evaluation of a category, by changing the category itself or by relabeling the category. Some time ago, American businessmen discovered that the public apparently believes that profits much over 6 per cent are exorbitant. Instead of trying to prove to the public that this belief is unrealistic, firms began reporting profits as a percentage of *sales* rather than a percentage of investment. This makes little sense to the traditional meaning of profit in economics, but it brought the percentage down to a range the public regarded as legitimate. Presumably those in the audience who were interested enough to note what had been done and able to recalculate profit in the usual meaning of the term were not likely to be hostile to a rate of over 6 per cent.

Symbols and Messages

In his attempts to influence people, the marketing communicator has available a great variety of symbols in each of several systems: spoken, written and printed language, pictures, and numbers. This is fortunate, since it enables him to communicate a great variety of meanings to widely differing audiences. By using only a part of the variety of symbols available to him, he can communicate effectively in very diverse situations and amidst a welter of competing communicators. Selecting symbols is only part of his task, however. He must also combine them into messages. How he does this is the subject of the next chapter.

SUMMARY

1. Through such symbols as words, pictures, and numbers, the communicator creates expectancies. He uses an attribute as the cue to a category and all its other attendant attributes. His aim is to use the smallest number of symbols necessary to create a given attitude in a given audience with a specified degree of precision and probability.
2. By using more than one cue and several symbol systems, the communicator achieves three ends: he overcomes interference or "noise," he conveys connotative meanings, and he can achieve very subtle distinctions.

3. Information theory provides a definition of the minimum number of cues needed to convey meaning; an example of computer language shows how "extra" cues, above this minimum, can prevent error caused by noise. This is done in four ways: by making cues neither independent nor equally likely, by accepting only part of the available cues as meaningful, and through context.

4. Different sets of symbols are needed to convey a given theme in marketing communications either because (1) different media are required to reach different audiences or (2) repetition-*with-variation* is needed.

5. Speech, the most universal symbol system, operates within two limits: the mouth's ability to produce sound and the ear's ability to receive it. Language imposes further limits, accepting only certain sounds and certain sound combinations as meaningful in a denotative or referential sense.

6. Differences in sound not required to convey denotative differences nevertheless convey information about the source: his age, his sex, his distance from the receiver, his social class, and so on.

7. The written word tends to less redundancy and brevity than the spoken word because it usually occurs under less noisy conditions.

8. The words one uses reveal a great deal about his personal characteristics, as well as the place and times in which he communicates. Indicators include vocabulary size and variation and sentence length and its variation.

9. The printed word has four devices to overcome noise or convey connotative meanings: type size, type family, type face, and the combination of type, illustration, and white space called layout.

10. Next to words themselves in importance are pictures, which run the gamut from highly denotative to highly connotative. They can help attract attention and create moods, aid product recognition, and express structure and process.

11. Although numbers are little used in consumer advertising, they are important in industrial communications as in business and science generally. For persons ill at ease with this symbol system, the communicator must provide simplified summaries. These summaries may express a central tendency (mean, mode, or median), a range of variation, or a relationship. The choice both of a figure and of the verbal label which is attached to it may have a good deal to do with the communicator's success.

Research Studies

People's attitudes will change to match their behavior, say *Festinger and Carlsmith*, and the less pressure one uses to change their behavior in the first place, the more subsequent change will occur in their attitudes.

Communications, of course, uses messages to change both behavior and attitudes, and messages are made up of symbols. Before a source can select symbols, he needs to know something about the way his receivers use them. *Woodrow and Lowell* report on word-association habits, and *Tannenbaum, Jacobson and Norris* on how the emotional responses to words vary with the type in which they are set. *Twedt* looks at 34 different variables and predicts readership of advertisements by the size of an advertisement, the size of its illustration, and the number of colors used.

shows how three different indices can be devised to answer a single question, and no two of them agree on the answer! Finally, an illustration suggested by *Zeisel* shows how percentages as well as indices must be figured with due respect both to the function one wants the percentage to perform and the data on which it is based.

Five

Tools of the Communicator
II: Messages

Before communication can occur, a source must combine the symbols he has chosen into larger structures such as sentences and messages. "Structure" is a relative term; what is structure at one level of analysis becomes an element for the next higher level. Thus to an engineer the typewriter which originally produced these words is a structure, made up of levers and screws and wheels and bits of type. To its user, however, the typewriter is an element in a larger structure. *What* structure the typewriter becomes a part of depends on the function one is interested in at the moment. The typewriter may, for example, be grouped with filing cabinet and desk as office equipment, or with tables and chairs as a taxable unit of personal property. My wife and children may regard it as a substitute for the frontiersman's rifle, in putting meat on the table, and my students, when I use it to design an examination, as an instrument of torture.

Words are the basic element of the communicator. He is seldom interested in breaking words down into their constituent sounds. His first task, therefore, is to select words. His second task is to combine these words into sentences and his third task is to combine these sentences into messages. We know some and are discovering more scientific regularities about words themselves.

We can measure the readability of a message, for example, with a computer (Danielson and Bryan). We know that short words and short sentences aid communications not only because they take less time to read and less effort to pronounce but because brevity is an index of familiarity. We find that frequently used phrases tend to telescope into "words" such as "UNESCO" (for United Nations Educational, Scientific and Cultural ·Organization) or "the TV" for television-receiving-set.

129

We know that it is usually easier to communicate at a specific and concrete level than an abstract level. If we provide an attribute, our audience will more easily and predictably supply the category we desire, and the evaluation we desire, than if we provide the category and hope they will supply the appropriate attribute.

We know that the same idea may need to be expressed in very different words, depending on the age, sex, social class, and attitudes of our audience. We know that words and phrases which get attention today, which set a product apart from its competition, and which challenge the audience's expectations are likely to lose their novelty quickly.

Ideas, Not Words

The key to successful communications, however, is not words at all, but ideas—to the marketer, such ideas as product features, consumer benefits, copy platforms. Unfortunately, since ideas must be expressed in symbols, many of us confuse the two and act as if writing advertisements were just a matter of juggling words. If it were, then computers would be writing advertisements for us, since they can juggle a lot more words a lot faster than we can.

A good idea can be expressed in dozens of different ways. One way to find such words or phrases to express an idea is to go back to the place we found the idea itself: to the people who use, or should use, the product. Good salesmen, if not strait jacketed by a canned pitch supplied by the front office, can catch these ideas and phrases as they fly by. Many advertisers and advertising agency people, however, are so far removed from the public, so different from their customers, and so insulated from them, that they have to depend upon market researchers who have been trained to listen for ideas.

(Incidentally, listening to the public does not involve less work or require less creative insight than dreaming up ideas at a typewriter in a cork-walled room. It requires a great ability to select; much of what the public has to say will be dull, repetitious, and an echo of what advertising itself has told them.) Some ideas or strategic insights require changes in product, in place or in price rather than, or in addition to, expression in messages.

Often a researcher will discover that the public has invented new uses for a product which expand its potential market. It was the public, for example, which decided that banana flakes really belong in the category of "baby food." Here was an idea that could be implemented by moving the product from one section of the supermarket to another. It was the public which discovered that Kleenex can be used for a lot of things other than removing facial cream. Advertising helped spread this news.

Sometimes pinning a new label on a product helps move it from a category which people reject to one they accept. This happened when "pool" was renamed "pocket billiards;" once renamed pool tables became acceptable in the home. Improving the image of bowling, on the other hand, required such technological innovations as pinsetters, a change of setting, and a variety of such accompanying features as women's leagues and babysitting services to make it acceptable to the whole family.

Attributes which an advertiser thinks are crucial to a category may be perceived quite differently by its users. Advertisers, for example, have been surprised to find people buying lemons not for their flavor but to cure constipation; luggage not for its strength but its style; and men's shoes not for their style but their comfort. One household product advertised that it "worked faster" (Hepner, 417). Yet a survey showed that only 2 per cent of the purchasers bought it for that reason. In contrast, 50 per cent bought it because it was easy on their hands, 20 per cent because it was not messy, and 18 per cent because it was "more effective."

The researcher may uncover felt needs which no existing product appears to meet; his employer can then produce a product to meet such needs, add an ingredient to his existing product, or claim that his product meets the need. Obviously the last method is often the cheapest. If the public has no better alternative, the "'mere words" of such a product claim can be highly effective, from the advertiser's point of view. People who worried because they could not brush their teeth after every meal or because their dogs did not get enough exercise were relieved of these worries, at least, when a toothpaste claimed it could take care of the first condition and a dog food promised to handle the second. They paid for relief of worry as well as clean teeth and well-fed dogs.

Where consumer benefits exist and products do differ, words can help more people discover the benefits and the differences more quickly than they would, if left to themselves. Words, of course, can also suggest benefits and differences which have little counterpart in objective reality, and such suggestions may lead to product purchase. Such illusions are always vulnerable, however, to user experience with the product and to a competitor's counterattack.

Connote or Denote?

Words differ, we have already noted, in the extent to which they identify a category or express a value for it. "Identification" implies that there is widespread agreement on the category, and is achieved by words which denote or point to, particularly the words that refer to specific, concrete, physical objects. "Value" suggests that there is difference of opinion, and it is expressed by words which connote, particularly those which refer to social, rather than physical reality. Most of us agree on the attributes of such physical realities as death, and agree that it is likely to follow a ten-story fall to a paved street. We are less likely to agree that winning a majority vote makes a candidate the "best" man for the job.

Connotative words usually are perceived as expressing the values of the person who uses them. They do not necessarily cause the receiver to accept those same values as his own. A source may find it most effective to use denotative words, selecting the details denoted so that when an audience supplies its own connotative, value-laden terms to the category being described, their evaluation will favor his goals.

Perhaps the most thorough study of connotative words and their meaning ever made is that of Charles Osgood, whose semantic differential technique presents a series of concepts, followed by pairs of adjectives of opposite meaning. Respondents make one check for each pair of adjectives, to indicate what the concept means to them (Osgood, Suci, Tannenbaum). Here is an example:

Mother

Good	:	X	:	:	:	:	:	Bad
Hard	:	:	:	:	X	:	:	Soft
Active	:	:	:	X	:	:	:	Passive

These ratings indicate that the respondent feels "mother" is very good, somewhat soft but neither active nor passive. (The middle of the scale represents the neutrality of either ambivalence or indifference or an inability to relate adjectives to the concept.)

In a typical Osgood experiment, eighteen students in an advertising class in copywriting sorted 289 sets of polar adjectives, drawn from a thesaurus, into seventeen categories, on the basis of their similarity (Osgood and others, 48–49). The seventy-six scales finally selected were then used by 100 other college students to rate twenty concepts, equally divided among nouns labeling persons, physical objects, such abstract concepts as modern art and sin, events as birth, and institutions as the United Nations.

A series of such studies showed that a strong evaluating factor, represented by good-bad in the scale above, accounts for 50 to 75 per cent of variance in individual ratings explained by all the scales combined (Osgood and others, 72–74). Second in importance, is a "potency" factor, represented by hard-soft above, which explains about half as much variance as the first factor. Third is an "activity" factor, about equal to potency in its explanatory ability. Additional factors—among them such things as stability, novelty, aggressiveness, and so on—vary with the concepts studied, and together explain only about half as much variance as potency and activity. Of course the relationship among scales varies with the concept being judged. A soft pillow may be good, a soft banana bad. We like our enemies to be weak and inactive and our friends to be strong and vigorous; the "good" qualities in an enemy are "bad" qualities in a friend!

Types of Sentences

Sentences, as well as words, differ in the extent to which they point to a category and attach a value to the category, and in the extent to which we find it easy or difficult to agree on them (Berlo, 217–277).

Judgments such as, "Too much money is spent on advertising in the United States," tell a good deal about the speaker. We can agree or disagree with the beliefs expressed in them, but we cannot say that the beliefs are either true or false. *Reports*, on the other hand, can be verified. "An average of 3 per cent of national income was spent on advertising during the 20 years preceding World War II," is a statement whose truth or falsity can be determined.

The difference is one of degree, however. There can be a great deal of disagreement on how "national income" and "advertising expenditures" are to be defined in testing the *report* statement just made. It may be fairly easy, on the other hand, in any specific audience, to reach agreement that the proposition "If 3 per cent of national income were spent on advertising, that is too much" is either acceptable or unacceptable.

Two kinds of reports are particularly hard to verify: the predictions and statements of an association between facts. To verify predictions, such as, "Advertising costs will double in the next decade," we must wait until the facts are available. Verifying a statement of cause and effect relationships is even more difficult. "Advertising expenditures are rising because of increasing competition" is an example. We must define what we mean by advertising expenditures and competition, determine whether each is, in fact, increasing, determine whether the two increases are causally related, and finally, specify in which direction causation operates.

Judgmental statements, like connotative words, are perceived as expressing the values of the user, and revealing his goals in communication. Since this revelation itself may make it easier for a receiver to resist, a source may want to avoid using them. In contrast, a receiver may accept statements which report on the grounds that their falsity is so easy to determine that no source would dare report what was not true. He may accept statements of causation for the opposite reason: because he himself finds it difficult to determine whether they are true or not or to provide any alternative explanation. Predictions may, like reports, be accepted because they appear easy to check in the future; a source may use them loosely, however, because he is sure that very few people will remember them or bother to check on their truthfulness. In short, we place different degrees of credibility on these several types of sentence; we apply different discount ratios to them.

Four Questions of Strategy

Most messages contain more than one idea. The effectiveness of a message depends not only on the ideas themselves but on the way they are put together—what we have called the structure of the message. Here are four questions we can ask about this structure:

1. Should only the points which favor the source's conclusion be mentioned, or should some of the "cons" be mentioned, too?
2. Is it better to speak our piece before or after the competition has its opportunity to be heard?
3. Should solutions to problems be provided before, or after, we have mentioned the problems themselves?
4. Is it enough to give all the facts, or must the source also draw a conclusion from the facts?

Let us start with the last point listed. From what we have said so far about connotative words and judgmental statements, it would seem to follow that drawing conclusions would cause resistance, by alerting receivers to the source's intent, and even resentment. What does the evidence suggest?

Conclusion Drawing

Two experiments suggest that if a source fails to draw a conclusion, the audiences may miss the point. In the first, college students in psychology were exposed to tape-recorded messages on devaluation of the currency (Hovland and Mandell). When the conclusion was stated, 48 per cent changed their opinions in the desired direction. When it was not, only 19 per cent did so. In another experiment, military recruits listened to speeches approving United States entry into the Korean War (Thistlethwaite and others). Educated subjects were equally affected by the version with conclusions and the version without. Other subjects, however, were more influenced by the version with conclusions.

Most advertising texts suggest that every advertisement should end with a specific request for action; some advertisements make the action easier by supplying a coupon or even attaching a prepaid, ready-to-mail postcard. Insurance salesmen make seven specific attempts to close a sale; they insist on getting seven "no's" before they will let the door close behind them.

If an audience is forced to sum up a message for itself, is the message more effective? This study suggests that some persons can not sum up the message and that those who can draw a conclusion for themselves show no more opinion change when they do so than when the source does so for them.

Was Decision to Fight a Limited War in Korea Wise?

Ten questions on United States policies in Korea were buried in a 62-item questionnaire given to 720 Air Force recruits. A week later, 4 groups were played tape-recorded messages 20 to 24 minutes long, accompanied by slides on the subject; a fifth control group listened to a program on tooth decay. Each experimental group then filled out an 18-item questionnaire, 4 questions of which measured subjects' comprehension of the speaker's overall conclusion. Scores on this were used to measure recruits' comprehension of the message. This was followed by a repeat of the opinion questionnaire given earlier.

For 2 groups, messages ended with a 1-minute conclusion by the speaker; for 2 others no conclusion was drawn. Each of these pairs, in turn, was further divided, with 1 group getting a "well-organized" message in which 2 minutes were devoted to a series of 23 statements to introduce and recapitulate issues and subtopics.

All 4 of the experimental programs changed attitudes toward the Korean war, as compared with the control group, differences being significant at the .05 level. Some of the differences were still significant 3 weeks later.

Three things influenced recruits' *comprehension* of the messages, as shown in the following table:

Analysis of Variance of Comprehension Scores (444 subjects matched on technician specialty aptitude index)

	F	p values
A. Conclusion drawing	3.84	.05
B. Good organization of message	3.84	.05
C. Higher IQ	28.61	.001

(None of the interactions—$A \times B$, $A \times C$, $B \times C$, and $A \times B \times C$—was significant.)

However, neither of the message variables—conclusion drawing and organization—produced significant differences in *attitude change*. A study was made of only those subjects who had answered at least 3 of the 5 comprehension questions correctly. Comparisons of conclusion drawing were made separately for subjects receiving poorly organized and well-organized messages. Differences favored no conclusion for 110 subjects getting the poorly organized messages and were not significant for the 118 receiving well-organized messages.

—Donald L. Thistlethwaite, Henry de-Haan, and Joseph Kamenetzky, "The Effects of 'Directive' and 'Nondirective' Communication Procedures on Attitudes," *Journal of Abnormal and Social Psychology*, 51:107–113.

Failure to draw a conclusion can aid a source by helping to conceal his intent. This may be useful in some forms of communication. In advertising and selling, however, the intent of the source is clear from the outset. The receiver expects to be asked to buy. He accepts this condition, and has been preparing to say yes or no throughout the communications encounter. If no conclusion is drawn, the encounter itself appears a waste of time.

Solutions or Problems?

In general, an audience must be motivated before it will pay attention to a message or learn its content. It does little good to provide solutions for problems an audience is unaware of. This was shown clearly when pairs of advertisements for twenty products, one emphasizing the need and the other its solution, were compared (Strong and Loveless).

The advertisements that emphasized need-arousal proved superior. It was also shown in an experiment with college students on the issue of grading on a curve (Hovland et al., 135–136). A need-arousing message changed more student opinion immediately and retained its superiority over a 3-month period.

The audience itself, however, must be studied before a message is prepared. Some audiences have such a strong need, and are so conscious of it, that the message itself need not waste time creating a problem for them. It can move directly to a solution.

Moreover, it is possible to go too far in need-arousal, as shown by studies of the so-called negative or "fear" appeal. In one experiment, a message threatening serious illness from tooth decay increased worry but did not improve behavior (Janis and Feshbach).

Can you get people to buy your product by showing them what will happen if they do not—or should you always stress the positive benefits?

"Scare Appeal" on Teeth Boomerangs

Four groups of 50 high school freshmen were formed in Connecticut. One group used a strong negative appeal, warning that poor care of teeth could lead to infections which could cause paralysis or blindness; 71 such "scare" items were included. A second group received a moderate message, with only 49 items. A third group received a "mild" message, with only 18 items, most of them talking about cavities rather than decay. Each of these three groups also saw slides, ranging from the gruesome, in the strong-appeal audience, to photographs of healthy teeth, in the mild-appeal group. (The fourth, control group heard a lecture on the human eye.)

The three messages seemed to be equally effective in transmitting information to the pupils, but the strong message had more effect upon their emotions:

	Percentage of Students Agreeing with Statement in Each Group		
	Strong Threat	Moderate Threat	Minimal Threat
I felt worried about care of teeth	66%	36%	34%
Talk does a good teaching job	62	50	40
Disliked something in the talk	28	8	2

A comparison of scores on a 5-point "not worried—very worried about decayed teeth" scale which was given a week before the messages showed that 42 per cent of the strong-threat group, 26 per cent of the moderate-threat group, 24 per cent of the minimal-threat group, and

8 per cent of the control group showed an increase in worry after the messages.

However, when a comparison was made of student's actual behavior, as reported in a measure taken a week before and week after the message, the low-threat message was found to be the most effective. Behavior was measured in two ways: conformity with such counsel as using a vertical stroke and brushing inner surface of teeth, and the number who went to dentist during the week after hearing the message.

	Strong Threat	Moderate Threat	Minimal Threat	Control
Net percentage increase	8%	22%	36%	—
Percentage who went to dentist	10	14	18	4

The authors suggest that when a message arouses fear but fails to relieve it, receivers will be motivated to forget the message or minimize the seriousness of the situation it deals with.

—Irving L. Janis and Seymour Feshbach, "Effects of Fear-Arousing Communications," *Journal of Abnormal and Social Psychology*, 48:78–92.

The same talks were used in another experiment in which subjects were asked to write down later as much of each message as they could remember (Janis and Milholland). The group that got the high-threat message recalled more of the unfavorable consequences; the low-threat group recalled more of the causes of such consequences.

In both these laboratory experiments, subjects were forced to listen to the talks. In real life, however, subjects may actually avoid exposure to high-threat messages. Smokers, for example, have been found to read fewer articles concerning the relationship between cigarettes and cancer than nonsmokers. In addition, they are less influenced by what they do read (Cannell and MacDonald).

Fear appeals seem to resemble punishment in learning, which may make an audience avoid or reject the source, rather than follow his suggestions on avoiding the undesirable effects themselves. Like punishment, fear appeals may increase anxiety to the point that persons fail to hear suggestions as to how they can avoid unpleasant results.

First or Last?

Except in the laboratory or a debate tournament, a source rarely has the opportunity to decide whether he will appear first or last. When he does, which is better? Apparently the second speaker has an advantage (Hovland et al., 130–131). In two out of three groups in one experiment, and three out of four groups in another, "recency" (appearing last) was superior to "primacy" (appearing first).

Extremes of "positive" and "negative" appeals are probably less pronounced in advertising than in the experiment just cited.

In Coupons, the Results Split 57 to 57

The number of coupons returned for 117 pairs of positive and negative advertisements for the same product, appearing in the same periodical at about the same season, were compared.

Number of pairs in which best ad was:

Product Advertising	Positive	Negative	No difference
Toothpaste	17	13	1
Food drink	19	17	1
Breakfast food	4	9	
Sanitation products	3	4	
Extension courses	14	14	1
	57	57	3

The authors concluded that variations within the two types of appeal were far more important than differences between them.

—D. B. Lucas and C. E. Benson, "The Relative Values of Positive and Negative Advertising Appeals as Measured by Coupons Returned," *Journal of Applied Psychology*, 13:274–300.

In Sales, Positive Appeals Show Superiority

Twenty-eight advertisements promoting a book to educate-by-mail were compared on the basis of the sales they produced. In terms of number of sales, 1 negative-appeal advertisement was only 36 per cent as effective as a matching positive appeal advertisement while another was 29 per cent more effective. In terms of costs, a negative advertisement was 49 per cent as effective as the positive member of the pair, while another was 325 per cent as effective. Overall, differences favored 16 positive advertisements, and 12 negative advertisements.

Another comparison involved sales of a proprietary drug in 5 groups of 3 test markets each over a 4-month period. A negative appeal here showed an increase of 71 per cent over the same period of the previous year; a positive appeal produced a decrease of 10 per cent.

—D. B. Lucas and C. E. Benson, "Some Sales Results for Positive and Negative Advertisements," *Journal of Applied Psychology*, 14:363–370.

This holds true only if the messages are presented by two different persons, however. In some experiments, the same person has presented both sides. When the source presents the second message, and so appears to contradict himself, students seem to suspect a trick and discount the second view (Hovland et al., 133–134). Much depends on what happens between the first and the second message. If the first message is preceded by a warning that first impressions are often erroneous, its advantage over the second is reduced (Hovland et al., 134–135). Its advantage is reduced even more if the warning follows the first message and reduced most of all if some unrelated activity intervenes between the first and second message. Such intervening activity, in fact, produces much the effect of having two different speakers give the message: the second message proves most effective.

Pros and Cons?

The first speaker does have one advantage: he can try to steal his opponent's thunder by mentioning some of his arguments—usually in weakened form and accompanied by his own answers. When does a source benefit by using a two-sided message, which includes both pros and cons, and when should he present only the arguments favoring his own position?

This question has been studied several times. Following Germany's surrender in World War II, some 400 American GIs were asked how long they thought the war with Japan would continue (Hovland, Lumsdaine, Sheffield). Then half the group was exposed to a one-sided 15-minute talk arguing that the war would last at least two more years. The other half got the same message but with some added material, citing Japanese weaknesses, to suggest that there was something to be said on the other side.

The results depended on the original attitudes of the men exposed to the messages. Among men originally opposed to the long-war conclusion, the two-sided message changed 48 per cent, and the one-sided message only 36 per cent. Among men who originally agreed with the long-war thesis, the one-sided message was superior, 52 to 23 per cent. A further breakdown by education showed that the two-sided message was more effective among men who had graduated from high school than with those who had not, regardless of their original position. In short, two-sided messages appear best with educated audiences and with audiences opposed to the source's point of view.

The two-sided message also is better with audiences which are likely to hear an opposing view at some time in the future. Several months before Russia set off its first atomic bomb, taped messages arguing that Russia would not be able to produce such bombs in quantity for at least 5 years were played for 197 high school pupils (Lumsdaine and Janis). One-sided messages changed the opinions of 64 per cent, about the same as two-sided messages, which changed the opinions of 69 per cent. A week later, however, half the pupils heard new

---

Research has shown that education and attitude affect probability of (a) being exposed to a message and (b) being influenced by it. Here are some hypothetical figures showing how this knowledge might affect an advertiser's decisions. (Figures in parentheses are products obtained by multiplying the two figures immediately preceding.)

Message Strategy Changes with Multiple Mailings

	High Education				Low Education			
	Like product		Dislike product		Like product		Dislike product	

Exposed

Figures on "exposure" reflect two facts: exposure rises with education, is higher for messages one agrees with. Percentage in each group exposed:

Like product		Dislike product		Like product		Dislike product	
90 %		75 %		70 %		50 %	
One-side	Two-side	One-side	Two-side	One-side	Two-side	One-side	Two-side

Affected

These figures show that educated persons and those opposed to the message tend to prefer two-sided messages.

Per cent in group affected:

One-side	Two-side	One-side	Two-side	One-side	Two-side	One-side	Two-side
40 %	50 %	20 %	40 %	60 %	40 %	40 %	50 %

Exposed and Affected

By multiplying the two percentages we find net effects of each message for each group:

(36 %)	(45 %)	(15 %)	(30 %)	(42 %)	(28 %)	(20 %)	(25 %)

Population

These percentages must now be applied to the actual population. (It is assumed that 30 % have high education and that attitudes are equally divided pro and con the product.)

15 %		15 %		35 %		35 %	

Effects of Message

Here are the actual per cents of the population favorably affected: those who liked the product buy it; those who didn't like it now do.

(5.4 %)	(6.7 %)	(2.3 %)	(4.5 %)	(14.7 %)	(9.8 %)	(7 %)	(8.7 %)
—Buy—		—Favor—		—Buy—		—Favor—	

We can now determine the *total effect* of the messages: 29.4% changed by one-sided and 29.7% by two-sided, or the *effect on sales:* 20.1% for one-sided and 16.5% by two-sided. But we can do something even more interesting. We can remove the actual purchasers from the population and send a second message; repeat the process and send a whole series of messages. Here is what happens with seven messages.

Cumulative proportion of population
purchasing the product—

Message No.	Type of Message One-sided	Two-sided
1	20.1%	16.5%
2	35.8	31.8
3	48.3	45.1
4	58.1	56.2
5	66.0	65.3
6	72.4	72.7
7	77.5	78.7

These figures show that the one-sided message is best for up to six mailings; the two-sided message beyond that point. If you can *change* your message, this shows *when* the best time for that is.

—Raymond A. Bauer and Robert D. Buzzell, "Mating Behavioral Science and Simulation," *Harvard Business Review*, 42:5:116–124.

---

messages describing four plants in Russia which were already supposed to be manufacturing bombs. Almost all of the change caused by the original one-sided messages was wiped out; only 2 per cent of the students in this group held to the belief that Russia lagged 5 years behind the United States. In contrast, 61 per cent of the group which originally heard a two-sided message held to the belief that Russia lagged. Even the actual explosion of Russia's first atomic bomb did not wipe out the effects of the two-sided message received months earlier.

This effect of the two-sided message is usually labeled "immunization." It is argued that exposing audiences to a "weakened dose" of an opponent's arguments immunizes them against those arguments when they are later presented in full force. To this extent the advantage of the second speaker, mentioned earlier, must be modified.

There are dangers in using a two-sided message, however. One danger is that we will thereby make persons aware of disadvantages, competitive or otherwise, of our product—disadvantages which they previously did not know existed. Another danger is that we will fail to mention an important disadvantage that they *are* aware of, and that this will cause them to discredit the source himself.

Immunity may work directly, by weakening the force of arguments. It may also work indirectly, either by increasing the prestige of the source, by making him appear fair minded, or by getting the audience to make up its mind now, under the impression that it has already considered both sides of the question.

Commitment?

Most salesmen know that a sale is more likely if the prospect can be induced to make a series of minor decisions and commitments along the way. And so they ask: "If you should decide to buy a refrigerator, what color would you prefer?" Or, "Which kind of binding do you think is most practical for an encyclopedia?"

The effect of commitment on immunizing against subsequent messages was shown in an experiment with high school pupils (Hovland et al., 131–132). Two speeches were used. One argued that the voting age be lowered and the other that it should be kept where it is. After hearing the first speech, each pupil wrote an essay stating his personal opinion. Half the pupils were told that their essays might be published in the school newspaper. This half, who thought their essays would put them on the record publicly, showed more resistance to the second speech than did pupils who did not expect their opinions to be published. Similarly, other experiments have shown that filling out an anonymous questionnaire does not tend to immunize (Hovland et al., 132–133).

In several respects, of course, the problems dealt with in these experiments differ from those which face the marketing communicator. The messages either had no identified source or the viewpoint of the source was not known in advance. Most of the messages involved several points, supporting arguments for the viewpoint being urged upon subjects. Clearcut public issues were involved; taking a position on them might involve a contradiction with a subject's previous viewpoint or mean rejecting a group of friends known to hold that viewpoint.

In contrast, the source of advertising and sales messages is known and his intentions are taken for granted. Most texts report and advocate use of a single central appeal in successful advertisement or even an advertising campaign. Most customers do not regard purchase of a brand today as representing a commitment to buy that brand tomorrow. They may exhibit brand loyalty, because it is easier, and they have no compelling reason to do otherwise, but they may also feel that rational puchasing behavior implies occasional sampling of other brands. They seldom feel that friendship requires that they buy the same make of automobile, soap or cake mix that their friends prefer. Unlike their decisions on social and political issues, most of their purchasing decisions do not affect what they think of themselves or what others think of them.

The "AIDA" Formula

Another way of looking at the structure of a marketing message is in terms of the AIDA formula. Some writers suggest that every message must cause every receiver to make a series of responses: to pay Attention, to show Interest, to believe the message, to Desire the product, and finally, to take Action. To the extent that this is true, they then can talk about the attention-getting and interest-arousing function of the headline and illustration, the way that the body of the copy can induce belief or conviction and desire, and the way the close of the advertisement, like that of the salesman, can induce action.

To us, the AIDA formula and its variants are more useful in distinguishing types of audiences than they are in analyzing the structure of a message. Some are inattentive and unaware and we must pick media and design messages which will get through to them. Others, however, strongly desire the product and have even had actual experience with it; our goals and techniques for these audiences must be different.

Moreover, the interplay of audience and our basic idea, whatever it is, will determine what symbols we must use. If the idea is simple and dramatic, the audience intelligent, and the source highly skilled, a headline, a picture, or a combination of the two may tell the whole story. In that case, no body of copy will be needed. The idea, the audience and the advertising man's skill—not a formula—determine structure. Except for point-of-purchase advertising, attitudes rather than action are the test of the successful message. Success depends upon (1) creating a favorable attitude now, which (2) will be elicited when the decision-to-buy is made and carried out.

Finally, the formula errs if it suggests that each step in it is necessary or that the steps must occur in a specific order. Buyers' behavior is influenced by messages which do not capture their attention, as attention is usually measured, and by messages which they do not understand, as understanding is usually measured. A change in attitudes, convictions, or beliefs can precede a change in behavior but it can also follow them. We often desire without action and act without desire. Let us take a close look at some of the elements in this formula, and some research which relates to them.

Attention

Nearly all writers recognize that attention alone is not enough, and that receivers may attend but no interest, desire, or action follow. Indeed, most textbooks warn that devices used to get attention may attract the wrong people to an advertisement and repel the right

---

Evidence that the effects of a message may extend to logically related attitude objects not discussed in the message is provided by this experiment.

Messages Offset Effects of Wishful Thinking

Thirty high school seniors and 90 college freshmen rated 48 statements as to their likelihood of being true, on a 0 to 100 scale, and then as to their desirability, on a 5-point scale.

Unknown to the students, each of the statements rated was taken from a syllogism, each of 16 syllogisms contributing 3 statements like the following to the rating sheet:

• Students who violate any regulation that has been made to safeguard the lives and property of other students will be expelled. (Major premise)

• The regulations against smoking in the classrooms and corridors were made to safeguard the lives and property of the student. (Minor premise)

• Students who violate the regulation against smoking in the classrooms and corridors will be expelled. (Conclusion)

The 3 statements in a syllogism were separated and interspersed with statements from other syllogisms. The students' modal grade was below the 30th percentile, and they had never studied logic.

As expected, wishful thinking showed up in the ratings. Conclusions which students rated as more desirable than their premises were also rated much more likely to be true than their premises, and vice versa, the difference being significant beyond the .01 level.

Desirability of Conclusions—	Joint Probability of Premises	Probability of Conclusions
Lower than premises	33.7	35.9
Higher than premises	30.1	47.3

One week later, students were given messages of 200 to 300 words which sought to raise probability ratings for 16 of the original premises. Messages increased ratings not only for the premises, but for the conclusions. Two weeks later, students repeated their ratings. Probability of the premises treated in the messages dropped sharply in the interim; but probability of the conclusions fell very little. In fact, although ratings for conclusions rose only 52% as far after one week as they would need for logical consistency with ratings of premises, in two weeks they had made 91% of the change. (The absolute rise was less, of course, since ratings for premises had dropped in the meantime.)

Increase over Original Probability Ratings

	After One Week	After Two Weeks
For premises treated in messages	17.56	9.13
For conclusions related to premises	5.96	4.47
Change required to make conclusions logically consistent with premises	11.57	4.89

The messages which were most effective in changing probability ratings were those concerning major premises or conclusions—those which contained the "predicate term" of the syllogisms.

> —William J. McGuire, "Cognitive Consistency and Attitude Change," *Journal of Abnormal and Social Psychology*, 60:345–353.

---

ones. (An example is that of the girl in a white bathing suit on a television commercial: 65 per cent of the test audience recalled the girl, but only 10 per cent what she was advertising.)

An analysis of readership figures for 2500 *Saturday Evening Post* advertisements, made by Harold J. Rudolph, shows that an illustration which is a good attention getter may not aid readership of copy (Hepner, 425). An index of attention gave these results:

Subject of Illustration	Attention Score
1. Bad results from not using product	123
2. Testimonials by users of product	110
*3. Product in use	106
4. Irrelevant, curiosity arousing	103
*5. Product itself	102
*6. Result of using product	97

The three starred types of picture were relatively ineffective in inducing readership; they retained only about 80 per cent of their readers, whereas the others retained nearly 90 per cent.

What writers often fail to add is that attention may be as unnecessary as it is insufficient. Many experiments have shown, on the basis of subsequent differences in behavior, that subjects have perceived

---

Even when persons' perceptions are distorted the distortion may lead to "rational" choices.

Consumers Are Right—for the Wrong Reasons

Can housewives detect shortweight packages? Three sets of packages of potato chips were prepared: 48 of the regular, 9-ounce weight; 48 with only 8 ounces; and 48 with 7 ounces. Anyone who purchased a package in either of 2 stores—an independent, suburban grocery and a metropolitan chain store—was then given one of the experimental packages, and asked to compare it with the one he had purchased. Dates for a follow-up interview were arranged at the time the free packages were handed out.

The last question asked in each interview was which pack had the most in it. Here are the results—differences were not significant, and most consumers perceived the 2 packages being equal.

Actual Weight of Experimental Pack	Pack Judged Heaviest Experimental	Regular	No Difference
9 ounces	9	4	30
8 ounces	5	8	22
7 ounces	7	8	25

Another question, however, asked consumers to rate each pack—the one purchased and the one given free—on a 9-point terrible-to-excellent scale. When both packs weighed 9 ounces, the free pack was preferred; when the free pack weighed only 7 ounces, however, the purchased pack was preferred, with significance by the F test at the .05 level.

A third question asked which pack persons would buy on their next shopping trip. Results were much the same, differences producing a chi square significant at the .05 level.

Pack I Would Buy Next Time

Actual Weight of Experimental Pack	Experimental	Either	Regular
9 ounces	22	7	11
8 ounces	13	14	6
7 ounces	12	8	15

The fourth question asked consumers to provide 3 words to describe each pack. The 109 words or phrases given were rated by 10 judges on a 5-point scale of favorability. The 8-ounce and 7-ounce packages were described less favorably than the 9-ounce package. Chips in short-weight packages, although identical with those in 9-ounce packages, were more likely to be described as greasy, bitter, stale, and limp and less likely to be described as crisp, delicious, and flavorful. Differences were not large enough to produce a significant F test, however.

In short, being both "new" and "free" the experimental 9-ounce pack was preferred to the regular 9-ounce pack; but the short-weight packs, even though consumers did not realize they were short-weight, were rejected.

—James C. Naylor, "Deceptive Packaging: Are the Deceivers Being Deceived?" *Journal of Applied Psychology,* 46:393–398.

---

messages, have formed categories, and learned reactions without being aware that they were perceiving, categorizing, or learning or, even after they were informed this had taken place, of being able to report what they had perceived and learned or how they had categorized.

Comprehension

There is a great deal of evidence, as we would expect, that understanding need not change attitudes. When groups of 500 to 1000 soldiers in World War II were shown a film, *Battle of Britain,* designed to increase their motivation to serve in the armed services, a familiar "funnel effect" was shown (Hovland, Lumsdaine, Sheffield). Some 78 per cent of those who saw the film, compared with 21 per cent who did not see it, learned the facts of how the British safeguarded planes on the ground from enemy attack. The film also caused an increase of 27 percentage points in those willing to agree that British resistance gave the United States time to build up its own military strength. Neither the facts of British resistance, nor the increased regard for their British allies, caused GIs to look more favorably upon their own involvement in the war, however. Other films on prejudice or socio-economic attitudes have shown similar results: learning of the facts, but failure to accept the conclusions which the facts were supposed to convey.

Attitudes

We take it for granted that not everyone who believes a message will take the action it advocates. Some cannot rush down to the corner drugstore at 10 P.M., because it closes at 9. Others would like a Coca-Cola, but do not have the money to buy it, or they have the money but refuse to walk that far. Although many like a message, they may not take action; interestingly enough, it is not always necessary that prospects like the message. The National Broad-

Here is another example of how a cue which the housewife cannot perceive affects her liking for a product.

In Hosiery, Narcissus Is Best

A house-to-house survey of 250 housewives in Utica, New York, asked them to judge 4 pairs of hosiery. Interviewers explained that the pairs were very much alike, of the same color, pattern, and style. They encouraged housewives to feel them, look through them, stretch them, examine the seams, and do anything else that they would ordinarily do in shopping.

In actuality, the 4 pairs were identical.

Housewives *explained* their choices on the grounds of texture, first of all, and then fineness of weave, feel, better wearing qualities, lack of sheen, heavier weight and firmer weave.

A truer explanation of their choices was provided by the experimenter, who had given each of the 4 pairs a different scent. One pair was left with the natural "rancid" scent from castor oil and sulphates used in lubricating yarns to facilitate weaving. Although only 6 housewives noticed the scents and commented on them, in actuality they gave views on scents not stockings:

Scent	Percentage of choices
Natural	8%
Sachet	18
Fruity	24
Narcissus	50

—Donald A. Laird, "How the Consumer Estimates Quality by Subconscious Sensory Impressions," *Journal of Applied Psychology*, 16:241–246.

casting Company sponsored 3270 interviews with matched groups of consumers, some of whom owned television sets and some of whom did not. It observed the changes that occurred when people entered the audience, by buying sets, or when a brand began to advertise on television. It studied purchases of twelve different products including gasoline, cigarettes, toothpaste, and coffee, and found that even when a viewer disliked a commercial he bought more of the product it advertised than did the nonviewer.

In another study, matched groups of soldiers were exposed to several messages which had been rated on a 100-point like-dislike scale urging them to take care of their shoes (Hepner, 430). A subsequent check of actual shoe care showed it improved most among men exposed to the best-liked messages and least among those who got messages ranked in the middle. An advertising man says that when consumer juries pick advertisements they like, positive appeals win out but coupon tests of the same advertisements show that actual buying behavior favors negative appeals (Weir, 126–127).

Mere repetition of a brand name, however irritating, may fix it so firmly in our minds that when someone says toothpaste we reply "Pepsodent" as automatically as we say "cold" when someone says "hot" or "cat" when someone says "dog." Neither awareness nor understanding nor belief seems to be involved. Memories will determine behavior and the very unpleasantness which produces memory may dissipate over time.

Behavior need not result from attitudes. It may be unrelated to them, and it may be their cause rather than their effect. Living in integrated housing has changed attitudes toward integration. Making speeches saying that college students face three years of military service has changed attitudes toward the draft (Hovland, Janis, Kelley). Pupils induced to argue in favor of a type of comic book they did not like have changed their comic-book preference (Kelman).

Face-to-Face Selling

All radio and television commercials and most print advertisements are so brief that there seems little value in trying to impose a several-stage formula like AIDA on them. The face-to-face encounter with an encyclopedia or insurance salesman is something else again. It usually lasts an hour or more, providing plenty of time for rather clear-cut stages to develop.

Some writers suggest that every sale must go through five stages, each of which ends when the prospect says "yes." The prospect first must admit to a need, they say, then agree that this product meets that need. The third stage ends when he agrees that this brand meets his need, the fourth when he agrees the price is acceptable, and the fifth when he agrees that the time to act is now. Like the AIDA formula, however, these "stages" are more useful in classifying audiences than in desciding the sales message itself.

The salesman making a "cold canvass" may have to use the first part of the interview to gather information which he can then use to convince the prospect that he does have a need. The salesman on duty at a builder's model home, on the other hand, can use the first few minutes to "qualify" the prospect—to make sure he has money for a down payment and sufficient income to get a mortgage. An encyclopedia or an insurance salesman may look at a house and perceive ability to pay, and interpret a tricycle at the door as indicat-

If a person or group is consistently associated with unpleasant things, sub-jects will find them unpleasant, and never know the reason.

The Swedes and Dutch: Do You Like Them Much?

Two groups of a dozen students each watched a screen to learn the names of 6 nationalities flashed upon it. After each name, the experimenter pronounced a word, which students also were to learn. The names were shown 18 times, in random order, but paired each time with a different spoken word. In each group, however, 2 of the nationalities were always paired with words of the same evaluative meaning. Thus, in Group I, "Swedish" was paired with words like "bitter" and "ugly" and "Dutch" with words like "gift" and "happy." In Group II, the situation was reversed.

After the 18 learning trials, students were given a list of 6 nationalities, asked to indicate which had been shown them, and to check on a 7-point pleasant-unpleasant scale how they felt about the word.

The same experiment was repeated with 2 groups of 24 students each, but this time with the names of persons rather than nationalities. Group I, for example, substituted "Bill" for "Swedish" and "Tom" for the positively evaluated "Dutch."

In both experiments, the mere association of undesirable words with a name of a nationality or a person made that name appear less pleasant; by analysis of variance, results were significant at the .05 level in the first experiment and the .01 in the second. Here are the results, with high scores representing the unpleasant end of the scale.

	Means	
	Dutch	Swedish
Group I: Swedish paired with negative words	2.67	3.42
Group II: Swedish paired with positive words	2.67	1.83
	Tom	Bill
Group I: Bill paired with negative words	2.71	4.12
Group II: Bill paired with positive words	3.42	1.79

Subjects were asked at the end of the experiment to write down what they thought its purpose was; none of those reported here showed an awareness of the nature of the evaluative pairings. (Seventeen who did show such awareness were dropped from the study.)

—Arthur W. Staats and Carolyn K. Staats, "Attitudes Established by Classical Conditioning," *Journal of Abnormal and Social Psychology,* 57:37–40.

ing need. If the salesman is following up an inquiry, or has made an appointment by telephone, the prospect has already acknowledged a need for a product.

As for the third and fourth stages in this sequence, the prospect gives up much chance to compare brands or prices when he agrees to a home interview. By doing so, he puts himself under an obligation to the salesman. To ask other salesmen to call appears unfair both to them and to the one already sitting in his living room. Moreover, an attempt to compare brands and prices will take more of the customer's time and increase the difficulty he has in making a decision (Crane, b).

A more functional way of looking at the salesman's message sees it as beginning with the conversation by which both salesmen and prospect acknowledge the social nature of the relationship and recognize that initiative in ending it has now passed to the guest, the salesman (Tucker, a). The ritual may be brief and perfunctory, involving only references to the weather. It may move on to the exchange of the names of mutual friends and acquaintances; an industrial salesman may find that this phase continues for an average of six calls, before he can make a sale.

As soon as feasible, however, the salesman tries to get feedback from the customer: responses which will indicate which product features and which sets of symbols which express them are most effective. He tries to get a series of commitments, by asking the prospect to choose between colors and sizes on an as-if basis. He encourages objections and questions, as pegs on which he can hang additional sales arguments, for these, too, represent commitments. Sometimes, in fact, objections represent conscious attempts by the prospect to help the salesman make a case for his product. If the salesman is successful, he will get a series of commitments before the matter of price is brought up. If it is brought up prematurely, he may sidestep it, for not only is price the chief restraining force on purchasing, but it threatens to evoke the very brand comparison which the salesman is trying to avoid, and in addition, it is the one socially acceptable way of rejecting the salesman's message.

A skillful series of commitments, the salesman perhaps noting them down on an order blank as he goes along, will shade imperceptibly into "the close" (Kirkpatrick). Each commitment is precipitated by a question which offers a choice of product features, so that no matter what choice the customer makes, the product and its purchase are taken for granted. Any of these choices could, in fact, terminate the salesman's message, if the prospect interpreted them as a close.

He is not allowed to interpret any of them in this fashion, however. If a sign of hostility or resistance appears, the salesman quickly shifts the discussion to safer areas. He may move back to the type of social conversation used at the start of the interview or pick up his briefcase and move to the door—only to stop at the threshhold with a new point that makes the sale.

If the customer shows his decision turns on a single feature, the salesman can praise the customer for his insight and emphasize why his brand is best for this feature. If one strong objection prevents a decision, the salesman may find it helpful to get the customer to acknowledge that this is all that stands in the way—and then demolish this objection, leaving the customer no line of retreat. The salesman may review the whole series of commitments which the customer has already made, perhaps bringing home to him for the first time how far along he is on the road to purchase. When all gentler means fail the salesman can be blunt: "We have spent two hours discussing these encyclopedias. I have answered all your questions. Shall I write up the order?" Or he can switch roles, in hopes that the prospect will turn salesman: "Of course, if you really cannot afford to give your children this protection . . ."

Messages and their Sources

A marketing communicator's success depends upon his ability to find compelling ideas, to express them in sentences, and to combine those sentences into messages which will lead the customer, step by step, to the marketer's goal.

Messages, however, cannot exist apart from their sources. The meaning of any message lies not only in the words it contains but in the source who is perceived as having chosen those words. It is this problem, that of how a receiver's image of the communicator affects his response to the communicator's message that we will examine next.

SUMMARY
1. Ideas, not words or other symbols, are the key to successful marketing communication. Both ideas and the words to express them are found by going to the prospect himself. Words can help people discover consumer benefits and product differences; they can also suggest benefits and differences that have little objective reality.
2. Connotative words tend to express a source's values for a category; they may not cause the receiver to share such values. Os-

good's studies of connotative meaning reveal a major evaluative (good-bad) factor; as well as potency (hard-soft), activity (fast-slow), and lesser factors.

3. Statements which judge, rather than report, tend to express a source's values, but do not necessarily induce a receiver to share those values. We apply different "discount ratios" to statements which report, judge, predict, or imply cause-effect relationships.

4. The effectiveness of a message depends on the ideas in a message and on the way they are related to one another:

   a. It is usually safer to draw a conclusion than to expect the receiver to do so.

   b. Solutions should be offered only after the audience has a felt need for them, aroused, if necessary, by the message itself. Too strong an arousal of fear, however, may cause receivers to reject the message and its source.

   c. The second of two speakers has a persuasive advantage—unless the first speaker can "immunize" the audience by giving a two-sided message.

   d. Public commitment by receivers may also immunize them against subsequent messages.

5. The AIDA formula is a better description of differences in audience than of the structure of a message. Not all AIDA elements are necessary to a message nor need they occur in the order suggested. Neither attention, nor comprehension, nor attitude change is either sufficient or necessary for changes in behavior.

6. The five stages of personal selling (admission of need, acceptance of product as meeting the need, brand preference, acceptance of price, and agreement to act now) also are audience rather than message concepts. A more functional analysis identifies the stage-setting phase of social conversation; the partial-commitment phase in which customer responses reveal high-valued product features and symbol choices; and the close.

Research Studies

Messages can change attitudes and behavior, whether a receiver is aware of them or not. Six of the articles summarized in this chapter deal with overt cues. *Thistlethwaite* and his co-authors find that conclusion drawing aids comprehension but does not affect attitudes. *Janis and Feshbach* report on a laboratory study in which strong fear appeals back-fired; *Lucas and Benson* report that positive appeals produced as many coupon returns and more sales than did negative appeals. *Bauer and Buzzell* indicate how the choice between two-sided and one-sided messages is affected by the number of messages transmitted, and the attitudes and education of the audience.

is affected by the number of messages transmitted, and the attitudes and education of the audience.

Four articles deal with responses to cues of which audiences were unaware. *Staats* and *Staats* show how evaluations of nationalities and men's names change as a result of their association with pleasant or unpleasant words. *McGuire* discovers that beliefs tend toward logical consistency over time and under the impact of messages; changes in evaluation of one statement affect related statements. Two studies concern responses to products. *Laird* shows how women distinguish between identical products on the basis of a cue which is irrelevant and of which they are not aware. *Naylor* shows how women can distinguish between products, although they attribute their ratings to nonexistent differences.

Six

The Communicator:
His Effects on Audience
Response

Let us take a quick look at the varied questions that a marketing communicator must wrestle with—

• One salesman is greeted with a cheery smile from the secretary and a hearty handclasp from her boss, while another cools his heels in the anteroom. What makes the difference—the salesman himself, or the firm he represents?

• "Goodwill—$1" reads the entry on the firm's books, but how much of a head start does a well-known brand name give a new product when it is competing with an unknown?

• Lady So-and-so endorses a facial cream and a professional football star testifies to the virtues of a cigarette or a razor blade. How much are their testimonials worth in increased sales?

• *Reader's Digest* prints a story about a new DuPont plastic that promises to drive leather out of the shoe business. How many advertisements would it take to duplicate the effects of that story? Can any number of advertisements duplicate the effects?

• An Arthur Godfrey kids his sponsor's product, and customers flock to buy. A Jack Benny sneaks into a commercial so smoothly that the television viewer finds he has missed his chance to raid the refrigerator. What are the advantages of humor and integrated commercials?

Many firms—and many college curricula—would assign these questions to a half dozen different experts. To the marketing communicator, however, they are all different facets of the same problem: the problem of the *source*.

Identity, Evaluation, Effects

This is a problem in three parts:

1. *Identity*. Who does the audience perceive as the source of a message—and how can one influence such perceptions?
2. *Evaluation*. How does the audience judge the source? Does it think the source can be trusted and knows what he's talking about? How can these evaluations be influenced?
3. *Effects*. What kinds of source increase the chances that a message will be perceived, understood, or accepted? To what extent do the words in a message change their meaning because of the source which is assumed to have produced the message?

Some writers try to sidestep the first of these problems by defining advertising as messages paid for by an identified sponsor. The marketing communicator cannot do this, however. First, because advertising is only one of the methods by which he transmits messages. The housewife is all too familiar with the salesman, particularly the telephone salesman, who dons the guise of a pollster, to get past her defenses. Although laws forbid such tactics in advertising (and reputable firms avoid them in selling), they are taken for granted in the third means of communication—public relations. This is the tool used when the writer does not want to be identified as a source; responsibility is shifted to the media.

Second, even where advertising and selling are involved there are multiple sources, and it is often not easy to determine how an audience divides responsibility among them. Jack Benny shares sourceship with Jello and the football star shares responsibility with Gillette. Indeed, the picture is more complicated than that, for television itself shares responsibility with Jack Benny and Jello. "How do you know that?" someone asks, and he gets the reply: "I read it in the newspaper" or "I saw it on television."

In the process of communication, as in any process, concepts tend to be arbitrary, merging into one another. Thus it is sometimes difficult to determine whether a salesman is primarily a source or a channel. His employer may view him as a channel and his customer as a source, and the salesman's view of himself may vary from moment to moment. In similar fashion, the source may so influence the response to a message that he becomes indistinguishable from it. Audiences respond to both source and message, and if a source is not provided, they are likely to supply one for themselves. If necessary, they will draw inferences about the source from the message itself.

The words used, for instance, may reveal a great deal about the place and times in which the source wrote, as well as his age, sex, education, and social class (Goldschmidt b). Language reveals *nationality:* An American rides a streetcar and walks on a sidewalk; an Englishman rides a tram and walks on the pavement. Language reveals *region:* In some parts of the United States men fish with earthworms or eat hotcakes; in others they fish with angledogs or eat pancakes. Language reveals *age and sex:* When we see the line, "I don't want to be catty, but, my deah, it was simply too terrible," we know the speaker was a woman, even if we cannot hear her voice.

We do not expect to see the sentence, "Innovations in demography are determined by the impingement of historical events," in a child's primer, or the sentence, "See Dick and Jane run," in a book intended for adults. Words change over time: we no longer pray, as did the Anglo-Saxons in 1000 A.D., "Faeder ure thu the eart on heofonum; si thin name gehalgod." Words change and so do their referents, and the words we use reflect the spirit of the *times*. Shakespeare's time produced many new words dealing with feeling and occupations; the new words we produce concern material objects.

When Englishmen depended on the hunt for their food they had extensive vocabularies for groups of animals—flock, herd, covey, brood, swarm, pack, skulk, gaggle. When Americans rode horses, our language was full of names for horses, harness, and carriages; today we distinguish between hardtop and convertible, station wagon and pickup.

Every trade has its jargon: the criminal his badger game, gunmoll, and stool pigeon; the printer his cold type, pages that bleed and stories that are killed. Words and the way they are combined can reveal how much education a man has had, where he got it, and even provide clues as to the neighborhood he grew up in and the origins of his parents.

Clues by Counting

If we want to go to the trouble of counting, content analysis provides further clues to the source of a written message. Among them are:

1. *Size of vocabulary.* On his first birthday, a child has about three words in his vocabulary; on his second, 270; and on his sixth, about 2500 (Miller, 149). College students can recognize 112,000 to

193,000 words, the average being about 156,000 (Miller, 121). As he grows older, a child strings these words into longer and longer sentences; a five-year-old averages sentences five words long (Miller, 151).

2. *Variation in word use.* A person with a small vocabulary must repeat words more often than a man with a large vocabulary. Repetition is also more likely to occur in speech than in writing. An *index of diversification* reflects the number of words appearing between repetitions of the most frequent word in a message. Written material averages ten to fifteen words between two appearances of the word "the" (Miller 122). We can also determine the ratio of different words ("types") to total words ("tokens") (Chotlos).

3. *Length of sentences.* Authors differ, one using sixty-word sentences and another using sentences a third as long (Miller, 125). Even when averages are similar, one author may vary length from one sentence to the next more than another.

Although experts, aided by a computer, can use subtle differences to determine whether Madison or Hamilton wrote a disputed passage, the usual audience is less interested in knowing the name of the person who wrote a message than in his age, sex, class, and so on. Why is the audience interested in these characteristics? Not for their own sake, but because they help answer the big question: How much can we trust this source?

Some sources can help a message get a hearing; they attract attention. This happens when the President of the United States speaks on television. It occasionally happens in marketing, and may help explain the proliferation of vice-presidents in advertising agencies. Usually, however, we depend on an audience's interest in the product or in the message to get attention. (Another reason for ignoring attention as something which the source can affect is that most of our knowledge about sources has been gained in experiments where attention was automatic.) The role of the source is to win acceptance of the message. The audience asks two questions: Does the source know what he is talking about? Will he be honest in telling me what he knows?

Most of us assume that our friends will be honest with us; if they mislead us it will be through their lack of knowledge. We assume the marketing communicator, on the other hand, has adequate knowledge, and that the question is whether he can be trusted. This depends upon two things: the situation within which he operates, including both his desire for our continued custom and the legal penalties for fraud, and the man himself. Our principal question about the man himself is to determine his intentions in communicating with us.

Cues to Credibility

This depends upon how his intentions are perceived. A source may declare his intentions openly, by saying, "I want you to like my product." Or he may hint at them by indicating how he feels about something: "I like this product. I am happy when I use this product. Brand X disappoints me." The implication, of course, is that he would like his audience to share his feelings. Needless to say, such statements need not represent his true feelings, and an audience does not always accept them as doing so.

A third cue to the intentions of a source, and one we feel he is less able to disguise, is his use of connotative words. A speaker may refer to one person as "firm and unyielding," to another as "fixed in his opinions," to a third as "stubborn," and to a fourth as "pigheaded." His audience may infer that all four persons are behaving identically; the words then reveal the attitude of the source toward the four persons. A source who wants to disguise his own feelings may use denotative words; by carefully selecting the details he will report, he can still express an opinion. A young woman thus may avoid describing her date as "tall, dark, and handsome," and convey this message more effectively by reporting that he is "six foot two, has black curly hair, and looks a little like Gregory Peck."

Some receivers feel it is easier to read the intentions of a source, when they are face-to-face. Human speech has a great many dimen-

---

A source who wants to change the opinions of a group on one topic may be more effective if he begins by emphasizing his identity with group views on some other, unrelated topic.

"Academic Freedom" Helps Foe of Fluoridation

If an "untrustworthy" source wants to advocate an unpopular view, does it help to precede his key message with another in which the source supports a view his audience accepts?

Yes, says Weiss, in a study of 4 groups of 30 undergraduates in Boston. He began with a survey which told him that students were in favor of academic freedom and fluoridation of water, and agreed that *The New York Daily Worker* was an untrustworthy source and *The New York Times* a trustworthy one.

Eight weeks later he had one group read 2 articles, supposedly taken from the *Daily Worker:* one favoring academic freedom and the other opposing fluoridation. The 3 other groups read the *Daily Worker* story on fluoridation, but preceded in each case either by an article concerning a topic on which they had no opinion (a description of Uganda) or purporting to come from a different publication (the *Times*). They then were asked their opinions on fluoridation again, on a 4-question scale permitting a 13-point range of response. Here is the percentage of each group whose scores, after reading the messages, indicated opposition to fluoridation:

Messages and sources		Percentage opposed
Academic freedom (DW)	Fluoridation (DW)	64%
Uganda (DW)	Fluoridation (DW)	39
Academic freedom (NYT)	Fluoridation (DW)	36
Uganda (DW)	Fluoridation (DW)	48

The fluoridation message for the last group was "weakened" by omitting internal attribution of content to government and professional sources. Differences between the first group and the second and third groups were significant at the .05 level. Although approval of academic freedom by the *Daily Worker* might be expected to lower subjects' evaluation of academic freedom (as well as raising their evaluation of the *Worker*) this effect was not found in this study.

—Walter Weiss, "Opinion Congruence with a Negative Source on One Issue as a Factor Influencing Agreement on Another Issue," *Journal of Abnormal and Social Psychology*, 54:180–186.

---

sions which, not being used to convey meaning about objects, can reveal the identity and intentions of the speaker. A high-pitched voice suggests youth and femininity; a quaver indicates age; a dialect may indicate foreign birth or the region in which the speaker grew up. Some of these cues are deliberately used by the speaker to convey subtle shades of meaning and attitude, even to the point of contradicting the surface meaning of his words themselves. Thus a sarcastic tone can turn words of praise into an insult, and a skeptical tone can indicate disbelief in a credo. Ordinarily, however, audiences feel the the speaker has less control over these variations than over his words, and therefore put more trust in such cues of a speaker's intentions.

The audience may, of course, be wrong. The salesman, like the actor, may through training and experience achieve a great deal of control over such cues. Unfortunately, we know very little about such cues. Notational systems which report these cues are a fairly recent development and usually have been used to describe language or dialects previously unavailable in printed form. Moreover, as the broadcast media standardize pronunciation and immigration quotas reduce the number of newcomers for whom English is a second language, dialects themselves disappear from the scene.

Channels Affect Credibility

An audience's ability to identify a source and read his intentions also varies with the channels used by the marketing communicator. The advertising message tends to be discounted because of the advertiser's obvious interest in making himself look good. Although this puts him at a disadvantage in any competition with nonmarketing communicators, the bulk of his competition is with other advertisers. Since all advertisers are assumed to be self-interested, this disadvantage may not be very serious. Self-interest is much less obvious, however, when the communicator employs a publicity story as his channel. Such stories must serve two interests: that of the marketing man and that of the medium itself. Generally, the higher the reputation of the medium, the more an audience will accept what it says, but the more difficult it is for the marketer to get his message into the channel.

In personal selling the audience perceives self-interest as being shared by the salesman and the firm which hires him. At the outset, a receiver will judge an unknown salesman's credibility by the firm he works for. As contacts continue, however, a good salesman becomes more a source and less a channel. Indeed, his employer must achieve a difficult balance between giving the salesman the freedom which will let him appear to be a source without actually being one.

Much of the salesman's success depends on his appearing to be a source. The weakness of the canned sales pitch is that it emphasizes that the salesman is only a channel. This causes the receiver to lose interest because, as a channel, the salesman has no power to negotiate terms, and any cues as to his credibility as a person are irrelevant to his behavior, which becomes that of some unseen source's puppet. The customer thus submits to all the disadvantages of face-to-face contact—personal pressure, inability to terminate the conversation easily, and lack of a permanent record—but gains none of its advantages.

It must be remembered that the source which actually originates the messages may never be perceived by the audience and, therefore, it will have no effect upon its responses. Subject to the advertiser's veto, many of the crucial decisions are made by the advertising agency. It selects the media, frames the messages, and may perform public relations functions as well. Thus, objectively, it is a source, but not one perceived by the audience. Audiences may know that there are "advertising men" in the picture, and even apply a pejorative term, "Madison Avenue" to them, but they do not know much about them, or which agency has produced a particular advertisement.

Uncontrolled Channels

Throughout this chapter, we are concerned with the source perceived by the audience. This means, for example, that we cannot limit ourselves to the channels under the direct control of the advertiser. If we look at marketing communication through the eyes of the customer, we discover that he has two additional sources of information, both of which he trusts more than advertising, selling, or publicity.

The first of these sources is his own experience. This experience may be limited and the customer may misinterpret it, crediting a product with qualities it lacks or blaming it for his own misuse. Moreover, all three of the marketer-controlled channels affect experience, whether the customer realizes it or not. They can produce experience, by persuading a customer to try products. A marketer can make use of this "source" of product information by encouraging experience through free samples and cents-off coupon deals, as well as by stimulating product trial through advertising, selling and publicity. The latter three channels can help insure that product experience is interpreted favorably by enabling a customer to use products properly and by creating expectations which influence his perception of his actual experiences.

Next to his own experience, the customer tends to trust the experience of his friends, relatives, and neighbors, although this experience, like his own, is not immune from advertising, selling, and publicity. A man's friends are likely to have needs similar to his own; if they like the product, he probably will also. Their experiences are relevant to his own purchasing decisions. Moreover, they are motivated to report honestly, since they want to keep his friendship. A marketer can sometimes use other persons' experience as a channel by using clever advertisements which people talk about. One advantage of doing so is that although the friends serve as a channel for the real source, the marketer, to the prospect the friends themselves appear as a source.

The importance of other consumers as a source of influence was revealed in a study of interviews with 800 women in Decatur, Illinois in 1945 (Katz and Lazarsfeld). Researchers found the women perceived their friends as being much more effective than other sources of information. Only 7 per cent of the women exposed to newspaper or magazine advertisements reported that such exposure influenced their purchase of cereal, coffee, and soap. This rose to 18 per cent of those exposed to sales clerks, 25 per cent of those exposed to radio commercials, and 39 per cent of those exposed to influence from friends.

As we would expect, most of these friends were in the same social class. An advertiser cannot count on his message "trickling down" from one class to the next via word-of-mouth. Some kinds of women were more influential than others, however, the kind varying with the product involved. Since one usually assumes all his friends are trustworthy, he turns for advice to those who have the most experience with the product itself and with messages about the product. He chooses those who are most *expert*.

Although only 12 per cent of the 800 women were young, single women, this group was frequently consulted about *fashions* and *movies*. Single women went to movies more often, 88 per cent of them at least once a month and 60 per cent said others had asked them about movies. Less than half of the wives over forty-five, the matrons, went that often, and only a fourth of them said anyone had asked their opinion about movies. Similarly, although the matrons made up 37 per cent of the total group, only a third of them said they were interested in fashions, compared with 80 per cent of the single women. The single women had the most influence on fashions, not only with their peers, but with older and married women as well.

When it came to *groceries*, older women tended to give advice to younger women and married women to single women. The more children a woman had, the more often she was asked for advice on buying cereal, coffee, and soap. In *politics*, however, women turned to men for advice; two-thirds of them consulted a husband or father. Interestingly enough, influence in presidential elections seemed to reflect socio-economic cleavages, seldom crossing class lines. On local, nonpartisan issues, however, wage earners tended to follow the lead of educated white-collar workers; here influence did "trickle down."

Self-Interested Sources

Sometimes customers are forced to turn to their friends or to such sources as *Consumer Reports*, not just because other sources are seen as biased but because sales clerks lack expert knowledge, and advertisements substitute adjectives or pictures of dogs and babies for the product information consumers want. In general, however, it is not the expertness of the marketer that is distrusted so much as his intentions. Indeed, if the customer does not trust his intentions, his expertness may repel rather than attract, since it puts the customer at a disadvantage. Why? Because expertness represents power and if the person who holds such power isn't perceived as sharing the consumer's interests, he may be perceived as likely to sacrifice those interests for his own.

How can the marketer overcome this attitude? One way to build source credibility is for the salesman and advertiser to admit the self-interested nature of their messages, which the customer takes for granted anyway, and then to point out that this very self-interest requires honesty on their part. The point is fairly easy to make when profit depends on repeat sales to satisfied customers, and it is easier for a retailer with a fixed location to make than for a door-to-door salesman. In advertising, self-interest is shared with the media as they recognize by policing their advertising and through such devices as the *Good Housekeeping* seal of acceptance. The consumer usually expects advertising to be more truthful than salesmanship, both because the media have a reputation of their own to maintain, and because the permanence of the advertising message, unlike the words of the salesmen, provides evidence useful in court, and with regulatory agencies, and the post office. Indeed, the customer seems to have a kind of flexible yardstick which applies a different "discount rate" to advertising and sales messages, to retail clerks and door-to-door salesmen, and to different products, such as new cars and used cars.

In short, the consumer's expectations vary with the source. This was demonstrated at Yale when history students rated sources on their trustworthiness (Hovland and Weiss). Four sources were rated as trustworthy by a minimum of 81 per cent of the students: a medical journal, a federal planning agency, Fortune magazine, and a nuclear scientist. Less than 25 per cent rated four other sources as trustworthy: the Russian newspaper *Pravda*, a picture magazine, a right-wing columnist, and a motion-picture columnist. Then students were given a series of messages arguing that certain drugs should or should not be sold over the counter, that a practical atomic submarine could or could not be built, that industry was or was not to blame for steel shortages, and that television would reduce the number of motion picture theaters. When messages were attributed to "trustworthy" sources, they produced more opinion change than when identical messages were attributed to "untrustworthy" sources.

Creating Credibility

How are such expectations created—what causes one source to be rated as "trustworthy" and another as suspect? In marketing, favorable experience with one product may build up a brand or corporate image which then encourages a housewife to try other products. Low prices, efficient service, and courteous handling of complaints may build a favorable image for a retailer, but these are not the only ways that source credibility is created. His very messages help build up a favorable image of the source that produced them.

How? One way is by identifying the source. This happened when 330 high school pupils listened to a tape-recorded message urging leniency for juvenile delinquents (Kelman and Hovland). For part of the audience, the speaker was identified as a juvenile court judge; for another group as a member of the studio audience; and for the remainder as a dope-peddling suspect out on bail. The judge's audience showed most opinion change, the suspect's audience least.

At first glance this appears irrational; the arguments were the same, why should it matter who made them? Subsequent investigation soon revealed that to the audience the arguments were not the same.

What causes us to regard one source as more credible than another, and how much is our response to a message affected by our rating of the source's credibility?

Credibility of 20 'Anonymous' News Sources

Many news stories are not attributed to any person but to "usually reliable sources" of one kind or another. Does it make any difference how these anonymous sources are described?

It did to 80 sociology students at the University of North Carolina, who were given a list of 20 different phrases to rate on a 1-to-7 scale of credibility. Thirteen of the sources ranked above the theoretical midpoint of the scale, which proved unidimensional. Differences in mean ratings of .44 or more were significant at the .05 level.

Here are ratings of some of the sources—a score of 1 representing complete acceptance of a source:

	Credibility Rating
U.S. Government	1.9
Official reports	2.4
Experts	3.0
Authorities	3.4
An announcement	4.0
Trustworthy indications	4.4
Indications	4.9

In a second experiment, another 104 sociology students were asked to indicate whether they accepted each of 4 news stories as true or false, on a 1-to-7 scale. The stories concerned a demonstration by African students in Russia, wheat negotiations between Red China and Canada, a Venezuelan resolution before the Organization of American States, and outflow of gold from the United States. By dividing the students into 4 groups, the experimenter was able to use each of the underlined sources with each story, as well as to use a fourth "no source" condition. Despite wide differences in the original credibility scores for sources, there were no significant differences when sources were linked to news stories.

Apparently enough cues to credibility were given in the news stories themselves so that readers did not have to depend upon the anonymous sources. Stories on gold and Venezuela, for example, had a joint mean of 3.06 compared with one of 3.88 for the Russia and China stories; the difference was significant at the .001 level.

> —John B. Adams, "The Relative Credibility of 20 Unnamed News Sources," *Journalism Quarterly,* 39:79–82, and "Unnamed Sources and the News," a paper given at the 1963 convention of the Association for Education in Journalism.

The word "revolution" from the mouths of Jefferson and Lincoln does not mean the same thing as it does from the mouths of Lenin and Stalin. "Leniency" means different things to a judge and a suspect. Meaning lies in both message and source. This, too, has been demonstrated several times. In one experiment student subjects rated occupations as to their social usefulness, the ability required, and so on. They were then told that 500 other students had put politics at the

---

The motives we attribute to a source affect our reception of his messages—or do they? Here are two views on the subject.

Men and Their Motives Make a Difference

Eighty-five college students were given booklets containing 10 statements, accompanied by the name of the man supposed to have made each statement and the motive he was assumed to have had in making it.

Four different versions were possible for each statement depending on whether the author named was viewed as "good" or "bad," and whether the motive attributed to him was "good" or "bad." (Each subject, of course, got only one author and one motive for any given statement.) Here is an example of the choices available:

Statement. Every artist should attempt to reflect and advance the social and economic aims of his society in his work.
Authors. Ernest Hemingway (good); Dmitri Shostakovich (bad).
Motives. To show an artist could advance desirable aims without

sacrificing his artistic ideals (good); to win wider approval for work criticized as unartistic (bad).

Each statement was followed by three 9-point rating scales, asking the student how much he accepted the statement, how much he accepted the author, and how praiseworthy he regarded the motive.

In only 3 out of 20 cases was the mean score of acceptance for a statement higher when accompanied by a "bad" motive than when accompanied by a good one, a result significant at the .01 level. In 19 out of 20 cases, the author was rated more acceptable when his motive was a good one than when it was bad.

—Nicholas Pastore and Milton W. Horowitz, "The Influence of Attributed Motive on the Acceptance of Statement," *Journal of Abnormal and Social Psychology*, 51:331–332.

Motives Affect Perceived Fairness—But Not Opinion Change

Some 242 undergraduates listened to taped messages favoring devaluation of the currency. To half the group the speaker was described as an importer, who would benefit from devaluation, and whose motives, therefore, might be perceived as suspect. To the other subjects, the speaker was described as a presumably impartial economist from a major university.

Many more subjects rated the economist as doing a good job of giving the facts and as being fair and honest—but the two were equally effective in changing opinions, as measured by net per cent changing answers to 2 questions in the direction favored by the messages.

Percentage of Subjects Giving
Favorable Response

	Importer	Economist
Source did a very good job of giving facts	21%	41%
Speaker was fair and honest	37	53
U.S. should devalue its currency	31	36

—Carl I. Hovland and Wallace Mandell, "An Experimental Comparison of Conclusion-Drawing by the Communicator and by the Audience," *Journal of Abnormal and Social Psychology*, 47:581–588.

top of their lists. The subjects thereupon raised politics on their own lists, explaining afterwards that it had become obvious to them, from ratings of the other students, that the word meant the work of congressmen and the president rather than that of the ward heeler, as they had originally supposed.

Self-interest alone does not necessarily reduce the effectiveness of an otherwise reputable source, however (Hovland and Mandell). Moreover, even if an untrustworthy source is less effective in the short run, this disadvantage may not last very long. In the study involving drugs, atom submarines and steel shortages, all difference in effects between good and bad sources had disappeared after four weeks. The same thing happened in the study on leniency toward juvenile delinquents.

A source who is trusted or expert is likely to be more effective—so long as the audience associates him with the message he is delivering.

Source Effects "Wash Out" Over Three-Week Period

Some 273 high school pupils in Brooklyn filled out an 8-item questionnaire concerning treatment of juvenile delinquents, then were exposed to messages favoring leniency—opposition to any form of punishment and treatment of the delinquent, regardless of age or offense, as a sick child. Each tape-recorded message began by introducing the speaker who was described to one group of pupils as a juvenile court judge, to another as a "neutral" member of the studio audience, and to a third as an ungrateful, ex-delinquent, and dope-peddling suspect.

As expected, more persons rated the judge as a credible source than the suspect:

	Percentage in Each Group Giving Favorable Rating to Source; Source Identified as—		
Basis of rating	Judge	Neutral	Suspect
Source "highly qualified"	78%	33%	9%
Source "fair"	73	63	29
Would trust source's judgment	87	66	25

Moreover, scores on a 16-item scale of leniency (possible range of 0 to 64 points) showed that the suspect was least effective in persuading the audience to his point of view:

	Mean Score Favoring Leniency		
	Judge	Neutral	Suspect
Immediate results	46.7	45.7	42.7

The "suspect" differed significantly from both judge and neutral source at or beyond the .01 level.

Three weeks later some of the subjects were reminded who had given the talk, by hearing the introduction replayed; other subjects were not.

Then each group filled out all of the leniency-scale items used previously. Scores for the group reminded of the source were much the same as before; those who heard the "judge" were more persuaded to his viewpoint. Groups *not* reminded of the source, however, were of much the same opinion, regardless of whom they had heard.

Mean Score Favoring Leniency

	Judge	Suspect
Reminded of source	45.3	41.5
Not reminded of source	43.5	43.4

Differences between the 2 figures in each column were significant at the .04 level.

—Herbert C. Kelman and Carl I. Hovland, " 'Reinstatement' of the Communicator in Delayed Measurement of Opinion Change," *Journal of Abnormal and Social Psychology*, 48:327–335.

Self-Interest Not Fatal

To summarize, there are at least four reasons why the self-interest of an advertiser may not reduce his effectiveness. First, the consumer perceives limits on the extent to which self-interest will allow a marketer to go. These limits may be external, in the form of laws or control exercised by the advertising media, or internal, in his desire for repeat sales of a product or a favorable image for a retail outlet or a product line. The advertising messages themselves may emphasize these limits. Second, self-interest alone will not reduce the effectiveness of a businessman's message if self-interest is accepted as a legitimate part of his role. Third, even if there are immediate effects, they may dissipate over time. Fourth, although advertising might be at a disadvantage as compared with other kinds of messages, most advertisements compete with other advertisements—all of them sponsored by persons with self-interested motives.

Recent research has raised still another question about source credibility. Most theorists have assumed that the most effective message was one which an audience accepted without question or thought. This may be true in debating public issues, where social acceptance determines reality. It may not always be true in marketing, however, where the advertisement seeks to get the audience to buy a product and "see for itself." The most effective message here may be one which engenders enough disbelief to challenge the consumer to check the product claims for himself (Maloney). An unusual-sounding claim which arouses curiosity may work best, always provided that the product itself can validate the claim.

Source vs. Object

So far we have discussed two aspects of the source. First, we have shown how changing the source can alter the meaning and the effectiveness of a message. Second, we have shown how information in a message relating to a source's expertness and interest in an issue can (a) affect attitudes toward the source which, in turn, (b) affect response to the combined source-message stimulus. There is a third aspect to be discussed, which requires that we pay attention to something that up to now we have ignored. The audience has attitudes about *both* the source of the message and about its object, about *Pravda* and atomic submarines and both of these attitudes may be changed. The question is: How much does each change and which changes most?

Recast in terms of the advertiser, this question becomes: How much does the firm's name affect acceptance of the message, producing *immediate* effects; and how much does the message affect attitudes toward the firm, producing *long-run* effects? (Long run in the sense, of course, that such attitudes can be used at some future date to win acceptance of other messages.)

One of the most insightful theories developed to answer this question is Osgood's congruity model (Osgood, Suci, Tannenbaum). It begins with three variables: a source, a product, and a message from the source about the product. It assumes that the consumer has attitudes about both the source and the object, attitudes which may be favorable or unfavorable.

For convenience, these attitudes may be measured by a seven-point sale that runs from strong dislike (−3) to strong like or approval (+3). Here is an example of what the author's scale of attitudes toward foods and people looks like:

		Product	Source
Like very much	3	Pecan pie	Wife
	2	Ice cream	Doctor
	1	Hamburger	Advertisement
Neutral	0	Bread	Stranger
	−1	Turnips	Waitress
	−2	Liver	Brother-in-law
Dislike very much	−3	Parsnips	Mother-in-law

Each source on this list may produce two kinds of messages; he may say he likes one of the products or that he dislikes one.

Balance is achieved when a source and the object treated in his message have identical point scores on my attitude scale. If the source says he *likes* an object, then the two scores will be on the same side of the neutral midpoint; if the source says he *dislikes* an object, then the two final scores must be on the opposite sides of the neutral midpoint, one positive and one negative.

In achieving balance, source and object do *not* necessarily move the same distance toward the midpoint. Osgood suggests that the one which is farthest from the midpoint—the one toward which I have most extreme opinions, either pro or con—will move *least*. He hypothesizes that the *source's* proportion of the total distance from the midpoint determines how far the *object* travels and vice versa. Predicting how far object and source will move on an attitude scale is a two-step process. One first figures the amount of movement necessary to achieve balance: this is the distance one item (source or object) on the scale is from the balance point. When linked positively, by a word such as "cause" or "like," this distance is equal to the original distance between the two items on the scale. When linked negatively, by a word such as "dislike" or "prevent," assume that one item remains fixed and that the other moves to the same value on the opposite side of the midpoint. This indicates the total distance to be shared between the two items.

We calculate what proportion of this distance each item must travel by adding the scale points of the two items, ignoring signs, to get the total distance from the midpoint. This represents 100 per cent. If an item's percentage of this total is labelled p, then the proportion of the distance it travels is represented by 100-p.

No movement occurs, of course, if the objects are already in balance. If my wife (3) praises pecan pie (3) or my brother-in-law (−2) praises liver (−2), I retain my opinions of both, since they are behaving just as I would expect them to. If the stranger, toward who I am neutral, praises ice cream, he takes on its value himself (2). Similarly, if he praises liver, he falls in my estimation to the level of liver (−2).

On the other hand, if my wife praises anything less desirable than herself, i.e., anything other than pecan pie, she falls slightly and it rises slightly. Let us suppose she praises hamburger; balance requires a total movement by both wife and hamburger of two points. My wife has a 3-point rating and hamburger rates 1-point distant, for a total of four points. My wife moves one-fourth (100–75 per cent) of the distance; since one-fourth of 2 is a half-point, she falls from a rating of 3 to $2\frac{1}{2}$, and hamburger rises to meet her.

If my doctor (2) praises liver (−2), they share the distance between them equally and both end up at the midpoint. However, if my doctor (2) praises turnips (−1), turnips benefit most: they move $\frac{2}{3}$ of the distance which separates the two, crossing the midpoint to a rating of 1.

The same method of sharing distance travelled applies when a source indicates a *dislike* for an object. In this instance, however, the distance travelled changes since source and object are in balance only if scores are equal in value but opposite in sign.

Balance exists and no change occurs if my doctor disapproves liver, my wife dislikes parsnips or my mother-in-law dislikes pecan pie. The stranger, however, who rose to 2 when he said he *likes* ice cream, falls to −2 if he decides he *dislikes* it. Similarly, the neutrally valued object, bread, falls to −2 if disapproved by my doctor (2) or rises to 2 if rejected by my brother-in-law (−2).

An interesting if somewhat unexpected result of the tendency toward balance when statements of disapproval or rejection are involved is that such statements may make me more favorable toward a source and an object I originally disliked, and less favorable toward a source and an object I liked.

Suppose, for example, that my mother-in-law (−3) were to turn up her nose at liver (−2). On the grounds that "A woman who dislikes liver cannot be all bad," my opinion of her would change. Since something my mother-in-law dislikes must have some good in it, so would my opinion of liver. In fact, liver, being in the less extreme position would gain most from the exchange. The total distance required for my attitudes to be in balance is the distance between the source's original position, and a position which represents the mirror opposite of the object's original position. Thus, when a mother-in-law (−3) rejects liver, liver must move from its original position of −2 across the midpoint to 3 or my mother-in-law must move to 2. In either case, a distance of 5 points. However, liver will move only three-fifths (100–40 per cent) of this distance to a scale reading of 1. My mother-in-law will move $\frac{2}{5}$ of 5, to a scale reading of −1 and balance, defined as equal-but-opposite scores is achieved.

Let my doctor (2) sneer at pecan pie (3), however, and both will fall: pie by $\frac{2}{5}$ of the distance, and the doctor by $\frac{3}{5}$, so that he arrives at a new reading of −1 and pie at a reading of 1. By similar reasoning, if an advertisement should attack pecan pie (3), the advertisement will suffer most; it will travel three-fourths of the 4-point distance, so that it lands at —2, while pie falls to 2.

Real-Life Complexities

In real life, of course, the situation becomes immensely more complex. Our attitudes, for example, probably cannot be contained within a mere seven-point scale, and messages concern many things other than products, such as people and issues. (We can, even in my simplified scale, calculate what would happen if the waitress (—1) made fun of the advertisement (1) or the doctor (2) praised my mother-in-law (—3).) Moreover, we frequently get messages from several sources about the same object, and messages about several objects from the same source. Osgood has made adjustments in the model for two such complications. One is an adjustment for sheer disbelief; I may disbelieve a message in which my doctor praises parsnips, or my mother-in-law rejects them or—to return to the "real world"—one in which an advertiser condemns his own product.

When a highly credible source is credited with a message that seems inconsistent with our knowledge of and attitude toward the source, we may suspect that a hoax is involved or that the source has been misquoted. We may explain away the apparent incongruity by saying the source was not himself or was speaking in special circumstances. Or we may reinterpret what was said. In similar fashion a message we approve of will not aid a source we distrust and dislike, if we explain away his apparent endorsement of our position.

The second adjustment Osgood made is the "assertion constant," which allows for the possibility that a message may change attitudes toward the object of the message more than toward its source. This would mean, for example, that my attitude toward the waitress is more affected—Osgood suggests .17 of a scale point more—when she is praised by my brother-in-law than when she praises him.

The important point to remember in the congruity model is that it illustrates how any message may change attitudes toward its source, as well as toward its object. Salesmen know this. Starting at a neutral position with a new customer, they gradually build up their own position by finding out what the housewife likes and indicating that they like it, too. Sharing customer dislikes will have similar effect. Then, in turn, the salesmen can transfer some of his attitude points toward new objects which are neutral or lower on the scale than he himself.

If the salesman finds himself disliked, this model suggests he would do well to suggest that he himself dislikes something the customer dislikes, in hopes of raising both the product and himself in the customer's estimation! Experiments have shown that a source who starts out by stating that he agrees with his audience has more effect than one who does not make this claim—even though both give the same message, one which is contrary to the original claim (Ewing). Apparently the claim is enough to create a perception of the source which alters audience perception of or response to his message.

Message Reacts on Source

So far in this chapter we have looked at source effects from the viewpoint of the audience, and we have seen how the right kind of source can make a message more effective and how the right kind of message can create such a source in the minds of the audience.

The source, however, affects himself in the very act of transmitting a message. He is part of his own audience, and the message may change his attitudes, too. This is seen most clearly, of course, when the source is persuaded to prepare a message on a topic about which he has no attitudes or very weak ones. In one study, fifty-nine college students argued that two-thirds of the nation's movie theaters would go out of business in three years or that civilian meat supply would be cut in half within two years, after being given three minutes to look over a canned outline and being told to play the role of a sincere advocate of these views in using a canned outline (Janis and King). Their opinions changed more than did the opinions of 104 other students who merely listened to the talks and read the outlines.

A follow-up study showed that the effect also could be obtained on an issue of personal importance to students—the likelihood that their military service would increase by a year. Moreover, the more freedom students had in presenting arguments, the greater the effect. In the group which read a script aloud, 54 per cent changed on three out of five opinion items related to the topic as compared with 87 per cent of the group which had to improvise a talk on what they could remember from the script (Hovland, Janis, Kelley). The same effect was found in younger students, when 250 seventh graders were induced to write essays favoring Tarzan-type comic books over Superman books (Kelman).

Interestingly enough, the *less* inducement a person is offered for playing a role inconsistent with his original attitudes (provided he does go ahead and plays such a role), the *more* his attitudes change.

Communications is a 2-way process. The source who sets out to influence an audience will find that he, in turn, is influenced by the reactions of that audience. Indeed, even if he has no opportunity to observe those reactions, he may still be influenced by what he expects them to be.

The Effects of an Anticipated Audience

This experiment was designed to test 2 hypotheses: first, that a person who expects to speak to an audience will be more likely to remember material which agrees with that audience's attitudes; second, that the training of professional communicators tends to increase this sensitivity to audience attitudes.

As subjects, the experimenters drew upon students from teachers' colleges and from schools of journalism, telling half in each group that they were to write a talk for The National Council of Teachers, who presumably would favor more pay for teachers, and the other half that the talk was intended for the American Taxpayers Economy League, a group that would oppose more pay for teachers.

Each half was then split again, so that 18 journalism students and 18 teachers college students who expected to talk to taxpayers heard a message containing 25 arguments favoring higher pay for teachers. Another 18 journalists and 18 education students also expecting to talk to taxpayers, heard 25 arguments against paying teachers more money. Eight groups, representing all possible combinations of audience, arguments, and students—2 × 2 × 2—were used.

Each set of arguments was read twice. Students were then given 15 minutes to write down all the points they could remember. A week later they were again asked to write down all the points they could remember. They then proceeded to write the talks themselves.

No significant differences showed up until a week had passed. Then both hypotheses were supported: subjects who heard arguments consistent with the attitudes of their expected audiences remembered more of them than did subjects who heard arguments opposed to the views of their audiences. And journalism students did prove more sensitive to "audience effect" than the teachers college students.

Average number of points recalled out of 25 originally presented were:

Expected Audience	Taxpayers		Teachers	
Arguments heard:	Raise pay	Do not raise pay	Raise pay	Do not raise pay
Type of student:				
Journalism	4.9	11.3	6.1	13.7
Teachers college	8.6	11.5	8.8	11.7

—Claire Zimmerman and Raymond A. Bauer, "The Effect of an Audience Upon What Is Remembered," *Public Opinion Quarterly*, 20:238–248.

Apparently an individual feels he must justify the commitment he has made by speaking, either to himself or others. If the rewards for doing so, or the penalties for not doing so, are big enough, this is justification enough and attitudes need not change. However, if rewards are small, the speaker tends to justify himself by actually changing his attitude in the direction of his public statements as shown in the theory of cognitive dissonance (Festinger).

Audience Affects Source

In preparing a message, a successful source will consider his audience, and select the material which he thinks will be most effective—playing up items it agrees with and playing down items it is likely to reject. A skillful source will choose language and other symbols which are congruent with an audience's dispositions and which it will understand—symbols related to its previous experiences. He will take account of its roles, reference groups, and the messages it has received from rival communicators. Thus the message itself is affected by the picture of its audience which the source carries in his mind.

Professional communicators such as journalists report that they have different audiences in mind while preparing their messages, and the type of audience affects the type of message they produce (Bauer and Pool). Newsmen who report thinking of hostile audiences are found to be most accurate in handling news such audiences would dislike—either for their own protection in anticipating criticism, or as a way of "getting even" with the hostile readers. Newsmen who imagine friendly audiences, on the other hand, tend to be accurate on news such audiences would like and to err on unpleasant news.

Graduate students in business at Harvard were asked whether they thought an advertising man should concentrate on keeping a client happy or be courageous in telling him unpleasant facts (Bauer and Pool). They then listened to two commercials—one for Lestoil, whose manufacturer was supposedly seeking their advice, and the other for a fictitious, competitive detergent named Lustre. Students who had taken the keep-the-client-happy position remembered more of the selling points for Lestoil than did those choosing a give-him-the-facts position.

Finally, the source may be affected not only by the anticipated reactions of his audience but by their actual responses. He may use such responses as feedback, adapting his message as he delivers it. However, he may also modify both the treatment and content of his message without being aware that he is doing so. This can happen without any conscious effort on the part of the audience to influence the source, although the effect has been demonstrated most clearly in the laboratory, where an experimenter, by a nod or an mmm-hmmm, has controlled the content of a subject's conversation, without the subject being aware of what was happening.

Reactions of an audience can control the content of a communicator's messages—without the communicator being aware of what is happening. This effect shows most clearly in a two-person, face-to-face situation.

Listener's Nod Affects Source's Behavior

Seventeen psychology students engaged 24 subjects—13 friends, 7 roommates, 1 date, 1 uncle, and 1 total stranger—in 30-minute conversations. The conversations took place in various settings: 17 in student dormitories, 2 in restaurants, 2 in private homes, and 1 each in a hospital ward, a public lounge, and over the telephone. Topics discussed included dates, vacations, Marxism, man's need for religion, Liberace, architecture, and the theory of music.

For the first 10 minutes, the psychology students counted the number of statements their subjects made, and the proportion which were opinion statements, beginning with such phrases as "It seems to me" or "I think." For the next 10 minutes, the students rewarded every opinion statement by agreeing with it, or paraphrasing and repeating it. Then, for a final 10 minutes, students "extinguished" opinion statements, either by making no response to them at all or by disagreeing with them. Seventeen subjects received this treatment. The remaining 7, a control group, were given the opposite treatment: rewarded for opinion statements for the first and last 10-minute periods, extinguished or punished for them during the middle period. As this table shows, frequency of opinion statements nearly doubled under "reward" conditions.

Median percentage of opinion statements

Experimental Group (N = 17)		Control Group (N = 7)	
No audience response	32%	Opinions rewarded	57%
Opinions rewarded	56	Opinions extinguished	30
Opinions extinguished	33	Opinions rewarded	60

Signed rank tests of the differences showed them to be statistically significant beyond the .01 level. Every subject increased the proportion of opinion statements when rewarded for them; 21 of the 24 subjects decreased the proportion when rewards were lacking. Paraphrasing appeared a more effective reward than agreement, although it did not attain the .05 level of significance. When students conducting the experiment began disagreeing or not responding to subjects, 7 subjects either stopped talking or left the room. Yet in no case did any subject indicate that he realized what was going on—that his behavior was being manipulated and his responses recorded.

> —William S. Verplanck, "The Control of the Content of Conversation: Reinforcement of Statements of Opinion," *Journal of Abnormal and Social Psychology*, 51:668–676.

Conflict in Roles

The effects of *anticipated* audiences are most important in advertising, where feedback is often nonexistent, requires specific research effort, and is, at best, delayed. The effects of *actual* audiences are more important in personal selling. They may enable the salesman to be more effective but there is also a danger that the customer will use feedback consciously to control the salesman, against the best interests of the firm he represents. The salesman receives two rewards from any sales interview. One is the formal reward, received from his employer for making a sale. The other is the informal reward, received in the form of pleasant social relations with a customer.

The salesman may err in two ways, either of which may occur without his being aware of it. One is to sacrifice the firm's interests, so that he may continue to receive the informal rewards. The other is to make an error of judgment by adapting his message further than he would have to. The firm tries to guard against these dangers through supervision and systems of compensation. It also tries to make sure the salesman accepts the firm's goals, and that he is aware of how customers' influence threatens these goals.

Our discussion to this point has assumed that, although the source might be a composite of several persons, and be perceived differently from different points of view, that source and audience could always be distinguished from one another. This is true in advertising, which is essentially one-way communication. It is also true if we limit communication to very brief, simple acts. In many two-person situations, however, and in nearly all group situations the distinction between source and audience becomes difficult to make, and rather useless even if made. We can call the person who initiates an encounter the source, but this includes both the salesman knocking at the door, and the customer asking a question of the sales clerk. We can label the person who does most of the talking as the source. If we regard communication as the exchange of influence attempts, rather than of information, then we can say that the person who makes the most attempts, or the person who has the highest ratio of success in his attempts is the source. But all of these have limited usefulness. An employee may go to the boss's office to ask for a raise, do most of the talking, and make a great many attempts to influence the boss—but a single grunt from the boss decides the issue.

Sources and Channels

The meaning of any message, we have said, lies not only in the message itself but in its source. Before a message reaches its audience, however, it must be transmitted through a channel. Throughout this chapter we have discussed the relationships that exist between sources and channels. Now it is time to take a closer look at the channels of marketing communications themselves.

We shall find, when we do so, that channels affect both messages and sources. We shall find that some messages cannot be transmitted on some channels, and that the amount of control which a source retains over his message varies widely from one channel to another.

SUMMARY

1. The meaning of any message depends both upon what is said, and who says it. If no source is named, then an audience will supply one, if necessary on the basis of cues contained in the message itself. Such cues include vocabulary: its size, variation, nature, and the way words are joined together in sentences. An audience puts particular faith in the cues of speech, on the grounds—not necessarily valid ones—that a communicator is less able to control these than he is to control his choice of words.

2. Although some sources help gain attention for a message, in marketing the chief function of a source is to win its acceptance. Consumers depend on two kinds of sources: their friends, who are trusted but not expert, and the marketing communicator, who is expert but may not be completely trusted.

3. As a source, the marketing communicator appears in three guises, depending on the channels he uses. As an *advertiser*, he is clearly identified as a source, and his self-interest is assumed; the media he uses share only a small part of the responsibility for his messages. Identification is also clear when *salesmen* are used; they and their employer share the role of source. The more a salesman appears to be a source, and the less a channel, the more likely he is to be accepted by the audience, but the greater the danger that he will stray from his employer's goals. When *publicity* is used, the medium itself is perceived as a source, and the marketer's role is

concealed. Consumer acceptance is high provided the marketer can first win acceptance by the media themselves.

4. The consumer is influenced by two additional sources: his own experience and his friends. Although consumers may not realize it, the marketer can use his own three channels to produce such experience and to influence the way it is perceived. Since all friends are trusted, by definition, consumers distinguish among them in terms of their perceived expertise. Similarly, they distinguish among marketing channels, all perceived as expert, on the basis of their trustworthiness.

5. Judgments of a source's trustworthiness may be influenced by varying his identity. Self-interest does not necessarily reduce a source's effectiveness, however, if it is consistent with a legitimate role. In any case, source effects are likely to disappear over time, as receivers remember messages but forget whence they came. Moreover, in advertising all communicators are seen as self-interested.

6. Although some communicators may desire complete, unquestioning acceptance of their messages, in marketing it may be better to use messages which stimulate the audience to test their veracity—assuming, of course, that the product will validate claims made for it.

7. A source may change audience attitudes toward the object of his message, but the message may also change attitudes toward the source. In facing an unknown or hostile audience, the first purpose of a message may be to create favorable attitudes toward its source, before the source tries to change attitudes toward other objects. Osgood's "congruity model," based on the assumption that extreme views, toward either sources or objects, are hardest to change makes specific predictions of reciprocal source-object effects. Messages which change attitudes toward sources may be seen as having a delayed pay-off.

8. In communicating, the source's own attitudes may be changed. This is seen most clearly when he is induced to advocate a view other than his own. The change, as predicted by Festinger's "dissonance theory" is greatest when extraneous rewards and penalties are least. Source behavior is also affected by the audiences he anticipates communicating with, and by audience reactions received when the message is transmitted. These effects may occur without the communicator being aware of them and may be beyond the ability of his employer to control them.

9. Just as it is sometimes difficult to distinguish between channel and source, so it is often difficult to distinguish between source and audience in any two-way communications situation, including many two-person (salesman-customer) situations and all group interaction.

Research Studies

"Consider the source," says the layman, and, indeed, it seems obvious that the effect of any message depends not only upon its content but upon who originated it.

Pastore and Horowitz found that "good" motives make an author and his message more acceptable. Three other studies, however, suggested that there are limits to source effects on messages. *Kelman and Hovland* discovered that original source effects disappear over a three-week period. *Hovland and Mandell* in one study and *Adams* in another reported that audiences evaluate sources differently but that this makes no impact on their attitudes.

Two more studies emphasized the two-way nature of all communications by pointing out how the views of the source himself may be changed. *Verplanck* showed that a listener's response alters a source's behavior. *Zimmerman and Bauer* demonstrated that the source is affected by the nature of the audience he expects to address.

Harking back to Chapter Two, which pointed out that an audience's evaluation of a source will be affected by his agreement with the audience's position, *Weiss* found that agreeing with the audience on one issue will help a source communicate more persuasively on another, unrelated issue.

Seven

Channels of Communications: Men and Media

Messages and audiences are linked by channels. Four channels carry the marketing communicator's message to his target audience.

- *Media*. Television and radio, newspapers and magazines, billboards and direct mail.
- *Face-to-face*. The salesman.
- *Publicity*. The news release or the event staged for its publicity value.
- *Informal channels*. The conversations over the backfence and at a business luncheon in which two members of the audience share their experience with products and messages about products.

The communicator's control over his message falls steadily as we go down this list. He has complete control over advertising messages transmitted by the media. He can specify exactly what words and pictures are used, when and to whom the messages are transmitted, and he has some control over the context which will surround his messages in the media. The marketer must share control with the salesman, however, and in the third type, control passes from the hands of the marketer to those of the media. The marketer influences decisions here but does not make them. The marketer exercises so little control over informal channels, the fourth type, that these might better be regarded as an environmental fact of life he must adjust to, rather than a variable he can manipulate, or even as an indirect test of his success in using the other channels.

Choosing Channels

The nature of the audience a communicator wants to reach and the nature of his message influence his choice of channel. His choice of channel, in turn, limits the audience he can reach and the types of symbols and messages he can use. Channels differ in the extent to which they can provide audiences which coincide, either geographically or demographically, with a target market. They differ in the proportion of nonprospects included. (The difference between costs per person exposed and costs per *prospect* exposed may vary widely with the channel (advertising), medium (television), or medium vehicle (*Life*).) Channels differ in the kind of context they provide for the marketing message. Most important of all, they differ in the speed with which audience responses to them can be observed by the communicator and used to modify his messages so as to make them more effective.

The best combination of channels may vary with each stage in the process of persuasion, with the audience and with the behavior being urged upon them. Here is an example from agriculture.

Word-of-Mouth Delays Innovation

Interviewers asked 175 Pennsylvania dairy farmers in 1957 about their adoption of 3 innovations: spittle bug control, use of grass silage, and artificial drying of hay.

They also asked what information channel the farmers had depended on. Farmers were classified for each practice on which of 5 stages they had attained: awareness, interest, acceptance, trial, and adoption. Here is the percentage of mentions which each channel received at each of the first 3 stages:

Stage	Awareness "Have heard of"			Interest "Will work in general"			Acceptance "Of value on my farm"		
Practice*	a	b	c	a	b	c	a	b	c
Source:									
Farm magazine	31%	36%	33%	23%	19%	17%	9%	22%	27%
Radio	5	3	2	2	2	0	0	0	0
Extension: print	36	17	21	14	15	13	16	10	18
Extension: oral	10	14	11	25	26	24	27	20	23
Peers	14	28	25	34	33	38	45	46	27
Commercial	1	0	4	1	2	6	2	2	5
Total†	97%	98%	96%	99%	97%	98%	99%	100%	100%

* *a* is spittle bug control, *b* grass silage, *c* hay drying.

† Failed to attain 100% through rounding errors and omission of "miscellaneous."

The researchers found, as expected, that magazines and extension agents had an early advantage in that their goal was to spread information, and they were most likely to have information to diffuse. Printed messages had an advantage in early stages, since a farmer could use them at his convenience. Face-to-face messages were important later, in legitimizing and making specific application to the individual's farm.

The researchers also suggested that peer influence, (word-of-mouth from friends and neighbors), was likely to retard adoption, since peers were themselves less well-informed than the media and extension workers and, if they had tried it without success, might advise against its use. Farmers were divided into two groups: those who mentioned peers as a source of information and those who did not. Each farmer was then scored from 1 to 5 on each practice, getting 5 if he had actually adopted the practice. Means for the two groups of farmers showed the expected differences. In five cases out of six, farmers who mentioned peers showed least progress.

Mean Progress Score on 1-to-5-Scale

	Cited peers	Did not cite peers	Statistical significance
Awareness of			
Spittle bug control	2.3	3.4	.001
Grass silage	3.2	3.7	.05
Hay dryer	1.2	2.2	.001
Interest in			
Spittle bug control	3.8	4.3	.05
Grass silage	3.9	4.5	.05
Hay dryer	3.6	3.3	Not significant

—James H. Copp, Maurice L. Sill, and Emory J. Brown, "The Function of Information Sources in the Farm Practice Adoption Process," *Rural Sociology*, 23:146–157.

Nearly every product sold depends upon both face-to-face and mediated communication. The marketer's choice is less a matter of "either-or" than it is one of "how much of which, when." Nearly every product uses more than one advertising medium; the marketer's problem is to find the media combination best suited to his target audience and message. Since 80 to 85 per cent of the money spent on advertising in the United States goes to buy time and space in the media, selection of the media mix is important, both to the advertiser and the media themselves. Indeed a large part of marketing communications consists of messages from media salesmen, of media advertising, and of research studies which media and the separate vehicles within each medium use as weapons in the competitive struggle for the advertiser's dollar.

The media differ among themselves in the context they provide for the sales message. Four media carry no messages other than advertising. One of these, direct mail, delivers its message to the customer. The other three—outdoor, transportation, and point-of-purchase advertising—let the audience come to them.

The remaining media differ in the nature of the nonadvertising context they provide for the sales message. In radio and television this context is one of entertainment (Crane, a). In newspapers it is primarily one of information. Magazines, which once represented a mixture of these two types of context, have shifted increasingly from fiction to nonfiction, so becoming more like newspapers.

The media differ in the extent to which they make it easy for an audience to escape exposure. Escape from media, other than magazines and newspapers, is difficult; escape from sales messages in the print media is relatively easy.

The media differ, finally, in the extent to which they accumulate a large, mass audience (many of whom are not prospects) at relatively low cost per person, or pinpoint a target audience at a higher cost per contact.

Media Effects on Messages

The limits which each medium places upon the messages it can transmit are obvious. All media can transmit words. All media except radio can transmit pictures. Radio and television can transmit sounds. Only television can transmit sound, pictures, and movement. The implications of these limits are less obvious and more debatable, however.

Most people can read silently faster than they can read aloud or listen, so that print is more efficient in transmitting a lot of words in a limited time. Print is also suited for audiences which vary widely in intelligence and reading skill, since each person can read at his own speed, providing he is willing to read at all, and can go back and reread the message as often as necessary.

Printed words, on the other hand, are useless with an illiterate audience, whether selling in an underdeveloped country or trying to interest five-year-olds in a breakfast cereal. Print is ineffective if the receivers dislike reading or are unwilling to pay for the newspapers or magazines that contain the advertisements. (Of course, print is also used in direct mail, bilboards, and point-of-purchase materials, which are free.) Advertising messages in the print media are easier to avoid than those on the broadcast media; it requires more ability and effort to understand print. As a result the print media tend to be selective in two ways: they select persons higher on the scale of income and education, and they select those with more interest in the product and more desire for information about it.

Since print media can carry pictures as well as words, pictures might seem to provide an escape from these limitations. We could argue that pictures transmit meaning to anyone, no matter what his intelligence or interest level. In fact, however, pictures are also a symbol system that has to be learned. This system may be more difficult to learn, and it may require more specialized experience than words themselves. Witness the number of us who have difficulty in "understanding" contemporary art and the number of persons who are as puzzled by *New Yorker* cartoons as they are by *New Yorker* fiction. On the other hand, pictures can express moods and impressions that it would be hard to reproduce in words. Since most of us are more adept in framing messages in words than in drawing pictures, we may find it easier to counter verbal than pictorial messages.

If color is important to a message, magazines have an advantage. The paper on which newspapers are printed and the printing processes used allow relatively poor reproduction, and color television is not yet, in 1965, a mass medium. Color is important to a message when we want to create a mood or want to show how food or textiles, wallpaper or house paint, really look. On the other hand, when color is used for its attention-getting qualities, newspapers or television may be more effective than magazines, because color contrasts with the predominant black-and-white of these two media.

The appeals an advertiser uses will affect the choice of a medium vehicle. A boat manufacturer, for example, may pick magazines as his medium. But he will use the *Saturday Evening Post,* family magazine, to suggest that you should buy a boat because it provides fun for the whole family. He will use *Esquire* to sell the same boat to the same purchaser by pointing out that a boat provides a good way to get *away* from the family.

Media Effects on Sources

Part of the meaning of any message depends on who is perceived as the source of the message, and the medium which carries the message is often perceived as part of this source.

The announcer who appears in a television commercial and the performer on whose program it appears are seen as part of the source. So are the television station, the television network, and even television in general: the advertiser who paid for the commercial may be seen as a less important part of the source than the sports star who reads a testimonial. The one reasonable certainty is that the copywriter who actually wrote the words and the art director who approved the storyboards will *not* be seen as the source. Most members of the audience are not aware they exist.

Each of the media has attempted to measure its significance as a source by asking such questions as: "If you could have only one of these media, which would you want?" or "If these two media disagreed in reporting the news, which one would you believe?" As we would expect, through careful selection of questions, each medium has been able to demonstrate that it is superior. The question which really interests an advertiser—which medium exerts more influence on purchasing decisions—is not one which can be asked directly. Most persons do not know the answer, and if they did they probably would not say, since few persons like to think of themselves as puppets of any medium.

In general, a direct question concerning influence probably has a bias in favor of the print media. There are two reasons for this. The first is that the media we seek out, which tend to be print media, are seen as being more likely to serve our interests than those which force themselves on us, such as radio, television, and outdoor advertising. The second is that many of us feel it is more respectable to be "informed" than to be entertained, so that we give media like radio and television, which put advertising content in a context of entertainment, lower prestige ratings. We do the same for media like billboards and direct mail which have no nonadvertising content and therefore represent persuasion in its purest form.

Images of the Media

Attempts to measure attitudes toward the media seem to assume that attitudes based largely on nonadvertising content will "rub off" on the advertising content itself. This is a pretty daring assumption, in view of the fact that most people seem to have little difficulty in distinguishing the two types of content! The assumption becomes a little more realistic when advertising messages deliberately imitate the content of the nonadvertising context. Newspaper advertisements, with their emphasis on price, are often perceived by the housewife as containing as much information as the news columns. *New Yorker* advertisements often show as much wry wit, or come as close to self-parody, as the editorial columns of the magazine. When the publication emphasizes the restrictions it places on its advertisers, by guaranteeing their performance through a *Good Housekeeping* seal of acceptance, the assumption becomes even more defensible.

Nonadvertising content creates an image for a medium and represents a challenge to its advertisers to match that image. The higher the standards of the medium, the harder the advertiser must work for acceptance. Sometimes the competition becomes too great; the television program or the magazine fiction becomes so exciting that the advertisements themselves are never perceived. What the advertiser would like is content exciting enough to attract an audience but bland enough not to distract people from his advertisements. On the other hand, if the audience begins to realize that the advertisements *are* more exciting than their context, its members may also begin to wonder why they bother to buy the publication or listen to the program.

Media Effects on Audience

Marketing management specifies the audience it would like to reach, and then asks which medium supplies an audience which comes closest to these specifications.

Product Channel

Firms use magazines and salesmen to communicate with other businessmen, with manufacturers who will process their products, or with retailers who will sell them. The magazines they use are of four types. They may be general magazines, such as *Time*, whose circulation has a high proportion of upper-income groups, including both professional men and business managers. They may be publications directed at businessmen in general, such as *Fortune, Business Week*, and the *Wall Street Journal*. Or they may be the more specialized magazines, usually called "business papers," which appeal to a horizontal group, such as comptrollers or marketing managers, or vertically, to an industry such as steel or fertilizer or supermarkets. Farm magazines, although usually classified separately, operate in much the same way to perform much the same function. Some have regional audiences and others collect audiences on the basis of an interest in cattle or pigs in general, or a specific breed. Many of them, however, recognize that the farm is both a production and a consumption unit by including material for the farm wife.

Messages which on the surface appear intended for customers may, in fact, be aimed at some prior target in the distribution chain. One supplier of automobile parts, for example, is said to have run an advertisement in the *Saturday Evening Post,* with no interest at all in the millions of *Post* readers. His target was one man—the President of General Motors. His reasoning was that the head of General Motors would be more likely to see the advertisement in such an unexpected context or that he would assume that a firm able to afford a campaign in such an expensive medium must be itself successful.

Some advertising campaigns are designed primarily to open up retail outlets. A manufacturer of milk cartons ran a campaign in a consumer magazines primarily so he could send copies of the issue to the nation's leading dairies. In such cases the advertisement and the medium in which it appears represent the message; the salesman who shows them to the retailer and points out that his customers are soon going to be demanding the advertised product, represents the channel. In such cases, the media confer status on the advertiser, and contribute to his image.

Geographically, we can distinguish between the print media, which face the distribution problems similar to those of the products advertised in them, and the broadcast media, which can ignore such physical limits of transportation in disseminating their messages. If a mail carrier or a railway express truck can deliver a product, it can deliver a publication. Another reason why print-media audiences tend to coincide with markets is that newspaper circulations tend to reflect political divisions; these divisions may affect both the news in them and physical distribution of products as well. The broadcast signal, on the other hand, extends varying distances in all directions from the station.

Both print and broadcast media may reach persons who are outside the geographic limits of a retailer's market. Historically, broadcast networks and magazines have delivered nationwide audiences; newspapers, billboards, and individual stations have delivered local audiences. We can accumulate a regional or national audience, of course, by collecting local audiences for newspapers, billboards and broadcasting stations. Media buyers have done this and the media themselves have assisted. More recently, large-circulation magazines, seeking to increase their flexibility in the face of competition from television, have begun to break their national audience into regional audiences. Thus *Life* offers twenty-six editions, each corresponding to an area in which A. C. Nielsen offers audience surveys, to serve the needs of the advertiser whose products are not distributed nationally, or the advertiser who wants to introduce a new product region by region, or the advertiser who wants to use different strategies in different areas of the country for research or other reasons (Magazine Advertising Bureau).

Demographically, we can distinguish two methods of audience selection: that which occurs between media vehicles and that which occurs within a given media vehicle. Magazines use the first method. *Jack and Jill* appeals to children, *Harper's Bazaar* to upper-income women, *Good Housekeeping* to the middle majority, and *True Confessions* to women of less education and income. Radio stations use this method also. One station attracts the teen-ager with rock and roll and another reaches an older, better-educated group with Mozart and Bach. Television and newspapers, on the other hand, tend to attract both sexes and all ages and classes, but with different content. Men, for example, watch baseball on television on evenings and week-ends, and concentrate on the sports pages of their newspapers. Women watch soap operas during the day and read the society pages of their newspapers. So important has demographic selection become that *Time* magazine, with a large, nationwide audience, in 1964 began offering three *demographic* editions: for physicians, or educators, or students.

Outdoor advertising is probably the least selective of the media, since anyone traveling by car in or near a city is exposed to its messages. Direct mail and personal selling can be the most precise, since they can choose their receivers, one by one. Business papers exercise selectivity both by their subscription rates and, with more precision, by refusing to accept subscriptions from persons outside a specific industry or below a given level of management. Usually, however, there is more than one way to reach any desired audience. Makers of band instruments, for example, have a choice of at least four magazines directed to the bandmasters who influence parents and children in purchase of an instrument. The radio station which broadcasts chamber music will probably reach many of the people who read *Harpers* magazine.

Audience selection is influenced not only by the men who control the media, but by the impact of outside events. When automobiles replaced the commuter train, morning newspapers lost their commuter audience. When commuting businessmen turned on their car radios, and teen-agers started carrying transistor sets, radio gained a new audience to replace the night-time, entertainment-seeking family audience it had lost to television.

Role and Mood

Every member of the audience has many roles to play. On any given day, for example, a woman is likely to shift back and forth between the roles of wife and of mother, of cook and of cleaning woman, of citizen and of purchasing agent for the family. Moreover, there are moods appropriate to each role. As mother, she may be indulgent or strict; as cleaning woman, woe-begone and self-pitying; as cook, proud; as purchasing agent, canny. The medium she turns to will vary with each role and each mood, as will the content she selects from that medium, and the kinds of messages to which she responds. A good housewife may not be comfortable watching a soap opera on television in the morning, for example, before the dishes are done and beds made (Crane, Talbott, Hume). She may be willing to work along with a radio quiz program, however; or feel that a homemaker program on television is consistent with her morning role.

Makers of fine perfume will neither advertise in *Parents* magazine, for its readers are more likely to be interested in powder for babies' bottoms, nor will they advertise on morning broadcasts when housewives' ears are attuned to talk about cake mixes. Makers of instant coffee ran into trouble when they tried to appeal to women in their role as keepers-of-the-family-budget, and stressed economy (Haire, a). They discovered that the role of hostess was a lot more important when housewives thought about coffee. A different vehicle may be appropriate to each role.

Stage of Persuasion

When a product is new and most persons are not aware that it exists or that they have any use for it, advertisers turn to a medium, like television, which is intrusive. On the other hand, news media and the publicity channel will be best for new products for which the prospect has a felt need. The person building a home is likely to see a news item about floor tile, roofing, or window screens in *Better Homes and Gardens* or in the housing section of his Sunday newspaper. The businessman is usually in an information-seeking mood when he leafs through his favorite business paper.

If prospects have such a strong preference for a brand that they will hunt for it, the yellow pages of the telephone book may provide the best medium for the advertiser. When a product is bought frequently, but brand preference is weak, the advertiser may try to put his brand name on the tip of the purchaser's tongue with a billboard that the buyer will see, a radio commercial that he will hear while driving to the store, or a point-of-purchase display in the store itself.

Delay in Response

The length of time which elapses between exposure to a message and a chance to purchase the product is an important factor in choice of media and design of a message. Of course, we would expect that the delay would be greater for the person in the unaware stage than for the person who has strong brand preferences already established. We would expect a big difference between expensive, rarely purchased and inexpensive, frequently purchased items. Allowing for such differences in people and products, we can ask which media are best when a message must be retained in the memory for a considerable period of time. Much depends on the message itself, rather than the media that carry it. Moreover, this problem involves more than a question of whether sight or sound is better in implanting memories. Psychologists advise that the more closely the conditions in which a message is learned approximate the conditions under which that message will be used, the better. If the purchaser must pluck a product off a shelf, then pictures which help him recognize the package, and media which can print such pictures, are best. If, on the other hand, he must ask for it by name, then a radio commercial which repeatedly links product and brand name may best serve the advertiser's goals. Repetition is good; rewarding the purchaser for repeated linking of stimulus and response is better.

Counting Noses

Under the pressure of media competition, which often takes the form of competitive media studies, counts of audience size have become increasingly refined. At first, newspapers and magazines merely reported the number of copies distributed, with an Audit Bureau of Circulation to police their counts. Broadcasters reported the number of receiving sets owned in the areas reached by their signals, and operators of outdoor advertising "plants" reported the number of persons passing their billboards.

Then the sample survey entered the picture. (Lucas and Britt, Chapters 10–16.) Broadcasting stations and networks began to report the share of sets tuned to their programs at half-hour and fifteen-minute intervals. Cameras in billboards snapped pictures, permitting the whites of the eyes of the passerby to be counted. Researchers reported the percentage of readers who claimed to recognize a magazine or a newspaper advertisement, or the percentage who could play back a description of an advertisement, given the name of the advertiser.

In addition to simple nose-counts, the surveys classified respondents by income, age, and sex, so that the extent to which a medium's audience coincided with the advertiser's target market could be approximated. As a further refinement, surveys identified prospects in the audience by means of product ownership, brand preference, or buying intentions. Simultaneous surveys of several magazines revealed the extent to which their circulation lists overlapped. Ingenious studies in depth counted not merely the number of persons who recognize a given advertisement, but the number of times a reader remembered having been exposed to a given advertisement in a given issue of a given magazine. Thus it became possible to compare the effects of repeated exposure in one magazine with repeated exposure in several magazines. *Life* counted its pass-along readers, pointing out that its accumulated audience was considerably larger than the number of copies printed. Other magazines rejoined that such pass-along readers were neither as rich nor as thorough in their reading as the subscribers themselves.

In both broadcasting and magazine publishing, studies showed that exposure to advertisements was associated with increased use of advertised products, the usual assumption being that exposure preceded and caused the increased use. Just as it appeared that the researchers' ingenuity in finding new ways to measure new aspects of media superiority was about to outrun the mind's capacity to process their data, the computer appeared.

Difficult decisions still must be made, as to which variables to include in a computer program, and what weight to give them. Is the viewer whose set was tuned in during a sixty-second commercial the equivalent of the reader who recognizes a full-page, four-color magazine advertisement? For that matter, is the person who buys a magazine at a newsstand a more devoted reader of a given issue, if a somewhat less consistent reader from one issue to the next, than the person who subscribes? How are we to measure the contribution which the medium vehicle makes to the credibility of the source? Are the readers' roles evoked by the medium appropriate to the message it carries? To what extent can advertisers and advertising agencies expect competing media to finance studies which aim not to sell a given medium or medium vehicle but to guide a space and time buyer in choosing among them? The great advantage of the computer in this situation is that it can apply several sets of alternative weights to the data fed into it when clearcut answers to such questions are lacking. It can apply varying assumptions and show how each alternative answer will affect overall results. (Text continued on p. 198.)

The complexity of media choice and the need for subjective judgment are revealed when one tries to program the selection for a computer—as this example illustrates.

Splitting $80,000 Among Three Magazines

Here is how an expert on mathematical models reaches a decision to apportion a four-month budget of $80,000, making 8 insertions of advertisements in 3 magazines. His decision-making process involves 10 steps. The first 5 of these consist of adjusting the magazine's audience upward or downward on the basis of 4 measures: The extent to which the audience's demographic characteristics match those of the advertiser's target market; the extent to which media and media vehicle are suited to the product being advertised; the effects of such message variables as size (time or space) and color upon the message's effectiveness and the effects of repetition.

1. *Audience.* The adjusted audience for Magazine X is arrived at by this formula, which represents an upward adjustment of 7.6%:

$$6,000,000 \times 1.09 \quad \times 1.05 \quad \times .94 \quad = 6,454,980$$

| (Actual audience) | (Age index) | (Income index) | (Regional index) | (Adjusted audience) |

These three indices look at segmentation of the magazine's audience along these 3 lines (age, income, geography), giving more weight to segments which show high purchase of the product and the brand in question. Here are the 3 steps by which the age index is obtained. First, these figures are taken from market and census reports:

Distribution of Women by Age

Age Group	In Population	For Product Sales	For Brand Sales
18–34	33%	35%	49%
35–49	30	40	36
50 and up	37	25	15

Second, these are converted to ratios. For each segment, one divides the population percentage by the product sales percentage (33%/35% = 1.06) and the brand sales percentage by the product sales percentage (49%/35% = 1.40). Then these two ratios are averaged for each segment. Multiplying by the average ratio then adjusts the actual audience figure either up or down to give more weight to high-purchase segments. Here is what happens:

Age Group	Product Index	Brand Index	Average Index	Actual Audience	Audience Adjusted for Age
	(Col. 1/ Col. 2)	(Col. 2/ Col. 3)			
18–34	1.06	1.40	1.23	3,000,000	3,690,000
35–49	1.33	.90	1.11	2,000,000	2,220,000
50 and up	.68	.60	.64	1,000,000	640,000
				6,000,000	6,550,000

Finally, one divides the adjusted audience (6,550,000) by the actual audience (6,000,000) to get the age index of 1.09 used in the formula shown above. A similar process is repeated for each index and for each magazine being considered.

2. *Medium.* Next, subjective weights are needed to reflect the fact that magazine color may be best suited to a product like food, and the live demonstration possible on TV to a new gadget. These are the subjective weights used for the unidentified product used in this example, which would be used to readjust the adjusted audience figure of 6,454,980 reached in step No. 1:

Media Weights		Readjusted Audience
Magazines	1.15	7,423,227
Television	1.00	6,454,980
Radio	.85	5,486,733
Newspapers	.80	5,163,984
Billboards	.60	3,872,988

3. *Vehicle.* Within any given medium such as magazines, vehicles such as *Good Housekeeping* and *McCall's* differ in the extent that their advertisements are noted, or believed, and in the extent to which the vehicle's prestige "rubs off" on the advertisement it carries. Subjective weights must be assigned to individual magazines and the readjusted audience readjusted all over again.

4. *Message variables.* The audience figures obtained in Step 3 must be multiplied by indices which reflect the relative effectiveness of 20-second vs. 60-second commercials, or full pages vs. half-pages, or color vs. black-and-white.

5. *Effect of repetition.* At some point, diminishing returns set in as an ad is repeated in the same vehicle. If we assume a 10% loss per issue, then the audience of Magazine X (which has been boosted from its actual audience of 6,000,000 to an adjusted audience of 7,500,000 by the four steps just described) would change over a period of four issues in this fashion:

Magazine X

Insertion	Adjusted Audience
First	7,500,000
Second	6,750,000
Third	6,075,000
Fourth	5,467,500

Up to this point, the example has dealt only with *people;* it is now time to discuss dollars; the final steps in this model of media selection involve budgeting problems: splitting an ad budget of $1,200,000 among media and among months of the year, while taking account of quantity discounts.

6. *Split among media.* The client or history or brand strategy dictate, for the sake of this example, spending 80% of the budget on television and 20% on magazines.

7. *Quantity discounts.* Magazine X has a constant rate of $9000 per insertion. Its three competitors, however, offer varying discounts as number of insertions rises:

Rate of Insertion

Number of Insertion	Magazine V	Magazine W	Magazine Y
First	$9,500	$10,000	$10,000
Second	9,000	10,000	9,000
Third	8,000	10,000	8,000
Fourth	8,000	7,000	7,000

8. *Readers per dollar.* The audience figures for each magazine illustrated in Step 5, which have gone through a series of five adjustments, are now divided by the cost figures of Step 7, to produce the following table, showing audience (number of persons) per dollar for each insertion in each of the four magazines being considered.

Magazine	1st Insertion	2nd Insertion	3rd Insertion	4th Insertion
V	737 (M.)	700 (A.)	709	638
W	800 (J.)	720 (M.)	648 (A.)	833
X	833 (J.)	750 (F.)	675 (A.)	607
Y	600	600	608	625

(Letters in parentheses indicate month in which this insertion occurred in this magazine as explained in Section 9.)

9. *Advertising schedule.* Some advertisers run heavy schedules in the months preceding the time they expect high-purchase rates; others try to counter such tendencies. In this illustration, $20,000 of the $240,000 magazine budget will be spent in January, $10,000 in February, $20,000 in March, $30,000 in April. Using the table in Step 8, these amounts will

be divided among the magazines as follows:

January. First insertions in Magazines X (833 persons per dollar) and
W (800). *Total cost: $19,000* (from Step 7).
February. Second insertion in X (750). *Total cost: $9000.*
March. First insertion in V (737) and second insertion in W (720).
Total cost: $19,500.
April. Second insertion in V (700); third insertions in X (675) and
W (648). *Total cost: $28,000.*

10. *Summary.* Here is a summary of the effects of this schedule over
these four months of January through April:

Month	Total Audience	Total Cost	Persons per Dollar
January	15,500,000	$19,000	816
February	6,750,000	9,000	750
March	14,200,000	19,500	728
April	18,855,000	28,000	673

The total audience, of course, does not take account of duplication that
occurs because one person may subscribe to two or three of the magazines used. If 30% saw both of the magazines used in January, the
audience in terms of different persons reached would be 10,850,000
instead of 15,500,000. Dividing the larger figure by the smaller gives
1.43 as an index of frequency—the number of times the average viewer
is exposed to the advertisement. Adjustments in the sequence of ten
steps just described could, of course, increase either reach or frequency,
depending on which was most desired.

—Philip Kotler, "Toward an Explicit
Model for Media Selection," *Journal of
Advertising Research*, 4:1:34–41.

The Salesman As Channel

The two most important advantages of the salesman are that he
has ears and eyes, and that each of his messages goes to fewer receivers
than do media messages. His ears and eyes mean that the salesman
can benefit from feedback. He can watch his listeners' faces, listen
to their voices, and modify his messages accordingly. He can do
this most successfully, of course, when he is facing a single receiver.
It becomes harder to observe and respond to several receivers at
a time.

Feedback seems more important to the salesman's success in communication than the fact that he uses many symbol systems at once. The television commercial, for example, engages the vision of his viewers as well as their hearing. The salesman on a telephone loses the visual symbols but more than compensates for this loss by his ability to get feedback from the other end of the line.

These two advantages—feedback and a smaller number of receivers —are purchased at a price. Personal selling is costly. One study reports that the average cost of an industrial salesman's call is thirty dollars, and that it takes six calls to sell a customer, compared with a media cost per receiver of as low as one-tenth of a cent (McGraw-Hill Research).

A third important difference between the media and a salesman is that the salesman is a person, not a machine. For the individual salesman, this is both an advantage and a disadvantage. It makes it more difficult for him to get a hearing. Prospects know that it is harder to get rid of a salesman than it is to switch off television or flip the page of a magazine. Realizing that once the salesman has crossed the threshhold they will find it hard to get rid of him, housewives tend to stand in the doorway and businessmen to barricade themselves behind a secretary. Having breached these defenses, however, the salesman has a good chance of having his message heard. He is not likely to be interrupted by a competitor, and the housewife will return after she has changed the diapers on a squawling baby. (That same squawl from a baby would blank out a television commercial completely.)

The fact that the salesman is a person means that his chances of success, already good because his message can be fashioned for an individual receiver and modified on the basis of feedback, are not dependent solely on the message itself. His receivers feel some obligation for taking up time during which he could have been talking to someone else. They may buy because they like him, or because they feel he needs the business. They may feel they can put more trust in a salesman, particularly if repeat sales are involved, than in an advertisement.

Because most of us have less ability to control our facial and bodily movements than the words we use, we tend to believe that such cues will reveal a source's intentions. Indeed, should the two sets of cues contradict one another, we tend to trust the visual and reject the verbal. (We may be wrong, of course. Skilled actors, skilled poker players, and skilled salesmen may be able to suppress or disguise cues which would reveal their intentions.)

If one could determine what kinds of attitudes and activities distinguish good salesmen, one could improve hiring and training practices.   Here are two attempts to do just that.

The human relations involved in salesman-customer communications represent an asset to the salesman. From the standpoint of his employer, however, these advantages are purchased at a rather high price. This price is not just the relatively high cost per receiver of this channel. It is more than the possibility that prospects may refuse to buy a product because they dislike the man selling it, since this difficulty can be overcome, in large part, by selecting salesmen, by training them, and through systems of compensation which make it to the salesman's own self-interest to make himself likeable.

To the employer, perhaps the most important cost of using a salesman as a communications channel is the loss of control which this involves. No two salesmen will deliver a message in exactly the same

---

Seven Test Scores: Three Types of Salesmen

Scores on the Strong Vocational Interest blanks were obtained from 22 firms for 300 salesmen whom sales managers said, after a year's service, they would be willing to rehire. Of the number, 100 were specialty salesmen, 100 route salesmen, and 100 sales engineers. Scores on 7 different Strong scales of the 3 groups were then compared.

Results showed that route men were highest on scores reflecting concern with business details: those for accountants, office workers, and purchasing agents. Sales engineers were most similar, in their scores, to production and personnel managers, and of the three groups, least like real estate and life insurance salesmen. None of the 3 groups ranked high on the advertising man scales.

	Mean Standard Strong Score for Salesman Type		
Strong Scale	Route	Specialty	Engineers
Accountant	39	36	33
Office worker	50	45	39
Purchasing agent	44	40	39
Production manager	40	39	45
Personnel manager	41	43	45
Real-estate salesman	48	48	44
Life-insurance salesman	50	49	43

In the 21 F tests obtained, by comparing 2 groups of salesmen at a time, all but 6 comparisons were significant at the .05 level or better.

—Arthur A. Witkin, "Differential Patterns in Salesmen," *Journal of Applied Psychology*, 40:338–340.

Activities, Adjectives, and Two Types of Salesmen

Using a checklist of 35 sales activities regarded as important to their jobs, the activities ranging from replenishing stocks to giving technical advice, researchers identified 50 "retail" salesmen, and 70 "industrial" salesmen for Minnesota Mining and Manufacturing Co. The groups were then compared as to Strong Vocational Interest Blank scores, scores on a personality test, the Edwards Personal Preference Schedule, and choices from 36 groups of 5 adjectives of those which each man perceived as best describing himself.

Industrial salesmen perceived themselves as high in ingenuity, inventiveness, and exercise of wits; retail salesmen emphasized planning, hard work, and the ability to persuade others. Success of industrial salesmen was related to verbal reasoning ability, that of retail salesmen to their motivation toward selling, as measured by Strong scores, and toward being dominant in relationships with others.

> —Marvin D. Dunnette and Wayne K. Kirchner, "Psychological Test Differences Between Industrial Salesmen and Retail Salesmen," *Journal of Applied Psychology*, 44:121–125.

way; no individual salesman will deliver the message in exactly the same way on two different occasions. The substitution-of-identical-parts implied by a system of mass marketing, similar to that which exists in mass production, becomes impossible when those parts are people.

Moreover, when human beings communicate, as in the salesman-customer situation, both are affected. The salesman's success depends upon his ability to create a sense of give-and-take, but it is hard for him to do this over any period of time if there is no reality behind the pretense. He may be able to act the role for a single sale of a house or a car, but such acting becomes more difficult when he expects repeated contacts with and repeat sales to a given buyer, whether he be selling Fuller brushes to housewives or stamping presses to manfacturers. An important part of a salesman's compensation consists of the nonmonetary rewards he receives in his work, the pleasure of communicating with other people. The salesman loses these rewards if he begins to look upon these contacts as entirely selfish and cynical, even if the customer himself is deceived. To the extent the salesman gets such rewards from his customers, he ceases to be dependent solely on his employer. Without realizing it, he may begin to take the side of the customer against the employer, modifying credit terms, delivery dates, or product features for the customer's benefit.

The key difficulty here is that the principal value of the salesman and the reason a marketer uses him as a channel rather than the mass media, is that the salesman can modify his message to suit a receiver. The skillful salesman is more likely to make these modifications without being aware that he has made them. At the same time the less aware he is of them, the more likely that an accumulation of such changes will pass beyond the limits permitted by company policy. Since a man's words cannot diverge too far from his actions without making the man himself uncomfortable and leaving his audience unconvinced, changes in the message are likely to be accompanied by changes in the conditions of sale and in product, price, and place.

The role of the salesman as employee and his role as friend to the customer come into conflict with one another. Although an employer can crack down in such cases and limit the salesman's freedom, this has its disadvantages. One is its effect on the salesman's morale. Another is on his standing with customers, who may not want to waste time talking to a man who has no freedom of action and cannot find a solution to their needs. Shifting the salesman to a new territory will break up such ties with his customers, but this, too, involves losses as well as gains. Closer supervision may destroy morale; exhortation may be ineffective.

Customers can punish salesmen as well as reward them. Refusal to buy may injure a salesman's morale. A firm, for example, might find it highly desirable and highly profitable if its salesmen managed to close only one sale in thirty attempts. The firm might be willing to pay its salesmen handsomely for such a ratio, but it is doubtful whether any salary could compensate for the lack of nonmonetary rewards in such a situation. A major part of a sales manager's job may be to maintain morale in a situation which the employer regards as satisfactory but the salesman does not.

Effects of Group Size

Two important variables studied in small-group research affect the salesman's performance. These are group size and the relative status of source and receiver. Many a sales manager has made points with one of his salesmen by saying, "Pick out your toughest customer, and come along, and I will show you how to sell him," and then has done just that. What he fails to point out is that the mere presence of a second salesman, even if he never says a word, tends to tip the balance against the customer.

Sometimes a customer can be led to believe that he and the salesmen are in coalition against a third antagonist. The salesman in a subdivision, for example, may promise a home buyer all sorts of changes, only to be overruled by the cost-conscious builder's architect. In a way, defeats are even better than victories, for they emphasize how far the salesman was willing to go for a "friend." To make his "fight" with the architect seem more real, the salesman may even insist that it go all the way up to the builder himself for a decision. (Learning theory suggests that a few, random victories for the salesman-customer coalition may do more to cement relations between them than would a 100 per cent record. See Chapter Fourteen).

Much the same type of drama occurs in the purchase of an automobile (Tucker, a). Salesman and prospect form a coalition against the hard-hearted appraiser who wants to allow only a fraction of what the old car is really worth on trade-in. Little wonder if the customer begins to feel a real tie of friendship with the salesman, to put high credibility in him as a source, and to feel an obligation to him.

A third kind of three-person group or triad, that in which an encyclopedia salesman communicates with husband and wife, involves a more complex strategy. Now the salesman constantly must shift sides, siding first with one and then with the other. When a buying decision is joint, as in this case, the salesman does well to work on both participants at the same time. To do otherwise would risk a veto by the spouse who has not heard his message. To talk to both separately would double the cost of the sales interview. Moreover, many of the advantages of the interview are lost if the sale is not completed in a single session. Delay allows the customer's sense of obligation to the salesman to dissipate. It gives the prospect a chance to compare brands and prices and to expose himself to competitive messages. As a result most salesmen press for an immediate decision. The insurance man, for example, will talk about the accident which could happen tomorrow morning, and the encyclopedia salesman has a "special rate" good for tonight only. One function of the salesman-customer "combat team" in home-buying and car-buying is to maintain this sense of obligation when a sale cannot be completed in a single session.

We suggested that one reason the sales manager so often succeeds in making the tough sale is the pressure which the presence of two salesmen puts on the customer. Another reason is that the manager's visit provides a subtle enhancement to the customer's status.

Effects of Status Differences

Selling involves a social relationship, and the most satisfactory social relationship is one between equals. If the salesman's status is clearly inferior to that of the customer, he is likely to lose control of the sales interview. Although we would think this would benefit the customer by giving him superior bargaining power, this is not necessarily true. The salesman's product knowledge and sales experience make him the best able to direct communications. If the salesman loses control, the whole communication process may break down. For this reason, a high status customer may insist on meeting with the salesman's superiors, to restore the equality of status necessary to communication and bargaining.

Through experience, most salesmen learn that they can communicate most successfully with persons like themselves and select their audiences accordingly, no matter how strongly their employers insist that "a good salesman can sell anybody." When this is difficult, as in a retail store where a clerk has little say about his audiences, communications difficulties are likely to arise. Three factors contribute to these difficulties. The first is that society prescribes roles for the participants: customer-as-king and salesman-as-suppliant. The second is the actual social status of the two role occupants. The third is the need for equality of status in two-way, face-to-face communications.

By definition, sales clerks are white-collar workers and members of the middle class. Little difficulty arises when their employer caters to a middle-class clientele, since the equality of status necessary for communication exists. Clerks in such stores can play a friendly, even informal role. If the shop caters to a wealthy clientele, the salesman finds it difficult to achieve the appearance of equality necessary to communication. He often does so by playing down the usual scale of wealth, occupation, or income on which status is based and emphasizing the special, limited area of product knowledge where he can hold his own as an expert. The store serving a lower-class clientele creates major status problems. Although the salesman could create the equality of status necessary to communication by "stepping down" temporarily to the customer's level, he find this so threatening and so punishing that he is likely to refuse. Instead, he emphasizes his own superiority by becoming brusque and impolite. His sales may suffer but his status is preserved.

Problems of status become even more complex in industrial selling, since both salesman and customer belong to more complex organizations which have more levels of status, more status symbols, and more competition for status. Social relationships, as a result, become even more important and more time is spent in establishing them. Talk about products may be delayed until the businessman's luncheon is ready to break up, or reserved for the nineteenth hole at the golf course. It may take six calls before an actual sale is made.

Varied Selling Functions

Many attempts have been made to determine what kind of person is most likely to succeed in selling or what kinds of sales techniques are most effective. Most such attempts have failed, for the same reason that attempts to determine what traits produce a leader have failed. Selling, like leadership, consists of a package of functions. Salesmen vary in their ability to perform each of these functions, and the need for each of these functions varies with product and prospect.

The salesman, for instance, often must determine what kinds of people are the best market for his product and audience for his message. He must then find individuals who fit in this category, and get them to listen to his message. He must know when several persons participate in the buying decision and, if he can, get them to meet with him as a group. He must combine symbols into messages. In addition he may find himself doing a lot of things that increase his influence as a source, from giving technical advice and trouble-shooting to providing a prospect news of his industry and gossip about his colleagues and competitors. Such activities reward both the salesman and his customer and make them willing to continue communicating.

In production, economies can be achieved through breaking up the production process into a series of specialized functions. In marketing, similar economies have been sought by eliminating the sales clerk in self-service stores, which means letting the customer perform some of the salesmen's functions; by letting advertising perform some of the salesman's functions; and by dividing these functions up among several specialists. These changes decrease the cost of selling. They may also increase its effectiveness:

". . . the mere presence of the salesman prevents large numbers of persons from looking at things that they are not seriously interested in, because of the presumed social obligation to buy . . . . Lack of such pressure in the self-service store allows the shopper to look around at his leisure, incurring no social debts . . . . Such leisurely perusal of merchandise seems to do as good a job of suggestive selling as many experienced salesmen, and accomplishes more than the mediocre sales clerk at less expense" (Tucker a, 76–77).

Advertising in business papers may open doors for the industrial salesman and give him high credibility before he opens his mouth. So many executives may influence a purchase that it is impossible for a salesman to determine who they are, much less talk to them. Some executives may have status so superior to the salesman that they would suffer a loss of status merely by talking to him. Advertising can reach and influence all these persons. This is why, to an increasing extent, marketing managers are needed to combine advertising and selling in a communications mix, rather than permitting the proportions to be determined by a battle between sales and advertising managers.

Economies in Specialization

Separating the several sales functions and assigning them to different persons involves costs of coordinating them and a risk that subgoals will subvert goals themselves. At the same time, the simpler functions can be assigned to cheaper help. This has beneficial side effects. An encyclopedia salesman can hire women to make a door-to-door cold canvass for prospects at a fraction of the cost of doing it himself. But that is not all. He also avoids the morale-destroying high rate of turndown associated with the cold canvass, and so do the women. By freeing them from the selling task itself, the salesman also frees them from the penalties of failing to make a sale.

In production, economies of scale can be achieved by standardizing products. Marketing, like production, has its standardized products and its standardized message—the canned sales pitch. The message, like the product, may be developed by the firm itself, or it may be fashioned by the salesman himself from his own experience. Again, standardization decreases the quality of salesman needed to carry the message—although a very high quality may be needed to develop the standardized package in the first place. It also shortens the length of time needed for communication. A good salesman can concentrate on prospects who are responsive to his package and messages, including the nonverbal messages of his own personality. The salesman who uses a canned pitch runs a risk, of course, since one reason people expose themselves to a salesman is the expectation that he will tailor both product and message to their individual needs. A good salesman may be able to preserve this illusion for them, even though in fact his presentation is a standard one.

Publicity as a Channel

The third communications channel is the channel of publicity via a story appearing in the space (or time) devoted to nonadvertising content in any of the major media. Often a medium will carry a message for the same product in both its advertising columns and its news columns. The publicity story often has two advantages over the advertisement. First, it may attract more attention or reach members of the audience who ignore the advertising. More important, the medium's share of source-ship is greater for the publicity story than for the advertisement. Since the medium is perceived as being less self-interested in the message than the advertiser, this means that the news story is more likely to be accepted than the advertisement.

Offsetting these advantages, the publicity story costs the firm control of its messages. Their fate depends upon the gatekeeper, the reporter or editor, just as the marketer's success in distribution of his product depends upon that other kind of middleman, the retailer. However, whereas financial inducements may sway the retailer, reputable media cannot be bribed. Instead, the firm must depend on the news or entertainment inherent in its message and its skill in persuading the gatekeeper. Many messages of great importance to the advertiser will fail to get through the gatekeeper; those that do may be greatly changed in form.

Role conflict, which works to the disadvantage of the firm when its salesmen take sides with the customer, may work to its advantage where publicity is concerned. The reporter may take sides with his news source, the manufacturer, with repeated contact. The manufacturer's interests exercise increasing weight on the reporter's decisions. The reporter, like the salesman, may originally take sides with his partner in communications (the news source) as a means to an end, but he may continue to do so because of the informal rewards he receives from the interaction itself.

Marketing management benefits from two kinds of publicity: direct or product and indirect or image building. Direct publicity is an excellent way to make persons aware of a new product. The very newness of the product is likely to appeal to the gatekeepers. The consumer, in turn, depends on the editorial columns (that is, nonadvertising content) to tell him of new products. Advertisers, he knows, are always claiming newness. Recognition by an editor separates the legitimate claims from the phony. Indirectly, publicity contributes to the firm's image, whether the publicity concerns a raise in employees' wages, an increase in dividends, or plans for a new plant.

Indirect publicity is usually assigned to a separate public relations department, which may report directly to the president. Direct product publicity is likely to play a small part in the activities of such a department, which is primarily concerned with the noncustomer publics of the firm; employees, stockholders, local communities, suppliers, the government, and the public-in-general. (Indeed, product publicity may be left to the firm's advertising agency.) However, on occasion, messages to each of these publics may include product messages. Employees, stockholders, and the local community may be urged to buy the firm's product as a sign of their "faith" and "loyalty." The volume of such sales may be less important to the firm than a hoped-for secondary effect. The firm may hope that, through these several publics, it can put a message in the informal channels of communication, such as conversations over the backfence and luncheon table.

Frequently the best communicator is a man who can talk the language of his receiver because he once filled that receiver's shoes. This is why publishers like to employ former superintendents in selling to schools and why drug companies like to use pharmacists as detail men. It also explains why most publicity men are ex-newspapermen. Former reporters can write a press release in newspaper langugage. Even more important, they can recognize a newsworthy idea when they see it, for they know the newsman's values.

Ideas and Events

Publicity resembles advertising in this sense: the basis of success is an idea and not a verbal formula. Ideas are even more important in publicity than in advertising, however, because a reporter takes greater pride and an editor is likely to give greater play to a news story written by the newsman than to a story, however well done, which has been written by an outsider. The publicity man who can feed ideas to the newsman can be a great success without ever writing a word. On occasion he may even want to write a release which "buries" the news, so that a reporter will have the thrill and self-satisfaction of appearing to discover it for himself.

Sometimes, of course, a public relations man really does want to bury the news, since publication would damage the firm's image. An outright attempt to do so, however, is likely to arouse the newsman's sense of independence and increase his conviction that news which is worth burying is worth printing. Diversionary tactics are more likely to be successful in such cases. The publicity man may subtly play down the importance of the item, provide details which mitigate its damaging effects, or come up with two or three news items of even greater news value which crowd the original item out of the paper. Publicity releases will take care of the routine new product. More significant news may employ the press conference so that reporters have a chance to ask questions and develop the story of their own.

A more advanced stage of public relations employs the staged or created event. The audience in the banquet room listening to a speech at an annual meeting of the Chamber of Commerce may be far less important to the chamber than the audience which reads a news story about that speech the next morning. (The bigger the audience and the bigger the name of the speaker, the more likely a newspaper is to report the speech in detail.) Every fund drive starts and ends with a ceremony, and it sprinkles progress-report meetings along the way. Presentation of an award for anything from life saving to longevity usually does more for the organization making the award than for the person who receives it.

Even more ingenious than these familiar events are the dramatizations that occur when an industry is in trouble. When charges of monopoly and even fraud smeared public utilities, a jubilee was staged honoring Edison's invention of the electric light. Even the government cooperated by issuing a special commemorative stamp. When motorists, angry after inching up a hill behind a truck, began demanding curbs on trucks in the name of safety, public relations men switched attention from the industry to individuals. They emphasized drivers' skill by staging annual "roadeos" and emphasized their safety records by requiring an accident-free history for entrants. Photographers and reporters for all the media covered the event, people began talking about it, and public opinion began to change. (Meanwhile, more direct tactics in the legislatures themselves slowed down the anti-truck campaign.)

Events of this kind not only have an intrinsic appeal to the newsman and the public, but are hard for the opposition to counter. The news columns of print media are a battleground to a much greater extent than the advertising columns. If the president of a truckers' trade association issues a statement, the railroads are likely to insist on a chance to reply. Usually, in fact, the reporter will ask them for it, both out of a sense of fairness and because a "fight" makes a better story. But what can a railroad do when truckers get columns of news and picture space with a "roadeo"?

Informal Channels, Pro and Con

Marketer control of the messages, which diminishes when a firm uses the channel of publicity, vanishes completely when the firm puts them on informal channels. In fact, it becomes very difficult for him to find what people are saying about his product to one another, much less influence what they say.

In return, however, he gains two advantages: one of audience, one as source. Persons whose defenses would ordinarily prevent exposure to an advertisement, a salesman, or even a publicity story are less able to protect themselves from the random comments of a friend. They are more likely to believe messages from a friend, partly because they feel he is more likely to understand their needs and partly because his interest in keeping their friendship is likely to keep his reports truthful. In addition, their knowledge of him enables them to judge where he is likely to err in knowledge or judgment, reducing the risks that arise from his lack of expertness.

A friend's messages are also likely to consist of reports of his experience with the product and so to reflect the variables of product, price, and place more than the marketer's message about these variables. Since these variables are more difficult to manipulate than messages about them, this is another reason why friends' messages have high credibility. Credibility aside, as with the salesman, we respond to a friend as a person—only more so. Even if we do not fully agree with his opinions, we may go along and buy the product a friend recommends, merely because we want the rewards of continued association with him.

The marketer who wants to use informal channels, faces two problems. One is how to get his message on those channels. Sometimes sheer weight of advertising can do it, since people tend to talk about prominent features of their environment. More often, the marketers will use the ingenious idea and the dramatic event-staging of publicity

or an unusual or clever advertising message. The other problem is
how to influence the nature of the messages which these channels
transmit.

Regardless of how much we may secretly enjoy an advertisement,
or how useful we may find it, many of us are reluctant to admit
that our behavior has actually been influenced by words on paper
or a salesman's spiel. To keep from admitting this to ourselves or
to others we may criticize advertising and boast of how we put one

---

*The advertiser has little control over backfence conversations among
housewives, but they represent a potent channel of information and influence.
This strength shows up clearly in the diffusion of a new product.*

Air Conditioners in Philadelphia

Fortune magazine sent a research crew into a sample of neighborhoods
in Philadelphia in 1954 to count the number of air conditioning units
jutting out of house windows. Whenever they found a neighborhood—
the blocks served by a single shopping center—with an above-average
number of units, they plotted them on a map. Then they questioned
10% of the owners, asking when they bought the units, whether a friend
had recommended them, what other appliances they owned, and how
long they had lived on the block.

At this time, air conditioners were just about to move out of the luxury
class. Nationally, about 3% of all homes had them. In Philadelphia, however, of 5000 houses counted, in the first part of the study, 20% had one
conditioner and 8% had two. Most of them were not found in either
high or low-income neighborhoods but in new, row-house neighborhoods
with young white-collar families in the $4000 to $7500 income brackets.

Young people, anticipating rising incomes, apparently were the best
prospects for a new product. This was confirmed when we looked at
ownership of other kinds of appliances, for the 55 persons who owned
conditioners ("innovators") and compared their rate with the national
average.

Appliances owned	Innovators	U.S. Average
Washer	84%	78%
Dryer	42	5
Garbage disposal	18	4
Freezer	16	14
Dishwasher	11	3

A closer look at the maps of air-conditioner owners, however, showed
that ownership was not spread evenly among even this income and age
group; in one block, 6% of the homes would have conditioners and in
another block 35%. In fact, one side of the street might have six times
the ownership of the other side. Air conditioners appeared to spread,
like a disease, from one house to those on each side, and to those across

the alley. Why? Because it is there children play and mothers gossip. Neighbors communicate with one another, learn about new products and brands, and develop group norms that say when a person *may* buy an air conditioner, without being considered "putting on airs" and when he *must* buy one if he is not to be considered out-of-step.

What better source of prospects for a new product like conditioners can there be, asks *Fortune*, than the neighbors of the man who has just bought one? None—unless it be to sell the man who has bought a unit for the master bedroom, another one for his children.

—William H. Whyte, Jr., "The Web of Word of Mouth," *Fortune*, 50:5 (November, 1954), 140–143, 204–212.

over on the salesman. On the other hand, all of us are constantly on the lookout for news that we can share with a friend, or for some common experience that we can share together in conversation. As a result, the role of informal communications is particularly important in encouraging purchase and use of a new product.

Innovation on the Farm

The role of informal channels in innovation has been studied in two settings, neither of which, interestingly enough, involved decisions by consumers. The first setting was that of the farm: decisions by the producer on the adoption of new farm practices. The other setting was that of the doctor's offices: what leads him to prescribe a new drug, which his patients will pay for and use.

Some practices are adopted a few hours after a farmer hears about them; others may take years. The time it takes depends on the practice (Lionberger a, 104–105). The more a practice *costs* and the more *complicated* it is, the slower people are to adopt it. If a practice can be adopted *piecemeal*, or *abandoned easily* if it does not work out, its adoption will be speeded up. If the practice fits into the *existing value system*, it will be adopted more quickly. Thus farmers were slow to terrace their fields, because the process was hard to reverse. And farmers, whose reputation had for years rested on their ability to plow straight rows and select good seed corn were slow to adopt contour plowing and hybrid seed corn, which discarded these two props to reputation. Scholars have found a gradient of complexity:

1. Changes in materials and equipment, which do not require farmers

to learn new techniques, are adpoted most quickly. *Example:* A new variety of seed.

2. Next come changes in techniques which do not also require new equipment. *Example:* A new type of crop rotation.
3. Then some entirely new techniques. *Example:* contour plowing.
4. Last of all some changes in the total enterprise, which involve complicated and far reaching changes. *Example:* A shift from crop to livestock farming.

The task for an advertiser is to see which of these changes most resemble the one he is trying to bring about. Is it a mere change in brand preference, or a new use for an old product, or such a new technique as shifting from driving a horse to driving an automobile?

Typically, researchers find that the individual being urged to adopt a new practice goes through five stages, similar to the advertising man's AIDA (Lionberger a, 21–24):

Awareness of practice.
Interest. The farmer begins seeking information about the practice.
Evaluation. He weighs the information and evidence he has.
Trial. He gives the product or practice a trial run.
Adoption. He makes the practice a permanent part of his operations.

Individuals do not go through these stages at the same pace; at any moment there are probably some in each stage. Some are quick to adopt, others are slow. Ordinarily adoptions are slow in the beginning, then speed up. During the first six years after hybrid seed corn was introduced, for example, only about 6 per cent of Iowa farmers adopted the practice; six years later, however, the adoption was almost universal.

Five Types of Farmers

It is possible to distinguish five types of persons, on the basis of when they respond to influence. When put in a normal curve they look like this (Lionberger a, 36–41).

1. Innovators   2.5%
2. Early adopters   13
3. Early majority   34
4. Late majority   34
5. Laggards   16

Why does a farmer fall into one type rather than another? In part, this depends upon his *location*. If his area is hit by a drought, he is likely to adopt grass sileage quickly. In part, it depends on his *situation*. A farmer with a sick wife, or children entering college, may lack the means to afford a new practice. In part, it depends on *demography*. An old man has different needs and abilities than a young man, and he is probably more interested in security in the short run than high profit in the long run; he is less likely to change. In part it depends upon his *personality*. Is he mentally rigid or flexible?

Farmers who adopt early are men able and willing to take risks, with larger farms and incomes (Lionberger a, 52–66). They do not hesitate to bypass the county agent and go directly to college research men for advice or by-pass a local dealer and go to a firm's headquarters. Late adopters tend to have smaller farms, often of subsistence nature, and tend to be elderly and vulnerable to risk. They tend not to belong to organizations, as do early adopters, but to associate with friends and relatives. They have unfavorable attitudes toward county agents. The middle majority operate average-sized farms, tend not to see their county agent, and to get information from neighboring farmers or dealers. Apart from these three main groups are certain special types.

Innovators. They are the first to adopt; their neighbors watch them but do not follow them. They provide the local trial which is needed to persuade more cautious persons. They may have low status-reputation, especially in communities whose norms favor traditional methods.*

Key communicators. These are farmers mentioned from two to five times by other farmers as sources of information. Where norms of the community favor change, they tend to be innovators. Elsewhere they tend to be only slightly ahead of their neighbors.

Influentials. These are farmers who other farmers say influenced them to adopt the change. Their farms tend to be bigger and their incomes higher. They tend to use more new farm practices and to use more sources of information. They provide others with information and their approval is often necessary to "legitimize" a new practice. Their influence tends to extend over many areas. This group is usually quite small.

---

* In purchase of consumer durables such as automobiles and kitchen appliances, the persons who adopt innovations first tend to be young and educated, to have incomes in the middle range, and to expect their incomes to rise (Katona).

Five Causal Factors

Five factors operate both as cause, leading farmers to adopt new practices, and as effect, since adoption of new practices tends in turn to affect them (Lionberger a, 100–106). A farmer is more likely to be aware of and to adopt new practices if his income is high, his farm large, he owns rather than rents, he has prestige, and he has close ties with such experts as his county agent or agricultural college. Since these factors themselves are closely related to one another, the most helpful approach is to consider combinations of them.

If we hold age and income constant, for example, the relation be-

---

Word-of-mouth messages in the form of rumors can upset morale in wartime or injure a product or brand. What determines the rate at which rumors spread and the amount of distortion that occurs as they spread?

Rumor Spreads in Girls' School—But without Distortion

Between 8:25 and 8:35 A.M., the principal of a private girls school stalked in turn into each of four classrooms, pointed a finger at one of the pupils, and said, "Get your hat and coat and come with me. You will be gone for the rest of the day."

Nothing like this had ever happened in the classrooms before, and each teacher was asked to keep a record of any questions asked. In all, 198 questions were reported from the 62 girls in the four classrooms; they came so thick and fast that two teachers were unable to keep a count of them.

The principal's action, in short, created intense curiosity, and a highly ambiguous situation—two factors in which rumors are supposed to spread rapidly.

Meanwhile, a rumor had already been planted which might serve as a plausible explanation. The groundwork for this had been laid a day or two earlier, when teachers set up routine appointments for 8:15 on the day of the experiment, with two girls each from two of the classrooms from which girls were to be removed, and with two girls each from two other classrooms in which no incident took place. In the course of these interviews, each teacher asked a planted question: "By the way, some exams have been taken from the office. Do you happen to know anything about this?" All the girls with whom this rumor had been planted were back in their seats before the principal appeared.

Thus the experiment created three different types of subjects: the U or unclear group of 29 girls who had seen the incident but in which no rumor had been planted, the R group of 30 who had not seen the incident but in which a rumor had been planted, and a U-R group of 29 in which both incident had occurred and rumor been planted.

Many opportunities for the rumor to spread were available during the rest of the day: a 15-minute morning recess, an hour lunch period, an hour gym period, and five-minute intervals while classes were changing. At

2 P.M. a check of the extent to which the rumor had spread was made by bringing each class in turn to the lunchroom to talk to a staff of 20 interviewers who asked whether they had heard the rumor, who had told them about it, and who they, in turn, had passed it on to.

Out of 96 girls interviewed, only two said they did not know of the principal's action, only one said she had not heard the rumor, and only 15% had failed to link the rumor and the principal's action.

Despite this widespread knowledge of what had happened, the *R* girls in the two classes who had not seen anyone removed, spent little time talking about the removal—an average of only 20 minutes compared with an average of 100 minutes for the others. Moreover, 93% of the *U-R* group mentioned the incident, without a probe question, during the interviews, but only 76 per cent of the *U* group and 26 per cent of the *R* group. Obviously, the incident was relatively unimportant to the group which had not seen it, only heard about it. The *U-R* group transmitted the rumor to an average of 2.9 others, the *U-R* group to 2.3, and the *R* group to 1.1.

Three weeks before the experiment, each of the girls had been asked to list her five best friends; girls whose friend was the one plucked out of the room by the principal originated more messages, sending them to 3.1 girls compared with two for any other girls.

Previous laboratory studies in which a chain of persons pass stories from one to the other have found a high degree of distortion occurring in the messages passed on. In this experiment, not one of the 96 interviews showed any evidence of distortion. New rumors did spring up—76 per cent of *U-R* girls reported them, 65 per cent of *U* girls and 15 per cent of *R* girls. But the original rumor was *not* distorted.

The author suggests that in the current situation accuracy was increased by the simplicity of the rumor, high motivation among subjects (who operated on their own initiative rather than an experimenter's instructions), and the fact that hearing a rumor from several sources rather than one would eliminate errors.

—Stanley Schachter and Harvey Burdick, "A Field Experiment on Rumor Transmission and Distortion," *Journal of Abnormal and Social Psychology*, 50:363–371.

---

tween education and adoption of new practices drops. In Missouri, age was negatively related to adoption of new practices for farms with gross incomes under $3000 but positively related for farms with incomes over that amount (Lionberger a, 106). Even the best combination, however, seems to explain only about 50 per cent of the variance in adoption scores. This was the finding for Kansas beef producers with predictions made on the basis of age, education, group membership, gross income, and scores on "mental flexibility" and "farm professionalism."

How a farmer is influenced depends upon (*a*) which type he falls into and (*b*) what stage of adoption he is in. The mass media make

most farmers *aware* of a new practice; the laggard, however, is more
likely to learn about it from other farmers. Messages from friends
and neighbors are the preferred source of information when a new
product is in the evaluation and trial stages. They are second in
importance at the initial stage, that of awareness, and at the final
stage, that of actual adoption. The type of personal contacts and
their effectiveness also varies with the type of farmer in terms of
his speed of adoption.

Innovation in Use of Drugs

A check of druggists' prescription files has revealed that physicians,
like farmers, fall into five types based on how soon they adopted
a new drug (Menzel and Katz). Like the farmer they have their
choice among commercial sources of information and influence, professional sources, and informal sources among their peers. Which channel of influence has most effect again depends both upon the nature
of the drug involved and of the physician who uses it. Colleagues
are important; doctors who exert the most influence upon their fellows
tend to pass on information gained from conventions and medical
journals. Physicians who see little of their colleagues, on the other
hand, rely more on drug salesmen not only for news about drugs
but for friendship and gossip as well.

Doctors are most influenced by colleagues in uncertain and
ambiguous conditions such as (1) the first six months after a drug
is introduced, when information about it is sparse, or (2) in diseases
where neither the physiology of the illness nor the nature of its treatment is well understood. They are also influenced primarily by
colleagues in high-risk conditions, such as severe illnesses or in using
drugs which have dangerous side effects (Bauer). Drug-firm images
in such ambiguous and risky situations influence both the trial and
the adoption of a new drug. Put another way, such highly credible
sources as a reputable firm and his colleagues determine a doctor's
decisions when other criteria are lacking and when the decision is
important and cannot be evaded.

Channels and Audiences

Choosing channels for his messages is a major task of the marketing
communicator and will probably remain one, even if research provides

better data about the media and computer programmers develop the ability to handle it.

Marketing itself is rooted in the recognition that business begins not with products but with people—with purchasers and prospective purchasers. Communications insists that only after a man has found and studied his audience can he begin to devise an effective message.

Most marketing communications deal with men in the mass, with the aggregates or collectivities we call markets and audiences. In the next section we examine such audiences, first asking what problems are involved in communicating with several receivers at one time. Then we turn to receivers who are collected into organizations. From there we move on to the effects on receivers of being assigned to specialized roles, and what happens when those roles are arranged in hierarchical systems of rank or status.

SUMMARY

1. The communicator's control over his message falls as he moves down this list of channels: mass media, face-to-face selling, publicity, and the informal channels of customers' conversation with one another.
2. Audience and message influence choice of channel and vice versa. Channels differ in the extent to which their audiences coincide with a target market and in the proportion of prospects they contain. They differ in the extent to which they permit observation of audience responses. Most marketing messages employ a combination of channels.

Media

3. Media differ in the kinds of symbol systems—speech or print, word or picture—which can be used on them; the implications of these differences for communications are not clear, however.
4. Each medium and medium vehicle affects receivers' responses to the extent that it is perceived as being a source of the messages it transmits. The image of a medium as source is affected by the nonadvertising content it carries, as well as the advertising.
5. Each of the audience definitions provided in an earlier chapter will affect media choices: distribution chain, geographic, demographic, stage-of-persuasion, etc. Nose-counting, as a preliminary to comparing costs of the several media, has become increasingly sophisticated under the pressure of media competition. Although many questions remain to be answered, the computer can provide alternative answers to the problem of media mix choice pending their answers.

The Salesman

6. The salesman's two advantages over the media are his ability to observe his receivers' reactions and that fact that he usually deals

with a much smaller audience. These two advantages enable him to change his message for increased effectiveness.

7. A third difference between these two channels is that the salesman is a person and that customers must treat him as one. In general, this represents an advantage to the salesman, in that his success ceases to be wholly dependent on his message. It represents a problem for the employer, however, in that it decreases his control over communications. Salesmen are not interchangeable; their morale affects their success; and they are subject to influence from customers which may be to the employer's disadvantage.

8. The salesman operates in a small-group situation; his behavior is influenced by such small-group variables as a tendency to form coalitions, role conflict, and status conflict.

9. Selling consists of several functions; men's ability to perform them varies as to an audience's or a product's demand for them. Money can be saved by letting the customer perform some of these functions, by assigning some of them to advertising and by dividing them up, so that simpler functions are assigned to cheaper help. Use of a standardized product and sales pitch may afford economies of scale, especially if this standardization can be concealed from the customer.

Publicity

10. The publicity story differs from the advertisement in that it is free, its attention-getting power may be different, the media, with less obvious self-interest in its content, play a greater part in sourceship, and the firm has less control over whether it will appear and in what form.

11. Publicity may work directly to make persons aware of a new product or aid sales indirectly by shaping the firm's image. Most messages to noncustomer publics of a firm have indirect effects, although some may aid sales directly. Messages may be transmitted through publicity releases, press conferences, and the staged event. These techniques vary in their ability to induce messages from receiver-to-receiver on informal channels.

Informal Channels

12. The marketer loses control of his message on informal channels but gains a chance to reach resistant audiences and an increase in source credibility. Heavy media use, a compelling idea, or an artful message may help the marketer get his message onto such channels.

13. The speed with which farm practices are adopted depends both on the practice itself and on the farmer. Farm audiences can be divided into five types, based on the speed with which they adopt new practices. Location, situation, demography, and personality all help push a farmer into one of these types.

14. Physicians, like farmers, can be typed on the basis of the speed with which they adopt new drugs. Informal channels—talks with colleagues—are important for early adopters and when conditions of high risk are involved, and highly credible sources of information are required.

Research Studies

Hundreds of studies, both academic and commercial, have been made of the mass media. The studies included in this chapter, however, concentrated on two channels about which much less is known: personal selling and the informal communications exchanged face-to-face in groups and among customers.

In contrast to laboratory studies which show a great deal of distortion in face-to-face transmission of rumors, *Schachter and Burdick* found no distortion in a real-life situation. *Whyte* showed how informal channels speeded the adoption of air conditioners in Philadelphia. *Copp, Sill, and Brown,* on the other hand, suggested that informal communications can slow down adoption of new farm practices. They also showed that different functions of communications are required at the several stages of innovation and that these, in turn, require different combinations of media.

Turning to personal selling, *Witkin* reported that we must first distinguish between selling functions before we can devise methods of predicting who will make a good salesman. *Dunnette and Kirchner* compared three methods of prediction: a vocational interest test, a personality test, and salesman's own selection of adjectives which best described themselves. Finally, the kinds of media evaluations made implicitly in selecting the media mix for our advertising were exposed by *Kotler,* as he outlined the kind of data needed for a computer program.

Contents of Section B

SECTION B

The Behavior of Aggregates: Markets and Audiences

THIS SECTION is concerned with the behavior of men in the mass—the aggregates which the marketing manager calls "markets" and the communicator calls audiences.

Before communications can take place, we must define *markets* and *audiences*. A useful device in planning market strategy is the grid which serves to identify different types of users and to suggest variations in product, place, price, and communications. Here is an example, adapted from a leading text in marketing (McCarthy 26–35).

In examining the market for furnaces or fuel, we may start by a three-way classification based on geographical area, type of fuel, and whether the installation is new or old.

MARKET FOR HEATING SYSTEMS

	Existing Buildings				New Buildings			
	Oil	*Gas*	*Electricity*	*Coal*	*Oil*	*Gas*	*Electricity*	*Coal*
Zone I							xx	
Zone II								
Zone III								
Zone IV								
Zone V								

We can put into each cell the number of units which have one of the forms of existing heating in the case of buildings already existing and compare these figures with those for current building or predictions for next year. The use made of the figures will vary with what is being sold—units, for example, to convert oil or coal furnaces to gas, or the fuels themselves. Each of the cells themselves can be broken down into a marketing grid of its own. The shaded portion above, for example, can be expanded thus:

MARKET FOR ELECTRIC HEATING IN ZONE I: NEW BUILDINGS

	Baseboard	Radiant	Hot-air Furnace	Hot Water	Heat Pump (Heating, Cooling)
Dwellings					
Apartment Houses					
Business Offices					
Public Buildings					

Differences in the extent to which a product is accepted may also be pictured in a diagram whose cells represent the various audiences that must be reached. Such "audience grids," adapted from Colley, can be used to depict present conditions, illustrate a communications plan, and report the effects of a campaign:

	Present Audience	Goal of Strategy A	Goal of Strategy B	Effects of Ad Campaign
A: Does not know product exists	A. 15%	A. 7%	A. 15%	A. 1%
		B. 20		B. 5
B: Know of brand, not its claims	B. 25		B. 5	C. 50
C: Know claims which brand makes		C. 25	C. 10	
D: Believe claims made by brand	C. 25		D. 40	
E: Prefer this brand to others	D. 15	D. 20	E. 20	D. 15
		E. 13		
F: Have sought to buy this brand	E. 10			E. 5
	F. 10	F. 15	F. 10	F. 15

The first column of the audience grid shows how a survey, conducted before a sales or advertising campaign begins, provides a benchmark for measuring progress. The next two columns contrast the goals of two different advertising campaigns. *A* seeks to push half of each audience segment one step further along. *B* neglects the hard core who do not know the product exists and concentrates on those who know the brand, those who know the claims, and those who already believe the claims. However, Campaign *B* does not expect advertising to trigger actual purchase—it does not anticipate any increase in stage *F*.

The fourth column thus represents the results of a hypothetical survey made after the campaign ends. It indicates that the campaign was high in attention value: an increase from 25 to 59% in the persons familiar with claims made by the brand. The campaign was low in credibility, however, since there was no increase in the proportion who believed the claims. However, the campaign induced half of those who had a preference for the brand to purchase it. When the marketing grid and the audience grid are combined we may get results like the following example taken from (Colley), which examines the market for household oils. Research shows this competitive stituation:

USE OF OILS AND FATS FOR HOUSEHOLD COOKING

	In Salads	In Baking	In Frying
Total industry (gallons or dollars)	10,000,000	5,000,000	25,000,000
Share by Brand "*A*" oil	50%	50%	10%
Competing brands of oil	30	30	10
Competing products: lard, butter, oleo, etc.	20	20	80

Consumer research has shown that housewives' principal demand in frying is for a substance that does not smoke, for smoke is the sign of a poor housekeeper and makes extra work for her as well. Laboratory studies have shown that Brand *A* can be heated several degrees higher than the competing fats before it begins to smoke. Consumer studies made before and after the campaign show these results:

SURVEY OF HOUSEWIFE AUDIENCE

	Before	After	Increase
Use some type of product for frying	25,000,000	25,000,000	
Associate Brand *A* with "no-smoke" claim	500,000	15,000,000	14,500,000
Have tried Brand *A* for frying	5,000,000	10,000,000	5,000,000
Use Brand *A* regularly for frying	2,500,000	5,000,000	2,500,000

Was the campaign represented in this imaginary figure a success? Not at first glance. The campaign cost five million dollars which is just equal to the gross profit of two dollars each made on the additional 2,500,000 regular users. But the increase in regular users was only one of the results. Remember that other persons were moved part way toward product use, future campaigns may move them the rest of the way. The campaign also enabled the firm to add 2000 retail outlets. Effects of the campaign on both regular users and on creation of outlets are likely to last more than one year. Finally, some advertising would have been necessary just to maintain the firm's previous share of volume against competitive inroads; its cost should be deducted from the five-million-dollar figure quoted above.

Eight

Communicating to
Plural Receivers:
An Example of Programed
Learning

This chapter differs from all the others in this textbook in its form: it is written as an example of *programed learning*. Each paragraph contains blanks which the student should fill in as he goes along. As soon as he has done so, he should check to see if he is correct, by looking at the correct answers which appear at the left, opposite the following paragraph. *To get the maximum benefit from this program, the student should mask these answers with an index card, sliding the card down to expose them only after he first has tried to fill in the blanks by himself.*

This program has been tested on a series of classes, to make sure that a student will be correct most of the time. Paragraphs which produced incorrect answers were rewritten.

Learning programs depend on giving students the immediate rewards of successful performance. To this end, cues as to the correct answers are provided by underlining key words, and by giving the initial and terminal letters, or indicating, with a series of dashes, the number of letters in the desired word. Gradually, as ideas are repeated, the number of such cues is reduced.

This chapter may take a little longer to read than other chapters in the book, but the student is also likely to find that he recalls most of its content on a single reading. Students who customarily get low grades in college probably will find the chapter takes longer to complete than will students who customarily get good grades. Both should have comparable numbers of "errors" during the learning process, however, and reach comparable levels of performance.

In addition to allowing a student to proceed at his own pace, learning programs of this kind are being widely used in industry because they permit learning to occur without instructors and save the cost of bringing students together in one place for instruction. Learning programs are sometimes placed in machines which prevent a student from peeking at the correct answer before he has provided his own answer. These are the so-called "teaching machines." The key to learning in this fashion, however, is not the machine but the program it contains.

Instead of providing blanks to be filled in, some programs offer a choice of answers. Programs of this kind often involve "branching": students follow a different sequence of paragraphs depending on whether they choose a wrong answer, and which wrong answer they choose. Students who choose the "worst" wrong answer presumably require the most retracing of steps. Branching programs of this kind are often printed in "scrambled textbooks," and have been adapted for computers. One criticism of multiple-choice programs is that the student may remember the wrong answers to which he has been exposed. Another is that they teach recognition instead of recall, the latter of which is more difficult to learn.

Here are the names of two brief paperbacks on programed learning. The first is, itself, in the form of a linear program; the second contains an example of branching and the scrambled text.

Susan Meyer Markle, Lewis D. Eigen and P. Kenneth Komoski, *A Programmed Primer on Programming* (New York: The Center for Programmed Instruction, Inc., 1961).

William A. Deterline, *An Introduction to Programmed Instruction* (Englewood Cliffs, N. J.: Prentice Hall, Inc., 1962).

Answers	
	1. When a source communicates, he attempts to influence the behavior of a receiver. We say communication is *successful* when the attempt succeeds and the receiver's behavior is_____.
1. influenced (or equivalent)	2. Similarly, we say that communication is not successful if the behavior of the receiver is_____.
2. not influenced	3. If a message succeeds in changing the behavior of the person who receives it in the way desired by the s_____, we say that successful c_____n has occurred.
3. source communication	4. In communication as defined here, it is the s_____ who defines the purpose of a message.

4. source

5. But it is the _____ whose reactions determine whether the message has communicated successfully.

5. receiver

6. The reactions produced by a message are more likely to be those desired by the source if he knows his r_____ well.

6. receiver

7. If the source knows his receiver, he may be able to _____ how the receiver will react to the message.

7. predict (or equivalent)

8. If a source does not know his receiver well, he may *not* be able to _____ how the receiver will _____.

8. predict react (or equivalent)

9. The reactions of a receiver themselves represent a kind of m_____e from the receiver to the source telling the source how skillful a communicator he is.

9. message

10. If the source observes the receiver's reactions and changes his message because of them, we call the reactions by a new name: *feedback*. Reactions by a receiver which change the behavior of the source are termed _____.

10. feedback

11. Feedback requires two kinds of behavior. The receiver must react to the source's message and the source, in turn, must r___t to the reactions of the receiver.

11. react

12. In a classroom, the lecturer is a _____ and his students are _____.

12. source receivers

13. If a student yawns, the yawn represents a _____ to the source.

13. message, If you said "feedback," re-read No. 11

14. If the lecturer sees the yawn, but does not react to it by changing his lecture, then we say that this m_____ from the student does not constitute _____.

14. message feedback

15. However, if the lecturer sees the yawn, thinks it signifies boredom, and stops to tell a funny story, then we say that the student's _____ does represent _____.

15. message
    feedback

16. Let's say it once more. When a receiver reacts to a message from a source, these reactions are a _____. When the source in turn reacts to the receiver's reactions, we have _____.

16. message
    feedback

17. Remember that we said earlier that a source who knows the receiver may be able to p_____ how the receiver will respond to a message. If the receiver is a stranger, successful communication is less likely, because the source cannot p_____ how the stranger will react.

17. predict
    predict

18. Although a source may not be able to predict how a stranger will respond to a message, he still can observe the stranger's _____ as he delivers the message.

18. reactions

19. While an ability to predict reactions helps in communicating with persons one knows, f_____ helps a source produce more effective messages to either friends or _____.

19. feedback
    strangers

20. When a source tries to communicate with more than one person, a new problem arises. The question then becomes: *Whose* r_____ does he try to predict? *Whose* r_____ does he observe?

20. reactions
    reactions

21. Suppose one student yawns as if bored and another student frowns as if he could not understand the lecture. Which of these two m_____ does a lecturer respond to?

21. messages

22. A lecturer can hardly respond to both. The reactions of only one student can serve as f_____.

22. feedback

23. A teacher may save time, effort, and money by transmitting messages to several students at a time, but he is less likely to i_____ their behavior.

23. influence

24. Therefore we may say that communication becomes cheaper but successful com-

munication becomes (less/more) likely as the number of receivers increases.

24. less

25. There are exceptions, of course. If the persons in an audience can be counted on to react similarly then transmitting a message to several persons may be cheaper and almost as _____ as speaking to them individually.

25. effective
(or equivalent)

26. If I write a letter to members of a taxpayers' league urging that taxes be cut, I can _____ their reactions. Since I cannot observe them, however, there is no chance for immediate _____. I can use only one of the two ways of improving my messages.

26. predict
(or equivalent)
feedback

27. On the other hand, if I hire a hall and address an audience of strangers, I can improve my message by _____ but I cannot _____ in advance how they will react.

27. feedback
predict

28. This is why face-to-face communication is usually superior to communication via the mass media (radio, television, newspapers, magazines, etc.). When we are face-to-face, we can get immediate _____. When we use the mass media we cannot.

28. feedback

29. Therefore, we would on the whole expect communication via the mass media to be _____ successful than face-to-face communication.

29. less

30. And we would expect a salesman to be _____ _____ in persuading us to buy something than the advertisement.

30. more successful

31. One advantage of the door-to-door salesman over the advertisement is that he can make use of _____. Another related advantage is that his audience is _____ than that of the typical advertisement.

31. feedback
smaller

32. Face-to-face communication thus tends to communicate more effectively because (1) there is immediate _____ and (2) audiences tend to be _____.

32. feedback
smaller

33. On the other hand, it is cheaper to send a form letter to a hundred persons than to write each of them individually. If the hundred are similar enough in their _____ to the letter, we may decide to use the _____ method.

33. reactions
(or responses)
cheaper

34. We can put people who are similar in some respect, such as their reactions to a message, into a *category*. Thus success in communications may depend upon our ability to put the right people into the right _____.

34. category

35. In marketing, we say that these _____ represent *markets*. We say that all of the persons who are prospective purchasers of a product constitute the _____ for that product.

35. categories
markets

36. In communications, we call these c_____ by a different name. We say that all of the persons who we would like to receive our message constitute its *audience*. But both of these terms—m_____ and a_____—are different names for c_____ of people.

36. categories
market
audience
categories

37. Products have _____. Messages have _____. Both terms represent _____ of people.

37. markets
audiences
categories

38. When an advertiser sends a form letter to a hundred people he hopes that the _____ for his letter coincides with the _____ for his product.

38. audience
market

39. If he hires a hall, instead of mailing a form letter, he hopes that the persons who constitute a _____ for his product are also in the _____ for his message.

39. market
audience

40. Cost aside, hiring a hall may be more effective because he can observe the _____ of the audience and _____ his message while he is delivering it.

40. reactions
    modify
    (or equivalent)

41. But the lecturer is not the only one who observes the reactions of the audience. Members of the _____ can observe one another. They hear one another's cheers—or jeers. They r_____ to one another's behavior.

41. audience
    react

42. In short, the hall includes three kinds of messages: speaker to audience, audience to speaker, and members of the audience to _____ _____.

42. each other
    (or equivalent)

43. The speaker can _____ in advance that this third type of communication will occur. If it is favorable, it may help him. If it is unfavorable, it may cause him to _____.

43. predict
    fail

44. When members of an audience i_____ one another's behavior in this way, we say that they *interact*. But persons can i_____t with one another outside the lecture hall as well as inside.

44. influence
    interact

45. When persons i_____ with one another frequently they soon become something more than a category. They become a *group*.

45. interact

46. Persons who are similar to one another constitute a _____. Persons who interact with one another constitute a _____.

46. category
    group

47. If a speaker's audience consists of a random sample of housewives aged 35 to 45, all strangers to one another, his audience is a _____. If he is speaking to the Tuesday Bridge Club, also made up of housewives 35 to 45, his audience is a _____.

47. category
    group

48. Housewives aged 35 to 45 may _____ in similar fashion to a message. A speaker can frame a more effective message if he can _____ in advance how they will react.

48. react
    predict

49. When these housewives _____ with one another, and so change from a category

to a _____ like the Tuesday Bridge Club, they become more similar.

49. interact
    group

50. This increase in _____ tends to aid a source, since it is often easier to _____ how a group will react to a message than it is to predict the _____ of a category.

50. similarity
    predict
    reactions

51. If a source knows groups or individuals, he can _____ how they will behave. If he does not _____ them, he cannot.

51. predict
    know

52. The fact that interaction in a group increases members' similarity makes it easier to _____ how they will behave. The similarity of their _____ also makes feedback more likely.

52. predict
    reactions
    (or equivalent)

53. There are still other reasons why a source may prefer a (group/category) as an audience to a (group/category).

53. group
    category

54. For one thing, a source does not have to round up his own audience when he talks to a group; the _____ will round up its members for him.

54. group

55. Even if all the members do not attend the lecture, the source's _____ will still reach them. Why? Because every group has a communications network of its own.

55. message

56. The next time two members of the _____ talk to one another, the one who heard the lecture is likely to tell the one who did not what the source said.

56. group

57. It is by using this communications n_____ within the group that the audience was recruited originally. And reports of the lecture pass along this same _____ after the lecture has been given.

57. network
    network

58. Sometimes a source does not even have to hire a hall. He can just give his message to a member of the _____ and count on its being transmitted to other members over the group's _____ of communication.

58. group
network

59. To summarize this _____ of communication can help a source in two ways: it can assemble an _____ to hear his message and it can _____ his message to members who fail to attend the lecture.

59. network
audience
transmit
(or equivalent)

60. Groups have still another advantage over _____, from the standpoint of a source. A message to a category may have to appeal to as many different values as there are m_____ of the category.

60. categories
members

61. Categories do not have v_____ of their own, but _____ do.

61. values
groups

62. In fact, these group _____ are such an important characteristic of groups, that they get a special name. They are called group *norms*.

62. values

63. If a source wants his message to get across, he will make sure that it is consistent with such group values or _____.

63. norms

64. He can _____ in advance that members of the group will pay more attention to parts of his message that *are* consistent with group _____.

64. predict
norms

65. He can be sure that members of the group not only will pay more _____ to such passages but that they are more likely to *remember* them afterward.

65. attention

66. These passages will attract more _____ when the lecture is given. Members of the group are more likely to _____ them after the lecture is over. And they are more likely to *transmit* them to other members who were not at the lecture.

66. attention
remember

67. Thus a source can predict that parts of his message consistent with group norms will get more _____, are more likely to be _____ by his audience, and more likely to be _____ to absent group members.

67. attention
remembered
transmitted

68. He also knows that parts of his message consistent with group _____ are likely to be greeted with applause. This applause represents a _____ from members of the audience to one another. It means that they approve of the speaker and *his* _____.

68. norms
message
message

69. Why do norms have so powerful an effect on members of a _____? Because the group regards its norms as necessary to survival and enforces them by *rewards* and *penalties*. Members obey the norms because they want the _____ and hope to avoid the _____.

69. group
rewards
penalties

70. One of the strongest sanctions a group has is *status*. By giving a member high status, a group can r_____ him. It can penalize him by _____ his status.

70. reward
reducing
(or equivalent)

71. Thus we can say that status can serve both as a _____ and as a _____. Reducing a member's _____ represents a _____.

71. reward
penalty
status
penalty

72. The most severe penalty which a group can inflict, however, is *expulsion*. The threat of _____ is one way groups see that members conform to its _____.

72. expulsion
norms

73. If a member deviates from the group norms, two things are likely to happen. The deviant's _____ will be reduced and, if this does not work, he may be threatened with _____.

73. status
expulsion

74. To predict how a member will react to a message we need to know the relevant _____ of the group, and how the group can enforce these _____.

74. norms
norms

75. We must also know how much the member values his s_____ and his m_____ in the group. Threats to _____ a member are unimportant if he does not care whether he belongs to the group or not.

75. status
    membership
    expel

76. One reason a member may not fear _____ from the group is that there are alternative groups he can join.

76. expulsion

77. Persons form _____ and join _____ because they think this will help them achieve some *goal* more quickly or with less effort than they could by themselves.

77. groups
    groups

78. A single group g_____ may satisfy several different individual _____.

78. goal
    goals
    (or equivalent)

79. Three teen-agers may form a dance combo. Tom joins because he likes to play drums. Dick joins because he wants to earn money. Harry joins because he enjoys being with the other two. Three different _____ goals, but a single _____ goal.

79. individual
    group

80. In this example the dance combo itself represents a _____ of (or for) the _____. A single activity satisfies three different _____ goals.

80. goal
    group
    individual

81. Each member is likely to remain in the combo so long as his individual _____ remains unchanged, so long as the group _____ remains unchanged, and so long as he sees no other _____ which can achieve his _____ goal more quickly.

81. goal
    goal
    group
    individual

82. Under these conditions each member will put a high value on his membership, and each is likely to be highly responsive to the _____ of the group.

82. norms

83. He will cease being responsive to the _____ of the _____ when he no longer fears expulsion.

83. norms
    group

84. He may cease to fear _____ under either of two circumstances. One circumstance is a *change* in his own personal _____. Another is appearance of a _____ which can do a better job of satisfying his _____ _____.

84. expulsion
    goals
    group
    personal goals

85. Sometimes groups are formed for the same reason that Harry joined the dance combo: because their _____ enjoy being together.

85. members

86. Even when this is not the original _____ of the group, members of most groups do find that they _____ being together.

86. goal
    enjoy

87. This may happen to Tom and Dick. Just being together may give them new _____ _____ which are not those that brought them into the group in the first place.

87. individual goals

88. The original goals for a group arise from individual goals. After a group exists, it may in turn produce new _____ for the _____.

88. goals individual

89. Most members of a group value two kinds of goals: (1) movement toward the original _____ _____ which brought them into the group and (2) the fun of being together, which helps keep the group going.

89. individual goals

90. Most groups must offer their members two kinds of satisfaction. They must perform some task, and so move toward a group _____. They must provide activities which are fun in themselves and so keep the _____ going.

90. goal
    group

91. We can describe members' activities under two headings: *task performance* and *group maintenance*. Activities which move the group toward its goals represent t_____ p_____. Activities which keep the group going represent g_____ m_____.

91. task performance
    group maintenance

92. Some members, like Harry, may put a high value on the activities that are fun in themselves and keep the group going: those we have called _____ _____.

92. group maintenance

93. Other members, like Tom and Dick, put a high value on the group's ability to

Decentralized networks produce the rewards of group maintenance but network effect on task performance varies with the task at hand.

Pinwheel or Comcon—Which Is More Fun?

In the laboratory, where subjects can be told who they may send messages to and receive messages from, a wide variety of communications networks have been tested. Here are a few of them:

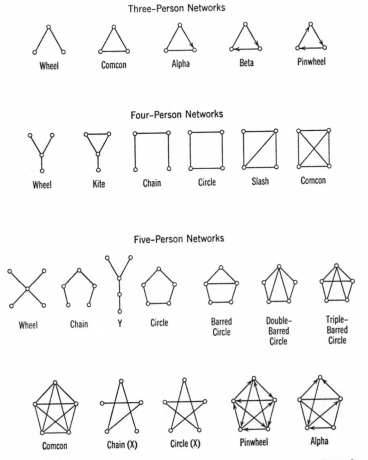

Three-Person Networks

Wheel Comcon Alpha Beta Pinwheel

Four-Person Networks

Wheel Kite Chain Circle Slash Comcon

Five-Person Networks

Wheel Chain Y Circle Barred Circle Double- Barred Circle Triple- Barred Circle

Comcon Chain (X) Circle (X) Pinwheel Alpha

Fig. 8.1. Dots represent positions, lines represent communication channels, and arrows indicate one-way channels.

All of them fall into two major types, however. The wheel, chain, and *Y* represent a *centralized* network, which often tends to put a single individual at the focus. The circle and "comcon" networks are decentralized, with greater equality of communications among members.

Similarly, scientists have looked at many different kinds of effects which networks have upon their members, but these, too, collapse into two major types. One is the autonomy or freedom of action which a network allows a member; the more choice he has, the more motivated he is to perform. The other is his vulnerability to demands from others; in general, the more demands made upon a position in a network, the less satisfied its occupant will be.

The effects of a network on group output vary with the nature of the task assigned to the network. Centralized networks are more efficient in collecting information in one place. Decentralized networks are more efficient, however, when the task requires that this information be processed. The nature of the task, however, does not affect members' satisfactions; whatever the task may be, they prefer the decentralized networks.

This table, summarizing a series of experiments, shows the percentage of trials in which centralized networks were superior on one of four dimensions, for tasks which called for the simple collection of information and for those such as sentence construction and discussion which demanded more complex processing.

	Simple Problems		Complex Problems	
	Percentage of Trials	Number of Trials	Percentage of Trials	Number of Trials
Faster in finishing task	78%	18	0	18
More messages sent	0	18	5%	18
Fewer errors	90	10	10	10
Higher satisfaction	12	8	9	11

—Marvin E. Shaw, "Communication Networks" in Leonard E. Berkowitz, ed., *Advances in Experimental Social Psychology, Vol. I* (New York: Academic Press, 1964).

---

achieve a goal: the activities we have called _____ _____ .

93. task performance

94. Groups also vary. Some are good at moving toward a goal; they do well in _____ _____ . Others are noted for the other kind of activity, that called _____ _____ .

**94. task performance
group maintenance**

95. To predict how a group will influence any individual member we must know how well the group performs each kind of _____ , and which kind of _____ the member values most highly.

95. activity
　　activity

96. predicting

97. group
　　goals

98. goals
　　members

99. members
　　members

100. membership
　　members

101. join

102. joining
　　quitting
　　(or equivalents)

103. belong
　　belong

104. reference
　　advice

96. Of course, a member may *change* once he's in the group, and the source must be aware of this if he is to be accurate in _____ the behavior of the member.

97. If a lot of members change as a result of being in a group, the goals of the _____ itself may change. But group _____ may change in another way, too.

98. This second way is not by a change of members' _____ but by a change in the _____ themselves.

99. Many groups have longer lives than do their individual _____. Since groups persist while their _____ change, groups' goals are likely to change, too.

100. One reason for changes in group m_____ is that members die and are replaced by new _____.

101. Another reason is that members quit one group and _____ another.

102. In trying to predict the behavior of such persons, who are on the point of changing groups, it may be more important to know the norms of the group they are _____ than those of the group they are _____.

103. For convenience, we call any groups which influence persons in this way *reference* groups. We say that they "refer" for advice to both groups they _____ to, and to those they would like to _____ to.

104. In addition to these two kinds of _____ groups, there is a third. These are groups to whom an individual turns for _____. Although he doesn't belong or hope to belong to them, he still "_____" to them.

105. To predict an individual's behavior, we must take account of all three kinds of

refers	_____ groups and of their respective norms.
105. reference	106. Let's go back for a moment to the communications *network* which exists in each group. We said that members who hear a lecture are likely to use this _____ to

---

Two kinds of groups influence individuals' attitudes—their membership groups and their reference groups—those they would like to belong to or regard as expert.

Freshmen Women Choose Rooms by Lot

An ingenious field experiment into the effect of groups on attitudes was made at Stanford University, which at that time required all freshmen women to live in a large dormitory. At the end of their first year, those who wished to move to high-status, ex-sorority houses were allowed to do so, if they drew winning numbers in a lottery.

Two things were known about Stanford women. One was that residents in the former sorority houses show higher scores on a scale of authoritarianism than do those who live elsewhere; the other is that scores tend to fall during the students' university career.

In a random sample of 95 Stanford freshmen women, 39 requested transfer to one of the former sorority houses. Of these, 9 got what they wanted. The remaining 19 had another chance to ask for such transfer at the end of their sophomore year—and 11 of them did so.

Thus there were 3 groups in all during the sophomore year: 9 women whose membership and reference groups were the same—an ex-sorority house. Another consisted of 8 women who changed their reference group from an original high-status house, to match the group they actually lived in. The third was the 11 women who lived outside a high-status house but whose persisting desire to move into one indicated it was still their reference group.

The question was whether scores for these 3 groups were affected differently. The answer was that they were. The 2 groups living outside the high-status houses showed more attitude change away from the original authoritarian position than did the group living in the high-status houses. Most change of all was shown by the group, living outside the high-status houses, which by the end of the sophomore year had lost its desire to move to them.

—Alberta Engvall Siegel and Sidney Siegel, "Reference Groups, Membership Groups, and Attitude Change," *Journal of Abnormal and Social Psychology*, 55:360–364.

---

tell members who didn't hear it what the lecturer said.

106. network

107. The whole lecture won't be transmitted—just parts of it. We suggested that parts selected will be those consistent with the _____ of the group.

107. norms

108. If a member of the PTA attends a meeting sponsored by the PTA and was surrounded by other PTA members while he listened, it is likely to be the _____ of the _____ which affect what he recalls.

108. norms
PTA

109. If this member repeats part of the lecture next day to a friend who is also a PTA member, the parts of the lecture he repeats are likely to be those parts consistent with the _____ of the _____.

109. norms
PTA

110. Not everyone belongs to the PTA, however. In fact, the person who heard the talk may report on it to a friend who belongs to a taxpayers league. In this case, what he repeats (and the way he repeats it) may be influenced by the norms of *both* the _____ and the _____ _____.

110. PTA
taxpayers
league

111. Few of us belong to only one group. Most of us can turn for advice to many different r_____ groups.

111. reference

112. Moreover, the values or _____ of these different groups are likely to differ from one another. They may even disagree with one another.

112. norms

113. If a source urges an increase in pay for teachers, persons may cheer, if they accept the _____ of the PTA. They are more likely to jeer, if they accept the _____ of the _____ _____.

113. norms
norms
taxpayers league

114. How can we predict which set of _____ will be most effective, when a member of the PTA gives a report of the talk to a friend who belongs to the taxpayers league?

114. norms

115. In fact, the member of the audience may himself belong to both groups. How can we predict which set of _____ will operate on a member of the audience while he is listening to the lecture itself?

115. norms

116. Much depends on the *situation* itself: on the sponsors of the lecture and its audience. But many messages are transmitted via newspapers and television, radio and magazines. Here there is no situation to tell us which set of g____n_____ will operate.

116. group norms

117. What we need is some way of predicting which group will come out ahead when two _____ with differing _____ are pitted against one another.

**117. groups
norms**

118. Are there any group characteristics which help us make such _____?

118. predictions

119. Yes, there are. We can measure five different characteristics which may help us predict which set of _____ will win out.

119. norms.

120. Society recognizes that some groups have *prior* claims. Such a phrase as "For God, for country, and for Yale" indicates that country is supposed to take p_____ over *college* and that the claims of God are supposed to take _____ over those of the country.

**120. priority
priority**

121. Thus we may say that the society often gives _____ to the norms of one group when there is a conflict between the _____ of this group and those of another.

**121. priority
norms**

122. A second characteristic which helps predict the group that will win out is *cohesion*. Some groups are more closely knit than others. They have greater c_____.

122. cohesion

123. Members of a group that has high c_____ put a high value on membership. They value the rewards of what we have called group _____ activities.

Cohesion in a group increases as members interact with one another and develop liking for one another.

Employees Like Groups Whose Members Like Them

The staff members of a Midwest child welfare agency—64 women and 8 men—filled out questionnaires, analysis of which permitted them to be assigned to one of 6 work groups. A month later, in their own homes, each received another questionnaire, on which he indicated, on a 6-place scale, how often he had contacts with each of his colleagues, the nature of them and their importance to him. Two months after the first survey, each member filled out a third questionnaire, in which he listed the 10 persons he felt were most valuable in the entire organization and checked the names of those persons he thought would nominate *him* as most valuable. At the end of this same questionnaire, he was given the names of persons in his work group (as determined in the very first questionnaire), asked to pick one-third of them he felt were "most valuable," and, again, to check the names of those in the work group who would pick him.

Each staff member was given three scores on the basis of these questionnaires: one on "social worth" (the extent to which he was valued by other employees), one on the "benefit" (the extent to which he felt he received a tremendous amount of benefit working in the agency), and one on amount of contact with others (the median being used to determine high and low scoring groups).

Staff members consisted of 44 social workers and two other professionals and 26 nonprofessional workers, such as typists, housemothers, and cooks. Professional workers who were rated highly by other members of their work groups or of the organization itself, were also likely to feel that they received "a tremendous amount of benefit from working here." Correlations between the two ratings, although low, were significant. This was not true of the nonprofessional workers.

Correlations between Benefit and Social Worth	Professionals		Nonprofessionals	
	r	*p*	*r*	*p*
Organization	.30	.04	.16	.53
Work group	.37	.01	.11	.67

However, within the professional group, significant correlations were found only for professionals who had a great deal of contact with other employees:

Correlation between Benefit and Social Worth	High Contact		Low Contact	
	r	*p*	*r*	*p*
Organization	.55	.006	.15	.49
Group	.66	.001	.15	.49

—Jay M. Jackson, "Reference Group Processes in a Formal Organization," *Sociometry*, 22:307–327.

123. cohesion
     maintenance

124. To get these _____, members of a group with high _____ will conform to its norms. Members of a group which is *not* characterized by high _____ are less likely to be influenced by its _____.

124. rewards
     cohesion
     cohesion
     norms

125. The remaining three characteristics which help predict which set of group _____ will influence behavior resemble one another. All three affect the number of individual acts covered by a group's set of _____.

125. norms
     norms

126. The more people there are in a group, the more individual acts covered by its norms. Thus the s___ of a group is important.

126. size

127. If a group is small, its _____ affect fewer individual acts than if it is _____. To repeat _____ is important.

127. norms
     large
     size

128. We get the same result, if a group is long-lived. The longer it lasts, the more individual _____ can occur. The duration of the group's life is important to the amount of influence it has.

128. acts

129. Thus both d_____ and s_____ help predict which group's norms will influence behavior.

129. duration
     size

130. Similar to both s_____ and d_____ in its effect is the *scope* of a group: the number of different kinds of activities which it covers.

130. size
     duration

131. A group whose norms cover a wide variety of activities has large s_____. Its norms are more likely to influence behavior than a group which has smaller s_____.

131. scope
     scope

132. To summarize, the five characteristics which help predict which of two groups will influence behavior are: p_____, c_____, d_____, s___ and s_____.

132. priority
cohesion
duration
size
scope

133. By studying these five characteristics, a source may be able to predict which of two groups will help him most. He may then construct his _____ so that it will be consistent with this group's _____.

133. message
norms

134. The source may also want to remind members of his _____ that this group is one of their important r_____ groups.

134. audience
reference

135. Up to now we have been concerned with the question of which set of group _____ will prevail, when an individual finds a conflict between two of his _____ _____.

135. norms
reference groups

136. Now let us turn the question "inside out." When there is a conflict between the views of individual members of a single group, how can we _____ which member's views will prevail?

136. predict

137. You may remember that we have said that a group may reward a member by giving him high s_____. But _____ is more than a reward; it has other functions.

137. status
status

138. The person with high _____ usually has more power to *influence* the behavior of others. We say that he is more i_____.

138. status
influential

139. A message is more likely to be accepted by other members when it is endorsed by a member of (high/low) status than when endorsed by a member of (high/low) status.

139. high
low

140. Not only does a person of high status have more _____ upon the behavior of others; he is also more likely to transmit _____ to them.

140. influence
messages
(or equivalent)

141. When messages come from outside, they usually flow within a group from a person of_____ _____ to one of _____ _____.

141. high status
low status

142. The person with high status often has power to do what an outside source wants without consulting other members. If he does not have p_____ to act on his own, he can still t_____ an outside message to others and he can add his e_____ to the message when he does so.

142. power
transmit
endorsement

143. Having found which of two groups can help him most, a source next needs to find which _____ of the chosen group can be of most help.

143. member
(or equivalent)

144. We have suggested that this is the person who has _____ _____. Are there any ways of identifying such persons in a group?

144. high status

145. And a still more basic question—why do such differences in _____ arise in the first place? Why are not all _____ equal?

145. status
members

146. To begin with, no sooner does a group form, than members begin to *specialize*. Abilities differ. One person has an a_____ to do one thing, another has an _____ for another.

146. ability
ability

147. And even if none of the jobs requires rare _____, it usually does not pay for persons to be shifting jobs all the time. They begin to _____ for this reason.

147. abilities
specialize

148. And, of course, when a man works at a job for some time he accumulates e_____. Even if he did not have greater ability to do the job originally, he acquires it through e_____.

148. experience
experience

149. The person who specializes is sometimes compared to the actor, and his specialty is compared to the r___ which an actor plays.

149. role

150. So it is that different r_____ come into existence in a group. These _____ persist even though the members who perform them change.

150. roles
     roles

151. This helps the group survive. When one member leaves and his _____ becomes vacant, a new member can be chosen to fill the _____.

151. role
     role

152. Since most persons belong to several groups, most persons have several _____ to play. Each role requires us to do certain things we m___ do.

152. roles
     must

153. At the same time, each role has certain prohibitions. There are some things which a person in such a role m___ NOT do.

153. must

154. In fact, a role is often viewed as a package of obligations or d____s and of certain r____s.

154. duties
     rights

155. The idea of a role as constituting a set of r_____ and of d_____ is crucial to understanding group behavior.

155. rights
     duties

156. Most men are simultaneously husbands and fathers, employees and citizens. Each of these may be regarded as a r_____. The d_____ involved in these roles may compete with one another for a man's time and energy.

156. role
     duties

157. A man cannot at one and the same time give all of his attention to his wife, in his role as a _____, and also give undivided attention to his children, in his role as a _____.

157. husband
     father

158. Different roles thus compete with one another for time and energy. They may also demand contradictory behavior. What one role says is a "m___" may be a "m_____ n_____" for another.

158. must
     must not

159. When this happens and a man faces *conflicting* demands, from two different r_____, it is said to be a case of r_____ c_____.

159. roles
     role conflict

160. Some types of r_____ c_____ result from a man's having two different roles which are relevant to a given decision.

160. role conflict

161. Sometimes c_____ is "built into" a role. A school superintendent, for example, must get along with teachers who want higher salaries and a school board which doesn't.

161. conflict

162. A superintendent is required as part of his role to get along with both his school board and his t_____. We call these two groups part of his role *set*.

162. teachers

163. Thus the "s_____" for any role is made up of the other roles that it must operate with, in this case teachers and

_____ _____.

163. set
board members

164. And r_____ c_____ arises because different members of the role _____ demand different things of the superintendent.

164. role conflict
set

165. Like the superintendent, the factory foreman must "get along" with both workers and management, who constitute members of his _____ _____.

165. role set

166. And the army sergeant must "get along" with both enlisted men and officers. Since enlisted men and officers want different things, this is an example of built-in

_____ _____.

166. role conflict

167. Earlier we pointed out that groups have n____ and that a person who has several reference groups may find that their n_____ conflict.

167. norms
norms

168. When this happens, when group _____ conflict, we said a communicator will try to remind his listeners of their reference group whose _____ are consistent with his message.

168. norms
norms

169. The communicator will do much the same thing when his listeners are involved in r_____ c_____.

169. role conflict

170. That is, he will emphasize the d_____ and the r_____ of the particular r___ which favors his message.

170. duties
     rights
     role

171. A crucial question in r_____ c_____ as it was in the case of a conflict of group n_____ was whether there is anything which predicts which side will come out on top in the conflict.

171. role conflict
     norms

172. Some roles tend to be more highly valued in a group than others. We said earlier that the most influential persons in a group are those with h_____ s_____.

172. high status

173. Strictly speaking, however, low and high s_____ are attached not to persons but to the r_____ they perform.

173. status
     roles

174. Is there any way of predicting *which* r_____ in a group are likely to have h_____ s_____?

174. roles
     high status

175. Roles which are vital to group survival and which only a few persons can fill tend to get _____ _____.

175. high status

176. Thus we can say that if the ability required by a role is r___ and if it helps the group s_____ it tends to be given (high/low) status.

176. rare
     (or equivalent)
     survive
     high

177. One role which has both qualities is that which requires one to coordinate the activities of others. Therefore the role of the coordinator has _____ _____.

177. high status

178. In fact, the coordinator is often recognized as a leader of the group. Note that we say "a" leader rather than "the" leader, because the activities which he c_____ may vary.

178. coordinates.

179. Earlier we said that every group exhibits two kinds of activities, which we termed t_____ p_____ and g_____ m_____.

179. task performance
     group maintenance

180. Group members necessarily exhibit two kinds of activities: group maintenance and _____ _____.

Many decisions in business are made by groups of men who may meet only once, or at best a few times. What types of leadership do such groups need and get? How can members be chosen who will get things done?

Types of Leadership in Small Groups

In a typical study at the Harvard laboratory in which Robert F. Bales studies group behavior, 5 freshmen, recruited by mail and paid $1.00 an hour, were given 40 minutes to arrive at a group recommendation concerning a solution to a human relations problem. As they worked toward a solution, their discussion was recorded on sound tape. Behind windows with one-way vision, a team of observers noted down, for each remark made, who it was made by and to and whether its purpose was to get the assigned task performed or to help maintain the group as a going organization. In addition members rated one another, after each session, on which participant had the most ideas, which one was best liked, and which one most disliked.

In the first of a series of 4 such sessions, about 56 % of the time the man ranked high as having ideas, tended also to be well liked. In subsequent sessions, however, having ideas and being liked tended to diverge. By the fourth session, the 2 ratings went together only about 8 % of the time.

Bales concluded that in general there are 3 separate, uncorrelated characteristics which a group member may have. He may be active in trying to solve the problem, he may be rated by other members as being very able in problem solving, or he may be rated as being likeable. If ratings on each of these qualities are split between high and low, theoretically there should be 8 different types (2 × 2 × 2) of persons in the group. Bales reports finding 5 of them. The *good leader*, high on all 3, is probably rare, he says, although the man who is low on all 3, a kind of *scapegoat*, may be fairly common. Two other types, who often operate as partners, are the *task specialist* low on likeability but high on activity and ability, and the *social specialist*, high on likeability but low on activity and ability. Bales also identifies the man who dominates rather than leads the group as one who is active, but low both on task ability and likeability.

To be recognized as having ideas, Bales suggests, a man may have to talk a lot. This may frustrate others, who also want to talk, and threaten their status. How, then, can the good leader, who is both active and likeable, exist? To answer this question Bales divided participants into 3 groups, depending on whether they had a high, medium, or low feedback ratio. (A low feedback ratio means a man received much less participation from others than he initiated.) The more such men talked the lower liking (and higher dislike) ratings they received. Men with a high feedback ratio, however, could talk as much as they wanted without causing others to dislike them.

—Robert F. Bales, "Task Roles and Social Roles in Problem-Solving Groups," in Eleanor Maccoby et al., *Readings in Social Psychology*, 437–447.

180. task performance

181. These two kinds of activities—_____ _____ and _____ _____ must be c_____.

**181. task performance
group maintenance
coordinated**

182. And each of these two activities may be c_____ by a different l_____.

**182. coordinated
leader**

183. This is why we are unlikely to find any single type of ability associated with "leadership." For there are different t____ of leadership each of which may require a different kind of a_____.

**183. types
ability**

SUMMARY

1. Successful communication occurs when a receiver responds to a message in a way desired by the source of that message. A source is more likely to succeed if he knows his receiver well or if he observes his reactions to the message and modifies the message accordingly.
2. When a message is modified as a result of the receiver's reactions, we say there has been "feedback."
3. Predicting the responses of a receiver, and benefiting from feedback becomes a problem when the source has more than one receiver. *Whose* responses does he try to predict, and whose reactions does he observe?
4. If several receivers are known to share an attitude, a source may be able to fashion a message consistent with that attitude. If the persons are not known to share any attitudes, but are face-to-face with a source, he can observe their reactions and modify his message accordingly.
5. We can group people into categories on the basis of some common attribute. If this attribute consists of readiness to buy a product we call the category a *market*. If it consists of sharing an attitude, or of being together where a source can observe their reactions, we call the category an *audience*. The more closely market and audience coincide, the more efficient marketing communications are likely to be.
6. When receivers are face-to-face with one another, they not only listen to a source and provide feedback by reacting to his message, but they also communicate with one another. This communication is called "interaction." Interaction may intensify, modify, or offset the efforts of the source.
7. Through interaction, receivers tend to become more like one

another; their responses to the source become more predictable as well as more resistant to change. Receivers who have interacted with one another before the source appeared are a *group*. Persons become a group through interacting.

8. Groups may aid a source in several ways. They may assemble an audience for him. They may provide a channel for his message when they communicate with one another outside of their meetings.

9. When receivers interact, groups form that develop values or *norms* of their own. By making his message consistent with these group norms, a source can sometimes be influential even when his message is not consistent with the values of individual members. Members often accept group norms that contradict their own values because the group will reward them with high status if they do, or punish them by expulsion if they do not.

10. Individuals with quite different aims may find them satisfied by the same group or group activity. A member is likely to stay in a group as long as it satisfies this aim better than any alternative group open to him.

11. Once a group comes into existence, it may provide new goals for its individual members. They may enjoy being together so much that they cease to care whether the original aims that brought them into the group are satisfied.

12. Every group has two kinds of activity: *task performance*, or activity directed toward some goals outside the group; *group maintenance*, or that activity involved in keeping the group together. The group's power over a member depends upon how much he values each type of activity, and how well the group performs in each area.

13. Group goals may change because their members' goals change, or because the members themselves change.

14. The influence of groups is not limited to their members. Some receivers are influenced by groups they would like to join; others are influenced by groups they regard as expert. Any group which influences a receiver's behavior is termed a "reference group."

15. Frequently an individual has two or more reference groups whose norms differ; one set of norms may agree with the intent of a source, whereas another set may oppose the source. Which set of norms will prevail? An answer to this question involves weighing five group qualities: priority, cohesion, size, duration, and scope. By definition, the group which includes more members, persists over a greater length of time, and has norms applying to a wider variety of human behavior will influence more acts. A cohesive group will have more power over its members. And some groups, everyone seems to agree, should take priority over others: the family is such a group.

16. Although the source has no control over these group qualities, no group can influence an individual unless he is aware, when he makes a decision, that the group norms are relevant to that decision. A source may remind a receiver of such norms as a means of getting the receiver to accept his message.

17. So far we have talked about how groups determine responses by the individuals in them. Sometimes, however, a source seeks a response from the group itself, or seeks to use the group network as a channel for his message. High-status members are more likely to transmit messages to others, and even when they do not have authority to decide for the group, may have a strong influence on group decisions.

18. How do status differences arise within a group? Specialization arises first, for two reasons: differences in abilities, and the increase in ability with experience. The specialized functions that develop in any group are called *roles*. In any group, roles persist although the persons who perform them change. Each role gives the person in it certain rights and requires certain duties.

19. Most persons belong to several groups and have a role in each of them. Sometimes his role in one group requires a member to do something, while his role in another forbids him to do it. Even when *role conflict* of so severe a nature does not arise, each role competes for a person's time and energy.

20. To perform any role, a person must work with other persons who are called members of the *role set*. Sometimes these other persons, in complementary roles, make conflicting demands upon the role occupant.

21. Specialization produces roles, and roles tend to be ranked on one or more value systems. Roles which require rare abilities or are necessary to group survival tend to get high status. Coordinating members' activities is a role which has both qualities; so coordinators tend to get high status, to be recognized as leaders.

22. Every group requires at least two different kinds of activities of its members: those directed toward task performance and those directed toward group maintenance. If two different persons are required to coordinate these two kinds of activities, then a group will have two different high-status, leadership roles.

Research Studies

Behind every message which a marketing communicator directs to a mass audience lies a great deal of communication within groups of persons. *Shaw* finds two major types of networks in groups, centralized and decentralized, and examines their impact on task performance and group maintenance—output and satisfaction.

Following up evidence that members who communicate a great deal with one another tend to create groups which are attractive to their members, and groups as a result control their behavior, *Jackson* shows that communications increase a group's liking for the individual and the individual's liking for the group. *Siegel and Siegel* then show how membership in a group, or even the desire to belong to a group, can slow down the process of attitude change among university students.

Leadership, which may result from a man's position in the communications network as well as from his behavior and personality, may be of several types. *Bales* reports finding five, the most important division being between experts in task performance and in group maintenance.

Nine

Communication
Within Organizations

• Meet Henry Maier, one of 30,000 students at a Midwestern state university. He is one pea in an enormous pod, a member of the audience identified as "student . . . male . . . state university . . . Midwest." If a communicator wants to zero in on this target a little more precisely, he can add more attributes to the definition, by asking what Henry's major is, for example, and how soon he will graduate. Henry is one item in a *category* which is sometimes labeled an aggregate or a collectivity.

• Meet Henry Maier, one of a gang that goes bowling once a week or sits around and swaps lies. They have been doing this for three years now, and some definite patterns of the kind we call roles have begun to appear. Henry, for example, is the one who is most likely to suggest something new when interest starts to lag. Joe has a gift for discovering ways to do it and Mike is the clown, with a joke ready if arguments get too hot. Three leaders, if you will, in a gang whose members have begun to think, and talk and even look alike; at least, if one finds a shirt he likes at a bargain, the others are likely to buy one, too. Here is both an audience and a channel for the marketing communicator: Henry's a member of a small, informal *group*.

• Meet Henry Maier, one of a hundred college men hired by a large corporation as a summer salesman. Henry is simultaneously source, channel, and receiver. He is at the receiving end, for example, of advice from the more experienced salesman who supervises him and a half dozen other summer employees. He is a channel which carries a sales pitch developed at the head office out to the firm's customers. And, as Henry picks up experience and begins to add a few twists of his own to this pitch, he becomes a source. Although he is low

The Human Structure of the Restaurant

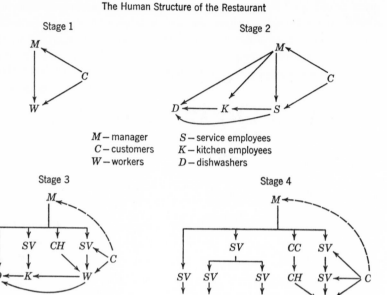

Stage 1

Stage 2

M — manager   S — service employees
C — customers   K — kitchen employees
W — workers   D — dishwashers

Stage 3

Stage 4

M — manager   W — waitresses
SV — supervisor   B — bartenders
CH — checker   P — pantry workers
CC — cost control supervisor   K — kitchen workers
C — customers   R — runners
                     D — dishwashers

Fig. 9.1. These four graphs, taken from a study of the restaurant industry*
(W. F. Whyte), show how a simple three-person group becomes a complex
organization with many different roles and status levels.

man on the firm's organizational chart, Henry has counted the levels
that separate him from the top job. He has started to figure, though
he would not admit this even to himself, how long it will take him to
get there. Henry's a member of an *organization*.

Three Labels for Sets of People

Category, group, organization—all names of sets of people. How
do they differ? Small groups and organizations consist of people who
influence one another's behavior through communication. The sociol-

* From *Human Relations in the Restaurant Industry* by William Foote Whyte.
Copyright 1948, McGraw-Hill Book Company. Used by permission.

ogist would say "they interact." Categories are made up of individuals who do not interact with one another, but have similar characteristics such as income or education, or similar behavior such as attitude toward a product or response to a message. Most of the definitions in our chapter on *audience*, for example, concerned categories, although the consumer decision-making unit, the family, represents one of society's most important groups.

The group and the organization: these are two extremes on a multi-dimensioned scale. Groups tend to be small. One definition, which says that each member must be able to communicate face-to-face with every other "regularly," imposes a practical ceiling on membership of fifteen to twenty, with the most effective groups appearing to be half that size. Groups tend to be short lived, to have less well-defined roles and statuses, and to have fewer of them. Organizations, on the other hand, tend to be more precise about their goals and the means to be used to attain them. Groups tend to put more emphasis on members having fun together than organizations do; sometimes this becomes their only goal. Organizations, on the other hand, are interested in members having fun—the technical label is "engaging in group-maintenance activities"—as a means to an end rather than an end in itself. Groups often grow up to become organizations; most organizations contain several groups within themselves.

From a communications standpoint, the convenient way of distinguishing the two is to say that channels of communication are an independent variable in the group, a dependent variable in the organization. If an individual is a member from the start, and through his communications with other members helps determine the rules and roles that develop, we have a group. If the patterns already exist, however, and Henry must learn what they are and how to adjust to them, he has joined an organization. Organizations have rules that, as we shall soon see, specify who may be a source and who a receiver for any given message.

The distinction between organizations and groups is one of degree, and one that sometimes varies with the individual member or the observer himself. If Henry leaves his gang of bowlers, for example, the other members may look for someone to take his place who is as much like Henry as possible—someone who has lots of new ideas, but will not try to compete with Mike in cracking jokes. To this new member, who must fit into patterns already established, the gang is an organization, as we have just defined it. If all the members try to insure the gang's survival despite their own graduation, by converting it into a club or society, then it becomes an organization. All organizations serve the needs of the decision makers within them. In addition, the functions they perform are supposed to serve other persons as well. For some organizations, like the police, these others are the public in general. For labor unions, the "others" to be served are their members; for schools, the pupils. In business organizations, the focus of this chapter, the others to be served are the owners.

Importance to Marketing

These are some of the differences between groups and organizations. Why are groups and organizations important to marketing communications?

To answer that question, let us meet another Henry Maier: a college graduate now, with a bachelor's degree in business administration, who wants to go into the advertising business, but he cannot decide what kind of organization he wants to work for. Should he try to get a job with an advertising agency, with one of the advertising media, or with the advertiser himself?

He has heard that most agencies are small. He has read somewhere that turnover is high. Men in their thirties switch jobs every three years, on the average, and a client stays with an agency for an average of only six years (Hepner, 37 and 662). (He realizes that the two changes may cancel out if an advertising man follows an account to its new agency.) Henry himself does not feel he is especially talented for creative work, which may be an advantage, since he has heard that some television commercials have to run a gauntlet of as many as forty different critics outside the agency itself before they can be put on the air, and Henry would find forty "bosses" hard to take. He has listened to all the arguments about being a big frog in a small organization, and vice versa.

None of these things really answer the questions, some of them only half formed, that bother him. He wonders how the rewards differ in these various organizations, for example, and by rewards Henry does not mean only money. He is also interested in the job itself, and the people he will associate with. What are his chances of getting ahead, and what personal qualities will help him most? What's best—to stay with one firm all his life or to change about?

This chapter will not answer any of Henry's questions directly, but it will tell him some of the things he needs to know about organizations and groups—things which may help him find an answer for himself.

Two Kinds of Reward

When Henry gets a job, he will find himself a member of an organization and that much of his time is spent in learning the rules, written and unwritten, which govern its activities. At the same time, Henry will find he is a member of a small group. This may be a group of fellow trainees, having lunch together. Some of the time they will talk about football and dates. But some of the time, if they are salesmen, they will talk about tough customers and how to cope with them, or discuss ways of getting around that latest ridiculous memo from the head office which has forgotten what a customer looks like. If Henry starts working for an advertising agency in New York or Chicago, he may lunch regularly with other "wet-behind-the-ears" beginners in other agencies, who help one another with the burdens of a beginner, and build ties which will enable some of them to switch employers in a year or two.

These are groups outside the organization itself, although the organization may not be aware such groups exist. Some of their activities, like the salesmen's exchange of tips on tough customers, help the firm. Some, like their discussion of ways to get around red tape, may hurt the firm. Many are irrelevant to any of the firm's goals. To Henry himself, however, these groups are good, for they provide two rewards. They are fun in themselves, providing the rewards of *group maintenance*, and they provide him with information he can get in no other way—information about his own department, other departments in the firm, and other firms. This information helps him do and get a better job of *task performance*. This is how things look to Henry in his first job.

As Henry begins to climb the organizational chart, however, he will find that more and more of his activities take place as the member of a group. If he becomes advertising manager, for instance, on Tuesday he may meet with the sales manager and the public relations director to decide on the best mix of channels. On Wednesday, he may meet with the account executive from his advertising agency to decide on a media mix or a message mix.

The rewards which Henry as a beginner received from informal groups outside the organization, he now as an executive receives from informal groups within the organization. Indeed, the formal rewards which the organization gives him for doing his job now depend on his skill in influencing other members in a group situation. This is generally true. Executives can satisfy more of their wants, both of task performance and group maintenance, within a single organization, the firm itself. As a result, they have less need for other groups.

Two Sources of Rewards

The group with which Henry, the advertising manager, meets on Tuesday differs in one important respect from the one with which he meets on Wednesday. On Tuesday, there was only one source of rewards, if Henry succeeded: his employer. To win the rewards offered by his employer, Henry had to compete with colleagues, the same colleagues whose cooperation he will need next week. On Wednesday, however, he was "in competition," to the extent that any decision making involved bargaining with and attempting to influence other persons, with outsiders. Although he must maintain good relations with them, too, over the long run, he does not have to work with them and exchange favors with them every day.

On Wednesday there were two sources of rewards for Henry. His employer, of course, will reward an able performance. At the same time, however, Henry makes himself highly visible to prospective employers; the harder he fights for his current employer, the more regard his "antagonists" may have for his ability. Thus Henry has an opportunity to rise both within his own firm and by changing firms.

This is true of any executive whose job requires him to communicate with outsiders. Indeed, it is true of any person who has "high visibility" in his work. It is true of the man who speaks or publishes and of the man who belongs to professional organizations. It is particularly true of the professional, whose superiors may be unable even to weigh the relative merits of two prospective employees by themselves, and so are forced to depend on the judgments of their fellow professionals.

Two Kinds of Controls

There are two ways of coping with uncertainty. One way uses organizations, which restrict the scope of decisions a man must make

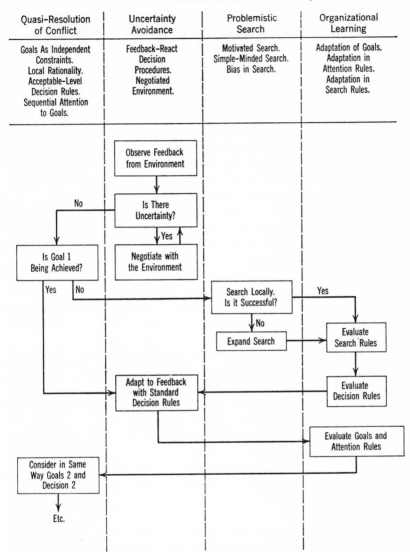

Quasi-Resolution of Conflict	Uncertainty Avoidance	Problemistic Search	Organizational Learning
Goals As Independent Constraints. Local Rationality. Acceptable-Level Decision Rules. Sequential Attention to Goals.	Feedback–React Decision Procedures. Negotiated Environment.	Motivated Search. Simple-Minded Search. Bias in Search.	Adaptation of Goals. Adaptation in Attention Rules. Adaptation in Search Rules.

Fig. 9.2. Here is a flow chart showing how Cyert and March conceptualize the decision-making process in an organization. (Richard M. Cyert and James G. March, *A Behavioral Theory of the Firm* (c) 1963, by permission of Prentice-Hall, Inc., Englewood Cliffs, New Jersey.)

by giving him a specific role and status in a chain of command. The other way increases the ability of the man himself, and makes him a professional with expert knowledge and support from his colleagues which relieve the tensions of decision making. The professional's authority comes from his expertness, rather than his position (Caplow and McGee). His loyalty is to his "clients" rather than to a specific organization. His performance is judged by his peers rather than his superiors. A professional orientation tends to distinguish "staff" from "line" and to characterize men at the top of an organization. Indeed, men at the top, who have no superiors in the organization itself, must be controlled, as the professional is, by their own internalized standards and by their peers.

Professionalism frees a man from organizational control. Such freedom has its price, however; it is obtained at the cost of receiving fewer "group-maintenance" rewards from the less mobile members of his firm. Peers may be envious. Superiors may hesitate to rely too much on someone who is mobile, and subordinates may see little value in relations with someone who may not be in a position to reward them tomorrow. At the same time, the mobile person himself is less motivated to seek such rewards within the firm and has less time to build up the relationships which provide such rewards.

To the men at the top, the business firm itself may appear as a coalition of individuals engaged in a continuous process of bargaining, working toward a set of individual goals which are often inconsistent with one another, and subject to change (Cyert and March).* This picture represents an alternative to the conventional view of decision making in which the top man in management considers all possible alternatives, chooses the best, and then selects and pays subordinates to conform to his choice. Cyert and March suggest, instead, a group decision-making process in which information is sought only when problems arise from the environment, or when an executive can bring a problem to the fore because he has a ready-made solution he wants adopted. Instead of searching for the best solution, they argue, the decision-making coalition drops its search as soon as a "feasible" solution is found. (A solution is "feasible" if it does not disturb members' individual goals or if it is made at the expense of the weakest members of the coalition.)

The extent to which bargaining is necessary is reduced by members' readiness to accept precedents, as failure reduces their level of aspirations or when prosperity produces enough excess resources ("organiza-

---

* This reference is the basis for much of the discussion of this chapter.

If business decisions are made by coalitions among executives, what rules determine how the coalitions themselves are formed?

Which Candidates Are Likely to Gang Up?

In some situations, every member of a group can benefit through coordinated effort. In pure conflict, there is no combination of members at all, since one person's gain is a loss for the others. But what of mixed situations, in which coalitions can form? What, for example, is likely to happen in a convention where candidate A has 48% of the votes, candidate B has 30% and candidate C 22%?

Reviewing experimental research, Gamson finds 3 different kinds of solution, each appropriate to a different set of circumstances:

1. *Parity norm.* In this case, each member's contribution to victory is fixed, and the winnings themselves are fixed, so each seeks to win with the smallest possible investment of resources. The prediction: candidates B and C would form a coalition, sharing the rewards in proportion to their contribution. This outcome is likely with competitive-minded males, especially if only 2 are allowed to bargain with first, second, and so on.

2. *Pivotal power.* Here power is decisive, and a member's power rises with the number of winning coalitions which he can form. In the present case, no prediction is possible since there are 2 such combinations for each candidate. High stakes lead to this solution, provided members' past (or future) relationships do not inhibit their ruthlessness.

3. *Good feeling.* Now the least invidious coalition is sought—that in which members can share rewards equally. Given 4 candidates—A 30%, B 24%, C 24%, and D 22%—this would mean a coalition by B and C. This solution is likely when women, sensitive to group maintenance needs, serve as subjects, when subjects are acquainted with one another, and norms of "sportsmanship" prevail.

—William A. Gamson, "Experimental Studies of Coalition Formation," in Leonard Berkowitz, ed., *Advances in Experimental Psychology, Vol. I* (New York: Academic Press, 1964).

tional slack") to allow everyone's minimum demands to be met. In bad times, however, bargaining becomes more intense and decisions are often made at the expense of the least powerful members of the coalition. Bargaining also becomes more intense when success raises individual members' levels of aspiration.

Two Functions of the Formal Network

Whether an executive is interested in rising within a single firm or in rising by strategic shifts from one firm to another, the processes of communication in a small group are of vital importance to him. Henry, however, must begin at the bottom, and his communications within the organization must flow through the channels prescribed on the organizational chart. Aside from fixing responsibility for decisions, the formal network of communications in an organization serves two functions: it prescribes the audience for each message, and it reduces tension created by the exercise of personal power.

Four Executives Spend 80 Per Cent of Time Talking

For 25 days, the department manager in a British factory and his 3 immediate subordinates kept records of all their communications,

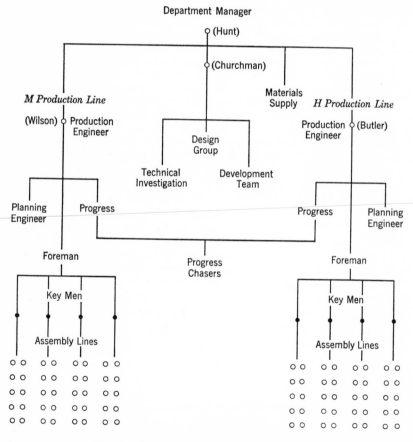

Fig. 9.3. Formal organization of department.

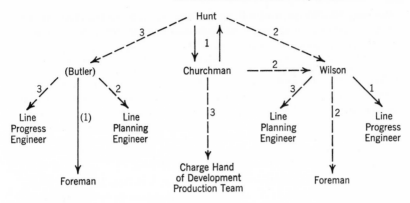

Fig. 9.4. Actual flow of communications (numbers indicate relative importance of messages).

face-to-face, written, and telephoned. They recorded from 25 to 40 "episodes" a day, noting down for each the following 5 characteristics:

1. Who initiated the interaction?
2. How long did it last?
3. Was the purpose to get, give, systematize, record, or interpret information? Was the information a decision, an instruction, advice, or information?
4. Did the interaction concern past, present, or future activity?
5. Did the activities concern sales, personnel, production, or what?

The reports showed that all 4 men spent 80 per cent of their time in conversations. They underestimated the amount of time they spent on personnel problems and research, and overestimated the amount of time spent on production:

	Time Spent on Activity:	Number of Episodes
Nature of Activity	Average of Estimates	Actually Recorded
Personnel	7.5	15
Research	10	16
Sales	5	3
Costs	8	7
Production	52.5	34
Office	8	12
Other	8.5	13

During the 5 weeks, none of the 4 saw more than a third of the 128 persons in the department involved and half of the 128 were not seen at all. Of the 217 persons seen in this time, 118 were in the factory but outside the department, 8 in the firm but outside the factory, and 31 outside the firm. The department manager, Hunt, top man on the chart, spent only 50 per cent of his time within the department itself; his 3 subordinates spent from 72 to 89 per cent of their time there.

The author concludes that wide differences in activities for individuals in the same role pointed to hidden forces at work. (Personality or esteem?) He also finds that most of the 4 men's communication was within a 14-member staff group and that 40 per cent of it was among the 4 men themselves. Perception of message content varied: what a superior reported as instructions were reported by his subordinates as information. Instead of flowing down the organizational chart, he found that many messages were shared with peers outside the department, then they "leaked" rather than "flowed" down the system.

—Tom Burns, "The Directions of Activity and Communication in a Departmental Executive Group," *Human Relations*, 7:73–97.

Since the organizational chart specifies who each source may communicate with, he can tailor his message for a known audience. Symbols can be chosen more precisely and less redundancy is needed. The recipient's position in the organization is assumed to motivate him to receive the message, so that motivational content can be omitted from the message itself.

Since less feedback is needed with a known audience than with strangers, this would suggest that low-feedback written messages would be used much more than spoken ones on the formal network. Written messages, however, outlast the immediate situation. The person who receives them may pass them on up the chain; knowing this, many an organizational source designs his messages for possible ultimate receivers, even if this reduces their effectiveness with the immediate receiver. Written messages also may show up in the files at an awkward time in the future. The canny executive keeps a file of written memos for his own protection, and, if he can, communicates face-to-face.

Less feedback is needed with persons who are known than with strangers, other things being equal. One of the things *not* equal, however, is the importance of the message to its source. Typically messages within an organization are much more important to the source than those he sends to strangers.

Rules Reduce Tension

As for reduction of tension, three factors make the exercise of power by one's superior a tension-creating situation. First, if the exercise itself does not punish the subordinate, it reminds him that the superior *can* punish. Second, exercise of power emphasizes a relationship, that of superior-and-subordinate, which is inconsistent with the general feeling in our society that men are or should be equal. Third, although our culture recognizes such grounds as age, sex (male), ability, or experience as justifying superior status, the superior may not always be older, not always obviously more able or experienced, and not always a male. By reducing the necessity for one person to give orders to another, the tension caused by these three factors is relieved.

Rules also relieve tension by emphasizing that power resides in roles, not in the persons who occupy them. Indeed, the superior can emphasize that he, as well as the subordinate, is subject to the same impersonal set of rules. Rules also focus attention on behavior that executives regard as important and provide the advance warning which makes penalties for their infraction appear legitimate. Moreover, it is often easier to detect violations of the rules themselves than it would be to detect the behavior they are meant to prevent. Finally, rules provide a superior with an additional set of rewards, since he can relax them as a special favor. (Although he runs the risk when he does so of throwing into question the very impersonality which represents the chief virtue of a rule, self-interest usually convinces the beneficiary that his case is, indeed, a special one.)

Rules reduce uncertainty. They protect the subordinate from inordinate or capricious demands, and they tell him what minimum behavior is necessary to avoid trouble. Rules also enable the superior to take a great many things for granted; his environment, too, becomes highly predictable. Predictability, however, is gained at the expense of initiative. Rigid rules and close supervision prevent an employee from devising new means to the firm's goal. They become dysfunctional when the prescribed means are not the best or when conditions change and the prescribed means no longer achieve the goal. (Rules, of course, are not the only means by which an employee's behavior can be controlled. The production assembly line, for example, is even more impersonal in its control of behavior than a formal rule; at the same time, it often reduces worker initiative and satisfaction, both by making the task he performs dull and reducing the chance to communicate with fellow workers in informal groups. Systems of reward based on performance records, on the other hand, increase the worker's satisfaction, since they prescribe goals but allow freedom as to means of achieving them.)

Functions of the Gatekeeper

The rules affecting communication, which are mapped by the organizational chart, reduce uncertainty by restricting the scope of each individual's communications. Every person on the organizational chart, except for those at the very bottom and the very top, is a "gatekeeper." Each gatekeeper is a receiver for orders coming down from above. These orders express the goals by which his performance will be judged. Each gatekeeper is also a source, since he must convert the goals given him into subgoals by which he will judge the performance of his subordinates.

As orders flow down the chain of command, gatekeepers tend to eliminate explanations, reasons why, and qualifying conditions as non-essential. Sometimes this is done deliberately; other times it is an inevitable part of the process of dividing a goal into subgoals and assigning them to different persons. Individual actions make sense only in the big picture, but the big picture is lacking. This process may lower morale in the ranks and lower the prestige of the superior. (A person who remains in the organization at all is likely to assume that the man at the top, the symbol of the organization, is sensible enough and that it is his subordinates who are at fault.) As a result, comments which a superior may have intended as suggestions become commands and *ad hoc* solutions become precedents.

Each gatekeeper is also a source of reports to his superior on how well those orders are being carried out. From the reports sent to him by his subordinates, each gatekeeper selects information to be passed on up the chain of communication. He must limit the amount of information he passes on, or his superiors will have to do the work (and take the responsibility) which is properly his. On the other hand, if he passes on too little information, he prevents them from doing their job.

Theoretically, each gatekeeper makes his selection objectively. In actuality, of course, no gatekeeper is likely to pass on information which puts him in a bad light if he can avoid it. Sometimes he can time a message so that bad news is coupled with good or so that a solution accompanies every message about a problem.

Length of Chain
The taller an organizational chart is, the longer the chain of communication and the more gatekeepers, the more possibilities there are of distortion occurring, in both directions. The chain can be

shortened by increasing a gatekeeper's "span of control"—the number of subordinates reporting to him. This means he can then spend less time in communicating with each of them and less time supervising them.

This may be good, since too close supervision by a superior prevents a subordinate from using and developing his own initiative. Or it may be bad, if the superior has so many subordinates under him that he lacks time needed to communicate adequately with any of them. Frequent interaction with a superior is rewarding to a subordinate, since such interaction raises his status. It may lower the status of the superior, however. Interaction may also reduce efficiency if it causes the subordinate to imitate his boss, so that he becomes an echo rather than an independent source of information.

Gatekeepers in a chain of command simplify decisions to be made at the top by reducing the amount of information or number of alternatives that have to be considered. A gatekeeper may try to consult the superior before he makes any decisions if he is insecure or thinks that by doing so he can gain rewards in the form of inter-action with or approval from the boss. A boss who has subordinates of this kind or encourages them in this sort of behavior (perhaps because of his own fear to delegate authority), is in trouble if he has many subordinates. He will not have time to communicate ade-quately with any of them, and decisions are likely to be delayed.

Span of Control

Specifying an appropriate span of control thus depends on the nature of both superior and subordinate, the number and kind of decisions that have to be made, and the extent to which new problems make standard routine decision-making impossible. One study, made in 1952, found that the presidents of 100 United States firms of over 5000 employees each had from one to twenty subordinates reporting directly to them (Longenecker, 177). Another study of 500 manufacturing plants in Ohio, found executives' span of control ranged from one to seventeen; 20 per cent of the firms reported a span of six sub-ordinates, and 18 per cent one of five, with top men in 94 per cent of headquarter plants having spans of less than nine (Longenecker, 177).

Poor communications can result from narrow or wide spans, tall or short charts, but the cause and the locus are different. In the tall chart they occur because of the limitations and self-interest of a long sequence of gatekeepers. In the flat chart, they occur because executives lack time for communications or cannot see their subordinates at the right time. The former type of distortion may be easier for an executive to control, since he is less involved in it. Although many gatekeepers mean more distortion each also provides a check on the others.

Here are 2 studies showing the importance of communications among peers within factory management: one made by an outside observer, the other by the executives themselves.

Horizontal Messages and Departmental Biases

For 14 hours, an observer watched the production manager in a factory, recording each telephone call and face-to-face contact. He repeated this process for 2 other department heads—the man in charge of sales liaison and the men in charge of production planning and control.

He then coded his observations according to Bales' system: counting the number of times each department head *gave* information, opinions or suggestions, and the number of times he *received* them. He also counted the number of negative or disapproving contacts and the number of positive ones.

Here is an example:

Production Manager	Personnel Manager
"Have you found a secretary for me yet?" (Request for information)	"No, I haven't." (Gives information)
"Look, Joe, this situation is intolerable. I've got to have one *now*." (Negative interaction)	
"Why don't you call that white-gloves outfit and see if they have someone?" (Gives suggestion)	"That's a good idea. I'll get on it right away." (Accepts suggestion)

Here are the results for one of the two plants studied:

	Percentage of Horizontal Interactions	
	Originated	Received
Production	17%	22%
Planning and control	31	31
Sales liaison	62	57

In short, horizontal communications were high in mediating between salesmen in the field and the factory. The planning and control group also mediated, but between fewer persons, and most of the production manager's time was taken up with supervision, that is, with *vertical* communication. Similar differences were found for the other plant, although the amount of horizontal communications was influenced by both differences between the plants, and differences in the personalities of the men filling similar roles.

A follow-up study asked 7 different department heads in 2 different plants to indicate on a 5-point favor-opposed scale what their position would be, and what they thought their 6 colleagues would feel, about 7 different issues. The results showed clearcut departmental differences, characteristic of both plants, and suggested ways in which departments form coalitions that differ from issue to issue. Identical departments in the 2 plants agreed 36 times out of a possible 49 (7 departments $\times$ 7 issues). The field sales department agreed with production, that "One should never cut down production before it is absolutely necessary," in opposition to purchasing which felt that, "There is no point in producing products beyond those that can definitely be sold."

The two departments disagreed, however, on the issue of design changes. Salesmen felt that "A lot of unnecessary fuss is made about the trouble caused by changes in design," but production said that design changes were "such a nuisance that they should hardly ever be introduced."

Underlying these policy disagreements, the author suggests were more basic differences in position on issues of flexibility vs. stability, shortrun versus long, organizational vs. societal goals, and consideration of measurable vs. imponderable variables.

> —Henry A. Landsberger, "The Horizontal Dimension in Bureaucracy," *Administrative Science Quarterly*, 6:299–332.

Bypassing the Gatekeeper

A gatekeeper's receivers, whether superiors or subordinates, are likely to wish that they had more information than the gatekeeper gives them. Subordinates often feel they could do a better job if they knew management's goals in addition to their own subgoals. They also would like to know that top management is aware of their contribution to the performance for which the gatekeeper will be credited. Superiors, of course, would like to know how the gatekeeper has tailored his messages to make himself look good. If either subordinates or superiors attempt to bypass the gatekeeper and communicate directly, however, he feels threatened. Indeed, his very existence becomes unnecessary, since his function is taken away from him. In addition, his subordinates will be confused since they will not know whether to follow the orders of their boss, or those of their boss' boss.

Salesmen can carry incoming as well as outgoing messages. How often do their reports get back to the firm and work their way through channels to the right executive?

Heard Any News About Widgets Lately?

At the request of an electrical manufacturing firm, but without the knowledge of the firm's salesmen, purchasing agents for its customers planted 6 rumors with the salesmen during their regular calls.

Three to 18 days later, the time varying with the salesman's call, the manufacturer than sent a questionnaire to its 615 employees: managers and staffs of 10 product sections, managers of the 57 operating units within these sections, and field personnel. Replies were received from 36 per cent.

The questions were general. Thus to check on a rumor that "all military radar will soon be converting to 1200 cycles," the questionnaire asked whether employees had heard anything during the past 2 or 3 weeks about the military planning to convert its radar.

In each case, the appropriate target for the rumors was Operating Unit A. Two of the rumors were planted with salesmen for this unit, 2 with salesmen for another section of the same branch, and 2 with salesmen for a different branch of the firm.

Only one of the rumors was passed on to the appropriate target without distortion. A salesman for operating unit *C* was told the Japanese had discovered an "electro-negative gas" to replace air in circuit breakers (produced by Unit *C*) which also could be used in widgets (produced by Unit *A*). He first queried his own unit to find out what the gas was, then wrote the sales manager of Unit *A*. The process took 10 days.

Two accidental factors probably explain this. The salesman had formerly sold widgets and was a personal friend of Unit *A*'s sales manager.

Another rumor was passed on in distorted fashion. The salesman was told the customer was using 30,000 overloads (made by another operating unit of the firm), but reported to the sales manager that the firm planned to buy 30,000 overload widgets a week (made by Unit *A*).

No trace was found of the other 4 rumors. Two concerned competitors: a low price quotation for a widget made by a Japanese company, and news that a competitor was to construct a new widget factory in California. Another concerned the conversion of military radar and the fourth the development of a competitive widget from a new, previously unused material.

> —Gerald Albaum, "Horizontal Information Flow: An Exploratory Study," *Journal of the Academy of Management*, 7:1, 21–33.

Instead of bypassing the gatekeeper, his receivers can check on his performance indirectly through informal groups of persons at their own level, made up of their equals or, in sociological jargon, their "peers." By comparing notes, subordinates with the same boss or even subordinates in different departments can get a better idea of what is going on overhead. Superiors have an added means of comparison, since they usually receive reports from several subordinate gatekeepers, who are in competition, either directly as when sales managers from different regions seek the same promotion, or indirectly, as when an advertising manager and a sales manager both want bigger budgets.

In addition to serving the ends of individual employees, informal communications of this kind may help the firm itself, by providing flexibility for situations not covered by the rules. Going from one department up to the top and then down again, to another part of the same firm or to another organization, is the time-consuming process. Informal messages between peers in different departments can short-circuit this process and help the firm function. They can, on the other hand, enable participants to circumvent control, restrict production, suppress information, and attain goals by disapproved methods.

Differences in Messages and Rewards

So far, in discussing informal groups as an alternative channel for communications, we have been concerned with audience differences. Formal channels supply audiences of superiors or subordinates; informal groups provide audiences made up of peers. The messages carried to the two audiences also differ, their content performing different functions and providing different rewards to the audiences.

Messages on formal channels are task centered. They are concerned with adjusting to the environment and with activities which advance the group toward a goal. Messages within informal groups are concerned with group maintenance, with holding members together, and relieving tension; often the interaction which maintains the group is rewarding in itself. Although hobby and sports clubs may have group maintenance as their sole goal, a business firm regards such interaction as a means to accomplish some specific task. This is one reason why informal groups exist within organizations; they provide the rewards of group maintenance which are necessary to keep a man in the organization and producing.

Organizations differ in their ability to supply these two kinds of rewards, and a given organization provides varying amounts of each kind of reward to different roles and status positions. Homogeneous groups, whose members are similar to one another, are likely to provide the rewards of group maintenance and make such rewards their major goal. Heterogeneous groups may be better at task performance, however, since they may provide the variety of skills and viewpoints needed to solve problems and achieve results.

From the standpoint of management, each role has a minimum amount of group-maintenance activities which it must provide if the group is to accomplish its task. If a role provides more than this amount, members gain the rewards of pleasurable interaction at the expense of goal achievement. It is the job of a leader to see that this does not happen.

Differences in Individuals

Individuals differ in the value they place upon these two kinds of reward. Those with a strong need to achieve are interested in moving toward the formal goal. Those with a need for affiliation are more interested in pleasurable interaction. Young men may league together in groups one writer calls "cabals" to exchange information which will help them advance in an organization. Older men, content with their positions, may form "cliques" which provide the alternative rewards of group maintenance.

Individuals also differ in their ability to perform the activities involved in task performance and in group maintenance. In an informal group which develops its own leadership each of these two functions tends to be best performed by a different man. The man who helps a group advance toward a goal by contributing ideas may be the one who is least liked. In a formal organization, where the leader is appointed, one man usually performs both functions. The successful leader in such an organization takes on a distinctive role. He plans, he assigns work, he rewards and penalizes, and his subordinates hope that he has influence higher up. At the same time, he seeks to motivate members and relieve tension. In general, he tries not to supervise too closely, since close supervision prevents the subordinate from using his initiative, makes him seek in small groups the group maintenance denied him by close supervision, reduces self-confidence, and tends to be perceived as punishing. Thus close supervision causes performance to deteriorate, requiring still closer supervision.

The amount of supervision a leader supplies reflects the amount his subordinates want. The amount they want increases as one descends the organizational chart, since employees at the bottom tend to have less interest in task performance and less confidence in their own ability. Even more important than the desires of a gatekeeper's subordinates in determining gatekeeper behavior is the behavior of his own superior. A gatekeeper tends to use the supervisory methods of his own superior as an index of what the organization wants and of what behavior on his part will be rewarded.

Effective Group Behavior

So far we have discussed groups and organizations from two different standpoints. First, we have discussed very briefly in this chapter (and at greater length in the previous chapter), how communication changes when the audience is an interacting group, rather than a category or aggregate. Second, we have compared the channels of communication in an organization, which tend to be strictly prescribed channels operating across several status levels, and those in a group, which tend to be less formal and to operate between peers. We have said that much of a top executive's activity involves group rather than organizational communication. The messages which organizations transmit to outside audiences usually are produced by group effort, but the problem is much broader than that. Most of the executive's activity involves solving problems and making decisions. He is influenced by and influences other persons of roughly equivalent status, whether members of his own or other organizations.

What are the conditions of effective decision-making and problem-solving? At this point we move to the field of small-group research, based partly on experiments in the field but more specifically on laboratory experiments. In most cases the groups were short-lived, and not part of any permanent, ongoing organization. The results, nevertheless, shed a good deal of light on the situation in which the executive must operate, light that must suffice until the day when the executive suite itself comes under the scholar's microscope.

Status Affects Productivity

A free flow of communications within a group performs three functions which increase productivity. Messages from persons similar to himself provide a man with the social support he needs before he can speak up and make suggestions. Messages from persons of differing viewpoints help the group detect errors in what he has to say. Competition among persons in the group provides an incentive to speak up, since a man can gain prestige by doing so. One study suggests that a man performs best when he has a like-minded person as a close colleague, to provide support, but has frequent contacts with others who challenge his statements. The gatekeepers in a formal organization obstruct the free flow of communications, and restrict all three of the functions just cited.

Moreover, the longer an informal group survives, the greater the tendency for it to develop differences in role and status similar to those of the organization. Such status differences obstruct communications in the informal group just as gatekeepers do in the formal organization. They affect productivity and, by changing the rewards which a group gives its members, affect attitudes of members toward the group.

Persons of low status in the informal group receive fewer rewards, are less motivated to participate and, in fact, participate less (Kelley and Thibaut, 772–776). When they do participate, they direct a high proportion of their messages to persons of high status, the messages often being irrelevant to the task at hand because they represent attempts to achieve status or to compensate for low status.

Persons of low status are reluctant to criticize persons of high status, even if the latter are wrong. When they do offer criticism, other members of the group are likely to pay no attention to them. Similarly, other members are likely to reject ideas offered by persons of low status, even when they are correct. Thus groups with status differences are likely to be less productive in many tasks. If low status members see a chance to increase their status by communication, they may communicate whether their messages are relevant to the task at hand or not. So groups with fixed status differences may be more productive than those in which status differences can be changed.

Status differences prevent equal participation by all members and this lack of participation in itself deprives low-status members of one of the major rewards of group membership. If the deprivation becomes acute, they may even leave the group. Participation tends to become unequal as the life of the group lengthens or as its size increases, since both factors tend to create status difference.

As soon as a group has as many as four members, some begin to participate more than others (Kelley and Thibaut, 762). The decline in equality is marked and consistent until the group has eight members; from then on no consistent trend is found. Interestingly enough, other experiments (Asch b, 181) suggest that the number four is critical from another standpoint. Group pressures upon a member reach their peak when he is faced with a unanimous trio. Increasing his opposition beyond that point appears to have no effect upon his behavior.

Similarity Increases

Equal participation by members representing a variety of abilities and viewpoints tend to increase productivity. But just as equality of participation tends to disappear from a group over time, so does variety among its members.

To begin with, the more voluntary membership in a group is, the more its members tend to be similar at the very outset. The business organization is likely to be more heterogeneous than the group, not only because it is bigger, and not only because its clearly defined roles call for clearly differentiated abilities, but because someone other than the members themselves decides who shall belong.

Once in a group, three additional factors tend to increase members' similarity. First, the group influences what members look for and what they see in their environment, what they think and talk about, what they learn and do. Second, if cues from the environment are ambiguous, members seek guidance and interpretation from one another. Finally, members can exert pressures to comform on one another in the form of rewards and penalties. In an organization, these sanctions may be administered by a leader; in a group with few status differences, the members themselves will exert them. Typically, they will step up their rate of communications to a member who is getting out of line, as long as they think he can be made to conform (Schachter). Beyond that point, they will communicate with him less and less until he is virtually ostracized.

The effectiveness of such pressure on an individual depends on how much he values membership. If the group has a clear goal, one that he values; if the group has the resources needed to attain the goal; and if it is following a path that seems likely to achieve that goal, the member is likely to value the group and respond to pressure from its members. If the member has available several alternative groups which can achieve this same goal, then the power which any single group can exert upon him will be less. Before a group can exert pressure on a member to conform, it must be able to observe that he is *not* conforming. Some roles in groups and organizations have low visibility; their occupants have a good deal of leeway.

Defining Task and Goal

In general, productivity and the rewards which productivity permits decrease over time as members of the group become more similar to one another in their thinking but become increasingly differentiated from one another in role and status. They have fewer different ideas to exchange with one another, and status differences inhibit the exchange of those they do have.

More specifically, productivity must be defined in terms of the task which the group is trying to accomplish. If the group is trying to agree on a decision, and one decision is as good as another, then both similar viewpoints and status differences will produce an early decision. If a "coalition" of executives is content with a "feasible" rather than an optimal solution, then the more similar the executives are the more quickly they are likely to agree on their decision. If a member values the rewards of group maintenance highly, he is likely to find them in a small group, where participation is equal and status differences are minimal. If he values the rewards of goal achievement highly, however, he may turn to a larger group which has more adequate resources.

The task must be defined before we can say what kind of group is most effective and before we can answer the related question of whether groups are more productive than individuals (Kelley and Thibaut, 750). Being in a group necessarily inhibits an individual, if only by the fact that only one person can talk, and be heard, at a time. Thus groups produce fewer ideas than the sum of ideas

---

Participation in setting goals is superior to discussion:

Garment Workers Set Own Goals

Ten office workers in a Midwestern garment factory met once a week for 5 weeks. Half of them discussed employee problems, company benefits and policy, and community relations. The others discussed these topics and also agreed on how many units per hour their members would try to produce the next week. Twelve swatchers from the factory, divided into the same two experimental groups, went through the same procedure.

The 2 groups which set their own production goals achieved increases in output, as compared with their average during a 5-week control period preceding the experiment, which were significant at the .05 level. Changes in the discussion group were not significant. Superiority of each goal-setting group over its matching discussion group was also significant at the .05 level. Attitudes of the 4 groups were very similar. About 70 per

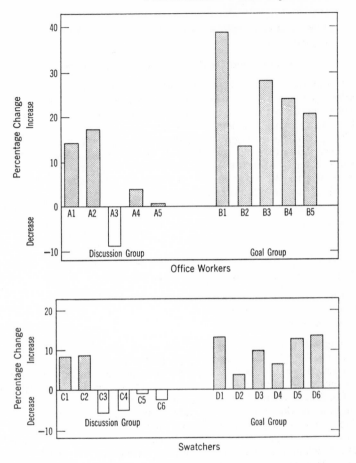

Fig. 9.5. Individual production change: percentage increase or decrease during experimental period as compared with control period.

cent felt the time in discussion had been well spent and that they had learned something new.

—Lois C. Lawrence and Patricia Cain
Smith, "Group Decision and Employee
Participation," Journal of Applied Psychology, 39:334–337.

that would be produced by their individual members. Groups converge upon a single solution much more quickly, however; indeed, it is hard to see how individuals would even happen upon a single solution without group pressures toward conformity. By dividing a job into

When persuasion fails, participation may succeed, this study in industry suggests.

Figures and Prestige Fail; Discussion Works

The stereotype that older workers are inferior to younger ones in skilled jobs had led many companies to refuse to hire women over 30. When war came, however, a garment factory faced an acute labor shortage—and a psychologist set about changing things.

The psychologist's arguments and actual production figures for over-30 workers failed to move management. So he tried an end-run: he persuaded them to make a study of the amount of money they were losing by employing older women. On each of the 4 areas where management perceived the over-30 group as being poorer, the group actually proved superior:

	Age Group		
	16–20	21–25	Over-30
Output achieved, as percentage of standard	95%	93%	112%
Output level reached after 96 hours training	40%		50
Average rate absenteeism	13	9	8
Percentage annual turnover	64	37	19–29

Management was convinced; it now faced the job of convincing its foremen. A typical supervisor, when questioned about each of the older workers in her unit, said they were among her best workers, but neither her own testimony nor the research itself could overcome her objections to the firm's new policy of hiring women over 30. It took several discussions among the foremen to get them to agree to an experiment in hiring older workers. A year later when a new engineer joined the staff, he showed the original stereotype—and clung to it despite the figures he was shown and the views of the firm's psychologist, personnel manager, plant manager and president.

—Alfred J. Marrow and John R. P. French, Jr., "Changing a Stereotype in Industry," *Journal of Social Issues*, 1:3: 33–37.

parts and assigning each part to a different person, one with special ability already or one who develops special ability through experience, groups can often produce more gadgets in a given period than the same number of individuals working separately. However, the time used in planning, assigning jobs, supervising, and coordinating must be added into the total for a fair comparison.

Effectiveness varies with the goal—and an outside observer, the head of an organization, and its members all may have different goals. Rewards can be defined only in relation to the goals of the person rewarded; both the amount of a reward and its nature depend on the individual. An individual's value for the reward received varies with the amount he expects. The amount he expects, in turn, depends upon three things. First of all, it depends upon his level of aspirations (Sears). Each time a person succeeds, he tends to raise his level of expectations; each time he fails, he tends to lower it, so that expectations tend to stay close to actual performance. Second, the rewards expected from a group depend upon the rewards which other organizations offer or the rewards which can be gained through alternative activities. Third, it depends on the rewards received by his peers. The individual who fails to receive rewards gained by his peers suffers from "relative deprivation" (Merton, 227–236). Thus it becomes important to know at any given moment who an individual is comparing himself to.

Most of us, for example, tend to compare ourselves with persons of higher rather than lower status. There is some evidence that persons with low status tend to compare themselves with high-status persons within the same organization (Krech, Crutchfield, Ballachey, 461). Since the gap is greater in large organizations, low-status persons within them tend to be less satisfied than persons at the bottom of small organizations. It also appears that persons of high status tend to compare themselves with persons of equivalent status outside the organization. Persons of high status in small organizations, viewing the sizable gap that separates them from the leaders of large organizations, tend to be relatively dissatisfied. Those at the head of large organizations, seeing no one much ahead of them, tend to be satisfied.

Costs and Expectations

Rewards, of course, cannot be measured apart from their costs. Although we have not said so, it is not rewards which determine man's behavior. A man may not seek the best advice available, because it would cost too much. He may avoid consulting a formal superior, because this involves the risk of acknowledging that he needs advice. He may avoid consulting a person of high status in his informal group, since this enhances the status of the person he consults and reduces his own status. Instead, he may go to a peer, someone who will both give and accept advice, since this minimizes the costs.

The problem of costs has two interesting and unexpected aspects. Given two activities with equal rewards, a man will choose the one with the lower costs. Once a man has made a choice, however, the process works in reverse. The higher the costs of the activity, the more he is likely to value its rewards; balance is achieved, says dissonance theory, by putting a higher value on the group which has high dues or a rigorous initiation (Aronson and Mills).

Moreover, the costs of an activity are not just the effort or time a man gives to it, but these costs as measured against the man's alternative uses of time and effort. A man with many opportunities expects higher rewards for a given activity than a man with few; not only does he expect them, but other members of society acknowledge his right to them. The situation is not without tension, however. Groups with few opportunities may feel that the rules of the game should be changed. Women and Negroes may feel that men and whites in general should not have more opportunities for employment. Nevertheless they tend to direct their resentment at the situation in general rather than an individual beneficiary of it. Tension also arises through conflict between different measures of cost. A man's experience, as reflected in seniority, may entitle a man to higher reward but his lack of mobility and of alternative opportunities may prevent him from getting it. The personal ability of a role occupant may not be congruent with the status of his role. Since organizations assign rewards on the basis of status, however, he may get appropriate rewards only by a change of role or status.

When rewards meet a member's expectations, he tends to identify with the organization. These rewards may be common to all members, as is likely when the organization is large, has an identifiable product, or has high prestige. Or they may be limited to some members, as when a member has high mobility within an organization, perceives that he is accepted by the other members, and engages in a good deal of interaction with them. Identification also increases with length of membership. An organization whose members identify with it and with one another is called "cohesive," and a cohesive organization is likely to be effective in task performance and, also, in providing the rewards of group maintenance. A cohesive group is one that is attractive to its members. A group may be attractive to a member because it has prestige, because he likes the other members (group maintenance), or because he finds the group helps him attain a personal goal (task performance). When these three sources of attraction are manipulated in the laboratory, members of cohesive groups show more influence on one another and make more effort to reach an agreement (Back). When cohesion is based on liking, members talk a lot. When it is based on prestige, they are more cautious. When it is based on task performance, they are more impersonal. Cohesion improves communication and communication clarifies the areas where the group expects conformity and serves as a channel for pressures which enforce conformity.

Three Focuses of Interest

There are three aspects of group-member relations which concern us. One is the effects which members have upon an individual. Group pressure to conform, seen most clearly when we look at the deviant member, is one such effect. If promises of reward fail to hold him in line, threats of punishment may. Punishment itself may drive him out of the group, however, unless he is prevented from leaving. Although a mixture of rewards and penalties may hold him in line by producing anxiety which makes him conform, anxiety may simultaneously make him a less productive member of the group.

Another effect, to be discussed in the next chapter, is that of role differentiation; through interaction with other members, the individual tends to specialize, engaging in fewer activities but becoming more expert in those he does engage in. A third effect is the control which members exercise over their leaders. A leader must be better than his members and ahead of them—but not too much better or too far ahead, lest his followers fail to understand him or despair of following in his footsteps. If a new leader is introduced into an existing group, he will have to spend a good deal of time learning the existing goals and methods of its members (Merei).

Another focus of interest is on the way an individual affects the members of a group. Such effects are most visible in the action of a leader. They are easy to see since most of us are source oriented and tend to take the influence of the leader for granted, failing to realize that he, in turn, is limited by his members. Although he cannot get members to perform tasks which are beyond them, he may be able to motivate and train individual members, or to encourage specialization which enables them to surpass their existing level of performance.

Interaction between a leader and a member represents a kind of bargaining process, again based on the ability of each to reward and penalize the other. Which side has more influence depends not only on the native ability of each but on other kinds of power as well. Members may have power to depose the leader, to resist without being detected, until he resigns or is removed, or to leave the group so that he ceases to be a leader because he has no one left to lead.

A third focus of interest may be in the *processes* by which one member of a group influences other members when the group must arrive at a decision. Peers bargain with one another as well as with group leaders. Since many persons assume that the dice are loaded in favor of a leader, however, the process is seen most clearly in groups which have no leader imposed on them from outside, in a group whose members start off on a formal plane of equality.

In an organization, members may remain equals in a formal sense because of external controls; predicting decisions, however, will require that one know which of the "equals" has won most decisions in the past and whose decisions have proved most rewarding to the group of decision makers. In effect, therefore, we will get two different status structures: one formal and one reflecting relative influence upon decisions. In a small group, which has no formal structure imposed from outside, status differences still arise; they reflect members' relative effectiveness in influencing decisions.

Decision Making

Each decision consists of a choice among alternatives, one or more of which are more or less consistent with the goals of each of the members of the coalition (Cyert and March). Two questions concerning the decision among these alternatives are of interest, although neither of them can be more than mentioned here.

First, what determines the number of alternatives that are considered? Of all the possible choices, which are actually discussed? The task itself limits the choice, as do the biases of the several members, the influence of their superiors, and the organization's incentive system. (Only those alternatives which will be rewarding under the payment schedules of the firm will be considered.)

Second, what kinds of influence can each member bring to bear in support of his favorite alternative? There are three major kinds of influence: First is the pressure inherent in his role and status. Some problems, for instance, are felt to fall mainly in the sphere of the controller. The vice president for marketing, on the other hand, will have more voice, by reason of his status, than the sales and advertising managers who are his subordinates. Second is the pressure involved in the member's personal attributes; one occupant of a given role may be able to exert more pressure than another. Third is the pressure which arises from a member's ability to form coalitions with other members of the decision-making group.

Ultimately, a member's influence rests on his ability to reward and punish. Either his contribution increases a group's chances to gain rewards, or he can influence the way in which rewards are divided among the members. The man who is recognized as an expert often exercises power within a limited range by his contribution to the rewards of task performance. The person who others like to associate with tends to have more pervasive influence, since he can provide group maintenance rewards no matter what task the group is engaged in performing. If the ability to bestow rewards is given the man by his general social status or by his specific role and status in the organization, such "legitimacy" tends to increase its influence.

Finally, the communications techniques by which this influence is expressed in decision making may enhance or diminish the effects. The extent to which a member builds support and feels out opposition before a meeting is part of the picture. So are his use of others as spokesmen in the meeting itself; his skill in listening to the feelings of others in the meeting, in separating what they say from why they say it; and his ability to persuade. His skill in assaying the relative power of each member of the group and each member's willingness to exert it at the moment are important. So is his ability to suggest solutions which satisfy enough of the needs of enough of the decision makers to get a majority of his side.

If the decision-making group includes members of a single organization, a man's influence depends in part on the role and status which he occupies and in part on the man himself. If the decision-making group includes members of different organizations, however, a member's influence depends on the role and status of his organization, as well as the man's own role and status and his personal qualities.

Size is one index to an organization's influence. In national consumer advertising, for example, the client firm is likely to be large. Advertising media vary greatly but tend to be smaller in terms of resources, than the national firms whose advertisements they carry. However, an individual advertiser tends to be less important to most media than that same advertiser is to its advertising agency. We would expect the agency to have the least influence on decisions, for this reason, if size were the only criterion. On the other hand, to the extent that the agency can limit communications between medium and advertiser, it will gain influence on advertiser decisions. A salesman, although relatively low on the organization chart of his own firm, may represent a company which is very much larger than the buyer's firm.

Organizations and Roles

Using the organizational chart as a map of communications channels within the firm, we have seen how each position on the chart represents a gatekeeper who controls the flow of messages up and down the chart. We have also taken a look at horizontal communications among peers and discussed how they are affected by restrictions on the free flow of messages. It is now time to ask why organizational charts exist, and why a firm's employees perform different functions or roles which require them to be mapped on such a chart.

Specialization, as we shall see in the next chapter, is basic not only to organizations but to communication itself, since coordination is necessary when men specialize, and coordination is accomplished through communication.

Specialization is a characteristic of all modern life, not just of the business firm, and each one of us performs several specialized roles. There are advantages in specialization, but there are problems, too, and it is time we examined them.

SUMMARY

1. Categories of individuals with similar characteristics make up audiences. If the individuals interact with one another they are either a group or an organization. Groups tend to be small, short lived, and emphasize group maintenance rather than task performance. Groups may become organizations; organizations contain groups within themselves. To a communicator, messages shape groups but organizations shape messages.

2. Groups facilitate communications among peers both within an organization and between organizations. When an executive communicates with outsiders, he has two channels of advancement: within his own firm and by employment elsewhere. These channels are open to any person of high visibility, including the man whose reputation is made within a profession rather than solely in his employer's own organization.

3. The organizational chart represents a map of communications channels permitted to the members of a firm. By prescribing the audience, it simplifies the messages that may be transmitted. Like other rules governing behavior, it tends to reduce the tension associated with the relationship of superior and subordinate.

4. Each position on such a chart represents a gatekeeper, who must modify the orders that he receives from above before passing them on and select from the reports he receives from below material to pass on to his superior. Since bypassing a gatekeeper would

threaten him, his receivers can do so only indirectly. Subordinates can do so through the peer group; superiors can use the same method and, in addition, depend on competition among their subordinate gatekeepers. Informal communications may aid or hurt the firm itself.

5. Audiences on informal channels tend to be peers, rather than persons of higher and lower status, as on the formal channels. Messages on formal channels tend to be task centered; those on informal, group channels tend to have group maintenance as their goal. Groups vary in their ability to provide these two kinds of rewards; homogeneous groups being better at group maintenance. Individuals vary in the value they place on these two kinds of rewards and in their ability to perform these two kinds of activities. Both functions tend to be united in a single leader in a formal organization, but split among two or more leaders in an informal group.

6. A free flow of communications enhances productivity by providing both support and criticism for members of a group and encouraging competition among them. Differences in status tend to inhibit communications by inducing unequal participation. Such differences increase with group size and longevity.

7. Size and longevity also decrease variety among members; variety is functional for tasks and dysfunctional for others. Groups induce conformity by screening cues, interpreting ambiguous cues, and putting direct pressure on deviants.

8. An effective group, from a member's standpoint, is one which provides him with the kind of reward he wants in an amount consistent with his level of aspirations, the amount received by his peers, and the amount available from alternative sources. A member is attracted to a group which rewards him; such a group is said to be cohesive.

9. Members of a group may affect an individual by forcing him to conform and by assigning him a role which limits the scope of his activities. The effects of an individual on other members are seen most clearly in the case of leaders who may raise the level of group performance. The freedom of any leader, whether imposed on a group from outside or emerging from the group itself, is limited by his members. The leader's power is exhibited in and affected by the decision-making history of the group. This history is best observed in a group of formal equals, typical of the top executives in a business firm.

10. Members of the decision-making group in a business organization tend to be in competition with one another; the alternative which rewards one member penalizes another. Students must ask what forces select the limited number of alternatives that are considered and what kinds of influence each member can exert on the group due to his role and status, his personal qualities, and his ability to form coalitions with other members. His influence may depend upon his position with a firm or the position of his organization *vis-a-vis* those of the other members.

Research Studies

Two kinds of face-to-face communications were examined in these studies: those among members of informal groups designed by an outsider to change attitudes and behavior and the messages exchanged by members of business firms in performing their jobs.

Marrow and French reported the use of discussion among supervisors in a garment factory to change attitudes toward hiring of older workers; *Lawrence and Smith* reported that goal setting but not discussion increased output of office workers.

Three different methods of studying communications in the firm were reported. *Burns* found that four executives, who recorded all their communications, spent 80 per cent of their time in conversation, only a third of it directly concerned with production. *Landsberger*, who depended on actual observations of three executives, found variations among departments, with horizontal communications (that is, to peers) highest among salesmen. *Albaum* reported a field experiment involving a rumor planted with a firm's customers, to find how good a channel for incoming information its salesmen were.

To those who view business decisions as the outcome of temporary coalitions among top executives, *Gamson* offered three different coalition-forming strategies and suggested the circumstances appropriate to each.

Ten

The Effects of Role
on Source and Receiver

• FOR AN HOUR, Don Dooley directs the drama. His cast is small: father, mother, and son. The scene is simple: a middle-class living room, the television screen momentarily dark, and the three actors seated around a coffee table. The plot is simple: Dooley has directed it hundreds of times before. The actors improvise their lines as they go along, as Dooley gives them their cues. But the responses are predictable; Dooley could speak them himself, and be right nine times out of ten.

The play begins with talk about the weather and reference to a mutual acquaintance, then shifts smoothly to talk of life and its hazards, of death and the complications it brings. The pace is varied: now hurried, now relaxed. Moods shift gradually: from indifference and reluctance to brief anxiety, to hope, to a sense of relief. A question from Dooley brings each of his actors into the conversation. Each answer—he knows them by heart—moves the actors toward a climax. Dooley brings them on stage and he takes them off again, so subtly that each actor thinks he himself has decided his entrances and his exits.

Every objection advances the plot: some are met head-on, others must wait for an answer until a more appropriate moment, and some are never answered. But the play moves inevitably to its conclusion. Son, wife, and husband balk, differ, question, object, only to concur, agree, come together, and make a decision. They buy—no Dooley sells them—a $20,000 insurance policy on the son's life.

• HALF AN HOUR LATER, Dooley is playing a part in a different kind of drama. This time the setting is an automobile dealer's salesroom. Two actors are on stage. Dooley and the automobile salesman, re-enacting the classic western drama of a fellow and his partner, threatened by a brooding offstage menace. The menace in this case, the sales manager, threatens to give Dooley a ridiculously low allowance on the car he plans to trade in on a new model. This play is briefer than the earlier one, for rapport builds up quickly as the two salesmen swap tales of their exploits with common enemies—customers and sales managers. It ends the same way, however: the prospect, Dooley, buys. Afterwards the car salesman and his manager agree they have just put on another successful performance of an ancient plot.

● AN HOUR LATER, Dooley takes part in still another play. This time he has few lines to speak, but he knows what is up the minute he steps through his front door. The hi-fi set is playing Mozart. There is no teen-aged son lounging in his favorite chair, and sounds from the kitchen tell him that shortly his wife will enter, stage left, with a cooling drink in her hand. This time it is the wife who provides the cues. She starts by giving Dooley a chance to brag a little about the sales he has made today. Then, with effortless transition, she compliments him on what a good father he is.

Fifteen minutes later, the suspense having built up to a high point, she announces that she has decided to buy their son a $395 saxophone so he can play in the school band. With that she and Dooley, he wondering whether this is the appropriate time to announce that he has just bought a new car, start for the supper table.

One Man, Many Roles

Salesman and customer, husband and father—four roles to play in half that number of hours. In the first role, Dooley was a source of messages which influenced a family's decision about insurance. In his second role, he was a receiver and decision-maker himself for messages from a car salesman. In his third role he was a silent partner in a decision-making group, being given a chance to veto his wife's decision—if he dared take it. Four roles in all, yet they represent only a small part of Dooley's repertoire.

All day long men play roles and the roles they play shift constantly. A marketing communicator will succeed to the extent that he makes his messages consistent with the roles his receivers are enacting at the moment of exposure. Sometimes a communicator can do this by context. He will broadcast a commercial for cake mixes during a woman's working hours and surround it with a program which emphasizes duty rather than self-indulgence. He will put an advertisement for diapers in a magazine whose editorial content makes the role of parent salient in its readers' minds. Sometimes he will do this in his message itself by addressing it to parents, or to men who want to get ahead, or to girls who, although often bridesmaids, have never achieved the role of bride.

Everyone plays many roles, some of which are more favorable to a given product than others. The advertiser needs to know how his prospects define their roles if he is to sell his product to them.

The Good Housewife versus Instant Coffee

One of the chief rewards a woman receives in her role as housewife is praise for her skill as a cook. One of the chief threats to her role as cook is the wave of products which require no skill at all to prepare.

She may say that prepared foods "do not taste as good" as others, although neither she nor anyone else may be able to tell them apart. But what she says may rest upon a half-sensed threat to her role from the "instant" foods and mixes.

One way to reach such hidden feelings is to ask questions not about products but about the people who *use* products. Mason Haire did this in 1950, when he asked 50 housewives to describe the woman who made out this shopping list:

> Pound and a half of hamburger
> 2 loaves of Wonder bread
> Bunch of carrots
> 1 can Rumford's Baking Powder
> Nescafe instant coffee
> 2 cans Del Monte peaches
> 5 lb potatoes

He compared their responses to the answers of another group of 50 housewives who got the same list with one substitution: 1 lb Maxwell House coffee (drip grind) instead of Nescafe.

Almost half of the women who saw the list with instant coffee on it described the woman who drew it up as being lazy and a poor planner; some added that she was a spendthrift and a poor wife. Very few of the women who got the list with drip grind coffee on it used such words about the hypothetical shopper.

Haire's next step was to ask whether housewives who themselves used instant coffee were more favorable to the hypothetical housewife of the shopping list. He checked respondents' pantries and found that 32 of the housewives who got the Nescafe list had instant coffee on their own shelves. And 72 per cent of the comments which these housewives made were favorable, compared with only 21 per cent of those made by the

18 housewives who did *not* have instant coffee on their shelves. (His study could not indicate whether use of instant coffee was a *result* or a *cause* of the favorable attitudes.)

—Mason Haire, "Projective Techniques in Marketing Research," *Journal of Marketing,* 14:649–656.

Seven years after Haire's study, 3 men at Northwestern University tackled the same problem by a slightly different method. They asked 177 housewives what kind of coffee they had made most recently— percolator, drip, vacuum, instant, or "other." Then they gave their subjects phrases describing 19 different types of housewives and asked them to pair each phrase with one of the various ways of making coffee. Again, the "good planner" who "cares for her family" was said not to use instant coffee, while the "worst cook I know" and the woman who "dislikes to cook" were said to use instant coffee. Although 58 per cent of the respondents who themselves used instant coffee called users "thrifty" only 28 per cent of nonusers agreed.

—Ralph L. Westfall, Harper W. Boyd, Jr., and Donald T. Campbell, "The Use of Structured Techniques in Motivation Research," *Journal of Marketing,* 22:134–139.

The success of a communicator can be seen by looking at any woman's shopping list. On it there will be the perfume of a manufacturer who succeeded in appealing to her in her role as wife and enchantress. There will be the brand of oatmeal which appealed to her in her role as mother. There will be olives, appropriate to her role as bridge club hostess. And when she leaves the shopping center, there may be an impulse item in her car, bought because she plays, when her other roles allow it, the role of an individual. All day long she and her husband play a variety of roles. Sometimes the roles they play are set by habit; sometimes they make a deliberate choice.

On the job, Dooley, who is talking to the sales manager, changes quickly from his role of employee, when the telephone rings and he hears a prospect's voice on the other end of the line. He changes again at lunchtime to become one of the boys with his fellow salesmen—all three roles, of course, are part of his job as salesman. On the way to lunch he meets a fellow board member of the Parent-Teacher Association and temporarily lapses into his roles as PTA-member-and-officer, with overtones of his role as parent. Sometimes he plays several roles at once; sometimes he plays them in sequence.

When Dooley's at work his job tends to limit the range of roles from which he must choose and to set priorities within his range. When Dooley comes home at night, however, his range of choice widens. He may act the role of an executive and retreat to his den with an attache case of papers until dinner is ready. He may become a father who plays softball with his son or a husband who sits down for a talk with his wife. He may act the role of a home owner, who looks over the month's bills, or that of a good neighbor, who gets out his lawnmower and starts to mow the backyard. The range is wide and the priorities are not clear.

Other Actors Define Role

Dooley is, in large part, the roles he plays. He has only limited freedom to determine what roles he will play or how he will play them, however. His setting and his audience limit this freedom. Even more important in limiting his freedom are the other actors in each scene he plays—the persons we call the "role set." In life, there are very few one-man performances; most roles can be performed only with the help, or the hindrance, of other persons. To be a mother, a woman must have a child; to be a wife, she must have a husband; to be a salesman, a person must have a customer.

No two performances of any given role are ever identical. No two salesmen operate in exactly the same way even with the same customers, and every salesman will adapt his presentation, however slightly, as he moves from one customer to the next. An observer can concentrate on the differences in role performances or he can ignore the differences and treat them as identical. A vice president for marketing, for example, will be interested in what salesmen have in common when he apportions a budget between selling and advertising. A sales manager, however, in screening applicants for sales positions, will concentrate on the differences in the ways in which individuals perform the role of salesman.

Arbitrary Definitions

The definition of what constitutes a role is an arbitrary one. If interested in comparing groups, an observer will note how the role of members of one group differs from the role of members of the other. In this case he will ignore role differences within either group. On the other hand, he may be interested in the differences in roles within a group: leader and follower, different types of leaders, and so on. In the former case, the role set of any given role occupant consists of persons performing similar roles. All are members. In the latter case, the role set consists of persons performing different roles. The leader must have followers, the salesman must have customers, the teacher must have students.

Earlier we suggested that Dooley, in his job as a life-insurance salesman, performed three different roles: employee, communicator, and member of a peer group with his fellow salesmen at lunch. Each of these roles can, in turn, be further subdivided. Within the peer group, for example, Dooley may play a role as leader or clown. On the other hand, if studying the life insurance company itself, he may want to speak of the role of the salesman in it, and ignore the salesman's subroles as employee, communicator, and peer-group member.

Three different sets of expectations influence Dooley's behavior: those of the members of his role set, as he perceives them; those of "outsiders," again as he perceives them; and what he expects of himself and others. As a child, Dooley's expectations concerning himself reflected the expectations of others—more or less accurately. In time, however his expectations become more independent of others and often a less accurate reflection of their views. Dooley himself changes. The scrawny youngster who becomes an athlete may still think himself unattractive to the opposite sex. Dooley's associates change or he moves into other groups, but his perceptions of what others expect of him may not change. If his family rejected him, he may anticipate rejection elsewhere; if his family accepted him, he may take acceptance in other groups for granted. Since his expectations of acceptance or rejection provide cues to his associates as to how they should behave toward Dooley, his prophecy of how they will behave toward him may become self-confirming.

Acts, Attitudes, Interaction

Expectations by self, by role set, and by outsiders vary with time and place, and they apply to three types of behavior: Dooley's acts, his attitudes, and his interaction with others. These expectations tend to be quantified. They permit a range of acts, attitudes, and interactions, rather than demanding a specific act, attitude, or interaction. In short, in discussing role performance we must determine the extent to which expectations overlap for three types of behavior among three participants (self, role set, outsiders) for a given time and place.

We must also know which acts, attitudes, and interactions are required, which are permitted, and which are forbidden to the occupants of a given role. And we must know how society specifies who is eligible to occupy a given role and how a choice is made from among those who are eligible. (An individual not content with the roles available to him may try to change the definition of a role itself, the listing of eligibles or the way an occupant is chosen.)

Eligibility for a Role

Eligibility is usually determined by three things: physiology, experience, and individual choice.

Physiology

Sex, of course, is basic. One must be a woman to be a wife and mother, although many women are neither. In most societies men tend to specialize in the functions of task performance and women in those of group maintenance, but societies differ in the way they assign occupational roles to the sexes. In the United States, for example, women are more likely than men to become typists, teachers, and dental technicians, but less likely than men to become lawyers, doctors, or sandhogs. In Russia, however, more women than men serve as physicians; Russian women also sweep streets, a job that in the United States is strictly for men. Eligibility differs with time as well as place. Early in this century, typists in the United States were men rather than women. With the return of veterans to the campus, after World War II, a temporary but drastic reversal of roles took place. Wives began working to support student husbands, and husbands combined cooking and baby sitting with their studies.

Age is significant because it forces a change of roles upon men as they pass out of childhood into adulthood and, finally, into retirement. This means that every individual is continually preparing for new roles. Sometimes he is taught them rather specifically. This tends to be true of the occupational roles within an organization, although even then some of the most important aspects of such roles may never be expressed in so many words. It also occurs when college students enroll in a course in marriage and the family. Sometimes, however, a person has little chance to learn a role until he actually begins to perform it. Sometimes he has a chance to learn by observing others in the role.

When this country was largely a farming country, boys and girls could learn their future occupational roles by watching their fathers and mothers. Indeed, they could and did assist them in their parents' work, so that there was no sharp change from childhood through adolescence to adulthood but continuity of roles (Benedict). At present this is, to some extent, still true of girls, but most boys have very little chance to see their fathers at work or to lend a hand. Many societies have more continuity of roles than ours does; our society used to have more continuity than it does today.

This lack of continuity applies to attitudes, too, of course, as well as to acts and interaction. A boy, who in his preschool years has been expected to inhibit his aggressive impulses in the home, now is expected to be reasonably aggressive with his playmates at school and to learn how place and time affect role behavior. The parents, who have tolerated careless work habits from a boy attending an undemanding high school, suddenly show alarm when a college, which expects a student to show self-disciplined study from the start, sends home his first grade reports.

If roles change drastically, a ceremony, which signalizes the change, makes the change easier. (Sociologists call such a ceremony a "rite of passage"—the passage being from one role and status to another.) Tribal initiation ceremonies represent such a rite; so does the marriage ceremony. Ceremonial induction following a formal period of training is characteristic of the military, medical, and legal professions. Most firms indoctrinate new employees, and most colleges orient freshmen. The first child, the first grandchild, or the first job are also fairly dramatic events that signalize a change in role.

Often, however, the change is less dramatic and less clearly marked. In the United States, for example, a teen-ager will not know where he stands for years. At home, he may have to behave like an adult, particularly where duties are involved. If he seeks adult privileges, however, he may suddenly discover that he is still regarded as a child. As home becomes unrewarding, he tends increasingly to turn to the society of his peers, to other teenagers who can help him learn the new role and give him the emotional support needed in such learning.

Experience

Two types of experience influence role eligibility. One is the experience of formal training. To an increasing extent American employers are requiring a high school diploma as a condition of employment, even on jobs where no objective need for it can be demonstrated.

Formal training both tests and influences the ability of an individual to perform the duties of the role, since the training process gives him a clearer picture of what those duties are. The second type of experience is informal contact with role occupants, and the chance such contact gives to observe their behavior. Experience of this kind informs an individual of the kind of roles available, their costs and rewards. It thus affects his level of aspirations for both jobs and the training necessary to achieve them. Anything which limits an individual's informal contacts with adults restricts his subsequent choice of adult roles. This tends to be true of all American males today, and it is true in an acute form of children in lower income families, particularly children in Negro families. Children whose parents and parents' friends have only unskilled jobs are unlikely to know that other jobs exist and to aspire to them or to know what abilities are required and whether they have such abilities.

What effect does social class have on a young man's desire to rise in the world? Does it give him the attitudes which will help or hinder his upward mobility?

Social Class Inspires, Aids Achievement

To answer this question, Rosen divided the students of two New Haven high schools into 5 social classes, on the basis of their fathers' occupation and education and the neighborhood in which they lived.

Then, using a slide projector, he showed groups of 20 to 30 students pictures of the Thematic Apperception Test type and asked students to write stories about the pictures. Students who wrote stories which evaluated performance and expressed an emotion in regard to it, were considered to be motivated to achieve. (*Example.* "The girl has failed in an exam and feels miserable as a result.")

Finally, students were asked to fill out a 14-item questionnaire, agreeing or disagreeing with 3 values assumed necessary to success. Here are examples:

Value. It is possible and necessary for an individual to improve his status in society.

Question. All I want out of life . . . is a secure, not too difficult job, with enough pay to afford a nice car . . . . (Disagreement indicates motivation to rise.)

Value. Present sacrifices are necessary to future gains.

Question. Nowadays with world conditions the way they are the wise person lives for today . . . .

Value. Family ties must give way to individual mobility.

Question. Nothing in life is worth the sacrifice of moving away from your parents.

Two judges scored student stories; high scores, indicating a high need to achieve, were characteristic of classes I and II, the higher social classes. Similarly, students in these classes had higher scores on all three of the values assumed necessary to success. Here are the percentages in each class with high scores:

Percentage in Class with High Scores on

	Achievement Motivation	Value Orientation
I and II	83%	77%
III	43	70
IV	30	33
V	23	17

Motivation scores, but not value scores, were related to school grades; value scores, but not motivation scores, were related to the desire to attend college.

Percentage in Group with High Scores

	Achievement Motivation	Value Orientation
High school average B or above	69%	54%
Desire to go to college	51	61

—Bernard C. Rosen, "The Achievement Syndrome: A Psychocultural Dimension of Social Stratification," *American Sociological Review*, 21:203–211.

To some extent the mass media can extend a child's horizons, but usually only deliberate efforts by teachers in face-to-face relationships can widen job horizons. To the extent that ability is a product of both physiology and experience it represents a mixture of these two kinds of limit on role eligibility.

It is never possible to teach formally all the rights and duties involved in any role. The more important a role, the less specific the teaching tends to be; important roles seem to be learned rather than taught. This is true of the roles of customer and of parent. Occasionally a home economics course will teach girls about textiles, but most college girls do not take such courses, and such courses rarely concern themselves with comparing brands. Publications such as Consumer Reports and Consumer Bulletin provide information about products and their prices, but their subscribers represent only a small part of the population—a part whose education already equips them to be better at bargaining than the ordinary customer, even without the aid of consumer organizations.

Perhaps such roles as customer and parent are too important to be trusted to an outside teacher. Perhaps an outside teacher is unnecessary, since we learn to be a parent and a customer continuously and from an early age so that teaching of the role cannot be restricted to a specific time or place. The scope of the rights and duties involved in such roles is so wide and the skills needed require so much practice that it would be difficult to include them all in any formal training. The very ambiguity with which the roles are defined permits flexibility, so that role definitions can adjust to the individual role occupant and change easily over time for society in general. Formal training and written specifications might reduce this flexibility.

Experience, we have said, differs in the degree to which it is organized into formal training. It also differs in its degree of generality. Some experiences are common to all members of a given society at a particular time in history; others are common to all members of a class within society. Still others are highly individual. The son of a dominating father may, in later years, perform the role of father in a domineering manner. Of two sons in the same family, the younger is likely to find his parents more relaxed, through what they have been taught about the parental role by their first child. Growing up in a relaxed atmosphere, the second child himself is likely to be more relaxed in later life. Meanwhile, the first son who now has to share parents he once had to himself, may become anxious and tense. In short, personal experience affects a person's eligibility for a role by the attitudes and behaviors it teaches him, and it also influences the way he will perform in that role. Older son and younger son both may become fathers, but they may become quite different types of fathers.

Choice

Experience also influences a person's attitudes, and these attitudes include his desires concerning role. Although both physiology and experience limit the choice of roles available to him, he does not aspire to all of the roles available. He may appear free to choose, but in actuality his choice may be determined for him by his experiences in ways of which he is unaware.

Roles differ from one another in several respects. Some have very specific and limited rights and duties attached to them; others are vague and unlimited. (The role of employee is specific as compared

to that of parent.) Some have a wide range of eligibility; others
have a narrow range. (Most persons can become parents, but not
many can become concert pianists.) Some roles combine easily; they
are "congruent." Others are not. (In the United States at present,
a priest of the Roman Catholic church cannot also be a husband
and a parent, but he can be a college president. We would be uneasy
if our physician were also an undertaker but find undertaking and
selling furniture congruent occupations.)

Four Major Roles

Four kinds of roles are of particular interest to the marketing
communicator. These are the roles associated with the family decision-making unit, those of husband and wife; the role of the employee;
roles in the informal group, and, above all, the role of customer.

Family

The roles of husband-father and wife-mother are difficult ones, because they involve highly diverse, virtually unlimited obligations.
Parents must feed and clothe their children, praise them and admonish
them, motivate them and teach them twenty-four hours a day, seven
days a week. The roles are also basic, in that others derive from
them. Most men would work less hard and less steadily, and some
would not work at all, if they were not husbands-and-fathers.

Society's survival depends upon communicating to each generation
the knowledge and values accumulated over time. Parents do much
of this job of communications and force the children to attend the
schools, churches, and other institutions which complete the job.
The family, the basic decision-making unit of society, interests both
politician and advertiser.

Employee

Although men and women take on the role of employee as a means
to an end, the means may become an end in itself. Dissonance operates,
and anything to which one gives a third of each day must be pretty
important. Over time, the value placed on rewards tends to increase,
even if the rewards themselves are unchanged.

Of course, as a man rises in a business organization, the rewards
become objectively as well as subjectively greater. The business may
demand more time, but whether or not it does, the executive is likely
to give more time to it and less time to his family. At upper levels,

there are increased opportunities for the firm to provide the rewards both of task performance and those of group maintenance which other men may receive from their families.

Informal Group Member

At lower levels in the firm, employees may seek rewards through membership in informal groups, either in the firm or outside. For some, informal groups may provide a chance to rise on the firm's organizational chart and a chance to gain the rewards of task performance. Others will seek the rewards of group maintenance by membership in informal groups, both within the firm and, after working hours, outside it.

Since most advertisements are prepared by one business organization (an advertising agency) on behalf of another business organization (a manufacturer) and transmitted through a third business organization (one of the mass media) to either households or a fourth business organization (a retailer or another manufacturer), the roles of employee and informal group member within the business organization are important to the marketing communicator. Such roles, however, were treated in the previous chapter, in the discussion of organizations. For that reason, let us turn now to the fourth role.

Customer

This role is of the greatest importance to the marketing communicator, who needs to know what customers expect of themselves and what they expect of the advertiser and the salesman. This is a role that involves bargaining over terms and price, and the making and meeting of contracts. An industrial society converts many of the role relationships that previously depended on kinship or friendship to relationships between a salesman and a customer. We expect people to do things not because they are friends or relatives, or because we have done them favors, but because we are willing to pay them for their services.

To an increasing extent, the group maintenance rewards obtainable through friendly interaction disappear from much of our daily life. Interaction becomes brief and impersonal. The housewife who in a more primitive society might spend an hour haggling in a market barely glances at the checkout girl in the supermarket. Relationships of this kind tend to extend to wider areas of human activity in a society such as ours and to be easily begun or ended so that the sheer number of buying transactions rises as the importance of any single transaction decreases.

How Much Interaction?

There are three different kinds of seller-buyer relationships, in two of which interaction is reduced to a minimum.

The first of these is that in which, due either to competition or administered prices, products and their prices are so uniform that no bargaining is possible. Buying skill is irrelevant. We might as well drop coins into a vending machine. The second is that in which each retail outlet has a fixed price, not subject to bargaining—but stores differ. A variant of this condition is that in which each store has a fixed price at any given moment, but prices change with the seasons. By waiting for clearance sales a canny customer can save money. Search and comparison by the customer is rewarding under such circumstances but again bargaining is impossible. Buying skills are relevant, but they are skills of knowing when and where bargains can be obtained and not the skills involved in bargaining.

The third kind of role relationships between buyer and seller appears in the purchase of appliances, automobiles, and other products whose prices are subject to bargaining. Here the hope of rewards is high, and these rewards include both those of rewarding interaction between buyer and seller (group maintenance) and obtaining increased satisfaction at decreased cost (task performance). But if the hope of rewards is high, so is the risk of penalties. Some customers may postpone a purchase or put it off altogether because of fear of unpleasant interaction or unsuccessful bargaining.

The eagerness with which a person assumes the role of buyer, when bargaining is possible, depends on two things: his definition of the situation and his perception of his own skill in bargaining. If he defines the relations between buyer and seller as representing a combat, in which anything goes, only the most aggressive and self-confident of persons is likely to assume the buyer's role. If he defines the relations as a friendly game, which tests the bargaining skills of each participant, a prospect's willingness to play reflects his perception of his ability. Most of us realize that the salesman has a stronger motivation to win, since his livelihood depends on "winning" most of the games he plays. He has the training, much of which consists of telling him how to seize and keep control of the sales interview. And he has the experience. It is an unusual customer who can come up with an objection the salesman has not heard, and turned to his advantage, a dozen times previously.

The basic role set in marketing communication is that of salesman and customer, each role being defined in terms of the other. Do variations in a customer's approach cause variations in the salesman's behavior? Here is a study dealing with the key question of price.

"Hard" Buy Wins Price Concessions

Customers trained to play 3 different roles called on all 30 new Ford dealers and all 28 new Chevrolet dealers within the Chicago city limits in a 10-day period in February 1959. One customer played a "soft" role, posing as someone who had just learned how to drive. Another played the role of a hardened shopper with a great deal of previous experience, whose only interest was in getting a good price. The third played an intermediate role, showing some experience and a moderate interest in price.

Of the 58 dealers visited, only 1 quoted the same price to all 3 shoppers. On the average, the "hard" approach got a lower price than the soft: $2577 versus $2610 for Fords and $2490 versus $2507 for Chevrolets. The difference was not statistically significant, however. It could have occurred by chance about 20% of the time.

Even more interesting, however, were the 23 cases in which the same salesman saw two test "customers." In 15 of these cases, the "harder" of the 2 approaches got lower prices, the direction of differences being statistically significant by the sign test. Four salesmen gave the same estimate to both customers. Four gave *lower* estimates to the "soft" approach; the "harder" message boomeranged—$5 to $10 for three Ford salesmen and $31 for a Chevrolet salesman.

Apparently the neighborhood in which the dealer was located and the number of years he had been in business did not affect his response to customers. Largest discounts were offered by the low-volume (500 cars a year) or high volume (over 1000 cars a year) dealers; those in-between averaged higher prices.

Neither customer nor salesman used the full range of bargaining techniques. Few salesmen offered demonstration rides or reasons for buying their make or from a particular dealer. They were least likely to do these things to the "hard" customers. Some 60% of salesmen took the prospect's telephone number, but only a third of these actually telephoned. Although salesmen might have tried to counter price bargaining by selling additional accessories, this happened in only 12 of the 174 sales interviews.

Customers, of course, could not bargain freely within the design of a controlled experiment. Each salesman had to be told that he was the first one who had been contacted, so the device of playing one dealer against another was not used. No trade-in was offered. Customers using the "hard" approach, however, countered the salesman's first offer with a counter-offer, set low enough so that it would be rejected, and then asked the salesman for his lowest price. In every case, this limited attempt at bargaining brought further reductions for the "hard" customer. In most cases, this customer had been offered a lower price to begin with; apparently salesmen did not boost their first offer, despite cues suggesting that they would have to bargain with this customer. (Dealers who quoted above-average prices to the "hard" customers were able to respond more generously to subsequent bargaining than those who quoted below-average prices: $94 compared with $33 for Ford dealers, $63 compared to $48 for Chevrolet dealers.) Markups for Ford dealers fell from 9.7%, the grand mean of all 90 prices obtained, (3 customers × 30 dealers) to 6.9% after bargaining by the "hard" customers. Chevrolet dealer markups fell from 8.3% to 6%. The author speculates that further bargaining would have meant still further price cuts and that a customer will gain more by bargaining with a dealer, after he has seen a few, than by continuing to see additional dealers.

To make sure that customers did not vary their approach from one dealer to the next, all three were given eight hours training in their roles. Each, of course, specified the same model. In the case of Chevrolet this was a $2969 factory-list V8 Bel Air four-door sedan with Powerglide transmission, airflow heater, manual radio, and 2-speed windshield washer. In the case of Ford, it was a $3043 factory-list Fairlane 500, 4-door sedan, V8, Ford-o-Matic transmission, with pushbutton radio, fresh-air heater, and windshield washer. Overall means were $2497 for Chevrolet and $2590 for Ford, medians were $2498 for Chevrolet and $2575 for Ford.

—Allen F. Jung, "Price Variations Among Automobile Dealers in Chicago, Illinois," *Journal of Business*, 32:315–326.

Skill in Bargaining

A customer's skill in bargaining depends on three things: his resources, his bargaining strategy, and his knowledge of the freedom of negotiation possessed by the seller.

The poor pay more because they have less freedom of action. They are less aware of alternative sources of supply, more dependent on credit, and lack the power and skills needed in bargaining. The rich pay more because they lack the time to bargain. They have resources and skills but alternative uses of their time are worth more than the savings they might achieve through bargaining. Thus it is the middle classes who have the resources and the motivation needed for bargaining.

As for strategy, several experiments have found that human beings and white rats often follow strategies which are not the best, whether they are aware of what they are doing or not. An experimenter may, for example, alter the proportions of red and black cards in a deck, so that numbers of the two colors are unequal. If he then turns the cards face up, one at a time, first asking the subject to predict which color will turn up next, the subject will soon start guessing "red" in a proportion equal to the actual proportion of red cards in the altered deck. The subject will not realize he is doing this, or, even if he is told, be able to say what proportion of his choices have been "red."

As a moment's thought will indicate, the optimum strategy given a deck in which red and black cards occur in unequal proportions and are presented in random order is to name the predominant card in every choice. Interestingly enough, if the subject is rewarded for his correct guesses by giving him small amounts of money and penalized by fining him small amounts, he does shift to this optimal strategy, without realizing he has shifted or how. Too little is known of most buyer-seller situations to specify what would be an optimal strategy, but it seems likely that many customers fail to employ it. Indeed, advertising and selling may seek to keep them from employing it!

Even given the resources needed for bargaining and a clearcut strategy, most customers lack the information needed for successful bargaining, particularly since the rules of the game themselves are vague and subject to frequent change. A customer, for example, rarely knows the amount of markup for an individual product, a class of products, or a type of retail outlet. Even if coded price tags contain this information, he cannot read them. Although the car is tagged with a factory-suggested list price, the automobile salesman still has room to maneuver both by adding accessories and by his evaluation of the trade-in. The home buyer faces an even more complicated mixture of location and structure, variations and accessories. Moreover, the range of maneuver open to the seller shifts with the season—new models are about to appear and the dealer's floor must be cleared—and with the year—building permits are down this year but overhead continues.

Motivation to Bargain and Buy

Finally, a customer's success in bargaining depends on the nature and intensity of his motivation to bargain and to buy. Low motivation to buy—the lack of any strong need or desire for the product—gives him an advantage, since he can always withdraw from the game without any serious loss to himself. High motivation to bargain, which causes him to use his resources and skill to the utmost, gives the buyer an advantage. Motivation to bargain is likely to be high if the customer regards the encounter with a salesman as a game of skill and a test of wits. Men, who in an earlier time might have gained prestige among their fellows by their skill in growing crops or fashioning spears with their own hands, now may boast of the bargains they bought and of how they outwitted the salesman on his own ground.

Less confident customers may fear to meet a salesman face-to-face; those who fear the "hidden persuasion" of an advertiser are even less likely to assume they have the skill to match wits with a salesman. The hesitant housewife makes a last-ditch defense on the threshhold of her home, fearing that if the salesman once gets inside she is a gone goose. Indeed, some of the advertising which is regarded as most unethical, such as the "bait" advertisement that offers a product which the store really does not plan to sell anyone, seeks to lure the prospect into waters where a salesman can hook him.

Salesmen's Skills and Limitations

The outcome of the bargaining encounter depends, of course, on the salesman's skill and resources, as well as those of the customer. Some sales clerks are mere order takers. In such cases, a self-service store which allows a customer to examine the merchandise at leisure, without feeling an obligation to buy, may find that the customer does a better job of selling himself than the inept clerk might do. Other retail salesmen show much skill in probing customers' preferences, in subtly directing them to a more expensive line than they originally planned to buy or to related merchandise so that a man who came in to buy a shirt, finds himself buying tie, socks, and handkerchief as well.

Marketing men seek to find and motivate such salesmen through selection, training, and methods of compensation. Some of them err, however, in failing to realize that selling involves several different functions, each of which requires different skills and techniques. Some err in supposing that a salesman should be selected to match a product rather than the customer who is being sold; they look for a man able to sell insurance, rather than a man who is able to sell insurance to physicians, lawyers, or other salesmen.

There are limits on the salesman's freedom to maneuver. If he is selling a product which is purchased frequently and whose qualities the customer feels competent to judge when he uses it, the salesman is likely to forego immediate shortrun gains in bargaining for the longrun advantage of repeat sales. If many competitors offer a similar product at a similar price, the customer's power in bargaining is increased. The customer who has many social contacts, a characteristic of middle- and upper-income groups, can use them as an information network, exchanging information about products and salesmen with other customers over these word-of-mouth channels. Talk about buying experiences make up a fair share of the social interaction among acquaintances, and trading buying tips constitutes much of the exchange of favors and mutual help through which friendships are built. The friend who really can "get it for you wholesale" is valued. The information friends give customers may be less accurate than that which the salesman provides through his formal channels, but the customer often trusts it more than he does the information that the salesman supplies. If so, it is more likely to influence the customer's bargaining behavior.

Congruence and Conflict

We said at the beginning of this chapter that successful communication requires that a source, advertiser, or salesman, know what roles are salient to his receiver at the time the marketing message is received. He must know more than this, however. He must know what roles the receiver has in his repertoire, which of the roles are consistent with the communicator's message, and how to evoke these roles in its support. One such role is the one that we have just explored—the role of customer. The communicator must know what the receiver, as prospective customer, expects both of himself and of the source. But this is only one of the roles to be evoked.

When an encyclopedia salesman calls on Don Dooley, for example, he hopes that Dooley's wife and children will be there, too. Their presence helps him remind Dooley of his obligations as husband and father; as a result, money that might have gone for fishing or hunting equipment ends up in the coffers of the encyclopedia publisher. Since the role of husband-and-parent involves so many obligations, and such obligations have such high priority, many communicators try to evoke this role. Membership in a Parent Teacher Association helps remind a man that he is a father who should vote for a school bond issue. Membership also exposes him to face-to-face messages, both at PTA meetings and from other members outside the meeting, and to printed messages which urge him to vote and to vote "the right way."

At the same time, there are other roles which are inconsistent with the aims of the communicator. At all costs, the encyclopedia salesman wants to keep Dooley from thinking of himself as a hunter or fisherman, and the advocate of the school bond issue wants to keep Dooley from thinking of his role as a taxpayer. This will be harder to do, of course, if Dooley is actually a member of a taxpayer association, as well as of PTA, and so exposed to messages which and people who urge defeat of the bond issue. Manufacturers of sports equipment are willing to spend a good deal of money, advertising in sportsmen's magazines and encouraging sportsmen's clubs, to remind Dooley that he likes to hunt and fish. They may even suggest that he owes it to his son to take him along—that this, too, is part of the duties of a parent. Too much conflict of this kind among sources is likely to make Dooley uncomfortable, to the point where he escapes by refusing to vote one way or the other, and is unwilling to spend his money for either encyclopedias or sports equipment.

Dooley has several devices by which he can minimize this conflict between roles (Breed). He may, for example, decide that bond issues are strictly a question of government finance and taxation, and have nothing to do with his obligations as a parent. Or he may have a very clear set of priorities, so that his obligations as parent automatically take precedence over all other duties. He may delay a decision hoping that the need for making a choice will go away, or that he can find a compromise which will satisfy the demands of both roles. Or he may make a choice, rejecting the claims of one of the roles.

The conflict between roles may occur within Dooley's mind, with only its outcome visible to an observer. On the other hand, it may be external. Members of the role set or of the group from which the role derives may bring pressure to bear on Dooley, as in the case of the PTA and the taxpayers league. Their effectiveness, of course, depends on the power which they possess and on the strength of their motivation to use such power. Their power over Dooley depends on how much Dooley values a particular role or membership in a particular group and on the extent to which its members can detect his failure to meet the obligations of that role or membership.

Dooley may be able to play off one group against the other, using the pressure from each to explain his deviant behavior to the other. He may join with other persons subject to similar pressures, thereby gaining the strength to resist them. He may be able to conceal his deviancy from others. Society itself throws a screen around some roles whose occupants might be unable to perform their functions if their performance could be observed. Thus the law recognizes privileged communications in law, medicine, and the ministry. The academic freedom of a college professor is protected by the comparative privacy of the classroom, as well as by the vigor of the American Association of University Professors.

"The Man in the Middle"

To some extent every role has conflict inherent in it since members of a role set are likely to disagree both among themselves and with the occupant of the role on how that occupant should act, interact, and feel. Some conflicts are avoidable: Dooley does not have to join both the taxpayers' association and the PTA. Others are not. The most acute form of conflict occurs when it is built into the role itself, as in the role of "the man in the middle," who must simultaneously belong to two groups if he is to perform the role at all. Most gatekeepers in the formal organization occupy such roles. The factory foreman, for example, must function both as a part of management and as one of the boys; the army sergeant is in a similar ambiguous position, not being fully accepted by either officers or by enlisted men.

Different kinds of power are brought to bear on the man in the middle (French and Raven). Superiors, for example, have formal authority to bestow rewards and penalties. Usually they are recognized as experts and the sanctions they exercise are usually regarded as legitimate. But subordinates are not without power of their own. They may offer the foreman and the sergeant the rewards of group maintenance; that is, friendly interaction. They may threaten him by withholding the cooperation he needs to accomplish the tasks his superiors have set for him; through "sabotage" subordinates can bring down upon the man in the middle punishment from his superiors.

Similar conflicts exist for another kind of "man in the middle"—the person who carries messages or mediates between the formal organization which employs him and outsiders. The newspaper reporter, the salesman, and the waitress are caught up in conflict of this kind. Each has an employer, from whom he may receive the rewards of task performance and, on occasion, those of group maintenance as well. The newspaper reporter must satisfy his editor, the salesman his employer, and the waitress the manager of the restaurant. Yet none of the three role occupants can meet these demands unless they also please outsiders. The reporter must gain the cooperation of his news source, the salesman that of his customer, and the waitress that of the hungry folk seated at her table.

These outsiders' demands are often at odds with those of the formal organization, yet they must be satisfied if the salesman, waitress, or reporter is to gain the rewards of task performance from his employer. Moreover, each of these "men in the middle" has more interaction with outsiders than with his employer. The immediate rewards of such interaction with outsiders may be higher than those of interaction with the employer, depending on the relative status of the two. (Interaction with persons of higher status, provided they are not the superiors in a formal organization, tends to be rewarding.)

The instrumental value of interaction with employer versus outsider as a means of improving one's own job status depends on whether the man-in-the-middle seeks to rise within his present organization or by shifting from one organization to another. Reporters can get jobs as public relations men with one of their news sources; salesmen can start working for one of their former customers; and waitresses may be able to marry the affluent patron. In such cases both types of reward are at a maximum when the role demands of the employer are flouted.

Two Sources of Conflict

Sometimes a distinction is made between the conflict which occurs because of differing expectations by members of one's role set and that which occurs because the role one occupies requires, as in the examples just cited, that one simultaneously be a member of two separate groups. This distinction is a tenuous one, however, because of the arbitrary nature of one's definition of role, which like any other definition, is a tool designed to perform a function. If the function varies, so must the definition.

A student who is also a proctor faces conflicting demands from the faculty which appoints him, since the faculty demands rigorous enforcement of rules against cheating, and from his fellow students, who favor leniency. A school board may expect a superintendent, as a member of the school administration, to keep teachers' salaries as low as possible; the teachers, in turn, expect him, as a member of the profession, to push them as high as possible. We can talk of a single student-proctor role, or of a single person who performs the two roles of student and proctor. Similarly, we can think of the superintendent as an occupant of one role, facing different demands from members of his role set, or as occupying two roles simultaneously, each involving different rights and duties. There is an important distinction in the two examples, however. The duties of student and proctor can be separated; we can and perhaps should use proctors who are not students. Splitting up the conflicting obligations of the superintendent is far more difficult. He needs the expert knowledge gained by being a member of the teaching profession. He needs the cooperation of the teachers and is rewarded by friendly interaction with them. (It seems safe to say, however, that the longer he is removed from teaching in time, and the further he is removed from teachers in space, that is, on an organizational chart, the less keenly

---

Occupants of many roles face conflicting demands. This study points out that these demands may overlap, but that individuals differ in the amount of overlap they perceive, and in their responses to it.

What Should a Proctor Do When He Detects Cheating?

In an anonymous questionnaire, 196 Harvard and Radcliffe students were asked to imagine they were proctoring an exam, saw a fellow student cheating, and that the student admitted it. They were asked to check a 5-point scale, indicating which of 5 actions they would take. These ranged in harshness from preventing him from completing the exam and reporting him for cheating to acting as if nothing had happened.

In all they answered this question 6 times:
1. The student was a stranger, and neither the authorities nor their own friends would know anything about the situation unless they themselves took action.
2. The student was a stranger and there was little chance their friends would find out—but a good chance that authorities would.
3. Next, they were asked how authorities and how their friends would feel about each of the 5 possible actions they might take.
4. Then they were asked how they would behave if the cheating student was their roommate and close friend.
5. Next the conditions of No. 2 were repeated but under the close-friend situation.
6. Finally question No. 3 was repeated under the close-friend condition.

The results showed that the students thought that the authorities would accept all but the 2 most-lenient positions (both of which let the cheating student finish the exam and failed to report him), but that authorities would take little account of the stranger-friend difference. Students indicated, however, that although few of their friends would expect them, as proctors, to take the most lenient course for a stranger, about 50% of them would expect them to follow this course for a cheating friend.

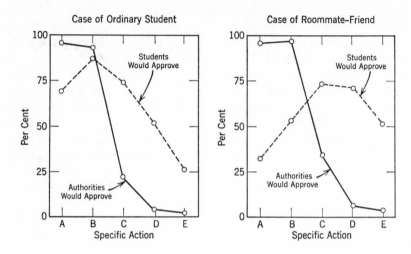

Fig. 10.1.

Most of the respondents fell into one of three types:

1. Twenty-one students thought the range of acts which authorities and their own friends would approve were identical; they perceived little conflict in the situation between demands of the 2 groups.
2. Fifty-six students saw no overlap at all between acts which authorities would approve and that which their friends would expect of them. Conflict for these students was extreme. All but 5 of this group said they would do what their friends expected, if authorities did not find out; 35 said they would do what their friends expected, even if authorities were likely to find out.
3. However, 119 students felt that there was at least one act they could perform, as proctor, which would be approved by both their friends and the authorities. However, only 36 of the 119 would actually choose this act if no one was able to observe the situation. If another proctor were present, however, 73 of the 119 said they would follow this course.

—Samuel A. Stouffer, "An Analysis of Conflicting Social Norms," *American Sociological Review*, 14:707–717.

he will feel pressures from them. The intensity of conflict diminishes but conflict itself is inherent in the role.) In marketing, a salesman may face conflicting demands from his customers and his employer and a system of compensation which serves the employer's ends may put the salesman at odds with his fellows. The account executive in the advertising agency is another man-in-the-middle, facing demands from superiors and subordinates within the agency, as well as demands from the client.

Two factors make the pressure upon a role occupant somewhat easier to live with than our discussion so far has suggested. The first is that the expectations of a role set are usually expressed as a range of behaviors, rather than as a specific act or attitude; the expectations are quantified. The other is that the persons in a role set, even those occupying the same role, differ in where their expectations fall within this range. Teachers, for example, differ among themselves in just how big an increase in teachers' pay they expect the superintendent to win for them, and how far they expect him to stick his neck out in fighting with the school board. Members of the school board, in turn, differ in their expectations. Somewhere within these two ranges, a superintendent can usually find some overlap, if necessary playing one teacher off against another, one board member against another, and using pressures from each group to justify his behavior to the other.

Most of us join organizations and groups after they have been formed and fill roles whose rights and duties have already been specified. The roles may change, and we may have a part in changing them, but our first task will be to learn them as they already exist. In the laboratory, however, groups can be brought into existence and the development of roles within them can be observed.

Observers find that specialization develops in such groups. Sometimes it is influenced by the native abilities or the previous affiliations of the members. Sometimes it arises because of the type of communications permitted to the group or the tasks assigned to it. If for no other reason, specialization develops because, within limits, it is more efficient for a person to stay with a task, and to learn by experience, than to jump from one to another. Three meetings of a group seem to be enough for the specialization of task performance and group maintenance to develop; the distinction between leaders and followers may come even more quickly (Bales).

Roles and Status

Roles aid group survival by enabling the group to replace a member without, at the same time, reassigning all the functions assigned to its members. Since each role designates who its occupant may communicate with, who he will influence and be influenced by, role implies status. Status, in turn, helps the group function by improving communication, since messages can be designed for specific receivers. Status also provides a system of automatically dividing rewards among members, so that it is not necessary, at the end of each week, for members to get together and, through a process of bargaining, decide who shall get what. If this were necessary, it would not only take a lot of time but it might very well create tensions which would break up the group and eliminate all of the rewards of group activity.

Men seem to have an invincible desire to attach values to the categories they use, and this is especially marked with the categories called roles. If a task requires that roles be performed in sequence, then men seem to put different values on the roles, depending on their place in the sequence. If some roles require rare abilities, their occupants tend to gain prestige. The direction in which orders or information flows will affect the values put on roles.

Every role has a rank or *status*, whether it is in as informal a group as a bridge club, as formal an organization as United States Steel, or as diffuse an aggregate as the United States itself. Moreover, status has important effects. It influences who says what to whom in communications. It affects the kind of things people desire to purchase. And, not least of all, it determines whether we have the money to buy the things we want, since rewards are directly related to the status of a man's role, often more than to his performance in the role.

In this chapter and the one that preceded it, we looked at status in groups and organizations. In the next chapter we will take a closer look at the function of status in society, where it is labeled "class" or "stratification."

SUMMARY

1. Every man plays many roles—salesman, customer, husband, father, and a score of others. A communicator must make his messages consistent with a receiver's role, at the moment of exposure, either by the way he frames the message or the context in which he places it.
2. A man's freedom in the choice of the roles he will occupy or the manner in which he will perform them is limited by the setting, audience, and the other persons in the role set, for few roles can be performed in isolation.

3. The observer's goal determines his definition of role, and whether he concentrates on the differences in the way occupants perform a given role or on their similarities. Similarity of roles within a group is important in making comparisons between groups.

4. A role consists of expectations concerning a man's acts, attitudes, and interactions with others by the man himself, members of his role set, and outsiders. Expectations include some things that are required, some that are permitted, some that are forbidden.

5. Society specifies who is eligible to perform a given role on the basis of physiology (sex and age) and experience. Physiology and experience both influence and limit the choices a man makes from the roles which he is eligible to perform. Role performance improves if continuity of roles is maintained, as a man ages; if roles change drastically with aging, then formal instruction and rites of passage ease the change.

6. Roles vary in the specificity and number of rights and duties they involve; in the number of persons eligible to perform them; and the number and kind of other roles they permit their occupants to hold.

7. Four roles are important to marketing communications. These are the role of spouse-and-parent found in the family, basic decision-making unit for consumer purchases; the roles of members of business organizations and of informal groups in business organizations, who may represent sources, channels, and receivers of marketing communications; and the role of customer. The latter, involving the buyer-seller role set, is of increasing importance in industrial society, where it takes over functions of kin and friends.

8. The role of customer is most highly developed in areas where bargaining occurs. The extent and nature of bargaining by the buyer depends on his definition of the process, and the resources, strategy, and knowledge he brings to bear upon it. His success in bargaining rises in direct proportion to his motivation to bargain and in inverse proportion to his motivation to buy. It also depends, of course, on the salesman's skill, resources, and motivation.

9. The salesman's freedom of maneuver is affected by the frequency of repurchase, customer ability to judge product quality in use, and the amount and intensity of competition. Customers seek information from one another to aid in bargaining, gain prestige by successful bargaining, and win friends by providing information to others.

10. The communicator tries to evoke roles consistent with his message and suppress those which are inconsistent. Conflict may arise because two roles compete for time and energy or pose antagonistic demands for the person who occupies them. Such demands may be backed up by members of the role set. The outcome of conflict depends upon the relative power of the conflicting members of the role set and of the role occupant's ability to conceal his choice, evade a decision, or resist the pressures.

11. Conflict becomes particularly acute for the "man in the middle" who may be a gatekeeper in a formal organization, like the foreman; or may be a member of one organization whose role requires him

to work with another, like the salesman or reporter. Conflict becomes easier to handle, however, to the extent that the expectations of members of a role set are quantifiable and to the extent that occupants of a given role in this role set differ among themselves.

12. Specialization of roles within a group increases productivity and enables a member to be replaced without having to reassign all of the activities within the group. The ranking of roles we call status aids communication within the group and provides a routine for allocating rewards among members, so that bargaining is not necessary at each such division.

Research Studies

A large part of human behavior resembles that of an actor on stage. The actor's role, however, is prescribed by the playwright's script; in life, we learn our roles from other people.

Two of these studies showed the influence of other members of the role set upon performance. *Jung* in a study which emphasized the two-way nature of all communication showed how variations in customer behavior affect the behavior of car salesmen. *Stouffer,* in a paper-and-pencil situation, found wide individual differences in the amount of overlap which students perceive in the demands made upon them by other students and by teachers.

Three studies then investigate the way in which role perceptions limit behavior. *Haire,* using a projective technique, found that purchase of a new product, instant coffee, was prevented by women's perception of how a housewife should perform her role. *Westfall* and others find similar effects seven years later, after use of the product had begun to spread. *Rosen* demonstrated the way in which values which determine the job roles a high school pupil aspires to are affected by social class.

Eleven

The Effects of Status
in Groups, Organizations,
and Society

Robert Crabb, sophomore, reports to a psychologist's laboratory for an experiment with six other student subjects, all strangers to one another. The psychologist opens a door to a seminar room, points to a conference table and says, "Please sit down."

If the group has never met before and does not expect to meet again, the seats students take may depend on who happens to come into the room first. If this is only the first of several meetings, however, the process may take a little longer. By sitting down a student stakes out a claim for future meetings and not all claims—not all seats around the table—are of equal value. Where a student sits affects whom he talks to, how often he talks, and how much influence he has on group decisions. By changing the shape of the table or by assigning men to specific seats, an experimenter can influence the status system which will emerge out of members' interaction.

If the student subjects are not strangers to one another, the process of seat taking will take even longer. If two of the students are good friends, they are likely to sit together and, perhaps, to form a coalition within the group. If coeds are included in the group, this will affect both seat taking and the who, what, and how of subsequent discussions. The status which emerges through interaction among strangers now is an independent variable which members bring with them from other groups; it influences the order in which they seat themselves and their subsequent interaction. A sophomore halfback may wait for his team's captain to seat himself. A long-distance runner may defer to a top-seeded tennis star, depending on how the college in question values the two sports, and the relative success of this year's tennis and track teams. The college's top debater, the vice president of the sophomore class, and the man who heads the dean's

319

list of honor students will have to sort themselves out along lines of status in the process of taking their seats. Over time, these status differences which are brought in from outside but are irrelevant to the present group will tend to disappear, and be replaced by new differences, related to students' roles and role performances in the discussion group itself. Their effects are not likely to disappear completely, however, since the original status differences give some students a head start toward valued roles in the new group, and the original status differences themselves may be based on differences in ability which are related to role performance in the new group.

Status in Organizations

Robert Crabb, vice president, arrives at a meeting on Madison Avenue, and now the matter of status becomes both critical and complex. Crabb's status, and the things that determine it, vary with the purpose of the meeting and the nature of its participants. The prestige of his occupational role, its position on the organizational chart, is a fairly good index of Crabb's status when the meeting consist of other employees of the firm. If the meeting is of peers, including only vice presidents of the firm, then Crabb's status will

---

When a "participant observer" immerses himself in the life of a primitive tribe, or a business firm, he often comes up with some interesting findings.

It's Better to Pluck Parsley Than to Peel Potatoes

Perhaps the most delightful introduction which a student can have to communications in a business firm is found in this study by William Foote Whyte. It begins like a novel: "It is 10:45 A.M. The chairs in Franklin's, one of Chicago's leading Loop restaurants, are still empty, but the customers are already beginning to line up outside the locked front door."

Whyte takes his readers through that front door and behind the scenes of the drama, telling what he and 3 research assistants found as participant observers, working in 12 Chicago restaurants during 1944 and 1945, and what they learned by interviewing workers in 13 other restaurants. He reports without using a single table or graph, but he tells the story of the bartender who let customers go thirsty, rather than take orders given him by a waitress, and of the waitress who suffered a nervous breakdown, caught between the conflicting demands of the management and the customers.

Using the four organizational charts on page 258, he sketches the rise of Mr. M, who started at the bottom, operating a lunch counter with two employees—all 3 of whom cooked, served customers, and washed dishes. He shows how, by stage 4, Mr. M—Whyte calls him "Tom Jones" —was surrounded by problems in human communications.

He puts a single symbol on this chart—the K that stands for kitchen workers—under the microscope and opens up worlds within worlds of role and status differences.

"K" in one restaurant, for example, included 45 workers arranged in a status chart like this, with highest status workers at the top:

Cooks at the range
↓
Salad preparation
↓
Preparation of chicken and meat
↓
Cleaning chicken; preparing vegetables

Each of these levels in turn had its own divisions:

Vegetable (8 persons)	*Chicken* (7 persons)
Cooks (Nos. 1 and 2)	Slice breasts for sandwiches (Nos. 1 and 2)
Halftime cook-preparation (No. 3)	Weigh slices (No. 3)
Supervision of preparation (No. 4)	Wrap slices (No. 4)
Others (Nos. 5, 6, 7, 8)	Pick white meat off carcass (No. 5)
	Pick dark meat off carcass (Nos. 6 and 7)

No. 4 on vegetables, Whyte found, was the only worker to handle the luxury, decorative vegetables like parsley and chives; Nos. 4 and 5 would handle vegetables as they neared the cooking stage—dicing carrots, for example, while Nos. 6, 7, and 8 sliced them. Clean vegetables without odor were the sign of high status: only 6, 7, and 8 ever handled potatoes and onions. In chicken, white meat had higher status than dark.

These were the things that determined the status of a given role in the kitchen; what determined who was assigned to a given role? Age and seniority were part of the explanation. Numbers 1 and 2 in the chicken hierarchy had been with the firm 9 years; Numbers 7 and 8, at the bottom of the vegetable hierarchy, were women of 72 and 65 who had to sit down while they worked. Education, social class, and marital status also played a part.

> —William Foote Whyte, *Human Relations in the Restaurant Industry* (New York: McGraw-Hill Book Company, 1948).

---

depend on two things—the prestige of his department and the esteem which his abilities win for him from his colleagues. The prestige of his department, in turn, may depend on how large a proportion of the firm's employees it has, or the size of its budget.

If Crabb represents his advertising agency at an industry-wide meeting which includes representatives of advertisers and the media, his status at the outset will reflect the standing of advertising agencies, *vis-a-vis* advertisers and the media; and the standing of his agency, *vis-a-vis* other agencies. The former will depend partly on who "initiates behavior" for whom (that is, who gives orders); both it and the latter will also depend on the resources of men and money which each controls. A large advertising agency, that is, will outweigh a small advertiser, but if both are the same size then the advertiser, as purchaser of the other's services, tends to have greater power and so higher status.

Crabb's status will change over a series of meetings. His personal contributions to the group's goals will give him esteem within this group some of which he may carry back with him to enhance his own esteem within the firm, or even to win a place in the firm that possesses more prestige. Indeed, some firms train and test their junior executives by having them serve on the boards of voluntary organizations and help fund-raising campaigns, where they can get experience in working with others without loss to the firm's own assets if they prove inept. Rising executives can practice the art of influencing group decisions, knowing that any enemies they make will not be around to cause trouble later, as they are when decision making occurs within the firm itself. At the same time, they learn how inter-organizational negotiations, a primary concern of any firm's top executives, differ from the intra-organizational processes with which they are already familiar.

Social Status

Robert Crabb, new resident of his suburb, is invited to serve on the planning committee for a United Fund campaign. As a newcomer, both to suburb and the committee, Crabb finds that his status depends upon his *occupation*. It is clear that an advertising man is not ranked as high here as are the physician and the lawyer, who sit beside him, or the man from Wall Street, who sits across the table from him. His status moves up a notch or two, however, when members discover that Crabb has a Ph. D. in psychology, heads the research division in his advertising agency, and teaches a course at Metropolitan University. Crabb's skill in negotiation, gained in his work as an advertising man, helps the committee reach its decisions. His skill in mass communication, also part of his equipment as an advertising man, helps the United Fund go over the top in its fund drive.

As a result, his esteem rises with committee members, and from them begins to diffuse throughout the community.

Gradually, his efforts on the committee begin to produce a new kind of pay-off. Not only is Crabb himself invited to play golf by the town's leading citizen, but his wife is invited to join the suburb's best bridge club, and his children start playing tennis on the best courts. Social status is essentially a family affair; wife and children both benefit from Crabb's achievements and, by their own efforts, help or hinder the family's rise on the ladder of status. The family's *associates* now begin to reflect and affect its status. High status comes to resemble a piece of property which Crabb can pass on to his children, as he can will them his house and his securities. The people we associate with are the people whose children our own children will marry.

The status which Crabb had to achieve, his children now gain by ascription. Moreover, this is status which Crabb can carry with him, should he move across the country. His friends in the suburb will give him an introduction to their friends in Texas or California. The persons he meets at the first cocktail party at his new location will engage in the game of search-and-comparison for the names of mutual friends, by which Crabb's status in his new environment will become fixed.

Crabb's status and men's common desire for permanent high status affect his behavior at every step along the way. Status affects his style of life. It determined his choice of an automobile, for example. When a friend in the agency reminded him that the boss drove a Buick, Crabb realized that he had better leave his Lincoln Continental at home and drive the family's second car to work. When he heard another vice president characterized as "unstable" on the strength of his bright red sports car, Crabb realized he had better choose something more conservative.

In the suburb, Crabb and his family soon find it inconvenient to travel so far to play tennis, golf, and bridge with their new friends. Even worse, when their new friends come to a party at the Crabbs', they usually arrive late, apologizing for having gotten lost driving in an unfamiliar part of town. Crabb takes the hint and moves across town. He finds two houses, a block away from one another. One is clearly superior, but he buys the other when his wife points out that the telephone number of the house they both prefer is listed in the "wrong" exchange.

Crabb used to be an ardent Democrat, but he does not talk much about politics these days. He listens more than he used to, and what he hears is mostly talk about Republicans. His reading material has changed. Magazines like *The Reporter* and *The New Republic* have moved from the living room to his study, and much of the time he is too tired, after reading the *Wall Street Journal,* to do more than glance at the two magazines' tables of contents. Crabb still votes Democratic through habit, but his *beliefs* seem to be changing. After all, neither his associates nor his reading material provide him with much ammunition, and his skills in political argument have become rusty through disuse.

Crabb has learned a lot and changed a lot along the way. His clothes, his tastes in recreation, his accent, his beliefs have changed. Some changes, however, are too great to accomplish in one generation, even in a society as mobile as our own. Only his children will have the self-assured poise of taking this way of life for granted, because they have never known any other; and Crabb's four-year-old will do a better job of this than his fourteen-year-old.

Status and Marketing

Let us stop for a moment, now, and try to sum up how Crabb's experiences can help the marketing communicator. All too often, advertising men talk about status as if it were something that only their customers possessed, something that affected the acts and attitudes of only the ignorant and weak-willed, something that the advertising man can manipulate at will.

It is true that much of Crabb's working day, as a psychologist doing research for an advertising agency, is spent in studying style of life, and the way that products come to represent life style and status. A brewer asks him, for example, how advertising can change the image of beer as a workingman's drink so that he can tap an upper-income market. A manufacturer wants to know how he can preserve his image as a maker of quality instruments for professional musicians, and yet sell to the mass-student market. Media buyers, as well as copy writers, need his help: Is this a product for the "young influentials," which one magazine claims to reach, or is its market the workingman's wives, claimed by Fawcett and MacFadden publications? Every time Crabb makes a survey, he has to decide whether to stratify it by social class or by one of the demographic indices of social class—income, occupation, education, and so on.

Moreover, Crabb must keep up-to-date on changes in style of life, for status symbols change more easily than other aspects of status.

Rising incomes and the advertiser's messages themselves may spread ownership so widely that a product ceases to carry any implication of high status. This happens to brands: Packard gives way to Cadillac. This happens to products: automobiles, a conspicuous symbol of income which accompany a man wherever he goes, have lost much of their significance. To some extent, a man's home and the frequency of his trips overseas have taken their place. Since both of these symbols help determine a man's associates, as the car he drove did not, their significance may be somewhat more enduring. In general, possessions seem a less useful index to status today than they used to be, now that the boats on trailers clutter the driveways of suburbia and the multiservanted homes of the wealthy have been torn down or turned into convents.

Crabb uses the status systems of his society, but he is also caught up in them, whether he wants to be or not, and whether he makes a conscious effort to improve his status, tries to ignore the issue, or attempts to resist the forces that bear upon him.

As a psychologist, Crabb is more likely than many men in advertising to be aware of what is going on, and to try to exert some control over the process rather than be its passive subject. He may, for example, make desperate attempts to be a good Democrat, even seeking support from dissident elements both on Madison Avenue and in the suburbs. As a Ph.D. in a staff job, research, he is to some extent outside the main arena of status seeking within the organization. Nevertheless, to communicate at all, he must talk the language of his associates; to win the facilities needed to do his job and to get the rewards that go with it, he must play the game according to the rules. Already set apart by the jargon of his trade, and the mixture of deference and hostility which his degree stimulates, Crabb may need to make special efforts to show that he is one of the boys and accepts the norms of the group.

We have concerned ourselves with Robert Crabb for three reasons. Our first purpose in telling Crabb's story was to point out that the marketing communicator as source is affected by status himself, and that status is not just something which other people have and value and which he uses to persuade them to buy the products he is selling.

Next, we wanted to show how prestige and esteem affect one another: how a man's role in an organization and his status in a community determine what groups he can become a member of and what his beginning role in such groups is likely to be. We wanted to show how his performance in the group may change his role within the group and how the esteem attached to his performance as a role occupant, and the prestige attached to his final role in the group, may then change his status in the organization or community from which he came. We showed this process working for Crabb, both on Madison Avenue and in the suburb where he lives. (Needless to say, the picture can become still more complicated; a neighbor in the suburb may become a client of Crabb's agency, a client of his agency may become an associate in the suburb.)

Third, we wanted to show that the dimensions of status vary greatly. The rest of this chapter will be concerned with exploring this variation in greater detail: discussing how each dimension is measured, when each is used and for what purpose and by whom, and what are the causes and the effects of each dimension.

Six Dimensions of Status

There are six dimensions of status, the first two of which are highly visible, and related to the work a man does (Kahl, 8–10).

Style of Life
A man's possessions reflect a man's income, which in turn is an index to the value of his occupational roles in society. They also provide subtle indicators as to whether the man's status is one he has achieved or one he was born into. Only by being inside a group can we know what the group regards as acceptable in terms of furniture, clothing, and dozens of other products. The purchaser's tastes are shaped by the group, and those of us who first "board" a horse in adulthood will probably never be fully at ease on its back. Originally valued because they are a symbol of membership in a group, possessions may become rewarding in themselves and for this reason be advertised and purchased by outsiders. Some possessions may be necessary to join a group and gain status through our associates, although they are seldom sufficient to win such membership.

Occupation
This is perhaps the most widely used and basic of status dimensions. Two aspects of an occupation affect its status: the amount of general, systematic knowledge which it requires and the number of other persons whom it controls. As a Ph.D. in business, where Ph.D's are rare, Crabb has a status comparable to that of the president of a firm with hundreds of employees who has status comparable to that of a government official with many subordinates. In academic circles,

however, Crabb's practical orientation may give him lower status than the experimental psychologist, who commands greater breadth and depth of theory—and the latter, in turn, may enjoy lower status than the physicist, who has a mass of highly developed mathematical theory and a nice governmental research grant to back up his claims to power. Such distinctions are less visible to an outsider than a man's possessions.

The second two dimensions of status are far less visible, since they concern a man's activities rather than the things he owns or the job he occupies.

The person who appears to have higher status may be more influential, even to strangers, than a person whose appearance suggests he has low status in society.

Status Symbols Affect Frequency of Jay-Walking

An observer, 100 feet from traffic lights at 3 different street corners in Austin, Texas, watched 2103 pedestrians as they faced a 40-second "wait" signal and a 15-second "walk" signal.

For 5 trials, a confederate of the experimenter wore a freshly pressed suit, white shirt, tie, and hat. Then 5 observations were made while the confederate was absent. Finally, 5 trials were made while he appeared in low-status garb: scuffed shoes, patched and soiled trousers, and an unpressed blue denim shirt. Sometimes, in his high-status garb, he would obey the signal; in another set of 5 trials, in the same garb, he would cross when the light said "wait."

Here are the results, showing percentage of pedestrians obeying the signal:

Dress of Confederate	Behavior of Confederate			
	Obeys	Absent	Disobeys	Total
High status	99%	99%	86%	95%
Low status	100	99	96	98

In short, most pedestrians were law abiding. A few apparently were encouraged to disobey the sign when a person in low-status garb did so; 14 per cent disobeyed when they saw a person in high-status garb do so.

—Monroe Lefkowitz, Robert R. Blake and Jane Srygley Mouton, "Status Factors in Pedestrian Violation of Traffic Signals," *Journal of Abnormal and Social Psychology,* 51:704–706.

Job Performance

How able is a man—how well does he perform his job? These are the differences which affect a man's reputation within an industry and his reputation and role within a business organization. Whereas occupations have prestige, a man's performance in an occupation has esteem, which often is known only to insiders. Within any group—lawyers, chiefs, or thieves, for example—comparisons can be made on the basis of reputation or income. Difficulty arises whenever reputation and income provide two sets of rankings. Greater difficulty arises, however, when we try to make comparisons between groups.

Income and reputation are poor indices to relative status for persons who cannot exchange jobs with one another. A sales manager may be paid more than a research director, businessmen in general earn more than educators, and gangsters become wealthier than anyone else in the society. The stars who perform on television and in the movies become widely known and even favorably thought of compared with most philosophers and college presidents. A rich gangster has higher status than a poor one, and a well-known singer higher status than an obscure one. We first must sort people as to occupation, then within any given occupation by job performance.

Associates

Occupation, job performance, and possessions often become means to this end. They determine who a man and his family associate with outside of working hours. Occasionally, this dimension becomes visible in the society pages of a newspaper or in a *Social Register* but the highly important within-group differences, crucial to an insider, are invisible from the outside. Tensions may become acute in such groups when members have very different goals for the group—some using the group to escape from business pressures as an end in itself, and others using it as a means of making a sale, a contact, or a deal. Great skill is needed to avert or relieve such tensions.

The final two dimensions and the least visible reflect men's attitudes. The other dimensions reflect the indices by which others judge a man's status and so determine their behavior toward him. The last two reflect the way a man perceives his own status and so influence the way he behaves toward others.

Beliefs

As we have seen in earlier chapters, groups induce conformity both by the original selection of members, by screening the cues its members may receive, and by direct pressures to conform. Our associates, both on the job and off, do just this. Some views are built into some occupations, so that we assume that a millionaire steelmaker will oppose higher taxes on millionaires, lower tariffs on steel, and higher tariffs on iron ore. We find it equally easy to predict the beliefs of a steelworker. However, a man is influenced not only by his associates but by what he perceives to be the views of groups he would like to associate with. The man who aspires to rise in an organization is likely to fashion his beliefs to match those of persons higher on the organizational chart, who become his reference group. Knowing a man's status, we can often predict his beliefs; knowing his beliefs, we can often specify both his present status and the status to which he aspires.

Class Identification

An alternative form of mobility is that in which a man tries to rise not as an individual, but as a member of a group, by lifting the status of the occupation or other group itself. Not only do persons in the group have similar beliefs, but they become conscious of both group and beliefs and tend to identify themselves with the group. If a new situation arises, they ask themselves what the group will think and do.

Varying Uses of Dimensions

In a small group, whose members have a good chance to observe one another, an individual's status depends on the extent to which he contributes to task performance and group maintenance in the activities the group regards as important. To Americans, occupation is the most important activity, so that a man is judged by how well he does and how important his job is (Kahl, 85–86). The job's importance, in turn, depends on the scarcity of the abilities and the amount of training it requires; the number of his subordinates, the wages; and the nature of the product.

In a small community, however, members may not be able to observe and evaluate all these elements. Instead, they will have to judge a man by his occupation; to them, one banker is pretty much like another and all druggists fall into a single category. As occupations increase in number and variety, men find it more and more difficult to rank them. As a result, they seek to rank them on the common denominator of the income they provide. Occupation thus is rated in income, just as income affects a man's style of life and his associates, and his style of life and associates affect his beliefs and class identification.

Since visibility is best in our immediate surroundings, persons tend to see finer distinctions in status at their own level in society than they do at more distant levels. This means that persons at either end of the status level tend to see two levels—their own level and that of everyone else (Bott). Persons in the middle, on the other hand, are likely to see at least three levels—their own, a higher level, and a lower one. Power appears to be the major variable used in judging status by persons at the bottom of the ladder. "They" have it and "we" do not. Prestige plays more of a part in judgments of status elsewhere in the system.

Measuring Status

A scientist observing status has three choices to make. He must choose which of these dimensions to observe, how much weight to give each of them in arriving at a score of general status, and what method to use in gathering his data.

He may gather data, for example, by letting respondents themselves decide how many social classes they need to classify people and what labels to pin on these classes, or he may supply both the number of classes and their labels. Given freedom to set up their own system of categories, 250 residents of Boston used an average of 6.9 categories to classify a list of seventy occupations in one study (Kahl, 78). Respondents varied greatly, however, in the number of categories they used, the number of occupations put into a category, and the number of categories assigned to a given status level. In general, they expanded the number of occupations at their own level, placing twenty-one there as compared to an average of thirteen occupations for all levels. Most market researchers and sociologists prefer to use five or six classes; of these, the middle two usually account for some 80 per cent of the population and the topmost class may include only 1 per cent of the population.

Having determined his social classes, a scientist must then decide how their occupants are to be chosen. He may ask individuals to rate themselves or to rate one another, or he may use an objective measure of status. In small communities, where everyone knows everybody else and in stable societies where the various dimensions of status have had a chance to crystallize, ratings based on a man's associates may be a very good index to status. Associates *are* important, since they influence a man's attitudes and acts, reflect group acceptance of his status, and tend to be more stable than other characteristics.

Since the isolated communities which an anthropologist studies are usually both small and stable, it is not surprising that the classic studies of Yankee City, made by W. Lloyd Warner, an anthropologist, used such a measure. He asked informants chosen from different levels in the community to report how many classes they perceived and to name representative members of each class. Warner's respondents agreed in identifying five classes, half the number which Warner himself had expected to find. Their agreement produced what he called the method of "evaluative participation" or EP (Warner 36–39).

Even in a small community, however, it is often easier to discover what a man does for a living and where he lives, than it is to find out who he dines and plays bridge with. In a society such as our own, in which one-fourth of the population changes residence each year, measures of interaction are seldom worth the trouble, since occupation and place of residence determine a man's associates. Moreover, a measure of interaction is hard to apply nationwide.

Thus Warner found it useful to supplement his measure of interaction with an "index of status characteristics" (ISC) which correlated .97 with EP (Warner, 168). Observers used seven-point scales to rate a man's source of income (investments, salary, and so on), his job, his neighborhood, and his type of house, then multiplied income source and house type by three, occupation by four, and neighborhood by two to arrive at a final score.

Scores of this kind are attractive to the marketing communicator because they can be made fairly objective for survey purposes and because data concerning markets as a whole is available without charge in census and other published reports. A man's occupation, given the heaviest weight in Warner's ISC is fairly public knowledge; fairly accurate information concerning it can be obtained either from the man himself or his neighbors, and we can compare the totals of our survey with census records.

Occupation is Basic

Intuitively, occupation seems basic to the other dimensions of status. A high-status job requires ability and education, and provides the income which permits a high-status style of living. Job, income, and possessions help a man gain access to groups of high-status associates and the groups which foster class identification and shape a man's beliefs. Empirically, occupation has been proved basic through the technique of centroid factor analysis (Kahl and Davis). Taking nineteen variables related to social class, Kahl and Davis extracted two factors. The largest included variables related to occupation—his education, income, the occupations of his best friends, and the interviewer's rating. The second factor centered on ratings for house and neighborhood. Most respondents saw a three- or four-level class system based on occupation and life style.

Measures of occupation have an added advantage. There is extensive data concerning prestige of occupation for both the United States and European nations. When the National Opinion Research Center

	Rank*	
1. Occupations requiring special technical knowledge or control over many subordinates:	1947	1963
United States supreme court justice	1	1
Physician	2.5	2
College professor	8	8
Banker	10.5	24.5
Lawyer	18	11
Civil engineer	23	21.5
2. Educated men who are not professionals; managers of medium-sized organizations:		
Owner of 100-employee factory	26.5	31.5
Accountant for large business	29	29.5
Teacher in public school	36	29.5
3. Owners of ten-employee firms; white-collar workers; highly skilled workers:		
Railroad engineer	37.5	39
Farmer	39	44
Bookkeeper	51.5	49.5
Automobile repairman	59.5	60
4. Owner of two-employee firm; less skilled white-collar and manual workers:		
Owner of lunch stand	62	62.5
Clerk in store	68	70
Farm hand	76	83
5. Unskilled laborers:		
Restaurant waiter	79.5	80.5
Night watchman	81.5	77.5
Shoe shiner	90	90

* Data from Hodge, Siegel, Rossi.

asked a sample of 2920 American adults in 1947 to rate ninety occupations on a five-point scale of prestige, it found considerable agreement on the rankings. On page 332 is a comparison of 1947 rankings with others made in 1963. Examples of occupations are given for each of five major intuitive categories suggested by Kahl (Kahl, 73).

Using the technique of Guttman scaling, this same list was divided empirically into eight groups, which produced scales with a "reproducibility" (a measure of predictive success) of .80 (Hatt). These eight groups were political occupations, professional, business, recreation-aesthetics, agriculture, manual work, military, and service trades. Predictability via Guttman scaling increased to a reproducibility of up to .90 when each of these groups was broken down still further. Separate scales were produced, for example, for four kinds of business occupations: big business, small business, labor organizations, and less-skilled white-collar workers.

Not only do people in the United States agree with one another, but their ratings of occupations agree with those of residents of other industrial nations as well. Although the data were scanty—ranging. from seven comparable occupations for Russia and Great Britain to thirty for Great Britain and New Zealand—a study (Inkeles and Rossi) found correlations range from .74 for ratings by Russians and Japanese to .97 for New Zealand and the United States. Here is a table showing correlations of ratings in each country with those in the United States, and average correlation for each country with the other five.

Correlation

	With U.S.	5-Nation Average
Russia	.90	.84
Japan	.93	.89
Great Britain	.94	.93
New Zealand	.97	.93
Germany	.96	.94
United States	—	.94

(Inkeles and Rossi, 339.)

Reprinted from the *American Journal of Sociology* by permission of the University of Chicago Press. Copyright 1956.

A man's education, like his occupation, is a useful index to status; it has been found particularly helpful in predicting a man's acts and his attitudes.

In one study, education alone predicted twelve out of twenty-two different kinds of behavior, ranging from frequency of church attendance to foreign travel and listening to news broadcasts (Haer). Education provided better predictions than a man's occupation, his answer to the question "What social class are you in?" or his self-assignment to one of four classes suggested by the interviewer: upper class, middle class, working class, and lower class. In fact, only one index was superior to education; this was Warner's four-part ISC.

How Class Affects Individuals

Social class, however measured, affects interaction. In the Roman Catholic church, class differences are reflected in the congregation to the extent that residential segregation affects parish lines. In

---

What kinds of farmers are most likely to influence their neighbors? This study finds those looked to for advice have high status and are more likely to follow more approved practices.

"Local Influentials" Are Active in Organizations

In a farming community in northeast Missouri, above average for the state, all the community's 279 farm operators were asked who they talked to about farm problems. Twenty-two out of the 279, labeled below as Group *A*, were mentioned by at least 5 other farmers. These 22 were the most active in 3 types of organizations: neighborhood, community, and extra-community. (Participation was scored by giving 1 point for membership or occasional attendance, 2 for regular attendance, 3 for committee membership, and 4 for holding office.)

Influence and Activity in Organizations

Mentioned by	A	B	C	D
	5 or more peers	2 to 4 peers	Single peer	Not mentioned
Number in group	22	60	72	125
Median participation score (local)	7.2	5.4	4.7	3.2
Percentage belonging to community organization	86%	65%	53%	39%
Percentage in extra-community organization	41	23	0	0

Group *A*'s likelihood of membership was higher across a variety of organizations: civic club, 41 per cent versus 4–10 per cent for the other

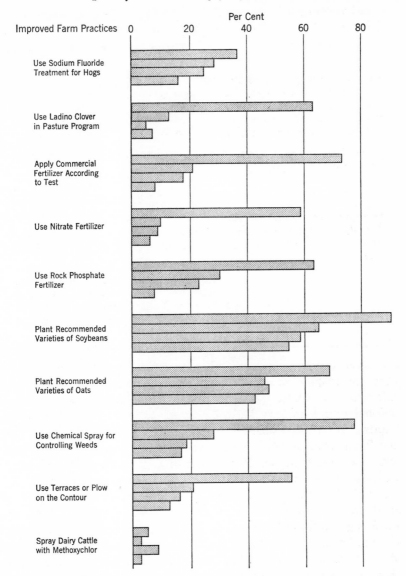

Fig. 11.1. Proportions of farm operations using designated improved farm practices. Bars in each set represent *A, B, C,* and *D* groups reading down.

groups; adult farm school, 59 per cent versus 4–13 per cent; grain marketing co-op, 45 per cent versus 4–12 per cent; farmers association, 64 per cent versus 28–40 per cent.

Although members of group *A* did not differ in age or education they did differ in other measures of status:

	Group *A*	Groups *B*, *C*, and *D*
Judge's ratings: percentage in group ranked in top two of six classes	86%	14–27%
Possessions: running water in home	77	17–30
Wealth: average farm size	380 acres	178–229 acres
Income: average annual gross	$8000	$2500 to $4455

Members of group *A* also were more exposed to outside sources of information:

	Group *A*	Groups *B*, *C*, *D*
Percentage taking daily newspaper	91%	52–65%
Average number of magazines taken	6.5	3.3 to 4.1

And they were more likely to follow improved farm practices as shown in Fig. 11.1.

> —Herbert F. Lionberger, "Some Characteristics of Farm Operators Sought as Sources of Farm Information in a Missouri Community," *Rural Sociology*, 18: 327–338.

Protestant churches, however, whose worshippers may be drawn from wider geographic areas, denominational memberships reflect class differences. A typical study in one California town found a Congregational church to have highest prestige, followed by the Methodist, Baptist, Adventist, Nazarene, the Assembly of God, Church of God, and Pentecostal churches (Goldschmidt a). Professional men and business managers made up 50 per cent of Congregational membership; unskilled labor made up 80 per cent of Pentecostal membership.

Social class affects men's acts. A comparison of fifteen studies of child-rearing practices made over a period of twenty-five years and involving a total of 11,000 cases, has shown clear-cut, but changing, class differences (Bronfenbrenner). From 1930 until the end of World War II, middle-class mothers were less permissive toward infants than working class mothers: less likely to breast feed or to feed a baby when it cried, and more insistent on early weaning and toilet training. Since then, middle-class mothers have become more permissive. (In both periods, prewar and postwar, middle-class mothers apparently were better informed and more susceptible to infant care fads currently fashionable among the experts.)

In dealing with older children, middle-class parents were more insistent than lower-class parents, over the whole twenty-five-year period, on good grades in school and acceptance of responsibility at home. They used less physical punishment, controlling children more by making the middle-class child feel guilty and afraid of losing his parents' love. At the same time, middle-class parents were more willing to treat the child as an equal and less insistent upon obedience. These practices, in turn, caused middle-class children to be more self-controlled than children of the lower class. High-status farmers are more likely to innovate and to induce others to innovate, too (Lionberger a).

Social class affects attitudes. In two studies, prejudice has been found to be related to mobility, the effects varying with the type of mobility: single generation or between generation. Among 150 war veterans in Chicago, those whose postwar occupations were lower in status than their prewar positions, a considerable prejudice was shown against Negroes and Jews (Bettelheim and Janowitz 57–61). The authors, hypothesizing that prejudice is the downward-mobile person's way of venting his frustration, found, as they expected, that upward-mobile veterans were less prejudiced than those whose status had not changed.

In contrast, two other authors (Greenblum and Pearlin) predicted that a man whose status is different from that of his father, whether higher or lower, will feel insecure and that this feeling will make him prejudiced. They, too, found what they expected, in an analysis of 664 residents of Elmira, New York. They used three measures of prejudice. They were dislike of having a member of a minority group as a neighbor ("keep out"), agreement that the minority in question is obtaining more power than "is good for the country" ("power"), and agreement with statements that Jews are dishonest in business and Negroes are ignorant and lazy ("stereotype"). Results of their analysis are shown in the following table:

| | | Percentage Taking Prejudiced Position toward: | | | | |
| | | Negroes | | | Jews | | |
Status of Son's Occupation:		Keep out	Power	Stereo-type	Keep out	Power	Stereo-type
Higher than father's	154	71%	9%	45%	15%	29%	36%
Same	415	59	7	39	11	20	28
Lower than father's	95	63	16	39	13	27	42

* Data reprinted from Reinhard Bendix and Seymour Martin Lipset, *Class, Status and Power,* Copyright 1953 by The Free Press and The Macmillan Co.

These are only a few of the effects that can be traced to social class. The effects of class on attitudes toward politics and on voting behavior are obvious, and the effects of class on media use and purchasing behavior are, of course, of major importance to the marketing communicator. We have chosen not to discuss these effects, however, for two reasons. One reason is that the student will become familiar with these aspects of social status in advanced courses in marketing just as the marketing communicator becomes familiar with them in his daily work. The other reason is that class effects, at the level of the status symbol, change quickly as fads ebb and flow, and are subject to manipulation by the communicator himself.

We have been concerned with more powerful and basic effects, such as the effects of class upon a man's religion and on the types of personality created by class differences in rearing children, and the effects of class and class mobility upon such intense and resistant attitudes as prejudice toward minority groups. These are part of the environment in which the communicator must operate and part of the facts of life to which he must adjust because he cannot change them.

Effects of Status on Society

We have seen the effects of status on the individual. What are the effects of status and of changes in status upon society itself? Status exists, in the first place, because individuals differ and because some of these differences inevitably tend to have values attached to them. Any recognizable difference can form the basis for a status or a ranking system and at some period in history, at some place on earth, most of them have. Some of these differences are basic to the human condition. In every group, organization and society, age and sex affect status. They limit the groups a man may belong to and they limit what roles and status he may acquire in the groups which accept him as a member. The values attached to age and sex vary markedly, however. In some societies, status rises with age; the United States, at this moment in history, seems to be a young man's country.

Other differences originate in the group itself. Chief among these are the specialized roles which develop in every group and every society and are built into every organization. By permitting specialization, roles increase efficiency. By allowing members to be replaced with a minimum of disturbance to the rest of the group, they aid group survival. Inevitably roles and their occupants tend to have different values attached to them, depending on the importance of the function assigned to the role and the difficulty of finding an occupant for it. These differences in ranking, or status, may improve efficiency by simplifying communication, flow-of-work, decision making, and division of rewards among members. If the status system is inappropriate to begin with or fails to adapt to changed conditions, however, it may hinder efficiency through these same limits it places on communication, flow-of-work, decision making, and division of rewards.

A status system which is appropriate for one function in society

---

Families and business firms make decisions—and so do communities. Who are the "influentials" who decide things for the community?

Decision Making: The Community

Sociologists at Syracuse University began a study of this question by interviewing 20 specialists in community study and 50 other persons representing various subgroups within the city of Syracuse. From the interviews they got a list of some 250 issues which had been decided between 1955 and 1960. They picked 39 of these and set out to see who had made the decisions.

From documents they first located the *formal authorities* involved in each decision. (In one case the decision group consisted of 2 persons and in another of 57.) Each of these authorities was asked which of the 39 decisions he had helped make and what other persons were involved in it. Any person named by 2 authorities was termed a "first-zone influential" and all such influentials were then interviewed. This gave another list of persons, those named by one authority and one first zone influential; such persons were added to the first zone group and interviewed. Finally, any person named by 2 first zone influentials was labeled a "second-zone influential."

In all 628 persons were interviewed, 550 qualified as participants, and 506 of the participants completed a questionnaire. The 32 persons named most often as *decision makers* were identified. This questionnaire asked participants if they belonged to 11 different kinds of organizations, including unions, clubs, business organizations, veterans groups, and so on. From the results, the 32 socially active persons, those belonging to the largest number of organizations, were identified. The questionnaire also asked each person to list the 8 most influential leaders in the community and again the 32 named most often were identified by reputation. Finally the titular heads of 32 large organizations were chosen on the basis of their *position:* about 60% from business organizations, 13% from the professions, 9% from government, and others from education, communication, labor, and religion.

Thus the researchers had 4 separate lists of influentials, each with

32 names on it. First identified were those actually participating in decisions, then those as active in organizations, then those with a reputation as leaders, and finally those at the head of major organizations. As the following table shows, only the last 2 lists—reputation and headship —showed much agreement:

Percentage of Agreement on Names of Influentials

	Participation	*Social Activity*	*Reputation*
Social activity	25		
Reputation	33	25	
Position	39	22	74

The authors then asked what would happen if one surmised that *reputations* were a property of organizations, not of individuals. So they credited the head of each organization with the sum of participation in decision making by all his employees. The new scores agreed 67 % of the time with reputation, and 80% with position. Persons with a reputation as leaders were not active participants in decisions themselves but headed the largest organizations whose personnel had high participation rates. These heads, however, were different from the persons mentioned most often as participating in actual decisions. Of these, 66% were government personnel or full-time executives of voluntary, community agencies.

The authors thus distinguish 3 types of leaders. First are the *institutional leaders*, head of the largest organizations, especially the business firms, identified by their reputation, their position, and the activity in decision making of their subordinates. They may lend prestige, legitimatize decisions, and place their subordinates in a position to influence decisions. Second are the *effectors*. These are the subordinates in the private firms, the government personnel, and the heads of voluntary organizations who actually make the decisions of the organizations. Third are the *activists*. Their part in decision making depends less upon the organizations behind them than upon the time and energy they spend on community affairs.

—Linton C. Freeman, Thomas J. Fararo, Warner Bloomberg, Jr., and Morris H. Sunshine, "Locating Leaders in Local Communities: A Comparison of Some Alternative Approaches," *American Sociological Review*, 28:791–798.

---

may be unsuited to another; that which rewards one group may penalize another. Only if we specify the function or the group, can we say whether a given status system is "good" or "bad," functional or disfunctional.

The family performs valuable functions for society but, at the same time, disturbs the distribution of roles according to ability and of rewards according to merit. Unequal rewards may be necessary to induce persons with rare skills to train for, accept, and perform roles society regards as vital. Rewards may also become unequal because someone of high status has the power to seize them, without regard to his contribution to the goals society has set for itself. To a wealthy father, inheritance taxes are bad because they limit him in sharing the rewards of his performance with his son. To the poor man's son, such taxes may be good, because they reduce the odds against his merits being recognized by the rewards of power and of wealth. To society itself, such taxes may be good, bad, or irrelevant. In some societies, for example, inheritance taxes may be necessary to prevent an idiot son from wrecking a firm; in our society, separation of ownership and control in the modern corporation shares this function with taxes themselves.

Status Is Complex

Not only can recognizable differences among individuals form the basis for a status system, but a great many such differences do affect the status of any given individual at a given point in time. Crabb, the sophomore, can be ranked on the basis of his height, weight, grade average, swimming ability, or dancing skill. Almost inevitably his ranks on these dimensions will be inconsistent with one another. They are not perfectly correlated with one another, nor are they completely independent of one another. An underweight, penniless student is not likely to rank high in prestige on the football-playing and car-owning scales; low rank on all four scales may give him low rank in a dating status system, too.

Crabb, the vice president, is similarly ranked on many different status systems. His occupation and income, education and style of life, job performance and associates, beliefs and class identification are seldom completely congruent. This inconsistency at once creates a problem and an opportunity. It creates a problem for his associates, who never know whether they are speaking to Crabb, the high-status football player, or to Crabb, the low-status student. It also creates an opportunity for Crabb to equalize his ranks, in an upward direction, and a strong motivation in him to do just that. The ease with which he can increase his status varies with each dimension of status. Money will buy possessions and a style of life, but associates must be won. The ease with which he can raise his status also varies from group to group and from society to society.

The extent to which prestige and esteem of a man's occupation coincides with his prestige as indicated by his associates has been studied by an ingenious use of published sources (Baltzell). Referring to the *Social Register* as an index of associates and *Who's Who* as a measure of occupational status, Baltzell compared listings in the two publications for thirteen major cities as of 1940. *Who's Who*, which showed a bias in favor of educators and the clergy, was the more exclusive of the two. It listed 12,530 individuals in these cities, compared with 28,450 who made the *Social Register*. The percentage of *Who's Who* listings also found in the *Social Register* ranged from a low of 11 per cent for Chicago to a high of 30 per cent for Washington, D.C. The overall average was 23 per cent.

In a society whose major decisions are made by financiers and businessmen, the author suggests, men in these occupations tend to be recruited from families at the top of the social structure—the kind listed in *Social Register*. In Philadelphia, for example, he finds that 75 per cent of the thirty-two bankers in *Who's Who* are also listed in the *Social Register*. Intellectual ability, however, is passed on from one generation to the next less easily than wealth. Occupations in which success depends on a man's own wits show less overlap between the two publications. Put another way, occupations of this kind represent a major channel of mobility by which a man whose ascribed status is low can, nevertheless, rise to the top.

Among such channels in Philadelphia are the church, only eight of the eighty *Who's Who* entries also being found in the *Social Register*, education (16 per cent overlap), and public office (21 per cent overlap). Physicians (37 per cent) and lawyers (51 per cent), perhaps as a reflection both of cost of their training and the wealth of their clientele, occupied a middle ground.

Caste and Class

Societies differ in the number of classes they contain, the clarity with which these classes are defined, and in the ease with which a man or his children can move from one to another. Ease of movement, in turn, affects both the efficiency of a society and the attitudes of its members.

In a closed or caste system, members tend to have the status they were born into. Status is *ascribed* rather than *achieved*. Although most such societies seem able to prevent incompetent occupants of high-status positions from doing as much damage as we might expect, they also prevent persons of high ability but low status from giving society the full use of their talents. (Although rewards are made on the basis of family rather than ability or performance, this does not cause unrest as long as members accept the justice or the inevitability of such a system of distribution.) This loss of efficiency is offset to the extent that high-status members of such a society can prepare for responsible positions with some assurance that they will get them. Such a society also provides high rewards of group maintenance since all members enjoy stable relationships with family and friends. (There are no leave-takings as my family, my friends or I climb up the status ladder.) If ambition is frustrated by lack of opportunity, members are also protected from the anxiety of failure.

In an open-class system such as our own, ability has an opportunity to show itself. The society gains in efficiency but at a price. Members who rise in status must leave friends and kin behind. Those who try to rise but fail are burdened with anxiety, disappointment, and self-blame.

Changes in Status

The changes in status which we call mobility are as important to the members of a group, an organization, or a society as are status differences themselves. What is the relevance of mobility to the problems of the marketing communicator?

Mobility affects markets, media, and messages. It affects people's use of the media, the products they buy, and their reasons for buying them. The marketer, for example, is interested in people's possessions; their possessions are part of their way of life, and their way of life is influenced by their associates.

If a man stays in the neighborhood of his youth, he may not be able to adopt the style of life which his income permits; to do so, would make it appear that he is "getting above himself." If a man moves into a higher-status neighborhood, on the other hand, he may be forced to spend more than he earns to keep up with his neighbors. The taste for some products and skill in using them take time to learn. A marketer must allow such time and assist such learning, if he is to sell as much of his product as incomes warrant. Business associates, too, affect what we must buy and what we must not. In short, the marketer needs to know how a man earns his income and how he spends it, as well as how large that income is.

Since mobility is important to marketing communications, we need to know how much mobility actually exists in the United States and how much is likely to exist in the future.

Experts estimate that over the last 100 years, both in the United States and the industrial countries of Europe, rates of mobility have been fairly constant. Between half and three-quarters of the men in professional, business, clerical, and skilled jobs have risen slightly in status compared to the occupations of their fathers. Only at the bottom of the ladder and at the top is mobility reduced. At the bottom are youths who represent the third generation of unemployed on relief. Sons of the wealthy, on the other hand, have five to eight times as much chance to stay at the top as would be expected if neither talent nor wealth could be inherited (Kahl, 272).

A survey made by the National Opinion Research Center in 1947 compared the occupations of 1334 men with those of their fathers. It found that two-thirds of the men in top positions had higher occupational status than their fathers and that most of the unskilled workers in the lowest group had lower status than they reported for their fathers.

Trends in Mobility

Is this situation likely to continue? An answer to that question depends on what causes social mobility and whether these causes are likely to continue to operate. Kahl estimates that in 1950 of the labor force 67 per cent held occupations at a different status level than those of their fathers. He attributes this change to four causes, giving the first three equal weight.

Cause of Mobility	Percentage Labor Force Affected
Technological	20%
Step-by-step	20
Individual	20
Reproductive	7

(Adapted from Kahl, 261–262.)

Technology has changed the shape of the American class system. Mechanization and automation have reduced the need for unskilled workers at the bottom and increased the need for technical and white-collar workers at the top. As a result, society begins to look less like a pyramid and more like a diamond. Between 1920 and 1950, as the labor force increased 27 per cent, the number of professionals increased by 58 per cent (Kahl, 255), but the number of farmers dropped by 32 per cent. Writing in 1956, Kahl predicted technology would continue to enlarge opportunities at upper levels of job status.

Step-by-step mobility occurs because each new professional position tends to be filled by someone whose father is in the next step down in the occupational structure. As he fails to follow in his father's footsteps, this creates a new opening at the owner-manager level and so on down the scale. Kahl predicts that this process will continue.

Reproductive mobility occurs when men in high-status jobs fail to have as many children as those further down the scale, and thus they create openings in high-status ranks. Kahl predicts that farm families will continue to be largest, urban blue-collar families next, and urban white-collar families smallest. The differences are small, however, and he predicts this source of upward mobility will disappear or even reverse itself, since within each occupational group high-income fathers tend to have more children than low-income fathers.

Individual mobility represents an exchange of job occupants, rather than an overall change in the job opportunities at any level; one father's son slips down a notch, making it possible for another father's son to move up to take his place. This source of mobility is expected to continue.

Immigration, which once introduced large numbers of unskilled workers from overseas at the bottom of the occupational pyramid, has ceased to affect mobility. Very few immigrants are admitted to the United States, and those few tend to enter at higher levels. A new factor in the picture is the internal migration of Negroes from the rural South to the urban North.

Mobility for the Communicator

Figures of the kind just presented help the marketing communicator envision his future audiences and markets. What of his own chances to rise, however? How much room *is* there at the top?

There are some signs that the chances improved between 1928 and 1952, although sons of professional men and businessmen still had an advantage. Four per cent of all men were professionals in 1920. By chance, therefore, 4 per cent of business leaders in 1952 should have been the sons of professional men, instead of the actual figure of 14 per cent. Thus sons of professional men were 3.5 times (14 ÷ 4) as likely to become business leaders as would have been true had they been unable to inherit either ability or improved opportunity. This ratio-of-advantage of 3.5, however, represented a decrease from the 1928 ratio of 4.3. Here are the figures*

Occupation	Ratio of Advantage	
	1928	1952
Professional	4.3	3.5
Business	9.7	4.7
Clerical, sales	.7	.8
Farmers	.3	.3
Laborers	.2	.3

Two factors seem to explain this increase in high-status mobility. One is the increasing size of business firms; in large firms ownership and management seem to be divorced. Another is the increasing number of college degrees obtained by the children of fathers lower on the status ladder, in a day when the degree has become a prerequisite to a job and advancement in the large corporation.

Society and the Individual

In the four chapters of this section, we have looked at men in aggregates and groups, for it is aggregates and groups that make up markets and audiences. Marketing men sell their products to markets and send product messages to audiences. Before the message of a marketing communicator can accomplish its purpose, however, it must reach the eyes and ears of individual members of these audiences and produce a response from them. If men-in-general are important in choosing channels for marketing messages, then man-the-individual is vital in choosing symbols and combining them into messages.

Therefore we must now turn to look at individuals. We shall ask first how they receive and interpret cues from the world about them, and then how their responses to such cues can be explained and

* W. Lloyd Warner and James C. Abegglen, *Occupational Mobility in American Business and Industry* (Minneapolis: University of Minnesota Press). Copyright 1955 by the University of Minnesota.

predicted, in terms of men's habits, their motives, and their personalities.

SUMMARY

1. In groups, status differences develop through interaction; they also reflect status which members bring with them from other, outside groups. These differences affect members' communication and the influence each member exerts upon group decisions.

2. In organizations, status depends both on a man's position on the organizational chart (the prestige of his role) and on his behavior (the esteem given his role performance). In group meetings involving several organizations, his status also is affected by the prestige of the organization he represents.

3. In society itself, status is attached to families rather than to individuals. Six major dimensions of status, which vary in their visibility, are: style of life and occupation, job performance and associates, beliefs and class identification.

4. A scientist must decide which of these dimensions he will observe, and the weight to give each of them in his final assessment of individuals' status. He must decide whether he is going to specify the number of status levels and their labels or let respondents do this. He must decide whether he is going to assign individuals to status positions by asking them to rate themselves, or one another or by using an objective measure of some variable, such as occupation, which is correlated with such ratings.

5. Both intuitively and empirically, occupation seems to be an important and useful index to status both in the United States and overseas. So is education, which helps predict men's acts, attitudes, and interaction. Social class affects such varied behaviors as church membership, child-rearing practices, and prejudice.

6. Roles increase group efficiency, longevity, and give rise to status differences. Status differences, in turn, may aid or hinder communication, decision making, and division of rewards. The status system which aids one function and benefits one group may harm another group and impede another function.

7. Inconsistency of an individual's simultaneous rankings on several different sets of values upsets both him and his associates and creates a desire for mobility. Some kinds of status can be changed more easily than others; societies differ in the kinds and amount of change they permit. High mobility may make a society more efficient at the cost of stress upon its members.

8. Two kinds of mobility are possible. One is a change in the proportions of occupants at various status levels in the society; technology has produced such a change in the United States and is likely to continue to do so. The other is a change in the occupants themselves; room at the top may open up because men at the top have a lower rate of biological reproduction or because inept sons of able fathers slip down a notch on the ladder of status.

Research Studies

The first of the studies in this chapter described how *Whyte* and three assistants worked backstage in a series of restaurants to find how status differences arise and what determines who is assigned to each position. Here you found how subtle distinctions arise among people on the basis of such variables as the food they handle: white meat of the chicken versus dark and why parsley is "better" than potatoes.

The remaining three studies showed how persons with high status influence others, not in the formal structure of the business firm but in less organized settings. *Freeman* and others looked at the community and found three kinds of leaders: men at the head of large organizations, who hold veto power; their subordinates, who actually do the work; and a third group who achieve leadership through sheer energy. *Lionberger* showed how high-status farmers influence their peers in the adoption of new farm practices. *Lefkowitz* and others demonstrated how a man's clothing can change his status and affect his ability to make others disobey a traffic light.

Contents of Section C

SECTION C

The Behavior of Individuals

THIS SECTION is concerned with the behavior of men as individuals, both what they have in common and how they differ from one another in the cues they receive from their environment and their responses to them.

Individuals differ—and this report of women's responses to the "message" conveyed by a display of women's coats in a store window serves as a delightful introduction to a more detailed examination of some of the ways in which persons differ, as explored by the behavioral scientist (Hepner).

How Doggy Is That Coat in the Window?*

Coed Henriette Fischer stationed herself by a store window that showed expensive women's coats and asked each woman who paused, "What do you think and feel when you look at this display?" Here are some of the answers she got:

1. *High school senior, age 17.* Could you see me in the black one? Check those puffy sleeves. I'd look like a woman of forty: I guess my mother would like it though. She'd like the sleeves too. I wonder why there are no cheery colors. How about jewelry or gloves? I think they'd look nice. You've got to have something pretty to wear with that coat. I think there should be more color here.
2. *Coed, age 18, English major.* What do I feel? That's an easy question. I feel like a million. Those black coats are simply exquisite. Just look at that one with the velvet collar . . . that's real style. Those black heels look expensive too. I like the use of the same coat on each figure. That's clever advertising. . . . I never thought

* From *Advertising*, 4th ed., by Harry Walker Hepner. Copyright, 1964, McGraw-Hill Book Company. Used by permission. (Pages 113–115.)

beige could be so attractive when used in such quantities. Any woman will fall in love with this display. I'd really like to see myself in that coat. That white light on their faces is good too . . . seems to be an expression of youth when there is such bright illumination.

3. *Teacher, age 45, married, 3 children.* I could walk right past and not even notice! I can't see what's appealing here. Who wants to see six coats, all the same? That was a poor move to make. What if I didn't like this one? What would make me want to go inside? Nothing. Who ever saw a window in a fine store like this that was so plain? Why not use accessories to brighten things up a bit. . . ?

4. *Saleswoman of department store, age 55, married.* Those sale signs got me. I love sales. What woman doesn't! I really don't need a coat. It's hard to turn away at these prices. How do you think that black one would look on me? Maybe I'm too heavy. Those puff sleeves are attractive. Those prices surely look inviting. I like to see prices in the window. At least you know what to expect when you get inside. If I don't see them, I usually won't go in. Seems too snobbish that way!

5. *Widow, age 57, 4 children, supported by them.* Oh, those coats are beautiful! My daughter would look stunning in that! I love fashions. That's what this looks like . . . a fashion show. Even the dummies look like they're modeling. I feel young looking at the pretty things and the bright coloring. I'm most partial to coats! They're so important in being well-dressed. . . .

6. *College student, age 21.* It doesn't impress me. The colors are dull. The coats are very ordinary. I want style in my clothes! The coats are too basic . . . they lack personality. I'd say they were for women with average tastes and interest in clothes. I'd look to *Mademoiselle* before I'd look here for the new fashions. . . .

7. *Retired school teacher, unmarried.* The color monotone effect is easy on the eye. That I like. I guess I've seen too much Picasso lately, that's why! I feel like splurging. Do need a coat badly. Don't you think I'd look younger in that black one . . . slimmer too! That'd really do a lot for my personality. . . .

8. *Landlady, age 54, married.* They look too country clubbish for me! What would an old lady like me want with such fancy clothes anyway? Don't really think I like the coats either. It sure looks like a nice store. Probably just for rich people. I hate snobbish places. I've heard they look down at you if you don't look ritzy. That's not right. Who can tell how much you have by what you're wearing? You don't know about me by just seeing me here.

9. *Librarian, age 50, married.* The window makes me feel young again. I guess it's the beige color. It's so pleasant to look at . . . so light and airy. I feel like spring is here. Bet you could wear one of those in the spring. A business person might like that black one for work and for social gatherings afterwards. I wish there were a few hats in the window. They're my mania. . . . I wouldn't go in to buy one though. Seems to be too late in the season to buy winter coats. Nice to see though.

Twelve

Receiving the Message:
Man's Senses

• A log blazes in the fireplace and peace reigns in the living room; in the kitchen, an automatic dishwasher grumbles at its evening chores. On one side of the fireplace, the housewife picks a magazine from a heap on an end table and begins leafing through it. Her husband, seated in an easy chair, turns the pages of his evening newspaper, looking for the sports pages. In the background, FM radio offers a string quartet, punctuated by occasional bursts of distant laughter from son and daughter, watching television in an adjoining room.

Peace reigns? Far from it. A bitter battle is being waged among advertising media and brands in the living room; the fate of a firm or a brand, a magazine or a radio program may be decided on what happens in the next ten seconds in this living room and hundreds like it across the nation. This battle begins each dawn, when a clock-radio wakens the housewife and ends only when sleep overtakes her. (Even then a Maidenform advertisement may continue to invade her dreams!)

At every moment of the day, the housewife's senses receive a dozen different signals. This evening, for example, her ears detect at least five: the snap and hiss of the burning log, the creak of her husband's chair, the string quartet, the children's laughter, and the mutter of an airplane passing overhead. And competing for attention with all these, are the advertisements—hundreds of them in a single day. Each advertisement aspires to the same goal: it wants to persuade her to buy something, probably by depositing a message in her memory, in hopes that message will affect her behavior when the opportunity arises.

To accomplish this, the advertiser must produce a message which one of man's ten senses can detect. This is not too hard in itself, for the senses are sensitive, able to report far more information than the individual can use. The problem, of course lies in this very competition.

The food manufacturer finds that his product is judged primarily by the senses of taste and smell, although color and texture have an effect. Cosmetic manufacturers may have to take account of one or more of the four skin senses—cold and warmth, pressure and pain. On occasion, airlines and auto dealers may need to think of two more senses: those of body position and bodily movement. In advertising, however, the men trying to sell other kinds of products and services depend on just two: sight and hearing. Fortunately, these are the two we know most about.

The senses report stimuli which the brain perceives as cues. The marketer needs to know what cues his customers depend on in making their judgments about his product.

How Do Housewives Judge the Freshness of Bread?

Having found that housewives want two qualities in bread—freshness, which they judge by feel, and flavor, which they judge by taste—Robert L. Brown then sought to discover whether bread wrappings affect judgments as to freshness.

He had 50 housewives in a supermarket feel loaves of varying degrees of freshness and in varied wrappings, using a screen so they couldn't see the bread itself. The method of "paired comparisons" was used, in which housewives said which of two loaves was fresher, all possible combinations being used. Proportion of judgments favoring each loaf was as follows:

Kind of Wrapping	Age of Bread			Average for Wrap
	Fresh	Day Old	2 Days Old	
Cellophane	42%	40%	42%	42%
Cellophane and wax	40	33	32	30
Wax paper	18	27	26	24

Difference in wrappers was statistically significant for each age of bread. Housewives could distinguish fresh bread but could not tell day-old from 2-day-old bread at an acceptable level of statistical significance.

—Robert L. Brown, "Wrapper Influence on the Perception of Freshness in Bread," *Journal of Applied Psychology*, 42:257–260.

Cues Are Many

Man's ~~ten~~ *five* senses themselves have several dimensions each. The sounds he hears differ in pitch, loudness, and timbre, for example, and the colors he sees vary in hue, intensity, and saturation. Just these dimensional variations alone—sound (3) $\times$ sight (3) $\times$ touch (4) $\times$ smell (6) $\times$ taste (4)—produce 864 combinations.

Man can distinguish many different degrees within each dimension so that the number of distinguishable combinations is, for all practical purposes, without limit. Slight discrepancies in reports from two receptors, such as eyes and ears, for the same degree and dimension, further increase the potential number of sensory cues.

At the same time, however, there are three factors which tend to limit this variety. First, the senses can detect only a small part of the physical events in the universe. Second, a change along any dimension must attain some minimum size to be detected. Third, every object is identified by many cues, rather than one. An apple, for example, has a distinctive color, taste, shape, size, and "feel." The sensations we feel may combine several cues. What we experience as taste may actually combine pressure, smell, pain, and temperature. We manage to stand upright not only because of cues in our ear, but also because of our eyes, muscles, and senses of hearing and touch. None of man's senses can report all the events that occur in his environment; laboratory instruments reveal many things going on around him which his unaided senses do not detect.

Sight

The electromagnetic spectrum runs from cosmic rays, with a wave length of 4/10,000,000,000,000 of an inch to radio waves nearly 19 miles in length. In this range man can see only a tiny portion in the area of 16 to 32 millionths of an inch. Visible frequencies range from 380 to 780 millionths of a millimeter (millimicrons), although some insects can see in the ultraviolet ray area below 400.

Hearing

Man can hear frequencies of between 15,000 to 20,000 cycles per second; bats can hear up to 40,000 or 50,000.

Smell

Man can detect as little as one-ten-billionth of an ounce of some substances when diluted in a quart of air, yet his sense of smell is inferior to that of a dog.

Taste

Sense of taste varies with the thing tasted, acid and bitter substances being easier to detect than sweet and salty substances. In general, however, man can taste substances that have been diluted from 25 to 1,000 times.

Touch

Sensitivity varies with the particular skin sense involved—pressure, cold, warmth, or pain—and the part of the body stimulated.

By moving his fingertip back and forth, man can detect surface irregularities of only 0.001 millimeter. He can feel two distinct pressure points on the tip of his finger or tongue if they are only 1 millimeter apart. On the middle of his back, however, two pressure points merge into a single sensation unless they are 68 millimeters apart (Woodworth and Schlosberg, 294).*

Sensory Dimensions

Although the senses detect only a small part of the signals available in the environment, the range they cover still contains a lot of information. By combining these reports from the senses, the brain can distinguish an almost infinite number of things. Thus taste buds make vinegar "smell" sour, and cold receptors in the nose can cause menthol to "smell" cool. Pain receptors in the nose give ammonia a biting "taste," and a loud noise can make a light "look" brighter. Much of what we think of as taste is actually smell; the tongue alone cannot distinguish apple from potato or ground coffee from cracker crumbs.

Only a few combinations are actually used to identify separate objects; extra or "redundant" cues are provided so that the "message" will penetrate despite noise and wide variation in the conditions under which the senses operate. This is true not only of combinations between senses, but of combinations among dimensions within each sense. Sight and hearing, for example, have three dimensions apiece; taste and touch four apiece, and smell a half dozen. Here is a summary of these dimensions, indicating for each the physical stimulus and its perceptual counterpart.

The color or *hue* we see is determined by *wave length*— the distance

---

* Because this chapter and the next refer so often to this source, it will be identified henceforth as WS.

between the peak of one wave and the peak of the next. Red appears at the "long" end of the visible spectrum with a length of 780 millimicrons, and violet appears at the short end with a length of 380 millimicrons. *Brightness* is determined by *intensity*—the height of a wave. The "purity" or *saturation* of a color—its freedom from gray—is determined by the *number of different wave lengths* it contains; the fewer wave lengths, the less gray and the more saturated. Gray is produced when we combine complementary colored lights—red and blue-green or yellow and blue—in the proper proportions. Varying the proportions can shift the balance toward yellow or blue with varying degrees of grayness.*

Ordinarily, people seldom distinguish between brightness and saturation and, in fact, the two are related. As intensity lowers, colors fade to gray; oddly enough, the same thing happens if intensity increases beyond a given point. The range of intensities in which gray, rather than color, is seen is widest for the short wave lengths. Within limits, increasing either the duration or retinal area of stimulation will increase the apparent brightness, although intensity itself does not change.

A vibrating object alternately pushes air molecules together and pulls them apart, creating a series of waves moving out from the object, in concentric circles, at a speed of 760 miles an hour. The *frequency* of such waves, the distance between peaks, is sensed as *pitch*. Their *intensity*, the height of the peaks, is sensed as *loudness*. And just as a mixture of complementary light waves produced a third visual dimension called saturation, so a *mixture of sound waves* produces a third dimension called *tonal quality*. It is this quality which enables us to tell a saxophone from a violin.

Again, an explanation requires a moment's digression. If a sound wave repeats itself, we call it a periodic wave. Several such waves may be combined into a complex wave, which can be described by giving the intensity and frequency of each of the parts. Such a wave might consist of 33 decibels at 400 cycles per second, 40 decibels at 800 cycles, and 54 decibels at 1600 cycles, for example. Note that both the higher frequencies are multiples of the lowest frequency. (The latter is called the fundamental and the former are its harmonics.) Such a complex wave, when shown on an oscilloscope or

* This is true only when lights are mixed or added. When paints are mixed, we have a subtracting process, in which yellow and blue produces green rather than gray. This is because yellow reflects red, yellow and green light, absorbing other wave lengths, and blue pigment reflects blue, violet and green light, absorbing all others. Thus the two paints, when mixed, absorb everything but green.

drawn on graph paper, will show a regular pattern. A wave which does not show this pattern, one in which the components are not multiples of one another, produces noise.

Pain, one of the four skin senses, seems to exist in two forms: a prickling sensation, which arises when a small area is stimulated and a dull ache, when larger areas are stimulated. A feeling of heat appears to come from simultaneous stimulation of nearby receptors for the three senses of warmth, cold, and pain.

Pain, of course, is not limited to the skin. Too-high an intensity of stimuli to any of the sense receptors, as well as to the internal organs, will produce a sensation of pain. There seems to be a gap or region of indifference between the maximum stimulation for pressure, cold, or warmth and the minimum for pain. Heat becomes pain when tissue damage begins at a skin temperature of about 113 degrees Fahrenheit. Pressure of 16 grams per square millimeter is sufficient to detect the pressure receptors on a human leg, but pain is not felt until pressure reaches 30 grams (WS, 274-275).

Of the 100-some chemical elements that have been discovered, only sixteen appear to affect the sense of smell. These can be put into five groups (WS, 319):

1. Hydrogen
2. Carbon, silicon
3. Nitrogen, phosphorus, arsenic, antimony, bismuth
4. Oxygen, sulphur, selenium, tellurium
5. Halogens: flourine, chlorine, bromine, iodine

Only the last four elements listed, the halogens, can be smelled in their pure state. Most of the substances we smell are a compound of carbon and one or more of the following: hydrogen, oxygen, or nitrogen.

There is no satisfactory agreement upon the dimensions of smell as a sensation. Indeed, two different classifications are favored, each by a different group:

Psychologists	Industrial Chemists
1. Flowery (violets)	1. Fragrant (musk)
2. Spicy (cloves)	2. Acid (vinegar)
3. Resinous (pine)	3. Burnt (roast coffee)
4. Fruity (lemons)	4. Goaty-sweaty (goats, sweat)
5. Putrid (bad fish)	(Crocker.)
6. Burnt (tar)	
(Stevens b, 1161)	

However, when fifteen subjects were asked to group odors into as many categories as they felt necessary, only one person used as few as four groups, about half needed five or six, and one subject used nineteen.

Generally speaking, taste seems much less sensitive than other senses, more dependent upon other senses, and what sensitivity there is seems most likely to disappear over time, either permanently, in aging, or temporarily, as we shall see later, in adaptation. Four dimensions of taste have been identified, each of which activates receptor organs (taste buds) at different points upon the tongue (Stevens b, 1148–1152):

1. Bitter tastes, produced by vegetable alkaloids like quinine—back of the tongue
2. Sweet tastes, produced by sugars and alcohols—tip of the tongue
3. Sour tastes, produced by acids—sides of the tongue
4. Salty tastes, produced by salts—tip and sides of the tongue

Taste organs seem more sensitive to sour and bitter tastes than to sweet and salty tastes. Note the variations in sensitivity and the existence of two kinds of sweet tastes (WS, 302).

Taste	Substance	Percentage of Concentration
Sweet	Sucrose	.7
Salt	Sodium chloride	.2
Sour	Hydrochloric acid	.007
Sweet	Saccharine	.0005
Bitter	Quinine sulphate	.00003

Combinations of Cues

These sensory dimensions, when combined, affect one another. They interact. In hearing, for example, the physical intensity of a sound tends to be perceived as loudness, and wave frequency as pitch. But a 1000 cycles-per-second wave sounds louder than a 100 cps wave of the same physical intensity. And as we increase the intensity, high pitches become higher and low pitches become lower, although wave frequency, which is primarily responsible for the sensation of pitch, remains unchanged.

There are three types of sensory cues which may be combined: the senses themselves, dimensions within a sense, or reports from different receptors for the same sense, such as reports from two ears, which tell us in what direction a moving object lies, and two eyes, which tell us how far away it is.

In nature, sound serves as an alarm (Kuhn). It does not travel far and it does not travel fast, but it tells us there is a moving object near at hand, and the nearer the object is, the larger it is, and the more violently it is moving, the louder the noise. Our ears can sense sound night or day; it travels around corners. As a result, sound serves the advertiser admirably as an attention getter, although it is poor in providing direction or detail. On the other hand, although we can "tune out" one conversation in a crowd and "tune in" another, man's ability to focus his ears is far less developed than his ability to focus his eyes. Once sound has aroused attention, sight provides cues to details, shapes, and directions. Unlike sound, light continues to carry messages about objects even when they are not moving. Indeed, even within the eye itself there is specialization with two kinds of cells. Some 125 million rods, which sense light and dark but not color, predominate on the outer rim of the retina, the field of receptors at the back of the eyeball which corresponds to film in a camera. They are sensitive to movement, which we can glimpse out of the corner of an eye. Our head turns, and light waves bouncing off the object are focused on the center of the eye, whose seven million cones can report color.

Ears Provide Five Cues

In all, there are five separate cues which our ears can provide as to the location of a moving object. Two of them are *monaural*—a single ear can provide them.

Intensity. Distant sounds are usually weaker than sounds which are near.

Frequency. Most sounds, as we have seen, are made up of several different frequencies. As sound travels, however, high frequencies are absorbed more readily than low; what began as a mixture of high notes and low reaches our ears as a low-pitched rumble.

In addition, there are three *binaural* cues (that is, cues which require both ears).

Time. Since sound waves travel at a rate of only 1100 feet per second, a mere shuffle compared with the 186,000 miles per second speed of light, the width of the head is enough to make a detectable difference of as much as $\frac{1}{2000}$ of a second between arrival of a sound at the near and the far ear. Although this cue does not work if the sound is produced directly overhead, ahead or behind us, we have learned to compensate for this by shifting our head, often unconscious we are doing so.

Intensity. A slight amount of sound is absorbed by the head or by the air as it travels around the head to get to the other side, telling which ear is nearest the sound.

Timing. Again frequencies enter the picture, provided they are low enough. If the distance between wave peaks is sufficient, the top of the wave, when pressure is greatest, will reach the near ear before it reaches the far ear.

Eyes Provide Seven Cues

As for distance, the eyes provide no less than seven cues (Stevens b, 870–871). Two are produced by *muscles* in focusing. For distances up to 20 feet, the muscles which make the lens of our eye thicker or thinner contribute to perception of distance. For distances up to 70 feet, the muscles which cause our eyes to turn toward one another aid perception of distance. More important than either of these cues, however, are four monocular (single eye) cues.

Overlap. When a bush blots out part of a tree, or a person masks part of a building, we know that the bush and the person must be between us and the objects they overlap.

Perspective. As every artist since the Renaissance knows, whether his art shows it or not, distant objects produce a smaller image on the retina than do objects of the same size nearby. Railroad tracks converge to a point on the horizon, detail blurs, brightness, decreases, and colors tend to "gray out" with distance. Objects in the distance appear to be "higher" than those near at hand. In a field or on a beach, the particles which make up texture become smaller and closer together at a distance, making the surface "smooth out." And since the air transmits light imperfectly, distant mountains become hazy and blue.

Shadows. Solid objects cast shadows, and shadows therefore suggest solid objects. Since light ordinarily comes from above, we can "see" three-dimensional, convex, and concave surfaces on a two-dimensional printed page, depending on the placement of shadows.

Movement. When a person moves his head, nearby objects appear to move backwards, but distant objects appear to move in the direction of the head. Thus telephone poles beside a railroad track fly backward as the train passes, but a tree in the distance or the moon overhead seems to "tag along."

In addition to these four cues, there is an important *binocular* cue to distance. Although our eyes are only about 2.5 inches apart, this is enough to give them slightly different views of an object, particularly one that is close. This slight disparity is interpreted as depth, as anyone who has used a stereopticon knows.

Other Cue Combinations

A third example of this kind of combination, in which two receptors for the same sense receive different messages is the sense of smell. Although man has only one nose, he has two nostrils to carry odors to receptor patches along the passageway between his nose and throat. If different odors are presented to the two nostrils, something unlikely to happen outside an experimental laboratory, one of four things may happen. The two may neutralize, so that nothing is smelled; the stronger substance may drown out the other; the two may combine into a new odor; or each may be smelled, one after the other.

Often products are so much alike that the only way customers can tell them apart is by their labels. Here are two experiments that demonstrate this point.

Beer: Remove Labels and Drinkers Cannot Tell Brands Apart

Five groups of 53 to 55 beer drinkers—326 in all—were given free six packs, from which all brand identifications had been removed. Each bottle bore a different lettered tag; each pack contained three out of the five brands, two regionals and three national, being compared. Drinkers rated each on a 10-point poor-to-excellent scale and, on three-point scales, for nine qualities such as aroma, lightness, and after-taste. After the empties were picked up, each participant then was given a pack with all five brands duly identified, plus one extra brand.

No significant differences showed up on the 10-point scale. As for the nine qualities, drinkers agreed that none of the beers had enough aroma, body, foam, or strength, and that all of them were too bitter. One brand stood out as having "just enough" carbonation. Nor did drinkers show any preference for the brand they drank regularly, when they had only its taste to go on.

But with the labels restored, all brands got higher ratings, significant differences appeared among four out of the five; regular users showed a clear-cut preference for their own brand. What is more, ratings for four of the qualities rose—body, foam, aroma, and strength all improved.

—Ralph I. Allison and Kenneth P. Uhl, "Influence of Beer Brand Identification on Taste Perception," *Journal of Marketing Research*, 1:3:36–39.

Bread: Put Different Labels on Identical Loaves and Choices Change

Forty-two women were asked to pick a loaf of bread from four marked only by letters: *L, M, P,* and *H,* being told that the study sought to find out how women make choices when they were faced with unfamiliar brands.

Each woman made twelve such choices. As soon as a woman showed "brand loyalty," by picking the same label three times in a row, the experimenter offered a premium by fixing a penny to the brand label of the brand she had picked least often earlier, and added another penny on each trial that followed until she picked the brand.

The experimenter assumed that early in the study, housewives would want to *compare* brands, and so they would be unlikely to pick the same brand twice; later, he hypothesized, they would tend to make a choice and take the same brand every time. In fact, 29 of the 42 women did try each brand in turn on the first four trials, and some never picked the same brand twice in a row during all of the twelve trials. On the other hand, one woman showed "brand loyalty" at the earliest possible moment, on the third trial, and twenty-one showed it by the end of twelve trials. Other women fluctuated between two favorite brands and six who did not pick a favorite did pick a "nonfavorite" by consistent rejection. Six women switched to the premium brand, when premiums reached anywhere from two to seven cents. Not all switched to the brand with the pennies on it, though; one said, "No wonder you put the special on brand *P.* It is the worst one of all."

In reality, each of the four loaves on every trial had been taken from the same oven on the morning it was delivered. The *only* difference in the loaves at any trial was the letter which appeared on their wrappings.

—W. T. Tucker, "The Development of Brand Loyalty," *Journal of Marketing Research*, 1:3:32–35.

The skin, of course, has a great many receptors. Those for pain are most numerous. The number varies, however, from one part of the body to another. Here are some typical figures, showing the number of sensitive spots per square centimeter (**WS, 276**).

	Pain	Pressure	Cold	Warmth
Tip of nose	44	100	13	1
Back of hand	188	14	7	½

As a result, sensitivity varies greatly. The tip of a tongue or a finger can detect as little as 2 or 3 grams pressure per square millimeter, but the sole of a foot requires 250 grams (WS, 274). The finger tip is very insensitive to pain, however. Although a fifth of a gram pressure on the cornea of the eye can be felt, one of 100 grams on the back of the hand and 200 grams on the sole of the foot, it takes a pressure of 300 grams on a sharp needle to make the finger tip feel pain.

Cues are Quantified

The number of different cues a man can receive thus depends upon the number of different sensory dimensions and the combinations they can produce. It also depends upon man's ability to detect different degrees of any given stimulus. How much does the intensity of a sound have to rise or fall, for example, before his ear can hear a difference?

More than 100 years ago, Weber suggested that to be "just noticeably different" (jnd) a stimulus must be increased by a constant fraction of its value (WS, 194). This rule seems to hold in the middle range of most senses. The least sensitive senses—taste, touch, and smell—require the largest increases, with fractions of one-fifth for salty tastes, one-seventh for skin pressure, and one-tenth for rubbery smells and loudness (WS, 223). A change of $\frac{1}{62}$ in visual brightness can be detected, however, and a change of $\frac{1}{333}$ in pitch. Color vision is sensitive in the 30-millimicron range that extends from 480 (blue) to 510 (green). The eye can detect many different hues here, but it reports very few differences in the 700 to 780 range of reds or the 380 to 450 range for violets.

More recently, it has been suggested that equal stimulus ratios correspond to equal ratios of sensation with each modality having a separate exponent, the range being from .33 for brightness to 3.5 for electric shock (Stevens a).

Decreases in Sensitivity

Although the senses can detect tiny changes, their ability to do so decreases under constant stimulation. *Adaptation* occurs, and time is needed to recover, both for the sense organs themselves and for the nerves that carry their reports to the brain. This temporary decrease in sense-organ sensitivity may serve two purposes. It may save the organs from damage due to overstimulation or it may increase the ability to detect changes, which are a more significant signal from the environment than the absolute level of stimulation.

Nerve impulses travel on the surface of the nerve, the speed varying with the circumference of the fiber—from 100 meters per second down to one meter per second for thin-fibered, cold-blooded animals (WS, 269). Before the nerve can fire again, surface energy must be replenished from inside the nerve, a process that may take 12 milliseconds for a large fiber. Meanwhile, other fibers, and there are several to serve each receptor, take over the communications job. The more intense a stimulus, and the larger the area stimulated, the longer recovery takes. Here are some typical figures.

Vision. When we move from the dark into the light, cones adjust in a minute, rods take 10 minutes (Osgood, 158–159). Sensitivity increases when we move from light into dark, cones taking 10 minutes to reach a level of sensitivity ten times greater than that in daylight, and rods 30 minutes to adapt to a level 10,000 times greater than that of daylight.

If the gaze is fixed on a single object in either light or dark, it will fade out after a brief time. If the eyes move so as to let the image fall on new areas of the retina and cortex, the image will reappear in a second. Three seconds are required if a new area of the retina but not the cortex is involved, and 10 seconds if both retina and cortex areas are unchanged (WS, Chapter 4).

Hearing. For a brief period at 200 to 300 milliseconds, loudness sensed for a given intensity increases over time. Then the ear fatigues so that after a pause of 80 milliseconds, a higher intensity is needed to produce the same loudness. This effect lasts only about half a second, however.

Touch. So far as *pressure* goes, the skin seems to report this sensation only while it is actually bending, a period varying from 2 to 20 seconds, depending upon the size of the weight used and the part of the body, hand, arm, forehead or cheek, being stimulated (WS, 287). Adaptation to *warmth* and *cold* operates primarily through varying the size of the neutral range in which neither sensation is felt (WS, 293). The time taken varies from one-half minute to 3 minutes, increasing as we move away from normal skin temperatures to points as extreme as 41°F and 113°F. On the other hand, if the changes take place slowly enough, at a rate of .36 degrees per minute, the temperature can move eighteen degrees up or down without producing any sensation (WS, 289). Surface skin *pain* produced by a single needle will cease in 10 to 100 seconds; when several needles are applied to a small area, the process may take as long as 5 minutes. Pain from heat does not adapt; it begins to be felt when tissue damage begins, at about 113 degrees Fahrenheit (WS, 293).

Smell. Most odors consist of chemical mixtures, whose parts adapt at varying rates, causing the odor smelled to vary over time (Stevens b, 1165). Nitrobenzol, which originally smells like bitter almonds, tends to take on a tarry odor over time. Both the kind of odor and its intensity affect speed of adaptation.

Taste. The decrease in sensitivity varies markedly with the substance involved (WS, 303–304). Acid shows least change, adaptation requiring an increase of only 1.6 times in the amount that can be used without detection. Bitter substances show a change of two to

---

Not only is the human being so constructed that he can receive dozens of reports simultaneously from his environment, but he seems to require them for his mental well being. This need for stimulation is shown at complex levels as curiosity and at the very simple levels studied in the following experiment.

Desire for Information Motivates Subjects

Eight male volunteers at the University of Pittsburgh were paid $12.50 a day to spend 12 hours lying quietly on a bed in a blacked-out room. Sound was cut off by earplugs and special ear muffs. By pressing a button, subjects could, at will, cause dim ceiling lights to flash 24 times, at one-second intervals.

Four different sets of lights were used; a different set for each of the five days in which volunteers stayed in the room, but unchanged on any given day. The sets varied in the amount of "information" (or novelty) they contained:

Zero information: All 24 flashes were the same color
One-third information: Two-thirds of a given color, the rest being randomly assigned to red or green.
Two-thirds information: One-thirds of a fixed color, the rest randomized.
Total information: All color selection was randomized (and, therefore, unpredictable from one trial to the next.)

As expected, subjects under the last condition pressed the button most often. Over all the conditions, button-pressing increased steadily for the first 9 hours, then fell off for the last three. It was higher on the first day than subsequently.

Experimenters realized that these results could be due to either of two things: a need for information, or an increase in habit strength with reinforcement. So they tried a second experiment, in which 26 undergraduates were paid $12 for a single 10-hour session. This time subjects were forced to spend some time in the room before they were allowed to push the button. Half of them had to wait one hour, and half had to wait five hours. And this time they were given a choice as to how much "information" would be contained in the lights they saw; a dial allowed them to pick the zero, one-third, two-thirds, or total information conditions, as well as a new condition—one in which red and green lights alternated. The question was whether subjects would choose this last condition, which contained the maximum of *variety* in stimulation, to the "total" condition, which included both variety and *novelty*, in that they would never be able to predict the order in which the lights would appear.

This time responses rose steadily with the amount of novelty in the light patterns; the average proportions of responses to each pattern were:

Zero information	10%
Alternating lights	15
One-third information	20
Two-thirds information	25
Total information	30

The group which had to wait five hours made many more responses than the other group—twice as many during the first hours, as shown in this graph. Researchers, who concealed the purpose of the study by calling it "a study of boredom," found they had to overcome two tendencies

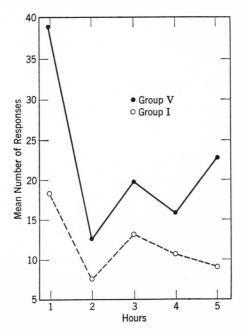

Fig. 12.1. Mean absolute numbers of responses during the first five hours of access to the incentive: Exp. II.

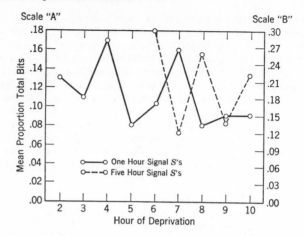

Scale "A"   Scale "B"

Fig. 12.2. Mean proportion of total bits received by *Ss* as a function of hours of deprivation: Exp. II. (For ease of comparison, Group I is plotted on Scale A, Group V on Scale B.)

by subjects. One was that of looking at the situation as a problem to be solved. This was done by telling them what the light patterns were. The other was to keep them from feeling that pushing the buttons was a sign of weakness, indicating that they "couldn't take it." Three subjects, who did spend 10 hours without once pushing the button, had to be eliminated.

—Austin Jones, H. Jean Wilkinson and
Ina Braden; "Information Deprivation as
a Motivational Variable," *Journal of Experimental Psychology,* 62:126–137.

three times, sugar a change of six to twenty times, and salt one of 300 times. The tongue ceases to report a salty taste from a 15 per cent salt solution in 30 seconds; sugar adapts almost as rapidly. Interestingly enough, as taste buds become less sensitive to salty or sour tastes, they become more sensitive to sweetness.

Awake or asleep, man receives dozens of cues through his senses from his environment. Not only does this constant stream of stimulation serve his needs, but it has itself created a need. If a man is placed in a secure, completely safe setting but deprived of all external stimulation, he begins to suffer hallucinations, supplying his system with nonexistent stimuli, and becomes emotionally disturbed.

Sensing and Perceiving

Throughout this chapter we have been concerned with the potential of men-in-general for receiving cues from the environment. Our interest has been in what men have in common and the differences between what their senses report and what is "actually out there."

Now we must turn to another kind of differences. This is not the difference between what men receive and the physical dimensions of sight, sound, and so on, but the differences that existence between one man and another or between Adam$_{today}$ and Adam$_{tomorrow}$.

These differences impose further limits on the cues which will be selected from those available, for only a few of those available actually influence behavior. These differences in perception limit the combinations of cues to which men respond. We move now, therefore, from what men's senses report to how man interprets the reports that he gets.

SUMMARY

1. Every waking moment, man is at the receiving end of dozens of cues from his ten senses. Marketing men may be concerned with all ten, but the advertiser depends primarily upon two: sight and hearing.
2. The number of cues which a man's senses can provide is *increased* by the possibility of using combinations of senses or intrasense dimensions or combinations of reports from two receptors (two eyes, two ears) for the same dimension.
3. The number of cues which a man's senses can provide is *decreased* by three factors: the senses inability to detect more than a small part of physical events along any dimension, their inability to detect changes in degree below some minimum size, and the use of multiple cues to identify objects.
4. Important dimensions are hue, brightness, and saturation in color vision; pitch, loudness, and tonal quality in hearing; warmth, cold, pressure, and pain in touch; sweet, salt, sour, and bitter in taste and four to six different categories of odor. Although each sensory dimension has a principal physical determinant, it often is influenced by other determinants as well. An example: the intensity of sound, as well as frequency, influence the pitch that is heard.
5. Sound serves an "alarm" or attention-getting function, reporting objects that are large, near, and in motion, despite intervening obstacles and darkness. The ears provide five cues as to the direction

of an object, the last three of them being binaural: intensity, frequency, and discrepancies in time, intensity, and timing.

6. Once attention has been aroused, the eyes can scan the object in great detail, providing seven cues as to its distance. Two are provided by eye muscles (changing shape of lens or causing eyes to converge); four are monocular (overlap, perspective, shadows, and movement), and one is the disparity of binocular images. Thus redundancy is built into the situation by using several cues to encode one piece of information.

7. Because the senses must report objects under many widely varying conditions, including the interference we call "noise," several cues are used to encode a single piece of information such as direction and distance. This reduces the number of combinations which can identify separate objects or such object characteristics as distance.

8. All sensory dimensions exist in degrees. However, the fact that a dimensional difference can be detected by laboratory instruments does not mean it can be detected by the unaided sense organs. Weber's rule, for example, calls for a constantly increasing increment of physical change if the senses are to detect any difference. This minimum size increases under continued stimulation, as nerves and sense organs become less sensitive.

Research Studies

The studies of this chapter varied greatly in the scope of their implications for marketing communications and in the nature of their subject matter. Thus *Jones* and others demonstrated that human beings desire variety in the cues which their senses report to them—and desire it to the point that they are willing to get it. They find variety rewarding—and the implications for advertising are obvious.

Brown examined a much more limited problem. He asked how the cues provided by a wrapper affect judgments about the freshness of the bread inside. *Tucker,* in turn, studied bread to show how labels can lead consumers to perceive sensory differences that do not really exist. *Allison and Uhl* showed a similar phenomenon for beer.

Thirteen

Interpreting the Message:
Man's Perceptions

• AN INSTRUCTOR MEETS a class of advertising students for the first time and asks them to write down "ten laws of advertising," based on their own experiences. Then the class proceeds to categorize and count the results. Two categories usually suffice. Many of the laws concern the advertising *message:* "Be brief. Use color. Select type suitable for your product." The others concentrate on the *market:* "Know your audience. Use appeals that interest your customers. Select media which will reach your prospects." Here are two ways of looking at the world, each of which has its adherents: emphasis on messages versus emphasis on receivers.

• AN ART DIRECTOR in an advertising agency leafs through a file of pictures. His success depends upon his skill in picking the illustration which will catch the attention of the largest possible number of prospects.

• A MACHINE TOOL SALESMAN pauses on the threshold of a purchasing agent's office, knowing that his success depends on an ability to size up the individual behind the desk. The prospect's hobbies, the names of his children, perhaps even his politics and his drinking habits all are relevant.

The art director is concerned with the perception of objects. The salesman is concerned with the perception of people—on how others perceive him and on how he perceives them. The art director must emphasize the similarity in the way people view objects. The salesman can concern himself with individual differences in perception.

In the laboratory an experimenter can produce messages so ambiguous and expectations or desires so powerful that the latter alone determines what is perceived. Or he can produce messages so strong, and for audiences so homogeneous that the messages alone determine responses. In real life, however, perceptions depend both on the thing perceived and upon the person perceiving.

Men tend to perceive objects rather than frequencies of light or sound. Sensations serve as cues to categories of objects. The more cues there are, the less perceptions are likely to be influenced by

---

Experts and laymen interpret cues differently in this study.

How Do Women Choose Gifts for Men?

Four groups of persons—80 women, 39 men, 7 package designers, and 8 employees of an advertiser—rated 18 different package designs. They used the "Q-sort" technique, with a 7-point scale "indicate appropriateness as a gift for a man," with quotas of 1-2-3-6-3-2-1 at steps of the scale. (Men and women also sorted designs as to their "masculinity" and "expensiveness.") The following table shows intercorrelations among the 18 designs, margins indicating the scale used and the group doing the rating. (Thus the circled figure, .92, represents a near-perfect correlation between the way men (#7) and women (#8) rated designs as to their apparent "expensiveness."

Scale: Rated by:	1 Mascu- line Men	2 Mascu- line Women	3 Gift De- signer	4 Gift Adv.	5 Gift Men	6 Gift Women	7 Cost Men
Scale **Rated by**							
1 Masc. Men							
2 Masc. Women	.70						
3 Gift Designer	.44	.65					
4 Gift Adv.	.14	.67	.55				
5 Gift Men	.23	−.08	.14	−.42			
6 Gift Women	−.23	−.21	−.48	−.21	.58		
7 Cost Men	−.47	−.61	−.29	−.44	.47	.47	
8 Cost Women	−.55	−.73	−.49	−.47	.41	.53	.92

Women perceived masculinity and expensiveness as being opposites, with a correlation of −.73. They perceived the appropriate gift as being expensive (correlation: .53) rather than masculine (correlation: −.21). Men tended to agree with women, and the advertiser's employees to agree with the designers. Both consumer groups disagreed with both management groups. In judging whether package designs were suitable for a gift, correlations were: −.48 between designers and women; −.42 between advertiser and men; −.21 between advertiser and women; −.14 between designers and men.

—Milton L. Blum and Valentine Appel, "Consumer versus Management Reaction in New Package Development," *Journal of Applied Psychology*, 45:222–224.

the perceiver. The fewer cues there are, and the more objects with which they are associated, the more influence is exerted by the perceiver's expectations and desires.

Only a small part of the physical events in a man's environment are sensed and a still smaller part of those which are sensed have any effect upon his awareness or behavior. A man may be aware of cues without responding to them. He may respond to cues he is not aware of. He may respond to irrelevant cues, perceiving objects that, in fact, are not present. He may misperceive and distort cues that are present.

Three questions concerning perception are, therefore, of importance

---

One way to determine the best combination of product attributes is to ask customers. Another way is to find out what customers have already bought and determine these attributes through examination of the articles themselves.

Housewives Know What They Like Even if They Do Not Know Why

Interviewers asked housewives to show them which pair of their children's boxer shorts she liked best and which pair she liked least of all those she owned. The interviewers then examined the shorts, using a checklist. They found, as one example, that 95 per cent of the "best" shorts but only 61 per cent of the "worst" shorts were made up of four pieces. Here was a clearcut difference, significant at the .01 level, that housewives probably were unaware of. They knew there was a difference in the shorts, but not why.

Here are some of the major ways in which "best" were superior, all of them significant beyond the .05 level:

Characteristic	Mean Difference in Percentage
Close-weave fabric	32%
Solid pattern	22
Sanforized	50
Double-needle stitch on sides	37

And here are some of the features characteristic of "worst" shorts:

Characteristic	Mean Difference in Percentage
Striped patterns	21%
Fading	50
Back seat too small	36
Crotch bind	56
Fabric ravel at seams	73

Five of these characteristics were converted into a discriminant function: 1.59 (close weave) plus .60 (solid color) plus 1.37 (absence of shrinkage) plus 1.01 (absence of fading) plus .97 (cut from 4 pieces). Since good qualities were scored as to presence (1) or absence (0) and bad qualities just the reverse, shorts with all of these good qualities would have a total score equal to the weights: 5.54. Interviewers then obtained 37 more pairs of shorts from housewives. A discriminant function split-off score of 4.50 had classified correctly 85 per cent of the shorts in the original study; it succeeded in identifying 80 per cent of the best and 65 per cent of the worst shorts in the second study.

As a next step, researchers correlated the prices charged for shorts with their discriminant function scores and got a coefficient of .88, indicating that 77 per cent (.88 × .88) of variations in prices were explained by variations in quality. The relationship between price and quality, the author suggests, can be used with sales data, to construct charts which show expected sales volume, given price on one axis and discriminant function scores on the other. This, in turn, can help him predict, for a given quality level, product sales at several different price levels, and from this calculate expected gross profits.

—E. L. Quenon, "A Method for Pre-evaluating Merchandise Offerings," *Journal of Marketing*, 16:158–171.

Data reprinted from the *Journal of Marketing*, national quarterly publication of the American Marketing Association.

---

to the communicator. How can we predict which sensations will be perceived? How can we predict how those perceived will be combined into perceptions of things and people? And when cues conflict, how can we predict which set will win out?

Why Cues Are Combined

Let us begin with the combining of cues and ask why these combinations occur. There are two reasons. The first is the sheer volume of sensations available. There are 100 million receptors in the eye capable of reacting 1000 times and pouring into the brain 100 billion bits of information a second (Kuhn, 113). In the nose, receptors can combine odors in 16 million different ways. In the brain, 10 billion cells of the cerebral cortex can provide a number of circuits that would take 8 billion digits to indicate. Here, in short, is a far greater range of stimulation than a man can respond to in a lifetime. Man must select and combine such sensations to detect a limited number of objects.

The second reason for selecting and combining sensations into perceptual categories is man's need for "object constancy"—his need to treat very different sensations and combinations of sensations as equivalent. A man looks for his car in the moonlight and at noon; he spots it from the front or the rear, at street level or from a fifth-story window; he learns to recognize it by sight or by hearing the crunch of its tires on the gravel of a driveway. He recognizes a friend's voice in a jungle's cacophony or the silence of an arctic waste; in the stillness of a soundproofed office or in the varied noisinesses of a cocktail party, a busy street or a boiler factory. By using several cues to identify an object, man protects himself against the widely varying circumstances in which those objects must be perceived, although occasionally, as in a laboratory, these safeguards may lead to error.

Thus sensations are grouped into categories, so that they simplify the variety of things to which man must respond, and enable him to respond in an unvarying manner to a given object, despite the variety of sensory messages used to report its presence. Some of these categories appear to be very uniform; individuals do not differ much in the way they form and use them. Others vary greatly from one individual to the next, being affected by culture and role, motivation and mood.

Patterns in Perceptions

The Gestalt psychologists have explored the first group of categories, those which appear uniform across individuals. Most of their work has been concerned with vision, which accounts for the great bulk of messages that concern the marketing communicator.

One of the "Gestalts" or patterns discovered by these psychologists is man's tendency to perceive two-dimensional pictures as representing three-dimensional objects against a background: the figure-ground phenomenon. This tendency appears unlearned, since it is found both among rats reared in darkness and in persons, blind from birth, who have gained vision. This phenomenon is found in hearing as well as in vision; a melody appears to "stand out" from its accompaniments. When experimental drawings are produced in which figure and ground are interchangeable, individuals find their perceptions fluctuating, with the part of the picture being seen as figure at any moment, being seen as nearer and as three-dimensional, with definite contours and even a surface texture.

Contrast makes an object stand out from its background and contrast may be of several different varieties. Stimuli which are large or intense, relative to others present, will be noticed. Moving objects will stand out against a static background, but if the background is in motion then it is the static object which will be noticed. If most of the stimuli occur at random intervals, then one which is repeated at regular intervals will stand out. If background sounds and sights are repetitious, however, the interruption will be noticed—the flaw in the border decoration, for example, or the missed beat of a ticking clock. Contrast has a time dimension, too. We hear the radio when it is turned on or turned off, but it fades into the background while it is on. (Perceptions, like sensations, "adapt.")

Another pattern of the Gestalt psychologists is the grouping of small objects, such as lines or dots, into larger units. Four factors cause stimuli to be grouped together:

Nearness. Objects or sounds near to one another tend to be perceived as a group.

Similarity. Objects which resemble one another tend to be grouped.

Continuity. Given a choice, subjects perceive continuous rather than interrupted patterns.

Closure. Missing parts in drawings of real objects or of geometrical figures tend to be filled in.

Grouping objects into patterns in these ways performs a function. It increases the number of stimuli which can be perceived in a given time. Thus subjects who at one-tenth of a second can correctly perceive from six to eleven dots (the average being about eight), can perceive *five groups* of five dots each or a total of twenty-five dots in the same time (WS, 90–105). (However, they probably will not notice if a dot is missing from one or two of the groups.) Subjects can see slightly only four or five unrelated letters on the average, but as many as twenty when put together in a familiar word. (Here, too, they are likely to overlook typographical errors.) They can read a four-word sentence in the same time it takes to read four unrelated letters. A similar phenomenon is observed when stimuli are grouped in time rather than space.

Tendencies to see figure-and-ground and groups of stimuli, of the kind just described, can be predicted without knowing anything about the subjects' previous experience. They seem to be characteristic of all human beings and some other animals as well. There are other perceptions, however, which depend on subjects' familiarity with various objects. These are learned and humans share them only so far as they share experience with the objects themselves.

Object Constancy

To survive in a world of objects, man must perceive objects rather than waves of light and sound. In ordinary life, multiple cues assist in accurate perception of objects. In an experimental laboratory, however, we can make cues conflict with one another and determine, as in the case of sound cues to direction and sight cues for distance, which of the cues are strongest. The most extensive studies of this kind have involved sight. We "see" objects despite partial or conflicting cues. We fail to see any change in objects, despite changes in the sensation-messages received from them, or we see a change in one aspect of an object although no physical change has occurred, merely because other aspects have changed. Here are four types of visual object constancy.

Shape

The top of a milk bottle or a drinking glass is perceived as round and a book or a door is seen as rectangular, whether it is viewed from the top or the side. Yet, every artist knows that when a glass is viewed from the side, he must draw its top as an ellipse, and when the door is swinging, it must be drawn as a trapezoid not a rectangle. So strong is our feeling that rooms and doors are rectangular that, even when we know they have been altered, our brain prefers to preserve object constancy at the expense of such physical impossibilities as shrinking human beings, in altered rooms, and rods that pass through oscillating windows.

Brightness

Coal looks black under a bright sun at high noon, and snow looks white even in the dim moonlight, although the high frequencies which coal is sending back should appear much lighter to our eyes. This is true, however, only so long as we *know* we are looking at coal and snow. Tell us, or let us assume that we are seeing a particular object and we can easily "see" cues that are not there; perception fills in the gaps. Bring the two substances into a laboratory, remove any cues as to what they are (including contrast with their background) and our brains will report the actual intensity reflected into our eyes. Coal then looks white and snow black. In practice we perceive what is called *albedo:* the percentage of light falling on a surface which that surface then reflects. And this, of course, is fixed by the nature of the object. An object with an albedo of 80 per cent will reflect 80 per cent of sunlight, however bright, and of moonlight, however dim. Adults and children have been able to pair off two sets of forty-eight different shades of gray paper, although one set had twenty times as much light thrown on it as the other (WS, 434). But they were able to do so only when they were judging concrete objects—pieces of paper. When the grays were produced by mixing various proportions of black and gray on a color wheel, judgments were much poorer.

Color

We can watch someone cut objects out of a single piece of orange paper then look away and pick colors to match them. So powerful are the meanings we have learned for objects, that the match we make for the piece of paper shaped like a tomato will be redder and that for the lemon yellower than the match we make for the cutout carrot (Bruner, Postman, Rorigues). Blue paper in a yellow light is seen as just that, so long as we know we are looking at a piece of paper against its surroundings. When viewed through a peephole, however, so that neither object nor background is known, the paper appears gray—just as the laws of color mixture indicate it should.

Size

If we see two men, one ten times as far away from us as the other, we do not report the man in the distance as being only one-tenth as tall as the man nearby. Instead we say that the "small" one is just farther away. This ability to interpret difference in retinal size as a difference in distance is clearly learned. Children of three and four have difficulty doing it. So do adults when they are shown unfamiliar objects at an indeterminate distance in the laboratory.

In each of these cases, some of the cues which ordinarily help us identify an object are altered, yet the object itself remains unchanged.

Where does such object constancy come from? It comes from experience; it is learned. This has been demonstrated in the laboratory. Even fish respond to objects. Having learned to pick their food from trays of a certain color, given twenty-four colors to choose from, fish will continue to pick the right tray even when a change in lighting changes the nature of the light reflected from the trays (WS, 437).

Ordinarily, every object provides many more cues than we need to put it into a category; most of our categories are based on several attributes. As a result, attributes can be removed or changed without destroying our ability to put an object into the correct category.

Perceptions Are Learned

In ordinary, everyday experience, we have learned that objects change position more often than they change size, shape, or the amount of light they reflect. This learning, however, is at the subverbal level; it is a habit that we are not aware of. Put us in a laboratory where a balloon can increase in size or brightness, and we are likely to interpret either change as movement toward us. Even when the trick is exposed and we "know better," the perceptual habit persists. We continue to see what experience has taught us to expect, when a single sensation may serve as a cue to two different phenomena. One important attribute of any category is, of course, the name or label attached to it. If the label changes, so does the thing we see or remember. The same line drawings, for example, are reproduced as bottles or stirrups, eyeglasses or dumbbells, depending on which labels were attached to the original drawings (Carmichael, Hogan, Walter).

Perceptual categories are created through the learning processes we call "generalization" and "discrimination." Pavlov's dog, induced to salivate to the ringing of a bell, at first tended to salivate to such similar sounds as the burr of a buzzer or the beat of a metronome. Its response generalized to other stimuli. A human subject's sweat glands can "learn" to react when a certain tone indicates that an electric shock would follow. At first, the glands react to similar sounds as well, although the strength of the response—its size, frequency, and so on—falls off as the similarity of stimuli falls off. Thus as the experimenter moves up or down the scale from the tone which was a cue for shock, the response strength falls off. As trial follows trial, and food rewards only the bell, or shock follows only the single tone, responses to nearby stimuli weaken and are "extinguished." Now, we say, the animal has learned to discriminate.

Through this technique of rewarding some responses and not rewarding others, we can increase or decrease the tendency to perceive objects rather than sensory data. An artist's training enables him to draw ellipses and trapezoids instead of circles and rectangles. When persons view his pictures, they see circular plates and rectangular books. The artist's ability to draw what he senses rather

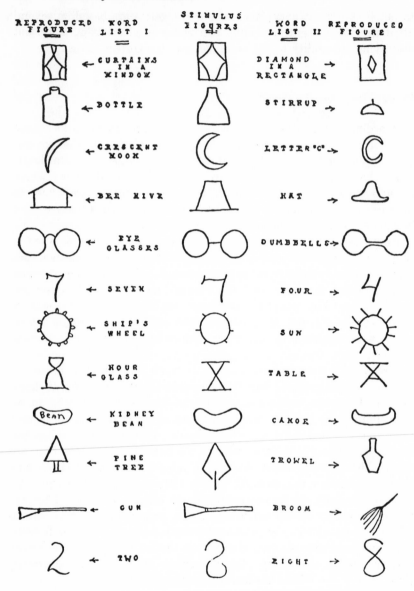

Fig. 13.1. The center column of figures represents those shown subjects. Columns on the side show figures which subjects later reproduced and effects of the labels attached to them (Carmichael, Hogan and Walter).

than what he perceives provides his viewers with information not as to the objects depicted but as to the position from which the artist viewed the objects.

Thus discrimination learning answers the question of qualitative perception—of how similar objects must be for us to be justified in treating them as identical. A series of rewarded and unrewarded trials narrows the limits of a category which originally was broad.

Perceiving Quantities

Other experiments in the perception of quantity have sought to determine how limits are set when we rank such varied phenomena as a set of weights or a collection of attitudes.

In some experiments, subjects are given a standard stimulus, somewhere in the middle of the range of objects being judged. In such cases, their judgments become less accurate as they move away from this standard, in either direction. On the other hand, if they are not given any such standard, after a few trials they supply standards for themselves in the form of the high and low ends of the series. Again, the farther they move away from these standards, the less accurate their judgments become, but in this case, errors pile up in the middle.

What happens when a subject has established for himself the limits of the set of stimuli and the experimenter introduces a new stimulus either above or below these limits? What kinds of error occur? If the new stimulus is near the old limit, the distance between the two will be underestimated. But as this new stimulus moves further and further from the original set, an opposite tendency sets in and the differences are exaggerated.

If a weight, a light, or a heated object is at the heavy, bright, or hot end of the set of objects being judged, it feels and looks heavy, bright, and hot. Extend the range, however, by adding heavier, brighter, or hotter objects, and the original object will begin to feel and look light, dull, and cold. If, on the other hand, the subject is handed a new kind of object during the judging process, its heaviness, brightness, or hotness will not affect those being judged. Comparison takes place only across similar objects, across objects falling within the same categories, whether these categories are the groupings of the Gestalt psychologist, the result of individual learning, or of temporary psychological set.

If a subject now divides the categorized objects into two classes, he will exaggerate the similarity of objects within a class and the difference between the classes. This is true not only of things like weight but even of attitudes. Prejudiced persons appear to be unusually sensitive in identifying members of groups they dislike but relatively insensitive to seeing differences within a group they dislike. Anti-Semites show superior ability to identify Jewish persons from a series of photographs; they are highly motivated to detect such cues (Allport and Kramer). Persons prejudiced against Negroes, on the other hand, find it difficult to tell one Negro from another; to them, these are distinctions without a difference (Seeleman). To keep our categories from merging into one another, we exaggerate inside similarities and outside differences.

The rewards of discrimination learning not only determine the limits of our perceptual categories; they also influence which of two objects we perceive, when given a choice. This has been demonstrated by showing four different outline faces (Schafer and Murphy). Subjects learned a name for each face, being rewarded with two to four cents each time they viewed two of the faces, and penalized the same amount each time the other two were exposed. After twenty-five exposures to each face, new drawings were shown, each of which combined one punished and one rewarded face. Subjects were told to call out the name of a face as soon as they recognized it; names of the rewarded faces won out, by a ratio of fifty-four to thirteen.

Evidence that a subject's eyes may report cues which do not get through to his awareness (or which he won't admit to another that he has seen) has established the phenomenon called "perceptual defense."

Sweating Palms Reveal What Tongue Denies

Sixteen students in Alabama, half of them coeds, were shown a series of 18 words. A tachistoscope exposed each word for .01 second to begin with, with exposure being increased .01 second on each trial, until subjects recognized the word.

In addition to measuring the time it took before a subject would repeat the word to the experimenter, electrodes on their palms reported their galvanic skin responses, a measure of emotional response outside the conscious control of a subject.

Seven of the words on the list were "emotionally toned," several of them having sexual implications and not ordinarily used in mixed company. A comparison of GSR readings and exposure times indicated that these seven words did produce more of an emotional response than the neutral words which followed or preceded them, and that longer

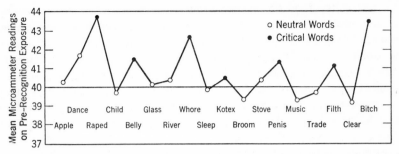

Fig. 13.2. Group averages of galvanic skin response to neutral and critical words during prerecognition exposures.

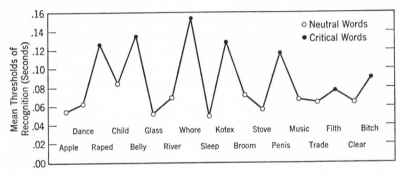

Fig. 13.3. Mean thresholds of recognition of the observers to the neutral and emotionally charged words.

exposures were needed before a subject would repeat them to the experimenter.

—Elliott McGinnies, "Emotionality and Perceptual Defense," *Psychological Review*, 56:244–251.

Role of Expectations

Given a choice of two figures, or a figure which is vague or ambiguous enough to be interpreted in two ways, one tends to see what he expects to see or what he would like to see. Expectations may be based on a lifetime of experience, as in object constancy, or on a very short period of activity, in the phenomenon called "psychological set." Thus if we have been looking at a series of letters, we are likely to interpret an ambiguous figure as the letter "*B*", whereas if the figure has been preceded by a series of numbers, we are likely to report seeing the number "13."

Just as we tend to see what we have been rewarded for seeing in the past, we tend, when given a choice, to see the reward most relevant to our current needs and desires. A hundred sailors were shown a dimly lit, smudged screen, and told that it showed a picture of "three objects on a table" or "a group of people enjoying themselves." Only 15 per cent of the sailors who had eaten an hour previously reported seeing pictures of food on the screen; but 23 per cent of sailors who had not eaten for sixteen hours reported seeing food (McClelland and Atkinson).

Suppose, now, that we are exposed to pictures which are threatening or unpleasant rather than rewarding. What happens then? Some exper-

---

But two critics point out flaws in this and similar experiments which cast doubt on the phenomenon.

Three Reasons to Doubt That "Perceptual Defense" Exists

A review of a wide variety of studies of perceptual defense suggested that so-called emotionally toned words, which subjects were slow to recognize, also tended to be longer, less familiar, or the kind which are not usually used in mixed company.

However, two studies in which word length was controlled, reported positive results. Of 25 studies in which both length and frequency was controlled, positive results were reported in 18. When all three factors—length, frequency, and the dirty-word dimension were controlled—only 5 out of 12 studies produced positive results.

A similar review was made of studies concerning the related phenomenon of subception. None of the 7 which found the phenomenon had controlled for partial recognition; the 3 which had all produced negative results.

—J. C. Naylor and C. H. Lawshe, "An Analytical Review of the Experimental Basis of Subception," *Journal of Psychology*, 46:75–96.

---

iments suggest that we are more likely to see such signs of danger than we are to see neutral cues. On the other hand, so many experiments show resistance to the perception of such stimuli that the resistance has been given a tag of its own—"perceptual defense." A smoker does not see newspaper stories about the relation between cigarettes and cancer (Cannell and MacDonald). If he sees them, he does not read them. If he reads them, he distorts the message. And if he understands the message, then he proceeds to forget it as rapidly as possible. The suggestion has been made that perceptual defense occurs when the threat is one that the subject is not ready to cope with, but that increased perceptual sensitivity occurs when

---

Are we more or less likely to recognize and remember an unpleasant experience? This study suggests that it depends on (1) how extreme the experience is and (2) whether we can escape or must endure it.

Clem and Rufus—A Shocking Pair

A squiggly line, marked "ambiguous" in the drawing below, was used as the basis for two faces—Clem, facing right and Rufus, facing left. Forty-nine coeds then were assigned to tracing the profiles with the fingers of their left hand. When their fingers reached the mouth, they were given an electric shock, half being shocked by Clem and half by Rufus. (Every so often Horace's face was introduced as a "set-breaker.")

Three different levels of shock were used (18, 25, and 50 volts) and some of the subjects were allowed to jerk their hands loose and escape the shock while others were not. (An additional 6 subjects received 75-volt shocks, but only under conditions of "escape.")

Combining these results with results in earlier experiments in which 40- and 60-volt shocks were used or in which shock was administered three-seconds after a profile had been traced, produced the following graphs.

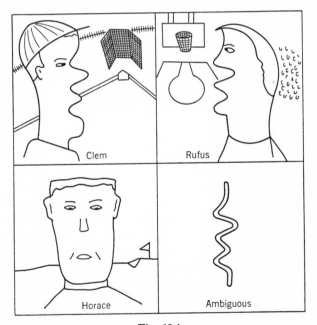

Fig. 13.4.

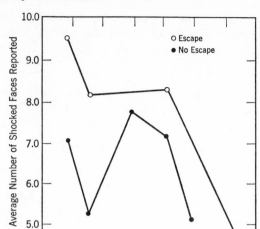

Fig. 13.5. Percentage of shocked faces recalled most vividly by subjects in each escape condition.

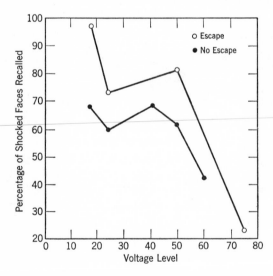

Fig. 13.6. Average number of shocked faces reported by each escape condition.

As the graphs show, subjects were more likely to recall the shocked profile more vividly in verbal reports after the test. In a subsequent series of tests, however, when the ambiguous line was shown 14 times, interspersed with views of Horace, they were less likely to recognize that the line was the profile which had shocked them earlier. When the shock was one they had been unable to escape, subjects tended to repress the shocking profile.

—Harold J. McNamara, Charles M. Solley and John Long, "The Effects of Punishment (Electric Shock) On Perceptual Learning," *Journal of Abnormal and Social Psychology*, 57:91–98.

the subject can do something to avert the danger. Perception thus aids survival. It mobilizes the individual for dangers he can do something about, but it keeps from him cues which would produce anxiety which, in turn, would make him less able to cope.

Details may be suppressed or distorted as a result of our desires, as in perceptual defense, and also as a result of our expectations. The inexperienced proofreader will miss a great many typographical errors; his eye sees what it expects to see. A black five-of-hearts in a trick deck will be seen either as red or, perhaps, as a five-of-clubs. Cues may also be overlooked for a third reason. Those which persist unchanged over time tend to fade into the background; it is the sudden silence, not the constant noise, which is heard.

Perceiving Persons

Predicting which cues will be selected and how they will be combined becomes even more difficult when we turn from the perception of objects, which interests the advertiser, to the perception of persons, which interests the salesman. Four things affect the salesman's perception: his own ability, the type of person being perceived, the particular trait or attitude being perceived, and the similarity between the situation in which cues are perceived and that in which perceptions will be used.

If the salesman is somewhat detached by nature, intelligent, and well-adjusted, his judgments are likely to be more accurate. It also helps if he makes an overall judgment rather than proceeding trait by trait. Similarity between salesman and customer makes the salesman's perceptions more accurate. One reason is that all of us tend to assume that other people resemble us; if in fact they do, then this tendency leads to accuracy in perception. Another reason is that we are likely to associate with people like ourselves and increased experience increases our ability to perceive them correctly. Traits which are expressed in overt behavior are easier to judge, the more so as the person being judged is uninhibited in his behavior. The man who can evoke significant behavior from another, as well as interpret the behavior correctly, forms more accurate perceptions.

The cues we look for depend on our relations with the person being perceived. Thus a salesman looks for cues of friendship from a fellow salesman, cues of praise or reproof from a sales manager, and of ability to take directions from a trainee. Moreover, the same act or comment will be perceived very differently depending on the status and role of the person who produces it. A slap on the back has different meaning if it comes from a superior, a subordinate, or a peer.

Gestures and pictures, like words themselves, convey meaning. People seem to agree on these meanings, although objective tests may indicate that they are wrong in doing so. Thus 800 visitors at a business exposition agreed fairly well on their estimates of the proficiency of ten salesmen, on being shown their photographs, but there was no relation between the rankings and the men's actual performance. This is somewhat surprising since we would expect so strong a stereotype to influence the salesmen's customers if not they themselves. Existence of such stereotypes was also demonstrated when 111 college students were asked to fill out a psychological inventory as they thought it would be completed by two men—one earning $42.50 a week and the other earning $250 (Luft). Students rated the low-income man as being maladjusted and unhappy—much more so than was indicated by similar forms completed by working men actually receiving such incomes.

Temporary conditions can alter these meanings, however. Students subject to military duty see more "threat" in pictures of military officers than students not so subject, and girls who have just played a game of "Murder" perceive more maliciousness in a set of photographs (Murray a).

Selecting Cues

None of us use all the cues available in judging another person. Typically, we make up our minds fairly soon after meeting him. We form an attitude about him, and from then on perceive those cues which are consistent with this attitude and distort or ignore those which contradict it.

In one experiment, for example, subjects were given a brief autobiography and, halfway through, asked to fill out a personality test as they thought the subject of the autobiography would have (Dailey). Having committed themselves, his subjects made few changes when they filled out a second personality test after completing the sketch. Their test results were further from those of the actual person involved than were the scores given him by a second group of subjects which read the complete autobiography before marking the test.

In another study subjects were given descriptions of two persons, one who was intelligent, industrious, and impulsive and another who was critical, stubborn, and envious. After writing down their impressions of the two individuals, they were then informed that all these traits actually belonged to one person. They found it very difficult to imagine such a person—much more so than did students who were told, from the start, that only one person was involved (Asch a).

Sometimes we form a general impression of like or dislike, and then rate all traits to conform to this, producing what has been called a "halo" effect. Or we judge one trait more or less accurately but then make other traits conform because of a "logical error"—we think the two are closely related to one another. Sometimes a single word is enough to color our perceptions. Two groups of subjects, for instance, were given a list of descriptive adjectives: "intelligent, skillful, industrious, determined, practical, cautious" (Wishner). There was only one difference in the lists. The word "warm" appeared on one and "cold" on the other. This was enough to make a difference. Such differences were big enough to persist even when subjects were face-to-face with a man described as "cold" or "warm." In a second experiment, students participated in a twenty-minute discussion with an instructor previously described as "warm" or "cold" (Kelley). Students in the "warm" half of the class participated more in a 20-minute class discussion, and rated the instructor afterward as being more considerate, informal, sociable, humorous, and humane.

When the description involves differences of *role and status*, similar differences in perception are found. Pictures of two middle-aged men were shown to seventy-six labor unionists and 108 personnel men, both men being described as family men who had held several jobs successfully, but had few outside interests or hobbies (Haire b). There was only one difference in the descriptions. One was described as the manager of a branch plant of a large manufacturer, and the other as secretary-treasurer of a union. The two groups looked at the pictures for a minute, then checked a list of 290 adjectives, some favorable and some unfavorable. By subtracting the number of unfavorable adjectives checked from the favorable, and summing the results by type of adjective, the following table was obtained:

Net Percentage of Favorable Adjectives in Area of—	Management Sees Manager	Labor Sees Unionist
Thinking	58%	55%
Feeling	62	56
Personal relations	71	65

Note that in each area each group saw its own "representative" as being superior.

In effect, of course, since the descriptions were identical and the pictures randomized, this study measures men's attitudes toward role descriptions—but one assumes that these attitudes would affect their perception of persons occupying such roles in real life.

Our stereotypes of roles are strong, sometimes so strong that we must devise ways of handling incongruent elements when they are brought to our attention.

When forty-five psychology students were given a list of seven phrases describing a factory worker, they found it easier to summarize the description than another forty-three students who were given the same list but with one added word, "intelligent." Five of the forty-three ignored the attribute completely. Some fourteen more explained it away by stating that he might be intelligent, but he must lack the ambition for schooling to benefit from it. Five more denied that he was a factory "worker"—they promoted him to foreman. Three students protested that the man's job and this trait, intelligence, were contradictory. Only fourteen students seemed to change the stereotyped views of factory workers by suggesting that his intelligence, which was denied outlet on the job, expressed itself in social activities. They described him as witty, interesting, well-liked, or fun to be around.

The *situation* in which perception occurs also will have an effect. By an ingenious use of tape recorders and screens, a number of students were given the impression that they were directing a dull task, in which one subject was supervised more closely than the other (Strickland). The output of both subjects was identical, and exceeded the supervisor's standard in nine periods out of ten. However, in

What a man perceives in a situation is influenced by what he expects to see—and his expectations derive from his job or role.

Each Man Sees Problems in His Own Area

A group of 23 executives enrolled in a manufacturing firm's executive training program wrote brief statements as to what they considered the most important problem facing a steel company, after reading a 10,000-word case study.

Here are the results. Column headings indicate the nature of the problem each identified; labels on the rows indicate what department of the firm the executives came from.

Department	Total Number Executives	Number of Executives Who Mentioned		
		"Sales"	"Organiza-tion"	"Human Relations"
Sales, accounting	10	8	1	0
Production	5	1	4	0
Other	8	1	3	3

—DeWitt C. Dearborn and Herbert A. Simon, "Selective Perception: A Note on the Departmental Identifications of Executives," *Sociometry*, 21:140–144.

subsequent ratings the student supervisors rated the subject who was given close supervision as being less trustworthy and dependable than the other. They justified the fact of close supervision by a feeling that this subject had worked only because he was closely supervised. Their perceptions of the other person were determined by their treatment of him, rather than the reverse, and in spite of his own behavior.

Perception and Learning

Men put the cues received from their environment into categories and perceive the cues as patterns. They ignore some of the differences that exist, treating the cues as equivalent, and they accentuate other differences. Some of the categories men use are shared by men in general, whereas others vary. These variations in individuals are the result of different experiences; men tend to use the categories they have found rewarding in the past.

This process of reusing categories which have brought reward is called learning; such perceptions, we say, are learned. Observations

**Do subordinate and superior see different things when they look at the firm?
Yes, says this study—**

Men in Management See the World Differently

Members of management in five firms—58 men who reported directly
to their firm's vice president—were asked to pick one of their subordinates with whom they had frequent contact and knew fairly well. Open-
end interviews with the 116 men were then studied by the two interviewers, plus a graduate student, who compared the answers of superiors
and subordinates.

Using a scale that ran from 0 (no agreement) to 4 (complete agreement), researchers concluded that only on the issue of job duties did their
superior-subordinate pairs agree even slightly more often than they
disagreed:

Issue: Subordinate's	Average agreement	Percentage of Pairs in which Agreement Occurred	
		Less than half	More than half
Duties	2.4	15%	46%
Qualifications	1.8	36	23
Future job changes	1.6	50	32
Job obstacles	1.0	68	8

The results raised the question of whether such disagreement is good
or bad, whether it aids or hinders the organization in reaching its goals.
A superior may conceal future job changes, to keep a subordinate from
becoming anxious. A subordinate may not tell a superior of all the
obstacles he faces, either because this might reflect on him or because
the superior does not want to be bothered. In short, perhaps the two
should not agree!

—Norman R. F. Maier, L. Richard
Hoffman, John J. Hooven, and William
H. Read, *Superior-Subordinate Communication in Management* (New York: American Management Association, 1961).

of a newborn baby will not enable us to predict such behavior in
the adult. Indeed, very little of the adult behavior which interests
the marketing communicator is innate. Most of it is learned. The
principles of learning, therefore, are of major importance to the communicator who wants his message to be understood and remembered.

Learning, as we shall see in the next chapter, deals with two kinds of behavior which, on the surface, appear very different. One is the almost-automatic response of brand loyalty; the other is the slow, deliberate choice of the person who carefully weighs brand against brand. One is habit and the other is problem solving and decision making on the basis of remembered messages.

Why do superior and subordinate see things differently? Because they have different goals and values, this study suggests.

How Do You Judge People: By Their Power or By Their Pay?

What kinds of categories do people use when they look at jobs and the men who perform them? To answer this question, Triandis gave employees at all levels in a firm a list of 3 jobs, and asked them to indicate which two belonged together. He gave them 13 such sets of jobs to choose from, and another 13 sets of people.

One set, for instance, consisted of "teacher, welder, clerk." A respondent could drop teacher from the list, as the only "professional," or welder, as the only manual worker, or clerk, as the only one involved in routine work.

Both top and middle management, he found, classified *jobs* on the basis of pay and power; workers classified jobs on the basis of pay and requirements of the job. The 3 differed markedly in the *people* categories, however: top management grouped people on the basis of class, middle management on the basis of power, and workers on the basis of authority and pay.

When he asked his subjects to rate 5 jobs and 6 kinds of people on a series of 8-point semantic differential scales ("clean-dirty, good-bad," etc.), he found women valued people on qualities such as honesty, politeness and marital status, but that men valued them on the basis of job knowledge and experience.

—Harry C. Triandis, "Similarity in Thought Processes and Boss-Employee Communication," in *Communication in Organizations* (Ann Arbor: Foundation for Research on Human Behavior, 1959).

SUMMARY

1. Men must perceive objects and people. What they perceive depends in part on sensation and in part on what they expect and desire to see. Perception that depends on sensation is of interest to the advertising man who must frame messages that appeal to large numbers of people. Perception that depends on the perceiver is of interest to a salesman who can deal with a few individuals at a time.
2. Perception involves three problems: which sensations will impinge

on our awareness or behavior; how will these sensations be grouped into meaningful categories; and when conflict occurs which perceptions will win out?

3. Why are sensations combined? To reduce the volume of cues man must attend to and to provide object constancy under widely differing contexts.

4. Gestalt psychology has discovered patterns which appear common to all humans. These include figure-and-ground, contrast, and grouping. These tendencies seem to exist in the stimuli themselves.

5. In addition, there are four types of selection of cues which seem to serve object constancy: shape, brightness, color, and size. Despite its apparent universality, such constancy appears to be learned; it can be produced in the laboratory in lower animals.

6. So much for methods of putting perceptions into categories. How are the categories themselves created? At first, rewards produce generalization; stimuli which resemble that to which response has been rewarded also call forth the response, although strength of the S-R relation decreases as stimuli are more distant. Failure to reward these related stimuli narrows the span of generalization, producing discrimination.

7. Within a category of qualitatively similar stimuli, subjective perceptions of a given stimulus vary with the upper and lower limits of its associated stimuli, but are unaffected by stimuli outside the category.

8. Rewards not only determine the limits of perceptual categories, through the process of discrimination learning, but also decide which of the two objects is perceived, when choice is necessary.

9. Expectations which influence perceptual choice may be life long and common to a culture, as in the case of object constancy, or they may be limited to a single individual and a brief time period, as in the phenomenon of psychological set.

10. In addition to perceiving what we expect, we also tend to perceive what we desire. Such desires may be deep rooted, as in beliefs, values, and attitudes, or they may be brief, reflecting temporary drive states and momentary moods.

11. Accurate perception of persons depends on the perceived, the person and trait perceived, and the similarity between the situation in which cues are perceived and that in which perceptions will be used. Role and status influence the cues that are looked for and the way they are interpreted. Labeling a person as "warm" or a union official can affect perceptions of him. The "halo effect" and "logical error" lead to inaccurate perceptions. First impressions are important and traits inconsistent with our expectations may be suppressed.

Research Studies

Three types of studies are included in this chapter: studies that deal with the fundamentals of perception, studies of perception by customers, and studies of perceptual differences among employees of business firms.

McNamara and others find that people throw up a barrier between themselves and unpleasant experiences, a barrier which makes them refuse to recognize or remember faces which have "shocked" them. *McGinnies* reports the same phenomenon when shocking words are involved, although *Naylor and Lawshe* suggest that factors of length and rarity also play a part in reducing recognition, immediate or delayed.

Quenon shows that housewives know what they like, but that it takes an expert to find out why in a study which reveals what five characteristics of boys' shorts win customer favor. *Blum and Appel,* in a study of gift packaging, on the other hand, point out why it is dangerous for business "experts" to assume that they know what the public wants.

Thre studies concern the business firm itself. *Dearborn and Simon* find that the work role which a man performs within the firm colors his perception of the firm's problems. *Maier* and others discover that perception of problems is influenced by the status a man occupies, and *Triandis* finds that status has an even greater effect upon the perception of people than it does on the perception of the jobs that people perform.

Fourteen

Responding to the Message I: Habits, Learning and Memory

A housewife pauses in front of a supermarket shelf. Her behavior in the next few seconds may decide the fate of a new product, an advertising campaign, or even an entire firm.

Two things may happen. The housewife's eye may sweep the shelf and her hand unerringly pluck from it a favorite brand of detergent, pretzels, or cake mix. Ask her a second later what she picked and she will not know until she looks into her shopping cart. Habit rules her behavior, to the point where she does not consciously make a choice at all: her eyes see and her hand moves. Something similar may happen when the woman picks up her telephone. To a clerk's query, "flour? she may respond "Pillsbury" and to his query, "toothpaste?" she may respond "Colgate's." Habit decides, not the housewife.

Another housewife may pause in front of the same supermarket shelf, but her eye sees the brands jostling one another for space. With a speed akin to that of a computer, her mind sorts out a series of memories: "Brand X? It did not turn out so well the last time I used it. Brand Y? They have been advertising a lot lately—maybe I ought to give them a try. Brand Z? Jane says there is nothing like it. Brand . . . Oh, there is that new kind of spaghetti that I have been looking for!" And, her attention diverted by a nearby display, she may pass up all three brands and go home without the cake mix, detergent, or pretzels she originally sought.

Two different housewives? Not necessarily. This may be the same housewife on two different days; indeed, the different behaviors just described may occur within a minute or two of one another, as the housewife walks from one aisle to the next.

Which type of behavior is "better"? That depends. The advertiser calls the first kind of behavior "brand loyalty" and, if he has a

396

major share of the market, regards such loyalty as a major asset; above all, he wants to know how to foster and preserve such habits. On the other hand, if the advertiser is just trying to break into the market, he regards existing loyalties as a major obstacle. His job is to get the housewife to compare the brands on the shelf—hoping, of course, that his product and his advertising will make her decide in his favor.

How about the housewife herself—which kind of behavior best serves her interests? Critics of American marketing sometimes talk as if *every* purchase a housewife makes should be preceded by careful comparison and a deliberate decision. If this were true, there would certainly be a lot fewer purchases, more hungry husbands, and more

---

Repeated purchase of a given brand or at a given store represents the important receiver habit which, viewed from the standpoint of the seller, is termed "loyalty".

Purchase Diaries of 66 Families Test Brand Loyalty

Purchasing records kept by 66 families for a 3-year period were analyzed to determine their loyalty to given brands of seven products, the inroads which bargain prices made on loyalty, and their loyalty to specific retail outlets.

The 66 families represented the "survivors" of an original Chicago Tribune consumer panel of some 700 families. First, not all the families returned records for the full 3-year period; this reduced the number to 402. Second, not all 402 families attained the "minimum purchase level" set for each product, as shown here:

Product	Minimum Purchase Level	Number of Families
Toilet soap	18 cakes	390
Scouring cleanser	15 cans	319
Regular coffee	20 pounds	359
Canned peas	13 cans	325
Margarine	10 pounds	290
Frozen orange juice	10 cans	211
Headache tablets	4 purchases	208

In fact, only 66 families achieved minimum purchase levels for all seven products. (Minimum levels were necessary for two reasons. First, low levels would inflate loyalty figures—the person who made only a single purchase by definition would be 100% loyal to the brand picked, and second, because low levels would be of little interest to the seller.)

The 66 families were divided into tenths on the basis of the amount of brand loyalty they showed. Here are figures for headache tablets and cleanser. Note that price deals for competing brands did reduce loyalty for cleanser but not for the tablets. (Figures for the most loyal tenth of families appear at the top of the table; figures for the least loyal tenth at the bottom.)

Percentage of Purchasers Loyal to Single Brand

Headache Tablet		Cleanser	
Price Deals Omitted	Price Deals	Price Deals Omitted	Price Deals
100%	100%	100%	95%
95	95	98	81
87	87	85	68
77	77	77	60
72	72	69	55
64	64	60	50
55	55	51	46
49	49	48	41
43	43	44	37
33	33	29	31

Apparently people cannot be split into two distinct types: the loyal and the disloyal. Brand preference is a matter of degree. Moreover, there was little evidence that a housewife who was loyal to one brand showed a general habit of loyalty to brands in other product groups. All of the correlation coefficients in the following table are low; even the highest, .30, was not statistically significant.

	Soap	Cleanser	Coffee	Peas	Margarine	Juice
Cleanser	.30					
Coffee	.23	.17				
Peas	.02	.12	.07			
Margarine	.14	.13	.12	.27		
Juice	−.06	.02	.06	.22	.19	
Headache tablets	—	.10	.09	.13	.08	.02

Loyalty to store was somewhat higher than loyalty to product. The tenth of the families showing most retail-outlet loyalty made more than 90% of their purchases of the seven products studied in a single store; the least loyal tenth made a third of their purchases in a single store. Loyalty to brands of coffee, canned peas, and frozen juice showed some correlation with single-store loyalty but headache tablets and cleanser did not.

	Correlation
Regular coffee	.43
Canned peas	.42
Frozen juice	.39
Margarine	.30
Soap	.20
Headache tablets	.05
Cleanser	−.05

—Ross M. Cunningham, "Brand Loyalty: What, Where, How Much," *Harvard Business Review*, 34:1:116–128.

Brand Loyalty after 12 Years

In a public school just outside Washington, D.C., Guest gave 813 pupils in grades 3 through 12 a list of brand names and asked them to indicate, for each of fifteen product categories, which one of five brands they preferred. That was in 1940–1941. Twelve years later, in 1953, he obtained responses to a mail questionnaire asking their brand preferences from 20% of the original group.

On a chance basis, he reported, he would have expected only about 3% agreement between 1940–1941 and 1953 preferences; he got an average of 32% for the 15 products. (Averages ranged from 23% for cereal to 38% for razors.) He also compared 1940–1941 preferences with the brand respondents reported buying most frequently in 1953, and found an agreement in 28% of the preference-and-use choices. (This compared with only 68% agreement between 1953 preference and 1953 use.) Age, sex, intelligence, and socio-economic status showed no effect on brand loyalty. However, respondents who were married in 1953 showed less agreement—presumably because a spouse's preference would affect their own preferences and use.

—Lester Guest, "Brand Loyalty—Twelve Years Later," *Journal of Applied Psychology*, 39:405–408.

---

nervous fatigue among housewives. Habits *are* useful; they save time and energy. Often there is little evidence on which a housewife can make a choice. Price is no guide, when brands do not differ in price. Product differences are no guide if she cannot detect them or does not think they are important. From her standpoint she might as well toss a coin. By buying the brand she has always bought, or the one whose name first pops into her mind, she saves the trouble of tossing a coin! Although a habit may persist beyond the point where it pays off, a shift to decision making is often more desired by the firm trying to increase market share than it is by the housewife herself.

Changing Habits

Sometimes accidents may help a firm get the housewife to break an old habit. A faulty oven or a telephone ringing at the wrong moment may spoil a cake, but if the cake mix is blamed, a new brand gets its chance. More often, a cents-off deal or a premium offer will make the housewife try a new brand. Advertising may switch the housewife from habitual to decision-making behavior, and then induce a new habit. Even the cents-off deal must be advertised. Moreover, advertising builds expectations concerning performance, and we know such expectations can influence the way a housewife perceives a performance. Point-of-purchase advertising then can remind the housewife of her success when the time for repurchase rolls around.

Point-of-purchase advertising can jog a housewife's memory at the moment she makes her decision; a colorful placard over a wire bin of cake mix can guide her hand unerringly to its destination. In somewhat similar fashion, the billboard that catches a driver's eye, the advertisement in a subway or bus and the commercial heard on a car radio may be followed minutes later by a purchase. Most advertising, however, has delayed effects, just as does most classroom learning. Most advertising has to be remembered if it is to be effective.

The housewife's memory may work at the level of unawareness, in the automatic verbal habit of a "flour?—Pillsbury" response or at the level of awareness, by providing the material for decision making. Thus memory links the two kinds of behavior—habit and a conscious choice among alternatives—which at first glance appeared very different.

Memory is the province of the learning psychologist. It is the residue of learning which itself is often described as the formation of habits. In a very real sense everything that an adult is and does is learned, including his attitudes and personality, his perceptions of the world, the motivations that stimulate him, and the way he groups objects into concepts and gives those concepts names. The discussion of learning in this chapter, therefore, is at the root of everything in this book, a key to the understanding of marketing communication. Marketing communications are, in fact, a kind of teaching process which we can divide into three elements—the learning that takes place at the moment of transmitting the message, the memory involved in "storing" and retrieving the message, and the performance evoked in the future. Of these three elements, the only one which can be observed is performance. Both learning and memory must be measured by performance; we can distinguish between them only by drawing an arbitrary line somewhere in time. Performance evoked before this point represents learning, and behavior evoked after this point represents memory.

This is true whether the habit involves the study of Sanskrit in a graduate seminar, or a five-year-old's insistence on cornflakes that look like ill-nourished doughnuts.

Classroom and Market Place

There are important differences in the way habits are formed in the classroom and in the market place, however. First, the student in the classroom usually has come there for the purpose of receiving the teacher's messages; he expects them and wants them. Second, the teacher's messages, both in theory and in practice, tend *not* to compete with one another. Most teachers suggest that there are "right" answers to questions, and correct solutions to problems. If a teacher offers several solutions or answers, it is often with an apology for the present state of the discipline, a hope that further study will disclose the special conditions under which each is appropriate, or a suggestion that the student extract the "best" elements from each answer. Third, when a student enters the classroom, he commits himself to listen and gives up his freedom to "turn off" the source.

In contrast, when a housewife views television or reads a woman's magazine the advertisements either must compete with the program and editorial content which she originally sought or slip their message across incidentally. Under such circumstances, the housewife may expect to see advertisements but does not particularly want them—her motivation to learn from them is relatively low. Moreover, the advertisements themselves compete with one another, each claiming to be "the" solution to the problem the advertisement itself has suggested, and "the" answer to the question the advertisement itself has had to raise. To the novice, many of the studies that come out of learning laboratories may appear to have little relevance to marketing. A great many learning experiments involve animals, such as the white rat, which lack the symbols of language that are so important in communications. Many studies of learning are made to guide the classroom teacher, who differs from the advertiser in the ways just described, and use children as subjects, in contrast to the adult targets of most advertisements. The laboratory settings used differ dramatically from the "real world" of the marketing man, and the tasks to which subjects are set often appear trivial and irrelevant. These differences may be less important than they first appear, however.

Measuring Learning

Learning has been defined as any relatively permanent change in performance resulting from past experience. This definition involves two difficulties. First, when we try to measure the kind and amount of change resulting from a particular past experience, we must first exclude all things other than experience which might affect present performance, things such as fatigue, drugs and drink, changes in motivation, and the physiological changes that occur as a child matures and an adult becomes senile. Second, we must rule out the effects of all the experiences which occurred *before* the particular experience we are interested in. This is why psychologists have had to invent novel tasks which no subject is likely to have had experience with.

Sometimes these tasks are perceptual-motor skills: running mazes, mirror-drawing, keeping a stylus in contact with a target on a turntable that revolves regularly, erratically, or at varying speeds. Sometimes the tasks consist of learning lists of nonsense syllables, either one by one or in pairs. (However much it may contribute to learning theory, a task such as memorizing lists of syllables such as "aij" and "zqj" and "vik" does appear both trivial and irrelevant to the marketing man. At least, it does until we remember that such studies have helped the makers of such products as "Fab" and "Vel" and "Duz" pick brand names that would be easily remembered and produce favorable feelings in the housewife.)

This is the first reason why, although we need to remember the differences between the learning laboratory and the market place and be cautious in generalizing from one to the other, the marketer does well to take a look at learning. He never knows when something from the field may become highly relevant to his own problems.

The marketing men can, of course, treat the literature of learning as a vast grab bag, turning to it for answers to such specific problems as these:

1. When six commercials are broadcast back-to-back, which will be best remembered—the first one, the last one, or the two middle ones?
2. Is it better to repeat the same commercial six times without a pause or, forgetting about any change in audience, at six widely separated times?
3. Under which circumstances is a message learned fastest and remembered longest—when every hearing of it is rewarded or only a few hearings?
4. What happens when a store switches to self-service—do the purchasing habits formed in one setting transfer to the new situation?

Each of these problems can be looked up in the index of any basic text in psychology. The first is under the label of *serial learning*, the second as an example of *distributed practice,* the third as *partial reinforcement,* and the fourth as *transfer.*

If the marketer treats learning as a grab bag, however, he will lose one of the greatest contributions of learning theory—the fact that it has achieved, to a degree unmatched elsewhere in psychology, a theoretical formulation which integrates and relates a wide variety of concepts and phenomena. And, of course, he will face the difficulty of finding the correct psychological labels for his problems, and the risk of generalizing from laboratory to market place mentioned earlier.

Four Basic Concepts

One way to look at learning theory is to start with four basic concepts. They are reinforcement, stimulus, response, and repetition as they appear in the phrase: "A *reinforcement* is anything which strengthens the relationship between a *stimulus* and a *response,* in a *repetition* of trials."

Of the three terms, response is the most basic: a rat, a pigeon, or a housewife does something. This behavior becomes a "response" if we can find some cue in the environment which set it off, and the cue itself becomes a "stimulus." The sight of a package of Duz causes the housewife to grasp it. A rat runs to a food-box; a pigeon pecks at a grain of wheat. If the relationship between cue and response increases in strength, or if the response increases in frequency, we ask what advantage housewife, rat, and pigeon gain from making the response and we call this advantage or reward a "reinforcement."

Let us take a look at two classic examples of how a reinforcement works.

• The first involves a dog—Pavlov's dog, strapped into a harness in the laboratory so that he cannot move. The amount of saliva flowing into the dog's mouth can be measured. Pavlov increased this flow by putting food into the dog's mouth then found that if he sounded a bell before providing the food, the sound alone produced saliva—and continued to do so for a few trials even when the cue of a ringing bell proved false and no food followed. Pavlov, in short, succeeded in attaching a new stimulus to an old response, and the food which was a stimulus in the original S-R pair became a reinforcement ("Anything which strengthens an S-R relationship . . .") in the new one.

• The second example involves a pigeon—Skinner's pigeon, enclosed in a glass box, and given a bit of grain whenever it did something the experimenter chose to reward, from pecking at triangles to twirling in counterclockwise circles. By skillfully providing rewards as the pigeon advanced closer and closer to the desired behavior, Skinner produced a new response. The reward of grain acted as a cue, "telling" the pigeon whether it was on the right track or not. In each case food acted as a reinforcement of the desired response. Thus Skinner succeeded in attaching a new response to an old stimulus.

Tests of Habit Strength

When a Pavlov "strengthens" the relationship between bell-and saliva, and a Skinner strengthens a whole series of responses which eventually may produce a counterclockwise twirl, how does one measure the strength of the new relationship between stimulus and response?

Pavlov had a convenient index. He measured the amount of saliva produced. This is one of six different measures of learning, the first three of which can be used with single subject:

Size. How *big* is the response? This is limited to situations such as the flow of saliva; it is used most often when trying to get individuals to perform an old response to a new stimulus.

Accuracy. How far or how long a time is the subject "off target"? This, of course, is best used when the habit involves a motor skill.

Delay. The response occurs much more quickly after the cue is given; the "latency" or delay decreases.

The other three measures of habit strength require several trials, or several subjects, or both:

Frequency. How many subjects give the desired response on a given trial, or how many times does a single subject give the response on a set of trials? The higher the frequency of response, or the fewer the errors, the greater the learning.

Practice to a criterion. How many minutes or how many trials does it take subjects to reach a standard, such as two successive repetitions of a list of words without error? This is useful for comparing different teaching methods or the learning abilities of different subjects.

Persistence without reinforcement. How long does a subject persist in behavior after withdrawal of the reinforcement which originally brought the behavior up to criterion?

This rise in the strength of a relationship between stimulus and response is what we mean by learning. Since the line between "learning" and "memory" is an arbitrary one, these four measures of memory are also measures of habit strength:

Recall. Can the subject reproduce what he has learned—can he supply the name, recite the list? This method takes a good deal of time and frequently scores are so low that comparisons between two advertisements are impossible. Various aids to recall can be provided. Instead of asking "What advertisements did you see in this magazine?" an interviewer may ask "What *soap* advertisements did you see?" Or he may name the product and a slogan and ask for the brand name.

Recognition. The subject is shown a list of words or a portfolio of advertisements and asked which he saw in the magazine. Scoring must take account of chance success, and make sure that subjects could have seen the ad only in the magazine being studied. Sometimes an ad not yet published is included. Subjects who claim to have seen the unpublished ad can be dropped from the study as unreliable.

Reconstruction. Scrambled parts of an original message are given the subject who is asked to put them back in their original order. The method, rarely used in advertising, works only when there is no natural or logical order which would be apparent even to someone who hadn't seen the message previously.

Relearning. When a subject relearns something he has forgotten, the "savings score"—the reduction in time or trials required for the second learning—is sensitive enough to reveal traces of learning where other measures will not. (Conversely, the savings score is inferior to recall if we want to discover small amounts of loss.)

These are ten ways in which we can detect a rise in the strength of a stimulus-response relationship, ten ways in which we can determine whether we have been successful in inducing learning.

Four elements are needed for learning. The customer must first have some *felt need*—what learning theorists call a "drive condition." This impels him to do something, but by itself does not determine exactly what. Second, there must be one or more *stimuli*—cues indicating that various acts will result in rewards relevant to the felt need. A very weak stimulus may not be sensed; a very strong one, such as a bright light or loud noise, may act as a drive—the subject will seek to escape. Third, the customer must anticipate a *reward* which is greater than the effort required to get it. Fourth, there will be some *previous experience* with drive, cue, and reward.

The more frequently a particular drive, cue, and reward have been associated with a given response in the past—the greater the habit strength—the more likely that response is to occur when drive and cue recur. Some minimum amount of each of these four elements must be present, since their relationship is multiplicative rather than additive. The difficult question, that must be answered in each specific instance, is how much one element must increase to offset a fall in another; how much habit strength it takes to compensate for a

---

It is easier to learn, and harder to forget information which lends support to our existing attitudes.

Mass Arrests or Clean Cottages: Two Points of View

Ten students in New York City, 5 of them pro-Communist and 5 anti-Communist, were asked to read two prose passages over twice. One of the passages was anti-Communist, referring to mass arrests, executions, and barbarous deportations. The other was somewhat pro-Communist, referring to Russian elections, its "bright clean cottages" and feeling of unity.

Students read one of the passages, spent 15 minutes chatting with the experimenter, and then were asked to reproduce the passage they had just read as accurately as possible, before going on to read the second message. The learning trials were repeated for 4 weeks at the end of which students' memories were tested for another five weeks.

The following graphs show that students tended to learn faster and retain longer messages which matched their own attitudes.

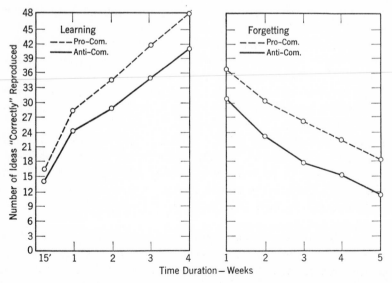

Fig. 14.1. Learning and forgetting curves for "correct" responses for pro-Communist and anti-Communist groups on the pro-Soviet Union selection.

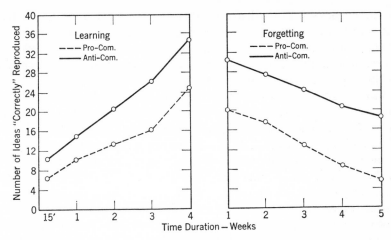

Fig. 14.2. Learning and forgetting curves for "correct" responses for pro-Communist and anti-Communist groups on the anti-Soviet Union selection.

—Jerome M. Levine and Gardner Murphy, "The Learning and Forgetting of Controversial Material," *Journal of Abnormal and Social Psychology*, 38:507–517.

drop in drive strength, or how much reward must rise as drive weakens.

An advertiser usually finds it easier to influence perceived reward than habit strength and felt need. Although he can predict fairly well whether a cue will be "sensed," it is harder to tell how it will be perceived—what response will follow. Rewards, therefore, are of great importance to the advertiser, as every writer of an advertising text recognizes when he tries to deal with them under the heading of "basic appeals." Unfortunately, almost anything that exists can be rewarding to someone. Most of the persons who make up an advertiser's prospects take satisfaction of the basic physiological needs for granted; no very satisfactory list of learned or secondary needs has ever been drawn up.

Six Decisions on Rewards

However, there are six decisions about rewards which can be listed and the listing of which can help an advertiser.

Source or receiver? It is the learner's goals, not those of the teacher, that determine what is learned; the customer's goals and not those of the advertiser. A teacher may seek to produce understanding, but the pupil will work for a passing grade. An advertiser may talk about shoes, when he should be selling comfort; toys, when he should be selling parents delight in happy children; or tires, when he should be talking about worry-free driving.

Timing. Every individual has many goals, some of which may conflict with one another; you have got to offer him the one he's interested in at the moment of choice. If you make cake mix then the rewards you can offer in an ad may mean picking a time to broadcast your commercials when individuals are likely to be hungry and interested in food. Individuals differ in their tolerance for delay; some will wait longer than others for a reward. Immediate rewards are more effective than delayed ones. Thus it is well to provide smaller rewards along the way—grades each term in college, not just a bachelor's degree at the end of four years, or trading stamps to paste in a book, not just a premium after the housewife has made enough purchases to fill twenty or thirty books.

Intrinsic or extrinsic? Children often learn things because of rewards which are extrinsic to (outside of) the learning itself. A boy practices piano so that he can play softball or he does his homework for a dish of ice cream. Let rain drown out the softball game or the store run out of ice cream, however, and the boy will stop playing the piano. Once the task itself becomes rewarding (that is, when rewards are intrinsic to the learning process), then learning maintains itself.

Complete or partial? Learning proceeds faster when every performance of the task being learned is followed by a reward, but under such a schedule performance also vanishes more quickly when rewards are cut off. The best strategy is to teach under a 100 per cent schedule of reinforcement, and then shift to partial reinforcement at random intervals. Performance then will persist long after the rewards themselves cease, or when the frequency of reward is very low. Skinner, for example, has taught pigeons to respond at the rate of 6000 pecks an hour for only twelve rewards—one for every 500 pecks (Hilgard, 92).

Random or regular? Reinforcement can be regular, with every nth trial being rewarded or with a reward being provided after every nth interval of time, or the rewards can be at irregular intervals, as indicated by a table of random numbers or the flip of a coin.

Positive or negative? So far we have talked only about positive rewards; what about punishment? Escape from the threat of punishment acts as a positive reward but actual punishment may interfere with learning. One reason is that although punishment acts as a cue to indicate what should not be done, it does not suggest any positive alternative types of behavior. It does cause the subject to engage in more variable behavior, during which he may stumble upon the desired behavior, but even then it does not tell him which of several alternatives is preferred. Punishment tends to suppress performance but doesn't cause a response to be unlearned; as a result, once punishment ceases the performance may return. Moreover, punishment may generalize, inhibiting more aspects of behavior than one intended, and inducing considerable emotional upset as a byproduct. A subject will try to avoid and escape punishment, but he may do so not by giving up the habit at which punishment is aimed, but by changing his attitude toward the source of punishment (rejecting the teacher or the advertiser who alarms him with scary symptoms), or by fleeing from the situation in which punishment occurs (giving up school rather than spitballs, turning off television rather than buying the sponsor's headache remedy).

Repetition. If a reward is received after an act is performed, then that response is strengthened; it is more likely to occur next time

---

If a category is always referred to in unflattering terms, its image becomes clear—but it is also easily reversed.

Students Assess the Traits of an Unknown Tribe

Eighty students in Massachusetts were told that anthropologists and missionaries who had visited a little-known people had agreed on their personality traits. They were then given a list of 50 personality traits; after each trait was shown, they were asked to indicate whether they thought it applied to the group.

In actuality, the list was equally divided between traits such as "active" and "gifted," which 90% of the students in an earlier study had indicated were desirable and traits such as "boastful" and "lazy" which 90% had termed undesirable. (The traits, of course, were presented in random order.)

Five 16-person groups, equally divided between men and women, were then formed. In one group, the experimenter confirmed every attribution of an undesirable trait to the group (a 100% schedule of reinforcement). The other groups were given schedules of 92%, 80%, 64%, and 50% reinforcement.

After 50 such trials, students then responded to 25 more traits, but without any comment by the experimenter; these responses were used to measure the strength of any tendency to describe the unknown group in undesirable terms. Finally, in a third series of 54 randomly ordered traits, the experimenter reversed his field, and indicated that desirable traits were characteristic of the group.

Here are the results, showing the proportion of "correct" responses—responses predictive of and confirmed by the experimenter, under each condition:

Proportion of Traits Confirmed	Mean Number of "Correct Responses" Under Various Levels of Reinforcement				
	100%	92%	80%	64%	50%
50 Training Trials (Negative confirmed)	44.6	36.6	29.2	25.4	25.5
25 Test Trials (No confirmation)	24.3	20.2	17.2	16.1	13.5
54 Habit-change Trials (Positive confirmed)	49.6	39.8	41.2	45.2	44.5

Reinforcement on every trial produced higher scores on training and test trials, the differences between groups being significant at the .001 level. The group receiving 100% reinforcement was also most easily reversed later, analysis of variance showing significance at the .025 level.

—Ramon J. Rhine and Betsy A. Silun, "Acquisition and Change of a Concept Attitude as a Function of Consistency of Reinforcement," *Journal of Experimental Psychology,* 55:524–529.

the opportunity offers, it occurs more quickly, and so on. If a reward is *not* received, then that response is weakened. The effects of repetition, therefore, depend upon whether it is repetition with reward or without reward. Repetition well beyond the point at which a criterion performance is reached greatly extends the length of time over which memory can operate. Such overlearning explains why such skills as swimming and riding a bicycle are never really forgotton; an adult who has not done either for years can quickly pick them up again. And it explains why we eventually learn such difficult sets of random digits as telephone numbers!

Task and Learner

In addition to rewards, there are two other things which affect the speed of learning. One is the state of the person doing the learning, and the other is the nature of the task being learned.

*Individual*s vary in their capacity to learn, which is measured by an intelligence test. At one time, it was assumed that these tests measured an inherited ability; increasingly, however, the effect of environment on these scores is being recognized. One of the most important aspects of environment, and one that affects performance both on an intelligence test itself and on a specific learning task, is the kind and amount of motivation it provides. Too intense a need can actually be distracting, and failure can discourage an individual from continued attempts to learn. A successful trial can be highly motivating to an individual who is accustomed to fail, just as an occasional failure can stimulate the individual who usually succeeds to greater effort. In many learning situations, success and failure depend upon what goals the learner sets for himself—on his *level of aspirations*. Therefore it helps to teach him to set goals that are high enough to stimulate continued effort but low enough to ensure frequent success.

As for the *nature of the task,* learning theorists have worked with several different kinds of tasks. Eventually, perhaps, all their findings may be reduced to a single theory. At present, however, and particularly for the person interested in relating their findings to market situations, it seems best to think of several types: serial learning, motor skills, problem solving, and such selective learning as perceptual discrimination.

Perceptual learning has already been best treated in our chapter on perception. Motor skills, whether of the advertising man's typist or the salesman's golf pro, are peripheral to communications *per se*. Problem solving, as found in decision-making by the household or business firm, is of very great importance to the marketing communicator, but up to now the leap from the laboratory finding to the board room application has been too hazardous for any but the very brave to attempt.

Serial learning comes closest to duplicating the conditions of communications as well as being a favorite subject for the psychologist, whether he is running rats through mazes, or getting human subjects to learn poems, word associations or lists of nonsense syllables.

In each of these examples, the subject's first response acts as a stimulus to his second, his second as a stimulus to his third, and so on. Note that although the second response becomes a stimulus for the third, and so on, there is no reason to expect the process to work in reverse, and indeed it does not. Most of us have overlearned the alphabet to the point where we can rattle it off without a thought—but we cannot recite it *backwards*. Indeed, the fact that "*g*" is a stimulus which suggests "*h*" tends to interfere with new learning when we try to work from "*g*" to "*f*" and "*f*" to "*e*".

Conditions That Aid Learning

Studies have shown serial learning goes best when rest periods break up learning sessions, when subjects recite as well as read, and when a teacher lets them know whether they are right or wrong. Breaking a memory task into parts and learning the parts separately sometimes helps, although learning to put the parts together will take time, too; from 30 to 80 per cent of learning errors occur at this stage (McGeoch and Irion, 504). In general, the more meaningful the material to be learned and the higher the intelligence of the student, the better it is to learn the whole rather than part by part. A chance to test ourselves by reciting what we are trying to learn should come early and may, with profit, take up to 80% of the total time spent in learning (McGeoch and Irion, 508). Recitation has several advantages: it provides partial rewards along the way, it gives subjects experience in taking the tests by which their final success will be measured, and, combined with prompting from a teacher, it helps students eliminate errors and concentrate their practice on the most difficult parts of the task.

The easiest parts of any word list or any maze are the beginning and the end; they are learned first and remembered longest. For this reason we would expect a customer's first impression of a salesman, the headline or illustration which is the first thing we see in an advertisement, or the first advertisement we see in a magazine or newspaper to have more effect than those that come afterward—except for those that come at the very end.

Frequent rest periods are very useful; one theory is that rests allow a subject to forget wrong stimulus-response relations faster than he forgets correct ones. Rests also allow physical fatigue and the fatigue of boredom to dissipate. As a result, a test may show a higher score following a rest than immediately before the rest, even though no learning has taken place during the interval. It is supposed that this is because the errors and fatigue which masked learning have been erased during the rest period. This phenomenon—it is called *reminiscence*—is especially likely with young subjects and meaningful material.

The proper length and spacing of practice and rest periods varies with subjects and task. It has been found, for instance, that subjects who can learn fifty words of prose in 2.25 minutes, take four times as long to learn twice as many words (McGeoch and Irion, 489). Subjects asked to add and subtract series of three, four, five, and six digits have found the time required for learning rises as the cube of the number of operations to be performed (McGeoch and Irion, 494). Rests as short as one minute between trials have been found helpful; periods of twenty minutes, twelve hours, and twenty-four hours have been found better than either shorter or longer periods in other experiments.

In studying the effects of rest periods we must make sure that subjects were not continuing to practice mentally while supposedly resting. One solution is to have subjects engage in some alternative activity during rest periods, but even this is likely to give them an advantage, by maintaining a learning set, or a disadvantage, by conflicting with their principal task. Other solutions are to compare a resting group with a control group which continued active practice; to use animals, presumably incapable of mental practice; or to study the effects of rest on learning of motor skills, where mental "exercise" during rest should be less help than in verbal learning.

If an individual's progress is plotted on a graph, in the form of a learning curve which shows an increase in proficiency or a decrease in errors, he makes rapid progress at first, gradually slowing down. Sometimes the graph shows periods of rest in which little improvement is shown. The sudden spurt that ends these "plateaus" may be a renewal of motivation, or a shift in learning strategy, as when an individual who has been translating a foreign language word by word begins to grasp the meaning of entire phrases. In this they resemble the sudden insights that occur in problem solving.

The more variable an individual's behavior, the more likely he is to stumble upon a solution. Being exposed to a lot of different stimuli helps; so does rapid abandonment of inadequate responses. Above all, it is necessary that the subject persist in his searching behavior. High motivation usually helps here—unless it is so high that it leads to persistence in inadequate responses rather than in trying new ones. Previous habits can both help and hurt problem solving. They hurt when they cause an individual to persist in inappropriate responses. Anything which can temporarily suspend the former habit, such as sleep, or engaging in another activity, or the help of another person, therefore will help. Habits help when problems can be solved by combining parts of old responses in new ways. The greater the variety of old responses, the more likely one is to have the parts needed. Moreover, experience in making new combinations itself can lead to a problem-solving habit called "learning to learn." The big question, of course, is how much transfer can occur between old and new.

Transfer of Learning

So far we have talked as if we were working with entirely new stimuli and responses. This is rare, however, for the adults with whom marketing communications is concerned. Adult learning is more likely to involve substituting a new stimulus or a new response in the old stimulus-response relationship. The question then becomes whether existence of the old relationship makes it easier or harder to learn the new one. In psychological terms, one asks whether *transfer* will be *positive* or *negative*.

Learning is aided when new stimuli and responses are similar to old ones—transfer is positive. Trouble arises, however, if the new response is opposed or antagonistic to the old one. Rats have learned to turn right when a light is on, and left when it is off, in an average of 286 trials (McGeoch and Irion, 323). When the signals are switched, it takes them an average of 603 trials to unlearn the old S-R relationship and substitute the new one. Similar difficulty has occurred in military airplanes where switches for communication and ordnance were located left-and-right for the pilot and right-and-left for the co-pilot; whenever the two men changed seats, trouble developed!

If such changes in S-R relations occur frequently enough, however, something new happens: we get nonspecific, positive transfer. Learning a specific action, such as stepping on the clutch, may cause one to tromp down meaninglessly in a car with an automatic transmission. But learning how to attack a new problem, or discovering a principle or rule that can be applied to a series of similar situations may speed up learning tremendously. In the short run of a single learning period we call such transfer "warming up" or "persistence of set." In the long run, we refer to it as "learning to learn." Such nonspecific transfer speeds up learning. Moreover, the rule or principle is much more economical than the variety of experiences which it covers; it is, therefore, much more easily remembered.

Transfer is important for three reasons. One is that the same task is never performed twice under identical circumstances; the conditions under which a task is learned and those under which it is used will always differ. Another reason is that almost all adult learning involves transfer since it requires taking parts of old habits and putting them together in new combinations. The third reason is that the phenomenon referred to as forgetting, or memory loss is itself an example of negative transfer. Mere passage of time does not produce forgetting, nor are the memories themselves totally wiped out. Ancient events long below the level of awareness can be brought to the surface of articulate speech again by hypnosis or electric stimulation of the brain. Passage of time gives a chance for new learning to occur which interferes with previous learning. This has been shown by comparing the memory losses that occur when subjects are put to sleep, immediately after learning trials, with the losses that occur when they engage in activity. The more this intervening activity resembles the new activities being learned, the greater the interference and memory loss. It is as if the mind had a series of shelves, with new memories jostling old ones for a place out front. This is why an advertiser seeks to make his message distinctive, his advertising media effective and experience with his product distinctive and why he repeats his message frequently. He hopes *his* message will be the first one to cross the threshold of awareness at the crucial moment when the housewife makes her purchase.

Observing Learning

So long as an individual responds by visible movement or audible speech to some observable event in his environment, it's easy to specify a stimulus (S) and a response (R). We can call the point-of-purchase advertisement an S and the housewife's grasping of a package an R. When thoughts and memories, which cannot be observed, serve as stimuli and responses they are symbolized by lowercase letters—s and r. When a television commercial causes a housewife to think, "I'll try that next time I shop," this is an S-r relationship. If the housewife recalls the television advertisement as she stands in front of the shelf, and reaches for the package, this is an s-R relationship. In the s-r relationship neither element is visible to an outside observer: the housewife, musing over her coffee cup, recalls the television commercial and makes a mental note to follow its advice.

How do we know that this s-r relationship exists? One way is through introspection—ours and that of others. Introspection fails, however, unless the housewife is aware of her s's and r's. If she is not aware of them, an observer can still infer their existence. He can divide subjects at random into two groups and expose one group to a series of ads. If he then finds that the exposed group purchases more of the advertised product than the unexposed control group, he can infer that an S-R, or an S-r-s-R relationship exists. From the standpoint of an advertiser, this unawareness of s-r relationships may be the best thing that can happen. Many persons do not like to admit they have been influenced, particularly by an advertisement, but if they aren't aware they have been influenced they cannot resist. This is why we question the dictum, common to many advertising texts, that the first job of an ad is to get attention, the implication usually being that the housewife should be aware of the advertisement at the time of exposure.

Little s's and r's which are verbal are of most interest to us in communication. However, the s and the r may be *muscular* or *sensory,* and in that form are of interest in such varied skills as learning to walk and learning to water ski. Every little movement has a meaning of its own—it is the "s" which calls for another movement as an "r" until, with practice, the movements smooth out into what appears to be a single, almost effortless sequence.

The longer the S-r-s-R chain—the more little s's and r's appear in the sequence—the more opportunity there is for a given S to produce very different R's, both in an individual and across a number of individuals. Frequent, reinforced repetition, of course, may strengthen a given sequence, producing a strong habit and what looks like an S-R relationship.

Problems in Research

Two problems in predicting are involved here. One is how likely a given individual is to show this S-R relationship; the other is how many individuals are likely to show it. The range is wide—from the very small number of individuals who can walk a tightrope across Niagara Falls to the almost universal habit in the United States of eating three meals a day. There is a basic question of communications strategy here. It is this: can we concentrate our attention on the message—or must we concentrate on the market? If an habitual S-R relationship is involved—if most of our prospects behave in this fashion—then we can concentrate on the message. If not, then we'd better base our predictions on a study of the different kinds of S-r-s-R chains occurring in our customers. It is often difficult to specify the stimulus, response or reward in a learning situation.

In the case of Skinner's pigeon, we can see the grain. For the pupil operating a Skinner learning machine, however, we must assume that the knowledge he has made a right answer is in itself rewarding. One "solution" to this problem is to talk about secondary reinforcement. The baby may begin to take pleasure in the sound of its mother's voice, because (like Pavlov's bell) it accompanies a primary reward, food; in time, even the name "Mother" may become rewarding. Trying to trace back the things adults find rewarding to their assumed origins in the physiological needs of infancy seems as unnecessary as it is difficult. Another "solution" is to talk about "incidental" or "latent" learning and suggest that learning can occur without reward, and that reward only evokes performance. An individual may wander through a town or a rat through a maze with no visible purpose or reward. Then, suddenly, a reward is offered for speedy movement to a specific destination and both rat and human get there much more quickly than if they had had no previous experience with the town or maze.

Since the only way of measuring learning is through improved performance, this "solution" is of more interest to the learning theorist than to the marketing man. Introspection by the learner is no sure solution since learning can occur without awareness. A person may not be aware that he is learning something or that he has learned

---

A cue may provide the solution to a problem without a subject being aware that it has done so. He "learns" without awareness.

Unaware of Cue, They Solve the Problem

Sixty-one students at the University of Chicago were put into a room in which two cords hung from the ceiling; their job: to tie the ends of the cords together.

There were three easy ways to bring the ends of the two cords close enough to tie them. One could be brought near the other, and anchored temporarily by putting a chair on top of it. One could be lengthened temporarily, by tying an extension cord to it. One could be pulled toward the other with a pole. There was one "difficult" way to do it—to set the cord in motion, like a pendulum, so that the subject could grab it while hanging on to the other.

Twenty-four of the subjects found the hard solution without any hints; one failed to find it even with the hints. The remaining 23 were given two kinds of hints: the experimenter brushed against the cord, "accidentally" getting it in motion, or, if this failed, he gave the subject a pair of pliers and told him they would solve the problem for him. Sixteen of these 23, saw the "pendulum" solution as a whole; but only *one* of these realized that the experimenter's brushing against it had helped him reach a solution. The remaining 7 said the experimenter's behavior did attract their attention, but the idea of attaching a weight to the cord to convert it into a pendulum occurred to them separately.

—Norman R. F. Maier, "Reasoning in Humans," *Journal of Comparative Psychology*, 12:181–194.

---

something. Moreover, through a system of rewards, an experimenter can condition a response so that it follows a given stimulus, even though that response is beyond the voluntary control of the individual.

This fact assumes more importance when we recall how much of human behavior is learned. Many perceptions are learned; most motivation is learned; personality is learned and the very categories man uses in thought and speech, and his methods of forming categories are learned. Indeed, some of these responses may be learned before man has acquired speech and they may, therefore, be harder for him or for others to control.

Learning and Motivation

Some motivations, we have said, are learned. At the same time, without motivation no learning can occur. Moreover, learning itself cannot be observed or measured until an individual is motivated to express his learning in behavior.

In concentrating on learning in this chapter, we have had to take motivation for granted. Now, having examined how men behave, we can ask why. In doing so, we must distinguish the goals which men set for themselves from the motives which determine those goals.

Motivation exists at many levels. The next chapter is concerned primarily with the level of physiology, with such problems as the chemistry which leads to a feeling of hunger and how the hungry man behaves. The chapter concentrates on motivations which men share—on those they have in common.

A later chapter on personality will deal with the differences in motivation from man to man—the learned differences, largely, which we give the name of personality.

SUMMARY

1. There are two kinds of purchasing behavior. One is the habit, sometimes called brand loyalty, which may be perceptual, motor or verbal, but usually operates below the level of awareness. The other is a conscious decision among alternatives, relying on memories, some of which may be memories of advertising messages.
2. Habits are useful to the housewife and to the advertiser with a large share of the market. The advertiser trying to break into a market, however, prefers purchases which depend upon conscious decision making.

3. Both habits and memory are part of the learning process, which underlies everything an adult is and does, and are the basis of communications. The distinction between "learning" and "memory" is an arbitrary one.

4. The conditions under which marketing communications typically occur, and the conditions obtained in the classroom or laboratory where learning usually is studied differ in terms of source (monopoly versus competition), subjects (animals and children versus adults), motivation (nature and amount), and tasks (artificial versus natural). Therefore caution is needed in trying to apply principles learned in the laboratory to conditions in the market place.

5. Four key concepts are contained in the sentence: A reinforcement is anything which strengthens the relationship between a stimulus and a response in a repetition of trials. A reinforcement—food—is shown operating in two conditions: substituting a new stimulus in an old S-R relationship for Pavlov and producing a new kind of response for Skinner.

6. There are ten different ways of measuring such a rise in strength: accuracy, size, delay, frequency, amount of practice, persistence without reinforcement, recall, recognition, reconstruction, and relearning. There are five decisions to be made about the kind of reinforcement used including definition from the standpoint of the learner, timing, intrinsic versus extrinsic, regularity, positive versus negative.

7. In addition to rewards, the speed of learning is affected by the state of the person doing the learning, his native ability and his motivation, and by the nature of the task being learned. In serial learning, a subject's response serves as the stimulus for his next response; rest periods and recitation speed such learning. Apparently rest periods allow fatigue to dissipate and incorrect S-R relations to be forgotten.

8. Most adult learning involves a change in the stimulus-response relationship—substituting a new stimulus or a new response. If the new response is opposite or antagonistic to the old one, the old habit interferes with learning the new one, and we say there is negative transfer. In other cases, transfer is positive. Forgetting is an example of negative transfer—the interference of new habits, learned since the one that is forgotten.

9. Difficulty arises for the observer because stimulus, response, and reward may not be visible or obvious in a learning situation. Through introspection we learn of the mental stimulus and response, usually designated by lowercase "s" and "r"; we may infer them, even when a subject is unaware of them and therefore unable to supply them through introspection, in an experiment.

Research Studies

Cunningham, using three-year records of family purchases to investigate the habit of repeat purchases, found brand loyalty higher for headache tablets than cleanser, and less susceptable to interference by special "deals." He also finds loyalty to store higher than loyalty to product. *Guest* showed that brand loyalty may persist for as long as twelve years, being eleven times as high as chance would predict.

Three other studies explored the conditions of learning under laboratory conditions. *Levine and Murphy* demonstrated that it is easier to learn and to remember messages we agree with. *Rhine and Silun*, however, illustrated the value of "intermittent reinforcement" by showing that a subject who is rewarded on every trial (by being told he is correct) learns faster—but forgets faster, too. *Maier* offered an experiment which reveals that subjects may use cues from their environment to solve problems without being aware that they perceived the cue.

Fifteen

Responding to the Message II: Emotions and Motives

Day after day, workers in the advertising agency toil at their desks. Night after night, lonely lights burn late in its offices. Interoffice memos flit back and forth like bats at dusk. Cigarette stubs pile up on conference table ashtrays. Media buyers juggle rates and circulations. Researchers punch away at their calculating machines. Product and prospect are poked and prodded for inspiration. Finally, a copywriter puts words on paper.

The campaign theme may be brilliant and the copywriter may have chosen symbols and combined them into messages with great skill, but all his work and all the work of the advertising agency will sink without a trace unless someone has determined what motivates the prospect to act.

"Motivation" is a label for three functions: the sensitizing of a receiver to certain stimuli, which increases the chance that he will receive a message; the triggering of action of some sort, and the selection of action appropriate to a specific goal. Hunger, we say, is a motive. The hungry person is more likely to perceive food; the hungry person is likely to be restless rather than lethargic; and, given any cues of the existence of food, he is likely to proceed in the appropriate direction, seize the food and eat it. With some motives, such as hunger, the mere passage of time without food sensitizes perception and induces restlessness. Messages only provide the cues necessary to the third function: the choice or direction of behavior toward a goal object. With other motives, such as the desire for higher status, messages may serve all three functions: they may sensitize, energize and direct. Most advertising messages can succeed only if they make a prospect want a product, want it enough to act now, and act in an appropriate fashion.

Prospects, of course, are not the only persons who have motives. As we pointed out in the first chapter, sources have goals which must be satisfied in communications.

Goals and Motives

To an economist, the goals of a firm tend to be few and comparatively simple. He has built a magnificent superstructure of theory by assuming that the aim of a firm is to maximize profit. Successive modifications of this theory, however, suggest that soon we will have to say, "If we assume, what we know to be false, that every person wants to maximize his profits, then it follows that . . . ."

Psychologists, in contrast, recognize that the goals of individuals tend to be multiple, complex, and contradictory and to vary greatly from one individual to the next. Behavior which appears irrational to anyone who supposes employees goals to be identical with the goals of the firm begins to make sense once one has determined what the individual's own goals are.

The firm assigns its employees goals which are means to serve the superordinate goals of the firm itself. The employee, however, brings with him from outside goals of his own; it is these goals, and his success in achieving them, which determine whether he stays with the firm and influence the quality and quantity of his output.

The employee's are often vaguer, less verbal, and more intense than in the economist's models: the component of attitude which we have called "feelings" or emotions is likely to be prominent in them. They are more persistent and less amenable to change by the individual or his associates than economic theory may suggest. These differences, characteristics of individual goals, are important enough to deserve a new name: we call them "motives" rather than "goals" to emphasize these differences.

Motives tend to be internal, goals external. That is, the individual may not bother or may not be able to express his motives in words. He expresses his goals in words but often uses words to conceal or disguise his motives. For this very reason, observers are not likely to take an individual's statement of his motives at face value. Instead they prefer to infer his motives from observation of what he says and does not say, what he does and does not do, and the manner of his saying and doing.

To communicate at all, an individual must express his feelings in terms another person can understand. This itself means modifying them. Further modification occurs if a source wants his receiver to accept him and society to regard him as "rational." Goals, *because* they are communicated, tend to appear more reasonable than motives.

Motives which are not communicated are subject to less control by other persons. If they are not verbalized, even in thought, motives also are subject to less control by the individual himself. Accidental juxtaposition of two events in time or space may cause an individual to respond as if one were cause and the other effect. A moment's thought might show that the two events are unrelated, but a man may never reduce his "theory" of cause and effect to the words which would make such thought possible. As a result, self-defeating and self-destructive behavior may occur, which only hours of skilled analysis can trace to their origins.

Audiences, Messages, Channels

Understanding human motives is difficult. It is also important.

Motives affect this text, for example, from the author's reasons for writing it in the first place, to the student's reasons for buying it. Motives have been present in every chapter in this text, although not always mentioned by name.

The demographic definition of *audiences*, for example, has value in communications only to the extent that demographic variables are correlated with differences in motives. These differences in motives may have some basis in physiology, as in the case of sex and age. Teen-agers and senior citizens, boys and girls do differ in some physical needs—but more of their differences arise from the *roles* they have learned to play. Persons in different occupations, income groups and educational level have different motives and those motives are aroused by different kinds of *symbols*. *Messages* begin with appeals, which are another name for motives. (Confusion sometimes arises when the word "appeal" is used to name both the motive and the symbols designed to influence that motive. This distinction between appeals and motives is important since arousing the same motive in different audiences may require the use of different symbols.)

A major difference in the *channels* of publicity and advertising is the extent to which they allow a receiver to infer the motives that lie behind a message by concealing, or revealing, the source of the message. *Learning* is impossible unless the student is motivated; the person who has learned will not perform unless he has motives

The middle class teaches its children to value success for its own sake. Working class children, on the other hand, learn to work for immediate rewards. Or so this study suggests.

To Motivate the Working Class, Try Money

High school pupils in this study were given two tasks—one involving anagrams and the other motor skills—and told that they'd be given a chance to compare their scores afterward with the high school average. In addition to this general motivation, a third of the pupils were told that those whose score reached a certain value would get a $10 prize.

The averages announced, however, were so high that none of the students had reached them. (This was done to arouse students' motivations to achieve, somewhat as 24 hours without food arouse a rat's motivation to run through a maze and reach a food box at the end.)

Following this, all students wrote stories concerning a series of pictures, the stories being scored on the amount of "motivation to achieve" which they showed—the extent to which the stories concerned success and failure and dealt with it in emotional terms.

Here are the results: scores were high for both middle class and working class children under the $10 prize condition. They remained high for middle class children even when no prize was offered, but fell markedly for the working class children.

Mean Scores on Achievement Motivation

	$10 Prize	No Prize
Working class	8.1	4.9
Middle class	8.3	7.6

Differences between means for the two groups under the no-prize condition were significant at the .02 level.

—Elizabeth Douvan, "Social Status and Success Strivings," *Journal of Abnormal and Social Psychology*, 52:219–223.

for so doing. Organizations provide special motives of their own, including the powerful motivation of *status*.

Prospects have motives. Sources have motives. So do all the persons involved in the three "human channels" of marketing communication: selling, publicity, and gossip. The sales manager's most important job may be to motivate his salesmen: to set goals and offer rewards which serve the more basic motives which led them to take up selling in the first place. The publicity man must know the motives of the reporter—his desire to get a "good story" and to avoid being wrong or a dupe. Even persons talking over the back fence have motives. They may want to help a friend who is trying to make a purchasing decision or impress a neighbor with their knowledge of bargaining skill.

Motives and Emotions

In discussing how messages reach receivers, we moved from the largely physiological level of sensation, where people are very similar to one another, to the level of perception, based on experience, where people tend to differ from one another. Motivation, too, can be discussed at two levels. One is the level of the emotions. Emotions are closely tied to physiology, and likely to be of fairly short duration. The other is the more complex level with which we have been dealing so far in this chapter, at which greater variety in individuals makes it hard to suggest any general principles. Studies of motivation at this level are less well developed than those of perception, so that most of the discussion in this chapter must remain at the lower level of the emotions.

Emotions are a major antecedent of motivation, but not the only antecedent. Usually they supply the energy necessary to action. In purchasing, however, habit and conscious problem solving may be more important than emotions in *directing* behavior. If emotions supply too much energy, they may actually interfere with both the first function of emotions (sensitizing the individual to cues) so that they impede rather than improve perception, and with the third function (directing action), so that they misdirect action toward a goal, or block it entirely.

In an earlier chapter we suggested that a distinction must be made between the use of connotative words by sources and by receivers. Use of such value-laden symbols by the receivers may indicate a source has been successful in his communications. We said that the source may find, however, that the best way to get receivers to use such terms, and to express judgments, is to avoid them himself. Similarly, although a communicator needs to know the emotions of his receivers, and how to arouse the emotions appropriate to his own goals, this does not necessarily mean that he will use language which reveals that he himself entertains those emotions. The very cold-blooded, logical terms of Swift's *Modest Proposal* to solve the problem of Irish population by peddling the flesh of Irish infants before they grew to adulthood and became tough and stringy added to its horror.

Three Functions of Motives

Motives sensitize, energize, and direct. The performance of these three functions can be seen most easily, perhaps, in the laboratory since most of our knowledge of the comparative strength of different motives and their interaction with one another is based on experiments with animals.

In real life, a desert rat, a prospector, plods across desert and mountain, hungry, thirsty, and alone. Is it the chance of finding gold that lures him on, or is he running away from a nagging wife, the police, or people in general? In the laboratory, a white rat dashes down a maze. What are its motives?

If we merely see the rat run from one end of a maze to the other, we do not know whether it is running away from an electric shock at the starting point or toward a reward at the other end. The racing rat itself tells us little. We need to see what the rat does at each end—to see it hop about in agitation at the start of the maze or munch food pellets at its end. We need to observe variations in its rate of running. If it slows down as it draws away from the starting box, we suspect it is running *away* from something. If it speeds up, we suspect it is running *toward* something. We need to see it in different situations. If it always runs to the same end point, regardless of where it starts, we suspect its goal lies in the end box. If, on the other hand, it runs in various directions from the same starting point, we suspect it is running away from rather than toward something.

The more we know about our rats, the better we can predict how they will behave. For the white rat it is usually enough to know these things:

Situation. A maze, with a food box at the end.

Drive state. The rat has had no food for twenty-four hours.

Behavior. Restlessness in the starting box, rapid running down the maze.

Goal box adjustment. Rat eats and becomes quiescent.

With this much information, we could *explain* the rat's behavior. We would probably say it was motivated by hunger. With a little more information, we could *predict* its behavior. It would help to know, for example, that the rat had previously been in this maze while hungry and had learned to run it and find food at the end.

In principle, the same is true of our prospector, with the difference that we may need to know a much longer chain of events to predict his behavior. He may be no more aware of some of these events or no better able to put them in words for us than the white rat. Some of the events which motivate his desert wanderings, for example, may have occurred sixty to seventy years ago when he was five years old. An even more important difference is the type of events which we must consider. For the white rat, these events tend to involve *things;* for the desert rat they tend to involve *people.*

Ten Points

To see these, and other differences in perspective, let us list some of the points we want to make in this chapter:

1. An animal may be uncomfortable because of internal conditions, such as the chemical changes and stomach movements which follow a period without food, or because of external conditions, such as intense stimuli (such as, an electric shock) which produce pain.
2. An uncomfortable animal is a restless animal. In moving about, such an animal may escape from the painful external stimuli or attain something, such as food, which puts an end to the painful internal stimuli. As a result we get two types of motivated behavior: avoidance and approach.
3. Through experience, an animal may learn to put an end to discomfort very quickly, and even to anticipate such conditions and take action to prevent them from having an effect. However, when placed in new situations that cause discomfort, or in situations where putting an end to discomfort is difficult, time-consuming, or problematic, restlessness recurs.
4. Visible restlessness and both internal and external discomfort are accompanied by internal responses which are not ordinarily visible, and which themselves act as stimuli. With experience, such internal stimuli may be set off by external cues, such as a hostile word or look, which originally would not themselves produce discomfort. Such invisible, internal stimuli tend to produce visible, motor responses which are quicker, stronger, and longer than would otherwise be true. This means that motor responses may occur in advance of physical stimuli which originally gave rise to them, or persist long after such stimuli have ceased.
5. These internal stimuli, which we term *"emotions,"* tend to involve the whole body, mobilizing it for action of a particular kind and in a particular direction, at the expense of alternatives. In en-

couraging quick, strong actions, emotions tend to inhibit the restraint of thought and memory.

6. With experience, a person greatly increases the variety of stimuli to which he can respond, and the variety of responses he can make. Predicting his behavior therefore becomes more difficult, since he has more freedom as to which stimuli he will pay attention to, and what responses he will make to them.

7. Not only are there many different stimuli which can call forth a particular response (as well as many different responses which can be made to any single stimulus), but in most instances a response results from a combination of stimuli.

8. Most of the motivations of people are learned, and most are attached to other people rather than to things.

9. Influencing human behavior requires that one offer a set of stimuli or goals, in the proper weight and order, appropriate to the internal state of the target individual and the situation in which communication takes place. This is difficult because it is complex (see No. 7 above) and because of the variations among individuals (see No. 8 above).

10. Although little is known about them, there appear to be behaviors not motivated by a desire to reduce discomfort. These include a desire to explore and manipulate and a seeking for pleasurable stimulation.

Hunger is an *internal condition* which causes discomfort. Apparently the hunger drive begins in biochemistry when the balance of sugar in the blood is upset. This sets off contractions of the stomach which we feel as hunger pangs. Asleep or awake, when our stomach moves, the rest of our body tends to become active. But hunger persists, even if our stomach is removed and can no longer contract, or when the nerve which reports its contractions to the brain is severed.

Hunger is a strong drive. After one day's deprivation, a female white rat's strongest drive is to reach her young. Next come thirst, sex, and hunger. After two days' deprivation, however, hunger becomes stronger than thirst or sex. Although humans have the habit of eating at regular intervals, few ever suffer real hunger. Those who do find hunger is a compelling drive.

Glands, Hormones, Nerves

Food materials and oxygen to burn them supply energy to our nervous system, sense organs, and muscles. The process is directed by hormones, chemicals poured into the blood by our glands. Five of the glands which produce these hormones are important for our discussion (Hilgard a, 25–27):

Pituitary, which controls the rate of growth and directs the others.

Thyroid, which controls the rate at which energy is produced (through the hormone thyroxin).

Parathyroids, important to nerve actvity, which keep the supply of calcium in the blood high and phosphorus low.

Pancreas, which controls the amount of blood sugar available to the tissues, including the brain, through the hormone insulin.

Adrenals, which produce two hormones: adrenaline, which stimulates the heart to beat faster, moves sugar from the liver to the blood and from the blood to the muscles and causes the smooth muscles to relax and makes blood clot more quickly; and noradrenaline, which occasionally acts in opposite fashion.

Adrenaline produces responses which are predominant in fear. Adrenaline increases the respiration rate, skin conductance and muscle tension. Noradrenaline is associated with responses in anger, when the response to danger is an aggressive approach. (Many other internal responses, of course, are common to both anger and fear.)

Adrenaline is similar in its effects to a substance released by the sympathetic nervous system called sympathin. This system itself is part of a system of nerves, called the autonomic system, linked to the viscera and the glands, relatively independent of the brain, and prominent in emotion. This system has two parts:

Sympathetic system tends to act as a unit, slowly and persistently. It is tied into the middle part of the spinal cord. It inhibits digestive processes, including flow of saliva and gastric juice and movements of the stomach. It raises blood pressure, causes sweating, makes the liver pour sugar into the blood, and increases the flow of adrenaline. In short, it mobilizes the body for emergency action.

Parasympathetic system acts more specifically to counteract effects of the sympathetic system and preserve "normal" functions. It is tied into the top and bottom of the spinal cord. It permits salivation, facilitates stomach contractions, slows down the heart.

Ten Measurable Responses

The autonomic system is linked to the brain, although indirectly, and tends to "take over" when the organism is most active. When the body is least active, as in sleep, brain, muscles, and sympathetic system are all at rest. A noise or other strong stimulus produces movement, which is reported to the brain. Adrenaline causes changes in the viscera which are reported through the hypothalamus, a kind of amplifier, to the brain. If the person becomes angry, muscle and sympathetic system activity increase and more impulses reach hypothalamus until and finally it tends to "take over," released from control of the brain. We say the person now is behaving "emotionally."

These changes within the body produce at least ten measurable responses (Lindsley, 473–481):

Galvanic skin response. A sharp change in the electrical conductance of the skin occurs.

Blood pressure. Vessels constrict and we turn pale in fright; blood floods to the surface and we flush in embarrassment and anger.

Heart. Rate of beating increases.

Two conditions, it is said, are necessary to an emotion: physiological arousal (via the autonomic nervous system or a hormone like adrenaline) and environmental cues which make emotional feelings appropriate.

Stooge Induces Glee or Anger in Subjects

Seventy-five students submitted to injections in what was described as a test of the effects of vitamins on vision. In actuality, all of them got shots of adrenaline, which increases heart beat, blood flow and respiration—all symptoms of physiological arousal.

A third of the subjects were told that these symptoms would occur as side-effects of the "vitamin injection." Another third were told nothing about side-effects and the remaining third were misinformed by being told that the side-effects would consist of numb feet, itching, and a headache.

After the injections half the subjects in each group were thrown together with a skylarking stooge who shot paper planes and hula-hooped, the intention being to create a general atmosphere of glee. The other half spent 20 minutes filling out an insulting questionnaire, with a stooge who got so mad that he stomped out of the room. Here the intent was to produce cues which would lead subjects to interpret the internal restlessness caused by the injection as being due to anger at the questionnaire.

Effects of the study were noted in two ways: an observer concealed by a one-way mirror recorded subjects' behavior, and each subject also filled out a five-point scale indicating how happy or how irritated he felt.

As predicted, subjects who had been told that the drug would make them feel uneasy did not need the explanation offered by environmental cues and were less likely to report or exhibit emotions of anger or glee than subjects who had not been told or had been misled.

Emotional Rating: High Values Indicate Emotionality

	Questionnaires		Behavioral Responses	
	Gleeful Stooge	Angry Stooge	Gleeful Stooge	Angry Stooge
Informed subjects	.98	1.91	12.7	.18
Uninformed subjects	1.78	1.39	18.3	2.28
Misinformed subjects	1.90	—	22.6	—

—Stanley Schachter and Jerome E. Singer, "Cognitive, Social and Psychological Determinants of Emotional State," *Psychological Review*, 69:379–399

Breathing. Rapid inspiration and expiration indicate excitement; a slow rate indicates tension.

Eyes. Pupils dilate (our "eyes widen") in anger, pain, or excitement; eyes may blink.

Salivation. Mouth becomes dry.

Goose pimples. The hairs of our skin bristle.

Visceral changes. We suffer nausea or diarrhea, and the flow of stomach acids may produce ulcers.

Muscles. When we cannot decide what to do, opposing muscles try to contract simultaneously and our muscles tremble.

Chemistry. The composition of the blood changes as adrenalin and blood sugar increase. Urine is affected.

Note, however, that many of these effects are observable only to the excited person himself or with the use of special instruments. Moreover, except for the differences between anger and fear mentioned above, these effects occur for all emotions, regardless of their nature.

Experience Changes Emotions

With experience a person greatly increases the variety of responses he can make, and the variety of stimuli to which he will respond. A newborn baby responds primarily to internal stimuli, and with a single response—general excitement. But then, as a study of 60 babies over a period of two years revealed, patterns of approach and avoidance begin to differentiate (Bridges). At three weeks, distress or excited avoidance appears and at about three months delight or excited approach. The process continues, until at the end of two years,

In a second study, cues from the environment were provided by one of the mass media rather than by a stooge.

Slapstick Produces Belly Laughs

"Vitamin injections" were given 126 students; this time some got adrenaline, some got a tranquilizer and some a saline solution, which would have no physiologic effect at all. They were told there would be *no* side-effects and then, individually, shown a 14-minute slapstick scene from a movie, *The Good Humor Man*. Every 10 seconds an observer reported the subject's response on a five-point scale, ranging from a completely straight face to the doubling-up of a belly laugh.

Not one of the subjects who received a saline injection produced a belly laugh—but 16% of the adrenaline group did. The mean number of amused reactions counted for the groups was:

Type of Injection	N	Amusement Score
Adrenaline	38	17.8
Saline	42	14.3
Tranquilizer	46	10.4

—Stanley Schachter and Ladd Wheeler "Epinephrine, Chlorpromazine and Amusement," *Journal of Abnormal and Social Psychology*, 65:121–128.

nearly a dozen different "emotions" of approach or avoidance can be identified by watching a baby's behavior.

At the same time, the baby begins to discriminate among stimuli. At first a baby will show no reaction to a sour substance in its mouth; by 18 months, however, the baby will spit it out. Not until about two to six months of age, does the infant smile at a face, and then it doesn't matter whether the face is strange or familiar, smiling or frowning. Even a mask will get a smile. But after six months, only a familiar face will evoke a smile.

At first, the child may show fear at any unusual, sudden and intense stimulation. Then he learns to fear things with which these have been associated; a loud noise, sounded when he sees a favorite toy, may make him fear the toy. The child also learns to fear things that he observes other people are afraid of. As an adult, he may fear failure on the job or in his relations with other people. At first, the child will show anger when he is physically restrained, as when he is being bathed or diapered. Then it will be when he is frustrated by being denied feed or attention or a toy.

All this time, of course, his responses are changing, too. As the child comes more under the influence of other people, direct physical aggression, when angry, is likely to be replaced by verbal aggression.

With an increase in the number of choices available, the chances also increase of conflict among them: which stimulus shall be responded to, and which of several responses should be made. This has implications for the outside observer, who finds prediction much more difficult. It also has implications for the person being observed, who finds choice much more difficult.

Four Types of Conflict

Basically there are four types of conflict as illustrated in an experiment in which subjects were instructed to draw a line *toward* a green light or *away* from a red light (Hovland and Sears):

Approach-approach

Such conflicts arise when two goals are equally attractive, and are fairly easily solved. The nearer one gets to a desirable object, like the rat nearer its food box, the more attractive it appears; a momentary advantage for one of the two attractive goals solves the problem.

Avoidance-Avoidance

Here both alternatives are undesirable—and a solution is difficult. Why? Because the nearer one gets to an unpleasant goal, the worse it appears. One chooses the lesser of evils, perhaps, and begins moving toward it; the nearer one gets, the worse it appears. One hesitates, stops, and moves back toward the more remote (and less frightening) alternative. If possible, one tries to escape, either physically or mentally, from choosing either. If not, his hesitation sets off the emotional responses we have already noted.

Approach-Avoidance

Often the same person or object has both pleasant and unpleasant aspects. A child may want a cookie—but knows it may be punished for taking it, or doesn't want to practice its piano lesson but does want the parental praise that practicing will bring. Unlike the previous example, escape from the situation itself is no solution.

Double Approach-Avoidance

This variation on No. 3 consists of two alternatives, with equally-strong desirable and undesirable features. This situation is particularly likely to produce hesitation, inability to act or attempts to escape the situation completely, and choose neither alternative.

Many such conflicts become internalized. The matter is not as simple as two lights one has been instructed to approach or avoid, but two desires, or a conflict between what one wants and fear of what others will think if one tries to get it, or between what one would like to do and fear that one lacks the ability to do it. Such conflicts arouse strong emotional responses, which tend to spread to stimuli that are remote from the original cause of conflict, and which tend to persist for a long time. Vague fears of what might happen arise, and because they are vague, we do not know what to do about them. Such a state, which we call anxiety, may even be produced by fears of one's own aggressive impulses—although aggression is one of the "natural" responses to frustration. This means that not only is one prevented from doing an aggressive act, which might end the frustration, but the very desire to aggress produces anxiety.

Avoidance is a strong kind of motivation, and it does not seem to extinguish. If we fail to give a monkey grapes in exchange for poker chips, he will eventually stop working to get poker chips. But a dog continues to avoid a grill where he has been shocked, even if the shock is turned off.

Avoidance-producing stimuli arouse strong emotions, which may spread widely to quite remote stimuli, so that it becomes increasingly difficult to predict when such behavior will occur. Avoidance-avoidance conflict, as we have just seen, is particularly likely to produce blocking, that is, no response at all. Subjects may try to escape not just the painful stimulus itself but the entire situation in which the stimulus occurs. (Instead of learning how to avoid halitosis, body odor and tooth decay, they *may* learn how to avoid television commercials that mention such topics!)

Learned Motivations

Most of the motivations of people are learned. When dealing with individuals, as in therapy where much of our knowledge of motivation has come from, it helps to know how motivations are learned in general as well as how those of the patient have been learned in particular. In communications and in marketing, however, one must work with motivations which are common to a group of people. Here we are concerned with finding motives which determine adult behavior now, without regard to the very different ways in which these motivations may have originated in the past. These vary too much to provide a basis for grouping adults in the present.

Making lists of motives is a common but dangerous practice since such lists seem to imply that all motives on the list are equally likely to occur, and equal in strength, and that each motive is separate and distinct from all of the others. In actuality most human behavior results from a mixture of motives. In this mixture some motives may be quite apparent to the observer or the person observed, but others may not. (Some persons assume that the motives we can't easily observe are more powerful.) There is also danger in isolating a motive from the situation in which it occurs, the behaviors it produces and the goals toward which motivated behavior is directed.

If we remember these dangers, lists of motives can be helpful. One of the most useful lists is this (Maslow):

1. Physiological needs. These are the needs which seem to exist in all cultures: hunger, thirst, sleep, elimination, breathing, activity.
2. Safety.
3. Love and belonging.
4. Esteem, in our own regard and in the regard of others.
5. Self-actualization, to become all one is capable of being.

The *order* is important. No need on the list can affect behavior until needs previous to it have been taken care of, Maslow argues. In our society, however, the physiological and safety needs have little effect; they are satisfied before they can be felt. Indeed, Maslow suggests that our society defines the person with major needs for love and esteem as psychologically sick and in need for therapy. Only the need for self-actualization then remains.

He illustrates this with a story of five men in a hostile jungle. The first of them is just able to stay alive but fearful of attack at any moment. The second can satisfy his need for food, drink, and sleep and also has a rifle and a cave, so that he feels safe. A third has all these things plus the companionship of two other men. The companions of the fourth man include his best friend, and the fifth man is chosen as a leader by the rest. Thus we have a hierachy of needs being met—survival for the first man, safety for the second, then belonging, love, and respect.

As a need at one level is partially satisfied, a need at the next level begins to be felt. If the need for food is 90 per cent satisfied, a need for safety, which is only 30 per cent satisfied, may dominate behavior. Meanwhile, a need for belonging is just beginning to make itself felt. As the need for safety is satisfied, the belonging needs take over.

When we say that a man desires something, in Maslow's schema, we imply that his more basic and powerful desires are, temporarily at least, satiated, renounced or suppressed. At any moment, an individual probably tends to put a high value upon the needs he currently feels and a lower value on needs which either are satisfied or have not yet begun to emerge.

There are critical periods in the life of an individual, however; needs not met at these times may persist intensely for long periods. A child whose need for safety is not satisfied may permanently lose the desire or the ability to give or receive affection (a higher need); safety needs may dominate his adult life. On the other hand, if the child's basic needs *are* satisfied, he may as an adult be able to tolerate a good deal of frustration of them.

Motives in Marketing

There are two reasons why a marketing communicator probably is less interested in the way in which motives are learned than is the therapist. One has just been mentioned—the fact that the communicator must deal with categories and groups of people rather than individuals. The other is that the communicator deals with them by manipulating goal objects, by promising the consumer that if he performs act A, he will get an object which satisfies desires A', B', or C'.

The marketer must work with goal objects, most of which have in them the capacity to appeal to many different submotives. If a checklist of motives is of any use to him, it begins as a list of things and services, each followed by a list of the motives which it can invoke. Obviously this is a very different interest than that of the scientist who is interested in comparing motives across cultures or across species, or in contrasting normal and abnormal motivational growth.

The communicator in marketing faces questions of strategy. Can he segregate his audiences, for example, so that he can appeal to this motive in one group and that in another? Or must all his messages appeal to several motives at once? If he appeals to several motives at once, is not this less effective than a single appeal to a homogeneous audience? What about conflicts among the several motives?

There is also the question of how close to basic needs the communicator wants to go—and how close his audiences will permit him

An advertiser may find attitudes toward his product affected by customers'
moods which, in turn, may be influenced by current experiences.

How Do Moods Affect Attitudes to Products?

Can a television program produce a mood which helps or hurts audience reactions to products advertised on the program? To answer this
question, 184 coeds at the University of Rochester filled out four
questionnaires:

1. *Attitudes toward 11 products.* Coeds used 10 semantic differential
   scales (bad-good, dirty-clean, etc.) to rate such behaviors as
   "drinking a Daiquiri" and "Depositing some money in your checking account." Other products were savings bonds, a sewing machine, a typewriter, sterling silver, a liqueur, a deodorant, silk
   stockings, vegetable oil and a pressure cooker.
2. *Desired Mood.* Using the same 10 scales, coeds then indicated how
   desirable they felt each of nine moods was: aggressiveness, depression, anxiety, etc.
3. *Present Mood.* On a 4-point scale, coeds indicated how appropriate
   each of 140 adjectives was in describing their present mood.
4. *Product and Mood.* On a 7-point scale coeds indicated for each
   product in turn whether it made them feel more or less anxious,
   depressed, etc.

After completing the 4 measures, coeds then were shown a government documentary on Nazi war crimes, *The Nuremburg Trial*. Then they
filled out the 4 measures all over again.

Moods changed, significant at the .05 level, on 8 of the 9 measures;
coeds become more depressed, anxious and aggressive and less affectionate and light-hearted. They also changed significantly in their ratings of moods they desired to have. Aggressiveness was rated more
highly; they were less interested in feeling light-hearted, energetic, self-
centered, and affectionate.

With the change in actual and desired moods, came a changed perception of the relationship between product and moods; the shift in moods
and shift in perception of the product-mood relationships correlated .87.

Each product had 2 attitude scores. One was taken directly (#1); the
other represented a predicted attitude, obtained by multiplying the
product's rating as a means to a mood by the desirability rating of that
mood itself. Two scores could be obtained for each product, therefore:
one based on the sum of the 10 scales noted in #1 above; the other based
on the sum of multiplications across nine dimensions of mood. Actual
and predicted attitudes correlated .54 before the movie and .53 afterward.

All 11 products were less liked after the movie than before, nine of the
changes being significant at the .05 level. Comparison of attitude predictions on the basis of mood, made before and after the movie, suggested
such a downward shift in all cases. Correlation between predicted and
actual shifts, however, was only .33, not significant statistically.

—Joel N. Axelrod, "Induced Moods and
Attitudes Toward Products," *Journal of
Advertising Research*, 3:2: 19–24.

to go. In an affluent society, it may be hard to arouse basic motives of safety except in insecure persons who are, in Maslow's terms, psychologically unhealthy. And with such persons the appeal may be so threatening that they will shut their ears, tuning out the commercial, and even the television set if necessary.

In discussing motives which are learned, we have already introduced the subject of the next chapter on personality, which is concerned with persistent differences in the motives that distinguish one man from another.

Advertisers, dealing with men in the mass, must work with common, pervasive types of motivation, for the most part. Salesmen, however, can concern themselves with individuals, and individuals of very divergent personalities. Of all the areas which interest the behavioral scientist, personality is in the least satisfactory state of development. One reason is that it is hard to generalize about a subject whose keynotes are specificity and diversity. Another reason is that much of what we know about personality has been discovered by therapists treating unusual, abnormal and emotionally-upset individuals.

SUMMARY

1. Motivation includes sensitizing a receiver to cues, energizing the receiver to act, and choosing among alternative courses of action. In contrast to goals, motives are less specific and more intense, internal, less easily observed and less subject to control by others. A single motive may lead to many different goals.

2. Motives are closely related to all the other concepts of this text, both as cause and as result. Thus we learn motives but learning, in turn, must be motivated; motives lead us to join groups, but groups in turn provide us with new motive-serving goals.

3. Human behavior is directed by habit as well as the emotions, although the emotions provide the energy for habit performance and problem-solving. If they supply too little energy, there will be no performance; if they supply too much, behavior may cease to be goal-directed or be blocked entirely.

4. Both internal and external causes may precipitate action. Important among the internal causes are the hormones produced by the body's glands, and the autonomic nervous system. The hormone adrenaline and a substance produced by the sympathetic nervous system act in similar fashion to mobilize the body for emergency action. The hormone noradrenaline and the parasympathetic nervous system tend to reverse this process.

5. Ten bodily changes associated with emotional behavior and introspective reports of feelings of emotion can be measured, among them respiration, heartbeat, and perspiration.

6. The behavior which results from internal causes seeks to end the situation which has produced unrest by moving toward objects such as food and drink which can satisfy needs and by moving away from objects which cause discomfort or pain.

7. With experience and the learning that accompanies it needs may be anticipated and satisfied and threats may be foreseen and avoided before the emotions are aroused; if so, no process of search and choice of appropriate behavior can be observed. As a result, emotional responses tend to be seen only in new or difficult situations.

8. By the age of two, the child has a dozen different emotional responses in his repertoire. With experience, the number of responses that can be made and the number of cues which will evoke them increase to the point that predicting human behavior becomes very difficult.

9. Motives of a white rat in a laboratory are inferred from knowledge of his immediate past (such as, twenty-four hours without food) and observation of the alternatives available in the present (such as, a maze with food or water at one end) and of the rat's choice among the alternatives (such as, whether he moves, how fast, and in what direction). Motives of men are more likely to depend on remote events and on events that involve people rather than things.

10. The therapist treating an individual is concerned with incidents in his personal history which explain how cues are linked to emotional responses. The marketing communicator, dealing with aggregates and manipulating goal objects, is concerned with similarity of motives. He must decide whether a single strong motive will attract a market for his product, or whether he must appeal to many motives.

11. Listing motives is dangerous if it implies that they are equal in strength, equally likely to occur, or occur independently of one another. A communicator needs to be aware that any given motive can be expressed in a variety of ways, and that any single act may be produced by a variety of motives. Also valuable is the point made by Maslow that in a society where fundamental bodily needs are usually satisfied as a matter of course day-to-day behavior may be directed toward less basic needs and needs which, as a result of divergent personal histories, are more various in their nature.

Research Studies

Three levels of human motivation, varying markedly in duration and intensity, are dealt with by the research studies included in this chapter.

Douvan deals with motives of a persistent, pervasive kind, akin to personality traits, but induced in the individual by the social class to which he and his parents belong. She finds that pupils of the middle class, who can assume there's enough money to care for their basic needs, value achievement for its own sake, while working-class children are more interested in money.

Axelrod, on the other hand, deals with the evanescent moods created by a war crimes movie, and finds that viewers' attitudes toward 11 products become less favorable after viewing the film.

Two studies demonstrate that emotional arousal requires both physiological change and environmental cues which provide both a direction for emotional expression and a reason for it. In an experiment by *Schachter and Singer* these cues are provided by a stooge, acting gay or angry; in the study by *Schachter and Wheeler,* they are provided by a slapstick film.

Sixteen

Responding to the Message III: Personality

• ONE CUSTOMER GREETS the sales clerk with a pleasant smile, and buys the first article she's shown; another snarls at the clerk, paws the merchandise, and stalks out of the store without buying anything. Why? The clerk has an explanation: the first customer has a pleasant personality, the second does not.

• One housewife lets an encyclopedia salesman into the house without a struggle, another slams the door in his face. The door-to-door salesman has a set of ready-made categories: the first housewife is "friendly" and the second is "hostile."

• One purchasing agent greets a manufacturer's representative with a hearty handshake and invites him out to lunch; another lets him cool his heels in the outer office for an hour and a half. Why? The salesman says that the first is a congenial, convivial sort of person; the second is a disgruntled sourpuss.

Explanations of this kind don't really explain men's acts, attitudes, and interactions—they just describe them. In a different setting, the snarling customer may be quite pleasant and when she's playing the role of mother, or wife, or bridge partner, the pleasant customer may turn sour. The housewife who slams the door in the salesman's face today, because she has just had a fight with her husband, may greet him cheerfully if he appears tomorrow.

Is Henry Maier, the advertising manager, a "creative personality" or is he motivated to creativity by the organization to which he belongs? Is Don Dooley, the insurance salesman, aggressive by nature or is this the behavior demanded by his role? Is Robert Crabb, advertising agency vice president, ambitious or do others perceive him as ambitious because of his status?

To the man in the street, personality "explains" most behavior:

people act the way they do because this is the kind of people they are. The behavioral scientist looks for explanations elsewhere. Often he finds that different people show similar responses to similar stimuli, or that an individual's behavior changes as he moves from one group to another.

Summary or Residue?

"Personality" serves two functions for the behavioral scientist; and these functions differ from one another. Sometimes the word is used to sum up the total effect of a man's habits and attitudes, his motives and perceptions, his roles and his statuses. At other times, the word is used to label all of the residue of human behavior which these other concepts have so far failed to explain or predict.

When used in the first sense, the area covered by personality constantly increases, with expanding knowledge of the concepts it embraces. When used in the second sense, the area covered by personality constantly diminishes, as the other concepts gain in explanatory and predictive power.

Used in either sense, personality is difficult to distinguish from the other concepts of behavioral science, for we are never quite sure where to draw the line. Habits, attitudes and the other concepts of this text merge imperceptibly into what we think of as personality. It may help, therefore, to think of personality as representing one extreme on a scale of *generality*. Attitudes, for example, are usually defined by their referent objects: we tend to like or dislike religion or politics or hot dogs or textbooks. When a person is friendly or hostile or indifferent to a wide variety of objects, we tend to say that he has a personality trait of friendliness, or aggressiveness or apathy.

Similarly, a person who is thoughtful of others, a personality trait, may express this trait by very different habits, depending on the setting: he may eat with both hands in one country, but with only his right hand in another; he may avoid belching in one country but belch out of courtesy to his host in another. A person may have a habit of deference to his parents, or the more general personality trait of submissiveness to many kinds of authority: parental, governmental, ecclesiastical, educational and peer group.

Personality also represents one extreme on a scale of *flexibility*. Messages alone may change attitudes, and habits may change with training or experience. Personality is harder to change. Ordinarily changes in personality require a close relationship between subject and therapist over a considerable period of time. Even then the therapist may limit himself to interpreting the patient's behavior to the patient himself, so that the patient re-evaluates it and understands why he behaves as he does. (His behavior remains as it was but his attitude toward it changes.) The therapist may help the patient find new means of nonverbal and verbal behavior, leaving the motives such behavior expresses untouched. Or he may try to weaken some motives and strengthen others.

Since personality is relatively inflexible, it serves the marketing communicator as neither an independent nor a dependent variable, but instead, represents part of the environment to which he must adjust. The industrial salesman, who sees a few customers regularly, can spend a good deal of time studying their personalities and re-shaping his communications to be most effective with them. The door-to-door salesman or the sales clerk who seldom sees the same customer twice, must develop a workable set of personality-type categories, a set of "symptoms" by which customers can be pigeon-holed into such categories, and messages for each of these categories.

Unfortunately, these are tasks in which the behavioral scientist can, at this point in history, offer little help. His own categories of personality are still being developed, and those he has developed are of little help in predicting responses to marketing communication or to any kind of nonpersonal communication. In part, this is because most of the work on personality has been done to aid the therapist, and in part it is because even in therapy there are few scientific, empirical, quantified tests of hypotheses.

Measures of personality, which provide an operational definition of the term, exist in great variety, measuring different things in different ways.

We are fortunate in having such variety. Personalities are not perfectly integrated, and methods of measuring them are not complete, and measures which work in one situation or at one moment in time do not always work equally well in other situations or at other times.

Moreover, the apparent discrepancies revealed when we use two different measures may themselves help explain or predict why an individual behaves as he does. An individual who is worried and upset and willing to say so in so many words, is very different from the person who our tests show is equally worried but is unwilling to admit it to himself or to others.

Three Types of Measures

Basically, there are three ways of measuring personality:

Observation. We can observe an individual's behavior in many different situations, either natural or created for the purpose of testing him. Since this method is a costly one, we are likely to use it only for important decisions about people or in research.

Ratings by others. These are especially useful in communications, since they tell us what personality an individual communicates to others. (Usually we also want to know what personality he thinks he is communicating or wants to communicate.)

Such ratings tell us something about the persons doing the rating, sometimes telling us more about them than about the person being rated. Friends may be too generous, strangers may be too uninformed, and all of us are likely to judge one or two of a person's most obvious traits and then assume that he has other traits which seem consistent with the obvious one. The role relationships between rater and person rated affect the accuracy of ratings. Students can best rate one another on traits like sociability, but teachers can do a better job in rating students on scholarship. A GI can do a better job of rating officers on leadership than their fellow officers can.

Self-ratings. These are perhaps the easiest, cheapest and therefore, the most common way of measuring personality. Usually they put the individual rated somewhere between what he "really" is (e.g., how he appears to others) and what he would like to be.

One Trait or Many?

Some measures involve only a single trait. One of the best-known traits which has led to such instruments is the introversion-extraversion scale. This distinguishes the person who is turned inward by his tendency to prefer to read about something rather than experience it, to have few rather than many acquaintances, and to be self-conscious and retiring in groups. Other measures, and controversial ones, measure a person's tendency to be authoritarian or dogmatic or distinguish between persons who tend to dominate and those who tend to be followers.

A major difficulty with such measures of single traits is that they permit users to divide persons into personality types, leading them to forget that everyone is a mixture of many different traits. Moreover, our language, which tends to deal with polar opposites, good and bad, dominant and submissive, provides a poor match for a world in which the extremes are rare, and most of us fall somewhere in the middle.* Thus such tests tend to divide a world of almost infinite gradations into only two groups.

In contrast, measures that involve several traits come closer to giving a complete picture of a personality, but make a personality harder to understand. They make it harder for us to decide how to act toward a person or determine what kind of messages will most influence his behavior.

Here are brief descriptions of three such multi-trait questionnaires:

California Psychological Inventory.† This consists of 480 items which in scoring produce eighteen different personality traits. An individual is asked to mark "true" or "false" on such statements as the following:

Lightning scares me.
I usually feel poised at parties.

Edwards Personal Preference Schedule.‡ This consists of 225 pairs of statements about things people like or feel which are reduced to fifteen traits in scoring. In each case, the individual must choose one of the pair:

• I feel depressed when I fail at something.
• I feel nervous when giving a talk before a group.

Cattell's Sixteen Personality Factor Form. This consists of 187 statements, each of which offers three responses, usually "yes," "in between," and "no," although occasionally other choices are offered:

• I prefer people who (a) are reserved, (b) are in between (c) make friends quickly.

* We fall in the middle because our tests are constructed to produce a bell-shaped curve. Tests are constructed to do this because of certain statistical advances in such a distribution. It is also true that many of us deliberately try to be "average" and that groups we belong to exert pressure on us to be "average."

† Reproduced by special permission from California Psychological Inventory by Harrison G. Gough. Copyright 1956. Published by Consulting Psychologists Press, Inc., Palo Alto, California.

‡ Reproduced by permission. Copyright 1953. The Psychological Corporation, New York, New York. All rights reserved.

• Money cannot bring happiness. (*a*) yes (true), (*b*) in between (*c*) no (false).

This form reduces in scoring to the sixteen traits mentioned in its title.

Since it is hard to keep sixteen or eighteen scores in mind, and even harder to compare one sixteen-trait person with another sixteen-trait person, psychologists often put the scores on a graph and compare personality "profiles." Such profiles are especially useful in guidance and counseling, since they enable us to compare an individual with other persons of his age, or with other members of the group or category to which he belongs.

Most of the multitrait questionnaires just described look to the person who is filling them out like a hodgepodge of unrelated questions. The questions *are* mixed up, of course. If all those for a given trait were grouped together, it would be too easy for the respondent to see what the measure is getting at and to conceal his true feelings in hopes of getting a "good score."

Many other devices are used to make it harder for persons to conceal their true responses, in hopes of making a good impression. One device is to force them to choose between two unflattering alternatives, only one of which research has found to be typical of a socially disfavored trait. (This is not apparent on the face of the questions and it is assumed persons who complete the questionnaire have not heard of the research.) Projective tests, in which a subject reacts to inkblots, or makes up a story to accompany a picture he is shown, or completes a sentence, reveal a great deal. One person, for example, may see a picture of a boy looking out a window and say that the boy is daydreaming about his future career, and another will say the boy is being punished by being kept in the house. Even physical responses can reveal personality; neurotics are likely to give up more quickly when asked to hold a dumbbell at arm's length or watch a flickering light (Shaffer and Shoben, 352–354).

Theory or Dictionary?

Psychologists go about constructing personality questionnaires in two different ways. Some begin with a theory and make up statements which reflect the traits called for in the theory. Others start with a dictionary and draw up questions to tap as many different words reflecting personality as possible. How many such words are there?

Cattell began his questionnaire with 4000 such terms. Allport estimates that of 18,000 words for distinctive forms of personal behavior, 4500 are relevant to measuring personality (Allport, 353–356). He arrived at this figure by omitting some 5500 evaluative words (angelic, disgusting) that describe a person's effects on others; another 4500 words that describe a temporary mood or activity (rejoicing, frantic); and some 3500 words that he calls metaphorical (alive, prolific).

How does the psychologist reduce such a list of 4000 or 4500 adjectives to the 480 items of the California inventory or the even small number of other questionnaires?

In general, there are two methods of reducing his original set of statements to manageable proportions. One way is to retain only those statements which differentiate between groups of persons known to differ in the particular trait being measured. We might construct a scale of conservatism, for example, by having die-hard Republicans and ardent Democrats, or monarchists and Socialists check a series of statements and then keep only those items which distinguish between the two polar groups.

The other way is through factor analysis. A computer, for example, can first correlate the responses to each statement with those given every other statement. If two statements are highly correlated with one another, this means either of them can be used to measure that trait. Through factor analysis, the original statements can be reduced to a much smaller number of dimensions or factors—sixteen in the case of Cattell—which explain the original results.

When a psychologist starts with a great many possible traits, he works to reduce them to a smaller, more manageable list in the ways just described. When he begins with a single trait, he often works in the opposite direction—to break up the trait he started with into several smaller parts. This happened, for example, with the introversion-extraversion dimension described earlier. Factor analysis of a test devised to measure this single trait, for example, has identified five different introvertive traits: a tendency to withdraw from social contacts, a preference for meditation and self-analysis, feelings of guilt, strong fluctuations in mood, and lack of a carefree, impulsive nature (Guilford). Some persons may show all of these to a high degree, but others may not; both the kind and the amount of introversion thus vary.

In either case, traits are likely to be grouped into categories or families—either because a trait, originally conceived as unitary, is broken up by subsequent research, or because several traits, originally conceived as being distinct, are found to be related to one another.

Categorizing Traits

Traits may be grouped on the basis of the kind of behavior which they call forth. Thus one theorist puts traits into three classes, based on the kind of response to other people they imply: movement *toward* other people, movement *away from* other people, and movement *against* other people. The sociable and gregarious person is classed as one who moves toward others. The hostile and aggressive personality moves against others, and the withdrawn and isolated personality moves away from others.

Another scheme distinguishes between traits shown in interactions with others, traits which describe feelings shown toward others, and noninteractive behavior exhibited in the presence of others. These are the three classes used in this system:

Role Dispositions. Ascendance, dominance, social initiative, independence. These represent the *behavior* one exhibits toward others.

What happens when men of varying personalities are put into similar positions in a communications network—does their subsequent behavior reflect personality or the demands of the situation?

Personality or Role: Which Is More Powerful?

Out of a pool of 200 volunteers, experimenters picked 20 men split equally between "high ascendance" and "low ascendance." (To be scored as high on ascendancy, a subject had to land in the upper-third of scores for this trait on the Guilford-Zimmerman Temperament Survey. Next, in a team made up of 2 high-ranking and 2 low-ranking subjects, which for 30 minutes worked on assembling precut lumber into the framework of a house, he had to meet 3 criteria. He had to be ranked by two observers as being one of the 2 subjects highest in "attempted leadership" and highest in recorded participations with others, and he had to be one of the top 2 in rankings by other team members on attempts to influence their behavior.)

From these subjects, experimenters picked one representative of each extreme, and added 2 subjects with moderate ratings to make up four-man teams. Three members of each team were seated in cubicles, with slots permitting them to communicate only with a fourth member: a "star" pattern, with this fourth member, designated as "Blue" at the center. In half of the teams, the center position was occupied by the high ascendant person; in half, by the low ascendant person.

Each team was then given 3 problems to solve, and 16 to 20 minutes to solve them in; each member of the team was given two of the eight pieces of information necessary to solve the problem. (A typical problem: How many trucks are needed to move a firm's chairs, desks, type-writers and files to a new office in a single trip?)

There were four measures of group performance: time to complete the problem, rate of communications, content of communications, and a questionnaire concerning subjects' satisfaction with their position in the message network.

On the first problem, personality differences made a difference: teams in which high-ascendant subjects occupied the central, controlling position reached solutions more quickly than teams where this position was occupied by a low-ascendant person. By the third problem, however, the ascendant behavior required by the central position had been evoked from its low-ascendant occupants. High ascendant subjects in one of the 3 peripheral positions (i.e., those not in the center) communicated more rapidly over all three trials than did low ascendant subjects, but even their rate was lower on the third trial than on the first.

As this table shows, low-ascendant occupants of center positions took much longer at the start, but no longer at the end, to solve problems.

Average No. of 10-second
Intervals to Complete Problems

	Center: High Ascendant	Center: Low Ascendant
Trial I	71	88
Trial II	45	35
Trial III	38	37

—Leonard Berkowitz, "Personality and Group Position," *Sociometry*, 19:210–222.

Sociometric Dispositions. Acceptance, sociability, friendliness, sympathy. These are essentially the *feelings* we have toward others.

Expressive Dispositions. These seem to be matters of individual style in behavior; a person may be competitive, aggressive, self-conscious, or exhibitionistic.

Both of these systems deal with the content of traits. Another system would classify traits in terms of the way they function on their stability and scope:

Stability. Some traits appear to change more easily under the impact of time and experience than others. In one study, 446 subjects were rated twice, with twenty years intervening between the two ratings. Self confidence appeared to be relatively stable; the two ratings produced a correlation of .60. Sociability appeared less stable, with a correlation of only .45. Similar studies have been made, twelve years after children were first studied in a nursery school, and of adults restudied from sixteen to twenty-seven years after they had been examined in a child guidance clinic.

Scope. Some traits seem to be exhibited only with specific situations or toward specific persons; others are more general. Some traits, such as poise, can be observed only in the presence of others. Some traits appear to be specific to a situation. Punctuality measured in four different tasks in a school setting: in returning a book, in handling course-change slips, in meeting class assignments, and in keeping appointments produced correlations which averaged only .19 (Dudycha). Similarly Guilford found three behaviors, commonly grouped under sociability, had an average correlation of only .44: being gregarious liking friends, and social affairs. Thus two persons could exhibit similar scores on "sociability" but exhibit very different behavior.

Persuasibility as a Trait

The personality questionnaire is a multi-purpose instrument, designed to help in therapy, in vocational and educational counseling, and for many other purposes. This means that it must be comprehensive enough to include all the personality traits relevant to these several purposes.

But we are concerned with *communication:* how many of these traits are important to the communicator—and which ones?

One trait that would be of great importance in communication, if it could be established, is that of persuasibility. If persons could be scored on the ease with which they can be influenced on any issue and regardless of variations in message, channels or source, a source could adjust his efforts to influence them to the exact kind and amount required.

This is a hard test, of course, since most of us are more easily persuaded on issues that are *not* ego-involved, and in areas where we lack information or the information we have is ambiguous. We are more easily persuaded by highly credible sources and by suggestions that conform with norms of a reference group.

Little wonder that although a great deal of effort has been spent in looking for such a trait, there has been little to show in the way of results. The results, in fact, can be summed up in three statements (Janis and others):

Girls tend to be more persuasible than boys. This appears to be a result of the sex roles which our society demands, rather that of innate, biological differences. As a corollary, since boys' sex role does not affect their persuasibility, personality variables can exert more effect on them than on girls.

The source of a message seems to have little effect upon young children. Children of seven, if persuasible at all, are equally responsive to persuasion from both peers and adults. By the age of thirteen, however, a general trait of persuasibility has disappeared: by this age the source does make a difference.

Persuasibility and low self esteem tend to accompany one another. The person who feels inadequate and socially inhibited tends to be easily influenced. Contrariwise, the person with high self esteem is little influenced by others but likely to make a great many attempts to influence others. However, we do not know which of these characteristics is the cause of the other. Indeed, it has been suggested that both may be the results of a third characteristic. Guilt feelings, produced by a variety of causes, might lead to both low self esteem and high persuasibility.

Even if a trait of general persuasibility could be identified, and persons scored upon it, there is question of how a communicator could use such scores. They would be of value if there were some way of gathering persons of similar scores together in an audience. It is of value to know that girls are more highly persuasible than boys, for it is possible to segregate audiences on sex lines. (There are, after all, schools for boys and schools for girls, even if most pupils in the United States are not enrolled in them.)

Age also segregates audiences. Some television programs do tend to draw an audience of seven-year-olds rather than of thirteen-year-olds.

Perception of Others

Another trait that would interest us in communication would be the ability to perceive the personality of others. The trait of persuasibility is essentially a trait we look for in an *audience,* its usefulness limited by the opportunity one has to direct a message, usually an advertising message, to persons with similar traits. Ability to perceive the personality traits of others, however, is a *source* trait and would be very valuable to a salesman.

What do we know about this ability?

The answer seems to be that this ability depends upon *whose per-*

sonality is being judged, *why* it is being judged, and *how* long the judge has known the person he is judging.

Some persons are good at judging themselves, others at judging friends, still others at judging strangers. In general, we would think that of these three abilities, the salesman would most need the ability to judge strangers. But even in judging strangers, there may be differences. The salesman may find it most important to judge what the *individual* he is talking to is like. His boss, the sales manager, will find it more useful to know what *customers in general* are like and to predict how they will behave.

Another important variable in personal selling is the length of time that the salesman is face-to-face with a customer, and the number of contacts he may expect to have. If he has only a single, brief contact then ability to judge correctly on the basis of first impressions may be very important. If there are many contacts, then the ability to revise first impressions may be much more important.

The roles which our society imposes on women tend to make them more sensitive to others and therefore better judges of personality. Four other qualities which tend to make one a good judge of personality are (Allport, 506–511):

Experience. Age improves one's ability to judge, and the more different kinds of persons one has known while he was aging, the better his judgements are likely to be.

Similarity. It is also easier to judge persons we are familiar with. Usually we are most familiar with people like ourselves.

Intelligence. Ability to judge others rises with intelligence. "It takes one to know one"—a person with a complicated mind cannot be understood by a person with a simple mental makeup. If a man can see all his own complex motives and contradictions, he may be more willing to credit others with similar complexity.

Social skill. Obviously no one can judge others if he is so concerned with himself that he projects his own feelings upon others. He must be willing to mix with others if he is to observe them. At the same time, he needs to remain detached enough to observe, and this is a difficult tightrope to walk, since people are not likely to behave naturally if they feel they *are* being observed! Part of this detachment, or linked closely to it, is an interest in the whole area of personality and feelings, motivation and emotion.

Aside from these two, how many traits are important in communication?

This question really can't be answered until one has first specified one's goals in communicating, and the other elements—source, issue, channels, audience and effects. A submissive person, for example, may be readily influenced by an authoritative source. A gregarious person may be influenced by a salesman at a neighborhood party.

Usually one trait is not enough to predict a receiver's response. The person who is dominant and hostile, for example, is likely to respond to a message in very different fashion than one who is dominant and friendly. On the other hand, it usually does not take all of the traits included in a typical questionnaire to classify a person, either. (Considering the number of possible combinations, this is mighty fortunate.) When students in one experiment were asked to write down the "essential characteristics" of someone they knew well, the average number of traits listed was 7.2, and only 10% of the students felt they needed more than ten (Allport, 366–367).

It's rare for us to have enough experience with anyone under varied enough circumstances to be able to judge his personality on a wide variety of traits. In one experiment, three teachers rated thirty pre-school children on 231 traits; the correlation among their ratings was only .48 (Conrad). But correlations of the same teachers for traits they considered important in a child's personality, reached .95. Probably this was because these traits "explained" overt behavior which teachers, sharing similar values, saw exhibited in similar situations.

Origin of Traits

In addition to knowing how personality is measured, it is also helpful to know how it originates. The answer, of course, is that, like other psychological variables, it is shaped by both heredity and environment. So many and so complex are the combinations of inherited and learned variations that any single act may originate in many different ways, and any given learned or inherited trait may, through the variety in combinations, lead to many different acts. Three children may steal, but for very different reasons: one because he wants to impress his peers, another to get even with the victim, and a third because of something he wants to buy with the money he steals.

Personality is only one of the forces which shape behavior; the "personality" at work in any act is never a single trait acting in isolation; and, even when we know which traits are at work, it is hard from knowledge of each by itself to predict how they will act in combination.

Nevertheless, there have been some interesting attempts to relate behavior to such things as body types, although the possibility of self-fulfilling prophecy enters here, too. The tall thin person may act like an intellectual and the short, fat person may be jolly not so much because their physique forces them to behave in this way but because they have learned that this is how everyone expects them to behave.

Importance of Learning

Three building blocks of personality seem to be inherited—intelligence, physique and response to emotional stimulation.

There have been some interesting attempts to determine how much of a person's behavior is determined by his genetic makeup, and how much by his experiences before and after birth.

One author suggests that if 10% of the population is incurably left-handed, that probably an equal percentage of the population would be incurably right-handed in a left-handed society (Allport, 69). The argument then is that the remaining 80 per cent will learn to be left-handed or right-handed, depending upon their society.

Studies of family members—ranging from twins to brothers and sisters to parent-child combinations—find members are most alike in physique, then in such abilities as intelligence, motor skills and the senses; then in emotion and mood; and least alike of all in attitudes, beliefs, values and interests (Allport, 70–71). Since it is this last area that most interests communication, learned aspects of personality should concern us most.

Two studies of persons with high intelligence scores emphasize this position. One represented a follow-up, twenty years later, of 750 gifted children (Terman and Oden). It found that the successful ones were those who were interested in their work, had integrated goals, were self-confident and persevering. All of these sound like learned characteristics, but how were they learned? Another study of leading scientists offers some clues (Roe). The scientists were persons who also showed high interest in their work. Where did this interest come from? Apparently it was strongest in persons who were striving to overcome early inferiority feelings, and who had marked success in their first experience with creative research in college.

Throughout life, experience shapes personality. A study found a wide variation among infants in their response to frustration in feeding, one child showing five times as much "bodily protest" as another (Marquis). The protesting child, it was found, was one who had been rejected psychologically by its mother, or one who had been hospitalized for a physical ailment in the first months of life and so deprived of a mother's care. There seems to be a critical period that shapes the whole later personality, during which such mothering is needed. The forms such mothering may take are comparatively unimportant, but the fact seems to be essential. In short, personality is learned, and learned through experience with people. Since it *is* learned, all the principles of learning, reinforcement, generalization, inhibition, and extinction, play a part in its formation.

Effects of Social Learning

Events in a child's life are far less important in shaping his personality than the way persons around him react to them. The timid child learns to fear lightning less from the light or from the noise

---

Evidence that a personality trait such as aggressiveness, like any other pattern of human response, is learned (and can be taught) is provided by this experiment on the results of frustration.

Just Like Taking Candy from a Child

Summer campers, 24 girls and 16 boys aged 6 to 9, were divided into four-person groups, and given seven half-hour training sessions. Half the groups were trained to be aggressive through games which involved competing for a goal, breaking other players' ping pong balls or tearing cloths tied around their arms. The rest were trained to be "constructive" and cooperative by drawing a joint mural or putting together a common jigsaw puzzle.

Then the groups were subjected to frustration—being forced to leave a room where a movie was being shown and having candy, given them earlier, snatched from their hands. Concealed cameras then recorded their behavior, during an 18-minute free-play period, for comparison with similar films taken before the experiment proper began. Two independent judges recorded the behavior of each subject, during subsequent viewing of the films, with no identification of which reel was "before" and which was "after." Four more judges then rated each of these records in terms of aggressiveness (20 records were dropped because no aggression was recorded) and in terms of constructiveness—with a coefficient of concordance, a measure of agreement among judges, of .90. By adding up ranks awarded by the four judges, each individual subject was given ranks for aggressiveness and constructiveness, both before and after the experiment. Constructively trained subjects lost rank in aggressiveness, increased rank in constructiveness. Here are the figures:

Changes in Rank

	Aggressiveness		Constructiveness	
	No. Gains	No. Loss	No. Gains	No. Loss
Aggressively trained	14	5	4	16
Constructively trained	6	11	12	8

Chi square tests showed that the aggressively trained groups proved more aggressive, following frustration, and the constructively-trained groups more constructive, at the .05 and .02 levels. Rank order correlation between aggressive and constructive ranks of the 40 subjects was −.83.

—Joel R. Davitz, "The Effects of Previous Training on Post-frustration Behavior," *Journal of Abnormal and Social Psychology*, 47:309–315.

that accompanies it, than from his mother's reaction to the light and noise. A depression which costs a father his job and his self-esteem affects a child one way; the same depression may have quite a different effect on the child in a family which is drawn closer together to withstand the hardships of a depression and unemployment.

Patterns of response of this kind are learned first of all *in the family*. One family has a warm and friendly atmosphere; another is cold and indifferent. Parents' attitudes toward aggression differ; some punish it, some tolerate it. Some parents encourage independence, whereas others seek to make their children dependent upon them.

If parents disagree with one another about discipline and other matters, are arbitrary and neglect the child, he may become very *aggressive*. When aggression becomes delinquency, however, (a typical result of poor supervision and inconsistent punishment), the child is *not* likely to be anxious. He does not fear punishment, and he is not in conflict with any internal standards of right or wring. Possessive parents, on the other hand, whether they indulge the child or dominate him, are likely to make the child *anxious*. In attempting to protect the child, they tend to make him fearful, and to feel guilty for worrying his parents. The indulged child becomes anxious when given more freedom than he is able to cope with.

Patterns are also learned *in the neighborhood* and, since United States neighborhoods tend to be segregated along class lines, class differences in child-raising practices become important. A child's playmates and the attitudes of his playmates' parents affect his personality. In general, lower class children are given more freedom to be angry and aggressive; they are more likely to band together in groups for protection. Middle class parents, on the other hand, emphasize self-reliance, control of aggression, the breaking of kinship ties that goes with social mobility, and preference for delayed rather than immediate rewards.

Finally, *society* itself will show certain common modes of adjustment, either directly or through the type of family it fosters. The nuclear family of parents and children, typical of the United States, emphasizes individual responsibility, strong affective relations and a sense of guilt. The extended joint family, which combines several nuclear families and generations, tends to induce more respect of authority since there are more elders whom the child must obey, but less initiative, and less feeling that an individual is in control of his environment.

Stages of Development

The child's first attempt to become independent of his parents, and establish a personality of his own, occurs at about the age of 2. His next move in this direction occurs when he enters school, and spends much of his waking hours with another adult. The third, and final move, comes at adolescence, as he becomes influenced by others of his own age. Allport sees seven stages in this growth toward self-hood, and points out that all seven may coexist in a student who is preparing for an exam. Such a student may be aware of several different aspects of self as he takes the exam (Allport, 137):

Bodily self. The student senses that his heart is beating faster.

Self-identity. He has a history; the student who takes the quiz today is the same one who studied yesterday and will study tomorrow.

Self-esteem. He has an attitude toward this person: he takes pride in his ability to handle the test.

Self-extension. He sees himself as part of a group; he wants to do well on the test to please his family.

Self-image. He also wants to do well on the test so that he can continue to think of himself as an intelligent person.

Rational agent. He can observe and compare his techniques in answering the exam questions.

Goal-directed. He realizes that success in this exam will help him achieve his goal of becoming a lawyer or doctor.

Roughly speaking, the first three of these aspects of self appear by the age of three; the next by the age of six. The sixth appears by the age of twelve, and the seventh during the teens.

Some of us are fortunate enough to have our needs satisfied as they develop during the process of growing up. If this happens, we tend to be confident and self-assured, although we may be at a loss when we face a problem or meet frustration for the first time, since we have had no experience in dealing with it. Many more of us have our wants met only in part. This may provide the energy and motivation for sustained action directed at satisfying our wants.

Something quite different happens, however, if our wants are completely and consistently frustrated. Such frustration may arise from physical conditions about us; from our own biological makeup; from the social environment, the people, in which we find ourselves; or because we simultaneously experience several conflicting wants. When this happens we may, depending upon what we have learned from other persons and previous experiences, attack the source of frustration, seek a way around whatever is blocking our way, or give up the effort to satisfy our wants. Or we may resort to one or more of several *defense mechanisms.* Resort to defense mechanisms is particularly likely when we feel threatened, but lack any clear sense of why we feel this way or what we can do about it. Sometimes this happens because we have roles or desires which we have learned persons we fear or respect to do like. Since it is far harder to deal with something inside ourselves than with an external object, frustration and anxiety are more likely to occur in response to internal than to external frustration. In such cases we may resort to one of these responses (Munroe, 243–266).

Projection. We may attribute to others aspects of ourselves which cause anxiety. Desiring public praise ourselves, we may accuse others of being vain and conceited.

Reaction Formation. We may react against the feeling that threatens us, by expressing a completely opposite attitude. Fear of our own sexual impulses may lead us to censor literature that arouses such impulses.

Rationalization. To conceal the real feelings that motivate us, we may seek to explain our behavior in reasons that we, or society find more acceptable.

Compartmentalization. We remove the conflict between two opposed feelings or tendencies by giving expression to them at different times and in different circumstances.

Denial and Withdrawal. We pretend that the feeling does not exist, or we refuse to think or talk about it.

All of us show each of these occasionally, to a mild degree, under suitable circumstances. When we tend to show a few of these responses frequently and under many circumstances, they become a part of

---

If products are different enough they will probably attract different kinds of personalities; books on philosophy and loaded dice might be an example! But how about different brands of such products as cigarets, cola drinks— and cars; can advertising differentiate them to the point that they attract different personality types?

Auto Buyers Take Personality Tests

From a list of 1639 purchasers of auto tax stamps in Park Forest, a suburb 30 miles south of the Chicago loop, researchers drew samples of 100 Chevrolet and 100 Ford owners. Of this sample, 70 per cent filled out psychological questionnaires and supplied data on 12 "objective" variables, such as home ownership, religion and politics, age, income, and miles driven per year.

The psychological test was based on Murray's list of manifest needs, which includes such personality traits as the needs for achievement, affiliation, dominance, deference and aggression. (This list has given rise to both a projective test of personality, the TAT picture test, and to a standardized personality inventory, Edwards' "Personal Preference Schedule.")

Items in the test consisted of 21 brief descriptions of people, drawn from Edwards' inventory: "likes to travel, aggressive driver, always telling jokes, thinks himself physically attractive to women." Each respondent checked the items which he felt applied to him and then responses of Chevrolet and Ford owners were compared. Later, respondents were given 21 phrases and asked which of the two cars would be better for each of the persons described. In this way the study was able to determine not only whether personalities of the two kinds of owners differed, but whether there was a stereotype, a brand image—a different question. (Such brand images, for example, may represent a feedback of advertising campaign themes.)

A linear discriminant function was calculated from test scores, then applied to the scores: it misclassified 37% of the sample, as compared with flipping a coin, which would have misclassified 50%. The function was "significant" at the 10% level—not good enough for most statisticians. Objective variables did slightly better; they produced a discriminant function which misclassified only 30% of the cases. It still did not reach the .05 level of statistical significance, however.

The study of brand images, the attempt to see whether owners perceived differences (even though such differences in owners did not attain statistical significance) also produced negative results, partly because 65% of the time an individual who rated a trait as typical of himself, also said it described whatever car he happened to own.

Owners of both cars picked 7 favorable traits as applying to their type of car: "loyal to friends, likes to travel, self-confidence, successful, etc." Only 5 traits showed significance at the .05 level: both groups of owners agreed that Chevrolets are for the very cautious person, and Fords for the aggressive, college boy, nonconformist, and someone who loves his car.

In addition, Ford owners thought their choice was for athletes and the man who was up-to-date, while Chevrolet owners were always seeking advice from others. Chevrolet owners, however, did not agree. They saw the Chevrolet owner as a dignified gentleman, a woman, or a person desiring job security—and sneered at the Ford owner as someone who thought himself attractive to women, wanted to be boss, and was always telling jokes. Needless to say, Ford owners did not agree that this uncomplimentary description fit them!

So far as objective variables went, the very uniformity of age and income within the suburb prevented any strong relationships from showing up, although this in itself meant more chance for psychological differences to be detected. On the other hand, the very popularity of the two makes chosen for study would reduce the chance of finding differences among their owners. In addition, it's possible that the 30% of the sample who did not take the personality test might have shown marked differences had they done so.

—Franklin B. Evans, "Psychological and Objective Factors in the Prediction of Brand Choice: Ford versus Chevrolet," *Journal of Business*, 32:340–369.

---

what we have called personality. In extreme form, when we use them inappropriately and lose control over these responses, they become symptoms of behavior which requires therapy.

Not only do we learn responses to conflict, but the conflict itself originates through experience. Experience may teach us to fear persons or situations which we cannot avoid, or to be anxious about desires or activities which we are likely to encounter frequently. Conflict also results if we learn to expect others to be unfriendly, or if we become dependent upon others.

Personality and the Advertiser

If, as we suggested earlier, advertisers must deal with men-in-the mass, with audiences rather than individuals, of what interest is personality to them?

To the extent that certain personality types are associated with a given social class, advertising media whose audiences are segregated along class lines do provide such audiences. We would, for example, expect to find appeals in the *New Yorker* magazine directed toward somewhat different personality types than appeals in *True Confessions*

Nine Products, Four Personality Traits

In Texas, 101 men students filled out questionnaires concerning the use of 9 different products and a 4-trait personality scale, the Gordon Personal Profile.

Subjects were divided into 2 groups on the basis of their use of each product in turn; there were 31 students, for example, who "never" used mouthwash versus 70 who used it, 4 of them more than once a day. Mean personality scores on each of the 4 traits—ascendancy, responsibility, emotional stability, and sociability—were then compared for each pair of product-use groups. Of 36 such comparisons, 13 were significant, as shown in the following table. (All correlation ratios significant at the .01 level, except those starred, at the .05 level.)

Correlation Ratios

	Ascendancy	Responsibility	Emotional stability	Sociability
Headache remedies	.46*		.32*	
Vitamins	.33*	.30	.09	.27*
Mouthwash		.22*		
Chewing gum		.29*	.33	
Alcoholic drinks		.36		
Automobiles		.28		
Accepting new fashions	.33			.57

Two products, cigarettes and deodorants, showed no significant relationship to any of the personality traits.

—W. T. Tucker and John J. Painter, "Personality and Product Use," *Journal of Applied Psychology*, 45:325–329.

---

or *True Detective*. Similarly, the advertiser whose appeals go to audiences in different parts of the world may find certain personality types more common in one society than in another.

Most media audiences, however, include a wide variety of personality types; only rarely are persons brought together into an audience on the basis of their scores on a personality measure. Perhaps the most useful conclusion to be drawn from this fact, and, indeed, this whole chapter on personality, appears in the form of a warning to the creative person in advertising.

If audiences and markets do contain such a wide variety of personality types, then anyone who designs a product or devises a message to appeal to a single type may not influence, or may even influence negatively, many persons in that audience. A variety of appeals may be needed; if not in a single advertisement, since this might lead to confusion, then perhaps in the series of ads which constitute an advertising campaign. The justification, then, of considering personality at all may be in that doing so helps to prevent a too narrow focus. It helps remind us of the wonderful variety of human nature!

As he comes to the end of this chapter, the reader must feel, and with good reason, that what we know about human behavior is only a small part of what we want and need to know.

Feeling thus, he is prepared for the two chapters which conclude this text, for these concern the opportunities and problems involved in extending the frontiers of knowledge about human behavior. We have raised more questions than we have answered, but ahead lie the tools with which answers may be sought.

SUMMARY

1. The layman uses the concept of personality to "explain": people behave the way they do because that's the kind of people they are. The scientist uses the concept in two contrasting ways: either as a general term to sum up an individual's habits, attitudes, roles, and so on; or as a residual term to indicate what such concepts as habits and attitudes are not able to explain.

2. Whether personality is used to label a very general category or a residual category it tends to merge with the other concepts of this book. It helps, therefore, to view it as being at the extreme end of two scales: more general than the other concepts, and harder to change than the others.

3. The difficulty of changing personality means that the marketing communicator must accept it as part of the environment to which he must adjust, rather than look at it as either an independent or a dependent variable.

4. From an operational viewpoint, there are as many definitions of personality as there are instruments to measure it. Basically, there are three ways of measuring personality: we can observe behavior (in natural or test situations), we can ask other persons to rate an individual, or we can have the individual rate himself. Others may be too generous or uninformed, or may let one or two traits influence their judgment on many others. An individual is likely to give us a picture of himself somewhere between what the "really" is and what he would like to be.

5. Some instruments measure single traits, with the risk that users will tend to put people into over-simplified personality "types." Instruments which measure several traits are harder to understand; their scores are often reported in the form of "profiles."

6. In devising a personality questionnaire, one may start with a theory or a dictionary; in the latter case, the number of traits may be reduced to manageable proportions through factor analysis or by choosing those that distinguish between known groups.

7. Traits have been grouped on the basis of three kinds of response to people; on whether interaction with others is involved, and on their stability over time and the scope of behavior covered.

8. Two traits, if established, would be of special interest to communications: a tendency to persuasibility, and an ability to perceive the personality of others. Women and persons of low self esteem appear to be persuasible. Ability to perceive others accurately varies with the trait being judged, the person being judged, and the length of time the judge has known the person he is judging.

9. If an advertiser could address an audience of persons with similar persuasibility scores, this would be an advantage; such a condition is rare. Ability to perceive the personalities of others, on the other hand, is important to the salesman.

10. The same end personality can be produced by many different combinations of inherited and learned traits. Social learning is important to personality: family, neighborhood and society teach patterns of adjustment to frustration. When frustration is protracted, the individual may resort to such defense mechanisms as projection, reaction formation, rationalization, compartmentalization, denial, and withdrawal.

Research Studies

Behavior which an onlooker might attribute to an "aggressive" personality can be produced in the laboratory, *Davitz* showed, if children who have been trained in aggressive responses are then subjected to a frustrating experience which evokes such responses. After training them for three and a half hours, he frustrated them by yanking them out of a movie and got the expected results.

Evans failed to find significant differences in the personalities of Ford and Chevrolet owners, at a time when the two automobiles had very different brand images; of course, as top-selling brands both cars had to appeal to a broad spectrum of the market. *Tucker and Painter,* on the other hand, found that such use of products as headache remedies and mouthwash are associated with personality differences.

Even such an important personality variable as the tendency to dominate others or be dominated by them can be altered significantly, *Berkowitz* found, if a man's position in a communications network calls for behavior other than the kind which he would normally exhibit.

Contents of Section D

SECTION D

Research as a Form of Communications

HAVING BEEN EXPOSED to some of the basic concepts and problems in the behavioral sciences, the student in this section faces the question of how those concepts were discovered and the methods by which those problems can be solved. Here he is introduced to the world of the researcher, in hopes that he may extend the frontiers of the behavioral sciences or seek to apply the insights of such sciences to the business world.

Two decisions must be made in engaging in that special form of communications called research. The researcher must, on the basis of the goals he wants his study to attain, decide on the method of analysis he will use. Having decided on the method of analysis, and examining both the circumstances under which the study must be made and the resources at his disposal, he then can determine the methods he will use in gathering his data.

The same problem can be approached by several different analytical techniques, although each will produce different results and may lead to different conclusions and policy or action decisions. Here is an illustration; Massy's original, of course, has much more detail, including the computational formulas used in arriving at the results shown here.

Predicting Sales of Coats for Dogs

The example began with real figures on income from the 1961 *Sales Management Survey of Buying Power* for 18 standard metropolitan areas;

real figures on temperatures from the 1958 *Rand McNally Commercial Atlas and Marketing Guide* and hypothetical figures on dog-coat sales.

	Coat Sales per 1000 Licensed Dogs	Effective Buying Income per Family ($000)	Average Jan. Temperature
Atlanta	2.9	7.15	44.0
Baltimore	4.5	7.31	35.5
. . . .			
Philadelphia	5.4	7.97	34.4

Then these figures were subjected, in turn, to four different kinds of analysis.

Cross-classification

By grouping the 18 SMAs into five classes on the basis of income, the marketer can see that sales of dog coats rise markedly with income. However, he find that in rural areas no such relationship holds; if he mixed the two types of areas the relationship to income shown in the last column, a weighted average of rural urban, would be obscured.

Average Sales per 1000 Dogs

Income Class	18 SMAs	Rural Areas	Total
$5500–5999	1.8	.2	1.5
$6000–6499	2.9	.3	2.0
$6500–6999	3.4	.4	2.2
$7000–7499	3.6	.5	2.3
$7500–7999	5.3	.7	2.0
$8000–8499	5.0	.8	2.2

Correlation

Now, using his original figures, the analyst obtains three correlation coefficients:

Income and sales:	.89
Temperature and sales:	−.45
Temperature and income:	−.57

The first two figures tell him that more dog coats are sold in high-income areas than in low, and fewer dog coats in cities with high temperatures than with low. But the third figure introduces a problem: for apparently incomes fall as temperatures rise. Does cold weather produce more sales of dog coats because the dogs are shivering or because their owners are wealthier? To answer this question, he resorted to partial correlation and got these figures:

Income and sales, with temperature held constant   .85
Temperature and sales, with income held constant   .16

Here is a surprise. Not only is the relationship of temperature to sales much lower when incomes are held constant, but the direction is reversed: the negative sign has changed to positive. In short, it appears that dog-coat sales *rise* with a rise in temperature! The analyst may have to look further to find an explanation for a result so at odds with common sense; one suggestion is that there are more sensitive dogs, such as Mexican hairless, in Southern climes. By squaring the correlation coefficients we find what proportion of variance in dog-coat sales is explained by temperatures and incomes: 74.8% (the sum of squares of the two partial coefficients) in contrast with the 99.5% suggested by the two earlier figures.

Multiple Regression

Moving from correlation, the analyst now seeks to predict how high sales will be for a new area, Kansas City, where they are not now sold. Using income figures for Kansas City (7.05) and the mean January temperature (26.7) he gets this prediction:

3.52 plus 1.51 (7.05–6.96) plus .0086 (26.7–40.9) equals *5.06*

So far, we have been able to assume that actual sales figures, even if hypothetical ones, were available for existing dog-coat markets. It is possible, however, that they are not and that the manufacturer is able to classify the 18 SMAs into "good" and "bad" markets. In this case, his question is whether Kansas City will fall into the good group or not. This requires a new technique.

Discriminant Analysis

Using his data on income and climate, the analyst now obtains a discriminant function: any city with a function above .809 is clearly a good market, and any below .746 is clearly a bad one. However, between these two points are some six SMAs: two bad markets and four good ones. Further computations allow him to specify a more precise breaking point of .762. Kansas City, he finds, has a function of .778—on the good side of his breaking point but within the twilight zone.

Factor Analysis

In this example, the analyst has been working with only two independent variables—temperature and income. If he had a dozen or more, as is often true in research in marketing communications, and if the distinction between independent and dependent variables was unclear, as is also often true, he might first want to reduce his variables to more manageable proportions. This, too, can be illustrated with the dog-coat data, although the small number of variables makes the illustration unrealistic:

	Rotated Factor Loadings		Communalities
	"Marketing"	"Climate"	
Sales	.959	−.195	96%
Income	.906	−.353	95%
Temperatures	.264	.964	100%
Percentage of total variance explained	60%	36%	96%

The loadings show that the first column represents what we have labeled a "marketing" factor—things like sales and income, expressed in dollars —and the second column a "climate" factor. With more variables, of course, it is possible that other geographical features might load onto this factor—and that additional factors might appear. (Ordinarily, one wants at least three variables heavily loaded on a column before he recognizes a factor.)

Next, one squares each of the loadings and adds across rows to determine the percentage of variance in each variable which is explained by all of the factors. (In this example, the "marketing" factor explains 96% of the variance in sales figures.) By adding down columns, he determines the percentage of variance in all of the variables which is explained by this factor.

—William F. Massy, "Statistical Analysis of Relations Between Variables," in Ronald E. Frank, et al, *Quantitative Techniques in Marketing Analysis*, (Homewood, Illinois: Richard D. Irwin, 1962).

Seventeen

Research as Communication
I: Analysis of Data

Six to eighteen months after they finish this text, most of the upper-classmen for whom it has been written will be at work on the lower rungs of some business organization. Those who start out as salesmen will have an immediate chance to check the principles of communication we've been talking about against their own observation and experience. Other graduates will have to wait for a chance to test and use the insights gained from the text; this is particularly true of those who have military service to complete.

Meanwhile, knowledge in the behavioral sciences will be advancing at an ever-increasing speed. A critical experiment may occur at any moment, or a new book appear which ties the bits and pieces of present knowledge together in an insightful new synthesis. These discoveries will be announced in the classroom, but today's student will not be there to hear about them. What is worse, from the viewpoint of today's student, is that his juniors will be there. Thus each new graduating class, equipped with the latest knowledge, makes each class that preceded it a little more obsolete.

This does not matter a great deal at the top of the ladder. Top executives can hire consultants to keep them up-to-date; junior executives can attend workshops. Moreover, the man at the top can substitute power for knowledge. There are fewer people breathing down his neck, able to observe the gaps in his knowledge; with power comes the ability to conceal what one is doing. Not many people are likely to say anything or be able to do anything even if they do observe lacks in knowledge which would be inexcusable in a more junior man. The man at the top is likely to be highly intuitive, thanks to the selective process by which he got there. He may be able to substitute more specific but less verbalized knowledge gained through

471

experience for the better-organized, more general knowledge gained in a classroom.

The problem of obsolescence is a serious one, however, for the student who has just graduated, and one that should concern him for that critical period of five or ten years which determines how far he rises in the business world.

What can he do about it? How can he keep his knowledge up-to-date in a rapidly changing world? To answer that question, let us take a look at another group of people who face this problem in its most acute form. These are the college student's teachers, and particularly the teachers who combine research with their teaching. A teacher who does not "keep up" is in a bad way, but his classroom is, nevertheless, a fairly protected environment compared with that of the researcher. The researcher, however, operates in a fishbowl, his words more or less permanently frozen in print for anyone to take potshots at. He has to keep up.

The researcher learns how to do this in graduate school; there he develops the skills and forms the habits needed to slow down the process of obsolescence. Specifically, he learns what channels bring news of recent discoveries, and how to read the messages they transmit.

Finding Channels and Messages

This text has introduced the student to these channels, perhaps without his realizing it. At the bottom of every summary of research study has appeared the name of the scholarly journal in which the original report appeared. In marketing communication, these have included the *Journal of Advertising Research,* the *Journal of Marketing Research,* the *Journal of Marketing,* the *Journal of Business,* the *Journal of Applied Psychology,* and, on occasion, the *Harvard Business Review.* In communications generally, the major journals are the *Public Opinion Quarterly,* the *Journalism Quarterly,* the *Journal of Abnormal and Social Psychology,** the *American Sociological Review,* and a variety of other journals in psychology and sociology.

Finding an article in any of these journals, however, is often a trickier task than finding a prospect for a million-dollar insurance policy. One friend of the student facing such a task is the fine print: the footnotes within each article, and the bibliography at its end. Given one article as a starting point, perhaps one of the articles summarized in this text, the student can soon locate dozens of others, by following the fine print.

* In 1965 this became the *Journal of Personality and Social Psychology.*

But how does the student find the first article? There are at least three ways. He may find it through a report in a trade journal or business paper, buried amidst the news of comings and goings of personnel and the outpourings of publicity men. *Printers' Ink, Media/Scope, Advertising Age,* and *Sales Management* all mention studies from time to time. Unfortunately, many of the studies they mention are not available in detail from their sponsors, being regarded as trade secrets and lack the technical detail one needs to appraise their worth and relate them to the general body of scholarly knowledge. Editors of trade papers do not screen and criticize research studies as does the editor of a scholarly journal, thus placing a greater burden on the reader himself.

A second way of starting a search is to turn to a systematic review. Two of the most valuable tools here are the *Annual Review of Psychology,* which brings together in more or less coherent fashion a year's output in major areas, and the quarterly *Psychological Abstracts,* which provides brief summaries of articles in thirty or forty different journals. The former is more selective, but always about twelve months behind the times. The latter places more burden upon the reader.

The third, and best way, to start the search is to use face-to-face communication and start with a person. This has two advantages. One is that the expert can help a businessman diagnose his problem. The breadth of the expert's experience, like that of the physician, and his training in theory and method, may reveal that the businessman's diagnosis of his problem is wrong. Although the businessman can tell where the pain is, finding the cause of the pain is something else again. The second advantage is that, having found the cause of the pain, the expert can translate it into the technical jargon used in the literature. Only after one knows whether the case is one of "relative deprivation" or "level of aspiration" can he use the index to any of the scholarly journals we have mentioned. Often, in fact, the expert can provide a list of equivalent labels for the same variable, one term preferred by sociologists and another by psychologists. Often each writer will have his own special term, competition not yet having decided which term the market itself will use.

Access to Experts

An expert can help one find the research reports one needs—but how does one find the expert? In communications, which is a form of social psychology, the best place to look is in the ranks of the two major societies to which social psychologists belong: the American

Psychological Association and the American Sociological Association. Although their memberships are large, only a few of their members are interested in marketing problems but those few members should be acquainted with the greatest amount and diversity of fundamental research of possible relevance to the businessman's problems. Experts with more specialized interests can be found in the Association for Education in Journalism, whose members are interested primarily in the mass media and only incidentally in advertising; in the American Association of Public Opinion Research, made up of academic and commercial survey researchers; and in the American Marketing Association. (The more of these organizations a professor belongs to, incidentally, the more likely he is to be interested in problems of the kind discussed in this text.)

Having found the expert, how does one get access to him? For a top executive, this is easy: he hires the expert as a consultant, or gives him a grant to conduct research. (College teachers achieve the same result by attending "workshops.") The recent graduate has two ways of gaining access to the expert. One way is by taking advanced courses, perhaps at night; the other is by attending one or two-week short courses or workshops, at a center for continuing education. He is most likely to find such courses at a public university, either state or city, which has a strong service-orientation.

Such short courses and workshops not only help the student find the research reports he needs, but also help him organize, integrate, relate and apply them. They give him a chance to discuss the articles with his peers, and with a teacher. For this reason, attendance at such workshops is helpful, at three or four-year intervals, even for the graduate who has been keeping up with the literature on his own.

Forming Habits, Learning Symbols

Finding a journal article is only the first step, however. Before a student can read it comfortably, understand and apply it, he must learn something about the categories used by behavioral scientists, the attributes of these categories, and the labels applied to them. Such background becomes even more important when a student wants to relate two or more journal articles. If they contradict one another, or contradict his own common sense and experience, he needs to know why. Is one article wrong and the other right? Or, more likely, have the two articles been gathering different kinds of data from different kinds of people by different methods, and analyzing them in different ways? This chapter and the next seek to provide the student with some of the background he will need. They can only introduce the subject, however. Undergraduate students will get further background in a course in statistics and graduate students from courses in research design. In neither case, however, will mere reading of a text fully equip a student to understand and use research data, much less enable him to perform research himself. These are skills which must be learned through practice, like figure skating and fancy diving.

A student who wants to develop such skills should re-read the summaries of journal articles in this text, this time not for content but for method. Next, he should go back and read, in their original form, the articles which interest him, and follow the footnotes to related articles. Finally, he should try to write summaries of his own, developing his skills both as a receiver and a source. He should be particularly alert to points which the author of this text has slighted or ignored, looking for alternative interpretations. Argumentativeness is a trait prescribed for the role of scholar!

The student must also learn some of the jargon of the behavioral scientist. For the most part, this book has tried to avoid using it, to make things easier for its readers. The serious reader who wants to read journal articles in their original form, however, will have to learn it. It is true that some of this jargon is unnecessary—the result of sloppy thinking, ignorance of or indifference to an audience, or poor skill in communications. Much of it, however, is necessary because the scientist makes finer discriminations in his concepts than the layman does, and cannot take time to describe frequently used concepts in a phrase, as the layman would, but must collapse them into a simpler term. Sometimes this is a barbarous word like "dyad" which designates a group of two persons, communicating face-to-face, and influencing one another's behavior. This type of word, annoying as it is to the layman, will cause him less trouble in the long run however, than a familiar word such as "group" which is given special meaning, as being not a collection of individual objects, but as a collection of persons who are "interacting" (communicating with and influencing one another). Similarly, purists object to talking about "causes" and "effects" if only because this seems to beg the question at issue. They prefer to talk about "independent variables," those which we manipulate or those which precede and therefore "cause" subsequent "dependent variables," or effects.

Two Goals of Research

Most students will find it easier to read research if they apply
to their reading the communications concepts used in this text. They
should, for example, begin by specifying their goal, whether they
are reading research or, at a later stage in their careers, paying
to have it done. Usually their goal is to find a solution to a problem.
They may have two very different reasons for wanting a solution,
however. They may want to make a decision themselves, or they
may want research to help them influence a decision which someone
else is making. Research of the former kind is highly respectable,
academically; it is the right and proper thing to do. Research of

---

*Many different relationships can be found in a single set of data, each being
represented by an index number constructed in a different way.*

One Variable Produces 8 Different Indices

Suppose we were to bring together six housewives, and allow each of
them to send a minimum of one written message and a maximum of five
messages to each of the others. In real life, the actual number of messages might depend on many things—on how near the housewives live
to one another, on how friendly each was with the others, and on which
ones are regarded as the most expert, etc. A simple table, like the following hypothetical one, might then report the actual number of messages
sent (read-down columns) and received (read-across rows).

Columns
Each housewife sent messages as shown in columns:

Rows— Each housewife received these messages from others	A	B	C	D	E	F	Total Received	Standard Deviation
A	—	5	3	3	3	4	18	.80
B	5	—	5	5	4	4	23	.49
C	3	3	—	3	3	4	16	.40
D	4	3	4	—	4	5	20	.63
E	3	4	2	1	—	5	15	1.41
F	3	4	2	1	3	—	13	1.02
Total sent	18	19	16	13	17	22	105	
Standard Deviation	.80	1.43	1.17	1.50	.49	.49		

How many different questions can be asked about these figures? There
are at least 7 comparisons which can be made among housewives in this
single hypothetical "neighborhood:"

1. *Which housewife got the most messages?* As totals in the next-to-last column indicate, Housewife *B* got the most, and Housewife *F* the fewest.
2. *Did housewives agree on their preferred receiver?* The standard deviations show that agreement was highest on Housewife *C*, lowest on Housewife *E*.
3. *Which housewife exerted the most pressure on her neighbors?* As the totals at the bottom of the table indicate, this was *F*, who sent 22 messages. *D* was least "talkative," sending only 13 messages.
4. *Which housewives picked their targets carefully, and which sent out an equal number of messages in all directions?* Standard deviation of ratings from these in the bottom row indicates that *D* was most careful in choosing her targets, whereas *E* tended to treat her neighbors more alike.
5. *How closely does the number of messages a housewife sends correspond to the number she receives?* This is shown by a coefficient of rank correlation between the 2 sets of scores. It is low and negative ($-.26$) for the group as a whole, and varies from one housewife to the next. Correlation coefficients for individual housewives are: *A* .69, *B* $-.22$, *C* $-.51$, *D* $-.85$, *E* $-.29$, *F* $-.48$.
6. *How closely do the messages which each housewife sends to others correspond with the total number of messages the others receive?* In short, does she rate her "targets" the same way other senders do? Another rank correlation coefficient answers this question. *A* .27, *B* .72, *C* $-.74$, *D* $-.63$, *E* $-.59$, and *F* $-.33$. These figures suggest that housewife *B* tends to get many messages from the housewives she herself sends messages to—there is a high positive correlation between the two. The reverse is true for *C*, *D*, and *E*.
7. *Do certain pairs of individuals tend to communicate a lot,* and others only a little? This is answered by taking each possible pair, and adding up the messages each sent to the other. On this basis, *A* and *B* are close knit, with the highest possible score (10); *CE* and *DE* are low with a mutual score of only 5. (Five pairs scored 8, four pairs scored 6, three pairs scored 7.) In addition to these seven indices for individuals, other indices can be computed if we want to compare this "neighborhood" of six housewives with other neighborhoods or to compare the neighborhood now with its state in the past or future—an example:
8. *How "communicative" is this group as a whole?* Its members could have sent 25 messages each, or a total of 150. Actually, they sent a total of 105, or an average of 17.5 each. (They attained 70% of possible.)

—Illustration suggested by pages 110–114 of Hans Zeisel, *Say it With Figures,* (New York: Harpers, 1957, 4th edition).

---

the latter kind is regarded by some academicians as disreputable. Yet research is often financed by persons who have already reached a decision and want to convince someone else that it is the right one. An advertising manager, for example, may want to convince the sales manager or the sales manager's boss, that a bigger advertising budget is needed. A media salesman may want his publication included in that ad budget. To many academicians, this kind of research is highly immoral, if not actually illegitimate. (The amount of such research being done suggests, however, that it is fattening a lot of bank accounts, some of them behind ivied walls.) In a way, the distinction between the two goals is unrealistic, since even the purest academician begins with some preconceptions, and starts looking for causes behind bushes of one type rather than another. The author of this text prefers to look upon research as a communications episode, involving at least two persons whose goals cannot be identical in all respects. By knowing what these goals are, one can understand why a problem was diagnosed the way it was, and why certain methods rather than others were used to seek a solution. For, of course, diagnosis and methods limit the conclusions one can obtain through research.

We should not expect the same methods to be used nor the same conclusions to result from research paid for by a decision-maker himself as one gets from research paid for by someone trying to influence those decisions. A decision maker cannot escape from this problem by deciding to pay for the research himself, since the researcher, too, has goals. The goals of the commercial and academic researcher differ; the businessman should choose between these two sources of research in terms of the type of research he needs, although to decide on the type he needs he may have to consult a researcher!

The rewards of the commercial researcher are similar to those of the businessman himself: profit, achieved by quick turnover of a standardized product. Exploratory studies rarely pay off for the commercial researcher; they are investments made in the expectation that the methods developed for one market or readership study can be applied over and over again. The rewards of the academic man are just the reverse: novel methods and original approaches produce the publications which pay off in prestige, promotions and pay increases. The academic man is less interested in speed, and more interested in methodological innovation. He is more interested in continuity of subject matter; the businessman's problem may excite him only if it is related to a long-continuing scholarly interest of his own, since depth helps build his reputation.

It is true that publication can increase prestige, and attract customers to the commercial researcher, too. He foregoes these rewards, if necessary, in return for money. The academic man may be willing to forego money because he puts a higher value on prestige, gained through publication. Sometimes a man wears both hats: gaining prestige in academic circles and becoming rich on private research. More often, he shows a two-stage life cycle: prestige first, then wealth. (Needless to say, the scale that runs from commercial to academic research identifies men and research, rather than the geographical spot where the man happens to have his office. The campus is not lacking in entrepreneurs.)

Knowing his goals and the goals of the sources of research a student then can look at meanings and symbols in research. The purpose of these two final chapters in this text are to help him do just that.

To an increasing extent, the symbols of research are the numbers and the concepts employed in mathematics and statistics. Fortunately, most business students have been exposed to these. (Unfortunately, in the opinion of the author at least, these disciplines are among the least audience-oriented of any on the modern university campus—the least willing to adjust to the needs and capabilities of the student.) These symbols have already been mentioned in an earlier chapter, where numbers were used descriptively. In research, however, numbers are used to infer a relationship of cause and effect. Some of the difficulties in doing this have already been mentioned. Chief among them is understanding the difference between cause-and-effect as seen by the businessman and as seen by the scientist.

Scientist versus Layman

The businessman may see two events as causally related merely because they occur together. The scientist will want to eliminate alternative explanations before he accepts occurrence together as causal. Among these alternatives are mere accident or chance, the possibility of both events being produced by a third cause, and the likelihood that either can cause the other. Although both businessman and scientist will agree that the event which occurs first cannot be the result of the one which occurs second, the scientist may be more precise in his observations and timing. He is also likely to be more conscious that events usually have several causes, and to be more interested in measuring the weight of each cause, and the degree of certainty involved in the cause-effect relationship.

In contrast to the businessman, the scientist may base his conclusions on a wider and more systematically varied sampling of times and places in which the event has occurred. The scientist will be aware of more alternatives in any research situation. He will, in the first instance, be aware of more possible causes for any given symptom; this makes him a good person to help in diagnosing the problem itself. He will be more aware of more different solutions to the problem, and of more different methods of determining which solution is most effective. The scope of the businessman's decision making power will help determine which solutions are relevant; the size of his budget and length of time he can wait for an answer will help determine which research methods are feasible. Choice of research methods, finally, will determine what data are to be gathered and how. Here again, the scientist is more likely than the businessman to know how the methods chosen to analyze data limit the methods used to collect it. If accidents occur in data gathering, the scientist knows best whether it can be analyzed at all and, if so, how we must change the original plans for analysis to fit the new conditions.

Every textbook ever written, including this one, contains a mixture of statements differing in the visibility of the cause-effect relationships concealed in them, and in the rigor with which those relationships have been determined. Some statements are at the rather primitive level of "in my experience," or "this authority says" or "the majority seem to agree." Others are expressed in more rigorous terms: these subjects performed these acts in this setting with these results, significant by this statistical test at a specified level of probability. Statements of the first kind represent the lore of the craft, hypotheses waiting for more rigorous testing. At the same time, every statement of the more rigorous type which seems to challenge common sense encourages one to look further, to see what elements in experience have not been adequately represented in the experiment. The student planning to do research and the student trying to get a foundation in the classroom for later learning outside school may find it useful to go back through this text, or any other he is using, and distinguish the plausible but untested statements from those supported by research. The merely plausible statements provide excellent hypotheses for the researcher, but a somewhat insecure foundation for the practitioner.

Three Limits on Observations

The concepts and categories of the scientist are like the neck of an hourglass, which is larger at the bottom than at the top. The top of the hourglass represents observations of human behavior; the bottom of the hourglass represents the scientist's predictions of human behavior. Observations produce predictions by funneling through a small number of concepts and a few summary figures and formulas; these concepts and formulas determine what is observed and limit what can be predicted. Thus the big decision which a scientist must make concerns the neck of the hourglass. Which set of concepts will allow him to decrease the number of observations, and therefore the cost of a study, while increasing the number of predictions which can be made, and the precision and probability attached to them?

The scientist imposes three limits on the observations he makes:

People. He usually observes a smaller number of persons than the number whose behavior he plans to predict—a *sample* of a *population*. He uses a probability sample; a sample in which the probability of any individual in the population being included is known. (In a simple random sample, every individual will have an equal chance of being included. In a stratified random sample, the probability will be identical within groups but may differ from one group to the next.) If the groups are based on some variable which is related to the dependent variable being studied, the random sample may mean better predictions at a lower cost.

If buying attitudes, for example, are related to income, then a sample which taps adequate numbers of persons at each income level is preferable to one which takes them in their actual proportions in the population. This may mean a 100 per cent sample of millionaires but a 5 per cent sample of lower income groups. In any case, the researcher wants the people he observes to be representative of the people whose behavior he plans to predict. He wants his sample to be representative as well as random. Getting representative consumers to cooperate in a laboratory study may be difficult; this is particularly true of the rich, the poor, the aged, and persons with little schooling. These are also the groups who are hardest to reach in a house-to-house survey and often the ones most likely to refuse.

Behaviors. The scientist usually observes a smaller number and variety of acts than those he plans to predict, although his predictions improve both as he observes more different acts, and acts which are more similar to those he wants to predict. In many instances, however, the acts he observes differ in kind from those he predicts. This may occur because the act he wants to predict can occur only once, or because he wants to predict its first occurrence. Or it may be because it is cheaper to observe verbal behavior than nonverbal, or easier for him to evoke verbal behavior from respondents at a time and place convenient to observe. A researcher could observe a housewife's behavior in a supermarket and predict how she would answer a questionnaire; he is more likely to do just the reverse.

Time. Enough observations of human behavior need to be made at enough different points in time to distinguish strong, permanent tendencies from more temporary ones. At the same time, the shorter the time which elapses between the events observed and the events predicted, the better the predictions tend to be. The long period of time permits observations under a variety of circumstances and separation of transient from stable phenomena. The short interval between observation and prediction allows less time for the "other things being equal" to become unequal.

The very factors which improve prediction, however, make prediction less useful. Presumably one invests money in research so that the predictions it produces will save money in subsequent decisions one makes. But a long period of observation may make the research cost more than its results are worth; too short a time lapse between observations and predictions may not allow time for one to incorporate the predictions in one's decisions. In short, the scientist must not obtain accuracy at the sacrifice of economy or usefulness. He could put limits on people, behaviors, and time which would make the probability and precision of his predictions very high. He might, for example, observe John Jones asleep at 12:01 A.M., so as to predict the behavior of John Jones at 12:02, but cost would be high and utility low. His predictions would be accurate but low in usefulness.

As we pointed out in Chapter One, a chain of causes precedes any effect; the question is how far back a researcher should go in this chain. One answer is that he should go back until he reaches a cause which the decision-maker can control. If the decision-maker can control several causal variables in the chain, he and the researcher again must balance utility and accuracy. The further back we go, the greater the gain in time and scope. More time elapses between decision and event, and any single decision covers more events. At the same time, the certainty that a given event will follow a given decision tends to decrease.

In addition to these limits on research in general, there are specific limits on the kind of events observed and the method of observing them in each research project. Most research reports don't indicate the variety of alternative methods that might have been used or indicate why *this* method was chosen for *this* problem. A few studies actually employ more than one method and compare the results. For the most part, however, the burden is on the reader, who should realize that alternative methods of analyzing data, and of gathering data, might have been used in every case. It would help if we knew what those alternatives were and could guess how their results might differ.

Group or Individual Variables?

One choice which the researcher must make is that between individual and group characteristics. Historically, most research in marketing communications has concerned itself with individual characteristics. Researchers have examined the reading habits and the buying habits, the attitudes and the personalities, the demography and the geographic locations of individuals. To an increasing extent, however, it is being recognized that many buying decisions result from group interaction, including that two-person group of husband and wife who make decisions for a household. The two types of characteristics are related, of course. Individuals can be given a score which represents their membership or their behavior in a group. Groups can be given a score based on the average score of its members or the dispersion of their scores. Groups also may be scored on the basis of relations that exist among its members or on the basis of some accomplishment of the group itself. Although the existence of group decisions is being recognized by researchers, both media buyers and the persons who prepare marketing messages have only begun to exploit channels of group communication, and only begun to enlist group norms and values in the influence process.

If a researcher is interested in groups, he can compare their averages or variances; if he is interested in individuals, he can use difference scores ("before" and "after") or compute correlations. His choice may also determine whether he finds statistically-significant (and publishable) results. A message may produce no change in a group's average score, for example, because some individuals move in one direction, and others move in the opposite direction, so that the two movements cancel one another. The actual effects of such a message can be detected by studying individuals, or by breaking the group up into smaller subgroups on the basis of some antecedent, independent variable. This is what was done in the study of two-sided messages: "educated" subjects reacted favorably, but "uneducated" subjects were more influenced by one-sided messages (Hovland, Lumsdaine Sheffield).

How Many Variables Are There?

In Chapter One, we suggested that very few independent variables in the behavioral sciences are both sufficient and necessary. It is seldom that one, and only one, cause produces an effect. Indeed, since multiple causation is the rule, it is seldom that any variable is sufficient, as would happen if one cause produced an effect all by itself, although that effect could also be produced in other ways. Moreover, since most variables have substitutes, it is rare that any variable is necessary; this would mean that an effect would fail to appear if this cause were absent from a package of causes. Finally, most variables are quantifiable; up to some minimum and beyond some maximum they may produce no observable effect at all.

In real life, causation is multiple, and multiple in two senses. Every event is preceded by several different series of causes. The researcher must decide how many of these series to study, and how far back

---

Given an effect, a decision as to which causes are most important will depend not only on which show the closest relationship to the effect, but which causes a communicator can best control. For this reason, he needs to be aware of the range of possible causes.

Group Variables or Individual Variables?

Sometimes we gather data about individuals so that we can characterize the groups to which they belong. Sometimes we collect data about groups so that we can characterize their members. And sometimes data about individuals is used to classify groups and then individuals are categorized on the basis of the classification of the groups they belong to.

Here is an illustration of these possibilities, based on a hypothetical exchange of communication by housewives over the back fence, which sought to assess the relative importance of the individual versus her neighborhood upon such effects as the number of back-fence messages produced, the kinds produced, and the influence they had on housewifely behavior.

One should note how data in one column may subsequently be used to characterize variables in the other. Thus the first four variables under "individuals" refer to the housewife, others in household, relationship among individuals, or the household itself. Each of these, in turn, can be used to characterize an aggregate or a neighborhood, and in the form of a type, a percentage, an average or a measure of variability.

To make it easier to contrast the two *columns*, no distinction is made within the "individuals" column between demographic variables, beliefs, feelings or behavior—important as these are. Nor is any distinction made between raw data, such as age and education, and such derived indices as the ratio between husband and wife in terms of education, age, and so on.

Independent Variables

Individuals	Aggregates
1. *Housewife.* What is her age, education, personality? What does she know about Brand X? Does she like it? Has she bought and used it? How often and how much?	1. *Nominal data.* How many types of personality are there in neighborhood? What is modal personality?
2. *Other persons.* What is husband's age, education, personality, occupation? What are his beliefs and feelings toward it? Has he used it? How many children and what ages?	2. *Percentages.* What per cent of families have children and own home? What per cent of wives have college degrees? What per cent have used Brand X? What per cent of husbands like Brand X? In what per cent of families do wives make decisions? In what per cent is husband older than wife?
3. *Interpersonal relations.* Who makes buying decisions about Brand X? How much weight does decision-maker give to others' feelings? How much difference in spouses' ages and education?	3. *Averages.* What is average age of housewives, average years schooling, average number of children? How much Brand X is used, on the average, during a year? What is average difference in spouse's years of schooling and age? What is average length of residence in neighborhood?
4. *a. Household.* How long has family lived in neighborhood? Does it own its home? *b.* Are housewife and household typical of neighborhood?	4. *Variation.* What is range of housewives' age and number of children, residence in neighborhood and use of Brand X?
5. *a. Demographic.* How is family classified along ethnic, racial and socio-economic lines? *b.* Does family live in a homogeneous or heterogeneous neighborhood?	5. Are one or several ethnic, racial and socio-economic categories represented in neighborhood?
6. Is household located in a neighborhood with many barriers to external communication, but few barriers to internal communication?	6. Does neighborhood aid or impede communication? *a.* Do highways, hills or rivers impede communication outside of neighborhood? *b.* Are houses close: Is there a lack of barriers within neighborhood? *c.* If present, do neighborhood facilities, such as schools, parks water supply, roads, facilitate? If lacking, does the lack create a motive for interaction?

Dependent Variables

7. *a.* Does the housewife see herself as influencing others or being influenced by back-fence communication? How many persons influence her? How many does she influence? How many of the influences in either direction are within and how many from outside the neighborhood?

b. Does housewife live in a neighborhood with a high or low rate of influence given or influence received?

7. What is average and range of influence given and received in neighborhood? Are most of messages given or received from inside or outside?

---

to go in each series. If he is interested in brand choice among beers, he must decide whether he wants to see if the strength of the beer-drinking habit itself is related to brand choice. If it is, he may then want to go back a step further and determine how the habit was formed originally or why it is stronger in some people than in others.

Trouble arises when a causal chain branches and a variable on one branch is seen as causing an event on another branch when, in fact, all they share is a common cause further back on the chain. Here are some examples, contrasting apparent relationships with genuine ones: "Highway locations with a lot of billboards cause a lot of accidents, because drivers, distracted by billboards, run into one another."

Appearance	*Reality*
Lot of billboards	Heavy traffic on highways
↓	↙ ↘
Distract drivers	Increases Attracts advertis-
↓	chance of ers who want high
And produce accidents	accidents ad exposure

"The more fire engines there are at a blaze, the more property damage results, proving that damage is caused by firemen, not fires."

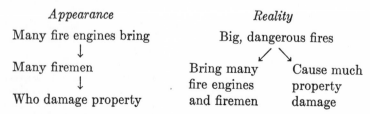

Appearance	*Reality*
Many fire engines bring	Big, dangerous fires
↓	↙ ↘
Many firemen	Bring many Cause much
↓	fire engines property
Who damage property	and firemen damage

In other instances, there are two possible causal chains; only research may be able to discover which of the two provides the better explanation. Here is an instance in which two personality traits or role behaviors of salesmen can be used to explain the same effect.

"Salesmen have more automobile accidents than men in other occupations. Apparently selling attracts aggressive and unstable personalities who are accident prone."

Explanation A	*Explanation B*
Salesmen are aggressive	Salesmen use their cars a lot
↓	↓
Aggressive persons tend to cause traffic accidents	Persons who use their cars a lot are more likely to have accidents
↓	↓
Salesmen cause traffic accidents	Salesmen are likely to be involved in accidents

How can we determine which of the two explanations is the correct one? One simple way is to classify salesmen both as to aggressiveness and the amount of driving they do:

Score on Aggressiveness	Amount of Driving	
	High	Low
High	40%	12%
Low	40	8
		100%

These hypothetical figures indicate that those who do a lot of driving tend to be involved in more accidents, regardless of their aggressiveness. In similar fashion, one can cross-tabulate fires on the basis of size and number of engines called out, or high-accident highway locations on amount of traffic and number of billboards.

In more general terms, this diagram shows how variables can be related to one another, without either being the cause of the other:

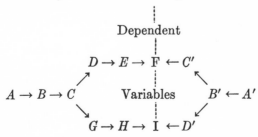

A simple example shows how introducing a third variable can eliminate or strengthen a causal relationship that appears to exist between two variables, or can show that the relationship holds for some people but not for others.

Effects of Age and Education on Program Choice

In the days before television, Lazarsfeld asked how choice of radio programs was affected by a person's age and his education. At first, it looked as if there were marked age differences in percentage listening to three types of programs:

Type of Program	Young	Old
Religious	17%	26%
Discussion	34	45
Classical music	30	29
	(N: 1000)	(N: 1300)

However, "old" persons were also less educated: only 30% of those over 40 were high school graduates compared with 60% of those under 40. Was it the difference in age or the associated difference in education which determined listening habits?

In the case of religious programs, apparently it was education; the proportion of listeners among the high school graduate group was only about a third of the proportion among persons with less education, but age had no effect.

Percentage Listening to Religious Programs

	Young	Old
High school graduate	9%	11%
Nongraduate	29	32

As for classical music, education made a difference but only among older people:

Percentage Listening to Classical Music

	Young	Old
High school graduate	32%	52%
Nongraduate	28	19

For discussion programs, age and education influenced listening:

	Young	Old
High school graduate	40%	55%
Nongraduate	25	40

In media-selection, as in all communications, one variable is seldom enough to explain an event or guide decision-making; an advertiser who chose his programs on the basis of age alone would have missed the mark.

> —Paul F. Lazarsfeld, "Interpretation of Statistical Relations as a Research Operation," pages 115–125.

Look first at the left of the dotted line. Depending on how far back one chooses to go in the causal chain, *A*, *B*, or *C* can be seen as the cause of all the remaining variables, *D* as a cause of *E* and *F*, and *G* as a cause of *H* and *I*. There is no causal relationship between *E-F* and *H-I*. Moreover, *C* is a "cause" of *E* if it is followed by *D*; if followed by *G*, the result is *H*, not *E*. Letters on these chains can represent any variables mentioned in this book. Frequently *C* represents a message, and *G* and *D* represent separate audiences for the message, which may react to it in different fashion.

The *A'* through *D'* variables on the right indicate a second set of causes which help produce the effects *"F"* and *"I"*. *C'* and *E* together may do a better job or a worse job of influencing *F* than the sum of each individually; when this happens we say that they "interact." The possibility of such interaction explains why a multivariate approach, in which all possible combinations of variables are tested, is usually preferable to a strategy which tests the variables one at a time.

How Many to Study?

As an example of multiple causation consider the simple decision to smoke a pipe which represents a balance between several pro's and several con's. The smoking habit, the advertiser's messages, the presence of an easy chair and a newspaper, news stories about cancer and cigarettes, an "oral" personality in the smoker, and his feeling that a pipe is the thinking man's smoke—all these favor smoking. Holding back the smoker are the cost of the pipe, his difficulty in keeping it lit and, perhaps, of keeping it clean. His wife's objection to the smell of the pipe and the ashes it produces may be a pro or a con—depending on the man's attitude toward his wife! All of these "causes" are important to a pipe manufacturer; he would like to know how much weight each has in a man's decision and how these weights differ for men of different demographic groups. Studying all of them, however, may be costly, particularly since the several causes are probably quantifiable and interdependent so that the researcher must study not merely the habit of smoking, but different strengths of this habit. Moreover each strength of habit must be combined in turn with varying degrees of each of the other variables. This is certain to be costly; probably too costly for even the wealthiest of cigar manufacturers. Selection is necessary.

Nor are costs the only reason why a researcher limits the number of variables he studies. Another reason, not unrelated to costs, is that as the number of variables rises, the number of subjects required rises even more rapidly. An advertiser who wants to study how sex, four different age levels, and three degrees of education affect responses to his messages must fill a table of twenty-four cells $(2 \times 3 \times 4)$. If we follow the rule of thumb that calls for thirty persons per cell, this will require 720 persons and some of the combinations called for, the Ph.D. aged twenty to twenty-five, for example, may be hard to find, and even harder to lure into a laboratory. Adding five income levels to the study would mean expanding the table to 120 cells and require 3600 subjects.

The difficulty of interpreting our results also increases with the number of variables studied. One statistician, for example, points out that using more than five or six independent variables in a multiple correlation formula does not increase its predictive power very much, and that the difficulty of interpreting interactions among variables in analysis of variance suggests that the number of variables used there, too, should be limited (McNemar, 186, 340).

In the past, many researchers have preferred to study a single independent variable at a time. There were three reasons for this: computation was simpler, statistical formulas for more complex analyses were lacking, and it was easier to understand what one was doing and communicate it to others. The first two of these problems have been solved: computers now perform the computations, and statisticians have developed techniques for multivariate analysis. The third remains: it is still hard to communicate complex research designs and their conclusions!

Four Ways to Present Results

Here are four of the most popular ways of presenting results when two or more independent variables are involved.

Cross-Tabulation

This method requires the least training on the part of the receiver, since it expands the simple table of results with which most persons are already familiar. In studying the effects of two-sided messages, for example, we can classify our subjects both as to the level of their education, and their previous attitudes. Multiple dependent variables can be reported, too, without much difficulty. We can compare the immediate effects of messages with the effects visible after some delay; usually delayed effects are less but sometimes they actually increase, producing significant results where none were originally

---

And here's another third-variable example to show why one needs to know why a man feels the way he does before one can design a message to influence his behavior:

Third Variable Can Make Original Effect Disappear

Here are figures showing the relationship found between education and willingness to serve in the military:

	Education	
	High (N: 1761)	Low (N: 1876)
I feel I should have been deferred.	12%	30%

Clearly, persons with low education were more likely to feel they shouldn't have been drafted. But why? Did their lack of education make them fail to appreciate the nation's war aims? Or was it the fact that many persons with low education couldn't pass screening tests and were deferred?

Here are hypothetical figures to show what might be the reason:

	Friends Were Deferred		Friends Were Drafted	
	Education		Education	
	High (N: 335)	Low (N: 1484)	High (N: 1426)	Low (N: 392)
I feel I should have been deferred	37%	37%	6%	5%

These figures suggest that men whose friends had escaped the draft were the ones who felt resentful. It is doubtful that any number of messages on war aims would overcome this feeling of "relative deprivation"—although other kinds of messages might.

—Based on Herbert Hyman, *Survey Design and Analysis* (Glencoe, Ill.: The Free Press, 1955), pp. 279–280. Reprinted with permission.

present. Or we can compare the effects of a message on attitudes and on other, nonverbal types of behavior. The method of cross-tabulation has its limits, however. If several variables are involved, a table or a series of tables may become too hard to understand. By using perspective, a three-dimensional table can be drawn on a two-dimensional page, but beyond that point other devices are needed.

Multiple Regression

This method produces a formula in which each independent variable is weighted so as to best predict the occurrence of a dependent variable. The formula tells what the relationship between the variables

---

Although computation formulas, available in any standard statistics text, are not included in this text, some of the factors which enter into the choice of a particular statistic are summarized below for the convenience of the student desiring to read journal articles in their original form.

Relations among Data, Measurement, and Statistics

The various devices described in Chapter Four, Symbol Systems, such as the mean, median and mode, and used to summarize data represent descriptive statistics. Those described in the present chapter are inferential statistics. When we use data from a sample to infer how a larger population will behave, we are using the latter. Some of the factors which govern our choice among several different inferential statistics are listed below.

Measurement. There are 4 types of measurement possible. Simplest is the mere identification of types, in a *nominal scale*. An example is the grouping of people or coffee into types. Through such techniques as *chi square* and the *contingency coefficient* we can then determine whether the number of individuals or cups of coffee observed is different from that we expected to find—including an expectation of equal distribution.

A more complex kind of scale is the *ordinal* in which one lists people and coffee in an order of preference. This permits use of so called "nonparametric" or "distribution-free" statistics, of which a common example is the *rank correlation coefficient*, also called "rho." On such a scale one knows that coffee *A* appears better than coffees *B*, *C*, or *D* which are ranked below it, but one has no idea how much better. The psychological distance between *C* and *D* may be very great, for example, or very small in comparison to the distances between *A*, *B*, and *C*.

A still higher type of scale is that which involves equal distances (or "equal-appearing intervals") between its scores. The statistics most commonly used in journal articles are of this kind, although it is questionable whether much communications data meet the requirements.

The most rigorous scale, the *ratio scale*, requires not only equal intervals but a zero point as well. This is true of such physical measurements as height and weight, and money but not of the behavioral data with which communications is concerned.

In addition, special techniques and special adjustments are needed depending upon the number of points on these scales. In general, it is recommended that data be grouped into between 12 to 20 classes. If both variables have only two classes each, such devices as tetrachoric correlation and fourfold point correlation are used. If one has two classes and the other is graduated (that is, has 12 to 20 classes), biserial or point biserial correlation can be used.

Normality. Many of the most powerful statistical techniques require, among other things, that one assume the trait being measured is distributed normally—that is, in a bell-shaped curve. Normality often can be attained by choosing items on a test to produce such a curve, and special techniques, such as *T* scaling, are available to convert skewed curves into normal ones. Or one can resort to the distribution-free methods which do not assume normal distribution.

Independence. Some formulas require that the two sets of data being collected be "independent." Others permit one to compare two scores for the same individual, or for pairs of matched individuals, and allow for the greater similarity to be expected in such scores. This consideration affects comparisons of proportions and averages, as well as more complex statistics.

Linearity. Many formulas assume that the relationship between two variables is a straight-line one, unchanged throughout the range of variation each can assume. For practical purposes this is often true although both threshold and ceiling effects exist for most behavioral variables, and special formulas are needed to handle the "curvilinearity" which occurs at the extremes.

Number of variables. In the laboratory tradition of allowing only one thing to vary at a time, many statistics permit a comparison of only two variables: two means, two proportions, two variances. To an increasing extent, however, multivariate techniques are being used. In part, this is because of the development of statistical theory. In part, it is because computers make possible the more complex manipulations of data which are required. Underlying these developments is the fact that causation of human behavior is multiple and that most decisions made by a communicator involve several independent variables. The use of multiple correlation coefficients in prediction, of factor analysis, and of analysis of variance are part of this trend. Many of the studies reported in this text, however, represent the older, one-variable-at-a-time, tradition.

---

is. The correlation coefficient, a different way of representing the same basic data, tells how large the relationship is, and so can be used to determine statistical significance. Squaring the multiple correlation coefficient in this formula will tell what per cent of variation all the independent variables together explain. Squaring the weights, once they are reduced to a common basis, will tell what per cent of each of the independent variables explains. These latter figures, when added up, usually will not equal the first percentage, since part of the explanation is due to the relationship or interaction among the independent variables themselves. Related to this device are *partial correlation*, which indicates the relationship which would obtain between variables if an additional variable were held constant, and the *discriminant function*, a formula which weights independent variables so as to index differences between groups of subjects on some dependent variable. These devices are used a great deal in business and survey research, with demographic data used for independent variables.

Analysis of Variance

This is a method for indicating which independent variables, and which combination of them, are making a contribution to variance which is "statistically significant"—that is, larger than could occur through chance. It does not indicate what proportion of the variance the independent variables explain, however. This device is primarily of use in the laboratory, since it requires that subjects be assigned to all possible combinations of the variables one is studying and this is often possible only in a laboratory. (Some combinations may be so rare in real life that finding subjects exposed to them may be too costly for the researcher.)

Factor Analysis

This is a method for identifying independent variables, rather than testing their effects, and so is often used in the exploratory stages of a research project. It serves the function of reducing the potential number of independent variables to manageable proportions. Factor analysis rests on the assumption that when subjects respond in similar fashion to different variables, these variables or these subjects have something in common. This something represents the "factor" in factor analysis. Factor analysis begins with a table in which scores on each of our variables, either questions or people, are correlated with scores on each of the others. As with multiple regression, one can determine what per cent of variance is explained by each individual factor or by all of them together.

Statistical Significance

All of these methods help answer the question of how close a relationship exists between our independent and our dependent variables.

In actuality, this is two questions rather than one. One question is whether the relationship found is strong enough to give any guidance to the decision maker that is worth more than the cost of demonstrating the existence of the relationship itself. The other question, and the one we will look at first, is whether our results are statistically significant—whether the relationship one finds is stronger than could occur by chance. The sample we are studying, for example, may be so small that the relationship one finds may be due to accident. The newcomer to experimental literature will find that the relationship between variables can be expressed in two different ways. We can compare independent and dependent variables throughout their entire range of values, and report how closely they are correlated with one another. Or we can group persons on the basis of their scores on an independent variable and show that these groups of persons differ significantly in their scores on the dependent variable. In using this method, the researcher hopes that members of a group will be as similar as possible in their scores on the dependent variable, but that the groups themselves will be as different as possible in such scores. As the "between groups" difference increases relative to the "within groups" difference, the independent variable increases in value as a predictor. In the first case we report whether the correlation coefficient obtained is large enough to be statistically significant. In the second case one reports whether the difference in scores is large enough to be statistically significant.

How large is "large enough?" Most behavioral scientists assume that if a relationship could occur by chance one (or five) times in 100, the current observation is not one of those rare times, and that chance has not been operating. Thus we get the phrase "significance at the .01 (or .05) level." In making this assumption, scientists run two risks. One is that even though there is only one chance in 100 that the relationship could occur by chance, this *is* one of those times. When this happens, they say a Type I error has occurred. The other risk is that even if this relationship could occur by chance one (or five) times in 100, this study is *not* one of those. If this happens, and one decides a relationship does not exist (even though it does), a Type II error has occurred. To the confusion of many readers, scientists do not actually assert that a relationship has been proven. Instead, they say that they have "disproved" the opposite possibility—the "null hypothesis" that there is no relationship between two events. This is a useful, if confusing, convention. If scientists have erred in defining their variables or the relationship between them, they are still correct in saying that the variables are not unrelated, but only later research can reveal the true nature of the relationship.

Practical Significance

Small differences between or low correlations within small samples are not likely to be statistically significant. By increasing the size of the samples, one can make even small differences or small correlations statistically significant. They may still not be significant from a decision-making point of view, or worth the cost of demonstrating their existence.

Correlation coefficients run from -1.00, indicating a perfect negative correlation, through the zero point of no relationship, to 1.00, indicating a perfect positive correlation. A coefficient of .60, regardless of sign, is fairly good (and not too common) in behavioral studies. However, since one must square it to determine what per cent of variance the coefficient explains and since $.60 \times .60$ equals 36 per cent, leaving two-thirds of the variance still to be explained, even a correlation of .60 leaves much to be desired. One often wants to compare two different alternatives. One independent variable may correlate .80 with the dependent variable, and another independent variable correlate .83. Both correlations are likely to be statistically significant, that is, higher than chance, but the difference between them may not be significant, so that question we started with remains unanswered.

Which is Cause, Which Effect?

To predict, one must know not only that two variables are closely related to one another, but also which of them is the independent variable ("cause") and which the dependent ("effect"). Sometimes the distinction is obvious; sometimes it appears obvious, but in reality is not. We can be sure, for example, that sex influences television viewing, rather than the reverse, provided we define sex as a biological variable. (If we are concerned with sex *role*, which is more likely in advertising, then television programs may be one means by which sex roles are learned.) In some instances, we know that the cause-effect sequence is highly probable; most persons in our society get married first and then set up households.

In still other instances, our study itself must determine or control the order of the variables. If income and age rise together, we know that age, rather than income, must be the independent variable. (Even then we must be careful, however, for income can provide medical care and other benefits which lengthen life.) If income and magazine readership rise together, we are likely to assume that income is the independent variable, even though it is possible that something a man reads may increase his income. We will feel safer in identifying income as the independent variable, if we can show the process by which it induces readership. We may find that income is correlated with education and that it is education which causes persons to read magazines. Or we may find that a certain income is necessary before a person is willing to spend money on magazines, or that income puts him into a social group where magazine reading is tolerated or even expected. Indeed, we are likely to find all of these factors operating, their importance varying, perhaps, from individual to individual. If brand purchase and readership of a magazine containing advertisements for that brand rise together, it is often assumed that readership causes purchase. The reverse, however, can and does happen.

To predict, one must also make sure that only the independent variables one is interested in can affect the results. In the laboratory this is most often done by eliminating extraneous variables or by holding them constant (that is, not allowing them to vary). Outside the laboratory, one does just the reverse: he introduces the independent variable that interests him, such as an advertising message, into the situation that already exists, and observes whether it makes a difference or not. He may do this by comparing two groups: an experimental group which is exposed to the message and comparable control group which is not exposed. He may do this by observing the same group before and after the introduction of a message. Or he may combine the two methods, taking "before" and "after" measures in both his control and his experimental group. If, in spite of all his efforts, extraneous variations do occur, then the researcher may use statistical tools to isolate their effects, so that he can estimate what would have happened had they not been present.

By using these same two methods, he can also make sure that his independent and dependent variables have not reversed positions. First, he assumes that an independent variable must precede a dependent variable in time. Then, in the laboratory, he controls the order in which the variables appear. Outside the laboratory he observes the order in which they occur.

Each of these methods involves problems. The experimental and

If measurements are made both "before" and "after" the antecedent variable whose effects one wants to study, changes may be due to the "before" measurement, the antecedent variable (also called the "experimental event"), unrelated outside events and the interaction of two or more of these. (Interaction: The effect of variables in combination may be different from the sum of their separate effects.) Various combinations of experimental and control groups may be used to overcome these difficulties.

Six Different Designs

The first design calls for four groups, with individuals assigned by random methods and an after-measure used in each group. It is assumed that if groups 3 and 4 had been given a "before" measure, their scores would equal the average of groups 1 and 2 on such a measure. Thus subtracting changes in Group 4, which was affected by only outside events (Y), will show effect of experimental event (Z) in group 3 and of the "before" measure (X) in group 2. Subtracting effects of X, Y, and Z from Group 1 will then reveal the extent of interaction effects (I).

Four Group Design

	Group 1 Experimental	Group 2 (Control)	Group 3 (Control)	Group 4 (Control)
	Measured before	Measured before	No before measure	No before measure
	Exposed to experimental event	Not exposed	Exposed to experimental event	Not exposed
Changes measured:	Before-after	Before-after	Before (average of scores of groups 1 and 2)	Before-after
Any changes found are due to:	Before measure (X) outside events, experimental event (Z) plus interaction (I)	Before (X) measure and outside events (Y)	Outside events (Y), experimental events (Z)	Outside (Y) events only.

Before-after design
(Two group)
Changes due to: Experimental event and its interaction with outside events and with "before" measure.

After-only design
Changes due to experimental event and its interaction with outside event

As indicated in the table, the 4-group design can be split into 2 halves: the after-only design and the before-after design. Neither design gets a "pure" measure of the effects of an experimental event since interaction enters into both.

There are 3 other possible designs:

One group. This is a "before-after" design corresponding to Group 1 in the table. It assumes that the "before" measure *will not* influence responses either to the experimental variable itself, or to the post measure, and that outside events will not affect the results.

Three groups. This design is attained by eliminating group 4 in the table, and assumes that outside events have no effect.

Two "interchangeable" groups. This design differs from the others just described in that each group is measured just once: the control group before exposure and the experimental group afterward. It is assumed that "before" scores in the experimental group would have been the same as those actually obtained for the control group. Thus any influence of the "before" measure is ruled out—but not an effect of outside events.

All 6 of the designs just described presuppose that one is able to assign individuals at random. This, however, isn't always possible. Sometimes one has to use so-called intact groups, either because the behavior is a group phenomenon, or because this is the only way subjects can be obtained. In this case giving groups a "before" test will help one adjust the final results on the basis of any original group differences, through the technique of covariance.

—Based on Section 4 of Claire Selltiz et al. *Research Methods in Social Relations* (New York: Holt, Rinehart, and Winston, 1961) rev. edition.

---

control groups, we have said, must be comparable. In the laboratory, a researcher can assign his subjects to the groups by random methods, which means that chance alone determines the assignment. He can make sure that the subjects themselves have no choice, since this would affect their responses in the group, and allow the same extraneous variables which influenced their choice to affect his dependent variables. Outside the laboratory, the researcher may have to work with whatever groups he can get, and depend on a "before" measure to compensate for differences in them. Such a measure, however, involves him in new difficulties.

First, the "before" measure itself may affect subjects. It may sensitize them to cake mix ads, for example, and so ruin an experiment in the attention-getting power of such ads. It may teach them a new attitude category, cause their attitudes to crystallize, or make them bored and indifferent to an after measure. Or they may try to make their answers on the "after" measure consistent with their earlier answers, regardless of their true feelings. Second, during the time which elapses between the "before" and "after" tests, outside events may occur which will intensify or weaken the impact of one's independent variable. If enough time passes, changes may occur in one's subjects which will affect their responses; this is particularly likely when studying children.

Third, all three factors—the "before" test, outside events, and the "after" test may interact with one another, producing results which could not be predicted just from knowing the separate effects of the factors. To overcome these difficulties, elaborate research designs have been developed, using as many as three control groups, as shown in the accompanying boxed summary.

In addition to these changes which occur in individuals when a "before-after" design is used, the panel survey, which employs a series of interviews with the same people, presents a new problem, that of *attrition*. Some subjects will drop out at each stage, through sickness, absence, lack of interest, or a change of residence. Unfortunately the very factors which cause a subject to drop out of a study are likely to be related to the dependent variable we are studying. Poorly motivated persons with little interest in the subject matter are likely to be among the dropouts; so are very busy and highly mobile individuals.

Summarizing with an Example

To summarize, the researcher's first job is to find out which variables are really related to one another and which only appear to be. Next, he determines the relative weight or importance of each of his predictive variables, and their different combinations. He checks to see whether the relationship is stronger than could occur by chance and whether it improves decisions enough to be worth the cost of establishing it—in advance of the research itself, if possible. He separates his independent, causal variables from his dependent, effect variables both on the basis of logic and by determining which occurred first. He tries to exclude alternative explanations, including an original difference or subsequent change in the subjects themselves and a change introduced by the measuring process itself.

Let us illustrate with an example. Sales of hi-fi sets in a retail store leap upward at the same time that the store begins heavy use of spot announcements on a local "good music" radio station. The advertising manager suspects that the spot announcements are responsible, and begins asking purchasers if they listen to this station. If he finds none of them do, he must look for another explanation.

Suppose, however, that he finds that 60 per cent of the purchasers *do* listen to this station. He then asks nonpurchasers whether they listen to the station and finds that 60 per cent of them do. Again it appears that his original hunch was mistaken. He may be wrong, of course. Listening to the station may induce persons with college degrees to purchase hi-fi sets; the commercials may interact with education and be *part* of a causal package, although not a complete explanation in themselves.

On the other hand, the advertising manager may find that only 10 per cent of nonpurchasers listen to the station; now his hunch that commercials have increased sales of hi-fi sets begins to look better. However, he must still make three more tests of his hunch.

First, he must determine which of the two types of behavior occurred first, since it is always possible that people began listening to the radio station *after* they bought a hi-fi set with a good FM tuner, or because they wanted to "preview" selections on radio before investing money in records.

Second, he must check his causal chain for branches. He may find that there is no causal relationship between listening to a good music station, and buying hi-fi sets. Instead, both are common effects of some third cause, such as introduction of a music appreciation course in the schools, which arouses children's interest in both hi-fi sets and good music stations.

Third, he may find that only one brand of hi-fi sets shows an increase in sales, and that this is a brand on which prices have been slashed, or one which has been heavily advertised nationally, in magazines and on television. Before the advertising manager decides that radio spots increase sales, and starts using radio to advertise other types of merchandise, he will need to see whether a price slash alone, or national advertising by itself will increase sales. He may find spot announcements increase customer traffic and the price cut makes the sale; or he may find that national advertising creates brand preference, and the spots bring prospects into his store to get the brand they want.

Even this example can describe only a few of the possibilities. The advertising manager could, at the very beginning, divide people into listeners and nonlisteners, and compare rates of hi-fi set purchase, rather than split them into purchasers and nonpurchasers and compare listening habits. Before he is through, he may want to examine all of the communications variables described in this entire text, including the type of persons most likely to buy hi-fi sets, the type of programs they are most likely to listen to, and the types of commercials which have greatest influence on them. All these, and such other marketing variables as store location, credit terms, parking facilities, competitors' prices, and so on, may affect sales.

A good advertising manager and a good researcher may find their own knowledge and existing data enough to provide answers, once they have devised a good "accounting scheme," which lists all the major factors which could increase sales, and come up with the right set of questions. They may not need to conduct research, or even have enough time and money left to make a study. On the other

---

How large an "audience" does one have to quiz in gathering data? Sometimes the number of decision makers is so few that one can take a complete census: they don't have to be sampled. Or a single member of each relevant audience may be sufficient to tell what each audience is thinking. Speed and economy may permit questioning only a few people; it is possible that this is enough to improve decisions and even that precision gained by extending the study to a lot more is not worth the additional cost.

The Role of "Qualitative" Research

A series of case histories, presented by Wilson, suggest the value of informal, "qualitative" research. These run the gamut from finding the single person, a man who rebuilds machinery to meet vibration problems, who is the nation's leading expert on nuts and bolts, to a study of the impact of television on family life.

•In the television study, interviewers asked 100 open-end questions of 135 families, varying in income, in 1959 when there were 450,000 television sets. The results pointed up a problem which the entertainment industry did not wake to until a year later, when the number of sets has nearly tripled. The question was how television had affected other kinds of leisure time activity. The results for a mere 135 families—

Went to movie	−64%
Went to theater	−32
Went to night clubs	−49
Went to boxing matches	−45
Went bowling	−12
Visited friends	−29
Entertained friends	81% up
Went to wrestling matches	22 up

•After the war, a firm wanted to know whether there was a postwar market for a device that adjusted the fuel supply in airplanes. Researchers began with the New York telephone directory, and interviewed engineering consultants. These produced so many suggestions that, after three weeks, the study was extended to Detroit. In all, 75 interviews turned up so many uses, including uses on railroads and in autos, that a device which management felt had no peacetime uses had soon boosted its wartime employees from 50 to 300.

•Another study, by a weekly news magazine, discovered the existence of two types of purchasing procedure on the basis of only 60 interviews in two cities. One type consisted of purchases which affected technical production standards and, indirectly, the reputations of specialists in design, development, production. So many persons were involved in these decisions—up to 20 for a single change in raw material specifications— that a technically skilled and persuasive salesman was needed to bring them together. Nobody seemed to care about other purchases, such as office equipment and floor coverings: anybody could initiate such a purchase and executive approval seemed a mere formality. Here advertising had a real role to play.

•The need for reaching a wide variety of audience types, rather than a large number of individuals of any single type, was illustrated by a study of surgical instruments. It included only 40 interviews, but they were made with hospital purchasing agents and superintendents, group purchasing agents, operating room supervisors, group insurance accountants, surgical chiefs of staff, resident surgeons, and makers of surgical equipment. The findings boiled down to this. Operating room supervisors did not like the stainless-steel instruments then in use, because they were hard to keep sharp. Surgeons did not like other kinds of instruments because their surfaces corroded. Researchers did not like the high cost of stainless steel instruments because the costs inhibited research. Surface corrosion was eventually traced to the use of unskilled personnel to handle sterilization. Better selection or training here and everyone was happy—with sharper, cheaper instruments.

> —Allan R. Wilson, "Qualitative Market Research," *Harvard Business Review,* 30:1:75–86.

---

hand, unless they *do* think through the possible causes in this fashion, the study itself is not likely to be very good or to be worth what it will cost them.

Only after he has gone through processes like those described in this chapter is he justified in embarking on the enterprise described in the next and final chapter of this text—the adventure of data collection. We said at the beginning that before a communicator can devise a message he must first specify his goal, saying what persons he wants to perform which behavior. Research itself is communication, and the scientist must specify in advance what circumstances he intends to find or create, and what effects he expects these circumstances to have upon a given audience.

SUMMARY

1. As new knowledge is discovered and transmitted through the classrooms, each year's graduates make those of previous years intel-

lectually obsolete, to a greater or lesser degree. To offset this, students need to learn the channels through which new discoveries are announced, how to find messages in them, and how to read those messages.

2. They need to know the sources of research and how goals differ: whether research is done to guide or influence decisions, whether it is performed by academic or commercial researchers. They need to know the symbols of research: numbers and statistical concepts.

3. The research scientist differs from the layman in his approach to problems of cause and effect. He examines alternative explanations more rigorously, is more aware of multiple causation, and more interested in quantifying relationships.

4. The scientist's categories limit and organize the events that he observes, so as to predict other events. They impose limits on the people who are observed, the types of behavior observed, and the time at which and during which observations are made. The sample of people he observes is representative of those whose behavior he wants to predict, and random. He usually finds it easier to evoke and observe verbal behavior to predict nonverbal behavior than the reverse. Accuracy of predictions increases with the length of time during which observations are made and nearness in time to events being predicted; but accuracy must be balanced against cost and utility.

5. The scientist may choose to observe individual or group characteristics; research in marketing communications is recognizing, to an increasing extent, the joint or group nature of purchase decisions. The choice made determines not only what data are gathered but may determine whether a significant relationship is found between independent and dependent variables.

6. The scientist must also decide how many independent variables to observe. In behavioral science, a single independent variable is seldom a sufficient *and* necessary cause, a sufficient cause or a necessary cause of another. Causation is multiple; the researcher must decide how many causal chains to examine and how far to go back in each chain. He must be alert to branching chains, which may suggest a causal relationship between two variables, only because they have a common origin, or may specify additional conditions necessary before a given cause can produce a given effect.

7. Computers and new developments in statistics make it easier to study several independent variables at once, but the difficulty of understanding and communicating such findings remains. Four ways of doing so are cross tabulation, multiple regression, analysis of variance, and factor analysis.

8. The relationship between independent and dependent variables can be expressed in two ways. One can compare them throughout their entire range by means of a correlation coefficient, or one can show how scores on a dependent variable differ for subjects grouped on the basis of their scores on an independent variable. One then must ask whether the relationship or difference is (*a*) greater than

that his questions themselves will have no impact at all upon his audience. Only thus can the question serve as a good measure of the impact of his message and other variables.

Despite his best efforts, however, the way a question is phrased

---

People will give different answers to the same question depending on what they perceive as the intent of the person asking it, argues this author.

Do Strangers Make YOU Feel Nervous and Inferior?

Every question, says Getzels, arouses two responses. The first is internal, and the respondent stops to think whether it will help or hurt him. What he actually says—his overt response—depends on how he appraises the situation; it depends on his anticipations of the reactions of his audience.

Question. How do you like meeting strangers?
Internal response. Strangers make me feel nervous and inferior.
Actual responses.
• To psychotherapist: Strangers make me feel nervous and inferior. (Respondent anticipates permissive reaction from therapist.)
• To pollster: It depends on the strangers. (Respondent realizes that the interviewer obviously doesn't object to meeting strangers and hesitates to admit his own weakness.)
• In job interview: Strangers are all right. Actually, I *enjoy* meeting them. (Respondent: Hmmm. They wouldn't want to hire me if they knew how I actually felt.)

This process of self-censoring, Getzels suggests, helps explain findings such as the following:

Interviewer effect. When Southern Negroes were asked during the war, "Do you think it more important to beat the Axis or to make democracy work here at home," white interviewers reported a 62% vote in favor of beating the Axis, Negro interviewers a 39% vote.
Perception of norms. When asked, "Have you cashed any war bonds in the past week?" 47% of upper-income respondents and 7% of lower-income respondents denied they'd done so. In actuality the list of persons involved included no one who had not cashed in his bonds that week.
Public versus private opinions. When Methodists in the state of New York were asked whether their bishop had made real efforts to help them, 92 per cent of those asked in public said he had—but only 31 per cent of the same people said yes when asked in private.

> —J. W. Getzels, "The Question-Answer Process: A Conceptualization and Some Derived Hypotheses for Empirical Examination," *Public Opinion Quarterly*, 18:80–91.

and the person who asks it do affect responses. These effects vary with the type of attitude being studied, and with the time period covered. If he knows what these effects are, a researcher can use methods which will reduce them to a minimum. He can learn what these effects are by using different methods and comparing the results. Using several different methods also will give him a much more complete picture of the phenomenon he is studying. Not all methods require that a researcher ask questions, although asking questions is the most common method. Perhaps the easiest way to introduce these methods is to ask a series of questions ourselves.

Does the Researcher Observe Behavior or Observe the Effects of Behavior?

An observer can stand in a supermarket and watch housewives remove items from the shelves. He will usually find it more efficient, however, to check invoices and take an inventory of the shelves at stated intervals. An interviewer can ask housewives what cake mix they use and which detergent they bought on their last trip to the supermarket. Their answers may reflect their attitudes, but an inventory of their pantry shelves may be a better check upon their behavior. Memory often errs. A housewife may not remember what she bought and name the brand which is heavily advertised, or the one she usually buys, or the one with a high-status image. If a researcher is interested in family power structure, he may be content with getting the private opinions of husband and wife, and then seeing whose opinions win out in terms of actual purchases. If he is interested in the methods by which the dominant member exerts his influence, then the researcher will want to observe the decision-making process itself, actual if possible, simulated if necessary.

Is the Fact of Observations and Its Purpose Known to the Persons being Observed?

A "participant observer" can mingle with a work group or a gang of delinquents and make observations without subjects' knowledge. In Britain, inconspicuous observers at news stands and on subways have studied the purchase and readership of publications in this fashion. By concealing themselves behind a one-way window which looks like a mirror to their subjects, psychologists have observed children at play and adults leafing through magazines, thus avoiding the disturbance of an outsider. Group conferences have been studied in the same way; even though members know there's an observer behind the glass, they usually report that after the first few minutes they get so absorbed in the meeting itself that they forget about the observer.

Even when the fact of observation is known, the purpose of an experiment is nearly always disguised, though ethical researchers make a point of removing the disguise at the end of the experiment, when it can no longer affect results. Similarly, most surveys do not reveal the names of their sponsors, since most persons will tell the interviewer what they think the sponsor would like to hear, regardless of their true feelings—and a few will do just the opposite. Both channels and the type of questions they transmit vary greatly in observability.

Does the Observer Merely Observe, or Does He Evoke The Behavior that He Observes?

By choosing time and place carefully, a researcher may need only stand by and observe. Some events recur regularly: the traffic jam at quitting time is an example. Other events are announced in advance: the student of mob behavior can count on sales at certain large stores in New York to produce grist for his mill. Some events occur with sufficient frequency that the researcher need wait only a brief period for one to come along, and then rush to the scene. Some events which occur rarely can be evoked in the laboratory, and some in the field.

How Does The Observer Evoke The Behavior Which Interests Him—by Asking Questions, or by Posing Problems and Creating Events?

If he asks questions, what symbol system does he use—words or pictures? And do his questions evoke responses in the form of verbal or nonverbal behavior?

Laboratory Experiments

Most research in marketing communications evokes the behavior that is observed by asking questions, and observes verbal responses. The questions which such research employs are transmitted through three basic channels which differ in the visibility of their source and the degree of control which the source exercises over the questions asked and the responses they evoke. These three channels are the laboratory experiment, the field experiment and the survey.

The *laboratory experiment* is a source-oriented communications situation, which gives the researcher a high degree of control. He can introduce and exclude stimuli at will and specify the order in which they will appear. Instead of asking questions, he can create laboratory analogues of real-life situations, and observe the ways his subjects respond to them. He can and does disguise the purpose of his experiments, often by giving a plausible but false explanation of their purpose. He can use novel tasks and novel situations, and so eliminate the effects of previous habits. He can use a great variety of techniques that would be impossible outside the laboratory.

He can, for instance, get subjects to play a role, such as giving a speech in favor of a point of view contrary to their own and see how action affects beliefs. He can induce feelings, through hypnotism, to see how they affect actions or he can create stressful situations and see how they affect feelings. He can observe behavior in a variety

---

Many variables in marketing are not subject to laboratory control. But a researcher can get clues to their effect if something temporarily removes them from the picture—if he can move fast enough.

A Clue to Impulse Buying

In the winter of 1948 a gas shortage forced retail firms in three Texas towns to close down for a day and then, a week later, for another day. Clover got sales data for retail stores for the two weeks in which stores were closed, the week between closings, and a week before and after the gas shortage.

He then said that any increase in sales, over the first or base week, in the week following a one-day closing would indicate planned purchases which could be postponed but not prevented. Sales not "made up" in the week following one-day closing, he said, would then represent impulse buying.

One-day closing represented a loss of 16% of the normal sales week. In 154 stores in the three towns sales dropped 18% in the first emergency week, were about half of 1% below base during the next week, dropped 14% in the third week (which had another one-day closing), and then were 3.6% below base in the final week studied. He estimated that the range of impulse buying, as per cent of total sales, ranged from 4 per cent in furniture stores to 60 per cent in variety stores, with groceries at 26 per cent. Among 19 types of retail outlet, he found four different kinds of impulse-buying situations:*

* Data reprinted from the *Journal of Marketing*, national quarterly publication of the American Marketing Association.

Change From Base Period During

	First "Holi-day" Week	Inter-vening Week	Second "Holi-day" Week	Final Week	Manager's Estimate of % of Impulse Sales
Book store (strong impulse)	−32%	+2%	−20%	+4%	15%
Variety store (medium impulse)	−16	+1	−16	−8	60
Grocery store (weak impulse)	−15	—	−10	−7	26
Department store (low impulse)	−25	+20	−12	+21	14

—Vernon T. Clover, "Relative Importance of Impulse Buying in Retail Stores," *Journal of Marketing*, 15:66–70.

Here is another example of how a researcher can take advantage of the lack of a variable: in this case, a newspaper.

A Clue to Advertising Effects

In Minneapolis, a newspaper strike closed down the afternoon *Star* and morning *Tribune* for 116 days, from April 12 to August 5, 1962. A telephone survey was made one week after newspapers resumed publication, of 198 business firms, chosen at random from the classified pages of the telephone directory.

In this survey, 11% of the firms, mostly furniture and general merchandise, reported they had cancelled promotions they had planned, and 30% cut advertising budgets. Advertising was shifted to a special strike newspaper, to suburban papers and to direct mail, rather than broadcast media. Some 40% of firms queried said sales had dropped. Most of the 40% who reported no change or the 20%—food and lumber-hardware outlets—that reported a rise in sales were suburban stores which because of their location or low volume had not advertised previously.

Secondary sources were also checked. The Federal Reserve Bank reported sales off $35 million from the previous year, and sales off $23 million. While weekly department store sales were rising 6.6% in the United States for the 9-week strike period, and 2.4% in the adjacent city of St. Paul, Minneapolis itself reported a 5.3% drop. Parking meter collections, which represent daytime, weekday traffic, fell 6.3% in May, 3.7% in June and 6.3% in July.

—William A. Mindak, Andrew Neibergs and Alfred Anderson, "Economic Effects of the Minneapolis Newspaper Strike," *Journalism Quarterly*, 40:213–218.

of laboratory situations and with special instruments; with a tachistoscope, he can determine the "readability" of a new brand name by exposing it for a few seconds, gradually increasing the length of exposure until it is perceived correctly. Once subjects have committed themselves by coming to the laboratory, there is almost no limit to what they are willing to undergo there. The major drawback

---

To what extent does the laboratory setting of an experiment influence the results? Here is a study of family decision-making in which the same subjects were studied in two settings: their homes and a laboratory.

Laboratory Reduces Emotion, Increases Disagreement

Twenty-four couples were obtained from 2 churches near Yale University, half the couples accompanied by a son 15–17 and the other half by a daughter of the same age. Each couple participated twice: Once in their own home, once at the university. Each session involved looking at a pair of TAT pictures for 20 seconds, spending 25 minutes discussing a "story" about the family shown in the pictures, and 10 minutes summarizing the story in writing. Each of the 3-person groups then was given 2 problems concerning the "family" in the TAT pictures, asked to discuss it and 6 alternative solutions. (The experimenter who also devised the hypotheses being tested, coded their comments into three categories: instrumental acts, and positive or negative social-emotional acts.) Then each individual was asked to rank the 6 solutions both for himself and for the other 2 members of his family.

One of the problems used concerned a 10-year-old child who left his homework until the last minute so that he frequently did it carelessly or didn't get it done at all. The six solutions suggested included: ignoring the problem, checking each day, explaining the importance of good work habits, setting a definite time each day for homework, helping the child with his work, and punishing him for not working harder.

The experimenter expected his coding of problem discussions to show three things: adults dominant over children; men as making task-centered comments and women concentrating on group maintenance; and more concentration upon task-centered comments generally in the unfamiliar setting of the laboratory than in the home. He also expected teen-age sons to compete with fathers and daughters with mothers, with such competition showing most markedly when the father's task roles or mother's group maintenance roles were emphasized. That is, he expected fathers to be most active in task performance in the laboratory— and most competitive with sons there.

The key to his analysis is an index of "positivity"—the *net* number of group maintenance responses (positive minus negative) expressed as a per cent of total verbal expressions. A rise in the index indicates relatively high group maintenance acts; a fall indicates task performance is being emphasized.

As the following tables show, positivity index scores summed for the

24 families were highest in the home, although mothers and daughters showed higher indices in the laboratory.

Scores of Individuals

	Fathers	Sons	Mothers	Daughters
Home	771	347	634	291
Laboratory	598	216	720	308

Scores for Groups

	Total	Couples with Sons	Couples with Daughters
Home	722	431	291
Laboratory	558	218	341

The author suggests that when daughters were present, the 3-family groups exchanged more separate verbal acts, but that a higher proportion of the acts were directed at group maintenance when sons were present. Fathers and sons tended to give emotional support to one another in the home, but became highly task centered in the laboratory. Presence of a daughter, on the other hand, tended to reduce the differences in laboratory and home, and reverse it. Change from home to laboratory had little effect on mothers. He also senses in his results a suggestion that fathers appeared to exercise their roles as if by right, perhaps as expressing a norm of their society, whereas the mother's priority in the home was exercised by permission of the other members. The father responds directly to a change in situation, such as a shift from home to laboratory, whereas the mother changes only if the members of the family themselves change. Such an interpretation would be consistent with the idea that fathers are task centered and mothers are person centered.

—John F. O'Rourke, "Field and Laboratory: The Decision-Making Behavior of Family Groups in Two Experimental Conditions," *Sociometry*, 26:422–435.

of the laboratory experiment, of course, is that many subjects cannot be induced to come. The great majority of laboratory subjects, in fact, are college sophomores, taking an introductory course in psychology, and white rats. This means that the experiment tends to be limited to studying problems in which audience differences, particularly demographic differences, are not important. A second drawback is the fact that some important independent variables cannot be brought into the laboratory.

Field Experiments

Both of these difficulties are reduced by the *field experiment,* in which an experimental message is delivered to real-life audiences in real-life settings by ordinary channels, usually without their knowing that anything unusual is going on. The "split-run," much used in marketing communications, is a good example of this technique. It consists of randomly dividing the mailing list of a newspaper or magazine into comparable audiences, and sending each audience an issue which contains a different advertisement. Interviewers then go into the field, and find out which advertisement has the higher recognition or recall score, the more favorable attitude score, or is associated with higher frequency of purchase.

If you are interested in comparing the advertisements' attention-getting ability, this is an excellent method. If, on the other hand, you are interested in an ad's credibility, a laboratory in which subjects can be forced to attend to the advertisements may be better, since it may take a great many interviews in real life to find anyone who remembers noticing the two advertisements.

Another difficulty with the real life situation is that allowing people to decide whether or not they will expose themselves to a message means that audience differences as well as variations in the message will affect the results. On the other hand, if we ask a random sample to act as receivers for a message, it becomes impossible to measure the attention-getting power of the message. In addition, the request is likely to change their attitudes to the message. They may start acting as they think "experts" are supposed to act, or tell the researcher what they think his supposed sponsor would like to hear. An ingenious solution to this problem is to ask a random sample *not* to receive the message. They then can act as a "control" group for the rest of the population. Both types of experiment, laboratory and field, help a researcher find which independent variables are most important from a cause-and-effect standpoint. To discover which variables are important from the standpoint of frequency or rarity, however, he must use the survey method.

Surveys

Most advertising research, in fact, has been *survey research.* One reason is that its goal is to assist in making a specific decision, or a specific prediction. The researcher needs to be sure that all relevant variables are present, but does not care too much whether he knows what they are, and isn't interested in testing different combinations or quantities of the variables. In short, he is not interested in establishing long-run principles but in settling an immediate problem. Another reason is that much of the research concerns and is sponsored by the media, which are difficult to study in a laboratory, and that much of the media research concerns self-selective exposure to messages by media audiences which the laboratory is designed to eliminate as a variable.

The survey itself is not free from the problem of obtaining representative audiences, which we identified as the major drawback of the laboratory experiment. Interviewers, whether face-to-face or telephone, have even more difficulty than salesmen in getting past

---

On the average, how effective are messages in changing attitudes? As the article summarized below points out, this depends on how effects are measured.

Disagreement between Experiments and Surveys

Why is it, asks the late Carl I. Hovland, that communications in a political campaign succeed in changing as few as 5 per cent of persons studied, whereas laboratory research commonly reports that a third to one-half of their subjects are affected by experimental messages?

He suggests 6 reasons for the difference:

1. The laboratory subject has no choice as to whether he will receive a message. In real life, however, persons have a choice and tend to expose themselves only to messages they already agree with. The "ceiling effect" appears: they can't move far because they are already close to the position advocated in the message.

2. Effects in the laboratory are measured minutes or hours after a message is received. In the field, however, measurement is usually delayed, giving time for forgetting to occur and for opposition messages to reduce the effect of the original message.

3. The experimental audience, all too often, consists of high school pupils and college sophomores, groups that may be easily persuaded, at least in a setting where they are used to accepting what they are told. Surveys commonly concentrate upon adults.

4. Similarly, the source of the laboratory message is a teacher or appears to have the approval of a teacher—someone who is highly credible as a source, and has rewards and penalties at his disposal. The sources whose messages are studied in surveys tend to be strangers.

5. The laboratory subject is usually an individual, isolated from the group affiliations which might provide information and influence that would counteract the effects of the experimental message. Such

groups have usually had a chance to operate upon persons responding to surveys.

6. The experimenter usually has freedom to select his own issues and
tends to select those sensitive enough to show an effect, often by a
screening study before his experiment. Issues used in a survey however, are chosen because of their intrinsic or social significance. As a
result they usually represent issues on which individuals, and the
groups they belong to have firm, longstanding commitment.

In addition to a difference in the size of effects found by the two methods, Hovland points out that the methods appear to disagree concerning
the conditions most likely to produce a change in attitudes.

In experiments, the further away a subject's attitude from that advocated in a message, the more room he has to change and the more he does
change. In surveys, however, too-extreme a message often has no effect
or boomerangs. Hovland explains this as due to a difference in issues:
Experiments deal with issues that are unimportant to the subject but
where expert opinion is relevant. Surveys are more likely to deal with
issues on which respondents have committed themselves.

In surveys, the first viewpoint presented appears to have an advantage, but this is not necessarily true in experiments. Why? Partly because of selective exposure in the field; the individual commits himself on
the basis of the first message and then avoids exposure to the other side.
Something similar happens in the laboratory when one person presents
both sides. The first side convinces, but when the source appears to
switch sides, subjects get suspicious and resist his second message. Even
in surveys, primacy—the chance to present one's position first—has
little effect if the situation is defined as controversial, if different communicators are used for each side and if communicators are identified as
partisans, conditions typical of debates, political campaigns generally,
and court trials.

—Carl I. Hovland, "Reconciling Conflicting Results Derived From Experimental and Survey Studies of Attitude
Change," *American Psychologist*, 14:8–17.

---

a secretary to see a business executive; a mail questionnaire may
land on his desk but this does not mean it will get answered.

Three Different Media

Just as advertising, one of the three major channels for communicating marketing messages, comprises several media, so does the
survey, the major channel for marketing research messages, employ
different media, one's choice among them varying with the function
to be performed. These are the face-to-face interview, the telephone
interview and the mail questionnaire.

Face-to-face interviewing, like personal selling, is useful when one expects considerable difficulty in getting a response from his receivers. There are several reasons why a researcher may expect difficulty. One is audience: persons of low income or little education are likely to have little interest in research per se and may find reading a questionnaire and responding in writing a difficult job. The aged may lack the flexibility or the hearing ability to respond. Another reason for difficulty is the nature of the questions. It may take the extra rewards and pressures of face-to-face influence to get answers to a questionnaire that is long, involves sensitive areas, or concerns subject matter that is not particularly interesting to the respondent.

Feedback is better when one is face-to-face with a respondent. An interviewer can observe the hesitations that suggest answers should not be taken at face value. He can follow-up with "probe" questions, or eliminate questions that don't apply to the respondent. He can observe the setting, which is a cue to a socio-economic status of the respondent. The major disadvantage of such interviews is their cost, about 5 dollars to get the interview and 10 dollars to get and process it.

The *mail questionnaire,* on the other hand, is quick and cheap. It works fairly well if the respondents one wants to reach are highly motivated, interested in the survey and if the questionnaire itself is neither long nor complicated. Its big disadvantage is that many persons don't answer, even after one has mailed persons three separate copies of a questionnaire, and offered various kinds of small incentives. It's usually safe to assume that the non-respondents differ in ways that are related to the subject matter of the study. (If nothing else, they seem to have less interest in its outcome.) A lesser but related difficulty is that even when a questionnaire is returned, one can never be certain who answered it. Many a boss turns his questionnaires over to a secretary to answer.

The *telephone survey* is fast, cheap, and suited to fairly brief schedules of questions. Although persons who do not have telephones are automatically eliminated from one's sample, leading to under-representation of lower economic groups and persons with unlisted numbers, such surveys usually have fewer respondent refusals than does the mail questionnaire. It is less polite to hang up a telephone than to throw away a questionnaire; at the same time, it is easier to hang up the telephone than to slam a door in the face of an interviewer. The greater anonymity of the telephone makes it easier to get honest answers to some sensitive questions than does the face-to-face interview.

Structured Versus Open-end Questions

In gathering data, as in communications generally, one's choice of channels and media limits what questions one can ask and the form in which one must ask them. The reverse is also true: questions limit choice of media and channels. The messages—questionnaires and interview schedules—used in gathering data vary in the extent to which the source forces a structure upon the respondent, or allows the respondent to use his own frame of reference. The source can impose his own structure upon the receiver both in the question itself, and in the response categories he provides for the receiver. Contrasting with such structured questions are open-end questions, which the receiver answers in his own words, and the diagnostic or therapeutic interview of the psychoanalyst, in which few questions may be asked and their nature depends upon previous comments of the patient.

Both extremes have their disadvantages. If the respondent has too much freedom, the interview is likely to be long. This alone may cause some respondents to give up before it is finished; it is certain to cost a good deal of money to collect the data and even more to analyze it afterward. On the other hand, if the respondent has too little freedom, he may quit answering. Even if he continues to the end, the choice of responses offered him may appear meaningless to him. He's likely to take the easiest course and check an answer, but the answer will be of little use in predicting his behavior. Eventually, even the answers to an open-end question must be crammed into categories of the researcher's devising. The question is whether he should do this before he goes to the respondent or afterward. If he does so afterward, then both his interviewers and the persons who code the finished questionnaires must be carefully selected, trained and supervised. An interviewer can seldom record verbatim the answers to an open-end question; what he does record may represent his opinion rather than that of the respondent. Coders, too, may impose their own categories upon answers; at least in the training phase it is well to have several coders analyze the same sample of questionnaires and compare results.

The respondent, of course, need not be limited to choosing a single response to any question. He can, instead, be asked to rank all the answers in order of preference. Since this becomes difficult, even when as few as ten items are involved, the method of "paired comparisons" can be used in which the respondent is presented in turn, with all possible combinations of two answers, each time picking one of them.

Each choice is easy, but the number of choices represents a problem. To get ranks for ten objects, a subject will have to judge forty-five pairs $N(N-1)/2$. The number of subjects needed drops, however; fifty persons using the method of paired comparisons will produce as stable a set of ranks as 100 using the rank order method.

The best strategy is often to use several different types of questions, all on the same general topic, but structured to different degrees. Here's an example, suggested by George Gallup, in which a series of five questions successively narrows the scope of the interview.

Will You Tell Me What The Term "Fair Trade Law" Means To You?

This is a screening question, much like the questions a salesman uses to qualify a prospect. If the term has no meaning for a respondent, then there is little point in asking him further questions about fair trade. On the other hand, if a great many respondents fall into this group in the exploratory interviews which precede a formal study, one may have to define the term or even drop the survey. Similar screening questions are used to eliminate persons who aren't familiar with the issue or event one wants their opinions on in a survey of public opinion or to drop persons who have not read the magazine in which one is measuring recognition or recall of advertisements.

What, If Anything, Do You Think Congress Should Do About Court Decisions Declaring such Laws Null and Void?

This is another open-end question, like the first, which the respondent is to answer in his own words. It is often used in the early stages of a study to find out what responses one should provide for a more structured questionnaire. It is also used to discover which idea is *salient* for a given respondent—which comes to mind first. The brand name which is salient is likely to be the brand which is bought; it is not necessarily true, however, that the belief which comes off the top of a respondent's head is the one he regards as most important.

It Has Been Suggested That Congress Pass an Amendment to The Constitution Permitting Such a Law. Do You Approve or Disapprove of Such An Amendment?

Here is a highly structured question. Like the courtroom lawyer's it insists upon a yes-or-no answer, forcing the evasive respondent to take a stand. The yes-or-no answer does not permit the "in-between" choice, which some respondents might like to make. Sometimes this is because the interviewer wants to force a choice upon them and is willing to risk a large number of "don't knows" or refusals by some subjects to go on. Another way to handle this problem is to ask the "undecided" group a follow-up question: "You say you have not decided which make of car you like best. But which would you say you tend to lean toward at this moment?" A variant is the multiple-choice question, or cafeteria question, in which the respondent is given a wider, but still limited, number of alternatives to choose from. To the extent that we eventually are forced to vote for one candidate or another, or to purchase one brand or another, such a question is useful. Since we always have a third alternative however—to refuse to vote and to delay a purchase indefinitely—the predictive power of such a question is increased if one follows it up by a fourth type.

How Strong Are Your Feelings? Or How Certain Are You of Your Reply: Very Certain, Fairly Certain, Not at All Certain?

Such an intensity question helps one predict whether approval or disapproval will be expressed in action, or how resistant a subject will be to pressure from other messages, other events, or other people.

Finally, there is a question which is of great importance to the communicator who wants to influence respondents' answers to question No. 3. It is this:

WHY Do You Feel This Way?

A return to the open-end type of question may disclose that there are several audiences, each of which arrives at its position by a different route and each of which, therefore, requires a different type of message. Again one can use the open-end question to determine saliency, and follow it up with a checklist of possible alternative responses for the sake of completeness and so one can compare respondents with one another. The open-end form itself is useful both in the exploratory phase of a study and at the end, to help explain the results one has obtained; the "explanations" then become hypotheses for another study.

Sequence Is Important

As this example suggests, the *order* in which questions are asked is important, even more so than the structure of the message designed to influence rather than measure attitudes. Most questions are so brief that context provides few cues of meaning of individual words; each question, however, may be interpreted in the context of the questionnaire as a whole, the setting in which it is asked, and its sponsor. Answers will vary from one administration of a questionnaire to the next if the setting or the mood of the individual changes. This can be overcome, in part, by increasing the length of the question-naire and by making the questions more homogeneous or unidimensional. Several unidimensional scales may be needed to measure an attitude which is made up of several parts. These parts may represent separate categories; an attitude toward food in general may be made up of separate attitudes toward meat, vegetables, and desserts. Or they may represent the familiar attitude types of belief, feeling, and action.

The first questions asked should be easy to answer, of interest to the respondent, and impress him with the seriousness and im-portance of the interview. Since they provide motivation and affect the rate of refusals itself, they should make the rewards of cooperation appear as large as possible and the effort as small as possible. Many interviews start by asking the respondent to express an opinion in an area where he is likely to have an opinion, since this is easy to do and most persons like to do it. Another way of making questions easy to answer is to group related items, so that a subject does not have to switch frequently from one frame of reference to another; grouping also permits individual questions to be briefer, since mean-ings carry over from one to the next.

Sensitive questions, such as those concerning the size of the re-spondent's income which help classify him demographically, are usu-ally buried in the interview. The respondent who has invested a good deal of his time in an interview will find it more difficult to refuse halfway through than at the outset. Delay also gives a chance for the interviewer to demonstrate his general trustworthiness and accep-tance of the respondent. Although a researcher arranges questions in an order which will encourage respondents to continue cooperating, he must avoid ordering them in a way which suggests any particular answer to respondents. He must, for example, avoid the salesman's technique of getting a series of partial commitments, in the form of decisions about style, color, price and credit terms, so that the final commitment becomes almost inevitable. This is a useful technique for *shaping* attitudes, and therefore must be avoided when one wants to *measure* them. If the purpose of a questionnaire is to gather facts, then starting with an opinion question may be unwise, since the subject may misperceive subsequent questions about facts as being requests for opinions.

Phrasing Affects Responses

Even more important than the order in which questions are asked is the phrasing of the questions themselves. Use of evaluative terms which indicate the source's attitude toward the object of his question is only one way of committing the error of influencing attitudes in the very act of measuring them. It is the most obvious way and, because of this, perhaps the least dangerous. A more subtle error occurs when a questionnaire puts together in a single category elements which the respondent feels are very different, or splits up elements he regards as identical. Although we have described this process earlier as one of the principal methods in which attitudes can be changed, it may occur in measuring attitudes because the researcher takes his category system for granted and assumes that everyone sees the world the way he does.

A similar error occurs when the set of responses provided for a question omits an alternative which the respondent feels is important. He may choose from those offered but his response will have poor predictive power. If the responses include response categories he has not thought of before, ones that would not spontaneously occur to him, the question may change his attitude, rather than measure it. Use of open-end questions and wording the same item in a variety of ways in the early stages of research can be helpful by disclosing whether source and receiver use the same frame of reference and define the situation in the same way.

Words may cause trouble because they mean different things to different respondents or because they have little meaning to any of them, and so produce a large number of "no opinion" and "don't know" answers. They may also cause trouble by appearing to favor one side of an issue.

Differences in wording so minor that they sound the same to an outside observer (or worse, to the survey researcher himself) may produce drastic differences in results. Here are three questions reported by Zeisel (Lucas and Britt, 224).

1. Which of these three magazines is your favorite?
2. If you could have but one of these three magazines, which would you keep for yourself?
3. Which one of these three magazines do you like best?

They sound almost the same—but the first question gave top score to magazine *A*, the second to magazine *B*, and the third to magazine *C!*

Changing a single word can change the meaning of a question and the responses to it as in this example (Payne, 9): "Do you think any-thing _____ be done to make it easier for people to pay doctor or hospital bills?" When "should" was inserted in the blank,

---

"Slanted" questions may be useful, if the person asking them and those reading the results know how and why they were slanted. Here are two views on the question of bias in opinion polls dealing with labor unions.

Three Kinds of Bias Charged

After studying 155 different questions on organized labor asked by seven different polling organizations between 1940 and 1945, Kornhauser found three kinds of bias.

First, was their subject matter: Of 155 questions, 81 were concerned with unfavorable aspects of unionism and only 8 with positive aspects. Many questions involved wartime strikes, feather-bedding, and curbs on unions. There were few if any questions on unions' fight for price controls, for their members, or their support of the President.

Second was the interpretation of results. A question asking attitudes toward war workers absent *without excuse* was reported as if it affected all absentees; 67 per cent of respondents were said to favor a law curbing labor—but only a third of respondents answered the question at all.

Most interesting kind of bias, however, was that involving wording of the questions themselves. Four different abuses were cited:

1. Double-barreled questions asked if respondents favored a particular solution to a problem, such as wartime strikes. The only way they could condemn the evil, strikes, was to vote for the solution—only one of several solutions available.
2. Technical questions were asked which respondents could answer only in terms of general attitudes, including such complex issues as piecework pay and the percentage of union leaders who handle union funds honestly.
3. Questions were ambiguous, over-simplified and based on hidden assumptions. They asked whether union leaders were "helping pro-duction," something they have no authority over. They asked whether there should be a ceiling on wages—without saying whether there would also be one on prices.
4. Only one side of an issue was stated, or prestige symbols favored one side. "Did *President Truman* do the right thing in having the navy take over strike-bound oil companies?"—almost forces a "yes" answer. "Do you think it is fair to keep prices down without also keeping wage rates down?"—almost forces a "no" answer, as

does the question as to whether any unions are run with "absolute" honesty.

Of the 155 questions asked, four appeared to be worded so as to favor labor, and eighty or ninety to be slanted against labor.

—Arthur Kornhauser, "Are Public Opinion Polls Fair to Organized Labor?," *Public Opinion Quarterly*, 10:484–500.

The Pollers Answer Kornhauser

Emotional words which are keys to respondents' biases *must* be used, Kornhauser's critics replied, if one is to predict behavior which these biases will determine. They pointed out that scientific polling requires eliminating bias in pollers, not people polled. They asked how many different viewpoints have to be represented in a question to be fair—management, union leaders, union members, nonunion members, other citizens? Or, in the case of politics—Republicans and Democrats, with all their variations, plus Communists, Prohibitionists and Vegetarians?

Another critic pointed out that one polling agency, three-fourths of whose questions involved negative subject matter, accounted for 40% of the 155 questions studied. Only a third of the questions asked by the six other agencies showed such bias. He also argued that concentration on negative aspects of labor cannot be blamed upon the pollsters but either (*a*) upon their sponsors, who determine subject matter, or (*b*) upon current popular interests.

A third rejoinder to Kornhauser reported the judgments of 38 students in a public opinion course in which they had themselves written and revised poll questions. They agreed with Kornhauser in 9 out of 14 instances, on six anti-labor, two prolabor and 1 neutral question. But the author pointed out that the significant question, still to be answered, was whether the public reading poll results interpreted them in the way that Kornhauser and these students did.

—Henry C. Link, Albert D. Freiberg, John H. Platten, Jr., and Kenneth E. Clark, "Is Dr. Kornhauser Fair to Organized Pollers?" *Public Opinion Quarterly*, 11:198–212.

---

82 per cent said yes; with "could" inserted, 77 per cent said yes; with "might" inserted, 63 per cent said yes. On another occasion, 92 per cent of respondents said hospital insurance was a good idea, but only 66 per cent said they themselves would like it. The choice one makes depends, of course, on why one is asking the question. The "good idea" question might be fine in a public opinion poll, but a salesman looking for prospects would certainly prefer the second.

Pronunciation Difficulties

Sometimes confusion occurs because words spelled differently lose their distinct identity when pronounced by an interviewer; this happened down South when rural farmers, asked their opinion about government control of *profits* in wartime, thought the interviewer was talking about *prophets*. Variations in stress may change the meaning of a question drastically, so that interviewers must be trained not to let such differences occur, either consciously or inadvertently. Words high on the ladder of abstraction, like industry and labor, permit a great deal of variation among respondents in the referents they include. And since abstract words often have a high evaluative content—either positive, like "freedom" and "American," or negative, like "dictatorship" and "Communism"—this adds to the difficulty.

Even denotative words may have very different meanings, although this may not always be clear from the brief context of a question. The word "country" for example, may mean the United States or it may mean rural areas of the United States. Words expressing quantity, such as near, about, much, most, more, many, are vague; their meaning will vary both with the object of the questions and the respondent. (However, as every student who has ever taken an exam. knows, it is usually safe to say "no" to any question stated in absolutes, any question which asserts that "all" or that "none" of something is true, or beautiful, or good.)

Some protection against bias is available if the questioner knows what words and what objects tend to have prestige and status implications. It seems likely, for example, that many people feel that everyone *should* have opinions about public issues, but that only weak-minded persons are influenced by advertising. If so, this will lead to an underestimate of the "don't knows—don't cares" in politics and an overestimate of the "never read advertisements—no advertisement has ever influenced me" groups in marketing. We know that people are likely to grade up their incomes, education, and occupations, and to underestimate their exposure to "cheap" magazine fiction, television programs, and brands. Various devices are available to get more accurate estimates. One is to give them an acceptable "out" by giving them the credit for good intentions or suggesting that other persons are in the same boat. It's easier to say no when the question asks, "Have you happened to read a book in the last month?" than when it bluntly demands, "Did you read a book last month?" The question, "Do you intend to give to the Community Chest?" gives those who have already given a chance to say so, and lets others save face by claiming good intentions. A man is more likely to give his correct occupational classification if one sets a factual atmosphere from the start by asking what firm he works for, or follows a question about his occupation with a probe question concerning his actual duties.

Four Rules of Thumb

Four rules of thumb can help one choose the "best" word for a question, as Payne illustrates in searching for a suitable middle term, in giving subjects a set of three responses: "good, _____, poor" (Payne, 141–147)

1. How many different meanings does each alternative have? Barnhart's American College Dictionary lists sixteen meanings for the adjective "fair," in addition to the one, "moderately good," in which we are interested, and the synonyms for this meaning of "passable, tolerable, average, middling." It lists one meaning for the adjective "medium," plus ten for the word as a noun. Payne's rule: *choose the word with the fewest meanings.*
2. What shades of meaning does each alternative term possess? The word "fair," for example, used as an adjective, may *denote* an equitable state of affairs or a blonde complexion. It may also be used as a noun, as in "state fair," or to indicate an evaluative state somewhere between good and bad. The synonym "ordinary" has something of a below-average connotation to it, while the synonym "normal" seems to carry a favorable connotation. Payne's rule: *Choose the word which is least likely to cause denotative confusion or connotative bias.*
3. How familiar is each alternative—how often do people use it? A count of 4.5 million words, taken from twelve issues of five popular magazines published from 1927 through 1938, found 1,526 uses of "fair" and 119 uses of "medium." Payne's rule: *Choose the most familiar word.*
4. How *long* is each alternative? Words of many syllables are usually harder to read and pronounce and usually appear well down on any list showing frequency of use. Payne's rule: *Choose the shortest word.*

Of course, these four rules are not independent of one another: short words tend to be frequently used, and to have many different meanings. The words we choose cannot score high on all four.

There is a fifth way to avoid trouble with words, and that is to use as few as possible—or none at all. Here are several variations of this method.

Use a Single Word

This is the *word association* technique, again used widely in therapy, in which respondents are given a series of words and asked to respond to each of them in turn with the first word that pops into their minds. This technique has been used in picking names for new products and new brands.

Use Pictures

This is the technique, later adapted for use in communications research, of the *Thematic Appreciation Test* (Murray) and the *Picture Frustration Test* (Rosenzweig), both used in psychotherapy. In the first of these the respondent is shown a rather ambiguous-looking picture and asked to describe the people and tell what they are doing—to make up a story. In the second, the respondent is shown a cartoon of persons in frustrating situations and asked what he thinks they are saying to one another. The respondent is given even less to go on in a third type of "picture" used by psychologists, the *Rorschach ink blots*. Here he is asked what he "sees" in the blots themselves.

The very thing that makes the word association and pictorial techniques useful in therapy—the fact that the respondent has to put meanings into a highly ambiguous stimulus—limits their use in marketing communications. These methods tell us a lot about the respondent and his personality, but less about how his attitudes are affected by the qualities of the products we want to sell him. Another difficulty is that they produce a large volume of verbal responses which have to be analyzed. Moreover, if an individual has a high rate of output, one can't be sure whether it is because the subject involved is important to him, or he is just highly articulate.

Evading Bias, Concealing Intent

Despite the problems involved, the word association and pictorial techniques serve two functions. They evade the problem of trying to phrase a sentence that is free of bias and they help disguise the purpose of the questionnaire itself. This is important, since many people show a "yea-saying" tendency; they tend to agree with the suggestion implied in the phrasing of a question or with what they perceive to be the desire of the interviewer and the sponsor (Wells). A few people, on the other hand, react just the opposite; they disagree, as a matter of habit, with the implications of a question, no matter what those may be. Respondents are likely to say what they believe they ought to feel and think. This is why privacy is necessary in an interview and the appearance of anonymity valuable in a mail survey. True anonymity in a mail survey, however, frustrates the need to know who has replied, so that second and third-wave questionnaires can be sent to the nonrespondents or phone and face-to-face interviews made with them. Moreover, if these fail, the researcher can still analyze the nonrespondent group on the basis of any available facts to see whether they differ consistently from the persons who have responded.

Still another type of question which tends to conceal intent, but controls the amount of respondent output and keeps his responses focussed on problems which the researcher is interested in is the *semantic differential* (Osgood, Suci, Tannenbaum).

To construct a semantic differential scale, one takes a pair of polar adjectives, uses them to represent the extremes on a seven-point scale, and asks each respondent to indicate by a check mark where he thinks each concept being rated belongs. Here is an example:

Coca Cola

Bad_____	:_____	:_____	:_____	:_____	:_____	:_____	Good
Strong_____	:_____	:_____	:_____	:_____	:_____	:_____	Weak
Active_____	:_____	:_____	:_____	:_____	:_____	:_____	Passive

A variety of adjectives can be used; in many studies they have been reduced, through factor analysis, to the three dimensions represented above: A strong evaluative dimension, and lesser activity and potency clusters. Subjects' scores can be averaged, and the resulting profiles of competing products compared. This measure taps connotative meanings and tends to disguise its purpose somewhat more than the usual attitude questionnaire. Like the other measures just mentioned it tends to reflect verbal habits, including that called thought, and the way an individual's verbal habits deviate from those of his language or society or subgroups within society.

The semantic differential provides at least partial concealment of its function as a measure of attitudes. Another disguise sometimes used is the *error-choice method* which, on the surface, appears to be a test of factual knowledge (Hammond). None of the responses it offers the interviewers, however, is correct; some err on one side of the truth and others on the opposite side. If a respondent consistently chooses responses which overestimate profits and underestimate wages, he is assumed to be showing a pro-labor (or anti-management) attitude.

Concealment in Experiments

Although we usually think of the laboratory experiment as being more "artificial" than a survey, it may do a better job of concealing the researcher's purposes and of reproducing the actual conditions under which buying decisions are influenced and made. An advertiser, trying to decide which of two commercials is better, can take a portable projector into the home and ask housewives to tell him. Their answers, however, may represent what they think they *should* like, rather than what actually influences them.

As an alternative, he can bring housewives into a theater, and ask them to judge some television "pilot" *programs*. In return for their cooperation, he says, there'll be a prize drawing; if they should win, which of these products would they prefer to take home with them? At the end of the showing, he asks the same question again. He can then determine how much their preferences have changed—and assume that if there is a change in preference for a product which happened to be featured on a commercial shown with the programs, the change must be due to the commercial. Given comparable audiences for two showings, in each of which a different commercial is featured, and audiences representative of the market for the product, this seems a better way of answering the advertiser's original question than the survey method.

At the beginning of this chapter we said that when a communicator does research he tries to make his questions as neutral as possible. There are exceptions to this rule, however. To prevent people from overclaiming socially approved behaviors, such as reading good books and giving to charity, we may have to ask questions which give them a way out without losing face: "Have you had time to read a book *in the last week?*" or "Have you made a gift to the United Fund *yet?*" Similarly, we may be able to prevent them from concealing disapproved activity through questions which indicate that many people *do* get parking tickets or argue with their wives, and that the interviewer takes this sort of thing in his stride.

If the behavior we are trying to predict will occur in an emotion-loaded situation, then the nearer one's questions can come to suggesting such a situation, the better. "You do not really expect a raise in pay this year, do you?" obviously suggests the answer "no"—but if that is the way the boss will phrase the question, then that's the way the interviewer may want to ask it. Here are three questions on an issue in international affairs:

1. Do you personally favor violent or nonviolent settlement of international disputes?
2. If war came, would you volunteer for military service, wait to be drafted, or seek alternative service as a conscientious objector?
3. Are you going to defend your country like a man or be a dirty draft dodger?

Which of these is the "best" question? The second, certainly, seems to be the least biased. The first would probably produce a 99 per cent majority in favor of nonviolence; nobody really favors violence, but some people think they have no alternative. If we are trying to predict the number of conscientious objectors during a war, however, the third question will probably produce the best results, since it's the kind of language a draft board is likely to use. The man who can't face a question like this, probably has not got what it takes to be a conscientious objector.

Beliefs, Feelings, or Actions?

The opening of this chapter suggested three types of attitudes which can be measured: beliefs, feelings, and actions. Most surveys try to measure *beliefs*. Uusally the questions used to elicit beliefs are not disguised, although privacy for the respondent and permissiveness by the interviewer may be required to elicit expression of unpopular beliefs. A yes-no or multiple choice question may allow a respondent to express an opinion on an issue he's never heard of before and knows nothing about. To prevent this, an interviewer may use an information-type question to screen out the uninformed; or may ask the question twice, in different ways, in hopes that self-contradiction will reveal who the uninformed are. In some circumstances, a question will provide information for the respondent; this is dangerous, how-ever, since the information which a researcher feels is adequate for a decision may differ from that which respondents actually use in making decisions.

Although an interviewer can ask a respondent what his *feelings* are, the interviewer is more likely to put credence in the hesitation, stammer or blush which accompany the answers, than in the answers themselves. Reading such cues takes skill and training on the part of the interviewer. In the laboratory, a variety of instruments, some of which have been combined into the "lie detector," are available to measure the physiological components of emotion. A major difficulty of taking verbal replies at face value as an index of feelings is that feelings are often diffuse. A respondent may not have the words needed to express them. In addition, of course, he may not accept the feelings himself, or feel that they would not be acceptable to a stranger.

Study of *actions*, the third type of "attitude," plunges us into the other major problem mentioned at the beginning of this chapter: that of time. Usually we want to predict what actions a respondent will perform sometime in the future. In fact, although the question usually is not phrased this way, we are asking the respondent to assume that he will not change and that he can foresee all the conditions which will be operating when the time for action comes. It would improve predictability if the respondent were to specify in detail what these conditions are, although even this will not prevent a crucial new condition which he does not now foresee from arising. The interviewer can specify alternative conditions by asking the same question several times, each time changing the conditions slightly. Even then, predictions are not likely to be very good if the respondent has never actually made a decision of the kind being studied. If he has made such a decision, his previous decision may be a better predictor than his present response.

Asking questions about what the respondent has done in the past presents new difficulties, however. If the question calls for a summary of behavior over a considerable period of time, he may not know. "How many tubes of toothpaste did you use last year?" is a question few persons can answer. If the question covers too remote a period, a respondent may not remember what he believed and felt or how he acted; his responses will be colored by his present beliefs and attitudes. Few of us remember what television programs we actually viewed a week or two weeks ago, since we do not place that much importance on viewing television. A skilled interviewer, however, can often revive respondents' memories by going back, day by day, or by starting with questions concerning events which they do remember, and around which they can reconstruct the events of the day.

Experts and Records

To determine what actually happened in the past, or to predict what is likely to happen in the future, a researcher may not want to interview a large, representative, random sample of persons, none of whom know what they're talking about, but to go to experts who are skilled in predicting the future, have the skills and training to play the role of historian, or possess the records needed to reconstruct the past. Since records themselves are based on somebody's observation, why are they better than going into the field oneself? There are several reasons. First, it is usually cheaper to go to the records. Second, the records were probably made at the time by skilled persons, reducing errors due to inaccurate perceptions and subsequent memory loss. Third, the audience for our research results may put more credence in a record than in a survey report.

Ultimately, all truth is social. Society itself, and subgroups within society, agree on who they'll recognize as experts and agree in advance to accept their consensus as representing the "facts" about stars and atoms, angels and fossils and consumer price indices. The user of records needs to know the methods used to collect them, and how these methods limit the conclusions he can draw from them. Ordinarily, however, his audience shows little interest in this problem, unless rival communicators present alternative versions of the past.

Although it is not what actually happened, but a respondent's present belief and feeling about it which is likely to govern his future behavior, it is helpful to compare a respondent's views with those of more objective, less involved observers. When we are concerned with relationships among persons, it helps to know how these relationships appear to each member of the group. The salesman can report his feelings toward his customers, and what he thinks their feelings are toward him. The customers, in turn, can report their feelings toward the salesman and what they perceive his feelings to be toward them. The nature and size of the differences in actual and perceived feelings can help predict how a sales interview will go. In short, the existence of different and even conflicting versions of past actions on present relationships is an asset rather than a liability for the person trying to understand, predict and influence human behavior.

If the most difficult question is one which asks a man how he will act in the future, the second most difficult must be the question of *why*, whether it is why he plans or expects to behave that way in the future, or why he behaved as he did in the past. To begin with, there probably are a great many reasons for his action: how many of them does the interviewer want? Some respondents will come up with a great many; others can do so only after considerable probing. Second, what weight is one to give a respondent's *first* response to this question? The first response may be the most important reason. It may, on the other hand, be comparatively unimportant; the respondent may be concealing from the interviewer, or from himself, his most compelling reasons. Much, of course, depends on the respondent, and on the subject of the question.

A series of "why" questions, including indirect and disguised questions, may be useful. A checklist of possible answers, usually developed in exploratory interviews early in the study, often will be helpful in comparing respondents, since it insures that each of them has considered all of the items on the list. The "accounting scheme" of possible causes, with which a researcher starts any study, will help insure that all the various "why's" are covered, including characteristics of the stimulus, which caused the respondent to act; the desires of the respondent; and the pressures of groups which influenced his response. Since the "why" question is a question of cause and effect, its answer may require a good deal of interpretation by a researcher of a variety of cues supplied by a respondent who himself has no clear or logical theory of cause and effect.

Process in Communication

Early in this chapter we suggested that gathering data is itself a form of communication, involving sources, channels, messages, and receivers. Gathering data is a process and all the matters dealt with in this text are relevant to it.

We have also suggested that a scientist's conclusions can be no better than the data on which they are based and that the quality of his data depends on the methods he uses to gather it. If this is true, then why has a text based on data collected by behavioral scientists chosen to end, rather than to begin, with a discussion of this problem?

There are two reasons for the choice. One was to emphasize that communications is a process and, as process, has neither end nor beginning. The chapters in this text, like the concepts they discuss, represent arbitrary (although conventional) divisions of a seamless subject matter. Learning and motivation and perception merge into one another; neither aggregates nor individuals can exist without the other. In real life, sources and channels become indistinguishable and the meaning in messages depends upon their sources and their receivers.

The second reason was that education may have a beginning, but can have no end. Let this chapter, then, serve as an introduction to one of the most exciting enterprises open to man—the discovery of new truths. The reader who, upon completing this text, can begin it again and apply to what he reads the ideas of this closing chapter should find much profit, and perhaps a few errors, along the way. (The profit he is welcome to; the errors, we hope, he will share with the author.)

The challenge of discovery is one which some students will carry with them into graduate school and, ultimately, into teaching and research. Many more readers, the author hopes, will find an opportunity in business to discover new insights into human behavior—and to share them with those of us in academic life.

SUMMARY

1. No one method of gathering data is best for all functions, but one rule applies to all. Unlike other messages, the question cannot influence attitudes if it is to measure them.
2. Five basic questions concerning data-gathering methods are: Does the researcher observe behavior or the effects of behavior? Are the persons being observed aware of the observation? Does the researcher evoke the behavior he observes? If he does, does he evoke it by asking questions? If by questions, then what kinds of symbols does he use and what kind does he desire in response?
3. Three basic channels for research, varying in the control over events and subjects which they give the researcher, are the laboratory experiment, the field experiment and the survey. The survey, in turn, transmits questions via three major media: mail surveys, telephone polls, and face-to-face interviews.
4. Two basic types of questions, varying in the freedom of response which they allow the receiver, are the open-end and the structured. Open-end questions are widely used in the early stages of a study, to feel out respondents' frames of reference. They may also be combined with more structured questions to measure saliency and probe for reasons why.
5. The order in which questions are asked will affect respondents' motivation, and the rate of refusal. It may also bias responses. Questions are usually brief, providing minimal contextual cues to the meanings of the words within them; the order of questions may provide additional contextual cues.
6. Questions may influence attitudes, rather than merely measure them,

through the use of evaluative terms and by imposing a category system upon the respondent.

7. Rules of thumb suggest one should choose the shortest word, the most familiar word, and the word with fewest meanings. Shortness and familiarity tend to be positively related, with one another and with number of meanings. A fourth rule is that words are best which avoid denotative confusion or connotative bias.

8. Problems in word choice can be reduced by using single-word questions, as in word association; by using pictures to evoke respondents' verbal responses; and by using the semantic differential, which requires only two polar adjectives for each "question." These techniques perform an added function: they help conceal the purpose of the study from the respondent. Error-choice questions disguise an attitude study as a study of factual knowledge; experiments can conceal the researcher's aims.

9. Neutral wording of questions is not always the best. Questions and interviewers may need to be very permissive in getting respondents to admit socially disapproved behavior or prevent them from over-claiming socially approved behavior. If an action requires a respondent to stand up against social pressure, then a question which seeks to predict such behavior may have to load the scales against too-easy acquiescence.

10. Beliefs can be studied through survey questions; feelings are more often measured by nonverbal symbols incidental to an expression of belief or, in the laboratory, by measuring the physiological components of emotion. Predicting future actions varies with the familiarity of the action being predicted and the skill of respondent and interviewer in anticipating the future circumstances of action. Memory loss affects the accuracy with which past action can be reported. "Why" questions are difficult to answer.

Research Studies

Having defined his problem and determined his overall research strategy, as discussed in Chapter 17, a scientist then can turn to the problem of how he is to gather the evidence which will test his hypotheses.

One decision he must make is whether he will make a field survey or try a laboratory experiment. *Hovland* offered six explanations of why laboratory studies usually find more significant results in communications studies than do field surveys. (One of his explanations, that of audience self-selection, was illustrated in Chapter Two by *Star and Hughes*.) *O'Rourke* illustrated Hovland's point by comparing family decision-making studies made in the home with those made in a laboratory. He found that traditional roles, which call for men to concentrate on task performance and women on group maintenance, tend to be emphasized in the more public (and short-run) conditions of the laboratory.

Two authors showed how a researcher can take advantage of natural events in the field, even when he cannot produce them on his own. Both instances involve the temporary removal of a variable which ordinarily affects behavior. *Clover* examined what happens when a gas shortage forces business firms to close and their customers to postpone their usual purchases. *Mindak* investigated the effects of a newspaper strike.

Finally, moving down to the level of decisions about details, *Getzels* explained why attitudes sometimes fail to predict behavior by a theory as to what goes on in a person's head between the time he hears a question and the time he answers it. *Kornhauser* charged that public opinion polls have used biased questions; *Link* and others responded by denying his charge or defending the need for "biased" questions.

8. Give number establishments with 20 or more em-   Akron: 233
ployees (P. 3, Col. 114).

Student Name	Qn. 1	Qn. 2	Qn. 3	Qn. 4	Qn. 5	Qn. 6	Qn. 7	Qn. 8

MARKET DATA #2

J. Walter Thompson: Population and Its Distribution, 8th edition, 1961.

1. Find 1958 sales in billions of dollars for "A" Market corresponding to your number. (Page 11.)   No. 1: 18.5 (New York, page 11)

2. Give food store sales for your state, as per cent of national total (Pages 2–3).   Maine: .59

Survey of Buying Power: Sales Management Magazine, June 10, 1963.

3. On page 54, for county matching your number, give number of households with income under $2500 in 1962; omit 000.   No. 1: 333 (Los Angeles)

4. Effective buying income per household in 1962, starting page 54.   No. 1: 55 (Akron: page 97)

Editor and Publisher Market Guide, 1964

5. For your SMSA, give total food sales in millions (Page 19).   Akron: 214.5

6. For your state, give estimate for 1975 of number of children 5 to 9 years, omitting 000.   1: Alabama 398 (Page 25)

Economic Almanac of National Industrial Conference Board, 1962.

7. For your state, number of employees in trade, 1960 (Page 46).   Alabama: 150

8. For your number, consumer price index in 1958 (Page 106; 1953 equals 100).   1: 107.6

Student Name	Qn. 1	Qn. 2	Qn. 3	Qn. 4	Qn. 5	Qn. 6	Qn. 7	Qn. 8

MARKET DATA #3

Survey of Current Business, Vol. 29, Dec. 1949

1. Use index to find product and page for data of entry corresponding to your number; if more than one, take first.   No. 1: 10 (Abrasive paper—38)

Business Statistics, 1963 Edition (U.S. Department of Commerce).

2. Use index on page 339; for entry corresponding to your number turn to that page and report first figure. Example No. 1: Acceptances, bankers (p. 86, Col. 1).   No. 1: 233

Study of Consumer Expenditures (University of Pennsylvania)

3. In Vol. 3, begin on page 23 and for your SMSA report per cent of 4-person families reporting expenditures for alcoholic beverages.   New York: 82%

4. In Vol. 18, start on page 163. For entry corresponding to your number note average expenditure on alcoholic beverages for families with head 25–35 years. Example: No. 1 (Self-employed, under $1000 incomes)   No. 1: $76

5. In Vol. 12, for your SMSA average dollars spent on wine served in home, rounding to nearest dollar.   New York: $9 (page 2)

6. In Vol. 12, for your SMSA report average price paid for pound of coffee in spring of 1951.   New York: 84¢ (page 200)

Life Study of Consumer Expenditures, Vol. I

7. On page 32, count down each data column in turn until you reach entry corresponding to your number. Report per cent of spending. Example: No. 1— Homes with no children, head under 40, spend for food and beverages how much of their income?   No. 1: 26%

8. On page 19, count down each data column to reach entry corresponding to your number. Report what share of purchases of this product are made by this group. Example: No. 1—Household with incomes under $2000 make up what per cent of U.S. households?   No. 1: 10%

Student Name	Qn. 1	Qn. 2	Qn. 3	Qn. 4	Qn. 5	Qn. 6	Qn. 7	Qn. 8

DATA ABOUT FIRMS

Poor's Register of Corporation Directors 1965—Firm

1. Name of person in charge of advertising   American Motors: Brogan

2. Number of employees   American Motors: 32,000

Standard Advertising Register, 1959—Firm

3. Name of firm's advertising agency. (If more than one, take first listed.)   American Motors: Geyer Morey

Moody's Industrial Manual, 1963—Firm

    4. Number of stockholders, common and preferred   American Motors: 137,000

Directory of National Associations of Businessmen, 1961
—Firm

    5. Starting on page 8, give number of page on which data concerning trade association corresponding to your entry is reported.   No. 1: 23 (Abrasive Grain)

PRODUCT INFORMATION

Consumer Reports: Buying Guide Issue for 1963

    6. Using index on page 413, find entry matching your number and report first brand listed for that product.   No. 1: Devcon (Epoxy adhesives, Page 202)

Student's Name	Qn. 1	Qn. 2	Qn. 3	Qn. 4	Qn. 5	Qn. 6

COMMERCIAL STUDIES

Each year the media—and, to a lesser extent manufacturers and commercial research agencies—emit a great many studies whose primary purpose is to sell something. If the student keeps in mind the sponsors of these studies and their probable goals, they can be quite useful.

Audits and Surveys Co. "The Audiences of Five Magazines" (1962) (Sponsored by *Newsweek*)   Example

    1. On page corresponding to your number, subtract percentage coverage by *Time* from percentage covered by *Newsweek*, including sign. (Nos. 1 through 12: add 20 to your number.)   No. 1: −1.4 (Page 21)

Reader's Digest: "Eight Leading Magazines" (1962)

    2. For region in which your state falls, report percentage of households covered by *Reader's Digest*.   Alabama: 18.3 (Page 53)

W. R. Simmons & Associates Research Inc. "The Women Behind the Market" (1962)

    3. On page corresponding to your number, note what percentage of MacFadden publication(s) readers were *not* included in audience of *Life*.   Page 3: 59%

Alfred Politz Research Inc. "A 12-Months' Study of Better Homes & Gardens Readers" (1956)

    4. On p. 20, count down each column in turn to reach number of your entry and report per cent listed.   No. 1: 50.2

(50.2% of readers who looked into back issues looked at building subjects.)

Magazine Advertising Bureau "Split-Run and Regional Advertising" (May 1964: 6th edition)

5. Starting with *Alabama Farmer*, count to publication corresponding to your number and report regional editions; if not indicated, leave blank.

No. 1: 2 (Alabama Farmer)

Advisory Service for Students of Advertising (1962)

6. On page corresponding to your number report brand name for which case history is given.

Page 2: Bayer

Milwaukee Journal 1963 Consumer Analysis (40th edition)

7. Using index for foods (facing p. 17) count down pages to your number, then report percentage of purchases in 1963 for top brand of this product.

No. 1: 58% (Reynolds aluminum foil)

Advertising Age, Jan. 15, 1963

8. Beginning on p. 155, count to your number and report the name of executive listed for advertising association listed.

No. 1: Collier (Advertising Association of the West)

Student's Name	Qn. 1	Qn. 2	Qn. 3	Qn. 4	Qn. 5	Qn. 6	Qn. 7	Qn. 8

Foundations

Overviews

Human Behavior by Bernard Berelson and Gary A. Steiner (Harcourt, Brace and World). 1045 findings based on research.
The Study of Society by Alfred Kuhn (Irwin). Harder to read; an attempt to synthesize.
Handbook of Social Psychology, Gardner Lindzey, ed. (Addison-Wesley). Two volumes of extensive essays; new edition being prepared.

Social Psychology

Texts: *Individual in Society* by David Krech and Richard S. Crutchfield (McGraw-Hill).
Fundamentals of Social Psychology by Eugene L. Hartley and Ruth E. Hartley (Knopf).
Reader: *Readings in Social Psychology,* 3rd ed., by Eleanor E. Maccoby, et al. (Holt, Rinehart and Winston). Best collection of original research articles; new two-volume edition in press.

Psychology

Texts: *Introduction to Psychology,* by Clifford T. Morgan (McGraw-Hill)
Introduction to Psychology by Ernest R. Hilgard, 2nd ed. (Harcourt, Brace and World).

Sociology

Text: *Sociology* by Harry M. Johnson (Harcourt, Brace and World).
Reader: *Sociology Today* by Robert K. Merton et al., editors (Basic Books).

Research

Design: *Research Methods in Social Relations* by Claire Selltiz, et al. (Holt, Rinehart and Winston).
Research Methods in the Behavioral Sciences by Leon Festinger and Daniel Katz (Holt, Rinehart and Winston).
Surveys: *Methods in Social Research* by William J. Goode and Paul K. Hatt (McGraw-Hill).
Statistics: *Statistics* by W. Allen Wallis and Harry V. Roberts (Free Press).
Psychological Statistics by Quinn McNemar (Wiley).

545

Applications

Marketing

Basic Marketing by E. Jerome McCarthy (Irwin).
Marketing: An Introductory Analysis by John B. Matthews, Jr. et al. (McGraw-Hill).

Advertising

Texts: *Advertising Theory and Practice* by C. H. Sandage and Vernon Fryburger (Irwin).
Advertising by Harry W. Hepner (McGraw-Hill).
Reader: *Cases in Advertising Management* by Harper W. Boyd, Jr., et al. (McGraw-Hill).

Public Relations

Effective Public Relations by Scott M. Cutlip and Allen H. Center (Prentice-Hall).

Salesmanship

Salesmanship by Carlton A. Pederson and Milburn D. Wright (Irwin).

Research

Measuring Advertising Effectiveness and *Advertising Psychology and Research* by Darrell Blaine Lucas and Steuart Henderson Britt (McGraw-Hill).

Bibliography

Abelson, Herbert I., *Persuasion* (New York: Springer Publishing Co., 1959).

*Adams, John B., "The Relative Credibility of 20 Unnamed News Sources," *Journalism Quarterly*, 39:79–82.

*Albaum, Gerald, "Horizontal Information Flow: An Exploratory Study," *Journal of the Academy of Management*, 7:1, 21–33.

*Allison, Ralph I. and Kenneth P. Uhl, "Influence of Beer Brand Identification on Taste Perception," *Journal of Marketing Research*, 1:3:36–39.

Allport, Gordon W., *Pattern and Growth in Personality* (New York: Holt, Rinehart and Winston, 1961).

Allport, Gordon W. and Bernard M. Kramer, "Some Roots of Prejudice," *Journal of Psychology*, 22:9–39.

Allport, Gordon W. and H. S. Odbert, "Trait-names: A Psycho-lexical Study," *Psychological Monographs*, 1936, No. 211.

Aronson, Elliot and Judson Mills, "The Effect of Severity of Initiation on Liking for a Group," *Journal of Abnormal and Social Psychology*, 59:177–181.

Asch, S. E. (a), "Forming Impressions of Personality," *Journal of Abnormal and Social Psychology*, 41:258–290.

Asch, S. E. (b), "Effects of Group Pressure Upon the Modification and Distortion of Judgments," in Eleanor E. Maccoby, Theodore M. Newcomb, and Eugene L. Hartley, *Readings in Social Psychology*, (3rd ed., New York: Holt, Rinehart and Winston, 1958).

*Axelrod, Joel N., "Induced Moods and Attidudes Toward Products," *Journal of Advertising Research*, 3:2, 19–24.

Back, Kurt W. "Influence Through Social Communication," *Journal of Abnormal and Social Psychology*, 46:9–23.

*Bales, Robert F., "Task Roles and Social Roles in Problem-Solving Groups," *Readings in Social Psychology*, (New York: Holt, Rinehart and Winston, 1958).

Baltzell, E. Digby, " 'Who's Who in America' and 'The Social Register': Elite and Upper Class Indexes in Metropolitan America," in Richard Bendix and Seymour Martin Lipset, *Class, Status and Power*, (Glencoe, Ill.: The Free Press, 1953).

*Banks, Seymour, "The Measurement of the Effect of a New Packaging Material Upon Preference and Sales," *Journal of Business*, 23:71–80.

*Banks, Seymour, "The Relationships Between Preference and Purchase of Brands," *Journal of Marketing*, 15:145–157.

*Bauer, Raymond A. and Robert D. Buzzell, "Mating Behavioral Science and Simulation," *Harvard Business Review*, 42:5:116–124.

Bauer, Raymond A. and Ithiel de Sola Pool, *The Effects of Audiences on*

Communicators (Cambridge: Harvard Graduate School of Business Administration, 1960).

*Becknell, James C., Jr., "Comment on Webb's Case for the Effectiveness Index," *Journal of Advertising Research*, 2:4, 42–43.

Benedict, Ruth, "Continuities and Discontinuities in Cultural Conditioning," *Psychiatry*, 1:161–167.

*Bennett, E. B., "Discussion, Decision, Commitment and Consensus in 'Group Decision,'" *Human Relations*, 8:251–274.

*Berkowitz, Leonard, "Personality and Group Position," *Sociometry*, 19:210–222.

Berkowitz, Leonard, *Advances in Experimental Social Psychology*, Vol. I (New York: Academic Press, 1964).

Berlo, David K., *The Process of Communication* (New York: Holt, Rinehart and Winston: 1960).

Bettelheim, Bruno and Morris Janowitz, *The Dynamics of Prejudice* (New York: Harper & Brothers, 1950).

*Blood, Robert O., Jr. and Donald M. Wolfe, *Husbands & Wives* (Glencoe, Ill.: The Free Press, 1960).

*Blum, Milton L. and Valentine Appel, "Consumer Versus Management Reaction in New Package Development," *Journal of Applied Psychology*, 45: 222–224.

Boder, D. P., "The Adjective-Verb Quotient: A Contribution to the Psychology of Language," *Psychological Record*, 3:309–343.

Bott, Elizabeth, "The Concept of Class as a Reference Group," *Human Relations*, 7:259–285.

Breed, Warren, "Social Control in the Newsroom: A Functional Analysis," *Social Forces*, 33:326–335.

Bridges, Katherine M. B., "Emotional Development in Early Infancy," *Child Development*, 3:324–341.

Bronfenbrenner, Urie, "Socialization and Social Class Through Time and Space," in Eleanor E. Maccoby, Theodore M. Newcomb and Eugene L. Hartley, *Readings in Social Psychology* (3rd ed., New York: Holt, Rinehart and Winston, 1958).

Brown, George H., "The Automobile Buying Decision Within the Family," in Nelson N. Foote, *Household Decision Making* (New York: New York University Press, 1961).

*Brown, Robert L., "Wrapper Influence on the Perception of Freshness in Bread," *Journal of Applied Psychology*, 42:257–260.

Brown, Roger, *Words and Things* (Glencoe, Ill.: Free Press, 1958).

Brown, Roger, "Models of Attitude Change," in Theodore M. Newcomb, ed., *New Directions in Psychology* (New York: Holt, Rinehart and Winston, 1962)—paperback.

Bruner, Jerome S., Leo Postman and John Rorigues, "Expectation and the Perception of Color," *American Journal of Psychology*, 64:216–227.

*Burns, Tom, "The Directions of Activity and Communication in a Departmental Executive Group," *Human Relations*, 7:73–97.

Cannell, Charles F. and James C. MacDonald, "The Impact of Health News on Attitudes and Behavior," *Journalism Quarterly*, 33:315–323.

Caplow, Theodore and Reece J. McGee, *The Academic Marketplace* (New York: Basic Books, 1958).

*Carlson, Earl R., "Attitude Change Through Modification of Attitude Structure," *Journal of Abnormal and Social Psychology,* 52:256–261.

*Carmichael, L., H. P. Hogan and A. A. Walter, "An Experimental Study of the Effect of Language on the Reproduction of Visually Perceived Form," *Journal of Experimental Psychology,* 15:73–86.

*Carroll, John B. and Joseph B. Casagrande, "The Function of Language Classifications in Behavior," in *Readings in Social Psychology* (New York: Holt, Rinehart and Winston, 1958).

Chase, Stuart, *Power of Words* (New York: Harcourt, Brace and Co., 1954).

Chotlos, J. W., "Studies in Language Behavior: IV, A Statistical and Comparative Analysis of Individual Written Language Samples," *Psychological Monographs,* 56:75–111.

Clark, Lincoln H., ed., *Consumer Behavior* (New York: Harper & Brothers, 1958).

*Clover, Vernon T., "Relative Importance of Impulse Buying in Retail Stores," *Journal of Marketing,* 15:66–70.

Colley, Russell H., *Defining Advertising Goals for Measured Advertising Results* (New York: Association of National Advertisers, 1961).

Conrad, Herbert S., "The Validity of Personality Ratings of Preschool Children," *Journal of Educational Psychology,* 23:671–680.

*Copp, James H., Maurice L. Sill and Emory J. Brown, "The Function of Information Sources in the Farm Practice Adoption Process," *Rural Sociology,* 23:146–157.

Crane, Edgar, Albert Talbott, and Rosarita Hume, "Time Use Profiles and Program Strategy," *Journal of Broadcasting,* Fall 1961, 335–343.

Crane (a), Lauren E. "How Product, Appeal and Program Affect Attitudes Toward Commercials," *Journal of Advertising Research,* 4:1:15–18.

Crane (b), Lauren Edgar, "The Salesman's Role in Household Decision Making," Proceedings of the American Marketing Association Winter Conference, 1964.

Crocker, E. C., *Flavor* (New York: McGraw-Hill, 1945).

*Cunningham, Ross M., "Brand Loyalty: What, Where, How Much," *Harvard Business Review,* 34:1, 116–128.

Cyert, Richard M. and James G. March, *A Behavioral Theory of the Firm* (Englewood Cliffs, N.J.: Prentice-Hall, 1963).

Dailey, Charles A., "The Effects of Premature Conclusion Upon the Acquisition of Understanding of a Person," *Journal of Psychology* 33:133–152.

*Danielson, Wayne A. and Sam Dunn Bryan, "Computer Automation of Two Readability Formulas," *Journalism Quarterly,* 39:201–206.

*Davitz, Joel R., "The Effects of Previous Training on Postfrustration Behavior," *Journal of Abnormal and Social Psychology,* 47:309–315.

*Dearborn, DeWitt C. and Herbert A. Simon, "Selective Perception: A Note on the Departmental Identifications of Executives," *Sociometry,* 21:140–144.

*Dennis, Wayne, "Uses of Common Objects as Indicators of Cultural Orientations," *Journal of Abnormal and Social Psychology,* 55:21–28.

*Dollard, John, "Under What Conditions Do Opinions Predict Behavior?" *Public Opinion Quarterly,* 12:623–632.

*Douvan, Elizabeth, "Social Status and Success Strivings," *Journal of Abnormal and Social Psychology,* 52:219–223.

Dudycha, G. J., "An Objective Study of Punctuality in Relation to Personality and Achievement," *Archives of Psychology,* 1936, No. 204.

*Dunnette, Marvin D. and Wayne K. Kirchner, "Psychological Test Differences Between Industrial Salesmen and Retail Salesmen," *Journal of Applied Psychology*, 44:121–125.

English, Earl, "Use of Split-Run Technique in Studying Advertising Typography," *Journalism Quarterly*, 23:66–68.

*Evans, Franklin B., "Psychological and Objective Factors in the Prediction of Brand Choice: Ford versus Chevrolet," *Journal of Business*, 32:340–369.

Ewing, T. N., "A Study of Certain Factors Involved in Changes of Opinion," *Journal of Social Psychology*, 16:63–88.

*Farr, James N., James J. Jenkins, and Donald G. Paterson, "Simplifications of Flesch Reading Ease Formula," *Journal of Applied Psychology*, 35:333–337.

Festinger, Leon, *A Theory of Cognitive Dissonance* (Stanford, Calif.: Stanford University Press, 1962).

*Festinger, Leon, and James M. Carlsmith, "Cognitive Consequences of Forced Compliance," *Journal of Abnormal and Social Psychology*, 58:203–210.

*Fiedler, Fred E. "A Contingency Model of Leadership Effectiveness," in Leonard Berkowitz, ed., *Advances in Experimental Social Psychology* (New York: Academic Press, 1964).

*Flesch, Rudolf, "A New Readability Yardstick," *Journal of Applied Psychology*, 32:221–233.

Foote, Nelson N., *Household Decision-Making* (New York: New York University Press, 1961).

*Freeman, Linton C., Thomas J. Fararo, Warner Bloomberg, Jr., and Morris H. Sunshine, "Locating Leaders in Local Communities: A Comparison of Some Alternative Approaches," *American Sociological Review*, 28:791–798.

French, John R. P., Jr., and Bertram Raven, "The Bases of Social Power," in Dorwin Cartwright, *Studies in Social Power* (Ann Arbor: The University of Michigan, 1959).

*Gamson, William A., "Experimental Studies of Coalition Formation," in Leonard Berkowitz, ed., *Advances in Experimental Psychology* (New York: Academic Press, 1964).

*Getzels, J. W., "The Question-Answer Process: A Conceptualization and Some Derived Hypotheses for Empirical Examination," *Public Opinion Quarterly*, 18:80–91.

Goldschmidt, Walter R., (a) "Class Denominationalism in Rural California Churches," *American Journal of Sociology*, 49:348–355.

Goldschmidt, Walter R., ed. (b) *Ways of Mankind* (Boston: The Beacon Press, 1954). (Also LP available National Association of Educational Broadcasters, University of Illinois, Urbana, Ill.)

Greenblum, Joseph and Leonard I. Pearlin, "Vertical Mobility and Prejudice: A Socio-Psychological Analysis," in Richard Bendix and Martin S. Lipset, *Class, Status and Power* (Glencoe, Ill.: The Free Press, 1953).

*Guest, Lester, "Brand Loyalty—Twelve Years Later," *Journal of Applied Psychology*, 39:405–408.

Guilford, J. P., *An Inventory of Factors STDCR* (Beverly Hills, Calif.: Sheridan Supply Co., 1940).

Haer, John L., "Predictive Utility of Five Indices of Social Stratification," *American Sociological Review*, 22:541–546.

*Haire, Mason (a), "Projective Techniques in Marketing Research," *Journal of Marketing*, 14:649–656.

Haire, Mason (b), "Role-Perceptions in Labor-Management Relations: An Experimental Approach," *Industrial and Labor Relations Review*, 8:204–216.

*Haire, Mason, Edwin E. Ghiselli, and Lyman W. Porter, "Cultural Patterns in the Role of Manager," *Industrial Relations*, 2:95–117.

Haire, Mason and Willa Freeman Grunes, "Perceptual Defenses: Processes Protecting an Original Perception of Another Personality," *Human Relations*, 3:403–412.

Hammond, K. R., "Measuring Attitude for Error-Choice: an Indirect Method," *Journal of Abnormal and Social Psychology*, 43:38–48.

Hatt, Paul K., "Occupation and Social Stratification," *American Journal of Sociology*, 55:533–543.

*Hepner, Harry Walker, *Advertising*, 4th ed., (New York: McGraw-Hill, 1964).

Hilgard (a), Ernest R., *Introduction to Psychology*, 2nd ed. (New York: Harcourt, Brace and World, 1957).

Hilgard (b), Ernest R., *Theories of Learning* (New York: Appleton-Century-Crofts, 1956, 2nd. ed.).

Hobart, Enid M. and Carl I. Hovland, "The Effect of 'Commitment' on Opinion Change Following Communication," *American Psychologist*, 9:394.

Hodge, Robert W., Paul M. Siegel, and Peter H. Rossi, "Occupational Prestige in the United States, 1925–63," *American Journal of Sociology*, 70:286–302.

*Hovland, Carl I., "Reconciling Conflicting Results Derived From Experimental and Survey Studies of Attitude Change," *American Psychologist*, 14:8–17.

Hovland, Carl I., Irving L. Janis, and Harold H. Kelley, *Communication and Persuasion* (New Haven: Yale University Press, 1953).

*Hovland, Carl I., O. J. Harvey, and Muzafer Sherif, "Assimilation and Contrast Effects in Reactions to Communication and Attitude Change," *Journal of Abnormal and Social Psychology*, 55:244–252.

Hovland, C. I., A. A. Lumsdaine, and F. D. Sheffield, *Experiments on Mass Communication* (Princeton: Princeton University Press, 1949).

*Hovland, Carl I. and Wallace Mandell, "An Experimental Comparison of Conclusion-Drawing by the Communicator and by the Audience," *Journal of Abnormal and Social Psychology*, 47:581–588.

*Hovland, Carl I. and Henry A. Pritzker, "Extent of Opinion Change as a Function of Amount of Change Advocated," *Journal of Abnormal and Social Psychology*, 54:257–261.

Hovland, Carl I. and Robert R. Sears, "Experiments on Motor Conflict I. Types of Conflict and Their Modes of Resolutions," *Journal of Experimental Psychology*, 23:477–493.

Hovland, Carl I. and Walter Weiss, "The Influence of Source Credibility on Communication Effectiveness," *Public Opinion Quarterly*, 15:635–650.

Hovland, Carl I. and others, *The Order of Presentation in Persuasion* (New Haven: Yale University Press, 1957).

Howells, Thomas H., "The Obsolete Dogmas of Heredity," *Psychological Review*, 52:23–34.

Huff, Darrell, *How to Lie with Statistics* (New York: W. W. Norton & Co., 1954).

*Hughes, J. L. and W. J. McNamara, "Limitations on the Use of Strong Sales Keys for Selection and Counseling," *Journal of Applied Psychology*, 42:93–96.

Hyman, Herbert, *Survey Design and Analysis* (Glencoe, Ill.: The Free Press, 1955).

Inkeles, Alex and Peter H. Rossi, "National Comparisons of Occupational Prestige," *American Journal of Sociology*, 61:329–339.

*Jackson, Jay M., "Reference Group Processes in a Formal Organization," *Sociometry*, 22:307–327.

*Janis, Irving L., and Seymour Feshbach, "Effects of Fear-Arousing Communications," *Journal of Abnormal and Social Psychology*, 48:78–92.

Janis, Irving L. and Bert T. King, "The Influence of Role Playing on Opinion Change," *Journal of Abnormal and Social Psychology*, 49:211–218.

Janis, Irving L. and W. Milholland "The Influence of Threat Appeals on Selective Learning of the Content of a Persuasive Communication," *Journal of Psychology*, 37:75–80.

Janis, Irving L., and others, *Personality and Persuasibility* (New Haven, Conn.: Yale University Press, 1959).

*Jones, Austin, H. Jean Wilkinson, and Ina Braden, "Information Deprivation as a Motivational Variable," *Journal of Experimental Psychology*, 62:126–137.

*Jung, Allen F., "Price Variations Among Automobile Dealers in Chicago, Illinois," *Journal of Business*, 32:315–326.

Kahl, Joseph A., *The American Class Structure* (New York: Holt, Rinehart and Winston, 1961).

Kahl, Joseph A. and James A. Davis, "A Comparison of Indexes of Socio-Economic Status," *American Sociological Review*, 20:317–325.

*Katona, George, *The Powerful Consumer* (New York: McGraw-Hill, 1960).

Katz, Elihu and Paul Lazarsfeld, *Personal Influence* (Glencoe, Ill.: The Free Press, 1955).

Kelley, Harold H., "The Warm-Cold Variable in First Impressions of Persons," *Journal of Personality*, 18:431–439.

Kelley, Harold H. and John W. Thibaut, "Experimental Studies of Group Problem Solving and Process," in Gardner Lindzey, ed., *Handbook of Social Psychology* (Cambridge: Addison-Wesley Publishing Co., 1954).

Kelman, Herbert C., "Attitude Change as a Function of Response Restriction," *Human Relations*, 6:185–214.

*Kelman, Herbert C. and Carl I. Hovland, " 'Reinstatement' of the Communicator in Delayed Measurement of Opinion Change," *Journal of Abnormal and Social Psychology*, 48:327–335.

*Kenkel, William F., "Husband-Wife Interaction in Decision Making and Decision Choices," *Journal of Social Psychology*, 54:255–262.

Kent, G. H. and A. J. Rosanoff, "A Study of Association in Insanity," *American Journal of Insanity*, 67:37–96, 317–390.

Kirkpatrick, Charles Atkinson, *Salesmanship* (3rd ed., Cincinnati: South-western Publishing Co., 1961).

*Kornhauser, Arthur, "Are Public Opinion Polls Fair to Organized Labor?" *Public Opinion Quarterly*, 10:484–500.

*Kotler, Philip, "On Methods: Toward an Explicit Model for Media Selection," *Journal of Advertising Research*, 4:1, 34–51.

Krech, David, Richard S. Crutchfield and Egerton L. Ballachey, *Individual in Society* (New York: McGraw-Hill, 1962).

Kuhn, Alfred, *The Study of Society* (Homewood, Ill.: Richard D. Irwin, 1963).

*Laird, Donald A. "How the Consumer Estimates Quality by Subconscious Sensory Impressions," *Journal of Applied Psychology,* 16:241–246.

*Landsberger, Henry A., "The Horizontal Dimension of Bureaucracy," *Administrative Science Quarterly,* 6:299–332.

*Lawrence, Lois C. and Patricia Cain Smith, "Group Decision and Employee Participation," *Journal of Applied Psychology,* 39:334–337.

*Lazarsfeld, Paul F., "Interpretation of Statistical Relations as a Research Operation," in Paul F. Lazarsfeld and Morris Rosenberg, eds., *The Language of Social Research* (Glencoe, Ill.: The Free Press, 1955).

*Lefkowitz, Monroe, Robert R. Black and Jane Srygley Mouton, "Status Factors in Pedestrian Violation of Traffic Signals," *Journal of Abnormal and Social Psychology,* 51:704–706.

*Levine, Jerome M. and Gardner Murphy, "The Learning and Forgetting of Controversial Material," *Journal of Abnormal and Social Psychology,* 38:507–517.

*Lewin, Kurt, "Group Decision and Social Change," in *Readings in Social Psychology* (New York: Holt, Rinehart and Winston, 1958).

Lindsley, Donald B., "Emotion" in S. S. Stevens, *Handbook of Experimental Psychology* (New York: Wiley, 1951).

*Link, Henry C., Albert D. Freiberg, John H. Platten, Jr., and Kenneth E. Clark, "Is Dr. Kornhauser Fair to Organized Pollers?" *Public Opinion Quarterly,* 11:198–212.

*Lionberger (a), Herbert F., *Adoption of New Ideas and Practices* (Ames, Iowa: Iowa State University Press, 1960).

*Lionberger, (b) Herbert F. "Some Characteristics of Farm Operators Sought as Sources of Farm Information in a Missouri Community," *Rural Sociology,* 18:327–338.

Longenecker, Justin G., *Principles of Management and Organizational Behavior* (Columbus, Ohio: Charles E. Merrill Books, 1964).

*Lucas, D. B. and C. E. Benson, "The Relative Values of Positive and Negative Advertising Appeals as Measured by Coupons Returned," *Journal of Applied Psychology,* 13:274–300.

*Lucas, D. B. and C. E. Benson, "Some Sales Results for Positive and Negative Advertisements," *Journal of Applied Psychology,* 14:363–370.

Lucas, Darrell Blaine and Steuart Henderson Britt, *Measuring Advertising Effectiveness* (New York: McGraw-Hill, 1963).

Luft, Joseph, "Monetary Value and the Perception of Persons," *Journal of Social Psychology.* 47:245–251.

Lumsdaine, Arthur A. and Irving L. Janis, "Resistance to 'Counter-Propaganda' Presentations," *Public Opinion Quarterly,* 17:311–318.

McCarthy, E. Jerome, *Basic Marketing* (Rev. ed., Homewood, Ill.: Richard D. Irwin, 1964).

McClelland, D. C. and J. W. Atkinson, "The Projective Expression of Needs: I, The Effect of Different Intensities of the Hunger Drive on Perception," *Journal of Psychology,* 25:205–222.

McGeoch, John A. and Arthur L. Irion, *The Psychology of Human Learning* (New York: Longmans, Green and Co., 1958, 2nd ed.).

*McGinnies, Elliott, "Emotionality and Perceptual Defense," *Psychological Review,* 56:244–251.

McGraw-Hill Research, *Laboratory of Advertising Performance* (New York: McGraw-Hill, undated).

*McGuire, William J., "Cognitive Consistency and Attitude Change," *Journal of Abnormal and Social Psychology,* 60:345–353.

*McNamara, Harold J., Charles M. Solley, and John Long, "The Effects of Punishment (Electric Shock) on Perceptual Learning," *Journal of Abnormal and Social Psychology,* 57:91–98.

McNemar, Quinn, *Psychological Statistics* (3rd ed., New York: John Wiley, 1962).

Magazine Advertising Bureau, *Split Run and Regional Advertising in Magazines,* 6th ed., (New York: Magazine Publishers Association, 1964).

*Maier, Norman R. F., "Reasoning in Humans," *Journal of Comparative Psychology,* 12:181–194.

*Maier, Norman R. F., L. Richard Hoffman, John J. Hooven, and William H. Read, *Superior-Subordinate Communication in Management* (New York: American Management Association, 1961).

Maloney, John C., "Curiosity versus Disbelief in Advertising," *Journal of Advertising Research,* 2:2, 2–8.

Marquis, Dorothy Postle, "Study of Frustration in Newborn Infants," *Journal of Experimental Psychology,* 32:123–138.

*Marrow, Alfred J. and John R. P. French, Jr., "Changing a Stereotype in Industry," *Journal of Social Issues,* I:3, 33–37.

Martineau, Pierre, *Motivation in Advertising* (New York: McGraw-Hill, 1957).

Maslow, A. H., *Motivation and Personality* (New York: Harper & Brothers, 1954).

*Massy, William F., "Statistical Analysis of Relations Between Variables," in Ronald E. Frank, et al, *Quantitative Techniques in Marketing Analysis* (Homewood, Ill.: Richard D. Irwin, 1962).

*Matthews, John B. Jr., Robert D. Buzzell, Theodore Levitt, and Ronald E. Frank, *Marketing: An Introductory Analysis* (New York: McGraw-Hill, 1964).

Menzel, Herbert and Elihu Katz, "Social Relations and Innovation in the Medical Profession: The Epidemiology of a New Drug," *Public Opinion Quarterly,* 19:337–352.

Merei, Ference, "Group Leadership and Institutionalization," *Human Relations,* 2:23–39.

Merton, Robert K., *Social Theory and Social Structure* (Glencoe, Ill.: The Free Press, 1957), rev. ed.

Miller, George A., *Language and Communication* (New York: McGraw-Hill, 1951).

*Mindak, William A., Andrew Neibergs and Alfred Anderson, "Economic Effects of the Minneapolis Newspaper Strike," *Journalism Quarterly,* 40:213–218.

Munroe, Ruth L., *Schools of Psychoanalytic Thought* (New York: The Dryden Press, 1955).

Murray, Henry A., "The Effect of Fear Upon Estimates of the Maliciousness of Other Personalities," *Journal of Social Psychology,* 4:310–329.

Murray, Henry A., *Explorations in Personality* (New York: Oxford University Press, 1938).

National Opinion Research Center, "Jobs and Occupations: A Popular Evaluation," in Richard Bendix and Seymour Martin Lipset, *Class, Status and Power* (Glencoe, Ill.: The Free Press, 1953).

*Naylor, James C., "Deceptive Packaging: Are The Deceivers Being Deceived?" *Journal of Applied Psychology,* 46:393–398.

*Naylor, J. C., and C. H. Lawshe, "An Analytical Review of the Experimental Basis of Subception," *Journal of Psychology,* 46:75–96.

*O'Rourke, John F., "Field and Laboratory: The Decision-Making Behavior of Family Groups in Two Experimental Conditions," *Sociometry,* 26:422–435.

Osgood, Charles E., *Method and Theory in Experimental Psychology* (New York: Oxford University Press, 1953).

Osgood, Charles E., George J. Suci and Percy H. Tannenbaum, *The Measurement of Meaning* (Urbana: University of Illinois Press, 1957).

*Pastore, Nicholas and Milton W. Horowitz, "The Influence of Attributed Motive on the Acceptance of Statement," *Journal of Abnormal and Social Psychology,* 51:331–332.

Payne, Stanley, L., *The Art of Asking Questions* (Princeton, N.J.: Princeton University Press, 1951).

*Pettigrew, Thomas F., "The Measurment and Correlates of Category Width as a Cognitive Variable," *Journal of Personality,* 26:532–533.

Politz, Alfred, *A 12-Months' Study of Better Homes & Gardens Readers* (Des Moines, Iowa: Meredith Publishing Co., 1956).

*Politz, Alfred, *Life Study of Consumer Expenditures, Vol. I* (New York: Time, 1957).

Politz, Alfred, *The Readers of the Saturday Evening Post, No. 2, Report A* (Philadelphia: The Curtis Publishing Co., 1958).

*Quenon, E. L., "A Method of Pre-evaluating Merchandise Offerings," *Journal of Marketing,* 16:158–171.

*Rhine, Ramon J. and Betsy A. Silun, "Acquisition and Change of a Concept Attitude as a Function of Consistency of Reinforcement," *Journal of Experimental Psychology,* 55:524–529.

Roe, Anne, *The Making of a Scientist* (New York: Dodd, Mead, 1953).

*Rogers, David A., "Personality of the Route Salesman in a Basic Food Industry," *Journal of Applied Psychology,* 43:235–239.

*Rosen, Bernard C., "The Achievement Syndrome: A Psychocultural Dimension of Social Stratification," *American Sociological Review,* 21:203–211.

*Rosenberg, Milton J., "Cognitive Structure and Attitudinal Affect," *Journal of Abnormal and Social Psychology,* 53:367–372.

Rosenzweig, Saul, "The Picture-Association Method and Its Application in a Study of Reactions to Frustration," *Journal of Personality,* 14:3–23.

Ruesch, Jurgen and Weldon Kees, *Nonverbal Communication* (Berkeley: University of California Press, 1956).

Schachter, Stanley, "Deviation, Rejection and Communication," *Journal of Abnormal and Social Psychology,* 46:190–207.

*Schachter, Stanley and Harvey Burdick, "A Field Experiment on Rumor Transmission and Distortion," *Journal of Abnormal and Social Psychology,* 50:363–371.

*Schachter, Stanley and Jerome E. Singer, "Cognitive, Social and Psychological Determinants of Emotional State," *Psychological Review,* 69:379–399.

*Schachter, Stanley and Ladd Wheeler, "Epinephrine, Chlorpromazine and Amusement," *Journal of Abnormal and Social Psychology,* 65:121–128.

Schafer, Ray and Gardner Murphy, "The Role of Autism in a Visual Figure-Ground Relationship," *Journal of Experimental Psychology,* 32:335–43.

Sears, P. S., "Levels of Aspiration in Academically Successful and Unsuccessful Children," *Journal of Abnormal and Social Psychology,* 35:498–536.

Seeleman, V., "The Influence of Attitude Upon the Remembering of Pictorial Material," *Archives of Psychology,* 36, No. 258.

*Selltiz, Claire, Marie Jahoda, Morton Deutsch and Stuart W. Cook, *Research Methods in Social Relations,* rev. ed. (New York: Holt, Rinehart and Winston, 1961).

Shaffer, Laurance Frederic and Edward Joseph Shoben, Jr., *The Psychology of Adjustment,* 2nd ed. (Boston: Houghton-Mifflin Co., 1956).

*Shaw, Marvin E., "Communication Networks," in Leonard E. Berkowitz, ed., *Advances in Experimental Social Psychology* (New York; Academic Press, 1964).

Sherif, Muzafer and Carl I. Hovland, *Social Judgment* (New Haven: Yale University Press, 1961).

*Siegel, Alberta Engvall and Sidney Siegel, "Reference Groups, Membership Groups, and Attitude Change," *Journal of Abnormal and Social Psychology,* 55:360–364.

*Staats, Arthur W. and Carolyn K. Staats, "Attitudes Established by Classical Conditioning," *Journal of Abnormal and Social Psychology,* 57:37–40.

*Star, Shirley, A. and Helen MacGill Hughes, "Report on an Educational Campaign: The Cincinnati Plan for the United Nations," *American Journal of Sociology,* 55:389–400.

*Starch, Daniel and Staff, *Measuring Product Sales Made by Advertising* (Mamaroneck, N.Y.: Starch and Staff, 1961).

Stevens, S. S. (a), "The Surprising Simplicity of Sensory Metrics," *American Psychologist,* 17:29–39. (p. 30)

Stevens, S. S. (b), ed., *Handbook of Experimental Psychology* (New York: Wiley, 1951).

*Stouffer, Samuel A., "An Analysis of Conflicting Social Norms," *American Sociological Review,* 14:10–26.

Stouffer, S. A. and others, *The American Soldier Vol. I, Adjustment During Army Life* (Princeton: Princeton University Press, 1949).

Strickland, Lloyd H., "Surveillance and Trust," *Journal of Personality,* 26:200–215.

*Strodtbeck, Fred L., "Husband-Wife Interaction Over Revealed Differences," *American Sociological Review,* 16:468–473.

Strong, Edward K., Jr., and J. E. Loveless, "'Want' and 'Solution' Advertisements," *Journal of Applied Psychology,* 10:346–366.

*Tannenbaum, Percy H., Harvey K. Jacobson, and Eleanor L. Norris, "An Experimental Investigation of Typeface Connotations," *Journalism Quarterly,* 41: 1, 65–73.

Terman, L. M. and M. H. Oden, *The Gifted Child Grows Up* (Stanford, Calif.: Stanford University Press, 1947).

*Thistlethwaite, Donald L., Henry deHaan, and Joseph Kamenetzky, "The Effects of 'Directive' and 'Nondirective' Communication Procedures on Attitudes," *Journal of Abnormal and Social Psychology,* 51:107–113.

Tinker, Miles Albert, *Legibility of Print* (Ames, Iowa: Iowa State University Press, 1963).

*Triandis, Harry C., "Similarity in Thought Processes and Boss-Employee Communication," in *Communication in Organizations* (Ann Arbor: Foundation for Research on Human Behavior, 1959).

*Triandis, Harry C., "Cultural Influences Upon Cognitive Processes," in Leonard Berkowitz, ed., *Advances in Experimental Social Psychology* (New York: Academic Press, 1964).

*Triandis, Harry C. and Martin Fishbein, "Cognitive Interaction in Person Perception," *Journal of Abnormal and Social Psychology,* 67:446–453.

*Triandis, Harry C. and Leigh Minturn Triandis, "Race, Social Class, Religion and Nationality as Determinants of Social Distance," *Journal of Abnormal and Social Psychology,* 41:110–118.

Tucker, W. T., *The Social Context of Economic Behavior* (New York: Holt, Rinehart and Winston, 1964).

*Tucker, W. T., "The Development of Brand Loyalty," *Journal of Marketing Research,* 1:3:32–35.

*Tucker, W. T. and John J. Painter, "Personality and Product Use," *Journal of Applied Psychology,* 45:325–329.

*Twedt, Dik Warren, "A Multiple Factor Analysis of Advertising Readership," *Journal of Applied Psychology,* 36:207–25.

*Verplanck, William S., "The Control of the Content of Conversation; Reinforcement of Statements of Opinion," *Journal of Abnormal and Social Psychology,* 51:668–676.

WS: *see* Woodworth and Schlosberg.

Warner, W. Lloyd and James C. Abegglen, *Occupational Mobility in American Business and Industry* (Minneapolis: University of Minnesota Press, 1955).

Warner, W. Lloyd, Marchia Meeker, and Kenneth Eells, *Social Class in America* (Gloucester, Mass.: Peter Smith, 1957).

Weir, Walter, *On The Writing of Advertising* (New York: McGraw-Hill, 1960).

*Weiss, Walter (a), "Opinion Congruence with a Negative Source on One Issue as a Factor Influencing Agreement on Another Issue," *Journal of Abnormal and Social Psychology,* 54:180–186.

*Weiss, Walter (b), "The Relationship Between Judgments of a Communicator's Position and Extent of Opinion Change," *Journal of Abnormal and Social Psychology,* 56:380–384.

Wells, William D., "The Influences of Yeasaying Response Style," *Journal of Advertising Research,* 1:4, 1–12.

*West, C. John, "Results of Two Years of Study into Impulse Buying," *Journal of Marketing,* 15:362–363.

*Westfall, Ralph L., Harper W. Boyd, Jr., and Donald T. Campbell, "The Use of Structured Techniques in Motivation Research," *Journal of Marketing,* 22: 134–139.

*Whyte, William Foote, *Human Relations in the Restaurant Industry* (New York: McGraw-Hill, 1948).

*Whyte, William H., Jr., "The Web of Word of Mouth," *Fortune,* 50:5 (November 1954) 140–143, 204–212.

*Wilson, Allan R., "Qualitative Market Research," *Harvard Business Review,* 30:1, 75–86.

Wishner, Julius, "Reanalysis of 'Impressions of Personality,'" *Psychological Review,* 67:96–112.

*Witkin, Arthur A., "Differential Patterns in Salesmen," *Journal of Applied Psychology,* 40:338–340.

*Wolgast, Elizabeth H., "Do Husbands or Wives Make the Purchasing Decisions?" *Journal of Marketing,* 23:151–158.

* Woodrow, Herbert and Frances Lowell, "Children's Association Frequency Tables," *Psychological Monographs,* Vol. 22: No. 5, Whole No. 97.

Woodworth, Robert S. and Harold Schlosberg, *Experimental Psychology,* rev. ed. (New York: Holt, Rinehart and Winston, 1964).

*Zeisel, Hans, *Say It With Figures* (New York: Harper & Brothers, 1947, 2nd ed.).

*Zimmerman, Claire and Raymond A. Bauer, "The Effect of an Audience on What Is Remembered," *Public Opinion Quarterly,* 20:238–248.

Index of Principal Authors

Index of Journals

Index of Subjects